Financial Market Regulations and Legal Challenges in South Asia

Amit K. Kashyap
Nirma University, India

Anjani Singh Tomar
Gujarat National Law University, India

A volume in the Advances in Finance, Accounting, and Economics (AFAE) Book Series

BUSINESS SCIENCE Reference
An Imprint of IGI Global

Published in the United States of America by
Business Science Reference (an imprint of IGI Global)
701 E. Chocolate Avenue
Hershey PA, USA 17033
Tel: 717-533-8845
Fax: 717-533-8661
E-mail: cust@igi-global.com
Web site: http://www.igi-global.com

Library of Congress Cataloging-in-Publication Data

Names: Kashyap, Amit K., 1982- editor. | Tomar, Anjani Singh, 1978- editor.
Title: Financial market regulations and legal challenges in South Asia / Amit K. Kashyap and Anjani Singh Tomar, editors.
Description: Hershey, PA : Business Science Reference, [2016] | Includes bibliographical references and index.
Identifiers: LCCN 2015050705| ISBN 9781522500049 (hardcover : alk. paper) | ISBN 9781522500056 (ebook : alk. paper)
Subjects: LCSH: Finance--South Asia. | Finance--Law and legislation--South Asia. | Capital market--South Asia. | Capital market--Law and legislation--South Asia. | Financial institutions--South Asia. | Financial institutions--South Asia.
Classification: LCC HG187.S64 F56 2016 | DDC 346.5407--dc23 LC record available at http://lccn.loc.gov/2015050705

This book is published in the IGI Global book series Advances in Finance, Accounting, and Economics (AFAE) (ISSN: 2327-5677; eISSN: 2327-5685)

British Cataloguing in Publication Data
A Cataloguing in Publication record for this book is available from the British Library.

For electronic access to this publication, please contact: eresources@igi-global.com.

Advances in Finance, Accounting, and Economics (AFAE) Book Series

Ahmed Driouchi
Al Akhawayn University, Morocco

ISSN: 2327-5677
EISSN: 2327-5685

Mission

In our changing economic and business environment, it is important to consider the financial changes occurring internationally as well as within individual organizations and business environments. Understanding these changes as well as the factors that influence them is crucial in preparing for our financial future and ensuring economic sustainability and growth.

The **Advances in Finance, Accounting, and Economics (AFAE)** book series aims to publish comprehensive and informative titles in all areas of economics and economic theory, finance, and accounting to assist in advancing the available knowledge and providing for further research development in these dynamic fields.

Coverage

- E-finance
- Finance
- Microeconomics
- Applied Finance
- Statistical Analysis
- Risk Analysis and Management
- Applied Accounting
- Economics of Migration and Spatial Mobility
- International Economics
- E-Accounting

IGI Global is currently accepting manuscripts for publication within this series. To submit a proposal for a volume in this series, please contact our Acquisition Editors at Acquisitions@igi-global.com or visit: http://www.igi-global.com/publish/.

The Advances in Finance, Accounting, and Economics (AFAE) Book Series (ISSN 2327-5677) is published by IGI Global, 701 E. Chocolate Avenue, Hershey, PA 17033-1240, USA, www.igi-global.com. This series is composed of titles available for purchase individually; each title is edited to be contextually exclusive from any other title within the series. For pricing and ordering information please visit http://www.igi-global.com/book-series/advances-finance-accounting-economics/73685. Postmaster: Send all address changes to above address.

Titles in this Series

For a list of additional titles in this series, please visit: www.igi-global.com

Handbook of Research on Impacts of International Business and Political Affairs on the Global Economy
Norhayati Zakaria (Universiti Utara Malaysia, Malaysia) Asmat-Nizam Abdul-Talib (Universiti Utara Malaysia, Malaysia) and Nazariah Osman (Universiti Utara Malaysia, Malaysia)
Business Science Reference • copyright 2016 • 450pp • H/C (ISBN: 9781466698062) • US $235.00 (our price)

Relational Methodologies and Epistemology in Economics and Management Sciences
Lucio Biggiero (Università dell' Aquila, Italy) Pier Paolo Angelini (Interuniversity Research Centre for Sustainable Development (CIRPS), Italy) Mario Basevi (Italian National Institute of Statistics, Italy) Nunzia Carbonara (Politecnico di Bari, Italy) Antonio Mastrogiorgio (Interuniversity Research Centre for Sustainable Development (CIRPS), Italy) Eliano Pessa (University of Pavia, Italy) Enrico Sevi (Università dell' Aquila, Italy) and Marco Valente (Università dell' Aquila, Italy)
Information Science Reference • copyright 2016 • 485pp • H/C (ISBN: 9781466697706) • US $200.00 (our price)

Global Perspectives on Risk Management and Accounting in the Public Sector
Augusta da Conceição Santos Ferreira (University of Aveiro, Portugal) Graça Maria do Carmo Azevedo (University of Aveiro, Portugal) Jonas da Silva Oliveira (Instituto Universitário de Lisboa (ISCTE-IUL), Portugal) and Rui Pedro Figueiredo Marques (University of Aveiro, Portugal)
Information Science Reference • copyright 2016 • 510pp • H/C (ISBN: 9781466698031) • US $225.00 (our price)

Handbook of Research on Comparative Economic Development Perspectives on Europe and the MENA Region
M. Mustafa Erdoğdu (Marmara University, Turkey) and Bryan Christiansen (PryMarke, LLC, USA)
Business Science Reference • copyright 2016 • 605pp • H/C (ISBN: 9781466695481) • US $440.00 (our price)

Handbook of Research on Financial and Banking Crisis Prediction through Early Warning Systems
Qaiser Munir (Universiti Malaysia Sabah, Malaysia)
Business Science Reference • copyright 2016 • 514pp • H/C (ISBN: 9781466694842) • US $265.00 (our price)

Comparative Economics and Regional Development in Turkey
Bryan Christiansen (PryMarke, LLC, USA) and M. Mustafa Erdoğdu (Marmara University, Turkey)
Business Science Reference • copyright 2016 • 451pp • H/C (ISBN: 9781466687295) • US $205.00 (our price)

Analyzing the Economics of Financial Market Infrastructures
Martin Diehl (Deutsche Bundesbank, Germany) Biliana Alexandrova-Kabadjova (Banco de México, Mexico) Richard Heuver (De Nederlandsche Bank, The Netherlands) and Serafín Martínez-Jaramillo (Banco de México, Mexico)
Business Science Reference • copyright 2016 • 410pp • H/C (ISBN: 9781466687455) • US $220.00 (our price)

Table of Contents

Detailed Table of Contents

Several far-reaching reforms to the financial sector were introduced by South Asian countries in early 1980. The nature and progress of these reforms vary from country to country. These reforms covered a number of areas such as promoting competition in the financial sector, developing payment and settlement systems, and strengthening regulations. So far, these reforms have not only helped South Asian countries to significantly raise domestic savings, attract foreign capital, and raise economic growth rates but also provided greater economic integration of South Asia. This chapter performs a close re-scrutiny of the reforms implemented in South Asian countries. Suggestion for further reforms for building efficient, competitive, and resilient financial sector is also provided.

This chapter studies the international market malpractice of insider trading where officials holding a fiduciary duty towards the company, violate the same to utilise company specific and price sensitive information to trade in company securities before such information is announced to the public investors. Information asymmetry, gross violation of ethical standards and abuse of fairness and market integrity are the underlining terms of this offence. The chapter studies four SAARC nations of India, Pakistan, Sri Lanka and Nepal to project their working against insider trading. While countries introduce law and yet fail to enforce it, SAARC countries are encouraged through this chapter to maintain strong ground against this malady. The author projects recommendations and observations to prompt periodic statutory review.

The chapter will extend upon the extant literature by considering the permissibility of crowdfunding practices within the South Asian region. There is a genuine dearth of research considering these matters, with little research considering the history and permissibility of crowdfunding methodologies within the noted nations. As such the contribution of the chapter is twofold, firstly it represents amongst the first coherent assessments of the use of crowdsourcing based fundraising methodologies within the South Asian region. Secondly it responds to the dearth of research considering the legal permissibility of such practices within the noted nations, while also contrasting the regulatory models of India, Bangladesh, and Sri Lanka with the regulatory models evidenced within selected OECD countries and pertinently the recently reformed model of regulation within the United States, specifically chapter 12 of the Jobs Act (2013).

The study compares the impact of the commercial environment on external financing of female- owned micro, small and medium enterprises (MSMEs) compared to those that are male owned in seven South Asian countries. The region exhibits weak institutional and regulatory regimes which result in expropriation of profits from MSMEs. It is likely that such commercial environments add to the risk of lending to MSMEs and this may further manifest a gender bias toward males. This study uses a unique dataset of over 5000 firms from World Bank Enterprise Surveys and combines this with additional information drawn from World Bank macro-economic data. Interval and logit regressions are used. Contrary other studies, this research indicates that once females have access to formal financing they use a higher proportion of formal financing in their firm capital structure than their male-counterparts. A gap in accessing external finance for female-owned MSMEs presents both a waste of human resource and a lost potential to lift standards of living, presenting an opportunity for reform.

The agency problem attributed to dispersed ownership is also principally regarded as being that of the control over powerful management. Whilst there are conflicting views in respect of the degree of agency problems which arise under dispersed and concentrated ownership structures, it appears that additional or greater agency problems will eventually necessitate the need for greater monitoring. In recommending the external auditor's expertise as appropriate for addressing agency problems, this chapter draws attention to the audit committee's roles, presenting them both as vital and complementary corporate governance tools.

In recent years, one of the most important topics related to stock market volatility which is attracting attention, is stock returns, or in other words, the relationship between stock price volatility and trading volume. The aim of this study was to obtain information about the financial market structure of Bangladesh, India, Pakistan by applying Granger Causality Analysis to the relationship of trading volume and stock returns volatility in the period 1980–2012. The study then examines some of the stock market regulations that have been proposed in South Asia to attenuate stock market volatility, which have usually included proposals to limit volatility by imposing temporary trading halts, limiting the legal leverage available to investors in financial assets, altering exchange trading practices to accommodate volume, and by raising the transactions costs of financial trading.

Chapter 9

The Nepalese financial sector is attributed of banking sector and non-banking sector. There is exponential growth in the number of financial institutions in Nepal in the last decade. The existing legal framework and institutional setup in Nepal is not conducive to the overall financial sector and private sector development and thus there is an urgent need for reformation in these sectors. The major impediments to private sector involvement in infrastructure development projects include the political and administrative instability; lack of consistent planning; lack of effective institutional support in designing and development of private sector infrastructure projects. Talking about the capital market and capital gains In Nepal, capital gains on securities transactions are taxed as ordinary income to corporations and individual investors while in most of the emerging markets capital gains on investments in stocks and bonds are not taxed, which need to be reformed as per the international practices.

Chapter 10

Financial market is the backbone of the economy, hence is crucial for the economic growth and development of any country. The financial sector also entails the seeds of financial crisis that can spill over across the rest of economy. Though the interaction between various economic sectors is crucial, it requires timely assessment of risks and redressed. This chapter attempts to capture the sequencing and implementation of financial market reforms in Nepal and briefly examine its consequences. The evidence confirms that reforms do not only mean the institutional and policy reforms but also manifests in terms of increase in the number of financial institutions, expansion in the outreach of financial services and products in terms of quality and quantity as well as improvement in the soundness of macroeconomic indicators. Finally, it argues for the continuation of reforms and consolidation in the financial markets to make the system resilient in changing contexts.

Chapter 11

In the following chapter, the authors have proposed to throw light on the scheme of financial sector prevalent in Afghanistan. The purpose of this chapter is to give the readers a brief insight on the financial background, policies and regulations in existence in Afghanistan. Adding upon, the authors have made an attempt to suggest a few recommendations to bring the Afghanistan's economy at par with the economy of other developing nations of the world. The authors received substantial amount of assistance from the top-managerial officials of Bakhtar Bank of Afghanistan and from a scholar named Abdul Samad Katawazy. The authors would like to thank AREU, AISA and ACCI for providing access to their published surveys and reports. This particular chapter as a whole focuses on ten basic factors which have the ability to make or break Afghanistan's financial structure and therefore aims to provide an insight into the same.

In order to provide financial services effectively to almost 1.21 billion people, India has adopted a comprehensive financial system governed under a number of financial regulations. These regulations, through regular amendments, are kept updated and inclusive of modern financial concepts that emerge in national and international markets. Islamic finance is one of such modern concepts emerged at global level. Growing with an annual growth rate of 15-20 percent the Islamic finance industry is holding total assets, value estimated to be more than USD 1.6 trillion. Hence, the authors, in this paper tried to study the feasibility of providing Islamic financial services in India, especially in the areas of Retail banking, Microfinance, Venture Capital financing. The objective of this paper is to identify the major regulatory challenges facing Islamic finance and to propose the possible solutions so as to make this emerging industry an internal part of the Indian financial system.

The capital market of Bangladesh perceived a self-important growth which is not in line with developed economy. The Securities and Exchange Commission (SEC) tried to correct the irregular behaviour observed in the market, lack of proper decisions from the regulator's side which has contributed to the creation of market instability. This study tried to identify the factors on market crash and regulatory failure. Government had reform SEC to soothe the market but unsuccessful as investors' confidence is in the bottom level. The reasons behind the stock market crash are found irrational market behavior, inconsistency in regulations, excess liquidity in the market, stock split by companies, faulty listing system, issuance of right shares and preference shares by companies at high price, stock manipulations by insider trading, serial trading and excessive greed of investors. Government and regulators should work together to detect the main speculators and should bring investors back to the market.

Many countries in the South Asia region are global players in many aspects due to the nature of emerging markets as well as being democratic countries irrespective of the fact that many people in the region are troubled by higher level of poverty. Many years of regulation in the South Asian region has hampered economic growth and reduced the level of efficiencies in almost all economic activities. However, implementation of market deregulations since the early 1980s in many sectors has benefited the majority

Preface

The Idea of editing a book on financial market regulatory structure and issues to the harmonization of financial structure in SAARC region germinated during my Doctoral studies on structured finance. After reading various authors I found lot of interesting resources and though of consolidating a piece of document which will serve as a study of discipline called 'South Asian financial market'. Today we are proud to offer to the research community an authentic piece of collected data on south Asian financial market, which will serve as a reference book for practitioners as well as students.

Financial Markets are the places of measuring development in modern era. The stabilized market of any country show the stability for the government, and prosperity of the people. There are different forms of the markets which is operating in the various countries. The major tasks of the market is enabling the trading of the primary or secondary securities. South Asian region is comprising of countries Sri Lanka, Bangladesh, Afghanistan, Nepal, Bhutan, India, Pakistan and Maldives. This Book have covered different countries of South Asia with different values, market standards and different investors with special reference to major countries having diverse issues in financial structure. But one thing is very clear that the south Asian countries are having diversified markets. The presence of different types of the investors make it imperative to study the markets very closely. Without the complete study of the markets it is impossible to advice the investment at all. These markets are being operated with several generations from now. Every time with the change in the polity and demography the trend in the investment changes. To meet out these challenges the changes in the markets is required. Sometime the positive and some time the negative incidents promote the changes in the structure of the markets in various countries. For an example the scandals in the Indian markets have promoted the coming up of the new Companies Act and SEBI as modulator of the Indian markets. Likewise presence of Islamic investors have promoted to various other institutes in different countries.

Several generations of financial market reforms in South Asia have resulted in extended prudential regulations, an improved soundness of financial systems, in particular the banking system, and in an increased diversification of risks. Policy makers, central bankers and supervisory authorities have made endeavours both to stabilize South Asian financial systems and to enable their economies to return to a sustainable growth path key issues in the South Asian financial market such as the national and global financial architecture including rules, infrastructure, and governance.

This book through its various chapters has deliberated that South Asia has witnessed the most diverse markets, as well as the biggest among the whole world. The Indian security market is the one of the most bulky market of the globe and it require hefty regulators like the SEBI and RBI. Similar on the lines there are definite markets in countries like Sri Lanka and Afghanistan. But all of them are facing some issues pertaining to the investment. The present work is just the summary of the different works, efforts which are going around the different countries to address the issues related to investment.

The present book is having different chapters which are discussing the market structure in different South Asian countries. It cover the matters related to the market structure, regulators, challenges and remedies that are offered at various level. The chapters are covering almost every financial market that is found in the south Asian countries. The maximum regulations and streamlining could be seen in those countries which are having set pattern of the governance and could also be co-related to the awareness to the investors. The development parameter is mentioned here because it is not a hidden factors that the countries like US and Germany are also having developed financial structure or markets which have paved way to their present status as developed countries of the world. The book is comprising of fourteen chapters which is covering various issues of the financial markets in South Asia. It opens with the brief introduction to overview of financial markets in south Asia through its first chapter and goes on to last chapter addressing various sectors of south Asian region with respect to challenges and issues.

The first chapter i.e. "Financial Market Regulatory Structure in South Asia: An Overview" is discussing about the regulatory framework in south Asia with a brief introduction about the financial market regulatory structure of major countries like India, Pakistan, Bangladesh, Nepal and Afghanistan. The international integration of financial markets of Asian countries sometimes leads to growth and sometimes leads to failure. This chapter have also analysed the issue of financial integration in south Asia and major challenges to the liberalising financial market of south Asia. Authors have discussed about the current laws and regulations governing capital markets of south Asian countries and what role is played by the financial market regulators in their respective country.

The second chapter i.e. "Regulatory Reforms in Indian Financial Market" among others. The chapters are covering the issues of the regulations at the financial markets of the different countries as well as in India. A recalibration of the overarching role of India's financial market regulators is critical given the imperative of reducing income inequality and ensuring rapid economic development. Indeed, the functions and mandate of the financial markets regulators must be made more holistic for enabling a robust capital market environment, by focusing on three key pillars. This chapter majorly covers the issues pertaining to the need of the regulations, challenges posed by non-observance of the rules and remedies thereafter and how regulators of financial market in India like SEBI, RBI and IRDA has played a very imperative role in its expansion. This chapter has discussed about all the regulators of financial market and major reforms done by the government of India in harmonisation of financial infrastructure of India to make it investor friendly and a better place for inflow of foreign currency.

Whereas the third chapter, "Financial Sector Reforms in South Asian Countries" is discussing the issue of reforms covered a number of areas such as promoting competition in the financial sector, developing payment and settlement systems, and strengthening regulations. So far, these reforms have not only helped South Asian countries to significantly raise domestic savings, attract foreign capital, and raise economic growth rates but also provided greater economic integration of South Asia. East Asian financial crisis resulted in providing greater space for these new reforms. Another round of reforms took place in the 1990s. The current financial crisis, which began in the U.S. sub-prime mortgage market in 2007, has already prompted a reassessment of financial sector policy making globally to address many of the weaknesses in supervisory, regulatory and prudential frameworks. The beginning of the current global crisis was associated with complex financial products. South Asian financial sector didn't have direct exposure to such products. Still the global financial crisis caused a considerable slowdown of South Asian economies as a result of contagion effects of global shocks. Some of the significant channels that affected South Asian economies were capital, remittances, credit and international trade. Capital outflow, reduced foreign remittances, dried up international credit markets, and reduced exports have had serious implications for these economies.

The chapter four, "Insider Trading - A South Asian Study" is covering the matters of the insider trading mechanism in the south Asian countries. It is comprising of different parts, part I, II and III respectively. Part I shall give the readers a brief background of the insider trading activity, its accepted definition and the development of this malady. Part II shall provide a synthesis of the insider trading regulations and enforcement procedures existing in the South Asian countries of India, Pakistan, Sri Lanka and Bangladesh. Part III shall describe the challenges faced by such jurisdictions in restraining insider trading and subsequently, the amendments required to be enacted in these countries. Part I Insider trading undermines investor confidence in the fairness and integrity of the financial markets. This accounts for the reason why nearly every jurisdiction has strictly prohibited insider trading. The majority of legislators adopting statutes relating to insider trading have addressed the following issues: What is inside information? Who can be considered an insider? What activities related to using inside information are prohibited? How to prevent insider trading? What sanctions and enforcement measures should be implemented? The author has studied the regulatory framework of the South Asian countries under Part II and suggested measures to overcome the gaps of challenges faced by such jurisdictions in containing insider trading under Part III. In 2003, IOSCO's Emerging Market Committee released a Report on Insider Trading analysing 41 jurisdictions all over the world. The Report has looked at the definitions of insider, unpublished information, and source of information, the materiality of information, the intent involved and finally the prohibited act of both dealing and tipping. Further, the regulatory structure surrounding this activity has been discussed in this Report. The chapter includes discussing the relevant parts of this Report, inter alia, the basic elements constituting insider trading; the power of supervisory bodies and civil and penal sanctions imposed.

The chapter five titled, "The permissibility of crowd funding within South Asia: a comparative analysis", discusses a new concept of crowd funding and its aspects. Crowdfunding is best understood as the process by which a web based organisation seeks to procure funding from the general public through a web portal, the web portal enables unrelated business enterprises seeking capital to make equity within their entities available to investors. This was not permissible given the restrictions placed on public fundraising by the SEC Act. As asserted, Crowdfunding was largely motivated by individuals and organisations promoting profit motivated initiatives through crowdsourcing platforms, and also by the potential benefits to entrepreneurs associated with creating more enabling pathways to accessing start-up capital. While it may not be apparent there is a critical distinction between individuals soliciting for support through web based portals, and offering items in exchange for such support and individuals and organisations making equity or profits from a venture available for distribution in exchange for monetary support. While many crowdsourcing models do not involve the issuance of securities in the conventional sense they may be in direct contravention with the Securities and Exchange Commission Act.

The sixth chapter titled, "The impact of institutional factors on firm financing: Evidence from South Asian Countries". The chapter is comprising of the study on the impact of the commercial environment on external financing of female owned small medium enterprises (SMEs) compared to those that are male owned in seven South Asian countries. The region exhibits weak institutional and regulatory regimes which result in expropriation of profits from SMEs. It is likely that such commercial environments add to the risk of lending to SMEs and this may further manifest in a gender bias toward males. An empirical investigation using a unique dataset of over 5000 firms from World Bank Enterprise Surveys is combined with additional information drawn from World Bank macro-economic data and these data are analysed using interval and logit regressions. Low access to formal external financing is identified as a constraint to female SME owners compared to male counterparts in the South Asia region. The findings indicate that once females have access to formal financing they use a high proportion of formal financing in their firm capital structure than their male-counterparts.

The very interesting chapter i.e. chapter seventh with a long title, "Why Credit Ratings Serve a Greater Role in Emerging Economies than Industrial Nations: A Comparative Analysis between Family Firms and Concentrated Ownership Structures in South Asia" has argued that South Asia being emerging an economy, which are also based on family firms (concentrated ownership structures), why corporate governance measures - including the operation of audit committees, as well as greater focus on audits as signalling mechanisms, is crucial for purposes of facilitating the achievement of regulatory aims - as well as the development of accounting and regulatory structures. Through this comparative analysis, this chapter also aims to investigate whether information provided through credit ratings agencies in South Asia, is superior to those of macroeconomic indicators. The chapter also seeks to address gaps in the literature - gaps in the current and previous literature which support the fact that family firms, concentrated ownership systems and structures suffer from less problems and issues associated with information asymmetries than pre-dominantly based dispersed ownership systems and structures, as well as the above claim relating to the worth and informational value of credit ratings agencies - in particular that relating to the negative impact of credit ratings announcements and their more "significant" impacts in emerging markets. Finally, the chapter seeks to propose rules and recommendations whereby the current legal and regulatory challenges faced by financial markets in South Asia could be addressed.

The eighth chapter titled, "Volatility and the Regulation of Stock Markets, Evidence from South Asia" has analysed, Volatility, which expresses the variability of the return of any financial asset, has a very important place in the estimation of financial asset returns. As volatility is a significant indicator of the degree of risk of an asset, option and derivative pricing, it has come to be used as a parameter. The simplest definition of volatility is the sudden movement of prices. In other words, the market volatility of stocks is an indicator which is used to describe the frequency and size of the waves occurring in the stock market index or a specfic stock price. The increasing volatility in recent years in the stock market as in all financial markets, has increased the interest of stock investors on this subject to a significant degree. The sources of the volatility of the stock market are important in terms of measurement and modelling as well as to specialists and portfolio investors.

The ninth Chapter titled, "Financial Market in Nepal: Challenges of the Financial Sector Development in Nepal" discuss about the overview of financial market regulatory structure of Nepal. This chapter have given a brief picture of financial market regulations of Nepal which is augmented by chapter tenth that has discussed about the reforms in Nepalese financial market.

The tenth chapter titled, "Financial Market Reforms in Nepal and its Presence in South Asia "covers, the financial market reforms in Nepal, it essentially starts with the discussion of conceptual issues and context of financial market reforms in the first part. The second part, basically reviews the sequencing of financial market reforms program in Nepal with detailed discussion on the past reform efforts and progress achieved on such programs. The third part deals with the issues and challenges of financial sector reforms in Nepal. The fourth part opens up the regional context of financial market reforms in South Asia whereas the last part concludes the chapter. Financial sector is considered to be important in most of the economies in order to pool and utilize financial resources, reduce costs and risks, expand and diversify opportunities, increase the allocative efficiency of resources and promote the productivity. It is equally important to facilitate the economic growth in the country through its intermediation activities.

The chapter eleven, "Regulatory Challenges in Financial Sector in Afghanistan" is discussing the challenges in the Afghanistan and also discussing the remedies to overcome the challenges. Some of the people in the financial sector of Afghanistan are being contacted to get their opinion on the issue of finance and its sources in Afghanistan. The chapter covers the Stock Exchanges in Kabul – The key role of Afghanistan Stock Exchange in the economic development of Afghanistan. The way State Owned Enterprises work there in reference to the Afghanistan Stock Exchange. The status of the Banking Sector in Afghanistan – The model of banking in Afghanistan with reference to the strengthening of the currency. Along with some work experience of the people working in Bakhtar Bank, Afghanistan like the Company Credit Officer working there. The issues pertaining to Foreign Investment Policy in Afghanistan – where it is found that it is not update. There is no proper mechanism and channel of foreign investment in Afghanistan. The fear of an international investor in investing in the companies located in Afghanistan. Whereas how the Governmental Regulations in Company Matters is also discussed at length. This gives the complete picture of the market in Afghanistan.

The chapter twelve titled, "Islamic Finance in India: Financial Regulations, Challenges and Possible Solutions" covers the issues related to the Islamic banking". Islamic finance is one of such modern concepts emerged at global level. Growing with an annual growth rate of 15-20 percent the Islamic finance industry is holding total assets, value estimated to be more than USD 1.6 trillion. Hence, the authors, in this paper tried to study the feasibility of providing Islamic financial services in India, especially in the areas of Retail banking, Microfinance, Venture Capital financing. The objective of this paper is to identify the major regulatory challenges facing Islamic finance and to propose the possible solutions so as to make this emerging industry an internal part of the Indian financial system.

The chapter thirteen titled, "Recent Status of Capital Market Regulations in Bangladesh", covers the issues of regulating the markets in state of Bangladesh. The capital market of Bangladesh perceived a self-important growth which is not in line with developed economy. The Securities and Exchange Commission (SEC) tried to correct the irregular behaviour observed in the market, lack of proper decisions from the regulator's side which has contributed to the creation of market instability. This study tried to identify the factors on market crash and regulatory failure. Government had reform SEC to soothe the market but unsuccessful as investors' confidence is in the bottom level. The reasons behind the stock market crash are found irrational market behaviour, inconsistency in regulations, excess liquidity in the market, and stock split by companies, faulty listing system, issuance of right shares and preference shares by companies at high price, stock manipulations by insider trading, serial trading and excessive greed of investors. Government and regulators should work together to detect the main speculators and should bring investors back to the market.

The last chapter i.e. Chapter fourteenth titled, "Economic and Financial Integration in South Asia" has discussed that going to that path of European union, counties in South Asia have formed an alliance called South Asian Association for Regional Corporation (SAARC) in 1985 with the objective of improving economic corporation and economic growth in the region. Going further in the path of economic integration, in 2002, leaders of SAARC have agreed to accelerate cooperation in the core areas of trade, finance and investment to realise the goal of an integrated South Asian economy in a step-by-step manner. They have also agreed to the vision of a phased and planned process eventually leading to a South Asian Economic Union (SAEU). Furthermore, they also have formed the SAARCFINANCE group which has been entrusted the responsibility of studying and making recommendations on the early and eventual realisation of SAEU, a development bank for the region, single payment system and a single currency. The objective of this study is to explore how feasible is such proposals and in particular what prospects are there to form a monetary corporation among countries in South Asia. The chapter has further discussed that, the major obstacle to economics and financial market integration in South Asia would be the underlying political factors in the region. For example, disputes among nations on many issues are substantial and ongoing discussions would not be able to give a clear solution in the immediate future. All countries in the region have internal political issues as well as issues with neighbouring nations. For instance, India, the largest economy of the region, has disputes with Pakistan, the second largest economy. Countries such as Sri Lanka and Nepal both have long-run ongoing ethnical issues within their countries. When there is no political stability in a country, it is a difficult task to introduce significant structural changes though such countries have democratic political systems. Many countries in Asia, specifically in East Asia, have been able to achieve remarkable economic growth during the past, irrespective of the political system they had. After achieving notable economic development, many of these countries have now introduced democratic political systems. Apart from political, religious, ethnical, cultural and social issues in each country in the region, other issues such as corruption, institutional deficiencies, lack of transparency, inefficiency and regulatory problems are needed to be looked at.

The objective of this study is to measure the financial market integration, so far, among South Asian countries and explore existing fundamental obstacles to achieve long term goals for significant economic benefits. Such a comprehensive analysis is followed by policy recommendations which may be useful to SAARCFINANCE group in its efforts to form an SAEU.

We thank all authors for the quality of their contributions, as well as all referees who carefully reviewed the chapters.

Amit K Kashyap
Nirma University, India

Anjani Singh Tomar
Gujarat National Law University, India

Acknowledgment

In many ways this volume has been a long time coming. Words cannot fathom the depth of gratitude that my heart is filled with to be associated with this prestigious publication House, IGI Global, USA. I am deeply indebted to them for their encouragement and support.

This publication is a concerted effort of the all the chapters contributors from various parts of the world for their efforts in collecting and verifying the information included in the publication all are well respected or rising stars in the discipline.

I acknowledge my gratitude to Prof (Dr.) Nisha Dubey, Vice Chancellor, Barkatullah University, Bhopal for her guidance in selecting the chapters for book.

I would also like to thank Mr. Anchit Bhandari & Miss Urvashi Jaswani, Research Scholars, Centre for Corporate Law Studies, Institute of Law Nirma University, Ahmedabad for their assistance in editing.

I am extremely grateful to the library staff of Gujarat National law University & Institute of Law, Nirma University for providing valuable intellectual resources, which was of great help in writing the introductory chapters & editing the book.

I would also like to thank Mr Raj Sandhu, Asst, Prof of law, Jammu University, Jammu & Kashmir, India, Miss Shail Shah, Advovate, Gujarat High Court, Marianne Ojo, North-West University, Filiz Eryilmaz, Uludağ Üniversitesi İİBF İktisat Bölümü, Narayan Paudel, Kathmandu University, Tanya Nayyar, Associate, AMSS, Mumbai, Stuart Locke, Waikato & Mr. Anchit Bhandari & Miss Urvashi Jaswani, Research Scholars, Centre for Corporate Law Studies, Institute of Law Nirma University, Ahmedabad for reviewing the chapters and providing valuable inputs.

I thank my parents, for their faith and encouragement which allowed me to be as ambitious as I wanted. It was under their watchful eye that I gained so much drive and an ability to tackle challenges head on. Also, I thank parents of my co-editor Dr. Anjani for provided us with unending encouragement and support.

Amit K. Kashyap
Nirma University, India

November 2015

Chapter 1
Financial Market Regulatory Structure in South Asia:
An Overview

Amit Kumar Kashyap
Nirma University, India

Anchit Bhandari
Nirma University, India

Urvashi Jaswani
Nirma University, India

ABSTRACT

South Asian region is comprising of countries Sri Lanka, Bangladesh, Afghanistan, Nepal, Bhutan, India, Pakistan & Maldives. The different countries are with different values, market standards & different investors. But one thing is very clear that the south Asian countries are having diversified markets. The presence of different types of the investors make it imperative to study the markets very closely. Without the complete study of the markets it is impossible to advice the investment at all. This chapter is dedication to the brief overview of financial market regulatory structure in all major south Asian countries in SAARC region.

FINANCIAL SYSTEM AND FINANCIAL MARKETS: INTRODUCTION

The financial system of any country consists of specialized and non- specialized financial institutions, of organized and unorganized financial markets, of financial instruments and services which facilitate transfer of funds. (Kinnon, 1973) Procedures and practices adopted in the markets, and financial interrelationships are also parts of the System. These parts are not always mutually exclusive. For example, financial institutions operate in financial markets and are, therefore a part of such markets. The word system", in the term "financial system" implies a Set of complex and closely connected or intermixed institutions, agents, Practices, transactions, claims, and liabilities in the economy (Gurney and Shaw,

DOI: 10.4018/978-1-5225-0004-9.ch001

1955). Financial institutions are business organizations that act as mobilizes and depositories of savings and as purveyors of credit or finance. They also provide various financial services to the community. (Pathak, 2003) They differ from non- financial (industrial and commercial) business organizations in respect of their wares, i.e. while the former deal in financial assets such as deposits, loans, securities, and so on, the latter deal in real assets such as machinery, equipment & so on. The activities of different financial institutions may be either specialized or they may overlap; quite often they overlap. Yet, we need to classify financial institutions and this is done on such bases as their primary activity or the degree of their specialization with relation to savers or borrowers with whom they customarily deal or the manner of their creation. (Shaw, 1973) In other words, the functional, geographic, sectoral scope of activity or the type of ownership is some of the criteria which are often used to' classify a large number and variety of financial institutions which exist in the economy. However, it should be kept in mind that classifications are likely to be imperfect and tentative. According to one classification, financial institutions are divided into the banking and non- banking ones.(Stiglitz, 1993) The banking institution have quite few things common with the non-banking ones, but their distinguishing character lies in the fact that, unlike other institutions, they participation the economy's payments mechanisms, that is, they provide transactions services, their deposit liabilities constitute a major part of national money supply, and they can, as a whole, create deposit or credit, which is money. Banks, subject to legal (Gurley, 1955) reserve requirements, can advance credit by creating claims against themselves, while other institutions can lend only out of resources put at their disposal by the savers. The distinction between the two has been highlighted Sayers by characterizing the former as "creators" of' credit, and the latter as mere "purveyors" of credit. Financial institutions are also classified as intermediaries and non-intermediaries. As the term indicates, intermediaries intermediate between savers and investors, they lend money as well as mobilize savings, their liabilities are towards the ultimate savers, while their assets are from the investors or borrowers. Non- intermediary institutions do the loan business but their resources are not directly obtained from the savers. Many non- banking institutions also act as intermediaries and when they do so they are known as Non- Banking Financial Intermediaries.

Financial markets are the centers or arrangements that provide facilities for buying and selling of financial claims and services. The participants on the demand and supply sides of these markets' are financial institutions, agents, brokers, dealers, borrower's lenders, savers, who are inter-linked by the laws, contracts, covenants, and communication networks of the land (Basyal, 2002).

Financial markets are sometimes classified as primary (direct) and secondary (indirect) markets. The primary markets deal in new financial claims and securities and therefore, they are also known as New Issue Markets. (Burton, Nesiba & Brown, 2015) On the other hand, secondary markets in Securities already issued or existing or outstanding. The Primary markets mobilize savings and they supply fresh or additional capital to business units. Although secondary markets do not contribute directly to the supply of additional capital, they do so indirectly by rendering securities issued the primary markets liquid. Stock markets have both the primary and secondary market segments. (Calvo and Mendoza, 2000)

More often financial markets are classified as money markets and capital markets, although there is no essential difference between the two because both perform the same function of transferring resources to the producers. (Obsfeld & Taylor, 2002)

This conventional distinction is based on the differences in the period of maturity of financial assets issued in these markets. While the money market deals in the short- term claims (with a period of maturity of one year or less), the capital market does so in the long- term (maturity period above 1 year) claims.

Contrary to the popular usage, the capital market is co- extensive not only with the stock market; it is much wider than the stock market. Similarly, it is not always possible to include a given participant only in either of the two (money and capital) markets. Commercial banks belong to both. While Treasury Bills Market, Call Money Market are examples of money market. Keeping in view different purposes, financial markets have also been classified into the following categories:

1. Organized and Unorganized
2. Formal and Informal
3. Official and Parallel
4. Domestic and Foreign

The wares financial systems deal in are financial services and claims or financial assets or securities or financial instruments. These services and claims are many and varied in character. This is so because of the diversity of motives behind borrowing and lending. The stage of development of a financial system can often be judged from the diversity of financial instruments that exist in the system (Goldsmith, 1969).

Financial asset represents a claim to the payment of a sum of money sometime in future and/or a periodic payment in the form of interest or dividend. (Bhole, 2004) With regard to bank deposit or Government bond or industrial debenture, the holder receives both the regular periodic payments, and the repayment of the principal at a fixed date. Whereas, with regard to the ordinary share or perpetual bond, only periodic payments are received.

Financial instruments differ from each other in respect of their investment characteristics which, of course, are interdependent and interrelated. Among the investment characteristics, of financial assets, the following are the important:

1. Liquidity
2. Marketability
3. Reversibility
4. Transferability
5. Transaction Costs
6. Risk of Default or the Degree of Capital and Income Uncertainty
7. Maturity Period
8. Tax Status
9. Options Such as, Call Back or Buy Back Option
10. Volatility of Prices
11. The Rate of Return- Nominal, Effective and Real

SOUTH ASIAN FINANCIAL MARKET

South Asia covers the entirety of the Indian subcontinent (Afghanistan, Bangladesh, Bhutan, India, Pakistan and Nepal) together with the island states of Maldives and Sri Lanka. It holds a quarter of the world's population within 4 per cent of the global landmass. Though confronting huge security and nation-building challenges, it has emerged as amongst the most dynamic regions in the world. Its projected growth rate of 7.2 per cent in 2015 is higher than in any other region.

South Asia has undoubtedly benefited greatly from globalization, with many countries of the region relying to a significant extent on international trade and investment as their main engine for economic growth and development. It has experienced a long period of robust economic growth, averaging 6% a year over the past 20 years. South Asia is Financial liberalization in south Asian countries started the in the early 1990's except Sri Lanka & Nepal. In Sri Lanka these reforms were introduced much earlier, and in Nepal, financial sector reform were not introduced until 2002. South Asian Association for Regional Cooperation (SAARC) is an organisation for Regional Corporation in south Asia.

One of the major problems for south Asian policy makers, supervisory authorities and regulators countries is lack of inclusiveness of the economic and financial system. Bangladesh is first in taking key steps in this field which has inspired India & Sri Lanka but still countries like Pakistan, Afghanistan & Bhutan are far behind.

The regulatory structure of financial markets in all the south Asian countries is almost similar with the difference of its progress. The evolution of south Asian financial market is not much hurt by global financial crises but rather was hurt through trade channels. South Asia is still struggling with how to make the financial system more efficient and responsive to real sector need. As the financial institutions and structures are less sophisticated. Financial market reforms in South Asia have resulted in stretched prudential regulations, improvement in particular the banking system, and in an increased diversification of risks. But financial sector reforms also resulted in a rising openness and integration of South Asian financial markets into the global economy. The front running countries toward integration with global financial market in south Asia are India, Bangladesh & Pakistan. One of the current major reform projects in South Asian countries is the implementation of Basel II which encourages pro-cyclical risk taking and thereby tends to accentuate boom-bust cycles. South Asian leaders has given priority to financial market expansion, liberalisation in FDI & harmonisation of regulatory students for doing business & market development in south Asian countries which is evident from the current regulatory structure of south Asian countries. Further, good governance is kept at highest priority in progress of financial market regulatory structure. Most South Asian countries have ample scope for improving corporate governance arrangements, for market regulators as well as for market participants. While most have introduced corporate governance standards. The financial market regulatory structure of major south Asian countries is discussed hereinafter.

FINANCIAL MARKET REGULATORY FRAMEWORK IN INDIA

Company Law Regulations

The major issues of securities, which are marketable in the securities market and in which the public are interested, are public limited companies. The companies act while providing for regulations of companies includes a general framework for the dealings in the securities of such enterprises. It mainly relates to share capital/issue of shares, prospectus/abridged prospectus, issues of shares on rights basis, issue of debentures, allotment of shares and issue of share certificates. Indian has introduces new companies Act in 2013 to promote market expansion & good governance practices.

Securities Contracts (Regulation) Act

In 1951, a draft bill on stock exchange regulation in India, based on the report of a committee, was prepared and referred to an expert committee under the chairmanship of A D Gorawala. The recommendations of the Gorawala Committee culminated the enactment of the securities contracts (regulation) Act, 1956 which has been amended from time to time. The SCRA provides the broader framework of the present scheme of stock exchange regulation in India (Mohan, 2007). The object of SCRA is to prevent undesirable transactions in securities by regulation the business of dealing therein, by providing for certain other matters connected herewith. It also seeks to regulate the buying and selling of securities outside the limits of stock exchanges through the licensing of security dealers. The SCRA sets up a general framework of control that makes the Government/SEBI influence all pervasive. At the same time, as an enabling legislative measure, it provides the Government/SEBI with a flexible apparatus for the regulation of the stock market in India (Reddy & Venugopal, 2006). The main scheme of regulation provided by the SCRA can broadly be divided under five main headings:

1. Constitution of Recognized Stock Exchanges
2. Contracts and Options in Securities
3. Listing of Securities
4. Penalties and Procedures
5. Other Matters

SECURITIES EXCHANGE BOARD OF INDIA

The SEBI has been set up under SEBI Act to:

1. To protect the interest of the investors in the securities
2. To promote the development of and regulate the securities market by much measures as it thinks fit.

SEBI's general superintendence and direction and management is vested in the Board of members which exercises all powers and do all acts which may be done by SEBI.

Powers and Functions of SEBI:

A. Regulating the business in stock exchanges and any other securities market.
B. Registering and regulating the working of stockbrokers, sub-brokers, share transfer agents, bankers to an issue, trustees of trust deeds, registrars to an issue, merchant bankers, underwriters, portfolio managers, investment advisors and such other intermediaries who may be associated with the securities market in any manner.
C. Registering and regulating the working of the depositories, participants, custodians of securities, foreign institutional investors, credit rating agencies and such other intermediaries as it may by notification specify in this behalf.
D. Promoting and regulating self-regulatory organizations.

E. Prohibiting fraudulent and unfair trade practices relating to the securities market.
F. Promoting investors education and training of intermediaries of the securities market.
G. Prohibiting insider trading in securities.
H. Regulating substantial acquisition of shares and takeovers of the companies.
I. Calling for information from, undertaking inspection, conducting inquiries and audits, of the stock exchanges, mutual funds, other persons associated with the securities market intermediaries and self-regulatory organizations in the securities market.
J. Calling for information and record from any bank or any other authority or board or corporation establishes or constituted by or under any central, state or provincial act in respect of any transaction in securities which is under investigation or inquiry by the SEBI
K. Performing such functions and exercise such powers under the provisions of Securities Contract Regulation Act as may be delegated to it by the Central Government.
L. Levying fees or other charges for carrying out the above purposes.
M. Conducting research of the above purposes.
N. Calling from or furnishing to any such agencies as may be specified by it, such information as may be considered necessary by it for the efficient discharge of its functions.
O. Performing such other functions as may be prescribed.

OMBUDSMAN/STIPENDARY OMBUDSMAN REGULATIONS, 2003

To address the grievances of investors in securities and for connected matters, the SEBI has established ombudsman/stipendiary ombudsman. The powers and functions of the ombudsman are-

A. To receive complaints against any intermediary of listed company or both.
B. To consider such complaints and facilitate their resolution by amicable settlement.
C. To approve the amicable settlement of the dispute between the parties.
D. To adjudicate such complaints in the event of failure of settlement by friendly or amicable settlement.

The ombudsman would submit to the SEBI within 3 months of the close of each financial year a report containing general review of its activities. It would also furnish from time to time such information as the SEBI may require.

SEBI INTERMEDIARIES REGULATIONS, 2008

Intermediaries are stock brokers, sub-brokers, share transfer agents, bankers to an issue, trustees of trust deeds, registrars to an issue, merchant bankers, underwriters, portfolio managers, investment advisers, depositories, custodians, credit rating agencies and other intermediaries associated with the securities market in any manner specified by the SEBI including an asset management company, a clearing member of a clearing corporation and trading member of a derivative stock exchange but does not include an FII, foreign venture capital investor, mutual fund, collective investment scheme and venture capital fund.

The obligations of intermediaries are:

A. Compliance certificate to SEBI
B. Redresses the investor grievances
C. Appointment of compliance officer
D. No investment advice without proper disclosure
E. To maintain the code of conduct
F. Inspection and disciplinary proceedings

SEBI PUBLIC OFFER AND LISTING OF SECURITISED DEBT INSTRUMENTS REGULATIONS, 2008

The main elements of these regulations relating to public offers of securitized debt instruments/listing of SDIs issued to public/any person on a recognized stock exchange are-

A. Registration of trustees
B. Constitution or management of special purpose distant entities
C. Schemes of specific purpose distant entities
D. Public offer of SDIs
E. Rights of investors
F. Listing of SDIs
G. Inspection and disciplinary proceedings
H. Action in case of defaults.

Reserve Bank of India

RBI was established on April 1935 in accordance with reserve bank of India act, 1934. RBI governs the banking sector & foreign invest in India. It acts as the apex monetary authority of the country.

The RBI is responsible for implementing monetary and credit policies, issuing currency notes, being banker to the government, regulator of the banking system, manager of foreign exchange, and regulator of payment & settlement systems while continuously working towards the development of Indian financial markets. The RBI regulates financial markets and systems through different legislations (Nseindia.com, 2015).

RBI regulates financial market while exercising powers under FEMA Act 1999 & RBI Act 1935.

FINANCIAL MARKET REGULATORY FRAMEWORK IN MALDIVES

The financial area in the Maldives is extremely constricted and is dominated by the banking business. There are 7 banks at present working in the Maldives which consist of one nearby owned commercial bank, branches of 4 foreign banks, one in the vicinity established subordinate of a foreign bank and an

Islamic bank. The Non-bank financial institutions in the nation comprises of a money leasing corporation, a specific housing finance organization, insurance companies, monetary services dealers and securities market mediators. All banks and the non-bank financial institutions, apart from the financial market mediators are certified, regulated and controlled by the Maldives Monetary Authority. The Capital Market Development Authority (CMDA) is the controller for the financial market in the Maldives (http://mma.gov.mv/, 2007). It has legal powers to certify securities market mediators comprising brokers, dealers, investment advisers, asset managers, custodians, credit rating agencies as well as stock exchanges and central depositories. The controlling powers are acquired under the Maldives Securities Act, 2006 and Maldives Pension Act 2009.

Financial Market

The Capital Market Development Authority (CMDA) was set up under the Maldives Securities Act (2006) and is accountable for controlling and increasing the capital market in the Maldives. The CMDA has been active in increasing the controlling surrounding in addition to the infrastructure for the institution of the financial market. Organizations that are controlled by the CMDA comprise of listed companies, dealing companies, brokers, the stock exchange and central depository.

In 2008, the Securities Trading Floor and the Securities Depository were alienated from the CMDA and accredited as a private area Stock Exchange and Depository. Then, on January 2008 Maldives Securities Depository (MSD) and Maldives Stock Exchange Company Private Limited were set up as private area organizations under the Maldives Securities Act.

Presently there are 6 companies with listed securities and 1 company with listed liability in Maldives Stock Exchange. The companies are; Maldives Tourism Development Corporation (MTDC), Maldives Transport and Contracting Company (MTCC), Bank of Maldives (BML), State Trading Organization (STO), Dhivehi Raajeyge Gulhun (DHIRAAGU), Amana Takaful Maldives (ATM) and Housing Development Finance Corporation (HDFC).

In expression of a primary market for debt securities, both government securities and private sector commercial debt mechanism are presently not accessible to the common public. However, the Housing Development Finance Corporation Plc (HDFC) has issued 3 corporate bonds which have been given to institutional investors comprising the commercial banks and few of the public activity. Moreover, Maldives Monetary Authority acting on behalf of the govt., issues Treasury bills to commercial banks and state acquired activities for the reason of investing in the budget shortfall.

An Islamic debt security was initiated to the financial market by HDFC in 2013 for the first time. Currently there are 2 certified dealing companies which comprise of Stock Brokers Maldives Private Limited and Aariya Securities Private Limited.

FINANCIAL MARKET REGULATORY FRAMEWORK IN AFGHANISTAN

- Afghanistan's fiscal market is going through a conversion phase because of the fact that the whole country is in a rebuilding stage. The financial system of Afghanistan has been getting better after the war. Afghanistan is a deprived country. Nevertheless, it holds a major quantity of natural resources and mineral deposits.

So it does have the potential to convert its economy into a steady state. The economy of Afghanistan is dependent on agriculture to a considerable extent. The national economy of Afghanistan has undergone a significant improvement after the year 2002 (World Finance, 2016).

- This resulted because of the influx of billions of United States dollar in the form of international aid. The agricultural production in Afghanistan has also gone up. Afghanistan is a country, which relies on foreign aids to a significant extent (Anand & Maimbo, 2003).
- The foreign aids come from various sources, for example, the World Bank, the Asian Development Bank (ADB), and International Monetary Fund (IMF). A significant portion of Afghanistan's revenue is generated from the export of opium, fruits, nuts, wheat, woolen and cotton goods, carpets, and valuable stones (World Finance, et al. 2016).
- The Asian Development Bank is playing a significant role in the reconstruction of Afghanistan. It is providing large volumes of grant in order to facilitate the growth of Afghanistan financial market and the private sector of Afghanistan World Finance, et al.

The Kabul Stock Exchange is also known as the Kabul International Stock Exchange would be regulating the first liquid exchange of Afghanistan with comprehensive variety of capital market products and services. .. This international stock exchange will have foreign currency exchanges and cash equity exchanges segments in its platform.

- It would be dealing in the following operations:
  1. Listing of securities
  2. Buying and selling of cash equities
  3. Interest rate and equity derivatives
  4. Buying and selling of bonds
  5. Supply of market data to various investors in Afghanistan

FINANCIAL MARKET REGULATORY FRAMEWORK IN BANGLADESH

Market Regulation

The Bangladesh Securities and Exchange Commission (BSEC) includes securities and mutual funds. It is associated to the Ministry of Finance and is mostly funded by government funds and listing fees for initial public offerings (IPOs). Staff has no authorized protection.

International brokers are allowed to work through a domestic subsidiary, which can be 100% alien owned. There are presently no international-owned brokers. Dealers are confined in the study they can put forward. Until lately, dealers were forbidden from giving investment suggestions to clients.

Preparation of proficient standards skill requirements for authorization of brokers are being measured by the SECB. Dealing beyond the stock exchange is allowed, but it needs BSEC consent. BSEC policy forbids market exploitation.

All stock exchanges have a surveillance system, though there is not much coordination of inquiry across the marketplace. Modern events and practitioner remarks put forward that abuse, mainly manipulation, is not unusual. The BSEC is in the course of acquiring an inspection system. The marketplace has been subject to quick variations in costs and capacity. The primary regulatory reply till now has focused on actions to help the market by, for instance, involve directors to keep up least holdings. The BSEC has been caught up in cheering applicants to hold up the market.

Subsidiaries of international companies working in Bangladesh can be listed. Presently, 11 are listed. Listings of an international subsidiary have to fulfill the free float necessities. There are no terms to list international companies as such. Domestic companies can be taken over by international companies.

Issuers are needed to let loose a least amount free float at IPO. For huge companies, the least amount is 10%. Issuers are needed to publicize a prospectus. The BSEC can enforce permit on issuers and their consultants and, as a severe measure, call off an IPO. Issuers are needed to make available annual financial report and unaudited quarterly reports. They are also needed to make available monthly statements of shareholdings by supporters and directors. Issuers are needed to make quick declaration of a broad and inclusive list of actions that may have an effect on the stock costs. Disclosure fulfillment (and observance of governance and accounting standards) is usually seen as not good, particularly in companies beyond the top fifty. Companies can have compound voting arrangement with conflicting rights. Safeguard of minorities is usually said as weak and insufficient. Approaches to permit directors to override additional shareholders at company gatherings are frequent. Corporate bonds are needed to be evaluated by a domestic CRA, but are not needed to be listed.

The stock exchanges control corporate governance. The rules are not clearly stand on a globally acknowledged code of control, but are being made domestically. It is explained as a work in progress and is at an initial stage of growth. Companies are needed to publicize their stages of observance in the annual statement.

Bangladesh accounting standards match to International Accounting Standards (IASs) with no major disparities. Standards and accounting firms are presently controlled by the Institute of Chartered Accountants of Bangladesh. International accountancy firms are not allowed to work.

FINANCIAL MARKET REGULATORY FRAMEWORK IN BHUTAN

The Financial market is controlled by a division of the RMA, which also controls insurance, banks, pensions, and nonbank financial institutions. The RMA's board members are government selected. The RMA charge fees on financial industry applicants and is self-funded inside the general RMA budget. Staff has lawful protection.

There is a bar on non-Bhutanese rights of Bhutanese companies, involving stockbrokers. International brokers are not permitted to turn into joint venture associates with domestic brokers or to set up domestic subsidiaries.

Dealing is limited to the stock exchange. The RMA and the stock exchange have combined accountability for supervising and implementation.

International companies are not allowed be listed in Bhutan, and are hardly allowed to work in the nation. Immunities involve the joint venture Druk PNB Bank. Companies with a path record of less than 3 years are mandatory to issue at face (book) value. In the nonexistence of a rating process for IPOs (e.g., book-building or auction), shares or companies with better track records seem also to be issued at book value. In either case, the shares go to a considerable post-IPO payment, which prevent listings.

Listing regulations and company law need precise prospectus. Non-compliant companies and their directors can be penalized. Companies are needed to make available semiannual financial reports for investors. Price-responsive information has to be made public within 24 hours of the company officers or directors becoming conscious of the information. There are no terms to defend the privileges of minority shareholders.

The RMA has issued the rules of corporate governance with which companies are estimated to conform, but there is no need to publicize information in their annual statements.

Bhutan has accepted the Indian Accounting Standards but is developing Bhutanese standards, which will match to International Financial Reporting Standards (IFRSs) and IASs. Practitioners are controlled by the Accounting and Auditing Standards Board of Bhutan.

FINANCIAL MARKET REGULATORY FRAMEWORK IN NEPAL

Nepal commenced its primary financial sector changes in the mid-1980s by liberalizing the banking structure to the private area and lined the way for the production of financial establishments since afterwards. Currently, Nepal has a logically expanded financial sector, with the many of the financial institutions approved by the nation's central bank, Nepal Rastra Bank (NRB), improved from 98 in 2000 to 242 in 2009. In financial year (FY) 2009, the banking structure conquered the Nepalese financial structure with assets reaching to 73% of the gross domestic product (GDP). The financial market has developed in latest years accounting for 53.4% of GDP but the local bond market, in comparison, has had no visible development at just 13% of GDP in FY2009, correspondingly.

Nepal's wealth market is yet at an initial stage of growth. The nation has 1 stock exchange, the Nepal Stock Exchange (NEPSE) with 23 member stockbroker. The bond market in Nepal comprises of a government financial market and a corporate financial market. The Securities Board of Nepal (SEBON) was setup in 1993 as a head regulator of financial markets, with accountabilities for the stock exchange and financial market applicants with regard to the Securities Exchange Act of 2006.

Nepal's bond market is small and conquered by government securities. To meet up short term funding needs, the government makes available short-term treasury bills and national savings certificates. The number of treasury bills in the local market has improved from 61% in FY2004 to 70% of outstanding local debt as of mid-April 2010. The government also issues extended sense instruments, the Development Bonds, and are adopted for dealing through NEPSE. Nevertheless, development bonds are hardly ever dealt and the range of the bond is very small to please the claim for dealing of institutional investors. Furthermore, in the existing market situation, fixed deposits with banks give the maximum rate of result than government securities and are thus an evident alternative for the fund's investment officer. Per se, the commercial banks are the major depositor in government securities having roughly 54% of outstanding government securities, which they utilize for maintaining legal liquidity conditions.

The government bond market require extent and deepness as issuance seems to be unpredictable, discouraging the government's trustworthiness as a borrower and not providing the bond market of the quantity of liquid debt tool which needed to build up a sovereign standard yield curve. By itself, there is no dynamic secondary market or standard yield curves, and thus, market rating of corporate bonds is lacking. As in mid-April 2010, corporate bonds composed just 5% of the whole bond market. Only 9 issues have taken place in the preceding 10 years, and were mostly issued on personal placements by banks to meet up tier-2 capital requisites (Basyal, 2001). There are approximately no corporate debentures because of a short of investor confidence, credited to the evasion on 2 earlier debenture issues of 2 major corporate bodies in the late 1980s and 1990s. The absence of corporate governance principles, reduced lucidity in companies' financial reports, and absence of a credit rating structure has made investing in corporate debt uncertain.

The growth of a liquid and profound bond market has significant spill out effects in a financial system. In the instance of Nepal, bond market growth will alleviate the possible maturity disparity of a bank-conquered financial division, decreasing the financial sector weakness and giving much-required long-term capital for infrastructure growth.

FINANCIAL MARKET REGULATORY FRAMEWORK IN PAKISTAN

The controlling structure in a particular nation has to be planned in background of the existing market arrangement, the condition of the financial institutions, the state of financial infrastructure and the general nature of macroeconomic plans. This structure should be wide enough to comprise of rules obligatory both for financial policy as well as reasonable purposes. The requirements of a sufficient controlling arrangement are if it can support confirming financial consistency by decreasing the possibility of bank breakdown and the prices of those that take place. Rules are mainly about transforming the actions of controlled organizations due to unhindered market actions seem to generate publicly most favorable results.

The controller thus has the accountability to take the structure to publicly favorable results. The plan that is pursued by the State Bank of Pakistan is multi-dimensional i.e. to improvise the market arrangement and rivalry, to toughen the domination and risk administration within financial establishments, to make a sufficient financial infrastructure and to give to sound macroeconomic administration through financial and exchange rate strategies. The limited or irregular accomplishment in gaining the most recent goal specifically in the preceding 3 years can be credited to the fault in the fiscal policy (Ministry of Finance, Government of Pakistan, 2007).

The measures that have been used to encourage competition and advance the market arrangement comprise of decreasing entry hurdles, eliminating interest rate upper limit, privatizing government acquired banks, encouraging mergers and consolidation of financial establishments, expanding the economy of capacity for banks, relaxing bank branching strategy and eliminating direct credit rules (Hameed, 2006).

In the area of financial establishments' growth, inspiration structure is so planned that the bank owners set to make considerable losses on the happening of bankruptcy arising from too much risk taking. Capital sufficiency requisites and loan loss conditions complete this task. Restraining bank holdings of extremely risky assets, avoiding the lending to associated parties, needing expansion and ensuring those banks have reasonable credit valuation, evaluation and regulating procedures in position are all motivated by this deliberation (Sbp.org.pk, 2015).

Corporate governance rules and finest practices have been prearranged for the financial institutions by the SBP. Unfavorable choice in bank entry is evaded and the individuals probable to exploit bank do not have bank licenses. Robust and correct criteria and quality stipulations, monetary back-up and previous path records are inspected cautiously for the regulating shareholders, directors of the boards, chief executives and senior management of the banks.

Among the constructive growth in Pakistan's financial arrangement has been the progression of the payment structure from the conventional cash and paper-based methods of payments to a set of connections of more urbane, scientifically driven structures. "Though cash continues to be the dominant mode of settlement of payments especially in rural areas, non-cash modes of payments have increased in volume over time". The banking segment has spent greatly in IT infrastructure in the last ten years that has answered in amplified approval of e-banking as the favored retail payment tool. At the end June 2010, the number of real-time on-line branches comprised of 73% of whole bank branches and 31% of total electronic Dealings. ATM-based dealings are gaining fame and now account for over 50% of electronic dealings. These electronic dealings comprise one third of the total dealings and have grown by 22 percent than paper dealings that grew at a rate of 2 percent only (Akhtar, 2006).

Similarly, the accomplishment of the Real Time Gross Settlement (RTGS) system by the SBP has made easy the automation of great value dealings therefore decreasing the settlement risk. The lawful infrastructure in Pakistan however remains fragile and is a hurdle to financial segment development. Changes and Lawful infrastructure and implementation are thus necessary (Kemal, Bilquees, and Malik 2002).

Finally, is the macroeconomic unevenness in monetary and external financial records spanning over last 3 years that cause system-wide dispute to financial consistency in Pakistan. Great public segment borrowing to fund budgetary shortfall in addition to losses of state-acquired endeavors has added to the liability of the banking structure ("Financial Sector Regulation in Pakistan: The Way Forward", 2011). The complacency of the banks which charge more than market costs for actions such as commodity funding have changed to low danger weighted assets in their range by providing it to the government and therefore showing more capital sufficiency ratios and greater profits could have grave repercussions on financial growth, employment, financial inclusion and price stability in the upcoming years. This is the tender point that has placed the financial consistency mainly at risk.

FINANCIAL MARKET REGULATORY FRAMEWORK IN SRI-LANKA

Sri Lanka has a long-standing but small capital market with 287 listed companies and a total market value of nearly $17 billion at the end of 2012. Sri Lanka has a large number of listed companies for the size of its economy (http://www.ibsl.gov.lk, 2007). Sri Lanka has 287 listed companies and a gross domestic product (GDP) of $59 billion (2010 World Bank) compared to Bangladesh with 229 companies and a GDP of $112 billion, and Pakistan with 573 companies and a GDP of $210 billion (Road Map: Monetary and Financial Sector Policies 2008 and beyond, 2008).

Investors Mutual funds are developing. Currently, seven companies are reported by the Unit Trust Association of Sri Lanka with funds available. They have struggled to attract retail investors and much of the business is tax-avoidance trading by companies. The government pension fund mainly invests in government stock, as do the private provident funds. Insurance companies—there are about 20 life companies—are permitted to invest up to 33% in equities. They mainly invest in the 25 largest companies.

The CSE runs the settlement system, which has a settlement cycle of T+2 but is not Delivery versus Payment. A central counterparty is planned as part of an overall upgrading of information technology. Foreign investors are active participants in the market, representing about 20% of trading. Unregulated margin lending by brokers against stock collateral is widespread—estimates give a total of $6 billion. The SECSL has recently required brokers to set up separate subsidiaries to handle margin lending. The SECSL announced in September 2012 that it was in the final stages of drafting a bill to demutualize.

There are, as yet, no derivatives. The government bond market is significant with an active issuance calendar. Bonds are issued in maturities of up to 10 years. Corporate bonds are much rarer with only some bank issues having a maturity of 5 years. Other The CSE has developed exchange-traded funds (Cbsl.gov.lk, 2007).

The capital market is controlled by the SECSL. This covers markets, brokers, and fund managers. The commissioners are appointed by the Minister of Finance or by virtue of their government position. The SECSL has income bases, but most of its revenues come from government transferals to meet the operating expenses.

Licensed brokers must be incorporated in Sri Lanka. There are no obstructions to foreign ownership and regulator of local broking subsidiaries. A number of brokers are foreign controlled, some by Indian firms.

Trading must be carried out on the CSE. Market abuse must be prohibited. The CSE has forefront monitoring charge and the SECSL has offline responsibility (Athulorala & Rajapatirana). The SECSL is endowed with a power to make settlements in abuse cases. There are plans to permit civil actions.

There are no hindrances, except in banking, to foreign ownership of listed companies. Sri Lankan integrated subsidiaries of foreign companies can be listed. All listed companies, including foreign subsidiaries, must have a minimum public float of 25%.

The CSE listing agreement specifies the requirements for prospectuses and quarterly reporting. The CSE is the regulator of corporate disclosures. Listed companies are also required to immediately notify the stock exchange of price-sensitive information including directors' dealing. Participants consider disclosure standards are quite good and above average for the region. (Cooray, 2015)

Since 2008, it has been a prerequisite that listed companies should conform to the corporate governance rules, which are part of the CSE listing rules. Companies are obligatory to publish their compliances or state the reasons for noncompliance in their annual report. The rules and regulations are based on the United Kingdom (UK) Corporate Governance Code.

Accounting standards are managed by the Sri Lankan Accounting and Auditing Standards Monitoring Board. The standards are moderately compliant with IFRSs. A number of substantial IFRSs will be adopted in 2013. Practitioners are governed by the Institute of Chartered Accountants of Sri Lanka (Edirisuriya, 2007).

During 2010, the Central Bank declared some relaxation of exchange controls. In particular, Sri Lankan individuals and companies now have general permission to acquire, hold, and transfer shares of companies outside Sri Lanka. This is to be accomplished through special outward investment accounts held at commercial banks. Each person has an annual allowance of $100,000 for investment in foreign equities.

The Sri Lankan taxation system is complex, though successful steps have been taken to make things easier. The issue of taxation of foreign companies or foreign-owned investments was not raised as a blockade in any of the fieldwork meetings.

SAARC MARKETS: INTEGRATION APPROACH

The South Asian Association for Regional Cooperation (SAARC) was set up in 1985. It is an economic and political organization of eight countries in Southern Asia. Capital market in this region have diversity in size, level of growth and importance in the national economy. SAARC being a very young regional cooperation project compared with similar arrangements in Africa, Asia or Latin America have long way

Table 1. SAARC members and their structurisation

SAARC Member	Structure	Dismissal of Senior Officials other than for Misconduct	Funding of Regulator	Legal Immunity of Staff
Bangladesh	Single regulator for capital market	No	Mixed, mainly government	No
Bhutan	Combined regulator for financial sector	Yes	Mixed, part of overall regulator	Yes
India	Single regulator for capital market	No	Industry	Yes
Maldives	Single regulator for capital market and pensions	Yes	Mixed, largely government	Yes
Nepal	Single regulator for capital market	No	Industry	Yes
Pakistan	Single regulator for capital market	No	Industry	Yes
Sri Lanka	Single regulator for capital market	No	Mixed, largely government	Yes

to go further for reforms in harmonization of financial regulations in the region. Since the inception of SAARC, regional cooperation has further advanced and extended especially in preferential trade areas but it has yet to contribute its major role in financial integration & harmonization as still there is lot of diversity in the region as shown in the Table 1.

The financial integration is a very challenging task in the region due to hue diversity in terms of geographical orientation, religion, political interference & historical background of the country. It is evident from the fact that, Nepal, Bhutan and Afghanistan are landlocked, whereas Bangladesh, India and Pakistan are located in the border areas and suffer from lack of market integration (Table 2).

The analysis has shown that while there is wide diversity in size and development level of the various SAARC capital markets, there is considerable structural similarity. This suggests that harmonization and integration are feasible and would potentially lead to significant benefits. The experience of integration both within countries and across regions is generally positive (Cowen, 2006). The Indian example is relevant. Until the early 1990s, the Indian capital market was very underdeveloped, similar to the current situation of the other SAARC markets (Atreya, 2005). At that time, there were many local stock markets, which made the capital market fragmented and inefficient from the early 1990s India undertook a transformation of its capital market (mainly but not exclusively its equity market) infrastructure, market structure, and regulation.

CONCLUSION

India has the most sophisticated financial market in the SAARC region with world class regulation and effective compliance. Other SAARC countries not only have a small financial market, they are poorly regulated as well. Harmonization of regulatory standards and uniformity in enforcement of rules and

Table 2. SAARC members and the associated barriers

SAARC Member	Main Barriers to Integration	Main Positive Factors	Readiness
Bangladesh	• Strict exchange control • Weak enforcement of market abuse rules • Poor enforcement of issuer disclosure rules •Lack of independence of regulator	• Regulation improving but many challenges remain • Some quality participants	Medium
Bhutan	• Strict exchange control • Complete barriers to foreign issuers and investors • Potentially nonviable national market • High level of government involvement in economy	Effective regulator	Low
India	• Already a large market • Barriers to foreign listings remain • Complex and rigid tax structure • Fragmented settlement system	• Effective, well-developed regulator • Progress in reducing exchange control • Foreign institutional investor structure permits foreign investors	Medium
Maldives	• Weak disclosure enforcement • Potentially nonviable national Market	Effective regulator	Low
Nepal	• Strict exchange control • Patchy regulatory structure • Potentially nonviable national market • Weak disclosure by listed Companies	Relatively low barriers to inward investment	Low
Pakistan	• Weak enforcement of market abuse rules • Lack of independence of regulator	Some relaxation of exchange control	Medium
Sri Lanka	Weak enforcement of market abuse rules • Obsolete settlement system • Potentially nonviable national Market	• Some relaxation of exchange control • Effective regulator • Disclosure fairly good	Medium

regulations would benefit these countries greatly. With the exception of Afghanistan the financial system in South Asia is dominated by the banking system in terms of assets, or finance of private households and domestic companies; major financial institutions are banks. Although many financial markets in SAARC countries are at developing stages, there exists a greater potential to become a regional financial hub.

REFERENCES

Ahmed, M. N., & Chowdhury, M. I. (2007). *Non-Bank Financial Institutions in Bangladesh: An Analytical Review.* Working Paper Series- WP 0709. Bangladesh Bank.

Akhtar, S. (2006). *Financial Sector of Pakistan – The Roadmap. Speech, Dawn Asia Finance Conference - Asian Banking: A Paradigm Shift*. Karachi, Pakistan: Academic Press.

Ariyarathna, T. W. (1993). Changes in the Banking and the Financial Sector in Sri Lanka Since 1985. *Sri Lanka Economic Journal*, *8*(1), 1–29.

Athukorala, P., & Rajapatirana, S. (2000). Liberalization and Industrial Transformation: Lessons from the Sri Lankan Experience. *Economic Development and Cultural Change*, *48*(3), 543–573. doi:10.1086/452610

Atreya, B. (2015). Financial Sector Regulation in SAARC Countries. In Research Department International Finance Division, Economic Integration in South Asia (pp. 41–49). Kathmandu, Nepal: Nepal Rastra Bank. Retrieved from http://red.nrb.org.np/publications/special_publication/Special_Publications--Economic_Integration_%20in_South_Asia_%282005%29.pdf

Bangladesh Bank (BB). (2008). Article. *Financial Sector Review, 3*(2).

Basyal, T. R. (2001). *Reforming Nepal's Financial System: Rationale and Measures. Nepal Rastra Bank Annual Bulletin*, 7–13.

Basyal, T. R. (2002). *Financial Sector Reform: Need and Strategy*. Arunodaya.

Bekaert, G., Harvey, C., & Lundblad, C. (2001). *Does Financial Liberalization Spur Growth?* NBER Working Paper No. 8245. Cambridge, MA: National Bureau of Economic Research.

Bhole, L. M. (2004). *Financial Institutions and Markets: Structure, Growth and Innovations*. Tata McGraw-Hill Education.

Burton, M., Nesiba, R. F., & Brown, B. (2015). *An Introduction to Financial Markets And Institutions*. Academic Press.

Calvo, G., & Mendoza, E. (2000). Rational Contagion and the Globalization of Securities Markets. *Journal of International Economics, 51*(June), 79–113. doi:10.1016/S0022-1996(99)00038-0

Cbsl.gov.lk. (2007). *Financial System Stability Review*. Retrieved 30 December 2015, from http://www.cbsl.gov.lk/pics_n_docs/latest_news/press_20071206e.doc

Cooray, A. (2015). *The Impact of Deregulation On Financial Market Efficiency In Sri Lanka*. Retrieved 30 December 2015, from https://www.researchgate.net/publication/268328371_

Cowen, D. (2006). *Financial Integration in Asia: Recent Development and Next Steps*. IMF Working Paper No. 169.

Edirisuriya, P. (2007). Effects of Financial Sector Reforms in Sri Lanka: Evidence from the Banking Sector. *Asia Pacific Journal of Finance and Banking Research, 1*(1), 45–64.

Financial Sector Regulation in Pakistan: The Way Forward. (2011). *SBP Research Bulletin, 1*(1), 31-44. Retrieved from http://iba.edu.pk/News/speechesarticles_drishrat/dec2011/Financial_sector_regulation.pdf

Goldsmith, R. W. (1969). *Financial Structure and Development*. New Haven, CT: Yale University Press.

Gurley, J., & Shaw, E. (1955). Financial Aspects of Development and Growth. *The American Economic Review*, (September), 515–538.

Hameed, F. (2006, December). Fostering the corporate bond market in Pakistan. In *IInd SBP International Conference on Fixed Income Market Development in Emerging Market Economies. State Bank of* Pakistan Learning Resource Center.

Har-An, & Maimbo, S. (2003). *The Money Exchange Dealers of Kabul: A study of the Hawala System in Afghanistan*. World Bank Working Paper No. 13.

http://www.ibsl.gov.lk. (2007). *Annual Report 2007: Strengthening. Regulating. Protecting. Colombo*. Retrieved 30 December 2015, from http://www.ibsl.gov.lk/images/annual_reports/IBSL%20Annual%20Report%202007.pdf

Kemal, A. R. (2002). Economy and the Government: Privatisation and Regulation in Pakistan. Islamabad: Pakistan Institute of Development Economics.

Map, R. (2008). *Monetary and Financial Sector Policies 2008 and beyond*. Colombo.

Masuduzzaman, M., Rahman, M. H., & Ahammed, S. (2013). *Integration of Financial Market and its implication of Stock Market Development in Bangladesh: An evaluation*. Working Paper Series- WP 1304. Policy Analysis Unit, Bangladesh Bank.

McKinnon, R. I. (1973). *Money and capital in economic development*. Brookings Institution Press.

Ministry of Finance, Government of Pakistan. (2007). Pakistan Economic Survey 2006-07. Islamabad: Finance Division, Economic Advisor's wing, Ministry of Finance, Government of Pakistan.

Mohan, R. (2007). India's Financial Sector Reforms: Fostering Growth While Containing Risk. BIS Review, 145, 1-24.

Mu, Y. (n.d.). *South Asia Bond Markets South Aisa Bond Markets: Bangladesh*. 10.2139/ssrn.999713

Nseindia.com. (2015). *NSE - National Stock Exchange of India Ltd*. Retrieved 30 December 2015, from http://www.nseindia.com/int_invest/content/regulatory_framework.htm

Obsfeld, M., & Taylor, M. A. (2002). *Globalization and Capital Markets*. National Bureau of Economic Research (Working Paper Number 8846).

Pathak, B. V. (2003). *Indian Financial System*. Pearson Education India.

Reddy, Y. V. (2006). Reforming India's Financial Sector – Changing Dimensions and Emerging Issues. Address at the International Centre for Monetary and Banking Studies. BIS Review, 39, 1-6.

Sbp.org.pk. (2015). *State Bank of Pakistan - Annual Report 2001-2002*. Retrieved 30 December 2015, from http://www.sbp.org.pk/Reports/Annual/arFY02/qtr-index-eng.htm

Shaw, E. S. (1973). *Financial Deepening in Economic Development*. New York: Oxford University Press.

Stiglitz, J. (1993). The Role of the State in Financial Matters. In *Proceedings of the World Bank Annual Conference on Development Economics*. Academic Press.

World Finance. (2016). *Afghanistan Financial Market*. Retrieved 12 January 2015, from http://finance.mapsofworld.com/finance/market/afghanistan.html

Chapter 2
Regulatory Reforms in Indian Financial Market

Amit Kumar Kashyap
Nirma University, India

Urvashi Jaswani
Nirma University, India

Anchit Bhandari
Nirma University, India

ABSTRACT

In India, Financial sector reforms are at the centre stage of the economic liberalization that was initiated in mid 1991. financial institutions and regulatory structures have been developing gradually & in this process SEBI, the capital market regulator & insurance watchdog IRDA has played a very significant role. On the other hand reserve Bank of Indian has built a strong regulatory environment which can be considered as backbone of Indian financial Industry. This chapter has discussed about the regulatory reforms initiated from 1990s till date in the evolution of Indian financial industry & harmonization of Indian laws to make it a investor friendly state for International Investors & safe platform for stock market trading for householders.

INTRODUCTION

Financial market is an important fragment of an economy making it probable for production, occupation and business to grow without any hindrance in relation to resources. Currently most markets around the globe are adjudged by the performance of their monetary markets. The financial markets ensure pointers in place which reveal the activities of businesses whose securities are transacted in those marketplaces. The financial markets, similarly, serve an important purpose in the progress and advancement of a business, which desires to grow. Such businesses with development plans and innovative ventures are in want of capital and the financial market functions as the greatest platform from where a business can regulate the viability of such opportunities (Joesph, 1989).

DOI: 10.4018/978-1-5225-0004-9.ch002

The economic writings recognize that effective and advanced financial markets can lead to improved economic development by promoting the productivity of distribution and use of investments in the economy. Well-functioning financial systems minimize the external funding restraints that obstruct strong and industrial development (Krishnan, 2011).

There is a growing body of empirical analyses, including firm-level studies, industry-level studies, individual country studies, and cross-country comparisons, which prove this strong, positive link between the functioning of the financial system and long-run economic growth. In addition, they better allocate resources, monitor managers and exert corporate control, mobilize savings, and facilitate the exchange of goods and services (Krishnan, 2011).

A capital market is a market for securities (debt or equity), where commercial enterprises (businesses) and governments can increase long-term resources. It is characterized as a marketplace in which currency is delivered for periods stretched than a year as the raising of short-term resources takes place on supplementary marketplaces (e.g., the money market). The capital market comprises of the stock market (equity securities) and the bond market (debt) (Jain & Bhanumurthy, 2005).

The capital market of a nation can be reflected as one of the principal pointer in shaping the development of its economy. *According to Professor Hicks, the industrial Revolution in England was ignited more by the presence of liquid financial market than the technological investment*" (Prasad, Rajan & Subramanian, 2016).

FINANCIAL MARKET IN INDIA

The economic system and setup of any nation at any interval can be measured as the outcome of its own particular historical growth. This growth is occasioned by constant communication among all the contributors prevailing in the system. The growth of Indian financial markets and the monitoring system has correspondingly followed a parallel path. India initiated with the principal bank, Reserve Bank of India (RBI), as the banking zone watchdog, and the Ministry of Finance as the controller for all supplementary financial segments (Singh, 1997).

Currently, maximum financial service sources and their governing agencies are present. The part of controllers has advanced over interval from that of advice for strategic growth in the primary phase to that of a mediator of a comparatively more contemporary and multifaceted financial sector existent. Over this phase, various financial sector improvement actions have been carried out in India, with numerous significant achievements. An imperative feature of these changes has been the endeavor of the specialists to line up the governing framework with global best practices, taking into account the requirements of the nation and internal factors (Gupta 2003). These changes can be broadly categorized as actions taken for:

1. Opening up the whole macroeconomic and governing background surrounded by which financial sector establishments will function.
2. Firming up the institutions and refining their efficacy and effectiveness.
3. Creating and strengthening the governing structure and institutions for supervision of the financial system.

The growth of financial markets ensues in its true nature simply if they are well-integrated; for it is merely then that the pecuniary policy desires are efficiently conveyed to the whole economy (Mohan, 2004). The role of financial markets in the process of a country's economic development needs no emphasis. At the same time, as the recent crisis has shown, financial markets can be the epicenter of crises that derail the growth process itself and unleash great misery (Thomas, 2006).

Thus, in countries like India, where financial markets are yet to achieve the size and sophistication as those of the more developed countries, perhaps there is merit in adopting a cautious approach to financial development (Khan, 2013). Financial market integration is witnessing a new wave of confidence in recent years; besides individual nations, some economic regions (such as the Arab countries) are also actively discussing the possibility of having integrated financial markets (Atyeh, 2012).

Financial markets and financial institutions are two important components of a financial system. A financial system's efficiency is reflected in the efficiency of both financial markets and financial institutions. Several steps have been undertaken to improve the efficiency of financial institutions and market. In case of financial markets, repealing of the Capital Issues (Control) Act, 1947, free pricing, rationalization of the process of price discovery in the form of book building and auctions, enhancing transparency through strict disclosure norms, improved trading and settlement practices, enlarging the number of participants, introduction of a transparent takeover code, encouraging the growth of firms both at home and abroad, rationalized tax structures, encouraging good market practices, introduction of real time gross settlement (RTGS) and other electronic payment mechanisms are some of the measures which have helped in improving information efficiency and bringing down transaction costs.

The money market, capital market and the foreign exchange market remained segmented till the early 1990s due to high level of regulation and restrictions. An integration of markets is necessary for effective transmission and implementation of policies and for facilitating better functioning of markets (Bhoi and Dhal, 1998). To enable integration, interest rates were freed, foreign capital flows and foreign participants were allowed entry, domestic companies were permitted to raise funds from outside, and participants were allowed to operate in different markets simultaneously (Ayuso and Blanco, 1999). Besides introduction of new products such as repos and derivatives and improvements in technology and payment and settlement infrastructure have facilitated integration of the domestic financial markets within themselves and with the foreign exchange market is reflected in trends in turnover and prices of securities in financial markets.

Besides this, an analysis of the transmission of volatility in one market to other markets also helps in knowing the extent of integration of financial markets. The linkage between the call money market and foreign exchange market is found during times of volatility in foreign market as commercial banks have a dominant presence in both the markets. An increase in foreign investment flows increases cross-border financial integration. The domestic integration of various segments of financial markets has been facilitated by the expansion of the online operations of two major stock exchanges- the BSE and NSE. The regional stock exchanges have been integrated with the Interconnected Stock Exchange of India Ltd. (ISE). In addition, many regional stock exchanges have become members of both the BSE and the NSE.

Subsequently, after the Indian economy started opening and the controls started to be undone or relieved, the securities market places observed a burst of IPOs that were propelled. This occasioned in several new businesses across various business segments to originate with innovative goods and services.

A notable point of the development of the Indian economy in current years has been due to working of Indian Financial Market. Financial Market engage in recreation by its securities markets in assisting and fuelling that growth with money rose within the economy. This was in marked disparity to the early stage of development in several of the fast developing economies of East Asia that observed massive measures of FDI (Foreign Direct Investment) stimulating progress in their early days of market deregulation. All through this time in India much of the structured segment has been affected by greater development as the financial markets played an wide-ranging role in supporting financial reserve utilization. Many PSUs (Public Sector Undertakings) that decided to discharge share of their equity were also assisted by the efficient securities market in India.

The introduction of the NSE (National Stock Exchange) and the OTCEI (Over the Counter Exchange of India) in the course of the mid-1990s by the GoI was intended to guide in a relaxed and more translucent form of dealing in securities. The NSE was considered as the market for dealing in the securities of businesses from the huge scale segment and the OTCEI for those from the moderate sector. Though the NSE has not just performed well to develop and progress into the practical support of capital markets in India the OTCEI fight back and is thus far to show any mark of development and improvement. The assimilation of IT into the capital market arrangement has been predominantly even in India owing to the nation's world class IT industry. This has pressed the operating efficacy of the Indian stock market to international criteria and as an outcome the nation has been competent to exploit on its better development and draw foreign funds like never before (Chakrabarti & Shankar, 2007).

The governing power for capital markets in India is the SEBI (Securities and Exchange Board of India). SEBI emanated into fame in the 1990s when the capital markets undergone some commotion. It had to proceed with severe actions to plug various gaps that were abused by some market powers to gain their assigned interests. After this early stage of tussle SEBI has developed in power as the controller of India's capital markets and as one of the nation's most significant organizations (Chakrabarti & Shankar, 2007).

REFORMS IN MONEY MARKET

The money market, the market for short-term funds has securities with maturities ranging from overnight to one year; therefore, its financial instruments are considered the closest substitute for money (Wikipedia, 2016). In order to achieve the ultimate goals of monetary policy growth and price stability the RBI had to modify its operational and intermediate objectives multiple times, primarily in response to the prevailing economic and financial environment (Mohanty, 2012).

The money market is divided into the formal and informal segments. One of the greatest achievements of the Indian Financial system over the last 50 years has been the decline in the relative importance of the informal segment and increasing presence of the informal segment upto the mid-1980s, money market was characterized by lack of depth, small number of instruments; and strict regulation on the interest rates. The money market consisted of the inter-bank call market, treasury bills, commercial bills and participation certificates.

Several steps were taken in the 1980s and 1990s to reform and develop the money market. The reforms in the money market were initiated in the latter half of the 1980s.

In the 1980s- A committee to review the working of the monetary system under the chairmanship of the Sukhamoy Chakravorty was set up in 1985. It underlined the need to develop money market instruments. As a follow up, the Reserve Bank set up a working group on the money market under the chairmanship of N Vagul which submitted its report in 1987. This committee laid the blueprint for the institution of a money market. Based on its recommendations, the Reserve Bank initiated a number of measures (Ray and Prabhu, 2013).

The discount and Finance House of India was set up as a money market institution jointly by the Reserve Bank, Public sector banks and financial institutions in 1988 to impart liquidity to money market instruments and help the development of a secondary market in such instruments. Money market instruments such as the 182-day Treasury bill, Certificate of Deposits and the inter-bank participation certificate were introduced in 1988-89. Commercial paper was introduced in January 1990. To enable price discovery, the interest rate ceiling on call money was freed in stages from October 1988 (Jain & Bhanumurthy, 2005). As a first step, operations of the DFHI in the call/notice money market were freed from the interest rate ceiling in 1988; interest rate ceiling on inter-bank term money (10.5% to 11.5%), rediscounting of commercial bills (12.5%), and inter-bank participation without risk (12.5%) were withdrawn effective May 1989. All the money market interest rates are, by and large, determined by market forces. There has been a gradual shift from a regime of administered interest rates to market based interest rates.

In the 1990s The government set up a high-level committee in August 1991 under the chairmanship of M Narsimham (the Narsimham Committee) to examine all aspects relating to structure, organization, functions and procedures of the financial system. The committee made several recommendations for the development of the money market. The Reserve Bank accepted many of its recommendations.

The Securities Trading Corporation of India was set up in June 1994 to provide an active secondary market in government dated securities and public sector bonds. Barriers to entry were gradually eased by-

1. Setting up the primary dealer system in 1995 and satellite dealer system in 1999 to inject liquidity in the market.
2. Relaxing issuance restrictions and subscription norms in respect of money market instruments.
3. Allowing the determination of yields based on the demand and supply of such paper.
4. Enabling market evaluation of associated risks by withdrawing regulatory restriction such as bank guarantees in respect of commercial papers.
5. Increasing the number of participants by allowing the entry of foreign institutional investors, non-bank financial institutions and mutual funds.

Several financial innovations in instruments and methods were introduced. Treasury Bills of varying maturities and RBI repos were introduced. Auctioned treasury bills were introduced leading to market-determined interest rates.

The development of a market for short term funds at market determined rates has been fostered by gradual switch from cash-credit system to a loan based system, shifting the onus of cash management from banks to borrowers. Ad-hoc and on-tap 91-day Treasury bills were discontinued. They were replaced by Ways and Means Advances (WMA) linked to the bank rate. The introduction of WMA led to the limiting of the almost automatic funding of the government (Rangarajan, 1998).

Indirect monetary control instruments such as the bank rate- reactivated in April 1997, strategy of combining auctions, private placements and open market operations- in 1998-99, and the Liquidity Adjustment Facility- in June 2000 were introduced. The minimum lock-in period for money market instruments was brought down to 7 days. The Reserve Bank started repos both on auction and fixed interest rate basis for liquidity management. Since June 5, 2000 the newly introduced liquidity adjustment facility has been effectively used to influence short-term rates by modulating day-to-day liquidity conditions.

The inter-bank liabilities were exempted from the cash reserve ratio and the statutory liquidity ratio stipulation for facilitating the development of a term money market. New money market derivatives such as certificate of deposits and commercial paper are freely accessible to non-bank participants. The payment system infrastructure was strengthened with the introduction of the negotiated dealing system (NDS) in February 2002, setting up of the Clearing corporation of India Limited in April 2002 and the implementation of real time gross settlement (RTGS) system from April 2004. Collateral Borrowing and Lending Obligation (CBLO) was operationalized as a money market instrument through the CCIL on January 20, 2003 (Saha, 2012).

The development and profile of the money market has changed in the nineties. A basic objective of the money market reforms in the recent years has been to facilitate the introduction of new instruments and their appropriate pricing. The Reserve bank endeavored to develop market segments which exclusively deal in specific assets and liabilities as well as participants. Accordingly the call or notice money market is now a pure inter-bank market. In order to ensure systematic stability, prudential limits on exposures to the call money market have been imposed. Standing liquidity support to banks from the Reserve Bank and facilities for exceptional liquidity support have been rationalized. The various segments of money market have integrated with the introduction and successful implementation of LAF. The RDS and CCIL have improved the functioning of money markets.

Research writings on the combination of Indian money markets with worldwide markets as an outcome of economic liberalization have generally informed adverse results. This shows the existence of a country risk premium, and/or obligatory rules on capital engagements, and/or compulsory constraints on interbank borrowing and lending (Buigut, 2011). The Indian currency markets have developed up to this point steadily. A prior study by means of CDs as the internal borrowing rate and the USD LIBOR as the foreign interest rate concluded that the covered interest parity (CIP) deviations for India were much higher than those reported for the markets belonging to the Organization for Economic Co-operation and Development (OECD) (Varma, 1997).

REFORMS IN CAPITAL MARKET

The history of Capital Market in India dates back to the eighteenth century when the East India company securities were traded in the country. Until the end of the nineteenth century, securities trading were unorganized and the main trading centers were Bombay and Calcutta. Of the two, Bombay was the chief trading centre wherein bank shares were the major trading stock. During the American Civil War (1860-61), Bombay was an important source of supply for cotton. Hence, trading activities flourished during the period, resulting in a boom in share prices. This boom, the first in the history of the Indian capital market, lasted for nearly half a decade. The bubble burst on July 1, 1865, when there was a tremendous slump in share prices.

Trading was at that time limited to a dozen brokers; their trading place was under a baniyan tree in front of the Town Hall in Bombay. These stock brokers organized an informal association in 1875- the Native Shares and Stock Brokers association, Bombay. The stock exchanges in Calcutta and Ahmedabad, also industrial and trading centers, materialized later. The Bombay Stock exchange was recognized in May 1927 under the Bombay Securities Contracts Control Act, 1925.

The capital market was not well-organized and developed during the British rule because the British government was not interested in the economic growth of the country. As a result, many foreign companies depended on the London capital market for funds rather than on the Indian capital market.

In the post-independence era also, the size of the capital market remained small. During the first and second five year plans, the government's emphasis was on the development of the agriculture sector and public sector undertakings. Public sector undertakings were healthier than private undertakings in terms of paid up capital but their shares were not listed on the Stock exchanges. Moreover, the controller of capital issues closely supervised and controlled the timing, composition, interest rates, pricing, allotment and floatation costs of new issues. These strict regulations demotivated many companies from going public for four and a half decades (Kaminshy and Schmukler, 2002).

In 1950s Century Textiles, Tata steel, Bombay Dyeing, National Rayon and Kohinoor mills were the favorite scrip of speculators. As speculation became rampant, the stock market came to be known as the *satta* bazaar. Despite speculation, non-payment or defaults were not frequent. The government enacted the Securities Contracts (Regulation) Act, 1956 to regulate stock markets. The Companies Act was also enacted. The decade of the 1950s was also characterized by the establishment of a network for the development of financial institutions and state financial corporations (Shah & Patnaik, 2011).

The 1960s was characterized by wars and droughts in the country which led to trends. These trends were aggravated by the ban in 1969 on forward trading and *badla*, technically called 'contracts for clearing'. *Badla* provided a mechanism for carrying forward positions as well as for borrowing funds. Financial institutions such as LIC and GIC helped revive the sentiment by emerging as the most important group of investors. The first Mutual fund of India, Unit Trust of India came into existence in 1964.

In 1970s, *badla* trading was resumed under the guise of 'hand-delivery contracts' a group. This revived the market. However, the capital market received another severe setback in 1974, when the government promulgated the Dividend Restriction Ordinance, restricting the payment of dividend by companies to 12 percent of the face value or one-third of the profits of the companies that can be distributed as computed under Section 369 of the Companies Act, 1956, whichever was lower. This led to a sharp in market capitalization at the BSE by about 20% overnight and the stock market did not open for nearly a fortnight.

Later came buoyancy in the stock markets when the multinational companies were forced to dilute their majority stocks in their Indian ventures in favor of the Indian pubic under FERA in 1973. Several MNCs opted out of India. One hundred and twenty three MNCs offered shares worth Rs. 150 Crore, creating 1.8 million shareholders within four years. The offer prices of FERA shares were lower than their intrinsic worth. Hence, for the first time, FERA dilution created an equity cult in India. It was the spate of FERA issues that gave a real filling to the Indian stock market. For the first time, many investors got an opportunity to invest in the stocks of such MNCs as Colgate and Hindustan Liver Limited. Then in 1977 a little known entrepreneur, Dhiruhai Ambani, tapped the capital market. The scrip, Reliance Textiles, is still a hot favorite and dominates trading at all stock exchanges.

The 1980s witnessed an explosive growth of the securities market in India, with millions if investors suddenly discovering lucrative opportunities. Many investors jumped into the stock market for the first time. The government's liberalization process initiated during the mid-1980s, spurred this growth. Participation by small investors, speculation, defaults, ban on *badla* and resumption of *badla* continued. Convertible debentures emerged as a popular instrument of resource mobilization in the primary market. The introduction of public sector bonds and the successful mega issues of Reliance Petrochemicals and Larsen & Turbo gave a new lease of life to the primary market. This, in turn, enlarged volumes in the secondary market. The decade of 1980s was characterized by an increase in the number of stock exchanges, listed companies, paid up capital and market capitalization (Gupta, 1998).

The 1990s will go down as the most important decade in the history of capital market of India. Liberalization and Globalization were the new terms coined and marketed during this decade. The Capital Issues (Control) Act, 1947 was repealed in May 1992. The decade was characterized by new players such as private sector mutual funds and private sector banks, and primary market boom and bust.

Major capital market scams in the history of the capital market. These shook the capital market and drove away small investors from the market. The securities scam of March 1992 involving brokers as well as bankers was one of the biggest scams in the history of the capital market. In the subsequent years owing to free pricing, many unscrupulous promoters, who raised money from the capital market, proved to be fly-by-night operators. This led to erosion in the investors' confidence. The M S Shoes case, one such scam which took place in March 1995, put a break on new issue activity (Khan, 1998).

The 1991-92 securities scam revealed the inadequacies in the financial system. It was the scam which prompted a reform of the equity market. The Indian stock market witnessed a sea change in terms of technology and market prices. Technology brought radical changes in the trading mechanism. The Bombay stock exchange was subject to nationwide competition by two new stock exchanges- National Stock Exchange, set up in 1994 and the Over the Counter Exchange of India, set up in 1992 (Kohli, 2001). The national stock clearing corporation (NSCC) and the National Depositories Limited (NSDL) were set up in April 1995 and November 1996 respectively for improved clearing and settlement and dematerialized trading. The Securities Contract (Regulation) Act, 1956 was amended in 1995-96 for the introduction of options trading. Moreover, rolling settlement was introduced in January 1998 for the dematerialized segment of all companies. With automation and geographical spread stock market participation increased (Kohli, 2001).

In late 1990s, Information Technology scrimps dominated the Indian market. These scrimp included Infosys, Wipro and Satyam. They were a part of the favorite scrimp of the period also known as new economy scrimps, along with telecommunication and media scrimps. The new economy companies were knowledge intensive unlike the old economy companies that were asset intensive.

The Indian Capital market catered the twenty first century with the Ketan Parekh scam. As a result of this scam, *badla* was discontinued from July 2001 and rolling settlement was introduced in all scrimps Trading of futures commenced from June 2000, and Internet trading was permitted in February 2000 (Sharma & Sharma, 2008). On July 2, 2001, the Unit Trust of India announced suspension of sale and repurchase of its flagship US-64 scheme due to heavy redemption leading to a panic on the bourses. The government's decision to privatize oil PSUs in 2003 fueled stock prices. One big divestment of international telephony major VSNL took place in early February 2002. Foreign institutional investors have emerged as major players on the Indian bourses. NSE has an upper hand over its rival BSE in terms of volumes not only in the equity markets but also in the derivatives market (Pethe & Karnik, 2000).

It has been a long journey for the Indian Capital Market. New capital market is organized, fairly integrated, mature, more global and modernized. The Indian equity market is one of the best in the world in terms of technology. Advances in computer and communication technology, coming together on internet and shattering geographic boundaries and enlarging the investor class. Internet trading has become a global phenomenon. Indian stock markets are now getting integrated with global markets.

Mr. L C Gupta has summarized the reforms as- "The great expansion of institutional financing facilities is indeed the most outstanding post-independence development in the sphere of industrial finance. A broad based and diversified institutional structure has gradually been built up for this purpose. Whereas before independence, intermediary financial institutions were hardly of any significance in the raising of long-term industrial finance, the position today is quite different with a variety of institutions providing substantial amounts by way of medium and long-term loans, playing a leading part in the underwriting of new issues, guaranteeing credit from other sources and also forming an influential class of buyers on the stock market. Also the whole financial system has come under the increasing control of public authorities, partly through extension of governmental and semi-governmental financial institutions and partly through more stringent regulations of private financial institutions"(Gupta, 1969).

It is to be taken into account that though several remarkable changes have been made, in this path, the capital market does not equate much satisfactorily with that of the technologically advanced nations. More concentrated efforts and activities are needed from the side of the government, stakeholders and industrialists, for a concrete foundation in the framework of the capital market.

REGULATORY REFORMS IN BANKING SECTOR

The technology that made industrial revolution in England possible was in existence for a long time before it was commercially exploited; it had to wait till the financial sector developed well enough to make the necessary resources available - John Hicks, A Theory of Economic History (1969)

Face of Global market has evolved and has undergone a significant transition. Banking is now considered to be a global issue and has a direct or indirect relation and connection with almost all the sectors which affects and covers the areas like insurance, taxation and finance. These sectors or catalyst play a very important role in strengthening the fundamentals of the Indian economy (The Indian Capital Market: Growth & Governance, 2010). Also there exists a direct relation between the topic and the reforms in banking sector. This can be said as the most primary objective of the financial sector will also include an efficient and effective banking sector.

The broader framework of reforms in banking sector can be elucidated as: modifying the old banking policy, creating and strengthening the new institutional framework, improve the faith, trust and credibility of the banks in India so that financial soundness in the economy could be maintained. At the beginning of the reform process, the banking system probably had a negative net worth when all financial assets and liabilities were restated at fair market values (Varma, 1992).

As far as reforms in banking sector are concerned; there are significant reforms which have taken place as compared to situation, what was prevalent prior to 1991. Prior to 1991, there was no such scope for any of the major sectors of the economy. Till this time, the Indian banking sector was characterized by low productivity of PSU banks, high and administered interest rate and reserve requirements, stringent regulations by RBI etc. But in the era of post-1991, Globalisation has played a vast and a multifaceted role in functioning and structuring the Indian economy.

Also deregulation has opened up new opportunities in the banking sector so as to increase the revenue by different modes of investment banking, issuance if credit card facilities, many facilities and benefits in the interest rate for a particular sector of the society, i.e., Senior citizens and children, depositary services, securitization etc. Since Globalisation opens and widens the ambit of credit flexibility and transferability throughout the world, these aspects have largely improved the situation. The most significant achievement of the financial sector reforms has been marked the marked improvement in the financial health of commercial banks in India in terms of capital adequacy, profitability and asset management quality, giving equal attention to the risk management (Vyas & Zaveri, 2016).

However, with advantages came the disadvantages in which the concept of liberalization brought with itself great competition among the banks, both domestic and international (Figure 1).

As far as the Indian economy is concerned, it has always been bank based where regular reforms had been brought out. "The assets of the banking sector have expanded nearly 11 times from '7.5 trillion at end-March 1998 to '83 trillion at end-March 2012. The non-food credit has expanded by more than 14 times from '3.1 trillion 1998 to '45.30 trillion during the same period. The credit to GDP ratio which stood at about five per cent in 1950-51 improved to about 25 per cent in 2000-01 and further to about 52 per cent at the end of 2011-12." (Khan, 2013)

To look into the effective functioning and to suggest reformative measures, one Narasimham Committee, was set up. One of the recommendations of Narasimham Committee was to bring a Uniform Prudential Norms and standards, broadly along the lines of the recommendations of Basle Committee I, on supervision of banking norms.

Few of the recommendations and till now the actions taken by the authorities are as follows (Table 1) (Singh, 1997):

The aim of Narasimham Committee (1991) was to bring about "operational flexibility" and "functional autonomy" to enhance efficiency, productivity and profitability of banks. Few of its other recommendations were:

- The private sector banks must be treated equally with the public banks and government should not hesitate to declare it a nationalized bank, if they are very efficient for the economy.
- The government of India should strengthen the prudential norms for the commercial banks.
- The interest rate must be deregulated as per the market conditions and must not be stringent for long. A mechanism of single lending rate was introduced known as 'Prime Lending Rate' over a period of five years. The aim was to devise multiple options and flexibility to their banks for asset liability management operations and shift towards indirect monetary control (Kohli, 2005).
- Licensing policy should be abolished and new foreign banks must be given a free entry.
- Each public sector bank should be setup atleast one rural bank as its subsidiary.

Figure 1. Bank credit as a percentage of GDP

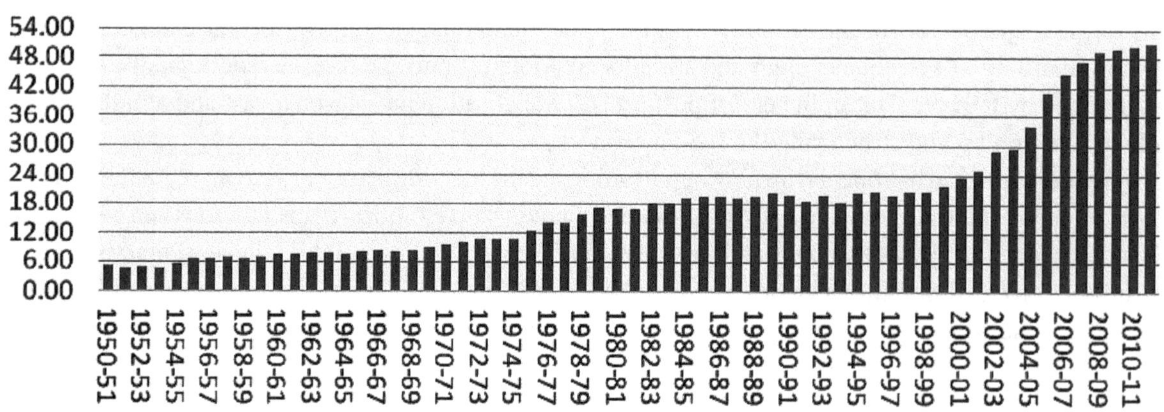

Table 1. Recommendations and action taken

Recommendation	Action Taken
Measures to strengthen the banking system: Capital Adequacy:	
3. *The Committee suggested that pending the emergence of markets in India where market risks can be covered, it would be desirable that capital adequacy requirements take into account market risks in addition to the credit risks.*	Banks are now required to assign capital for market risk. A risk weight of 2.5% for market risk has been introduced on investments in Govt. and other approved securities with effect from the year ending 31st March, 2000. For investments in securities outside SLR, a risk weight of 2.5% for market risk has been introduced with effect from the year ending 31st March, 2001.
4. *In the next three years, the entire portfolio of Government securities should be marked to market and this schedule of adjustment should be announced at the earliest. It would be appropriate that there should be a 5% weight for market risk for Govt. and approved securities.*	The percentage of banks' portfolio of Govt. and approved securities which is required to be marked to market has progressively been increased. For the year ending 31st March, 2000, banks were required to mark to market 75% of their investments. In order to align the Indian accounting standards with the international best practices and taking into consideration the evolving international developments, the norms for classification and valuation of investments have been modified with effect from September 30, 2000. The entire investment portfolio of banks is required to be classified under three categories, viz., Held to Maturity, Available for Sale and Held for Trading. While the securities 'Held for Trading' and 'Available for Sale' should be marked to market periodically, the securities 'Held to Maturity', which should not exceed 25% of total investments are carried at acquisition cost unless it is more than the face value, in which case, the premium should be amortised over a period of time.

These reforms were so significant that till today, most of the Indian banks are maintaining the capital adequacy ratio. However, the substantial contribution of the government and the amount from the internal reserves cannot be forgotten (Ahluwalia, 2000). And because of the reason to bring this reform, new investors were attracted, but the most important reason was that because the capital adequacy ratio was to be maintained, all the balance sheet and profit and loss account was to be kept up to dated, which in a way gave an insight as to maintain the asset quality and quantity, as required.

However, after the financial collapse of East Asia, the expectation of working from a financial institution around the world increased and so as a result, in the year 1997, the government, to meet the demands being a developing country, appointed a committee known as 'Committee on Banking Sector Reforms' to review the progress of the changes brought in the banking reforms and have thus submitted a second report, thus further suggesting the changes which could be brought and outlined the same.

"In order to initiate a second stage scrutiny of the Financial Reforms, a committee on banking Sector Reforms was again set up under the chairmanship of M. Narasimham in 1998. The major change brought was that the central bank's should not be just restricted to monetary control but must also be given the authority to regulate. Also, the committee favored the merger of strong public banks and closure of weaker banks whose rehabilitation was not at all possible."

PRUDENTIAL STANDARDS TO MEET THE INTERNATIONAL STANDARDS

Indian banks have proved to be robust time and again to prove its international standards and most importantly, to maintain it. It is quite evident from the global financial crises, where every financial institution in major countries found difficulty to maintain it. However, Indian banking sector have proved to be resilient. These regulations consists of literature broadly consists of capital adequacy norms and restrictions on banking activities (Sen and Vaidya, 1997).

REGULATORY FRAMEWORK IN FOREIGN EXCHANGE IN INDIA

India is now a well-integrated nation which is always moving in tandem with all the global developments which includes both economic and financial front. From the time of 1990s, with the advent of liberalization, it has opened gates and had huge impact on the financial sector of India. And one of the factors which form part of Indian Financial Sector is the foreign Exchange. The large inflows and outflows of the foreign exchange including the financial investment leads to increase in the substantial amount in the economy.

During the era of pre 1991, there was huge barrier on the companies where they were not allowed to maintain co-operative relations with the foreign nations. But after the advent of 1991 LPG policy, the whole scenario in the nation changed, where the economic prosperity grew on a very fast pace. As soon as the trade barriers were dismantled, the companies started to approach and make investment in the foreign countries and made direct investments there. This lead to establishment of organizations, which are even leading the global market in different industries. Since inflow and outflows of currencies are continuous with regards to different countries, the individuals have come to know and understand about the usage of different currencies as compared to the usage of Indian rupee.

"In India, there has been an increasing awareness for the need to introduce financial derivatives in order to enable hedging against market risks in a cost effective way. A dynamic foreign exchange market provides businesses with a spectrum of hedging products for effectively managing their foreign exchange risk exposures." (Srivastava, 2013)

The most important reform which took place in this sector is shifting to a market development with built in prudential norms and safeguards so that the market won't stabilize in this process (Krishnan, 2011).

The desire to accumulate Foreign Exchange Reserve has many reasons with it. In today's time, it is more for a precautionary purpose (Singh, 2005), as large Foreign Exchange can be a source of flexibility and protection from crises as well to maintain the stability in the economy.

The most important development in Foreign Exchange was the shift to a market based development where exchange program took place and where the current account convertibility (Overview of Fuller Capital Account Convertibility and the Committee's Approach, 2011), concept arose. With the government having its control over the economy, after 1991, because of the LPG policy, new players came into the market in which foreign players too played an important role. Few other reforms were that banks were allowed greater autonomy in their foreign exchange program.

An unparalleled and unimagined rise in the Foreign Exchange Reserves in India, and its different ways to utilize it, particularly the finance infrastructure is often debated. It is quite presumed that as India's infrastructure will grow, it will hold a strong GDP. Infrastructure includes transportation and communication which in India is facing a huge fiscal problem. The reason noted for this is that there is no structure or policy laid down for tariff structures and also no sort of subsidies could be gathered out of it. Also, as a domestic player, we are not able to anticipate the capacity of foreign/ private participants as to what all policies and regulations, they are coming with, which in a way will solve not only social obligations but will also fulfill societal expectations and meet the standards.

The basic setback for India is that it lacks proper labor laws, further, There are about 40-50 Central Acts directly relating to Labor laws and in some ways there are indirect connection to those. So many laws had led to so many inconsistencies. And has no proper infrastructure for dispute resolution. In a study it was shown, 23 million or more cases are pending in Courts in contrast to number of judges to 10 million or even less. In OECD countries, they have around 70-80 judges per million. The cases keep on piling up and get backlogged steadily. In the recent years, the exchange traded currency future market has been introduced which lays down the limited transaction between Indian rupee and US dollar with a ban of Non-Resident Indians, including FIIs. However, the liquidity has grown with a steady pace in India. Also the companies, in order to indulge themselves in the big market, they started to enter into an agreement with the bank, which have been the Authorized dealers in this market. For many years, India has been using cautious approach on 'Capital Account Convertibility.'

THE WAY FORWARD

India has been putting great efforts in maintain the capital account liberalization, but to reach at an optimum level, a more liberalized capital account would be needed along with different types of instruments so as to maintain a balanced situation so as to reduce volatility. Also huge influx of foreign exchange in the economy of India will in a way give an international standard to Indian Rupee, which is a good sign for our economy. To bring this idea into effect, it will be the responsibility of central as well as subsidiary banks to popularize the benefits of rupee in front of global investors, if they want to have an unending rupee based assets.

Further, in the cases of currency future markets in India, since at times they donot have a mandate requirement for instant delivery, there is no regulatory relation between OTC and exchange traded segments of the currency futures market. It is generally presumed that exchange traded currency futures, rather than being used by real sector are mostly driven by speculative interest (Mahalingam, 2015).

Moving forward, development of forex management and exchange would include more instruments, participation of more market players which had with it the risk management systems. Also there is a need to increase the liquidity for long run to maintain the assets of the concerned company and also, on a larger picture, for the economy to give a reputed picture abroad. Since this is an ongoing process as the forex exchange buildup cannot stop at any level, it will need small improvements to maintain and build up a big image. However, there will be a macroeconomic environment needed in the economy for the development of not just forex exchange sector but also for the development of other market infrastructure in the financial market, which includes equity, money and securities market, all together in just one.

CONCLUSION

The Indian methodology to growth of financial markets has concentrated on steady, phased, and regulated introduction of the internal monetary and external sectors, keeping in view the changes in other segments of the economy. This stays to be the entire stand on changes, even when there was worldwide crisis; however rules for the financial sector appear to be a slightly more vigilant. However, agreed that a much of the purpose of financial sector changes in India has comprised of allowing previously barred financial markets, firming up regulation, working on regulatory breaches, and firming up of regulatory synchronization, contemporary global advances in no manner have weakened this plan.

Midst the accurate instructions that can be taken from the emergency are:

1. Novelty in financial markets must not be suppressed. Nonetheless, it must be warranted that the complications of new goods are understood, specifically if they are transacted off exchanges, as OTC products. When extensively disseminated and weakly implicit, such goods are hazardous to systemic firmness.
2. Excessive risk abhorrence on side of controllers can hinder progress and improvement.
3. There is no flawless supervisory structure, but established strategy must be in harmony with marketplaces and necessities (Krishnan, 2009).

Inclusion, development, and steadiness are the three aims of any transformation procedure, and these goals are conflicting. With the accurate changes, the financial sector can be a massive cause of job formation both openly as well as secondarily, through the initiative and consumption it can help with sponsoring. Without changes, though, the financial sector might convert into a collective cause of risk, as the disparities between the ability and requirements of the actual economy and the competences of the monetary sector broaden. India has been a case study of how financial sector changes can play an ancillary character in the development of an emergent market economy. The test is how to bootstrap from these past achievements to heighten to the succeeding level of financial sector growth, so that it can endure to upkeep the development that India faces while going forward. As Joan Robinson remarked, economic growth creates demand for financial instruments, and, where enterprise leads, finance follows (Robinson, 1952

REFERENCES

Ahluwalia, M. S. (1999). Reforming India's Financial Sector: An Overview. *India: A financial sector for the twenty-first century*, 29-54.

Allen, F., Chakrabarti, R., & Shanker, D. (2007). *India's Financial System*. Available at: http://fic.wharton.upenn.edu/fic/papers/07/0736.pdf

Aruna Kumar, D. (n.d.). *An Overview of Indian Financial System*. Available at: http://ww.indianmba.com/Faculty_Column/FC177/fc177.html

Atyeh, M. H. (2012). The Theoretical Considerations of Financial Markets Integration: The case of Arab countries. *Journal of Economics and Sustainable Development*.

Ayuso, J., & Blanco, R. (1999). *Has financial market integration increased during the nineties?* Research Department, Banco de Espana.

Bhoi, B. K., & Dhal, S. C. (1998). Integration of Financial Markets in India: An empirical evaluation. *RBI Occasional Papers, 19*(4), 345–380.

Bhoi, B. K., & Dhal, S. C. (1998). Integration of Financial Markets in India: An empirical evaluation. *RBI Occasional Papers, 19*(4), 345–380.

Buigut, S., & Rao, V. K. (2011). International Financial Integration of the Indian Money Markets. *International Journal of Economics and Finance, 3*(4). doi:10.5539/ijef.v3n4p170

Committee on Financial Sector Assessment. (2009). *India's Financial Sector - An Assessment*. Mumbai: RBI and GoI Database on Indian Economy. Available at: http://www.rbi.org.in

Gopinath, S. (2008). Financial Markets in India: Recent Developments and Challenges. Cairo: RBI and FIMMDA-PDAI. Available at http://rbidocs.rbi.org.in/rdocs/Speeches/PDFs/85236.pdf

Gupta, L. C. (1969). *The changing structure of Industrial Finance in India*. Oxford University Press.

Gupta, L. C. (1998). What Ails the Indian Capital Market? *Economic and Political Weekly, 23*(29-30).

Gupta, S. C. (2003). Banking Industry Vision 2010. *Risk Management, 23*, 25.

Jain, S., & Bhanumurthy, N. R. (2005). Financial Markets Integration in India. Asia-Pacific Development Journal, 10(2).

Joseph, E. (1989). Financial Markets and Development. *Oxford Review of Economic Policy, 5*(4).

Kaminsky, G., & Schmukler, S. (2002). *Short and Long-Run Integration: Do capital controls matter*. Publication at World Bank Discussion.

Khan, H. (2013). *Indian Financial Markets: Fuelling the Growth of the Indian Economy*. Speech, inaugural session of the conference on Indian Financial Markets: Fuelling the Growth of the Indian Economy organized by the Confederation of Indian Industry at the ADB Annual Conference, Delhi, India.

Khan, M. Y. (1997). *Financial Services*. New Delhi: Tata Mc-Graw Hill.

Kohli, R. (2001). *Capital Flows and their Macroeconomic effects in India*. Indian Council for Research on International Economic Relations. Available at http://www.icrier.org/pdf/renu64.pdf

Kohli, R. (2001). *Capital Flows and their Macroeconomic effects in India*. Indian Council for Research on International Economic.

Krishnan, K. P. (2011). *Financial Development in Emerging Markets: The Indian Experience*. ADBI Working Paper 276. Tokyo: Asian Development Bank Institute.

Kuchhal, S C. (n.d.). *Industrial Economy of India* (18th ed.). Chaitanya Publications.

Kumar, M. (n.d.). Banking Sector reforms in India. *International Research Journal of Commerce Arts and Science*.

Kumar, M. (n.d.). Banking Sector reforms in India. *International Research Journal of Commerce Arts and Science*. Available at http:www.casirj.com

Mahalingam, G. (2015). *Some Thoughts on Forex Markets in India*. Speech, Key Note Address on February 25, 2015 at the India Treasury Summit, Mumbai, India.

Mishra, S. K. (n.d.). *Money, Income and Financial Institutions* (5th ed.). Pragati Publications.

Mohan, R. (2007). *Development of Financial Markets in India*. Mumbai: Reserve Bank of India. Retrieved from http://rbidocs.rbi.org.in/rdocs/Speeches/PDFs/77375.pdf

Mohan, R. (2004). *A Decade of Reforms in Government Securities Market in India and the Road Ahead*. Mumbai: Reserve Bank of India. Available at: http://rbidocs.rbi.org.in/rdocs/Speeches/PDFs/60551.pdf

Mohanty, D. (2012). *Money Market and Monetary Operations in India*. Mumbai: RBI. Available at: http://rbidocs.rbi.org.in/rdocs/Speeches/PDFs/SMMIED171212.pdf

Overview of Fuller Capital Account Convertibility and the Committee's Approach. (2011). Retrieved from https://rbidocs.rbi.org.in/rdocs/PublicationReport/Pdfs/72252.pdf2007

Padmanabhan, G. (2011). *Forex market development: Issues and challenges—Thoughts of a returning forex market regulator*. Singapore: RBI and Forex Association of India. Retrieved from http://rbidocs.rbi.org.in/rdocs/Speeches/PDFs/EDGPS110811.pdf

Pethe, A., & Karnik, A. (2000). Do Indian Stock Market Indices and Macro Economic Variables. *Economic and Political Weekly*, *35*(5), 349-356.

Chadrasekhar, C. P. (2013, May 18). Redistributing Regulatory Power: Financial Sector Legislative Reform Commission. *Economic and Political Weekly*.

Prakash, B. A. (n.d.). The Indian Economy Since 1991: Economic Reforms and Performance. Pearson Education.

Prasad, E., Rajan, R., & Subramanian, A. (2016). *Finance and Development. Finance and Development F&D*. Retrieved on 8 August 2015, from http://www.imf.org/external/pubs/ft/fandd/2007/03/prasad.htm

Rangarajan, C. (1998). *India's Financial Markets changes and challenges*. Available at: http://www.iief.com/Research/tushar_chp1.pdf

Ray, P., & Prabhu, E. (2013). *Financial Development and Monetary Policy Transmission Across Financial Markets: What Do Daily Data Tell for India?* Mumbai: Department of Economic and Policy Research, Reserve Bank of India.

Renu, K. (2005). *Liberalizing Capital Flows: India's Experience and Policy Issues*. Oxford University Press.

Saha, M. (2012). *Indian Economy and Growth of Financial Market in the Contemporary Phase of the Globalization Era*. Academic Press.

Sen Kunal and Vaidya R.R. (1997). *The process of Financial Liberalisation in India*. Oxford University Press.

Shah, A., & Patnaik I. (2011). *Reforming the Indian financial System and India's Financial Globalization*. Academic Press.

Sharma, R., & Sharma, D. (2008). *Role of Stock Exchange in the Development of Indian Capital Market: A Study of National Stock Exchange*. Indianmba.com. Retrieved 4 April 2015, from http://www.indianmba.com/Faculty_Column/FC708/fc708.html

Singh, A. (1997). Financial liberalisation and economic development. *The Economic Journal*, *107*(May), 771–782. doi:10.1111/j.1468-0297.1997.tb00042.x

Smithies, A. (1953). Review of The Rate of Interest and Other Essays. *The American Economic Review*, *43*(4), 636–641. Retrieved from http://www.jstor.org/stable/1812414

Srivastava, A. (2013). *Foreign Exchange Risk Management in India - FICCI Blog*. FICCI blog. Retrieved 19 September 2016, from http://blog.ficci.com/foreign-exchange-india/2834/

The Indian Capital Market. (2010). *Growth & Governance*. Retrieved from https://www.pwc.in/assets/pdfs/publications-2010/india-captial-market.pdf

Thomas, S. (2006). How the Financial Sector Was Reformed. In Documenting Reforms: Case Studies from India (S. Narayan, ed.). Bangalore, India: Macmillan Publishing India.

Varma, J. R. (1992). *Commercial Banking; New Vistas and New Priorities*. Paper presented at the seminar on Reforming Commercial Banking, New Delhi, India.

Varma, J. R. (1997). *Indian money market: market structure, covered parity and term structure*. Academic Press.

Varma, J. R. (1997). *Indian Money Market: Market Structure*. Covered Parity and Term Structure.

Vyas, P., & Zaveri, B. (2016). Banking sector reforms in India: Some reflections. Varanasi: School of Management Studies. Retrieved from http://www.smsvaranasi.com/insight/banking_sector_reforms_in_india_some_reflections.pdf

Wikipedia. (2016). *Money market in India*. Retrieved 19 July 2015, from https://en.wikipedia.org/wiki/Money_market_in_India

Chapter 3
Financial Sector Reforms in South Asian Countries

Amir Manzoor
Bahria University, Pakistan

ABSTRACT

Several far-reaching reforms to the financial sector were introduced by South Asian countries in early 1980. The nature and progress of these reforms vary from country to country. These reforms covered a number of areas such as promoting competition in the financial sector, developing payment and settlement systems, and strengthening regulations. So far, these reforms have not only helped South Asian countries to significantly raise domestic savings, attract foreign capital, and raise economic growth rates but also provided greater economic integration of South Asia. This chapter performs a close re-scrutiny of the reforms implemented in South Asian countries. Suggestion for further reforms for building efficient, competitive, and resilient financial sector is also provided.

INTRODUCTION

Several far reaching reforms to the financial sector were introduced by South Asian countries in early 1980. The nature and progress of these reforms vary from country to country. These reforms covered a number of areas such as promoting competition in the financial sector, developing payment and settlement systems, and strengthening regulations. So far, these reforms have not only helped South Asian countries to significantly raise domestic savings, attract foreign capital, and raise economic growth rates but also provided greater economic integration of South Asia.

East Asian financial crisis resulted in providing greater space for these new reforms. Another round of reforms took place in the 1990s. The 2007 financial crisis, which began in the U.S. sub-prime mortgage market, has already prompted a reassessment of financial sector policy making globally to address many of the weaknesses in supervisory, regulatory and prudential frameworks (Berkmen, Gelos, Rennhack, & Walsh, 2009).

The beginning of the current global crisis was associated with complex financial products. South Asian financial sector didn't have direct exposure to such products. Still the global financial crisis caused

DOI: 10.4018/978-1-5225-0004-9.ch003

a considerable slowdown of South Asian economies as a result of contagion effects of global shocks. Some of the significant channels that affected South Asian economies were capital, remittances, credit and international trade. Capital outflow, reduced foreign remittances, dried up international credit markets, and reduced exports have had serious implications for these economies (Griffith-Jones & Ocampo, 2009).

The objective of this chapter is to perform a close re-scrutiny of the reforms implemented in South Asian countries in the context of developments that took place after global financial crisis. The chapter also examines the room for further reforms that might be necessary for building efficient, competitive and resilient financial sector. Such a sector would play a key role in putting South Asian economies to the path of sustainable high growth. According to (World Bank, 2014), India set the pace for regulatory reform in South Asia in 2013/14 India with 20 - the region's largest reforms during the period. India was followed by Sri Lanka with 16 reforms while three countries - Bangladesh, Nepal, and Pakistan - focused their efforts on adopting modern electronic systems to facilitate business activity. Therefore, many examples, with respect to various reforms, provided in this chapter will be from India as it is expected that other south Asian countries will follow the similar path.

STRENGTHS AND FLAWS OF SOUTH ASIAN FINANCIAL SECTOR

Various strengths of current South Asian financial structure were pivotal in lessening the direct impact of the global financial crisis on South Asia. Some of the notable strengths were healthy reserves, improved export performance and enhanced risk-taking capabilities of financial institutions. These strengths were supported by previous financial reforms. The outlook over the next years for South Asia indicates broad economic stability and a pick-up in growth with potential risks concentrated on the fiscal and structural reform side. Future growth will increasingly depend on strong investment and export performance (Griffith-Jones & Ocampo, 2009).

Exports have recently shown a strong export performance in many South Asian countries, growing in the double digits in several of them. While sales abroad were boosted by favorable tailwinds, such as the depreciation of the Indian rupee in 2013, there are also deeper trends at play. Export diversification by type of product increased, as did the share of emerging markets in total exports. These are manifestations of an increasingly stronger position of the region in global markets (World Bank, 2014). In Bangladesh, A rise in export growth helped to lower the trade deficit, and foreign exchange reserves continued to accumulate despite the 1.6 percent decline in remittance. In Bhutan, Hydropower generation (river-flow dependent) in the first half of 2014 was 2 percent (annualized) down on the same period of 2013 due to weaker rainfall. As a result, export revenues from the sale of electricity declined. In India, the exchange rate has remained stable since last year's depreciation, which stimulated exports and slowed imports. In Sri Lanka, robust performance of exports contracted the trade deficit for the first half of the year to 4.6 percent of GDP.

Most South Asian countries solidified their foreign reserve positions. Benefitting from strong capital account inflows and a stable and manageable current account balance, India saw its foreign exchange (FX) reserves increase from an estimated US$ 276.4 billion in FY2013/14 to 321.1 billion projected for FY2014/15. Bhutan built up an impressive 17 months of import coverage reserve by June 2014, with the only caveat that 83 percent of them are in convertible currencies while it is mainly Indian rupees which are required for trade settlement and debt service. Nepal continues to maintain extraordinarily high reserve levels, most recently above 10 months of import coverage. Afghanistan's FX reserves stood slightly higher than a year ago at US$ 7.3 billion or around 8 months of imports at the end of 2014. Bangladesh further bumped up its FX reserves to around 6 months of import coverage by June 2014. Similarly, Sri Lanka saw its gross official reserves reach around 6 months of imports by end July 2014. However, there are weak spots as well. In Pakistan, official reserves regained ground and stood at 2.1 months of import coverage by June 30, 2014, only to slightly drop again to 1.9 months by the end of August. Maldives saw its international gross reserves benefit from higher than expected revenue collection and tourism receipts, but remains in a precarious external position (World Bank, 2014).

At the same time, some reforms were effective and yielded desired results while some didn't. Some effective reforms include opening up of the financial sector for domestic and foreign competition, expanding the availability of credit information, and significant change in the conduct of monetary policy over the years. Some ineffective reforms include a large share of the banking sector is still state-owned and requires to be better managed, non-availability of an appropriate regulatory environment, non-availability of an institutional investor base, and Underdeveloped derivative and securitization markets (Mohan, 2013).

In beginning, many South Asian banking reforms started by opening up the financial sector for domestic and foreign competition (Mohan, 2013). With low entry barriers, many foreign banks setup branches in South Asia thereby increasing competition among banks. The total number of branches of the 32 foreign banks operating in India as on March 31, 2010, stood at 306 (The Economic Times, 2011; Gopalan & Rajan, 2015). This also resulted in a sharp reduction in the market shares of state owned banks. In India, Shares of state-owned banks rallied up to 12% in 2014 after a Reserve Bank of India-appointed panel recommended that the government bring down its stake in these banks to below 50% to improve competitiveness and governance (The Economic Times, 2014). The liberalization of financial markets has also changed the ownership pattern of the financial institutions (Molyneux, Nguyen, & Xie, 2013). Table 1 shows the ownership pattern of financial institutions in India at the end of March 2013.

In the mean time, banks engaged in various fee-based activities to expand their base of financial services. To remain competitive, both private and state-owned banks made heavy investments in state-of-the-art technology to increase efficiency of financial services. In India, IT has made a visible difference in the functioning of banks and conduct of banking operations. Banks have scaled up their businesses and

Table 1. Ownership Pattern of Financial Institutions in India (As of March 2013)

Institution	Ownership	Percent
1	2	3
EXIM Bank	Government of India	100
NABARD	Government of India	99.3
	Reserve Bank of India	0.7
NHB	Reserve Bank of India	100
SIDBI*	Public Sector Banks	62.5
	Insurance Companies	21.9
	Financial Institutions	5.3
	Others	10.3

*: Three major shareholders of SIDBI were - IDBI Bank Ltd. (19.2%), State Bank of India (15.5%) and Life Insurance Corporation of India (14.4%).

Source: (Reserve Bank of India, 2013)

grown successfully using technology. This technology adoption by banks has also benefited customers in terms of improved customer service quality. For large banks, the IT capital expense to total IT expense ratio stands at approximately 18%. For small banks, this ratio stands at approximately 54%, which shows significant investments by small banks in IT. Most banks have also put up a robust mechanism for governance and management of IT assets with board level committees and alignment of functional and technical teams for IT implementation. Initiatives taken by banks have been in multiple areas both to augment business services as well as the control functions and include up-gradation of core banking system, data center migration, incident management command center, upgrade of ATM switches and virtualization of servers among others. These initiatives will have a significant impact on the business of banking in the coming years (Institute for Development and Research in Banking Technology, 2014).

For growth of banking industry, the availability of credit information is critical. Non-availability of credible credit information can deprive many credit-worthy borrowers access to credit. Therefore, many South Asian countries have established credit information bureaus that, in some cases, also include additional information such as history of utility bills payment. In India, Credit information bureaus found a new way to expand their footprint: credit counselling. Companies such as home-bred Credit Information Bureau India and US-based Experian offer services to consumers that range from tips to improve credit score to advice on how to deal with loans after losing a job or following divorce. These services are often free for consumers. However, improved public awareness may lead to more loan demand and higher business for these companies, which compile information on borrowers' credit history (Nayak, 2014).

Recently, regulators required banks to obtain credit ratings from acceptable credit rating agencies. The purpose was to enhance transparency and investor awareness of banks. These ratings also helped borrowers in selecting banking products and rehabilitate to increase credit quality. Accordingly, many South Asian countries setup credit councils. The objective of these credit councils was to increase credit quality, promote banking products, and introduced credit discipline among customers (Ciccaglione, 2014). In India, a National Credit Council was set up in 1968 to assess the demand for credit by these sectors and determine resource allocations. The National Credit Council of India has three sectors of investment, i.e., agriculture, small- scale industries and exports (Gupta, 2015).

The monetary policy operations in South Asia have seen significant changes over the years. The focus of monetary policy is to achieve a sustainable path of low inflation and central banks are now using primarily the market-oriented instruments. Therefore, Open-Market Operations have become mainstream in in the management of market liquidity. In India, the market operations are conducted by the Reserve Bank of India by way of sale/ purchase of Government securities to/ from the market with an objective to adjust the rupee liquidity conditions in the market on a durable basis. In line with a market-oriented monetary management approach, South Asian regulators have implemented measures to enhance the transparency, predictability, and credibility of monetary policy. Mechanisms have been setup to disseminate information on the monetary policy framework including any changes in the monetary. In Sri Lanka, developments in the government bond market have facilitated the Central Bank further strengthen the market oriented monetary management strategy (Muzaffar & Chowdhury, 2014; Indian Council for Research on International Economic Relations, 2013).

For efficient functioning of financial system, an efficient and secure system of payment and settlement is essential. In many South Asian countries, payment and settlement systems have been upgraded and modernized. Many South Asian countries have implemented the Real-time Gross Settlement Systems to facilitate the payment and settlement of large value and time of critical transactions. Electronic Funds Transfer (EFT) mechanisms have been implemented to provide modern retail payment systems (Indian

Council for Research on International Economic Relations, 2013). A cheque imaging and transaction system has been introduced to improve efficiency of payment system. The long-term objective of this system is to adopt electronic cheque transaction. Cheque Truncation System (CTS) or Image-based Clearing System (ICS) is a project of Reserve Bank of India RBI. The objective of the system is faster clearing of cheques. CTS is an online image-based cheque clearing system that uses cheque images and Magnetic Ink Character Recognition (MICR) data to transmit cheques electronically. The physical instrument is truncated at some point en route to the drawee branch and an electronic image of the cheque is sent to the drawee branch along with the relevant information like the MICR fields, date of presentation, presenting banks etc. Cheque truncation eliminates the need to move the physical instruments across branches and provides effective reduction in the time required for payment of cheques and associated costs of transit and delays in processing. This system speeds up the process of collection or realization of cheques (Akshatha, 2014). The SAARC payments initiative (SPI) is a step taken by central banks in South Asia for collective reform of regional and national payment and settlement systems. The SAARC Payments Initiative (SPI) is a regional forum developed to have common understanding and cooperation to help South Asian countries to move forward in reforming their national payment and settlement systems (PSS). Another objective of this initiative is to establish an appropriate regional payment system that facilitates trade and investment in the region. SPI is a very significant initiative due to various reasons. First, the national payment and settlement system (PSS) reforms to have a regional forum under the SPI for SAARC countries to help and learn from each other. Second, the SPI would provide an effective institutional arrangement for working towards an efficient payment system mechanism to promote trade and investment in the region. Third, with SPI, the South Asian central banks get an opportunity to become a regional partner of the global payment system community and upgrade the region's payment systems to international standards (Metzger, 2010).

Enhanced access to finance increases opportunities available to small and medium enterprises (SEMs) and low-income groups. Since increased access to finance fosters economic growth, many South Asian countries have taken steps to expand and strengthen the systems of development finance delivery and to create a conducive environment for establishing financial institutions.in remote areas (Ferrarini, Ramayandi, & Jha, 2012). Credit guarantee schemes have been introduced to encourage bankers to provide facilities related to micro-finance projects. In Sri Lanka, SMEs faced many constraints in their access to credit on commercial terms. The credit secured on movable assets was heavily underutilized due to high risks and transaction costs. Sri Lankan regulators planned a Secured Transaction Registry that aimed to facilitate the credit extension by SMEs that was secured on the basis of movable and intangible assets (Hommes, Khan, Gerber, Kipnis, & Hamm, 2014; Indian Council for Research on International Economic Relations, 2013).

South Asian countries introduced various new regulatory measures to strengthen the regulatory and supervisory framework. South Asian central banks have shifted their focus to risk-based supervision. The Reserve Bank of India, scrapping its age-old practice of CAMELS inspection, switched 30 banks to risk-based supervision, indicating what could be the beginning of the regulator's micro management of banks (India Times, 2014). There is renewed interest in fiduciary responsibilities of board of directors and central banks have issued directions on corporate governance requiring banks to streamline their governance practices. At a time when several corporates and finance companies were aspiring for banking license, the Reserve Bank of India (RBI) formed a panel to review the governance practice followed by banks. RBI formed this expert panel chaired by P. J. Nayak, former chairman and CEO of Axis Bank. This panel was tasked with review, among other things, of central bank's regulatory guidelines on bank's ownership, ownership concentration and representation in the board. Several corporates like Birlas and L&T and large finance companies like IDFC and LIC Housing Finance were among the 25 applicants for banking license (India Times, 2014).

The implementation of Basel II framework has contributed to improved risk management mechanisms of financial sector and enhanced regulatory structures. A large number of leading South Asian banks setup independent risk management/compliance units to monitor bank-wide risks. Major banks are now focusing on implementing advanced approaches provided by Basel II framework. These banks have leveraged technology to establish high-tech systems in their bid for better risk management and compliance. Similarly, the adoption of Basel II framework by banks will enhance disclosures, presentation, and measurement practices related to financial instruments (Cho, 2013). In 2012, The Reserve Bank of India (RBI), issued the final guidelines for implementation of Basel III capital regulation in India, to be effective from January 1, 2013, in a phased manner. The Basel III capital ratios were to be fully implemented on March 31, 2018 (The Hindu, 2012).

We witness several improvements in the financial systems of many South Asian countries. These improvements include improved institutional structures, developed money and capital markets, and extension of facilities and products offered. Still, there are several weaknesses such as low financial depth, high costs of intermediation, low levels of access to finance, and less developed derivative and securitization markets. That clearly indicates that some reforms have not produced their desired results (Kumari, 2014).

In many of the South Asian countries, state still owns a large share (ranging from 20% to 70% of all assets) of the banking sector (Indian Council for Research on International Economic Relations, 2013). This is a much higher proportion as compared to the rest of the world. Increased state ownership can provide financial system stability in uncertain environments due to high levels of public confidence on state-owned institutions. However, state-owned banks in South Asia are considered less competitive, less profitable, and less efficient when compared to privately-held and foreign-owned banks (Kumari, 2014). One significant reason for this is high operating expenses of state-owned banks attributed to overstaffing and higher loan loss expenses due to directed or priority sector lending by these banks. Politically influenced credit decisions by these banks deteriorates quality of assets held (Ibrahim & Shuaibu, 2013).

In South Asia, non-banking institutions and markets face a significant constraint in their development: non-availability of appropriate regulatory regime. While stock markets have expanded and developed in many South Asian countries, bond markets have not developed. As a result, derivative investors have limited choice of financial instruments. Unstable macroeconomic environment has also limited the foreign investors access to local bonds markets. There is a need to develop liquid corporate bond markets that could also help prevent asset price bubbles. Many factors have constrained the development of local bonds markets. These factors include high government borrowings from non-banking sector, in-effective disclosure standards, and insufficient credit rights and investor protection (Goyal, 2012; Indian Council for Research on International Economic Relations, 2013).

The limited development of capital and money markets can be attributed to non-availability of institutional investor-base that is essential to obtain funds for long-term investments. In this regard, there is a need to promote pension funds and insurance companies as important agents of mobilizing long-term funds (Hussain, 2013). Underdeveloped derivative and securities markets can limit the expansion of financial markets and financial depth. Non-developed market cannot provide the requisite products (such as credit derivatives) that financial system need to allocate risks (such as credit risk and interest rate risk) among market participants as per their preferences (Goyal, 2012).

PRACTICAL/MANAGERIAL IMPLICATIONS AND RECOMMENDATIONS

To provide financial system stability, the economic policies and regulatory frameworks need great coordination and consistency in order provide stability of financial system. The macroeconomic imbalances (such as sharp decline in exchange rate and significant increase in inflation) are regarded major causes of financial crises (Indian Council for Research on International Economic Relations, 2013). Prudent management of fiscal and monetary policies is important to prevent buildup of factors that could trigger a crisis.

Banking sector should be further strengthened by healthy consolidation of small and weak banks through mergers and acquisitions (M&As). In this regard, the regulators should consider rationalizing regulatory standards that permit such consolidation. Such consolidation would promote a healthy banking sector. Prevailing regulatory regime needs to be expanded to cover unregulated shadow banking system and the significant build-up of off-balance sheet leverage. Shadow banking system in most South Asian countries is not subject to the same rigorous prudential regulatory requirements applicable to licensed financial institutions (Indian Council for Research on International Economic Relations, 2013). In addition, the increasing use of structured investments results in excessive increase in off-balance sheet leverage. With a large number of financial scams coming up in recent years, the Reserve Bank of India (RBI) decided to take the growing phenomenon of shadow banking head on. The RBI set up a 15-membered committee comprising officials of the RBI, Securities and Exchange Board of India (Sebi), Central Economic Intelligence Bureau and the National Housing Bank. The committee's role was to find out the volume of money in shadow banks, who the investors are and direction of the money flow, and to look very meticulously into real estate dealings (Hindustan Times, 2014).

There is a need to develop non-banking financial institutions (NBFIs). NBFIs can provide vital financial services. They can expand their role in areas where banks may not be competitive. Well-developed capital markets can help raise long-term funds and share the risk of raising capital. A developed bond market can help improve the efficiency of financial markets and promote sustainable economic growth (Indian Council for Research on International Economic Relations, 2013). These expanded opportunities of large-scale financing can help provide better allocation of capital and facilitate public debt management. A developed bond market can be significantly helpful in the progress of a country. The institutional infrastructure should be strengthened and impediments should be removed in order foster efficient working and sustained growth of the bond market. A special focus is needed to enhance the institutional infrastructures, develop rating agencies/trading platforms/clearing and payment systems, and strengthen the regulator environment.

Policies are needed to help build a diversified institutional investor base. This investor base will help create sustainable demand for bonds. Pension funds and mutual funds can help create demand for bonds. These funds can also promote financial innovation and enhance corporate governance/competition in the bond market. Strengthened disclosure standards, credit rights, and investor protection can also contribute to the smooth functioning of bond market by removing impediments. Micro finance is an important instrument in poverty reduction. Micro finance institutions (MFIs) promote economic activities because they provide relatively easy and flexible financing options. However, the presence of a large number of unregulated MFIs can jeopardize the stability of financial system. MFIs require an appropriate regulatory mechanism to provide a strong environment for operation of MFIs. Such regulatory mechanism will foster public confidence in the financial system. The central bank of Sri Lanka a two-tier regulatory approach for MFIs. The existing regulatory and legal framework is used to regulate existing MFIs and also used to develop a comprehensive legal/regulatory/supervisory framework for types of MFIs that are not currently under regulator supervision of any institution (Indian Council for Research on International Economic Relations, 2013).

Lack of coordination and consolidated supervision are two key risk factors that had contributed to global financial crisis. Coordination among different regulatory agencies within countries and amongst countries needs improvement. By establishing regional alliances, regulators can establish a mechanism of effective monitoring of cross-border financial activities that could threaten stability of financial system. Consistent with the practices of developed financial markets, the South Asian markets vary with respect to the responsibilities of regulators. In some countries, regulatory bodies are integrated that perform prudential supervision of a full range of financial activities. In some countries, the regulators supervise diversified financial groups at the parent company level. In certain countries, there is no integrated regulatory body mandated with supervision of the entire financial system. In some cases, regulators supervise non-licensed holding companies (Indian Council for Research on International Economic Relations, 2013). To ensure financial system stability, regulators need a collaborative 'group approach' of supervision of licensed financial institutions. This approach would take account all possible effects of all risks within the group of licensed financial institutions irrespective of where the risk reside within the group.

Bank failures can be a source of significant direct and indirect costs to economies. As a result, all segments of the society face enormous economic and business hardships. At a macro level, bank failures put into risk the maintenance of financial system stability and public confidence in the financial system. The regulatory/supervisory frameworks need to provide measures to avoid bank failures and provide a buffer to minimize impact of failing or failed banks. Adequate contingency plans are needed to deal with weak banks. Regulators need good understanding of the tools available for handling weak banks and NBFIs. Appropriate measures are needed to facilitate the identification of weak banks and NBFIs. Once weak institutions are identified, corrective measures should be taken to turn around these weak institutions. In many cases, regulators would need to develop an appropriate exit strategy for these institutions. The task is challenging but successful identification of weak banks and NBFIs would ensure that undetected losses do not increase further. Sound corporate governance standards and practices would be needed to ensure that management practices of licensed banking institutions are safe and sound. The financial institutions with strong governance and compliance processes will be in a much better position to gain public confidence, attract investors, improve corporate reputation, and efficiency. These institutions will also contribute towards increasing financial system stability. To promote such practices within banking sector, regulators need to prepare and implement principle-based rules on corporate governance. These rules should emphasize the role and responsibility of board of directors to maintain proper stewardship of the institutions. These rules would also ensure adoption of sound and prudent policies and procedures by banking institutions that are adhered to at all organization levels and at all times.

Analysis of past financial crises have shown that lapses in financial reporting system resulted in non-compliance with accounting standards and adoption of creative accounting practices by companies to boost profits and hide material risks. There is a strong need to put in place effective and sufficient internal controls and processes to ensure compliance with accounting standards. There is an urgent need to improve disclosure standards and a mechanism to monitor and ensure that these standards are complied with. There exist many bodies and mechanisms in various South Asian regions to facilitate and promote intra-trade and excess funds investments. However, what is needed is a strong mechanism to promote domestic bond market. This mechanism is very important due to significance of a developed bond market for sustainable regional development.

Market credibility and reputation among foreign investors greatly depends on information disclosures. Effective or sufficient disclosures standards are needed. These standards should be based on consolidated accounts and well established auditing/accounting standards (such as IAS). In this regard, promoting listing of companies can also produce positive impact on information disclosures and help markets and regulators both. If both issuers and investors have enhanced understanding of the capital markets, it can help them make educated decisions and contribute to long-term development of financial markets.

It is argued that current financial system contains a number of pro-cyclical features that induce banks to take excessive risk and Basel II framework has actually reinforced these pro-cyclical features by increasing risk sensitivity of financial regulation (Indian Council for Research on International Economic Relations, 2013). The large expansion in private sector credit and overheated economy in South Asia during 2005-2007 fueled this pro-cyclical behavior. Many South Asian countries tool several measures to contain the pro-cyclical risk taking behavior of banks. These measures even included provision on performing loans and risk weightages in the calculation of capital adequacy. Measures are needed to contain this pro-cyclical behavior and provide negative feedback loops, at both micro and macro level, to discourage excessive risk taking. Following are some such measures/suggestions.

For banks, sound capital buffer is critical. This is because it provides cushion against shocks and promote financial stability. It is argued that Basel II framework does not adequately capture risks in relation to complex credit products. In addition, the minimum capital requirement and the quality of capital did not provide adequate buffer during the crisis. Some of the measures that can be considered in this regard include counter-cyclical capital buffer and improve quality of Tier 1 capital. Counter-cyclical capital buffers can be provided by increasing the coverage of capital requirements. This increased coverage should take into account the asset-backed securities, off-balance sheet risk exposures and trading account activities. A fixed minimum leverage ratio for capital can be introduced. This ratio would put a limit on the size of bank assets and hence would discourage excessive risk taking by banks. The risks arisen due to rapid loan growth can be mitigated by introducing dynamic forward-looking provisions. These provisions would aim at capturing the levels of default risk over time. To mitigate risks due to moral hazards and fraudulent loan underwriting, financial institutions can be bound to retain a fixed share of the underlying assets of their balance sheets. It is argued that fair value accounting was an important factor behind global financial crisis that exacerbated the crisis and amplified the market fluctuations. Despite the fact that fair value approach can show the real time value of financial instruments the risks of magnification in the changes in the asset values can increase the volatility of returns of banking and other financial institutions. Therefore, a guided approach should be followed in implementation of fair value accounting. External rating agencies can act as a pro-cyclical measure. This was evident in the recent global financial crisis. This is due to the fact that all major credit rating agencies follow similar assessment models. And this is also a very fact that public and financial institutions use the ratings of these agencies as a yardstick to assess the operations and performance of financial institutions. To counter excessive risks taken by banks, regulators should encourage banks to have their own risk assessment mechanisms rather than solely relying upon the risk assessment provided by the rating agencies. The Basel II framework allows financial institutions to apply their own rating approaches in pricing and assessing risks associated with complex products. Banks can use their own internal ratings to derive risk weights to be used in capital adequacy calculations. Currently, risk weighs are generally low in South Asian countries (Indian Council for Research on International Economic Relations, 2013). As such, the capital adequacy ratio (CAR) is high when economy is booming and vice versa. As a result, financial institutions enjoy high leverage ratios during economic booms and we see an amplified bubble builds up. During economic downturn, the situation is changed and we see credit squeeze and asset dumping. As a result, we see strong pro-cyclicity. The pillar II of Basel framework includes implementation of Internal Capital Adequacy Assessment Process (ICAPP) (Indian Council for Research on International Economic Relations, 2013). Therefore implementation of pillar II of Basel framework can provide the right balance of economic capital and mitigates all risks not covered in pillar I. Pillar II implementation enables banks to determine whether their degree of leverage is appropriate given the amount of risk taken and the institutions' risk appetite. Many financial institutions outsource the development of their own internal control systems and models used by both banks and traders. The problem with this approach is that banking industry relies on few known experts of quantitative analysis to develop these systems and models. As such, these models tend to produce similar directional results and do not account for certain prevailing conditions that promote pro-cyclicity. Regulators should provide incentives to financial institutions for improvements in their risk assessment of structured products.

FUTURE RESEARCH AREAS

The policy problems South Asian countries face today have changed considerably over past decade. This is partly because of external factors (such as international capital flows) but the major factor is the progress made with macroeconomic and trade reforms and a more complex set of issues. Future research is needed as to how governments can diagnose where specifically their problems lie, design, and build institutions and programs to address the weaknesses, and get continuous feedback on whether services are improving. In these financial sector reforms, the norms of behavior of both public officials and private agents must be included. One important future research area is the examination of the interactions between policy reforms, institutional change, and norms of behavior.

CONCLUSION

The financial landscape is continuously evolving and financial markets are integrating at global level. Therefore, it is critical that financial sector reforms are pursued with a focus to develop an efficient, competitive, and resilient financial sector in South Asia. For sustainable containment of inflation, South Asian economies need prudent monetary policies. These monetary policies need supported by fiscal policies and adjustments in exchange rate regimes. This would provide a conducive environment for the development/stability of financial sector. The efficient working of financial markets and development of strong institutional infrastructures would need many policy initiatives and reforms. Structural issues need to be addressed to remove impediments in efficient working of labor, capital, and product markets. In this regard, the cooperation of stakeholders from other sectors would also be needed.

REFERENCES

Akshatha, B. G. (2014). Cheque truncation system: Innovative mechanisms for effective payment. *International Journal of Logistics & Supply Chain Management Perspectives*, 2(4), 767–771.

Ang, J. B. (2010). Finance and Inequality: The Case of India. *Southern Economic Journal, 76*(3), 738–761. doi:10.4284/sej.2010.76.3.738

Anwar, S., & Cooray, A. (2012). Financial development, political rights, civil liberties and economic growth: Evidence from South Asia. *Economic Modelling, 29*(3), 974–981. doi:10.1016/j.econmod.2012.02.009

Berkmen, P., Gelos, G., Rennhack, R., & Walsh, J. P. (2009). *The global financial crisis: Explaining cross-country differences in the output impact*. International Monetary Fund.

Burki, A. A., & Niazi, G. S. K. (2010). Impact of financial reforms on efficiency of state-owned, private and foreign banks in Pakistan. *Applied Economics, 42*(24), 3147–3160. doi:10.1080/00036840802112315

Cho, Y. (2013). *Why do countries implement Basel II? An analysis of the global diffusion of Basel II implementation. The London School of Economics and Political Science*. LSE.

Ciccaglione, K. R. (2014). *From Inclusion to Empowerment: The Political Implications of Microfinance*. Academic Press.

Dee, P. (2012). *Economic Reform Processes in South Asia: Toward Policy Efficiency*. Abingdon, UK: Routledge.

Dee, P. (2012). *Economic Reform Processes in South Asia: Toward Policy Efficiency*. Abingdon, UK: Routledge.

Delis, M. D. (2012). Bank competition, financial reform, and institutions: The importance of being developed. *Journal of Development Economics, 97*(2), 450–465. doi:10.1016/j.jdeveco.2011.05.012

Edirisuriya, P. (2007). Effects of Financial Sector Reforms in Sri Lanka: Evidence from the Banking Sector (SSRN Scholarly Paper No. ID 1536035). Rochester, NY: Social Science Research Network; Retrieved from http://papers.ssrn.com/abstract=1536035

Ferrarini, B., Ramayandi, A., & Jha, R. (2012). *Public debt sustainability in developing Asia*. Routledge.

Financial reforms in Sri Lanka and their influence on the banking industry. (n.d.). Academic Press.

Ganesh Kumar Shrestha. (n.d.). *Financial Sector Reforms in Nepal*. Retrieved from http://www.nrb.org.np/ecorev/pdffiles/vol16_art3.pdf

Gill, S. S., & Madaan, D. K. (2015). *Understanding Non-Tariff Trade Barriers between India and Pakistan*. Academic Press.

Gopalan, S., & Rajan, R. S. (2015). *How Does Foreign Bank Entry Affect Financial Inclusion in Emerging and Developing Economies?* HKUST Institute for Emerging Market Studies.

Goyal, A. (2012). *The future of financial liberalization in South Asia*. Academic Press.

Griffith-Jones, S., & Ocampo, J. A. (2009). *The financial crisis and its impact on developing countries*. Working Paper. International Policy Centre for Inclusive Growth.

Gupta, D. (2015). *Key Barriers Faced in Implementing Financial Inclusion*. Academic Press.

Hassan, M. K., Sanchez, B., & Yu, J.-S. (2011). Financial development and economic growth: New evidence from panel data. *The Quarterly Review of Economics and Finance*, *51*(1), 88–104. doi:10.1016/j.qref.2010.09.001

Hindustan Times. (2014, August 17). *RBI forms committee to monitor shadow banking; realty in focus.* Retrieved from http://www.hindustantimes.com/business-news/rbi-forms-committee-to-monitor-shadow-banking-realty-in-focus/article1-1253148.aspx

Hommes, M., Khan, A., Gerber, C., Kipnis, H., & Hamm, K. (2014). Out of the shadows and into the banks: Financing very small and informal enterprises. *Enterprise Development and Microfinance*, *25*(3), 211–225. doi:10.3362/1755-1986.2014.020

Hussain, M. A. (2013). *Effect of Dividend Policy on Market Return Empirical Evidence from South Asia.* Available at SSRN 2206819.

Ibrahim, T. M., & Shuaibu, M. I. (2013). Financial Development: A Fillip or Impediment to Nigeria's Economic Growth. *International Journal of Economics and Financial Issues*, *3*(2), 305–318.

India Times. (2014a, January 20). *RBI sets up a panel to review banks' corporate governance.* Retrieved October 31, 2014, from http://articles.economictimes.indiatimes.com/2014-01-20/news/46374817_1_private-banks-banking-licence-shubhalakshmi-panse

India Times. (2014b, March 3). *RBI switches 30 banks to risk-based supervision.* Retrieved October 31, 2014, from http://articles.economictimes.indiatimes.com/2014-05-03/news/49594370_1_risk-based-supervision-riskbased-supervision-asset-quality

Indian Council for Research on International Economic Relations. (2013). *Reforms to the Financial Sector in South Asian Countries to Promote Economic Growth with Financial System Stability.* Retrieved from http://icrier.org/pdf/DeepakMohanty-PPT.pdf

Institute for Development and Research in Banking Technology. (2014). *Technology in Banking Towards Improving Business Performance and Customer Engagement.* Retrieved from http://www.idrbt.ac.in/publications/Frameworks/Technology%20in%20Banking%20(2013).pdf

Jadhav, N. (2003). *Financial Sector Reforms and Role of RBI.* Retrieved from http://drnarendrajadhav.info/drnjadhav_web_files/speeches/NDC-speech.pdf

Jain, R. (2013). *Overview of the International Financial Instruments Issued from Sri Lanka.* Available at SSRN 2312253.

Jalil, A., & Feridun, M. (2011). Impact of financial development on economic growth: Empirical evidence from Pakistan. *Journal of the Asia Pacific Economy*, *16*(1), 71–80. doi:10.1080/13547860.2011.539403

Kumari, S. S. M. (2014). Determinants of Interest Margins of Banks in Sri Lanka. *South Asia Economic Journal*, *15*(2), 265–280. doi:10.1177/1391561414548952

Kutan, A. M., Muradoglu, G., & Sudjana, B. G. (2012). IMF programs, financial and real sector performance, and the Asian crisis. *Journal of Banking & Finance*, *36*(1), 164–182. doi:10.1016/j.jbankfin.2011.06.015

Metzger, M. (2010). *Trends in Financial market development in South Asia.* Available at: http://www.icrier.org/pdf/martina%20metzger-paper.pdf

Ministry of Finance and Planning. Sri Lanka. (2012). *Annual Report*. Retrieved from http://www.treasury.gov.lk/reports/annualreport/2012/7-Rerorms.pdf

Mohan, R. (2005). Financial sector reforms in India: Policies and performance analysis. *Economic and Political Weekly*, 1106–1121.

Mohan, R. (2011). Growth with Financial Stability: Central Banking in an Emerging Market (OUP Catalogue). Oxford University Press. Retrieved from http://ideas.repec.org/b/oxp/obooks/9780198070207.html

Mohan, R. (2013). Financial Sector Reforms and monetary policy. *Economic Reform in India: Challenges, Prospects, and Lessons*, 139.

Molyneux, P., Nguyen, L. H., & Xie, R. (2013). Foreign bank entry in South East Asia. *International Review of Financial Analysis, 30*, 26–35. doi:10.1016/j.irfa.2013.05.004

Muzaffar, A. T., & Chowdhury, A. (2014). The IMF and the policy of low inflation: A review of Article IV consultations for selected Asian developing countries. *Economic and Labour Relations Review, 25*(3), 435–454. doi:10.1177/1035304614544272

Nayak, G. (2014, October 22). *Credit information bureaus rely on counselling to expand footprint.* Retrieved October 30, 2014, from http://economictimes.indiatimes.com/industry/banking/finance/banking/credit-information-bureaus-rely-on-counselling-to-expand-footprint/articleshow/44903908.cms

Nguyen, C. V., Islam, A. M., & Ali, M. M. (2011). *The Current State of the Financial Sector of Bangladesh: An Analysis* (AIUB Bus Econ Working Paper Series No. AIUB-BUS-ECON-2011-03). American International University-Bangladesh, Office of Research and Publications (ORP). Retrieved from http://econpapers.repec.org/paper/aiuabewps/89.htm

Nicholas, C., et al. (n.d.). *Economic Reform India Challenges Prospects And Lessons | Economic development and growth | Cambridge University Press.* Retrieved July 28, 2014, from http://www.cambridge.org/us/academic/subjects/economics/economic-development-and-growth/economic-reform-india-challenges-prospects-and-lessons

Prasad, E. S. (2010). *Financial Sector Regulation and Reforms in Emerging Markets: An Overview* (Working Paper No. 16428). National Bureau of Economic Research. Retrieved from http://www.nber.org/papers/w16428

Rajan. (2009). The Global Crisis and Financial Sector Reforms in India. *Business Standard India, 2009*, 142.

Reserve Bank of India. (2013). *Non-Banking Financial Institutions*. Retrieved October 29, 2014, from http://www.rbi.org.in/scripts/PublicationsView.aspx?id=15442

Sahoo, P., & Dash, R. K. (2013). Financial sector development and domestic savings in South Asia. *Economic Modelling, 33*, 388–397. doi:10.1016/j.econmod.2013.04.018

Seelanatha, L. (2010). Market structure, efficiency and performance of banking industry in Sri Lanka. *Banks and Bank Systems*, *5*(1), 20–31.

Seelanatha, L., & Wickremasinghe. (2009). Financial reforms in Sri Lanka and their influence on the banking industry. *Banks and Bank Systems, 4*(4).

Shahbaz, M., & Islam, F. (2011, January 15). *Financial development and income inequality in Pakistan: An application of ARDL approach.* MPRA Paper. Retrieved July 28, 2014, from http://mpra.ub.uni-muenchen.de/28222/

Shrestha, G. K. (2004). Financial Sector Reforms in Nepal. *NRB Economic Review*, *16*, 75–90.

Siddiqui, J., & Ferdous, C. S. (2014). The Regulatory Conundrum: Achieving Corporate Governance Reforms in Developing Countries. In S. Boubaker & D. K. Nguyen (Eds.), *Corporate Governance in Emerging Markets* (pp. 445–464). Springer Berlin Heidelberg. doi:10.1007/978-3-642-44955-0_18

Sofia, A., Ghulam, S., & Zakir, H. (2011). Relationship between Financial Sector Development and Sustainable Economic Development: Time Series Analysis from Pakistan. *International Journal of Economics and Finance*, *3*(1). doi:10.5539/ijef.v3n1p262

Special Inspector General for Afghanistan Reconstruction. (2014). *Afghanistan's banking sector: The central bank's capacity to regulate commercial banks remains weak.* Author.

State Bank of Pakistan. (2007). *Pakistan Banking Sector Reforms: Performance and Challenges*. Retrieved from http://www.sbp.org.pk/about/speech/governors/dr.shamshad/2007/Banking-Reforms-01-Feb-07.pdf

The Economic Times. (2011, March 13). *Number of foreign banks' branches up in India in FY10.* Retrieved October 29, 2014, from http://articles.economictimes.indiatimes.com/2011-03-13/news/28686069_1_new-branches-foreign-banks-royal-bank

The Economic Times. (2014, May 15). *Shares of state-owned banks rally up to 12% after RBI panel moots lower government stake.* Retrieved October 29, 2014, from http://articles.economictimes.indiatimes.com/2014-05-15/news/49873347_1_psu-banks-state-run-banks-public-sector-banks

The Hindu. (2012, May 3). RBI to implement Basel III from January 1, 2013. *The Hindu*. Retrieved from http://www.thehindu.com/business/rbi-to-implement-basel-iii-from-january-1-2013/article3377762.ece

Uddin, S. M. S., & Suzuki, Y. (2011). Financial Reform, Ownership and Performance in Banking Industry: The Case of Bangladesh. *International Journal of Business and Management*, *6*(7), 28. doi:10.5539/ijbm.v6n7p28

Williams, J., & Nguyen, N. (2005). Financial liberalisation, crisis, and restructuring: A comparative study of bank performance and bank governance in South East Asia. *Journal of Banking & Finance*, *29*(8–9), 2119–2154. doi:10.1016/j.jbankfin.2005.03.011

World Bank. (2014a, October 6). *Led by India, South Asia Economic Growth to Accelerate, World Bank*. Retrieved October 29, 2014, from http://www.worldbank.org/en/news/press-release/2014/10/06/led-india-south-asia-economic-growth-accelerate

World Bank. (2014b, October 29). *India leads South Asian countries in "doing business" easier: World Bank*. Retrieved October 30, 2014, from http://news.oneindia.in/international/india-leads-south-asian-countries-doing-business-easier-world-bank-1548324.html

World Bank. (2014c). *South Asia Economic Focus Fall 2014: The Export Opportunity*. World Bank Publications.

Chapter 4
Insider Trading:
A South Asian Study

Tanya Nayyar
Gujarat National Law University, India

ABSTRACT

This chapter studies the international market malpractice of insider trading where officials holding a fiduciary duty towards the company, violate the same to utilise company specific and price sensitive information to trade in company securities before such information is announced to the public investors. Information asymmetry, gross violation of ethical standards and abuse of fairness and market integrity are the underlining terms of this offence. The chapter studies four SAARC nations of India, Pakistan, Sri Lanka and Nepal to project their working against insider trading. While countries introduce law and yet fail to enforce it, SAARC countries are encouraged through this chapter to maintain strong ground against this malady. The author projects recommendations and observations to prompt periodic statutory review.

INTRODUCTION

The author will be dividing the chapter into three parts – Part I, II & III respectively. Part I shall give the readers a brief background of the insider trading activity, its accepted definition and the development of this malady. Part II shall provide a synthesis of the insider trading regulations and enforcement procedures existing in the South Asian countries of India, Pakistan, Sri Lanka and Nepal. Part III shall offer the author's observations and recommendations to each nation on curbing this wide spread practice.

INSIDER TRADING AND ITS DYNAMICS

Regulation for insider trading is a recent phenomenon. The first country to enact insider trading law was United States of America, the inspiration of which was the Securities Act of 1934 which prohibited other kinds of stock manipulation (Barnardo, 2001). France was the second country followed by UK, Japan, Australia and Korea. 1989, EU passed a Directive requiring all member countries to pass legislation

DOI: 10.4018/978-1-5225-0004-9.ch004

prohibiting insider trading (Gevurtz, 2002). By 1991, Sri Lanka was the first SAARC Nation to amend its securities Act of 1987 to include insider trading prohibitive sections (Akhter & Ghani, 2010). Thus, the author points out that SAARC has been behind in the regulatory race to snatch and kill the offensive practice. This chapter shall individually study each country's regulatory activities and bring out the stand taken on insider trading. Before that, a general background and reading on the concept of insider trading and the need of prohibition is advised.

In simple words, insider trading is the illegal trading in the shares of a company whilst in the possession of unpublished, price sensitive information in respect of the securities of the said Company, with a view to the making of a profit, or the avoidance of a loss. As Lord Lane puts it: "the rationale behind the prohibition on insider trading is "the obvious and understandable concern about the damage to public confidence which insider dealing is likely to cause and the clear intention to prevent so far as possible what amounts to cheating when those with inside knowledge use that knowledge to make profit in their dealings with others."

Under insider trading, the restriction is on corporate insiders directly or indirectly using the price sensitive information that they hold to the exclusion of the other shareholders in arriving at trading decisions. Such illegal insider trading undermines investor confidence in the fairness and integrity of the financial markets. This accounts for the reason why nearly every jurisdiction has strictly prohibited this activity.

It has been observed that insider trading is an evocative subject. Drafting regulations for this practice, in precise and unambiguous terms entails balancing multiple and conflicting perceptions of various stakeholders in the market system. For example, the High Level Committee under the chairmanship of Justice N.K. Sodhi set up in India to suggest insider trading regulatory reforms held a view that ideally, the easiest but most simplistic approach would be to prohibit any trading by an insider (SEBI, 2013) . However, such an approach would not only be as ineffective as any blanket prohibition policy but would also be unrealistic and out of sync with economic and regulatory realities.

The general offence of insider trading requires the fulfilment of the following components:

1. The person responsible for committing the offence must be an insider;
2. The insider must hold material unpublished price sensitive information;
3. The insider must use this knowledge to trade in the company's securities;
4. The insider must consequently, earn profits at the expense of the public investors.

The materiality of a fact depends upon the circumstances. A fact is considered "material" if there is a substantial likelihood that a reasonable investor would consider it important in making a decision to buy, sell or hold a security or where the fact is likely to have a significant effect on the market price of the security. Material information can be positive or negative and can relate to virtually any aspect of a company's business or to any type of security – debt or equity.

Information is "unpublished price sensitive information" if it is not available to the general public and it could potentially have any effect on the price of the Company securities. In order for information to be considered public, it must be widely disseminated in a manner making it generally available to investors through such media as the website of the Stock Exchange, newspapers or other media outlets. The circulation of rumors, even if accurate and reported in the media, does not constitute effective public dissemination.

This defines the second requirement of "material unpublished price sensitive information". Any person who possesses such material, unpublished price sensitive information is considered an "insider" as to that information (SEBI, 2002). Insiders include the Company's directors, officers, employees, independent contractors, and those persons in a special relationship with the Company, e.g., its auditors, consultants, attorneys and also include the family members of the above in some circumstances. The definition of insider is transaction specific; that is, an individual is an insider with respect to each material, unpublished information of which he or she is aware.

The next element of committing this offence is the "use" of such information. However, this use must be between the duration of the insider receiving the price sensitive information and the public disclosure of the information. In such circumstances, the insider receives the "undue advantage" of the market reaction that is about to follow the public announcement by the Company. Any trading transaction backed or based on such private information is a gross misuse of the information as well as the position held in the Company. Infact, the courts of USA have clearly laid down the view that "the insiders who receive unpublished price sensitive inormation by virtue of their connection with the company and for corporate purposes only, such insiders owe a fiduciary duty to the company not to misuse or misappropriate such information for an unlawful purpose i.e. to make secret profits or personal gains for themselves." (Chiarella v. US 455 US 222) Thus, any such misuse is a gross violation of corporate governance and in turns behaves as a fraud on public shareholders who legitimately expect the management to run the company in the best interests.

In light of the above studied components of the mal practice, it is noted that the majority of global legislators adopting statutes relating to insider trading have addressed the following issues: What is inside information? Who can be considered an insider? What activities related to using inside information are prohibited? How to prevent insider trading? What sanctions and enforcement measures should be implemented? These questions shall be similarly studied by the author in respect South Asian regulatory frameworks.

SYNTHESIS OF SOUTH ASIAN REGULATORY FRAMEWORK

Historical Development of Insider Trading Regulations in India

This section tracks the evolution of insider trading laws in India, and the events forcing enactment of such regulations.

The 18th century marks the earliest record of security dealings in India. By 1840, there were only 6 brokers in stocks and shares recognized by merchants and banks in Bombay and by 1887, the Native Share and Stock Brokers Association of Bombay was formally constituted which was later renamed as the Bombay Stock Exchange, the first exchange in India.

By the time India got independence in 1947, the Defense of India Act, 1943 was in force. This Act imposed restrictions on capital issues and was continued to be incorporated in the Capital Issues (Control) Act of 1947. Besides other restrictions, this 1947 Act provided for the establishment of a Controller of Capital Issues who was the authority to approve the issue of securities, amount, type and price of such securities. However, as a part of the liberalization process in India, this Act was repealed in 1992.

Between 1946 & 1947, the stock market faced few impediments in its development. There was a phase where trading was bringing large profits to speculators whereas huge losses were being incurred by interested investors. The Government realized a need to tighten control over the stock market.

Thus, the first concrete attempt to regulate insider trading was the constitution of the Thomas Committee in 1948(Insider Trading Regulations - A Primer, 2013) . The agenda of this Committee was to frame a law regulating such stock market activities. The Committee's recommendations were highly influenced by the US Model. The Report founded that officers like directors, agents, auditors were found to be using inside information for profitably speculating in the securities of their own companies. On analyzing these instances, it was observed that insider trading occurred due to:

1. Possession of inside information by company officials;
2. Such possession before it became public knowledge;
3. Information pertaining to changes in economic conditions of the company, specifically, issue of shares, amount of dividend; or entering into a favourable contract.

Pursuant to the recommendations of the Thomas Committee, Sections 307 and 308 were introduced in the Companies Act 1956. This change paved the way for certain mandatory disclosures by directors and managers, but failed to be effective enough in achieving the objective of preventing insider trading. The need for the introduction of these Sections was similarly felt post the speech of Bombay Stock Exchange President where he noted that many leading companies failed to provide prompt declaration of dividends and issue of bonus shares, as a result of which information of such activities was to the knowledge of only officials before it became an official announcement. This resulted in reaping of unjust profits by company officials.

In 1979, the Sachar Committee reiterated in its Report that company employees like directors, auditors, company secretaries etc. hold price sensitive information that could be used to as a tool to manipulate stock prices, causing financial misfortunes to the public investors. This Report suggested amendments to the Companies Act, 1956 to restrict or prohibit the dealings of employees and officials constituting insiders of the Company. The Report recommended penalties to prevent insider trading as well.

In 1986, the Patel Committee recommended that the Securities Contracts (Regulations) Act, 1956 should be amended to make stock exchanges regulated by this Act, curb insider trading through the means of a regulatory mechanism. The Committee suggested penalties by way of heavy fines including imprisonment, apart from refunding the profit made or the losses averted to the stock exchanges. It was the first time that the term "insider trading" was defined comprehensively in the following words:

Trading in the shares of a company by the person who are in the management of the company or are close to them on the basis of undisclosed price sensitive information regarding the working of the company, which they possess but which is not available to others

In 1989 the Abid Hussain Committee recommended that the insider trading activities should be penalized by civil and criminal proceedings. The Committee put forth a recommendation suggesting the formulation of separate regulations and a governing code to prevent such unfair dealings.

In compliance with the above studied Committee Reports, India sought to prohibit the mal practice of insider trading by the introduction and enforcement of the Securities and Exchange Board of India (Insider Trading) Regulations 1992.

This dire need to curb insider trading through SEBI Regulations was felt due to the following reasons:

1. To make the Indian Securities Market fair and transparent for all public investors;
2. To boost the investor confidence;
3. To maintain integrity in price discovery;
4. To have a level playing field for all investors and market participants; and
5. To prevent Insiders from earning a profit or causing detrimental loss to the public.

Over two decades of the 1992 Regulations in force, the Justice N. K. Sodhi Committee released a Report capturing the public deliberations and confusion caused over the provisions in force and as a consequence, recommended a new set of regulations termed as the Proposed Regulations. These Regulations saw the light on 15th January, 2015 when SEBI notified he SEBI (Prohibition of Insider Trading Regulations) 2015.

The regulatory power and prohibition is reiterated in the recently revised Companies Act, 2013 which takes a bold step by clearly defining the offence of "insider trading" in the following words: *an act of subscribing, buying, selling, dealing or agreeing to subscribe, buy, sell or deal in any securities by any director or key managerial personnel or any other officer of a company either as principal or agent if such director or key managerial personnel or any other officer of the company is reasonably expected to have access to any non-public price sensitive information in respect of securities of company, or an act of counselling about procuring or communicating directly or indirectly any non-public price-sensitive information to any person;* (Section 195 (1), Explanation (a)). This is the only legislative instrument which prohibits insider trading in an iron clad manner. The power to regulate this activity still lies with SEBI.

Regulatory Body and its Functioning

The Securities & Exchange Board of India ("SEBI") was established under the SEBI Act of 1992. Section 11 of this Act enlists the functions of the Board, the primary being investor protection. This task of promoting investors' interest and development provides for the strict prohibition of insider trading in securities (Section 11(2)(g), SEBI Act, 1992). Statutory powers given to SEBI include investigation and inspection of books or registers or any documents (Section 11(2A), SEBI Act, 1992), suspension of trading, restraining any person from accessing the securities market or selling and dealing in securities (Section 11(4), SEBI Act, 1992).

SEBI Act, 1992

SEBI fully understands the rising issue of insider trading and the fraudulent activities attached to it with the impact such activities hold on investor confidence. Thus, the Act has dedicated Chapter VA to the prohibition of such manipulative and deceptive devices vide an amendment in 2002. The Act repeats its stand on the strict prohibition of insider trading in securities under Section 12A wherein its states that no person shall directly or indirectly engage in the activity of insider trading (Section 12A(d), SEBI Act, 1992) or deal in securities while in possession of material or non-public information or communicate such information to any other person (Section 12A(e), SEBI Act, 1992).

The presence of the penalty clause under the SEBI Act explains SEBI's firm stance on its illegality. Any person, held to be an insider, who deals in securities based on unpublished information, communicates any non-public price sensitive information or counsels or procures for any other person to deal in securities, shall be held liable to a penalty of a sum not less than ten lakh rupees but which may extend to twenty-five crore rupees (Clause 12, Securities Law (Amendment) Bill, 2014, Bill No. 88 of 2014) or three times the amount of the profits made out of insider trading, whichever is deemed to be a higher sum (Section 15G, SEBI Act, 1992). The adjudicatory powers of SEBI are provided in the Act (Section 15I and 15J, SEBI Act, 1992).

SEBI (Insider Trading) Regulations, 1992

Under the SEBI Act, Section 11(2)(g) empowers SEBI to take such measures, *inter alia*, for the prevention insider trading; protection of investor interests and promotion of the development and regulation of securities market. The power to make Regulations for the promotion of the above mentioned aims is derived from Section 30 of the Act. Pursuant to such powers, SEBI introduced the Insider Trading Regulations on November 19, 1992.

The 1992 Regulations simply prohibited any insider from dealing in securities of a company on any stock exchange either by himself or on behalf of any other person. Further, communication of any unpublished price sensitive information to any person, with or without his request for such information, except as required in the ordinary course of business or under any law, was also prohibited. Any person guilty of this offence was liable under Section 15G and 24 of the SEBI Act, 1992.

These Regulations were drastically amended vide the 2002 Amendment and renamed as SEBI (Prohibition of Insider Trading) Regulations, 1992.

SEBI (Prohibition of Insider Trading) Regulations, 1992 [Post 2002 Amendment]

These Regulations even though successful in imposing stringent norms, fails to define the term "insider trading". On a comprehensive study of the Regulations, it is noted that the practice of insider trading comprises of three elements:

1. Involvement of insider or connected person;
2. Presence of unpublished price sensitive information; and
3. Use of such information for dealing in securities

In 2013, India constituted a High Level Committee to review the SEBI (Prohibition of Insider Trading) Regulations, 1992 under the chairmanship of Justice N.K. Sodhi ("Sodhi Committee"). This Committee submitted the report on December 7, 2013 with a proposed revision to the existing Regulations. In the section below, the author shall be discussing the recently notified SEBI (Prohibition of Insider Trading Regulations) 2015, and shall lay out a detailed comparison between the the pre-existing 1992 Regulations ("1992 Regulations") along with notified Regulations ("2015 Regulations").

SEBI (Prohibition of Insider Trading Regulations), 2015

I. Applicability of the Regulatory Framework

The 1992 Regulations limit their scope to companies listed on a stock exchange in India (Regulation 3). However, the 2015 Regulations extend the applicability of the Regulations to any entity that has issued securities which are listed on a stock exchange or intended to be so listed, as stated under Regulation 3 of the SEBI (Prohibition of Insider Trading Regulations), 2015. By amending and expanding the definition of 'company' to include any entity that issues securities listed on stock exchanges, the Sodhi Committee has been mindful to include entities like mutual funds, trusts etc. within the scope of this malpractice.

Further, the pre-existing 1992 Regulations related to securities of a company. The term "securities" has been defined under the Securities Contracts (Regulation) Act, 1956 as shares, scrips, stocks, bonds, debentures, debenture stock or other marketable securities of a like nature in or of any incorporated company or other body corporate; derivative; units of collective investment scheme; security receipts; mutual fund units; Government securities; and such other instruments as may be declared by the Central Government (Section 2(h)). Since this definition is wide in its ambit, the 2015 Regulations defines "securities" as the meaning assigned under Regulation 2(i) of SEBI (Prohibition of Insider Trading Regulations), 2015.

II. Who is an Insider?

At the very outset, it is pertinent to understand the term "person" who may be treated as an Insider within the scope of these Regulations. SEBI clarified in the matter of Mr. Naval Choudhary (via its Adjudication Order No. PB/AO-15/2011 dated February 28, 2011) that the word *'person'* is a generic term and it may take in its ambit, when construed in common parlance, not only individuals but also firms, associations or bodies corporate. This view is backed by Section 3(42) of the Indian General Clauses Act, 1987 which gives an inclusive definition of the term "person" including any company or association or body of individuals, whether incorporated or not.

Regulation 2(e) of the previously existing 1992 Regulations defined an 'insider' as any person who:

- Is or was connected with the company or is deemed to have been connected with the company and who is reasonably expected to have access to unpublished price sensitive information in respect of securities of a company; or
- Has received or has had access to such unpublished price sensitive information.

In the Hindustan Lever case [March 11, 1998], the interpretation of the term 'insider' under regulation 2(e) was one of the key issues under consideration before the appellate authority. In this regard, the appellate authority observed that the definition of "insider" should have three ingredients:

1. The person should be a natural person or legal entity;
2. The person should be a connected person or a deemed connected person; and
3. Acquisition of the unpublished price sensitive information should be by virtue of the connection.

The Securities Appellate Tribunal supported the above view through the cases of Rajiv B. Gandhi, Sandhya R. Gandhi, Amishi B. Gandhi v. SEBI (Appeal Number 50 of 2007) and Dr. Anjali Beke v. SEBI (Appeal No.148 of 2005) by clarifying that, "a person who has received unpublished price sensitive information or who has had access to such information, becomes an insider".

Now the 2015 Regulations simplify the definition of an "insider" (under Regulation 2(g) of SEBI (Prohibition of Insider Trading Regulations), 2015 to mean any person who is a "connected person" or those in possession of or having access to "unpublished price sensitive information". Thus, the definition has been tailored down to two categories: i) connected persons; and ii) those persons that have possession or access to unpublished price sensitive information. The definition of an "insider" under the 1992 Regulations included "a person deemed to be a connected person". This category included a company under the same management or group or a subsidiary; intermediaries, members or board of directors or employees of a public financial institution, officers or employees of self-regulatory organizations, relatives of the aforementioned persons, bankers of the company, relatives of the connected persons etc. With the simplification of the definition of an insider, the category of 'persons deemed to be connected persons' has been done away with.

The 2015 Regulations explains the burden of proof scenario in case to prove the possession or access to such unpublished information, to state that the onus of showing that a certain person was in possession of or had access to unpublished price sensitive information at the time of trading would be on the person leveling the charge after which the person who has traded when in possession of or having access to unpublished price sensitive information may demonstrate that he was not in such possession or that he has not traded or or he could not access or that his trading when in possession of such information was squarely covered by the exonerating circumstances.

a. Connected Persons

The definition of connected person is crucial for purposes of defining an insider. The 1992 Regulations envisaged a connected person to be an integral determinant of insider trading as observed under the definition of "insider". Regulation 2(c) included any person who had temporary and permanent professional or business relationship with the company within the ambit of a "connected person". The definition under the 1992 Regulations read as any person who is connected 6 months prior to the offence of insider trading and:

- Is a director of a company, or is deemed to be a director of that company by virtue of section 307(10) of the Companies Act, 1956; or
- Occupies the position as an officer or an employee of the company or holds a position involving a professional or business relationship between himself and the company whether temporary or permanent and who may reasonably be expected to have an access to unpublished price sensitive information in relation to that company.

In an event a person is not a connected person as per the given definition, then the test of establishing the liability lies in the factual determination of whether such person has received or has had access to unpublished price sensitive information relating to the company. In the matter of SEBI v. Shri A. L. Shilotri, the Appellate Tribunal clarified that a person who is not a connected person will be an insider if he had access to unpublished price sensitive information. It is to be noted that the access of a person to unpublished price sensitive information is highly relevant and essential but in cases where there is proven connected or deemed connected person, the test is stricter. Mere reasonable expectation of access to unpublished price sensitive information can make connected person or deemed connected person an insider.

In Chandrakala v. Adjudicating Officer ([2012] 107 CLA 55 (SAT)), the definition of 'connected person' has been discussed. The Appellant's husband was the promoter of the Company and brother of the Managing Director of the Company. Thus, SEBI held that the Appellant was deemed to be a connected person with the Company.

The recently introduced 2015 Regulations widen this definition of connected persons (as stipulated under Regulation 2(d) of (Prohibition of Insider Trading Regulations), 2015. It includes any person who is or has during the 6 months prior to the concerned act been associated with a company, directly or indirectly, in any capacity including by reason of frequent communication with its officers or by being in any contractual, fiduciary or employment relationship or by being a director, officer or an employee of the company or holds any position including a professional or business relationship between himself and the company whether temporary or permanent, that allows such person, directly or indirectly, access to unpublished price sensitive information or is reasonably expected to allow such access. The definition provides an exhaustive category of persons falling under the term 'connected persons' by reason of their relationship with the company. The persons deemed to be connected persons are:

1. Immediate relative of connected persons.
2. Holding company or associate company or subsidiary company.
3. Investment company, trustee company, asset management company or an employee or director thereof.
4. Official of a stock exchange or of clearing house or corporation.
5. Member of board of trustees of a mutual fund or a member of the board of directors of the asset management company of a mutual fund or is an employee thereof.
6. Official or an employee of a self-regulatory organization recognised or authorized by SEBI.
7. Banker of the company.
8. A concern, firm, trust, Hindu undivided family, company or association of persons wherein a director of a company or his immediate relative or banker of the company, has more than 10% of the holding or interest.

Thus, the extension of this term is not only limited to persons that occupy responsible positions in the company or those having professional / business relations with the company but also those who are associated with a company in any manner. The Regulations are careful to clarify in the note appended to the definition that immediate relatives and other categories of persons specified above are presumed to be connected persons but such a presumption is a deeming legal fiction and is rebuttable.

III. Unpublished Price Sensitive Information

With the 2002 Amendment to the 1992 Regulations, the definition of 'unpublished price sensitive information' was bifurcated into "unpublished" and "price-sensitive information" in the Regulations. The definition for 'price-sensitive information' was inserted at Regulation 2(ha) and the term 'unpublished' was defined at Regulation 2(k).

Under the 1992 Regulations, "price sensitive information" (Regulation 2(ha)) is information which fulfils the following two requirements:

1. has to relate to the company, directly or indirectly; and
2. should have the capability to materially affect the price of the securities of the company when published and disclosed to the public.

The Explanation appended to this definition lays out examples which shall be deemed to be price sensitive information. They include:

1. Periodical financial results of the company.
2. Intended declaration of dividends (both interim and final).
3. Issue of securities or buy-back of securities.
4. Any major expansion plans or execution of new projects.
5. Amalgamation, mergers or takeovers.
6. Disposal of the whole or substantial part of the undertaking.
7. Significant changes in policies, plans or operations of the company.

Further, the Equity Listing Agreement released by SEBI, applicable to all companies listed on the stock exchanges of India, requires all such companies to immediately inform Stock Exchange(s) in respect of the some events which are considered to be price sensitive such as:

1. Disruption of operations due to natural calamity;
2. Commencement of Commercial Production/ Commercial Operations;
3. Developments with respect to pricing/ realization arising out of change in the regulatory framework;
4. Issue of any class of securities;
5. Acquisition, merger, de-merger, amalgamation, restructuring, scheme of arrangement, spin off or setting division of the company, etc.;
6. Change in market lot of company's shares, sub-divisions of equity shares of the company;
7. Voluntary delisting by the company from the Stock Exchange(s);
8. Forfeiture of shares;
9. Any action which will result in alteration in the terms regarding redemption/ cancellation/ retirement in whole or in part of any securities issued by the company;
10. Information regarding opening, closing or status of ADR, GDR or any other class of securities to be issued abroad;
11. Cancellation of dividend/ rights/ bonus, etc.
12. Litigation/ dispute with aerial impact; and
13. Any other information having bearing on the operation/ performance of the company as well as price sensitive information.

For such price sensitive information to be a determinant of insider trading, it must be unpublished, not privy to public knowledge, consequently, created an asymmetry of information. The term 'unpublished' (Regulation 2(k) under 1992 Regulations) has been defined as: "information which has not been published by the Company or its agents and is not specific in nature." The Regulations have clarified in the Explanation attached that speculative reports in media cannot be considered as published information.

The 2015 Regulations reverts to the position existing before the 2002 Amendment made to the previously existing 1992 Regulations by defining "unpublished price sensitive information" as a singular term with the meaning: "any information, relating to a company or its securities, directly or indirectly, that is not generally available which upon becoming generally available, is likely to materially affect the price of the securities", which has been explained under Regulation 2(n) of SEBI (Prohibition of

Insider Trading Regulations), 2015. It goes on to explain that such information shall ordinarily include information relating to the following activities:

1. Financial results;
2. Dividends;
3. Change in capital structure;
4. Mergers, de-mergers, acquisitions, delistings, disposals and expansion in business and such other transactions; and,
5. Changes in key managerial personnel.

Under the effective 2015 Regulations, the reliance has shifted to generally available information which includes information that is accessible to the public on a non-discriminatory basis. Any information that is not generally available shall account for unpublished price sensitive information. The essence of the definition remains as given under the 1992 Regulations, however, the new addition of the "generally available information" determines the malpractice, where information which is not generally available on public forum, and which may affect the price of securities shall mean unpublished price sensitive information.

IV. Charging Provision

The 1992 Regulations prohibit insider trading by holding that no Insider shall:

1. Either on his own behalf or on behalf of any other person, deal in securities of a company listed on any stock exchange when in possession of any unpublished price sensitive information; or
2. Communicate or counsel or procure directly or indirectly any unpublished price sensitive information to any person who while in possession of such unpublished price sensitive information shall not deal in securities. This is not applicable in case any communication required in the ordinary course of business or profession or employment or under any law (Regulation 3 of SEBI (Prohibition of Insider Trading Regulations), 2015 states this.

Thus, any insider dealing in securities in contravention of the above provisions shall be guilty of insider trading. Thus, the prohibition is twofold, in terms of prohibition by all insiders in general and specific prohibition on insider trading by companies.

The 2015 Regulations has expanded the liability clause to two Regulations – Regulation 3 pertaining to communication or procurement of unpublished price sensitive information relating to a company or securities listed or proposed to be listed, to any person including other insiders except where such communication is in furtherance of legitimate purposes, performance of duties or discharge of legal obligations; and, Regulation 4 relating to trading when in possession of such unpublished price sensitive information. These new regulations have adopted the term "trading" instead of "dealing" in securities under the charging provision. This change was introduced based on the Sodhi Committee recommendation which held a view that each and every act of doing something with securities would constitute dealing, for example, getting securities dematerialized, creating an encumbrance, agreeing not to dispose of the securities without another person's consent such as a lender, would all be acts of dealing in securities.

Since the mandate of the Parliament is to prohibit insider trading and the regulations ought to focus on such a prohibition and not inflict unintended and untold prohibitions on any and every activity connected with securities, it is advisable to restrict the prohibition to "trading". Thus the charging principle of the 2015 Regulations has been modified to prohibition of trading when in possession of unpublished price sensitive information. The general rule backing this principle is that no insider should gain undue benefit by trading with the benefit of possessing unpublished price sensitive information which the rest of the market does not have and therefore, gain an advantage over the market.

The 2015 Regulations has retained the general prohibition on communication or counselling unpublished price sensitive information as the second primary charging provision, modifying it slightly to be read as the insider is not allowed to communicate, provide or allow access of any unpublished price sensitive information to any person including other insiders. In such circumstances, communication is only permissible when in furtherance of legitimate purposes. The 2015 Regulations attempt to protect this clause by insisting on execution of confidentiality and non-disclosure agreements by parties.

V. Liability Clause

In India, insider trading is not only a tort but also a crime. A person convicted of insider trading is punishable under Section 24 and Section 15G of the SEBI Act 1992. Under these provisions, SEBI may impose a penalty not be less than ten lakh rupees but which may extend to twenty-five crore rupees or three times the amount of profits made out of insider trading, whichever is higher.[1] Besides the imposition of such penalty, the regulatory authority may also initiate criminal prosecution looking at the gravity of the offence. In the interests of investors and market confidence, SEBI may also issue orders prohibiting an insider or refraining an insider from dealing in the securities of the company.

The recently introduced Companies Act, 2013 contains a clause prohibiting insider trading which states that any person contravening the given section 195 will be punishable with imprisonment for a term which may extend to five years or with fine which shall not be less than five lakh rupees but which may extend to twenty-five crore rupees or three times the amount of profits made out of insider trading, whichever is higher, or with both.[2] The difference in standards of punishment – imposition of imprisonment and fine under the Companies Act and imposition of only higher fine under Insider Trading Regulations points out the ambiguity in regulation of this offence.

Under the previously effective 1992 Regulations, the authority was given investigative powers (Regulation 4A) to conduct inquiries and inspections of books and records of insider(s). However, before undertaking any investigation, SEBI is bound to give a reasonable notice to the insider. Where SEBI is satisfied that in the interest of investors or in public interest no such notice should be given, it may by an order in writing direct that the investigation be taken up without such notice.

VI. Disclosures for Prohibition in Insider Trading

These 2015 Regulations require companies to provide the following types of disclosures during their working:

- **Initial Disclosure[3]:** Required by every promoter, key managerial personnel and director of every company whose securities are listed on any recognised stock exchange to mandatorily disclose his holding of securities of the company as on the date of these regulations taking effect, to the company within thirty days of these regulations taking effect. Further, every person on appointment as a key managerial personnel or a director of the company or upon becoming a promoter shall disclose his holding of securities of the company as on the date of appointment or becoming a promoter, to the company within seven days of such appointment or becoming a promoter.

- **Continuous Disclosure[4]:** Required by every promoter, employee and director of every company to mandatorily disclose to the company the number of such securities acquired or disposed of within two trading days of such transaction if the value of the securities traded, whether in onc transaction or a series of transactions over any calendar quarter, aggregates to a traded value in excess of ten lakh rupees or such other value as may be specified. Such mandatorily disclosure shall be notified to the stock exchange within two trading days of receipt of the disclosure or from becoming aware of such information.
- **Additional Disclosure[5]:** Are required for all holdings in securities of that company held by any other connected person or class of connected persons. Such disclosures shall be made at the periodic frequency as determined by the company with the purpose of monitoring compliance with the present 2015 Regulations.

VII. Statutory Defences

Valid defences for an insider who has traded when in possession of unpublished price sensitive information have been set out under the SEBI 2015 Regulations as:

1. Communication, access or procurement of unpublished price sensitive information in connection with takeovers, mergers and acquisitions involving trading in securities and change of control to assess a potential investment involving an open offer under the takeover regulations where the board of directors of the company is of informed opinion that the proposed transaction is in the best interests of thc company[6];
2. Communication, access or procurement of unpublished price sensitive information, not attracting the provisions of the takeover regulations, but made in the best interests of the company within 2 days prior to the proposed transaction;
3. Trading in securities while in possession of unpublished price sensitive information where the transaction is an off-market inter-se transfer between promoters who were in possession of the same unpublished price sensitive information and both the parties have made a conscious, informed trade decision[7];
4. The individuals in possession of unpublished price sensitive information were different from the individuals who factually traded in securities and took trading decisions, and such individuals trading were not in possession of the same unpublished price sensitive information;
5. Evidence of adequate arrangements been taken to protect the unpublished price sensitive information and that no unpublished price sensitive information has been communicated to persons trading in securities, and no regulations have been violated;
6. That the trades were pursuant to a Trading Plan devised under Regulation 5. India has now initiated a provision of trading plans on the lines of US practice providing safeguards to the company. A trading plan allows and enables persons perpetually in possession of unpublished price sensitive information to trade in a compliant manner. By doing so, the possession of unpublished price sensitive information when a trade under a pre-scheduled trading plan is actually executed would not prohibit the execution of such trades that he had pre-decided even before the unpublished price sensitive information came into being.

While the regulators lay out defences, they must also formulate a strong framework for investigation and enforcement to ensure that the perpetrators do not falsely use such defences to their wrongful benefit.

PAKISTAN

Regulatory Body and its Functioning

The regulator, Securities and Exchange Corporation of Pakistan ("**SECP**"), undertook drastic efforts during the first 20 months of its operation to lay down the foundations of a sound and effective regulatory body to govern and supervise the capital markets in Pakistan.

The history of the SECP began formally in 1970. The Securities and Exchange Authority of Pakistan (SEAP), a precursor to the Corporate Law Authority, was set up in November 1970, with the approval of the President of Pakistan. Since then, this Commission has taken bold initiatives to bring the capital markets, into an effective discipline specially to protect the interests and rights of small investors and minority share holders.

The Securities and Exchange Commission of Pakistan Act was passed by the Parliament and promulgated in December 1997. In pursuance of this Act, the SECP, having autonomous status, became operational on January 1 1999. The Act gives the Commission the administrative authority and financial independence to carry out the reform program of Pakistan's capital market.

This Commission is supported by a Security and Policy Board, consisting of nine members appointed by the Federal Government. The Board may constitute such number of its committees as it considers necessary or expedient to assist it in the performance of its functions under this Act.

The powers and functions of the Commission and the Board are enlisted in the SECP Act, 1997, broadly covering areas to uphold the mission and vision of the Commission.

The mission of the Commission has been laid down as: To develop a fair, efficient and transparent regulatory framework, based on international legal standards and best practices, for the protection of investors and mitigation of systemic risk aimed at fostering growth of a robust corporate sector and broad based capital market in Pakistan. It is in pursuance of such best practices that Pakistan has provided for regulations prohibiting insider trading.

Securities and Exchange Ordinance, 1969 (Ordinance No. XVII of 1969) and Listed Companies (Prohibition of Insider Trading) Guidelines, 2001

I. Applicability of the Regulatory Framework

Chapter III-A (Section 15A to 15E, introduced vide Finance Act, 2008) of the Securities and Exchange Ordinance, 1969 (Ordinance No. XVII of 1969, June 28, 1969) ("Ordinance") provides exclusively for insider trading. The primary legal point put down is that no person shall indulge in insider trading activity.

Pakistan has separately issued the Listed Companies (Prohibition of Insider Trading) Guidelines, 2001 exclusively applicable to those companies dealing in securities which have been allowed to be traded on the stock exchange (Section 2(h)). Thus, this SAARC Nation provides separately yet covering both listed companies and companies yet to list their securities.

The author will be studying both the regulatory frameworks simultaneously and comparatively under each sub-heading.

II. Who is an Insider?

The Ordinance defines Insiders (Section 15C) to include the following persons –

A. Sponsors, executive officers and directors of an issuer;
B. Sponsors, executive officers, directors and partners of a legal person or unincorporated business association, in which the issuer holds shares or voting rights, directly or indirectly, of twenty per cent or more;
C. Sponsors, executive officers, directors and partners of a legal person or unincorporated business association who holds, directly or indirectly, shares or voting rights of ten per cent or more in an issuer;
D. Sponsors, executive officers and directors of an organization, that has been engaged in the placement of listed securities or the public offer of securities or the issuing and marketing of such securities, who has had access to insider information during his employment till a period of one year after leaving employment;
E. Any natural person holding, directly or indirectly, ten per cent or more shares of an issuer;
F. Sponsors, executive officers and directors of credit institutions in which the issuer has an account;
G. Any person obtaining inside information as part of his employment or when discharging his usual duties in an official capacity, or in any other way relating to work performed under contract of employment or otherwise;
H. Any person obtaining inside information through unlawful means; and
I. A spouse, lineal ascendant or descendant, partner or nominee of a person referred to in clauses (a) to (h).

It is worth discussing that Pakistan Ordinance includes a provision terming any natural person holding ten per cent or more shares of the issuer company as an insider. Addition of the phrase 'holding, directly or indirectly' further widens the scope of the insider category. While a plain reading of the clause may sound beneficial to the financial markets, scrutinising and investigating charges of the offence may turn out cumbersome. Further, the Ordinance holds that insiders may even include persons of credit institutions where the issuer has an account or business associations in which the issuer company holds a share. It is advisable that the securities regulator provides for periodic reporting norms of such details including relatives and ascendants and descendants of the persons referred in the clause so as to ensure effective redressal of insider trading charges and investigation procedures.

The Listed Companies' Guidelines provides a more basic yet expansive definition pointing out who the insider (Clause 2 (g)) is, in such cases. The definition provides:

1. Person who is a director, chief executive, managing agent, chief accountant, secretary or auditor of a listed company or the beneficial owner holding directly or indirectly not less than 10% of the shares of a listed company; or
2. A person who, is or was connected with the company or is deemed to have been connected with the company, and who is reasonably expected to have access, by virtue of such connection, to

unpublished price sensitive information in respect of securities of the company who has received or has had access to such unpublished price sensitive information.

For the purpose of comprehensive understanding, the Guidelines defines "connected person" as any person who-

1. Is a director; or
2. Occupies the position as an officer or an employee of the company or holds a position involving a professional or business relationship between himself and the company and who may reasonably be expected to have an access to unpublished price sensitive information in relation to that company.

Thus, the insiders in a listed company are essentially the top management and key managerial personnel, holding a position of trust in the professional relationship and deemed to have access to unpublished price sensitive information.

III. Unpublished Price Sensitive Information

The Ordinance uses the term "inside information" (Section 15B). It is explained as:

A. Information which has not been made public relating, directly or indirectly, to listed securities or one or more issuers and which, if it were made public, would be likely to have an effect on the prices of those listed securities or on the price of related securities;
B. In relation to derivatives on commodities or information which has not been made public, relating, directly or indirectly, to one or more such derivatives and which are traded in accordance with accepted market practices on those markets; or
C. In relation to persons responsible for the execution of orders concerning listed securities, information which is conveyed by a client to such person and related to the client's pending orders.

Clause 2(m) of the Guidelines for listed companies defines "unpublished price sensitive information" in a similar yet not inclusive manner as the Ordinance, as any information which relates to the following matters or is of concern, directly or indirectly, to a company, and is not generally known or published by such company for general information, but which if published or known, is likely to materially affect the price, of securities of that company in the market, like:

A. Financial results (both half-yearly and annual) of the company;
B. Intended declaration of dividends (both interim and final);
C. Issue of shares by way of rights, bonus, etc.;
D. Any major expansion plans or execution of new projects;
E. Amalgamation, mergers and takeovers;
F. Disposal of the whole or substantially the whole of the undertaking;
G. Such other information as may affect the earnings of the company; and
H. Any changes in policies, plans or operations of the company.

The Guidelines of 2001 will help individuals understand what events and actions of the company shall fall under price sensitive information.

IV. Charging Provision

Section 15A (1) of the Ordinance proves to be a general prohibitory provision wherein it states that no person shall indulge in insider trading. Sub-clause (2) continues to say that the offence of insider trading shall include the following components:

A. an insider person transacting any deal, directly or indirectly, using inside information involving listed securities to which the inside information pertains, or using others to transact such deals;
B. any other person to whom inside information has been passed or disclosed by an insider person transacting any deal, directly or indirectly, using inside information involving listed securities to which the inside information pertains, or using others to transact such deals;
C. transaction by any person as specified in clauses (a) and (b), or any other person who knows, or ought to have known under normal and reasonable circumstances, that the information possessed and used for transacting any deal is inside information;
D. an insider person suggesting or recommending to another person to engage in dealing in any listed securities to which the inside information possessed by the insider person pertains, without the inside information being disclosed to the person who has dealt in such securities.

The two essential ingredients of establishing an offence of insider trading are that the person dealing in a scrip should be 'insider' as defined under Section 15C of the Ordinance and the information used by him must fulfil the criteria laid down in Section 15B of the Ordinance.

In other words, the Ordinance prohibits an insider or any other person to whom information has been passed on from transacting any deal in listed securities based on insider information or suggesting or recommending to another person to engage in any deal in securities based on the insider information obtained by the insider. As found in other SAARC nations, Pakistan too prohibits dealing in securities, counselling, procuring, or communicating any insider information to any other person who may engage in dealing of the same.

It ought to be noted that the Ordinance has clearly clarified that no agreement shall be held to be void or unenforceable only because such a prohibited activity has taken place (Section 15A(4)).

Under the Guidelines for listed companies, Clause 3 reads that no person who is or has been, at any time during the preceding six months associated with a company undertake either on his own behalf or on behalf of any other person, deal in securities of a company listed on a stock exchange on the basis of any unpublished price sensitive information; or communicate any unpublished price sensitive information to any person, with or without his request for such information; or counsel or procure any other person to deal in securities of any company on the basis of unpublished price sensitive information.

The author points out that India's Regulations of 1992 lays out the charging provision in the exact manner as above. This proves the common stand taken by SAARC Nations on the offence of insider trading.

It is observed that insider trading has been looked down upon with strong emotions. Lahore Stock Exchange has issued the Regulations for Proprietary Trading of the Lahore Stock Exchange (Guarantee) Limited wherein under the clause for maintaining 'Market Integrity', the offence of insider trading has been prohibited. The clause provides that no broker shall, directly or indirectly, deal in any listed security or cause any other person to deal in securities of such company if he has inside information which is not generally available; and would, if it were so available, be likely to materially affect the price of those securities. Further, the clause also mandates the brokers to maintain a separate book of accounts displaying the money received and paid separately. The efforts on part of the regulators to maintain integrity and curb the offence are well appreciated.

V. Liability Clause

Pakistan has in unambiguous terms laid out the enforcement and penalty charges on insider trading under both the Ordinance and the Guidelines for Listed Companies.

Under the Ordinance, any person liable under the charging provision explained above, will be liable to fine, which may extend to ten million rupees or three times the amount of gain made or loss avoided by such person, or loss suffered by another person, whichever amount is higher (Section 15E (1)). Where an insider person discloses inside information to any other person who is not required to possess such information for any reason, the insider person shall be liable to fine, to be imposed by the Commission, which may extend to thirty million rupees (Section 15E (3)).

In addition to the fine, the Commission may direct the person to surrender to the Commission, an amount equivalent to the gain made or loss avoided by him; or pay any other person who has suffered a loss, an amount equivalent to the loss so suffered by such person; and in cases where the person guilty is an executive officer, director, auditor, advisor, consultant of a listed company, he shall be removed from such office by an order of the Commission and debarred from auditing any listed company for a period of upto three years; or where such person is registered as a broker or agent, shall be liable to cancellation of registration.

The Ordinance has been successful in categorising punishment for each type of professional. This shall prove to be a deterrent measure for such persons.

It is observed that Pakistan provides for the most comprehensive liability clause (Clause 5) under the Listed Companies' Guidelines. Since Guidelines provide for connected persons and their access to insider information, the liability of every connected person who purchases, sells or otherwise deals in and with securities of an issuer with the knowledge of unpublished price sensitive information is liable to compensate the seller or purchaser of the securities, as the case may be, for damages. Further, every insider who informs another person of unpublished price sensitive information shall also be liable to compensate for damages.

The Guidelines provide regulatory assistance to the Commission by stating that in the process of assessing damages, the Court may consider the following elements:

A. if the plaintiff is a purchaser, the price paid by the plaintiff for the security less the average market price of the security in the twenty trading days following general disclosure of the unpublished price sensitive information; or
B. if the plaintiff is a vendor, the average market price of the security in the twenty trading days following general disclosure of the unpublished price sensitive information less the price received by the plaintiff for the security.

In addition to the above, the Court may also consider such other measures of damages as may be relevant in the circumstances (Clause 5(6)).

Clause 7 of the Guidelines provide for the investigatory powers of the Commission where based on the information available, it may investigate and inspect the books of account, other records and documents of an insider and that of the member of a stock exchange. For such purposes, it may even appoint an enquiry officer.

VI. Disclosures for Prohibition in Insider Trading

Recently in 2013, the Commission issued a notification under Section 15D of the Ordinance of 1969, specifying that all listed companies must follow the given manner and form of disclosure of inside information. It also described the obligation of stock exchanges with respect to dissemination of information so that no person takes undue advantage of the inside information.

It is believed that the Commission will be in a better position to prosecute the persons involved in insider trading as the presence of newly introduced statutory obligations will restrain the persons alleged of insider trading from citing legal justifications for their illegal acts in the presence of clear requirements.

The notification issued by the apex regulator states that all the listed companies as well as the persons specified shall immediately file with the Commission and communicate the same simultaneously to the stock exchange(s) on which these are listed, the details as to the inside information and ancillary matters in the Form annexed to the notification upon the occurrence of any one or more of the events which may affect the price of a listed security. The stock exchanges shall immediately disseminate the material information and ensure posting of same on their website (SECP, February 13, PR Release)

VII. Statutory Defences

Since the Listed Companies' Guidelines provides for connected persons and their access to insider information, the liability of every connected person who purchases, sells or otherwise deals in and with securities of an issuer with the knowledge of unpublished price sensitive information is liable to compensate the seller or purchaser of the securities, as the case may be, for damages unless they prove the following defences:

A. That the connected person reasonably believed that the unpublished price sensitive information had been generally disclosed; or
B. That the unpublished price sensitive information was known or ought reasonably to have been known to the seller or purchaser, as the case may be (Clause 5 (1)).

Similarly, where the insider informs another person of unpublished price sensitive information shall be liable to compensate for damages, unless he proves the following defences:

1. That the person who informed the other person proves that the informing person reasonably believed the unpublished price sensitive information had been generally disclosed;
2. That the unpublished price sensitive information was known or ought reasonably to have been known to the seller or purchaser, as the case may be; or
3. In the case of an action against an issuer or a person in special relationship with the issuer, the information was given in the necessary course of business (Section 5(2)).

SRI LANKA

Sri Lanka, which was earlier known as Ceylon, is an emerging and developing economy in South Asia with a comparatively small population of 20 million. Since the end of the civil war in 2009, Sri Lanka's financial system has been growing at an average growth rate of 5.3%. As a result, its economy has been very resilient to both internal and external shocks over the last two decades (Gunathilake, Zoysa, & Chandrakumara, 2011).

Regulatory Body and its Functioning

The Securities and Exchange Commission of Sri Lanka ("SEC") is the financial market regulator of this SAARC nation. SEC was established in pursuance of the Securities and Exchange Commission of Sri Lanka Act (No. 36 of 1987) ("SEC Act"). The vision of this regulator is "to become the benchmark regulator in South Asia for effective, efficient and proactive capital market regulation". Accordingly, the objectives of the Commission include the protection of the interests of investors, and further, to maintain professional standards in the market (Section 12, SEC Act).

The independence of Commission and avoidance of conflict of interest is visible under Section 9 of the Act. While all questions for decision at any meeting of Commission shall be decided by the vote of the majority of the members present (Section 7(3), SEC Act), in cases where any member is directly or indirectly interested in any decision that is to be taken on any matter by the Commission, shall disclose the nature of such interest at the meeting and consequently, shall not take part in any deliberation or decision of the Commission with regard to that matter, and shall withdraw from such meeting while such deliberation is in progress or such decision is being made.

Securities and Exchange Commission of Sri Lanka Act, Act No. 36 of 1987 as amended by Act No. 26 of 1991, Act No. 18 of 2003 and Act No. 47 of 2009

The prohibition on insider trading is articulated in Part IV (Sections 32-34, SEC Act) of Securities and Exchange Commission of Sri Lanka Act in the following words:

Trading in the shares of a Listed Company whilst in the possession of unpublished, price sensitive information in respect of the securities of the said Company, with a view to the making of a profit, or the avoidance of a loss.

I. Applicability of the Regulatory Framework

Sections 32-34 of the Act states that an individual is prohibited from indulging in insider dealing of listed securities. A plain reading of Section 34 (3) states that a "*company*" means a listed public company, clarifying the applicability of the legal provisions. Whereas, the ambit of Companies Act No. 07 of 2007 is wider as its provisions apply to both listed companies and companies looking forward to being listed.

II. Who is an Insider?

The persons holding unpublished price sensitive information are liable under this Act (Section 34(1)(a)-(c), SEC Act) if they fall under the following categories:

A. Any person who is the director of that company or related company; or
B. Any person who occupies a position as an officer (other than director) or employee of that company or a related company; or
C. Any person holding a position involving a professional or business relationship between himself (or his employer or a company of which he is a director) and the first company or a related company, which in either case may reasonably be expected to give him access to information which, in relation to listed securities of either company, is unpublished price sensitive information and which it would be reasonable to expect (a person in his position not to disclose except) for the proper performance of his function; or
D. Any person having access to information in relation to listed securities, which he knows, is unpublished price sensitive information and which it would be reasonable to expect him not to disclose except in the course of performing his duties.

In the mother Act, it was understood that the concept of an insider was premised on the traditional regulatory approach based on fiduciary duties of an insider or a connected person. Directors and corporate officers of a corporation are viewed as persons who owe a fiduciary duty to the corporation because of the special relationship between them and the corporation. This traditional approach has influenced the development of insider trading laws where insiders are limited to only directors and officers of the corporation. This approach is reflected in section 32(1), 32(3), 33 and 34(1)(a) and (b) of the SEC Act. In 2003 however, the SEC Act was amended to include another category of a person connected to the company in section 34(1)(c) namely when, *"he has access to information in relation to listed securities, which he knows is unpublished price sensitive information and which it would be reasonable to expect him not to disclose except in the course of performing his duties."* SEC has widened the scope of insiders post the 2003 amendment.

III. Unpublished Price Sensitive Information

Individuals holding unpublished price sensitive information with respect to listed securities are liable under these provisions if they deal, counsel, procure or communicate such information as defined below (Section 34(2), SEC Act):

A. Information describing specific matters relating, or of concern, (directly or indirectly) to that company, i.e. matters which are not of a general nature relating to that company; and
B. Information not generally known to those persons who are accustomed or would be likely to deal in those listed securities but which would if it were generally known to them be likely to affect materially the price of those securities.

It is noteworthy that the SEC Act extends its application to a special category of persons, not otherwise regulated by securities market regulator. The provisions of this section are also applicable to information held by the following persons (Section 33(1)(a)-(c), SEC Act):

A. Public servant or former public servant by virtue of his position or former position as a public servant, or
B. Knowingly obtained by an individual (directly or indirectly) from a public servant or former public servant who he knows or has reasonable cause to believe, held the information by virtue of any such position; and
C. It is reasonable to expect an individual in the position of the public servant or former position of the public servant not to disclose except for the proper performance of the functions attaching to that position.

Colombo Stock Exchange's Listing Rules defines unpublished price sensitive information as including, but not limited to information known to the company, concerning the company's property, assets, business, financial condition and prospects; mergers and acquisitions; and dealings with employees, suppliers and customers; material contracts or development projects, whether entered into in the ordinary course of business or otherwise; as well as information concerning a significant change in ownership of the company's securities owned by insiders, or a change in effective or voting control of the issuer, and any developments that affect materially the present or potential rights or interests of the issuer's shareholders (Clause 8.1, Section 8, Listing Rules, as amended upto April 24, 2013).

IV. Charging Provision

This Act lays out situations and circumstances (Section 32) under which an individual is prohibited from trading in securities of a listed company:

1. An individual who is, or at any time during the six months immediately preceding the date on which the Act was brought into force, connected with a company and has information by virtue of being connected with the company or is reasonably expected of a person so connected to hold such information by virtue of his position and not to disclose the same except for the proper execution of official duties, shall not trade in the securities of the company being reasonably expected to know unpublished price sensitive information in respect of those securities (Section 32(1), SEC Act);
2. An individual who is or at any time during the six months immediately preceding the date on which the Act was brought into force, been connected with a company, shall not trade in the securities of any other company on the basis of information held by virtue of being connected with the first mentioned company or is reasonably expected to know unpublished price sensitive information in relation to those securities of that other company (Section 32(2), SEC Act);
3. An individual, who has obtained information, or has reasonable cause to believe that it is obtained, whether directly or indirectly, from another individual who is connected with a particular company or has been at any time in the six months immediately preceding the date of obtaining of the information so connected with such particular company, shall not trade in listed securities of that company or any other company if he can reasonably be expected to know that the information is unpublished price sensitive information in relation to those securities (Section 32(3), SEC Act);

4. An individual who is contemplating, or has contemplated, making, whether with or without another person, a take over offer for a company in a particular capacity, shall not trade in listed securities of that company in another capacity if he can reasonably be expected to know that the information that the offer is contemplated or is no longer contemplated is unpublished price sensitive information in relation to those securities (Section 32(4), SEC Act);
5. An individual who has obtained information or has reasonable cause to believe he has obtained from an individual falling under the above clause, information about a take over offer being contemplated or no longer contemplated, shall not trade in listed securities of that company if he can reasonably be expected to know that the information is unpublished price sensitive information in relation to those securities (Section 32(5), SEC Act); and
6. An individual is prohibited from communicating any information to any other person if he knows or has reasonable cause to believe that some other person will make use of the information for the purpose of counselling or procuring any other person to trade in such listed securities; or, counselling or procuring himself any other person to deal in those securities (Section 32(6), (7), SEC Act).

SEC Act also extends the application of insider dealing prohibition to public servants who are restricted from use of information by virtue of his position or former position as a public servant or is knowingly obtained by an individual (Section 33, SEC Act). Such person is prohibited from dealing, counseling, procuring any other person to trade in securities, or communicating information held or obtained by him if he knows or has reasonable cause to believe that such person or any other person will make use of that information for the purpose of counselling or procuring any other person to trade in such relevant securities.

V. Liability Clause

Section 33A of the SEC Act provides for a criminal offence for breach of the aforesaid insider trading provisions. It states that a person convicted after summary trial by a Magistrate shall be liable to a fine not less than one million rupees or to imprisonment for a term not less than two years and not exceeding five years or to both such fine and imprisonment.

It is evident that SEC has taken a strong stand on insider trading. The SEC Act does not empower the SEC to take any civil enforcement action to disgorge the profits made by the insider or to impose a civil penalty for the breach. There is also no provision conferring a statutory right of action to investors who have traded with the insider to sue for losses incurred by them as a result of the breach (SEC Consultation Paper No. 10 – Proposal to amend the SEC Act to introduce a range of administrative and civil enforcement powers to deal with capital market offences).

VI. Disclosures for Prohibition in Insider Trading

In order to maintain fairness and investor confidence in the securities market, it is essential that a company discloses at periodic intervals financial information with respect to its securities.

The Colombo Stock Exchange Listing Rules states that a listed company shall make an immediate announcement to the Exchange of disclosures made by a director in terms of Section 200 of the Companies Act (*Disclosure of share dealing by directors*), of any acquisition or disposal of a relevant interest in shares issued by the company.

Further, Section 8 of the Listing Rules (as amended upto April 24, 2013) provides for '*Corporate Disclosures*'. Clause 8.1 states that a listed company shall make immediate disclosure of price sensitive information to the Exchange in order to ensure the maintenance of a fair and orderly securities market. This clause marks the foundation of the SEC's objectives and vision instituted on its establishment.

Appendix 8A of this Listing Rules enlists events which require immediate disclosure on part of the company, *inter alia*, full details of any trade which amounts to 10% or more of the voting rights of the company; change in control of company; joint ventures, mergers, acquisitions or take-overs, etc. which can materially affect the prices of the securities. On immediate written announcements to the Exchange, the regulators can keep a watch on any irregular insider trading.

VII. Statutory Defences

It is extra-ordinary to note that a SAARC nation has provided for statutory defences in the SEC Act itself:

1. Where the act is done not with a view to make a profit or avoid a loss (section 32(8)(a));
2. Where the transaction is entered into in good faith by a liquidator, receiver or trustee in a bankruptcy (section 32(8)(b));
3. Where the information is obtained in the ordinary course of business as a stock broker or stock dealer and the act is done in good faith (section 32(8)(c));
4. Where the act is done in order to facilitate the completion or carrying out of a transaction such as a takeover offer (section 32(9)).

Company Take-overs and Mergers Code, 1995

The rules made by the Securities and Exchange Commission of Sri Lanka under section 53 of the Securities and Exchange Commission of Sri Lanka Act, No. 36 of 1987 are called as Company Take-overs and Mergers Code 1995, as amended in 2003.

Rule 28 states that every person privy to confidential price sensitive information concerning an offer or proposed offer shall treat that information as secret and shall not divulge such information to any other person unless it is necessary to do so for the purpose of preparing the offer document. Any such person privy to confidential information shall not make any recommendation to any other person with respect to dealings in the securities. Further, the time period during which dealings of securities of the offeree are prohibited by any person, who is privy to confidential price sensitive information concerning an offer or proposed offer is between the time when there is reason to believe that a proposed offer is being contemplated and the announcement of an offer.

Rule 28(4) defines a person to be privy to confidential price sensitive information concerning an offer or proposed offer, if he is:-

A. A director or employee of any one of the companies involved in the proposed offer; or
B. A professional advisor either to one of the companies involved in the proposed offer or to any director of any such company; or
C. In a position to have received information in the context of a confidential relationship; or
D. A close relation of, any person referred to in paragraph (a), (b), or (c).

Companies Act, No. 7 of 2007

The Companies Act is the most significant regulation governing companies in Sri Lanka. This Act replaces the existing Companies Act No. 17 of 1982 which was based on the English Companies Act of 1948. The new Act was necessary to respond to the significant increase in commercial and economic activities in the country and its capital and financial markets in 1980s and 1990s.

In the Companies Act No 7 of 2007, section 197 (*Use of Company* information) provides that a director of a company who has obtained information in his capacity as a director or employee is prohibited from disclosing, making use of or acting on the information except for the company's purpose, when he is authorised to do so by the Board or the company or as required by law.

While the SEC Act contains a total prohibition on the use of the inside information except in certain circumstances, the Companies Act No. 07 of 2007 gives the discretion to the Board to authorise the director to use unpublished confidential information if it is satisfied that such use will not prejudice the company. It is believed that such regulatory overlap is not uncommon given that the regulatory thinking for prohibiting serious capital market offences may be different from that in regulating director's fiduciary duties via-a-vis the company.

NEPAL

Regulatory Body and its Functioning

Securities Board of Nepal (SEBON) was established on June 7, 1993 as the regulator of securities markets in Nepal. The Board derives its duties, and powers from the Securities Act, 2007 ("Securities Act"), with an objective to regulate and manage the activities of the securities markets and persons involved in securities business by regulating the issue, purchase, sale and exchange of securities in order to develop capital market and protect the interests of investors in securities (Section 3, Chapter 2, Securities Act). In pursuance of these objectives, the Act specifies that the functions of the Board includes, *inter alia*, to make such arrangements as may be necessary to prevent insider trading or any other offense relating to securities transactions (Section 5(o), Securities Act).

Chapter 9 (*Offenses Relating to Insider Trading in Securities and Transactions of Securities and Punishment*) is the only legal provision defining insider trading and making the individual guilty of an offence in the country of Nepal. It is acknowledged that it is one of the last few SAARC nations to bring out securities regulations for a mal practice like insider trading been practicing in countries like USA since the early 1800s.

The Securities Act, 2007

I. Applicability of the Regulatory Framework

Section 2(c) of the Securities Act, defines "Company" to mean a company incorporated under the company laws in force in Nepal. Since Chapter 9 (*Offenses Relating to Insider Trading in Securities and Transactions of Securities and Punishment*) is contained in this very statutory instrument, it is understood that the insider trading provisions are applicable to all companies with the requisite of being listed on a stock exchange.

II. Who is an Insider?

The Securities Act has devoted Section 92 on defining the persons likely to be involved in insider trading. The following persons shall be deemed to have access to the insider information or notice not published by any body corporate, and likely to affect the price of securities:

A. A director, employee or a person, who can obtain any information or a notice in the capacity of a shareholder of that body corporate;
B. A person who can obtain any information or a notice in the capacity of a professional service provider to that body corporate; and
C. A person who can obtain any information or a notice having a direct or indirect contact with the person or source as specified in clauses (a) and (b).

These clauses are wide and vague in nature. No other SAARC Nation provides for "a professional service provider" as an insider. Sri Lanka extends its ambit to stock broker or stock dealer. It is appreciated that Nepal is strongly against this practice that it has widened the jurisdictional scope of the Securities Board to hold any service provider, including lawyers and investment managers, under the offence of insider trading. However, in case of such expanded scope, the Securities Board must be prepared with a iron clad framework to penalize the offender.

III. Unpublished Price Sensitive Information

Section 91, Securities Act, is the charging provision making insider trading a capital market offence. In the Explanation appended to the Section, the legislators have defined "insider information or notice" to mean any specific information or notice not yet published by a body corporate issuing any securities as may be capable of affecting the price of such securities if such information or notice is disclosed.

IV. Charging Provision

Section 91(1) of Securities Act, lays out the prohibition on insider trading in the following words: "if any person deals in securities or causes any other person to deal in securities on the basis of any insider information or notice that are unpublished or communicates any information or notice known to such a person in the course of the discharge of his or her duties in manner likely to affect the price of securities such a person shall be deemed to have been committed an insider trading in securities".

This section, though short in words, establishes a strong ground against insider trading. No person shall deal in securities; cause any other person to deal in securities on the basis and reliance on unpublished price sensitive information; or communicate such unpublished information, likely to affect the price of securities, obtained in the course of duties.

V. Liability Clause

Though Section 91-92 of the Securities Act has been drafted solely for the purpose of curbing insider trading, it fails to provide for a penalty or offence.

Section 101, Securities Act, is a common section on punishments for all the mal practices being committed in the securities market. Clause (1) of the given Section states that a person guilty of committing insider trading under Section 91 shall, upon being convicted of the offense of insider trading, be liable to the punishment with a fine equal to the amount in controversy or with imprisonment for a term not exceeding one year or with both, fine and imprisonment.

VI. Disclosures for Prohibition in Insider Trading

Securities Registration and Issue Regulations, 2008 with its first amendment in 2010, states that a body corporate that has got its securities listed shall inform the Securities Board with material information on the events or transactions that are likely to affect the price of security listed within three days of such occurrence.

VII. Statutory Defences

Section 91(2) of Securities Act, provides a defense or exception to insider trading liability by holding that notwithstanding anything contained in the charging provision, being Section 92(1), any transactions already carried out shall not be deemed to be affected merely by the reason that an insider trading offence has been committed, thus, making the transaction out of the purview of the Securities Act on the ground of retrospective effect.

OBSERVATIONS AND RECOMMENDATIONS

The underlying reason for initiating this study on SAARC nations is fairness. Each financial market should be fair and maintain integrity to all its participants. It must be level playing field. In cases where insider trading is not regulated, there is a prevalent asymmetry of information in the market benefiting only a section. Though a level playing field is not possible in the sense of perfect economics, yet providing comparative advantage to a few over the majority participants may affect the confidence of all.

The introduction of such law also answers the question on ethics in financial markets. It is the ethical duty on part of the professionals exposed to price sensitive information to not only avoid utilisation of such information for their selfish interests causing loss to others but also to avoid communicating it to others causing indirect benefits. While ethical behaviour is an onus on the market participants and those professionals privy to the unpublished price sensitive information, it is the responsibility of the securities regulator to maintain high enforcement standards to curb such malpractice. Below is a comparative SAARC table with the mean of English countries undertaken by Rafael La Porta, Florencio Lopez-De-Silanes, and Andrei Shleifer in 2006. This Table 1 proves whether the regulatory practice of the SAARC nations are at par with countries or whether they ought to consider a review of their existing practices. While India is under process of introducing new and tighter insider trading regulations,

Table 1. Comparative study of enforcement action against insider trading

Jurisdiction	Disclosure requirement	Public enforcement	Supervisor attributes	Investigative powers	Orders	Criminal sanctions
	Mean value of English Countries =0.78	Mean value of English Countries =0.62	Mean value of English Countries =0.48	Mean value of English Countries =0.75	Mean value of English Countries=0.57	Mean value of English Countries =0.65
India	0.92	0.72	0.38	1.00	0.67	0.83
Sri Lanka	0.75	0.33	0.50	0.50	0.00	0.33
Pakistan	0.58	0.50	0.75	1.00	0.17	0.08

(Source: Rafael La Porta, Florencio Lopez-De-Silanes, and Andrei Shleifer, 2006, "What Works in Securities Laws?", The Journal of Finance, Vol. LXI, No. 1, pp. 1-32)

SAARC nations Pakistan and Sri Lanka must focus on criminal sanctions and stringent orders issued against market participants indulging in the offence.

Post a thorough study of four SAARC nations, the author has the following recommendations from a practitioner's point of view:

1. Insider trading is not only limited to companies with securities listed on stock exchanges. Professionals like brokers, investment managers, attorneys are also privy to unpublished price sensitive information which if disclosed, are most likely to affect the price of securities. While most of the regulations are limited to listed companies, minimal extend to other professionals. The author recommends SAARC nations to implement Chinese Walls as a measure to avoid conflict of interest and act as a prophylactic activity. Chinese Walls are policies and procedures designed to stop the passage of information, especially price sensitive information operating between departments within a firm or a financial group. India includes this concept under a Model Code of Conduct appended to its Regulations, yet it is only directory and not mandatory for companies and entities to institute the same (Tomar & Kashyap 2013) . Further, only implementation of Chinese Walls will not be helpful in curbing the malpractice, regular monitoring by independent persons and consequently, reporting will evaluate the effectiveness of the structure. If the Chinese Walls between various departments of the securities firm are porous, then much of the material, non-public financial information gathered by its board representative will also find its way to other departments of the securities firm including the research desk, proprietary and retails trading desks, and market-making operations.
2. Another prophylactic act that companies can adopt to minimise insider trading is the maintenance of whistle blower hotline where company personnel or shareholders or other market participants can inform the company of potential insider trading malpractice being committed. These instances can help the company investigate and look into the ethical behaviour of such persons. Alternatively, companies must institute a Ethics and Compliance Committee comprising of majority of Independent Directors. The Compliance Officer shall report to this Committee in monitoring the adherence to the company's code on insider trading.
3. India has recently taken strong steps in this path. The author suggests other SAARC nations to study the concept of related parties, including relatives and associate companies and note its scope to regulate the same. Related parties, their details, standard of control and present shareholding in the company must be periodically reported and the company must monitor that such related par-

ties are not at the receiving end of insider information and consequently, illegally gaining profits. It is the duty of every company employee to inform the company of related parties, and connected persons. Any supply of information to them must be accordingly regulated.

4. The author encourages the supply of unpublished price sensitive information on the "need to know" basis only. Price sensitive information should be disclosed only to those within the company who need the information to discharge their duty and whose possession of such information will not give rise to a conflict of interest or appearance of misuse of information. Limited access to such information shall be guarded by the appropriate efficient use of technology and security measures.
5. Further, the author emphasises on the avoidance of selective disclosures which shall benefit only a section of the recipients. Material information should be publicly disclosed promptly by news release to prevent selective, unauthorized disclosures prior to broad disclosure. The Company should look into research reports, rumours and press articles which may leak inside information before the official public announcement.
6. The author appreciates India's efforts into reviewing their insider trading regulations based on the growing market strength and need for investor confidence. The author encourages other nations to follow suit, and provide stringent penalties and enforcement standards acting as a deterrent to company officials. In fact, as followed in Sri Lanka, both the tipper and the tippee should be held liable in such offences.

India believes that for insiders who have access to unpublished price sensitive information all the time, such as the CEO or Chairman, any trade by them may prove hazardous to the company's security prices. Completely prohibiting them from trading in securities may also prove to be an unfair limitation. Thus, India has initiated the concept of trading plans on the lines of US practice. Under these plans, the insiders may trade at pre-scheduled times for bona fide transactions and has to be mandatorily informed to the stock exchange concerned in advance. Disclosure of pre-scheduled trading plans by high level officials will pacify the investors of any suspicious trading activity causing wrongful losses. Other SAARC nations are encourages to introduce such measures which safeguard investor confidence in the market and economy and yet, assist in maintaining integrity and fairness.

At the end of this study, the author highlights a quote by an US Attorney for the Sudden District of New York (Preet Bahara, 2010), which shall help readers gain an insight on the imminent struggle of nations to curb insider trading. He states:

But for them (insiders), material non-public information is akin to a performance-enhancing drug that provides the illegal "edge" to outpace their rivals and make even more money. In some respects, inside information is a form of financial steroid. It is unfair; it is offensive; it is unlawful; and it puts a black mark on the entire enterprise.

REFERENCES

Akhter, N., & Ghani, E. (2010). Regional Integration in South Asia: An Analysis of Trade Flows Using the Gravity Model. *Pakistan Development Review*, 105–118.

Ali, M. J., & Ahmed, K. (2007). The legal and institutional framework for corporate financial reporting practices in South Asia. *Research in Accounting Regulation*, *19*, 175–205. doi:10.1016/S1052-0457(06)19009-8

Bernardo, A. E. (2001). Contractual Restrictions on Insider Trading: A Welfare Analysis. *Economic Theory*, *18*(1), 7–35. doi:10.1007/PL00004135

Chandratre, K. (1993). *Bharat's law relating to insider trading*. New Delhi: Bharat Law House.

Gevurtz, F. A. (2002). Globalization of Insider Trading Prohibitions. *The. Transnat'l Law*, *15*, 63.

Government of Nepal. (2007). *Securities Act, 2007*. Kathmandu: Government of Nepal.

Gunathilake, W., De Zoysa, A., & Chandrakumara, P. M. K. (2011). *Corporate governance in Sri Lanka: the status quo*. Academic Press.

Insider Trading Regulations - A Primer. (2013). Retrieved from http://www.nishithdesai.com/fileadmin/user_upload/pdfs/Research%20Papers/Insider_Trading_Regulations_-_A_Primer.pdf

Kapadia, J. (1992). Insider Trading: SEBI on Test. *Economic and Political Weekly*, 2571–2572.

Preet Bharara. (2010). *The Future of White Collar Enforcement: A Prosecutor's View*. New York Bar Association.

SEBI. (2002). Securities and exchange board of India (prohibition of insider trading). *Regulations, 1992*, 1–21.

SEBI. (2013). Report of the high level committee to review the SEBI (prohibition of insider trading). *Regulations, 1992*, 1–78.

SEBI. (2015). Securities and exchange board of India (prohibition of insider trading). *Regulations, 2015*, 1–21.

Securities and Exchange Commission Sri Lanka. (2003). Company Take-overs and Mergers Code 1995, as amended in 2003. Colombo: Securities and Exchange Commission, Sri Lanka.

Securities and Exchange Commission of Pakistan. (2001). *Listed companies (prohibition of insiders trading) guidelines*. Islamabad: Securities and Exchange Commission of Pakistan.

Tomar, A. S., & Kashyap, A. K. (2013). Corporate Governance In Indian Capital Market: An Appraisal. *Journal of Business Management & Social Sciences Research*, *2*(5), 5–12.

ENDNOTES

1 Securities Laws (Amendment) Act, 2014, No. 27 of 2014.
2 Section 195(2) of Companies Act, 2013.
3 Regulation 7(1) of SEBI (Prohibition of Insider Trading Regulations), 2015.
4 Regulation 7(2) of SEBI (Prohibition of Insider Trading Regulations), 2015.
5 Regulation 7(3) of SEBI (Prohibition of Insider Trading Regulations), 2015.
6 Regulation 3(3) of SEBI (Prohibition of Insider Trading Regulations), 2015.
7 Regulation 4(1)(i) of SEBI (Prohibition of Insider Trading Regulations), 2015.

Chapter 5
The Permissibility of Crowd Funding within South Asia:
A Comparative Analysis of South Asian Jurisdictions

Michael D'Rosario
Deakin University, Australia

Aaron Busary
Hyveminds Pty Ltd., Australia

Kairav Raval
Hyveminds Pty Ltd., Australia

ABSTRACT

The chapter will extend upon the extant literature by considering the permissibility of crowdfunding practices within the South Asian region. There is a genuine dearth of research considering these matters, with little research considering the history and permissibility of crowdfunding methodologies within the noted nations. As such the contribution of the chapter is twofold, firstly it represents amongst the first coherent assessments of the use of crowdsourcing based fundraising methodologies within the South Asian region. Secondly it responds to the dearth of research considering the legal permissibility of such practices within the noted nations, while also contrasting the regulatory models of India, Bangladesh, and Sri Lanka with the regulatory models evidenced within selected OECD countries and pertinently the recently reformed model of regulation within the United States, specifically chapter 12 of the Jobs Act (2013).

AN INTRODUCTION TO CROWDFUNDING

Crowdfunding is best understood as the process by which a web based organisation seeks to procure funding from the general public through a web portal, the web portal enables unrelated business enterprises seeking capital to make equity within their entities available to investors. This was not permissible given the restrictions placed on public fundraising by the SEC Act.

DOI: 10.4018/978-1-5225-0004-9.ch005

As asserted, Crowdfunding was largely motivated by individuals and organisations promoting profit motivated initiatives through crowdsourcing platforms, and also by the potential benefits to entrepreneurs associated with creating more enabling pathways to accessing startup capital. The existing crowdsourcing platforms (consider Kickstarter, IndiGoGo and similar platforms) limited promoters to accepting donated monies, or selling items for defined sums, with the provision of equity or profit sharing impermissible. However many treaded a unfamiliar and perhaps unexplored path between soliciting general support on behalf of project owners, and offering the possibility of equity sharing which may be conceived to be a security offering, under the technical definition.

The Need for Crowdfunding Provisions and the Howey Test

While it may not be apparent there is a critical distinction between individuals soliciting for support through web based portals, and offering items in exchange for such support and individuals and organisations making equity or profits from a venture available for distribution in exchange for monetary support (Securities and Exchange Commission v. W. J. Howey Co, 1946) . While many crowdsourcing models do not involve the issuance of securities in the conventional sense they may be in direct contravention with the Securities and Exchange Commission Act. N D Pope in 2010 noted that some for profit crowdfunding models may be in contravention of the SEC Act, under the rubric of Howey (Pope, 2010).

Additionally prior to the enactment of the JOBS Act, firms wanting to employ crowdfunding techniques when acting in accordance with SEC legislation faced an additional set of challenges. As such the impact of such reforms within the U.S. cannot be understated. The proposed chapter shall consider the permissibility of crowdfunding within the South Asian region with a pertinent focus on India, Sri Lanka and Bangladesh. The chapter is best described as a study in comparative law, considering the regulator provisions enacted within the United States and Australia, and contrasting the evidenced approaches within India, Bangladesh, Nepal and Sri Lanka.

Introduction to Title III of the Jobs Act (2013)

The introduction of the Jumpstart our Business Startups (JOBS) Act was a response to a significant economic slowdown evidenced in the United States. The Act while seemingly focused on job creation is in reality focused on enabling smaller enterprises to avoid onerous securities provisions enacted post the depression. Though the primary motivation behind the act was the easing of regulatory burdens for smaller enterprises, the act provides significant relieve to both small and large enterprises by exempting them from a broad range of seemingly burdensome regulatory pronouncements.

The bill received strong bipartisan support notwithstanding its' significant ramifications, and its unique nature. Proponents of the Jobs Act believe that it will bring much needed system liquidity to emerging organisations starved of capital due to the restrictive lending practices of the banks brought about by sectors recent conservatism. Title III of the Jobs Act is referred to as the Crowdfund Act, and represents perhaps the most intriguing part of the reform program. The provisions found within title III of the Act, enable the use of crowdsourcing methodologies in procuring start-up capital. While such methodologies have been employed within other sectors, to procure resources to address defined needs, perhaps most notably in the charitable sector, and more recently ingeniously in funding artistic works and consumer products, such approaches would be considered unlawful under the Securities Act (1933) and the Securities Exchange Act (1934). As such procuring capital has been a problematic exercise for start-up entities.

The recently enacted crowdfunding exemptions make the use of crowdsourcing methodologies possible within the capital market. The enacted provisions enable small start-up entities to procure capital through crowdfund offerings that exempt such offerings from registration. The provisions also exempt qualifying websites from broker registration, thus enabling the qualifying website to facilitate the collection of capital on behalf of the entity. The crowdfunding simplification provisions (herewith the Crowdfund Act) attempt to facilitate and actively support the use of crowdfunding techniques for capital raising through the enactment of section 4(6) offering registration exemption for capital raisings of equal to or less than $1 million. This exemption is enabled to the extent that individual investor restrictions are maintained; essentially that no investor exceeds the investment cap placed upon their crowdfund investments. The investment caps are based on net worth of prospective investors as well as income levels, though some ambiguity exists about which threshold prevails.

In facilitating these significant changes, the provisions create a regulated new entity form; the so called 'funding portal'. This new regulated entity sits somewhere between a broker, a closely regulated and scrutinized professional and a crowdsourcing website. The new intermediary must register as a funding portal, unless a registered broker. This new entity classification will undoubtedly bring with it a significant amount of ambiguity, given the 'broker like' role such intermediaries will play in the marketplace.

Bradford notes that the new provisions leave many ambiguities and inconsistencies for the courts to resolve. The mandatory disclosure requirements are asserted to be far too onerous and needlessly complicated and expensive for the small offerings that they are designed to facilitate. It is evident that these new provisions necessitate critical analysis; as such analysis is necessary to further understanding of this pertinent set of reforms. The current study shall afford a critical analysis of the most recent reforms considering a number of the ambiguities that exist in relation to the Acts in their present form.

The Origins of Crowdsourcing

Jeff Howe broadly considered the originator of the term crowdsourcing, describes crowdsourcing as a movement akin outsourcing, a source of low cost labour, whereby everyday people use their spare time and capacity to address problems, generate new content and even engage in high level R&D activities (Howe, 2006). Crowdsourcing is perhaps best understood as a distributed problem solving process. While under the original Howe (2006) definition the terminology was taken to mean the procurement of various services employing the internet as a form of replacement labour market, crowdsourcing is generally associated with the creation of content, ideas and solutions through the internet, though is not always associated with a replacement source of labour.

Crowdsourcing models have been used within a number of different sectors in response to a number of unique challenges. The models have been employed successfully within the music industry (Bandfund), to fund the fabrication of consumer electronics (Kickstarter) and to enable the competitive analysis of complex datasets (Kaggle). However to highlight only recent examples of the use of crowdsourcing models alone, would appear to pay scant regard to the use of such models prior to the advent of the internet. Charitable organisations have employed crowdfunding models to respond to a number of charitable causes, while political entities have used comparable models to raise funds for political causes. Crowdsourcing models existed well before the advent of the internet, but the internet has certainly served as a powerful enabling force, with such models now ubiquitous on the internet, and creating 'disruption' within a number of industries. Prior to the enactment of the JOBS Act, crowdsourcing models were limited in the manner with which they could procure funds. (Taku 2012) asserts that current crowdfunding platforms have generally adopted business models designed to avoid characterisation as a sale of security.

Kickstarter is arguably the most well-known of the crowdsourcing platforms, originally conceived as a web hosting service for what could be described as creative projects, but grew into something much larger, incorporating journalism, technology, and consumer products. Individuals seeking support lodge projects with Kickstarter that are evaluated based on the criteria set but the platform. If accepted the projects are listed publically on the entity's website and the site users can make contributions to the project. The platform requires that the project conveners offer something to the users that contribute to their project. The platform does not allow the parties raising money on the platform to share the proceeds of the projects with donors, nor can they provide equity to donors. Yet increasing a fine line was evident between the activities of crowdsourcing websites that enabled parties to raise development funds and early venture capital providers. Consider crowdsourcing websites for musicians such as Sellaband.com, promoters of this venture asserted that 'bands might let you get a cut of revenues'. Such claims draw into question whether the activities of the users of the platform constitute selling services, goods or whether they would be considered investments under the Howey test. This is highly likely given the broad applicability of the Howey test.

It is arguably this collection of issues that generated political interest in crowdfunding models, and their potential use as capital funding models, or equity raising models (and consequently their potentially deleterious impacts if left unregulated).

Reward-Based Crowdfunding

Reward based crowdfunding ranks amongst the most common forms of crowdfunding. Reward based crowdfunding entails the provision of non-monetary rewards being provided to crowd funders for their participation.

Equity-Based Crowdfunding

Unlike reward based crowdfunding, equity-based crowdfunding entails the raising of financial funding through crowd based mechanism. The funds raised bestow ownership rights onto the holders of equity funding.

Credit-Based Crowdfunding

Credit-based crowdfunding links Prospective borrowers with lenders. Lenders and Borrowers join lending clubs/platforms first lodging their credit requirements, which are then matched with groups of lenders/investors willing to meet their credit terms.

Equity vs. Non-Equity Crowdfunding

Crowdfunding is best understood as the process by which a web based organisation seeks to procure funding from the general public through a web portal, the web portal enables unrelated business enterprises seeking capital to make equity within their entities available to investors. This was not permissible given the restrictions placed on public fundraising by the SEC Act. For the purposes of disambiguation it should be duly noted that, this chapter is concerned with equity based crowdfunding.

As asserted, Crowdfunding was largely motivated by individuals and organisations promoting profit motivated initiatives through crowdsourcing platforms, and also by the potential benefits to entrepreneurs associated with creating more enabling pathways to accessing startup capital. The existing crowdsourcing platforms (consider Kickstarter) limited promoters to accepting donated monies, or selling items for defined sums, with the provision of equity or profit sharing impermissible. However many treaded a unfamiliar and perhaps unexplored path between soliciting general support on behalf of project owners, and offering the possibility of equity sharing which may be conceived to be a security offering, under the technical definition (see Sellaband).

The Need for Crowdfunding Provisions and the Howey Test

While it may not be apparent there is a critical distinction between individuals soliciting for support through web based portals, and offering items in exchange for such support and individuals and organisations making equity or profits from a venture available for distribution in exchange for monetary support. While many crowdsourcing models do not involve the issuance of securities in the conventional sense they may be in direct contravention with the Securities and Exchange Commission Act. Pope (2011) noted that some for profit crowdfunding models may be in contravention of the SEC Act, under the rubric of Howey.

Additionally, prior to the enactment of the JOBS Act, firms wanting to employ crowdfunding techniques when acting in accordance with SEC legislation faced an additional set of challenges. Spring Street Brewing Company, sought to raise fund from the public through a DPO under regulation A of the Securities Act. The entity sought to raise USD 5 million and eventually raised approximately 2 million. Alan Klein the founder of the brewer Spring Street claimed that the entity faced a number of challenges when seeking to sell equity through a direct public offering over the internet. Klein's claimed the entity's experience could only be claimed to be a qualified success, noting the relatively poor conversion rate from those perusing the firm's prospectus online and eventually agreeing to participate in the DPO (Pope 2011). Klein asserted that the issues associated with the rate of conversion could be attributed to a number of critical factors, but they could be broadly defined as issues associated with information asymmetries, trust and reputational challenges, all of which could be addressed through the participation of trusted partners. Klein asserted that the absence of "an intermediary that is in the business of evaluating a company, doing due diligence, and putting its reputation on the line with the company reputation" was in part the reason for the outcome (ibid, 2011).

Pope (2011), claims that the most significant lesson to be taken from the Spring Street experience is that intermediation is not critical to the success of small fundraising activities, of less than 1 million. On the contrary it is asserted herein that the moderation of information asymmetries is critical to the ongoing participation of micro-venture capitalists, and that the role of intermediaries is critical to this. Moreover, the reporting standard associated with a Regulation A listing appears to assign greater responsibilities than the new crowdfunding provisions. While intermediation may not be critical to the procurement of a smaller quantum of capital, this should not diminish the onus placed on entities to ensure adequate disclosure. Failure to do so would potentially encourage 'boiler room' type scenarios that may have a deleterious impact on the overall model and prospects of crowdfunding under its current guise, in the long term. The pertinent securities' provisions and critical new crowdfunding provisions are considered presently.

AN ANALYSIS OF THE KEY PROVISIONS

The Securities Act (1933)

The existing securities provisions were enacted largely as consumer protections in the aftermath of a major financial crisis. The Securities Act (1933), arguably the first major regulatory apparatus concerned with the sale of securities, came in response to the stock market crash of 1929. The legislation sought to ensure that investors were adequately informed about investment opportunities; emphasizing disclosures aimed at helping investors make informed decisions. Prior to its enactment the sale of securities within the U.S. was governed by state laws. The adequacy of such provisions was called into question by the crisis that ensued, and the enacted provision sought to restore investor confidence in the financial system and in particular in the securities market.

The provisions sought to protect consumer interests by mandating higher levels of disclosure than were commonplace at the time of enactment. The 1933 Act necessitated that firms register a formal disclosure document to investors where securities were to be made available to the public. This meant that investors could access consistent high quality information from firms and make more informed investment decisions. The Act made unlawful any security offering that was made absent of the full disclosure document. Exemptions to the key provisions (Section 5) were possible under certain circumstances.

The Securities Exchange Act (1934)

The Securities Exchange Act (1934) gave rise to the Securities and Exchange Commission (SEC). In comparison to the 1933 Act, the 1934 Act is concerned more with periodic disclosures than the matter of registration. The critical change that came with the 1934 Act was the need for ongoing disclosures. The Securities Act, was concerned with the registration of securities and a formal disclosure document, the prospectus, and as such targeted at disclosures relating to fundraising and the conception of the company. The 1934 Act went further to consider secondary market trading activity.

Any company listed on a national securities exchange must find accord with the Act. In addition companies not listed on a national exchange may be required to be compliant with the 1934 Act, if they exceed certain shareholder or asset threshold levels. The asset threshold for triggering compliance was revised from $5 million to $10 million. The additional shareholder trigger remains at 500 shareholders (s12, s13, & s15). The act necessitates that companies lodge information with the SEC periodically (the quarterly 10-Q, and the annual 10-K), in addition to making known any matters deemed material to the entity, in an ongoing manner (Form 8K reporting). The 1934 Act also increased the obligations placed on entities serving as an intermediary in relation to the purchase or sale of securities. As such brokers and other intermediaries involved in the sale of securities must find accord with the Act.

The Sarbanes Oxley Act

The Sarbanes Oxley Act (2002) (SOX) sought to improve standards associated with public companies, boards, management groups and accounting firms. The bill was seen largely as a response to a number of corporate failures, and accounting and financial scandals. The frequency with which these scandals arose, caused investors and regulators much consideration and served and the impetus for the reviews which led to the SOX reforms.

While the Act brought with it a significant number of sweeping reforms, for the sake of brevity, herein the provisions relevant to reporting requirements assigned to newly registered entities shall be considered. The relevant reporting provisions contained within s.404b, were the source of much debate given that they were perceived to be unnecessarily onerous by many, particularly in relation to smaller 'start-up' entities. Title 3 of the JOBS Act responds directly to s.404b.

Consider s.404 (b) "With respect to the internal control assessment required by subsection (a), each registered public accounting firm that prepares or issues the audit report for the issuer shall attest to, and report on, the assessment made by the management of the issuer. An attestation made under this subsection shall be made in accordance with standards for attestation engagements issued or adopted by the Board. Any such attestation shall not be the subject of a separate engagement." The provisions necessitate those newly conceived entities' meet significant initial reporting requirements presenting significant fixed compliance costs on such entities. These regulations are claimed to present significant operational headaches to the organisational leaders of newly created entities. Moreover, the pronouncements are claimed to unduly expensive for smaller entities.

THE CROWDFUND ACT (2012)

Title three of the JOBS Act, the CROWDFUND Act ranks amongst the most controversial in recent memory. Depending on the jurist consulted the act will have minimal impact or rank amongst the most impactful and disruptive. While the bill received strong bipartisan support there appears to be little consensus about the value of the reforms.

The motivation for the legislative reforms remain clear, the supporters of the bill, believe that it will serve as an enabling force helping smaller entities secure much needed capital during what has been a challenging time for global capital markets. The reforms seek to make the procuring capital by emerging enterprises more straightforward while also lessen the burdens placed on smaller public entities through recent consumer protections reforms. Specifically, the reforms respond directly to the specific capital raising restrictions within the Securities Act (1933) and the Securities Exchange Act (1934), and the reporting requirements associated with Sarbanes Oxley (2002). The reforms also enable non broker entities to serve as intermediaries, with a new entity classification conceived, affording a unique delineation to this new status of entity differentiating it from a 'broker' as defined by the Securities and Exchange Commission Act (1934).

Exemption from Registration under the Securities Act

The new exempt entity may make use of crowdsourcing methodologies, enabling the creation of crowdsourcing micro-capital platforms. Critically section 4(6) of the act specifically exempts from registration entities raising equal to or less than $1 million. Exemption is only available to the extent that specific restrictions on private investor's caps are maintained, where investor caps are a function of either income level or an asset threshold level.

Exemption from s.404 of the Sarbanes Oxley Act (2002)

Another key reform is the roll back of the requirements of Sarbanes Oxley for smaller entities with revenues of less than 1 billion from the noted requirements of s.404 (b). This represents amongst the most significant changes to securities and company law emanating from the Act. The reform reduces the burden placed on new entities

Adequacy of Disclosure, and Consumer Protections

The Securities Act (1933) and Securities Exchange Act (1934) were both motivated by a desire to protect investors and promote enhanced disclosure. The provisions do however place a number of onerous requirements on entities trying to procure start-up capital, serving as an impediment to many start-up entities. The enacted reforms seek to respond to the challenges faced by start-up entities by creating simpler mechanisms through which capital can be procured.

However a number of theorists remain critical about the enacted reforms. Many fear that by diminishing the requirements placed on entities engaged in capital raising activities, and by enabling the participation of non-broker entities in capital raising activities, the potential for misconduct is greater. Of particular concern is the potential for boiler room type effects that would undermine any confidence engendered in the market mechanism and have a deleterious impact on investors generally. Further concerns relate to the adequacy of due diligence conducted in the first instance by 'funding portals' the non-broker intermediaries critical to the new scheme. Many are wary about the capacity of funding portals to complete this important task. Clearly given that such entities are not required to be brokers, and possess broker registration, this is certainly not an unwarranted concern. Further concerned parlayed by theorists and foreign regulator bodies include the uncertainties associated with returns from crowd funded investments given that there will be limited disclosure information released by entities seeking funding through crowdfunding initiatives, than entities securing funding through non crowdfunding based capital raisings.

The Potential Impact of Equity Crowdfunding Models on Capital Markets Beyond the U.S.

Sorrenson & Stuart (2001) assert that venture capitalists focusing of the provision of early stage funding focus their attention largely on local markets, given their comparative advantage in local markets. As such some theorists might contend that the impact of crowdfunding provisions within the U.S. will have a limited impact beyond U.S. markets, however such an assertion appears to be flawed. The claims of Sorrenson & Stuart (2001) are largely based on the advantage venture capitalists possess within their own geographic region, and a corollary of this assertion would be that the search costs associated with accessing opportunities beyond their own market make broader searches prohibitively expensive. Their advantage diminishes within different geographic territories because their knowledge is likely greatest within their own territory.

As such it is plausible that the recent enactment of the crowdfunding provisions will have an impact on the venture capital market beyond the U.S. One possible implication is that many companies registered in less developed markets will find it more challenging to procure venture funding, within their own polities and as such may feel a greater pull to the U.S. market where opportunities to raise early stage funding are greater. While it is certainly true that such a draw already exists particularly in relation to many high technology companies, the implementation of crowdfunding provisions would appear to incentivize such movement further.

Firms operating within markets where limited venture capital is available might find themselves squeezed out by rival firms incorporated within the U.S. This is because the crowdfunding provisions reduce the discover costs associated with startup enterprises incorporated in the U.S. thus affording U.S. startups a distinct advantage over foreign firms. Foreign venture capitalists can now access opportunities within U.S. markets, with discover costs substantially lower than costs associated with investing in other markets.

EQUITY CROWDFUNDING WITHIN SELECTED OECD COUNTRIES

Australia

In light of the significant discussions taking place globally in relation to crowdfunding models, ASIC released guidance to clarify arrangements that may be regulated by ASIC under the Corporations Act (2001) and the Australian Securities and Investments Commission Act (2001). The commentaries suggested that a number of posited crowdfunding models may be unlawful under the Corporations Act and ASIC Act.

ASIC Commissioner Tanzer asserts that "Crowd funding, as a discrete activity, is not prohibited in Australia nor is it generally regulated by ASIC'. 'However, depending on the particular crowd funding arrangement, ASIC's view is that some types of crowd funding could involve offering or advertising a financial product, providing a financial service or fundraising through securities requiring a complying disclosure document. These activities are regulated by ASIC under the Corporations Act and ASIC Act and may impose legal obligations on operators of crowd funding sites and on people using those sites to raise funds. 'We want to make sure anyone involved in crowd funding is aware of these obligations to ensure they operate within the law and don't potentially expose themselves to penalties under the Corporations Act or ASIC Act'

The briefing also emphasised a number of risks associated with crowdfunding, and served as a cautionary note to those seeking to avail themselves to opportunities within the market. As part of its broader crowdfunding monitoring activities, ASIC detailed a number of risks associated with crowdfunding activities;

1. A risk of fraud being carried out through crowd funding websites. Website operators can help manage this risk by doing background and credentials checks on project creators to help minimise the opportunity for fraud.
2. A risk that funded projects are not completed and the project sponsors do not receive the rewards promised. As well as background and credentials checks, the website operators can manage this risk by assessing the viability of the project before it is posted on their website, requiring the project creator to provide more information on how and when they complete the project and consider requiring the project creator to report periodically through the website on their progress in implementing the project.

3. A risk that the money collected is lost due to the fraud or bankruptcy of the website operator before the money is passed on to the project creator. The website operator can manage this risk by holding all crowd funding money in a trust account separate from its own assets, avoiding excessive holding periods and implementing appropriate internal controls to ensure withdrawals are appropriate.

In relation to whether a crowd funding initiative is considered lawful the following appears pertinent. A crowdfunding initiative that merely procures gifted or donated sums without the possibility of a return may not be considered unlawful under the ASIC Act (Indeed a number of such vehicles/entities exist and operate within Australia, such as IndeGoGo and Kickstarter). This factor is amongst the most pertinent, the nature of the reward provided by the project promoter would be critical to whether an initiative would be considered unlawful. The nature of the reward offered and the structure of the crowdfunding offering would determine whether the arrangement would require an Australian Financial Services license, whether it constitutes a managed investment scheme pursuant to Chapter 5C of the Corporations Act, or whether it constitutes a fundraising activity under Chapter 6D of the Corporations Act.

Given the underlying realities of the Australian regulatory framework in relation to fundraising the CAMAC released a number of commentaries, most notably an exposure draft pertaining to the viability of crowdfunding models within Australia. Their proposal called for a change in the regulatory model. Essentially their proposition entailed changing Chapter 5C and 6D of the Corporations Act, to enable crowdfunding. More specifically, the CAMAC posited the following amendments to regulatory pronouncements;

1. That investors are permitted to invest a maximum of AUD $2500 into a company; with the sum of crowdfunding investment not exceeding an annual investment cap quantum of AUD $10000.
2. That companies are allowed to lawfully raise up to AUD 2 million during any 12 month interval.
3. That the issuing entity be required to change its entity status, from the conventional Pty Ltd status, to a new Exempt Public status as a precursor to fundraising.
4. That only "exempt public companies" would be able to raise equity capital through equity crowdfunding based mechanisms.

EQUITY CROWDFUNDING WITHIN SOUTH ASIA

Sri Lanka

The Securities and Exchange Commission of Sri Lanka is the primary financial markets regulator. The Sri Lankan SEC first established under Securities and Exchange Commission of Sri Lanka Act No. 36 of 1987, and is the main regulator of the Colombo Stock Exchange (CSE), as well as Stock brokering firms and brokers directly. The entity also regulates financial market intermediaries, as well as publically listed companies and agencies providing ratings services. While no formal guidance has been offered by the Sri Lankan Securities and Exchange Commission, given the regulatory apparatus in effect, it is evident that crowdfunding as a discrete activity is unlawful under the Securities Act (2008) and the Securities Exchange Commission Act (2007).

The Securities Act (2008) is modelled on judicial pronouncements from the UK. In respect to the matter of the legality of crowdfunding within Sri Lanka the following is pertinent. A crowdfunding initiative that merely procures gifted or donated sums without the possibility of a return may not be considered unlawful under the Securities Act (2008). This factor is amongst the most pertinent, the nature of the reward provided by the project promoter would be critical to whether an initiative would be considered unlawful. The nature of the reward offered and the structure of the crowdfunding offering would determine whether the arrangement would require licensing, and whether it constitutes a managed investment scheme pursuant to the Companies Act, or whether it constitutes a fundraising activity under the Companies Act.

In relation to non-equity and non-debt based crowdfunding there have been a number of examples. The New York based Crimso has launched in Sri Lanka, and as received much positive press, with several funded initiatives. Additionally a number of Kickstarter and IndeGogo listings originate from within Sri Lanka indicative of the general level of interest in this new model of fundraising. There has been a dearth of discussion within Sri Lankan parliamentary dialogue in relation to crowdfunding activities. The Sri Lankan securities agency has not released commentary on equity crowdfunding.

Nepal

The major financial sector reforms within Nepal occurred in the 1980s. HMG/N and Nepal Rastra Bank have been implementing comprehensive Financial Sector Reform Program since 2001. HMG/N has strongly pursued financial sector reform across all aspects of the financial services sector. Nepali securities regulations do not provide for the permissibility of crowdfunding. The Companies Act, 2063 (2006) does not consider the matter of crowd based funding or posit alternative models of disclosure. The relevant Act, the Securities Act 2007 does not permit non broker intermediaries to engage in capital raising related activities as is permissible under U.S. securities legislation. The act was framed at a time when alternative fundraising methods such as equity crowdfunding were envisaged. In exercise of the power assigned through section 116 of the Securities Act, 2007, the Securities regulations and issue registration legislation was established. The legislation is silent in relation to crowd based fundraising methodologies. Equity crowdfunding as a discrete activity remains prohibited within Nepal.

The Foreign Investment and Technology Transfer Act, 1992 was formulated to promote the mobilization of capital to increase the competitiveness of Nepal's workforce and natural resources endowment. The act was amended in 2000, though the matter of equity based fundraising was not considered.

There has been little dialogue within Nepali Hansard in relation to crowdfunding activities. Moreover there has been little conjecture of such matters within the popular media within Nepal. Unlike the Indian securities agency SEBI, the Nepali agency has not issued any exposure drafts or memorandums in relation to equity crowdfunding. The absence of a local equity crowdfunding portal has meant that there is unlikely to be the same level of awareness and consequently impetus for equity crowdfunding.

Bangladesh

Within Bangladesh, the Securities and Exchange Commission (SEC) was established in 1993 under the Securities and Exchange Commission Act, 1993. The enacted model entails the Chairman and Members of the Commission being appointed by government, with the afforded respopnsibility to manage and administer securities legislation, notablty the Securities Act 1993. The Bangladeshi Securities and Exchage Commission is a statutory body, under the auspices of the Ministry of Finance.

The primary exchange, the Dhaka Stock Exchange was estabhished in 1954 (generally known as DSE). Post independence with the establishment of Dhaka Stock Exchange (previously known as the East Pakistan Stock Exchange) capital mrket indermediaries commenced activities within Bangladesh. The conception of the Investment Corporation of Bangladesh paved the way for fourther development and reform within the Bangladeshi financial services sector, and increased participation within the capital markets.

The Securities Act (1993) is silent in relation to crowdfunding type methods. The Securities Act (1993) is modelled on judicial pronouncements from the UK. In respect to the matter of the legality of crowdfunding within Bangladesh the following is of particular importance. A crowdfunding initiative that merely procures gifted or donated sums without the possibility of a return may not be considered unlawful under the Securities Act (1993). This most pertinent consideration is the nature of the reward provided by the project promoter would be critical to whether an initiative would be considered unlawful. The nature of the reward offered and the structure of the crowdfunding offering would determine whether the arrangement would require licensing, and whether it constitutes a managed investment scheme pursuant to the Companies Act, or whether it constitutes a fundraising activity under the Companies Act.

India

India has actively pursued financial liberalization for the past three decades. The current governor of the Indian Central Bank, Mr. has been championing financial sector liberalization since accepting the office in September. The Governor has frequently asserted that financial sector reform serves as a mechanism through which greater economic growth and pro poor advancement can be achieved. "Change is risky", he has asserted, "But as India develops, not changing is even riskier."

Indeed SEBI have been advancing such arguments as well. SEBI the Indian Securities agency has been the most proactive regulatory agency within the South Asian region in relation to equity based crowdfunding, encouraging dialogue and requesting public commentary. It is evident that crowdfunding as a discrete activity would be prohibited under Indian securities legislation. Pursuant to the Companies Act 2013 and additional SEBI regulations pertaining to disclosure; the SEBI (Issue of Capital and Disclosure Requirements) Regulations, 2009 (ICDR), the raising of funds through a crowdfunding based mechanism would be considered unlawful. In light of recent development globally, SEBI asserted a desire in elicit more comment and discussion from within the Indian business community in relation to crowdfunding. The drafting of the discussion paper titled "Consultation Paper on Crowdfunding in India" is the first step in this regard, with SEBI asserting that no clear determination has been made in relation to either the desirability of crowdfunding provisions, and their potential enactment in the future. Rather SEBI has sought to stimulate debate into whether further revisions to the Companies Act 2013 would be amiable, and support economic growth and development, in line with the position of the Minister of Finance.

The actions of SEBI appear to be the most proactive, and consultative of any agency within the South Asian region. The move is pertinent in light of recent changes to the Companies Act 2013, which arguably make fundraisinbg through private placements more challenging and rigourious. The revisions to the Companies Act 2013 appear pragmatic in light of events light the Sahara Ltd fundraising effort, but they do have the unintended consequence of making smaller fundraising efforts more challenging. The SEBI exposure draft in many respects is a response both to the global movement pertaining to crowdfunding and equity crowdfunding in particular, but it also serves as a counterpoint to the revisions to the Companies Act 2013 pertaining to private placements.

It is noteworthy to acknowledge that the Companies Act 2013 does afford mechanisms through which securities offers can be extended to Qualified Institutional Buyers. Ostensibly these provisions may prima facie, provide for the raising of equity capital through crowdfunding type schemes, albiet the existing provisions do no specifically address crowdfunding mechanisms. As such reform is required for crowdfunding to be formally enabled.

Under the SEBI introduced proposal SEBI would register approved platforms to operate as crowdfunding platforms, akin to the non-broker entity model enacted in the U.S. Firms would then be permitted to raise to Rs 10 crore during a given financial year through listing on the crowdfunding platform. Again in line with the U.S. framework and the CAMAC proposal, given the underlying risk associated with such mechanisms the mechanism will not be available to all investors, with only accredited investors permitted to participate in any equity fundraising. Logically the agency will permit institutional investors, companies, High Net worth Individuals and financial sound investors to participate in a fundraising call. The crowdfunding investment level would be capped consistent with the CROWDFUND Act and the CAMAC proposal albeit at a lower investment level of Rs 60,000 or 10 per cent of individual/entity's net worth.

As such, this study has evidenced that crowdfunding legislation has not been enacted within any South Asian jurisdiction, with India the only nation to strongly conjecture and post draft legislation for public comment. Given this fact it is pertinent for policymakers within other South Asian jurisdictions to consider the potential viability of crowdfunding legislation within their polities. It would appear that only SEBI has afforded due credence to these matters, having released an exposure draft for public comment modelled on the U.S. pronouncements. Moreover the Indian markets have a greater level of understanding of crowdsourcing methodologies given the success of crowdsourcing entities within India, and more recently the success of non-equity based crowd funders such as Kickstarter within India.

CONCLUDING REMARKS

Herein it is contended that much can be learnt from the American experience, and while some hesitation may exist in relation to the adoption of similar provisions with Australia, to not afford due consideration to such provisions would be inapt. The implementation of the crowdfunding provisions will be closely followed by jurists and policymakers alike. If the crowdfunding legislative reforms have little to no impact on capital raisings and the market for venture capital, then the it is unlikely that analogous pronouncements would be impactful abroad, but the U.S. experience presents South Asian policymakers and regulators with a worthwhile opportunity to observe the impact of what is arguably one of the most significant small business reforms in living memory.

There will always be a regulatory contest between innovators and regulators appearing as a dialectic process. The process of innovation and regulatory cycle may be steadily gaining pace, as information and communications technologies continue to disrupt an ever increasing number of industries.

Edward Kane employed a Hegel (Kantian) dialectic approach in when describing the divergence and convergence that occurred between regulators and those the laws intend to regulate. Kane essential claim was that the dialectic process commenced with a regulatory framework, to which there was a response of regulatory avoidance, and subsequently regulatory change. We then observe a series of repeat iterations potentially going through an infinite number of cycles. As such in the view of Kane regulations are merely artefacts that motivate regulatory avoidance, and innovative new approaches to enable avoidance.

Kane (1972) asserts that creativity tends to be more evident amongst those seeking to avoid regulation, and that regulation is arguably a reactive device rather than a proactive mechanism. Essentially the core thesis proffered by Kane (1972) is that "regulation immediately begets avoidance… and there's much more creativity on the avoidance side, much more opportunity to play, to make moves that the regulators have to address. So we're always behind, until we get new regulation, which addresses some of the problems of the past, but that immediately starts the process all over again."

This situation is certainly true of the matters discussed within this paper. The Securities Act (1933) and Securities Exchange Act (1934) as regulatory apparatuses served their purposes well, however also served to stifle capital raising activities amongst SMEs, to the extent that the costs associated with raisings made the use of certain capital raising techniques.

Information and communications technologies have served as an enabling force, responding to this regulatory cycle from a bygone era. The internet and platform based crowdsourcing models have created alternative mechanisms through which resources can be procured.

The U.S. congress has sought to use these potential sources of disruption to the financial services sector as enabling tools to create employment opportunities and fund innovation. The JOBS Act notwithstanding some procedural uncertainties represents a remarkably forward thinking approach to the unique practices being adopted by platform sellers. Crowdsourcing models had the potential to supplant and potentially contravene securities legislation and rather that allow this to happen unabated, the lawmakers have enacted a policy that will seek to define how such practices are manifest in society.

The potential economic benefits are clear; if the increased costs associated with restricted/limited information disclosure are greater than the economic benefits associated with entities securing funding then then policy will have a deleterious impact on society. But the policymakers should be lauded for working with innovators to ensure the best outcome for emergent entities, and society as a whole. Striking a balance between the often dichotomous demands of commercial innovators, their rivals and the interests of consumers can be particularly problematic, and while the pronouncements enacted may be contentious they appear to strike the correct balance, finding that appropriate middle ground. While the policy appears to reside on the equidistant point along the spectrum that represents the interests of innovators/emergent entities and broader society, its effect remains to be seen, and will be followed with close interest.

REFERENCES

Federal Government of United States of America. (2012). *Securities exchange act of 1934*. Washington, DC: Federal Government of United States of America.

Federal Government of USA. (2002). *Sarbanes–Oxley Act*. Washington, DC: Federal Government of USA.

Federal Government of USA. (2013). *Jumpstart Our Business Startups (JOBS) Act* (pp. 1–22). Washington, DC: Federal Government of USA.

Howe, J. (2006). The rise of crowdsourcing. *Wired Magazine, 14*(6), 1-4.

Kane, M. T. (1983). Evidence that protease action is not specifically involved in hatching of rabbit blastocysts caused by commercial bovine serum albumin in culture. *Journal of Reproduction and Fertility, 68*(2), 471–475. doi:10.1530/jrf.0.0680471 PMID:6688094

Pope, N. D. (2010). Crowdfunding Microstartups: It's Time for the Securities and Exchange Commission to Approve a Small Offering Exemption. *U. Pa. J. Bus. L.*, *13*, 973.

Securities and Exchange Commission v. W. J. Howey Co, 163 A.L.R 1043 (US Supreme Court 1946).

Sorenson, O., & Stuart, T. E. (2001). Syndication Networks and the Spatial Dis-tribution of Venture Capital Investments. *American Journal of Sociology*, *106*(6), 1546–1588. doi:10.1086/321301

Stemler, A. R. (2013). The JOBS Act and crowdfunding: Harnessing the power—and money—of the masses. *Business Horizons*, *56*(3), 271–275. doi:10.1016/j.bushor.2013.01.007

Taku, Y. (2012). Crowdfunding: Its Practical Effect May Be Unclear Until SEC Rulemaking is Complete. *Bus. L. Today*, 1.

Chapter 6
The Impact of Institutional Factors on Female and Male Owned Firm Financing:
Evidence from South Asian Countries

Stuart Murrin Locke
University of Waikato, New Zealand

Nirosha Hewa-Wellalage
University of Waikato, New Zealand

ABSTRACT

The study compares the impact of the commercial environment on external financing of female- owned micro, small and medium enterprises (MSMEs) compared to those that are male owned in seven South Asian countries. The region exhibits weak institutional and regulatory regimes which result in expropriation of profits from MSMEs. It is likely that such commercial environments add to the risk of lending to MSMEs and this may further manifest a gender bias toward males. This study uses a unique dataset of over 5000 firms from World Bank Enterprise Surveys and combines this with additional information drawn from World Bank macro-economic data. Interval and logit regressions are used. Contrary other studies, this research indicates that once females have access to formal financing they use a higher proportion of formal financing in their firm capital structure than their male-counterparts. A gap in accessing external finance for female-owned MSMEs presents both a waste of human resource and a lost potential to lift standards of living, presenting an opportunity for reform.

I. INTRODUCTION

The study compares the impact of the commercial environment on external financing of female- owned micro, small and medium enterprises (MSMEs) compared to those that are male owned in seven South Asian countries. South Asia[1] poses a number of institutional obstacles for accessing external finance and in many cases, access is even harder for women. An empirical comparison of the impediments, for the South Asian countries excepting Maldives, provides a base from which policies may be formulated

DOI: 10.4018/978-1-5225-0004-9.ch006

to facilitate participation of small businesses in obtaining finance and encouraging business formation. One important dimension in the access to finance debate and which is relatively less analysed, is gender gap (Aterido, Beck, & Iacovone, 2011).

Women make up more than half of the population in Asia, and the United Nations estimates that the Asia-Pacific economy would earn an additional $89 billion annually if women were able to achieve their full economic potential ("UN Women's flagship report: 2011-2012 Progress of the World's Women: In Pursuit of Justice," 2013). Initiatives in the microfinance area, have focussed on making money available to women and it is of interest to observe what traction these initiatives are achieving. The extent to which institutional development has a differentiated effect on female- and male-owned MSMEs warrants serious attention given the magnitude of additional GDP that may be generated and the related impact on per capita income.

The importance of the institutional environment for corporates making choices regarding financing is well established. Using cross-country analysis, La Porta et al. (1997), Demirguc-Kunt and Maksimovic (2001), Booth, Aivazian, Demirguc-Kunt, & Maksimovic (2001), Rajan & Zingales (1995) and Beck et al. (2008) present evidence that a country's legal and financial environment influences a firm's use of external financing. The heterogeneity of both form and magnitude of institutional imperfections existing in each country varies widely and according to Carvalho (2008) depends on the level of its institutional development. The inclusion of measures relating to gender may indicate even less uniformity across the nations of South Asia. While the literature on gender and entrepreneurship is extensive, it is predominantly associated with mature economies and little work exists in relation to emerging economies and low income countries (LICs). Although, there are reports and studies that touch on gender and MSMEs, these do not explicitly explore the issue of external financing.

There is a need for a context specific study in South Asia to generate baseline stylised facts to help policymakers design better credit programmes for these smaller enterprises. Similar to La-Porta, Silanes, Shleifer, & Vishny (1997) and Demirg-Kunta & Maksimovic, (2001), institutional theory is well suited to investigate differences in the factors that have potential to impact on a firm's accessibility to external financing. In the South Asia region, the World Bank Enterprise surveys, conducted by the World Bank, provide data relating to female and male led firms.

MSMEs in South Asia

Enterprises owned by women, as mentioned in the UN (2013) report, have tremendous potential for adding to the economic output of economies in South Asia. This will necessarily involve social change, empowering women and transforming society through the removal of constraints or barriers that effectively stymie such potential. Currently, this potential remains largely untapped, with fewer than 10% of the entrepreneurs in South Asian countries being women (Sinhal, 2005). While this Sinhal evidence is a little dated, there is no significant evidence to suggest that the figures have moved dramatically. Accordingly, the potential to raise living standards across the region remain latent. Consistent with this perspective is an Asian Development Bank study, which observes that there are only 8%-9% formal MSME enterprises owned by women in South Asia, compared to 38% -47% formal MSME enterprises owned by women in East Asia, Central Asia and Eastern Europe (*Women Entrepreneurs in Asia and the Pacific*, 2013).

An earlier Indian-based study by Kaur and Bawa (1992) finds that only 10% of female entrepreneurs received funds from government agencies and nationalised banks while 54% of women entrepreneurs started their business with their own personal savings and with some financial assistance from their spouse. Their numbers are consistent with the more recent pan South Asia numbers above (World Development Bank, 2013) reflecting little change in 20 years. A Pakistan MSMEs study by Das (2000) indicates that middle-level female entrepreneurs in Pakistan were financed by their own savings or borrowings from their relatives with more than 50% of Pakistan female entrepreneurs using their own funds or funds borrowed from their spouse or family to set up their business.

The available evidence points to MSMEs in South Asia being severely restricted by the slow development of supporting institutions, the banking system, the legal framework and, most of all, by the government's regulatory processes in a weak institutional environment. The weak rules and regulations push entrepreneurs to the informal sector of the economy, which negatively impacts upon growth. When capital markets are not well developed there is inefficient pricing of risk and this consequently distorts the market for goods and services. Business opportunities that might be successful cannot obtain finance and consequently a poverty trap is maintained. Such situations give rise to other social problems, such as crime, and more valuable resources are expended on policing, etc. than would otherwise be the case.

When there are undeveloped rules of the game and a business environment which lacks transparency and at best might be termed non-conducive, then all economic agents, MSMEs in particular, have to decide whether, and to what extent, they wish to operate in the formal economy. Their decisions are based on the incentive system generated by the legal and institutional mechanisms operating in different countries. In many cases, firms in South Asia operate under weak legal and institutional structures, a wide variety of rules and regulations, corruption and informal payments, all of which create the incentive for MSMEs to restrict access to formal external financing.

II. REVIEW OF LITERATURE

The importance of gender in ownership is receiving attention across many areas of small business and larger business research. Within the literature there has been a reluctance to address some of the more contentious matters. The two most obvious relate culture and religion. If the religious precepts preclude women from engaging in commerce or venturing out of the home then this is final statement in terms of the published data. In areas where religion is not the main issue there remains a cultural matter. The coauthor experience an issue in Sri Lanka where a side payment was necessary to get a permit for a business but a male was needed to hand over the money as the male clerk could not take a side payment from a woman.

Issues relating to decision style, organisational performance and governance have illuminated the existence of unique gender impacts. Not surprisingly, the gender of the owner is an important issue impacting access to external financing. A number of studies extensively examine the gender of MSME owners and the impact of this on firms' external financing (Cavalluzzo & Wolken, 2005; Cavalluzzo, Cavalluzzo, & Wolken, 2002; Jones & Tullous, 2002). Credit constraint is observed as the major barrier to the growth of female-owned small businesses in developing countries, including South Asia ("Strengthening Access to Finance for Women-Owned SMEs in Developing Countries," 2011). It is suggested that in addition to the greater likelihood that women are more likely to be working part-time and earning less than men, they find it more difficult to accumulate personal savings (Marlow & Patton, 2007).

It is also noted that women typically try to access smaller amounts of funding because so-called ''feminine'' occupations are less capital-intensive (D'Espallier, Guérin, & Mersland, 2010; Guérin &

Palier, 2006). Nevertheless, a perception of higher risk and cultural bias amongst loan officers is often reported among local banks which limit female MSME owners' access to external finance (Muravyev, Talavera, & Schäfer, 2009). A consequence of the uneven playing field in terms of access to funds is that the average quality of the businesses run by women is lower, leading to a self-reinforcing discrimination mechanism (Scalera & Zazzaro, 2001).

There have been several attempts to investigate access to finance for female MSME owners (Carter & Rosa, 1998; Green, Brush, Hart, & Saparito, 2001; Read, 1998) and issues other than gender that affect access to external financing (Carter & Rosa, 1998). Differential access to credit may be a reflection of differences in the choice of sector, education level and the amount of loan requested (Sinhal, 2005). However, sector choices, education level and risk aversion tend to be influenced by gender and multivariate analysis is required to determine more clearly the key issues. It is tempting to assert that differences in accessibility to external financing are at least indirectly motivated by gender.

Women, in particular those who are less educated in South Asia[2,] also find it more difficult to get financing from banks because of inadequate information and information asymmetry in a weak institutional environment. Sometimes in developing countries with weak institutional environments, credit may be available for women through several schemes but there are bottlenecks and gaps, and the multiplicity of schemes is often not adequately listed and nor is there adequate networking among agencies (Vishwananthan, 2001).

Women may face unequal inheritance practices and laws, discriminatory laws on ownership of property, access to bank loans, and other discriminatory practices by banks. In more rural areas the power of local custom is stronger than in the more cosmopolitan centres. The patriarchal system of village leader and council may enforce overtly, or through customary process, approaches that are not supported by law or regulation. Such forms of bias are more difficult to document and analyse. The spread of technology may help to redress imbalances with all Indians now to have a bank account under a new government policy (2014) and the greater potential to apply online to open an account and simplified identification requirements announced by Reserve Bank of India, may over time ameliorate discriminatory influences, but this will not happen overnight.

Institutions have governance structures based on rules, norms, understandings and routines (March & Olsen, 1989) where social patterns are characterised by a standard sequence of interactions (Ronald & Meyer, 1991). Consequently, a firm's borrowing access depends on its legitimacy to institutional structures rather than on the efficiency to which it co-ordinates and controls its productivity. As an example, factors that can influence a firm's legitimacy also have potential to improve a firm's accessibility to external financing (Le, Venkatesh, & Nguyen, 2006). Prior research emphasises the importance of using an institutional perspective for better understanding of firm behaviour in transitional and developing economies (Hoskisson, Lau, & Wright, 2000; Meyer & Nguyen, 2005).

It has been assumed that the institutional context will influence the nature, pace of development and behaviour of the business owners (Welter & Smallbone, 2011). For example, in countries with low GDP growth rates the mainstream commercial banks tend to focus on the most solid and typically low risk businesses, thus reducing the opportunity for small-scale firms to access bank credit. Corporations and businesses often deal and/or negotiate with governments (Rodriguez, Uhlenbruck, & Eden, 2005) regarding public sector contracts, lobbying activities, negotiating loans and other issues of interest (Faccio, 2006). Chakravarty and Xiang (2011) and Firth, Lin, Liu and Wong (2009) report that in some countries political connections also play a significant role in allocating capital or credit by financial institutions to micro-firms. Not surprisingly, in the absence of effective institutional structures, firms in developing and transitional economies tend to rely on alternative strategies, such as connections with political parties and/or networking with friends who are in high places or have power to influence decision makers in order to gain legitimacy, criminal syndicates and the shadow finance communities (Peng & Heath, 1996; Tsang, 1994).

In countries where the regulatory environment is more supportive of start-up and operating new businesses, firms enjoy better or easier access to external financing (Cull and Xu, 2005). Using firm-level data from 40 countries, Beck et al.(2008) report that the development of a country's legal system is a good indicator of firms' accessibility to external finance. La-Porta et al.(1997) using data from 49 countries report that countries that have weak investor protection also have a smaller and less developed capital market. The level of financial intermediation existing in those countries is low. The positive role of banks in monitoring performance (Levine, 1997; Levine, Loayza, & Beck, 2000) and the existence of an efficient financial market (where information is revealed quickly to liquidity holders) are a necessary condition for enhancing accessibility to external sources of financing.

Political stability is also an important institutional index which impacts on private entrepreneurs' growth and accessibility to finance (Lemmon, 2012). Most of the literature analysing the effects of conflict deals with issues of security and reconstruction at the macro level and with the role of the state agency (Collier, 1999; Cramer, 2006). Conflict might indirectly affect the potential to start entrepreneurial activities through the destruction of social capital, e.g. networks due to forced displacements and migration (Amuedo-Dorantes & Pozo, 2006) Migrant refugees are likely to lose collateral and resources they owned before a forced move to leave. These issues are likely to lead to limited access to formal finance.

III. DATA AND METHODOLOGY

The methodological underpinning for the study is positivist with an intention to analyse the data in a manner that discerns relationships between variables. The choice of observations flows from the literature on equilibrium asset pricing views of financial markets. These markets price risk and impediments to the accurate assessment of returns from institutional and cultural barriers means the markets will not clear and anomalous results will avail. Typically, where there is a lack of transparency and information is not readily available or may not be used, such as through the result of not allowing certain parties to participate, then the risk pricing signals for forecast returns are distorted. Resource allocation is sub-optimal and gross domestic product per person does not advance as quickly as would otherwise be the case.

The method of analysis is empirical and based on linear regression methods. The research question provides a number of testable hypotheses and the statistical processes are used to test these.

H_1: There is no significant relationship between MSME owner's gender and types of external financing through bank financing, non-bank financing, trade credit and other sources).

H_2: There is no significant relationship between MSME owner's gender and proportion of external financing through bank financing, non-bank financing, trade credit and other sources.

To explore the relationship between gender and enterprise access to credit, we use data collated from the Enterprise Surveys conducted by the World Bank in 2006-2011 (*Enterprise Surveys: What Businesses Experience*, 2012) for seven South Asia countries (Afghanistan-2008 survey edition, Bangladesh-2007 survey edition, Bhutan-2009 survey edition, India-2006 survey edition Nepal-2009 survey edition,

Pakistan- survey edition, Sri Lanka-2011 survey edition)[3]. Following a uniform and stratified random sampling method and survey instruments, the Enterprise Surveys collect information on the investment environment of individual economies across the globe.

The general form of a regression-based study is to investigate the links between one variable, known as the Dependant Variable and other variables, the Independent Variables, which from a theoretical perspective are thought likely to be correlated with it. The analysis will indicate the strength of the relationship and whether there is a positive or negative relationship. For example Qualifications and Experience might be expected to be positively correlated with ease of access to finance while a Criminal Record might be thought to be likely to be negatively correlated.

Data

World Bank (*Enterprise Surveys: What Businesses Experience*, 2012) provided micro level information on gender and access to finance. Macro level economic data used are collected from various sources. The information regarding "ease of doing business" in different countries is drawn from the World Bank website (*Economy Rankings*, 2012). Each country's GDP growth rate is available from the Central Intelligence Agency (CIA) Factbook reports (*The World Factbook*, 2012), while countries' interest rates are collated on the World Bank website (*Real interest rate (%)*, 2013).

Dependent Variables

The dependent variables used for this study are concerned with the source of finance and the amount of finance obtained. These attributes are captured by the following question in the world Bank Enterprise Survey:

Over the fiscal year, please estimate the proportion of this establishment's working capital that was financed from each of the following sources: borrowed from banks (private and state-owned), borrowed from non-bank financial institutions, purchases on credit from suppliers and advances from customers, other (money lenders, friends, relatives, bonds, commercial papers etc.)

Dependent variables are divided into two groups relating to the accessibility of financing and proportion of financing by each source. This will help to find out both accessibility of financial sources and the limit of accessibility of proportion of each financing source. This is important, because access to and use of financial services by entrepreneurs is of increasing concern to policy makers across the globe. From a policy maker's perspective the amount of money going through the formal financial sector vis à vis the informal sector is important.

Dependent Variable for Accessibility of External Financing

To capture the accessibility of external financing in a particular year, a dichotomous variable is created from responses to a question about sources of money. Over a fiscal year, if the firm's working capital was financed from a bank the A_BANK variable takes value "1". If a firm has access to non-bank financing, A_NONBANK takes value "1". If the firm has access to credit, A_CREDIT takes value "1". Finally if firm has access to other methods of financing,, A_OTHER, takes value "1", otherwise 0.

Dependent Variable for Proportion of Financing

The dependent variable P_BANK is used as a metric for the bank finance obtained by the firm. This variable takes the percentage of bank financing used by the firm in the last fiscal year as working capital. Similarly, P_NONBANK is used as a measure for the non-bank finance obtained by the firm. P_CREDIT is used to record the credit finance obtained by the firm and P_OTHER is used for any other finance obtained by the firm.

Explanatory Variables

We use two categories of independent variables, viz. firm-level characteristics and country-level indicators.

Firm–Level Characteristics

This study uses the Female (FEMALE) variable as a primary explanatory variable taking the value "1"if the firm has a female owner. We use three dummy variables to represent small, medium and large type of business. This study assumes a relationship between firm financing accessibility and business age. The natural log of firm age (ln (AGE)) is used as the metric for age.

The conflict impact on MSMEs' financing is captured using a variable denoted as CONFLICT. The CONFLICT variable is recorded as "1" if firms are from conflict affected areas. Further, to identify the geographical location impact on firm financing/proportion, this study uses the CAPITAL variable. The Enterprise Survey only categorises firms as manufacturing, retail and other. Hence, this study uses an industry variable as a categorical variable.

Government relationship (GOVERNMENT) encodes the percentage of proprietor's time spent and, for larger businesses, senior management's time spent dealing with requirements imposed by government regulations. This study categorises "legal form of business" variable into 6 categories, i.e. Shareholding company with shares traded on the stock market, Shareholding company with non-traded shares or shares traded privately (public or private), sole proprietorship, partnership firms and limited liability companies. Finally, government support (SUPPORT) as explanatory variable is recorded as "1" if government or other institutions provide start-up funds.

Country-Level Indicators

The World Bank Report ranks economies on the "ease of doing business" (EASE) from 1 – 183. A high ranking means that the regulatory environment is more conducive to the start-up and operation of businesses. We propose that a positive relationship would exist between EASE and firm external financing in each country. We use GDP growth rate as a proxy for growth (GDP). GDP is obtained from the CIA website (*The World Factbook*, 2012). The real interest rates (INTEREST) of South Asian countries are sourced from the World Bank website (*Real interest rate (%)*, 2013) computed as the lending interest rate adjusted for inflation as measured by the respective GDP deflator. The World Bank Survey data includes fairness of court system as a categorical variable. Based on the above information, three dummy variables are created as FAIR equal to "1" when owners feel the court system is fair, MODERATE is equal to "1" if the firm owners feel the court system is moderate and UNFAIR equals "1" when firm owners feel the court system is unfair.

Descriptive statistics for all variables are presented in Table 1. The first column of Table 1 provides mean figures on debt with banking institutions providing approximately 3.25% of MSMEs' external financing needs, followed by trade credit (2.25%) which contributes to the normal source of the sales cycle in financing working capital. The minimum and maximum helps confirm the distribution of the data in conjunction with the mean and standard deviation; which is important for subsequent analysis where normal variates are important. It is apparent that MSMEs appear to face a great constraint in obtaining external financing. Interestingly, firms with only male owners show a much lower component of bank financing in their MSMEs' capital structure when compared to MSMEs with both male and female owners. Results indicate that MSMEs with only male owners engage a high proportion of trade credit compared with MSMEs having female owners. The figures also indicate that female-owned MSMEs use quasi debt (debt from family and friends) twice as much as those that are male owned.

Potentially, it may be that female-owned MSMEs in developing countries are more likely to be home based and operate within the household more than male led enterprises (Bruhn, 2009; Mead & Liedholm, 1998), and that they actually prefer informal sources of financing. It is apparent from Table 1 that the majority of MSMEs in conflict affected areas are female owned. This may be that women are often the only survivors left to support their families when male relatives are killed or injured in battle (Lemmon, 2012). Overall statistics indicate approximately 70% of MSMEs are from outside the capital city or cities with populations of more than one million in South Asian countries, indicating the vital role of MSMEs in rural economic development. Consistent with prior research, the results point to female MSME owners as being highly engaged in retail and other industry sectors compared to male owners. Male MSME owners are dominant in the manufacturing sector. Finally, the judiciary system variable indicates that a larger percentage of female MSME owners compared with male MSME owners consider their country's judiciary system is moderate or unfair for them .

Model

An analysis of variance (ANOVA) is used to test whether the external financing accessibility and external financing proportion variables are the same between firms with no female owners and firms with female owners. The testable hypothesis for ANOVA proposed is:

H_0: There is no difference in the external finance accessibility/proportion of the female group and male group.

The results are presented in Table 2. The F statistic provides an indication of the confidence level at which the hypothesis can be accepted. The $F > F_{critical}$ and $p < \alpha$; so the null hypothesis is not accepted, suggesting the two groups' means are different. Further analysis is necessary to determine if there are any significant relationships between MSME owners' gender and external finance accessibility or the external finance proportion in the firms' capital structure.

To investigate the gender impact on both financing accessibility and financing proportion a logit regression is an appropriate form of analysis to estimate the relationship between gender impacts on financing accessibility. The lower bound of financing proportion (%) for each selected mode is zero and the upper bound is 100. Following Beck et al., (2010) an interval form of regression is applied to discern the relationship between gender impacts and financing proportion of each external financing source.

Table 1. Descriptive statistics

	All Sample (A)					With Female Owners (B)					Male Owners Only (C)				
Variable	**Obs**	**Mean**	**Std.D**	**Min**	**Max**	**Obs**	**Mean**	**Std.D**	**Min**	**Max**	**Obs**	**Mean**	**Std.D**	**Min**	**Max**
Dependent variables															
P_BANK	5775	.0325	.1319	0	1	1196	.0491	.1651	0	1	4555	.0283	.1217	0	1
P_NONBANK	5763	.0032	.0392	0	.95	1196	.0039	.0441	0	.75	4543	.0030	.0379	0	.95
P_CREDIT	5763	.0225	.0965	0	1	1196	.0165	0940	0	1	4543	.0240	.0971	0	1
P_OTHER	5775	.0041	.0378	0	1	1196	.0064	.0522	0	1	4553	.0036	.0332	0	.75
Independent variables															
SMALL	5775	.6001	.4899	0	1	1196	.4757	.4996	0	1	4555	.6335	.4818	0	1
MEDIUM	5775	.3206	.5214	0	1	1196	.3620	.5505	0	1	4555	.3086	.5129	0	1
FEMALE	5775	.2079	.4058	0	1										
Age	5772	21.90	13.62	2	164	1195	19.21	14.6	2	164	4553	22.62	13.277	2	135
LnAGE	5772	2.902	.6302	.6931	5.099	1195	2.71	.7039	.6931	5.099	4553	2.951	.6007	.6931	4.905
CONFLICT	5775	.0924	.2897	0	1	1196	.0978	.2972	0	1	4553	.0911	.2877	0	1
CAPITAL	5775	.3189	.4661	0	1	1196	.5242	.4996	0	1	4555	.2656	.4417	0	1
Industry															
MANU	5775	.6893	.4627	0	1	1196	.6145	.4869	0	1	4555	.7108	.4534	0	1
RETAIL	5775	.1390	.3460	0	1	1196	.1421	.3493	0	1	4555	.1361	.3429	0	1
OTHER	5775	.1037	.3049	0	1	1196	.1847	.3882	0	1	4555	.0823	.2748	0	1
GOVERNMENT	4389	-1.6739	2.148	-99.210	4.605	842	-1.221	2.42	-6.907	4.605	3529	-1.789	2.062	-9.21	4.605
Legal form of Business															
LISTED	5775	.0706	.2562	0	1	1196	.1195	.3245	0	1	4555	.0559	.2299	0	1
NONTRADE	5775	.2008	.4006	0	1	1196	.2976	.4574	0	1	4555	.1762	.3811	0	1
SOLE	5775	.5277	.4992	0	1	1196	.3745	.4842	0	1	4555	.5694	.4952	0	1
PARTNERSHIP	5775	.1664	.3724	0	1	1196	.1789	.3834	0	1	4555	.1626	.3691	0	1
LIMITED	5775	.0117	.1078	0	1	1196	.0242	.1538	0	1	4555	.0085	.0921	0	1
OTHER	5775	.0219	.1466	0	1	1196	.0050	.0706	0	1	4555	.0263	.1601	0	1
SUPPORT	5775	.4469	.4972	0	1	1196	.4331	.4957	0	1	4555	.4498	.4975	0	1
Judiciary system															
FAIR	5775	.2819	.4499	0	1	1196	.2734	.4458	0	1	4555	.2843	.4511	0	1
MODERATE	5775	.4905	.4999	0	1	1196	.5083	.5001	0	1	4555	.4849	.4998	0	1
UNFAIR	5775	.1954	.3966	0	1	1196	.1964	.3975	0	1	4555	.1958	.3968	0	1

Table 2. ANOVA Results

Agency Costs	F	P-Value	F-Critical
External financing accessibility	4.143	0.009	3.865
External financing proportion	4.653	0.040	3.865

IV. RESULTS

Results for the analysis of determinants of external financing for female and male groupings are reported in Tables 3 and 4 respectively. It is interesting to observe the differences in the coefficient values. Logit regression reports "accessibility of finance" and interval regression reports "proportion of finance by cach source". In both tables, Column II refers to the bank financing, Column III reports non-bank financing, Column IV reports trade credits and Column V reports other sources of external financing. Furthermore, we divided each column into two sub-columns which indicate external financing accessibility and external financing proportion from each of the sources. External financing accessibility by each source is denoted in CAPITAL such as (percentage having trade credit in MSME's capital structure). External financing proportion by each source is denoted as follows: P_BANK (percentage of having bank financing in MSME's capital structure), P_NONBANK (percentage of having non-bank financing in MSME's capital structure), P_CREDIT (percentage of having trade credit in MSME's capital structure and A_OTHERS (percentage of having other financing (finance from friends and families in MSME's capital structure). In each table standard errors are in parenthesis. The significance level is denoted using an asterisk and shows one percent, five percent and ten percent significance levels.

Female-owned MSMEs report greater financing obstacles when endeavoring to access external financing from banks and non-bank institutions. It is therefore not surprising to observe that for female-owned MSMEs the bank/non-bank financing accessibility is approximately 13% / 18% less than for their male counterparts. Evidence presented by Coleman (2000) reveals that female-owned businesses pay higher interest rates and need to provide higher collateral requirements than those businesses owned by men. This may compound the difficulty of accessing finance from the formal financial sector (bank and non-bank).

The gender of MSME owners is not a significant influencing factor for trade credit accessibility and other modes of external financing (quasi-debt) accessibility. Although owners' gender does have a significant impact on bank and non-bank financing accessibility for MSMEs, the results indicate that gender is not associated with external financing proportion by formal and informal financing sources. This suggests that loan size is not influenced by owners' gender but is more related to factors more directly related to the business. It appears reasonable to infer that while a weak institutional environment creates barriers to access external financing for female-owned MSMEs, once a MSME owner satisfies the external financing criteria, then gender is not a significant factor in determining loan size.

The CONFLICT variable captures the impact of conflict on the financing accessibility of firms. There is no significant statistical correlation between male accessibility to finance and conflict. However, for female MSME owners the sign on the coefficient is negative and there is a statistical significance at the 10% level. The relationship is not strong but, not surprisingly, indicates that in regions experiencing conflict female business owners find it more difficult to access external financing. There may be a lack of alternative sources of finance available in violence- and conflict-affected areas and consequently MSME owners are more dependent on formal bank financing to meet their external financing requirements.

The pattern of financing for female and male MSME owners in relation to the capital city/larger urban areas is interesting. The coefficient for the capital city variable is positively related to the non-bank and credit financing accessibility and the proportion. However the capital city variable is at the 10% significance level, negatively related with bank finance proportion. An interpretation is that female-owned MSMEs from capital cities have more opportunity to access external financing from other sources and they may prefer not to have a high proportion of bank financing in their capital structure. However, for

Table 3: Determinants of external finance (Female Group)

(COLUMN I)	BANK (COLUMN II)		NONBANK (COLUMN III)		CREDIT(COLUMN IV)		OTHER(COLUMN V)	
	A_ BANK	P_BANK	A_ NONBANK	P_ NONBANK	A_ CREDIT	P_ CREDIT	A_ OTHER	P_ OTHER
SMALL	-.48153* (.1180)	-3.560*** (1.081)	.2292* (.2132)	.7459 (1.399)	.4946*** (.1424)	3.081** (1.366)	.3295* (.1940)	4.342 (4.575)
MEDIUM								
CONFLICT	.2111 (.1343)	2.155* (1.191)	.2309 (.1900)	1.545 (1.353)	.0864 (.1516)	.6459 (1.336)	-.2993 (.2328)	.6515 (4.561)
CAPITAL	-.0679 (.1775)	-3.946** (1.642)	.7557** (.2918)	6.204*** (1.799)	.5684*** (.2170)	8.269*** (1.595)	-.2486 (.4164)	-14.96 (9.710)
Industry								
MANU	-.0581 (.1620)	-.4484** (1.543)	-.3265* (.1808)	-1.137 (1.7519)	.0549 (.1662)	-.2627 (1.521)	.1802 (.2685)	6.549 (5.712)
RETAIL	-.4221 (.3215)	7.329** (3.507)	-.0699 (.4960)	2.007 (4.059)	.5912** (.2905)	.1107 (.1706)	.3914* (.2205)	61.55 (3.021)
OTHER								
GOVERNMENT	-.0358 (.04280)	.1745 (.3948)	.1264* (.0734)	.6620 (.5256)	.0489 (.0488)	.5214 (4631)	.1075 (.0766)	5.058 (3.330)
Legal form of Business								
LISTED	4.574*** (.2935)	3.864 (11.47)	3.306*** (.3913)	2.199 (.7861)	3.485*** (.3113)	2.884 (1.111)	-5.645 (1.223)	5.767 (6.394)
NONTRADE	4.368*** (.2684)	3.880 (11.47)	3.582*** (.3103)	2.433 (.7861)	3.687*** (.2816)	3.142 (1.009)	-5.344 (.3499)	6.157 (4.122)
SOLE	4.226 (.2623)	3.852 (11.47)	3.789 (.2985)	2.583 (.7861)	3.689*** (3.689)	3.068 (2.263)	-5.555 (.3564)	5.613 (8.246)
PARTNERSHIP	4.349 (.2726)	3.892 (11.47)	3.327*** (.3264)	2.260 (.7861)	3.672*** (.2862)	3.067 (2.489)	-5.609 (.4113)	5.817 (6.601)
LIMITED	3.619 (.7718)	1.536 (11.47)	3.862*** (.5947)	-7.661 (8412)	4.799*** (.7294)	3.922 (2.586)	-4.961 (.3508)	-1.190 (6.340)
OTHER								
Ln(AGE)	-.0812 (.0776)	.2374 (.7148)	-.1991 (.1249)	-.7808 (.8934)	-.0650 (.0890)	-.3443 (.7964)	-.1958 (.1276)	-1.259 (2.745)
Judiciary system								
UNFAIR	-.1426** (.1342)	-.4838** (1.256)	-.2547* (.2111)	-1.455** (1.4517)	.2456 (.1762)	1.960 (1.641)	.0469 (.1967)	-3.11 (4.929)
MODERATE SUPPORT	-.1447 (.2051)	-1.711 (1.762)	.4214 (.3569)	3.668 (2.327)	-.0589 (.2209)	-2.884* (1.702)	.7415* (.4280)	-1.168 (1.617)
EASE	.2892*** (.5068)	.6633*** (5.626)	.1010* (.5367)	.1130** (5.623)	-.746*** (.5231)	-.2179*** (4.399)	-.2030 (.7819)	-..0067 (3.116)
GDP	.1914*** (.4715)	.5310*** (4.112)	-.4923 (.9217)	.8673* (5.197)	-.7759 (.5261)	.1168** (5.113)	.2693** (.8677)	-8.270 (6.756)
INTEREST	.2276*** (.6964)	.2607*** (4.345)	.7748 (5930)	5.740 (8.700)	.7758 (..3237)	-9.595 (3.339)	.6209 (5664)	-1.332 (4.631)
Regression summary								

continued on following page

Table 3. Continued

(COLUMN I)	BANK (COLUMN II)		NONBANK (COLUMN III)		CREDIT(COLUMN IV)		OTHER(COLUMN V)	
	A_ BANK	P_BANK	A_ NONBANK	P_ NONBANK	A_ CREDIT	P_ CREDIT	A_ OTHER	P_ OTHER
No of observations	4389	4389	4389	4389	4389	4389	4389	4389
Log likelihood	-722.8	-2262.2	-209.8	-2262.2	-490.54	-997.8	-259.72	-163.4
sigma		10.1146		10.1146		8.9782		14.73
Pseudo R2	.9730		.9030		.9170		.633	

Standard errors are in parenthesis. * denotes significant at 10% level, ** denotes significant at 5% level and *** denote significant at 1% level.

This table reports relationship between firm characteristics and firm financial accessibility and their proportion.

Logit regression reports "accessibility of finance". The purpose model for accessibility of finance:

$$Finacing\,dummy = \propto + \beta\ \ firm\,ownership + \gamma\,firm\,individual\,charaterisitcs + \delta\ \ country\,dummy + \mu,$$

Interval regression reports "proportion of finance by each source". The proposed model for proportion of finance:

$$Finacing\ proportion = \propto + \beta\ \ frim\,ownership + \gamma\ firm\,individual\ charaterisitcs + \delta\ \ country\,dummy + \mu,$$

Firm ownership is dummy variable which takes value 1 if a firm has female owners.

Table 4. Determinants of external finance (Male Group)

(Column I)	BANK (Column II)		NONBANK (Column III)		CREDIT(Column IV)		OTHER(Column V)	
	A_BANK	P_BANK	A_ NONBANK	P_NONBANK	A_CREDIT	P_CREDIT	A_OTHER	P_OTHER
SMALL	-.3490** (.1901)	.2905 (.4693)	.4007* (.4384)	-.2104 (.3086)	.8226*** (.2693)	1.774** (.6539)	.5108 (.6603)	4.250 (4.566)
FEMALE	-.2512** (.1698)	2.001*** (.4248)	-.4605*** (.4114)	.8564* (.3383)	-.4197* (.2354)	1.115** (.5642)	-.1914 (.5592)	-.7066 (3.822)
CONFLICT	.3110 (.2161)	.4545 (.5267)	.4127 (.4002)	-.1125 (.3166)	.1393 (.2705)	.5443 (.6905)	.3727 (.6844)	.7363 (4.566)
CAPITAL	-.8094 (.2521)	8.081*** (.6676)	.2082 (.4842)	2.343*** (.3765)	.3218 (.2780)	4.413*** (.7338)	-2.12 (1.522)	-15.24 (9.918)
Industry								
MANU	.1982 (.2064)	-.8588* (.5118)	-.6099 (.3928)	.3516 (.3082)	-.3201 (.2480)	-.3824 (.6314)	3.015*** (1.286)	1.6405** (7.829)
RETAIL	.0084 (.2568)	-1.340** (.6305)	-.5570 (.4979)	.2425 (.3883)	.2270 (.2972)	-1.541** (.7514)	2.517** (1.325)	1.234 (8.078)
OTHER								
GOVERNMENT	-.1910 (.0639)	1.425*** (.1499)	-.0159 (.1318)	.2880*** (.0926)	-.0804 (.0781)	.4226** (.1933)	1.132 (.7103)	-1.119 (1.6151)
Legal form of Business								

continued on following page

Table 4. Continued

(Column I)	BANK (Column II)		NONBANK (Column III)		CREDIT(Column IV)		OTHER(Column V)	
	A_BANK	P_BANK	A_ NONBANK	P_NONBANK	A_CREDIT	P_CREDIT	A_OTHER	P_OTHER
LISTED	12.22 (4.677)	-1.555 (.8132)	9.071* (5.541)	-3.501 (6.457)	10.35 (4.857)	-1.336 (5.097)	1.030 (1.080)	5.683 (.5565)
NONTRADE	11.91* (4.403)	-1.662 (8.336)	9.783* (8.891)	-4.557 (5.855)	10.81 (6.982)	-1.364 (7.325)	10.88 (2.955)	6.086 (.6553)
SOLE	11.62 (9.809)	-1.555 (8.132)	9.783 (8.850)	-4.339 (6.455)	10.69 (9.829)	-1.353 (7.319)	9.852 (8.295)	5.547 (.5538)
PARTNERSHIP	11.85 (8.414)	-1.647 (7.889)	10.01 (9.986)	-4.021 (8.599)	10.77 (7.206)	1.382 (7.320)	10.39 (9.926)	5.748 (.8399)
LIMITED	10.87 (8.101)	-1.384 (2.344)	9.1605 (7.677)	1.167 (6.669)	12.29 (.7271)	-1.382 (7.388)	10.80 (9.930)	-1.1469 (.3899)
OTHER								
LnAGE	-.0819 (.1279)	.2413* (.3095)	-.3909 (.2730)	.0625** (.2155)	-.0432 (.1578)	.0566 (.3924)	-.1911 (.4137)	-1.375 (2.730)
Judiciary system								
FAIR	-.2990** (.3846)	-.3384*** (1.006)	-.6777 (.7082)	-.2764 (.5372)	1.223*** (.4619)	.0900 (1.114)	-1.750 (.9274)	-7.599 (6.288)
UNFAIR	-.3228 (.2155)	.1410*** (.5258)	-.7269 (.4461)	.8497** (.3371)	.3233 (.3387)	-.2027 (.7599)	-.5035 (.7546)	-3.13 (4.927)
MODERATE SUPPORT	.0072 (.3306)	3.494*** (.8833)	.1942 (.5989)	.6478 (.4657)	-.2020 (.3490)	-1.978** (.8814)	1.132 (.7103)	3.9610 (4.815)
EASE	.0463*** (.0169)	.6791*** (.0408)	.0090 (.0299)	.6985 (.0406)	-.0105 (.0181)	-.2737*** (.0571)	-.1279*** (.0454)	-1.121*** (.3286)
GDP	-3.394 (.7399)	6.051*** (.2161)	-2.002 (.1382)	9.386*** (.1272)	-6.537 (8.557)	1.294*** (.2373)	7.384*** (2.722)	5.957*** (1.958)
INTEREST	-2.830 (7.795)	-3.158*** (.1987)	-3.598** (1.572)	-7.511*** (1.001)	-6.658 (9.9924)	-6.581*** (2.440)	-1.111 (.4324)	-8.748*** (3.071)
Regression summary								
No of observations	4389	4389	4389	4389	4389	4389	4389	4389
Log likelihood	-734.3	-1732.8	-218.51	-215.2	-500.51	-791.32	-193.20	-163.54
sigma		4.188		1.422		4.117		14.745
Pseudo R2	0.8300		0.6263		0.732		0.205	

Standard errors are in parenthesis. * denotes significant at 10% level, ** denotes significant at 5% level and *** denote significant at 1% level.

This table reports relationship between firm characteristics and firm financial accessibility and their proportion.

Logit regression reports "accessibility of finance". The purpose model for accessibility of finance:

$$Finacing\,dummy = \propto + \beta\ frim\,ownership + \gamma\,firm\,individual\,charaterisitcs + \delta\ country\,specific\,instituional\,factors + \mu,$$

Interval regression reports "proportion of finance by each source". The proposed model for proportion of finance:

$$Finacing\ proportion = \propto + \beta\ frim\,ownership + \gamma\ firm\,individual\ charaterisitcs + \delta\ country\,specifc\,instituional\ factors + \mu,$$

the male-owned MSME group, the coefficient for the capital city variable is positively related to bank, non-bank and credit financing proportions.

The figures also indicate that the female-owned MSMEs in the manufacturing sector are reluctant to access formal financing sources compared with their female counterparts in retail firms. Similarly, for male-owned MSMEs there is an industry difference between the manufacturing and retail industries.

Government relationship is important, i.e. the percentage of total senior management time spent dealing with requirements imposed by government regulations. For the male group the variables are statistically significant at the 10% level and the sign on the coefficient is positive for non-bank financing accessibility, suggesting that when South Asian MSMEs follow government regulations they have more access to external financing sources.

The form of the business structure is important. The smallest businesses tend to be sole proprietorships and slightly larger businesses may take the form of a partnership in some loose form. Generally, but not always, the company structure relates to more medium sized businesses. Female-owned listed MSMEs show significant positive access to bank financing, non-bank financing and trade credit, while sole-proprietorships show a significant positive relationship with trade credit. This result indicates that when firms move from sole-proprietorship/partnership to listed companies they can have high access to both formal and informal financing. Considering female MSME groups, the coefficient of the variable FAIR is positive and is statistically significant with bank financing, non-bank financing and trade credit financing accessibility. It is also statistically significantly related with bank, non-bank and trade credit financing proportion. When MSME female owners feel their court system is fair, they tend to have greater access to trade credit and it also comprises a larger proportion of their capital structure. Interestingly, the male MSME owner group shows that when the judiciary system is unfair males have high access to external financing. Finally, the government support variable is negatively correlated and statistically significant at the 10% level with the trade credit proportion in female-owned MSMEs. It appears that for those MSMEs, government support is a substitute for trade credit finance.

Ease of doing business and growth in the economy are both important. In an environment where it is relatively simpler to establish and operate a business the EASE variable is statistically significant and positively correlated with bank financing accessibility and negatively related with the OTHER variable. When the regulatory environment is more conducive to the start-up and operation of business, both male and female MSME owners in South Asia have high access to formal financing, avoiding the requirement for quasi-debt. The overall levels of debt are not extended, implying that even though the regulatory environment is more conducive to accessing external financing, MSMEs are reluctant to have debt in their capital structure. In times when a country shows a high GDP growth rate, MSMEs accept more external financing in their capital structures. Not surprisingly, a high real interest rate has a significant negative impact on the male group external financing proportion, with contradictory results for the female MSME group. There appears to be a substitution effect; as males stop borrowing females move in to use the available funding.

V. CONCLUSION AND IMPLEMENTATIONS

The discussion and analysis focuses on whether weak institutional and regulatory regimes in South Asia impede female-owned MSMEs in accessing external finance. The findings reported are consistent with prior research based in South Asia, which demonstrates that the low access to formal external financing is a significant constraint for female MSME owners compared to their male counterparts. However, an important extension to these earlier studies is the finding that once females have access to formal financing they use a higher proportion of formal financing (bank and non-bank debt) in their capital structure than their male-counterparts. What is also important is that the more robust quantitative analysis, using newer, more recently available data and econometric software supports the prior findings. The additional insights offer a timely signal to South Asian countries to promulgate rules to strengthen institutional structures and regulatory regimes that will enhance the opportunities for growth and development of female-owned MSMEs.

The argument for gender equality may be presented from many perspectives. The discussion in this chapter relates to finance and makes no assumptions about ethical rights to equality. The effective pricing of risk in capital markets for both equity and debt is essential to raise living standards. Artificial constraints based on gender result in less than optimal growth and promote additional market failure through adverse selection of projects by both male and female entrepreneurs.

This study points to several actions and policy-related recommendations to enhance female MSME owners' access to external financing. First and foremost is the potential to enhance access to financial services by creating and strengthening the legal framework. Female-owned firms require the establishment of supportive regulatory environments to strengthen female property rights, legal capacity to enter contracts in their own name, and reduction in cultural constraints and barriers to networking, etc. Nevertheless, steps along the path are likely to require amending constitutional provisions of non-gender discrimination in relation to assets, property rights and property inheritance.

An expanded financial infrastructure and increased availability of financial intermediaries may promote the prospect of women-owned enterprises having enhanced financial access. Specialised institutions e.g. credit information registries have evolved over the years which to some extent address the asymmetric information problem existing for the female-owned MSME sector. These agencies now collect and distribute information which helps lenders to better assess the risks and accordingly lower the costs of processing loan applications. As an example, Africa Credit Bureau Program is providing advisory services to central banks, national bankers' associations, and other private sector stakeholders in six countries. The credit information on individuals or small business borrowers they provide to lenders helps remove the uncertainty that has traditionally been associated with lending. Accurate and timely credit information also allows financial institutions to reduce risks, loan processing times, costs, and default rates.

Further, to avoid the lack of traditional collateral held by female owners, introducing collateral registries and secure transaction systems will further contribute to better allocations of finance. Facilitating the use of movable collateral, i.e. non-fixed assets, such as land and buildings which are less frequently vested in the name of females, for borrowing will promote access to finance for female-owned MSMEs.

Enhanced financial institutions should better serve women entrepreneurs; ensuring female entrepreneurs have external financing accessibility. Local and foreign financial institutions, especially micro-finance institutions, have a big role to play in female-entrepreneurs' access to external financing accessibility. There is potential merit in introducing more opportunities for female education especially in the domain of financial literacy, management and leadership training to enhance their skills and this will assist women entrepreneurs to reduce bank-loan rejections and bankruptcies.

As a final observation, further work is required to explore the balance between the formal and informal financial sectors. In LICs and emerging economies the balance may be less than optimal. The impact of these lower levels of financial inclusiveness will not be neutral with respect to impact upon female-owned businesses accessing finance. At this point in time the answer as to which direction the pendulum is weighted requires further work. There is a degree of uniformity of impacts detected in our research, as reported above, but the extent to which this will be true in West Africa or Pacifica requires further empirical investigation and the model proposed developed here should be of assistance to scholars in wishing to expand the generalisability of our results.

REFERENCES

Amuedo-Dorantes, C., & Pozo, S. (2006). Migration, Remittances, and Male and Female Employment Patterns. *The American Economic Review*, *96*(2), 222–226. doi:10.1257/000282806777211946

Aterido, R., Beck, T., & Iacovone, L. (2011). *Gender and Finance in Sub-Sahran Africa: Are Women Disadvantaged?* Policy Research Working Paper: 5571.

Beck, T., Demirguc-Kunt, A., & Maksimovic, V. (2008). Financing Patterns Around the World: The Role of Institutions. *Journal of Financial Economics*, *90*, 467–487.

Beck, T., Demirgüç-Kunt, A., Soledad, M., & Pería, M. (2010). Bank Financing for SMEs: Evidence Across Countries and Bank Ownership Types. *Journal of Financial Services Research*.

Booth, L., Aivazian, V., Demirg¨uc¸-Kunt, A., & Maksimovic, V. (2001). Capital Structures in Developing Countries. *The Journal of Finance*, *56*(1), 87–130. doi:10.1111/0022-1082.00320

Carter, S., & Rosa, P. (1998). The Financing of Male- and Female-owned Businesses. *Entrepreneurship & Regional Development*, *10*(3), 225–241. doi:10.1080/08985629800000013

Carvalho, A. (2008). *The Effect of Institutions on the External Financing of Brazilian Firms*. Academic Press.

Cavalluzzo, K., & Wolken, J. (2005). Small Business Loan Turndowns, Personal Wealth, and Discrimination. *The Journal of Business*, *78*(6), 2153–2177. doi:10.1086/497045

Cavalluzzo, K. S., Cavalluzzo, L. C., & Wolken, J. D. (2002). Competition, Small Business Financing, and Discrimination: Evidence from a New Survey. *The Journal of Business*, *75*(4), 641–676. doi:10.1086/341638

Chakravarty, S., & Xiang, M. (2011). Determinenets of profit reinvestment by small business in emerging economies. *Financial Management*, *40*(3), 553–590. doi:10.1111/j.1755-053X.2011.01153.x

Ciarli, T., Parto, S., & Savona, M. (2010). *Entrepreneurship under conflict in Afghanistan: Determinants and Motivations of Small Business Owners*. Retrieved from http://pagesperso.dial.prd.fr/dial_pagesperso/dial_eve_shocks/pdf/59_Ciarli%20Tommaso.pdf

Coleman, S. (2000). Access to Capital and Terms of Credit: A Comparison of Men- and Women-Owned Small Businesses. *Journal of Small Business Management*, *38*(3), 37–52.

Collier, P. (1999). On Economic Consequences of Civil War. *Oxford Economic Papers*, *5*(1), 168–183. doi:10.1093/oep/51.1.168

Cull, R., & Xu, L. C. (2005). Institutions, Ownership, & Finance: The Determinants of Profit Reinvestment Among Chinese Firms. *Journal of Financial Economics*, *77*(1), 117–146. doi:10.1016/j.jfineco.2004.05.010

D'Espallier, B., Guérin, I., & Mersland, R. (2010). Women and Repayment in Microfinance: A Global Analysis. *World Development*, *39*(5), 758–772. doi:10.1016/j.worlddev.2010.10.008

Das, D. J. (2000). *Problems Faced by Women Entrepreneurs* (K. Sasikumar, Ed.). Women Entrepreneurship.

Demirguc-Kunt, A., & Maksimovic, V. (2001). *Firms and financial intermediaries: Evidence from Trade Credit Data*. Research Working Paper 2696: The World Bank Development Research Group.

Doing Business. (2011). Retrieved from http://www.doingbusiness.org/rankings/

Enterprise Surveys. (2013). Retrieved from http://www.enterprisesurveys.org/

Faccio, M. (2006). Politically Connected firms. *The American Economic Review*, *96*(1), 369–386. doi:10.1257/000282806776157704

Firth, M., Lin, C., Liu, P., & Wong, S. (2009). Inside the black box: Bank credit allocation in China's private sector. *Journal of Banking & Finance*, *33*(6), 1144–1155. doi:10.1016/j.jbankfin.2008.12.008

Green, P. G., Brush, C. G., Hart, M. M., & Saparito, P. (2001). Patterns of Venture Capital Funding: Is Gender a Factor? *Venture Capital*, *3*(1), 63–83. doi:10.1080/13691060118175

Guérin, I., & Palier, J. (Eds.). (2006). *MicroFinance Challenges: Empowerment or Disempowerment of the Poor?*

Hoskisson, R. E., Lau, L., & Wright, M. (2000). Strategy in emerging economies. *Academy of Management Journal*, *43*(3), 249–267. doi:10.2307/1556394

Jones, K., & Tullous, R. (2002). Behaviours of Pre-Venture Entrepreneurs and Perceptions of Their Financial Needs. *Journal of Small Business Management*, *40*(3), 233–249. doi:10.1111/1540-627X.00053

Judge, W. Q., Douglas, T. J., & Kutan, A. M. (2008). Institutional antecedents of corporate governance legitimacy. *Journal of Management*, *34*(4), 765–785. doi:10.1177/0149206308318615

Kaur, R., & Bawa, S. (1992). Psychological Correlates of Entrepreneurial Performance among Women. *The Journal of Entrepreneurship*, *8*(2), 195–205. doi:10.1177/097135579900800204

Klapper, L., Laeven, L., & Rajan, R. (2006). Entry regulation as a barrier to entrepreneurship. *Journal of Financial Economics*, *82*(3), 591–629. doi:10.1016/j.jfineco.2005.09.006

La-Porta, R., Silanes, F. L., Shleifer, A., & Vishny, R. W. (1997). Legal Determinants of External Finance. *The Journal of Finance*, *52*(3), 1131–1150. doi:10.1111/j.1540-6261.1997.tb02727.x

Le, V., Venkatesh, S., & Nguyen, T. V. (2006). Getting bank financing: A study of Vietnamese private firms. *Asia Pacific Journal of Management*, *23*(2), 209–227. doi:10.1007/s10490-006-7167-8

Lemmon, G. T. (2012). *Entrepreneurship in Postconflict Zones*. Working Paper.

Levine, R. (1997). Financial development and economic growth: Views and agenda. *Journal of Economic Literature*, *35*, 688–726.

Levine, R., Loayza, N., & Beck, T. (2000). Financial intermediation and growth: Causality and causes. *Journal of Monetary Economics*, *46*(1), 31–77. doi:10.1016/S0304-3932(00)00017-9

March, J., & Olsen, J. P. (1989). *The Organizational Basis of Politics*. New York: The Free Press.

Marlow, S., & Patton, D. (2007). All Credit to Men? Entrepreneurship,Finance and Gender. *Entrepreneurship Theory and Practice*, *29*(6), 717–735. doi:10.1111/j.1540-6520.2005.00105.x

Mead, D., & Liedholm, C. (1998). The Dynamics of Micro and Small Enterprises in Developing Countries. *World Development*, *26*(1), 61–74. doi:10.1016/S0305-750X(97)10010-9

Meyer, K., & Nguyen, V. H. (2005). Foreign investment strategies and sub-national institutions in emerging market: Evidence from Vietnam. *Journal of Management Studies*, *42*(1), 63–93. doi:10.1111/j.1467-6486.2005.00489.x

Muravyev, A., Talavera, O., & Schäfer, D. (2009). Entrepreneurs' gender and financial constraints: Evidence from international data. *Journal of Comparative Economics*, *37*(2), 270–286. doi:10.1016/j.jce.2008.12.001

Peng, M. W., & Heath, P. S. (1996). The growth of the firm in planned economies in transition: Institutions, organizations, and strategic choice. *Academy of Management Review*, *21*(2), 492–528.

Rajan, R. G., & Zingales, L. (1995). What Do We Know about Capital Structure? Some Evidence from International Data. *The Journal of Finance*, *50*(5), 1421–1460. doi:10.1111/j.1540-6261.1995.tb05184.x

Read, L. (1998). *The Financing of Small Business: a Comparative Study of Male and Female Business Owners*. New York: Routledge. doi:10.4324/9780203024942

Real Interest Rate (%). (2013). Retrieved from http://data.worldbank.org/indicator/FR.INR.RINR

Rodriguez, P., Uhlenbruck, K., & Eden, L. (2005). Government corruption and the entry strtergies of multinationals. *Academy of Management Review*, *30*(2), 383–396. doi:10.5465/AMR.2005.16387894

Ronald, J. L., & Meyer, J. W. (1991). *The Public Order and the Construction of Formal Organizations*. Chicago: University of Chicago Press.

Scalera, D., & Zazzaro, A. (2001). Group reputation and persistent (or permanent) discrimination in credit markets. *Journal of Multinational Financial Management*, *11*(4-5), 483–496. doi:10.1016/S1042-444X(01)00037-8

Sinhal, S. (2005). *Developing Women Entrepreneurs in South Asia: Issues, Initiatives and Experiences*. Trade and Investment Division: ST/ESCAP/2401.

Tsang, E. (1994). In Search of legitimacy: The private entrepreneur in China. Entrepreneurship Theory and Practice, 21(1), 21–30.

UN Women's flagship report: 2011-2012 Progress of the World's Women: In Pursuit of Justice. (2013). Retrieved from http://progress.unwomen.org/

Vishwananthan, R. (2001). *Opportunities and challenges for women in business*. Retrieved from http://indiatogether.org/women/business/renuka.htm

Welter, F., & Smallbone, D. (2011). Institutional Perspectives on Entrepreneurial Behavior in Challenging Environments. *Journal of Small Business Management*, *49*(1), 107–125. doi:10.1111/j.1540-627X.2010.00317.x

Women Entrepreneurs in Asia and the Pacific. (2013). Academic Press.

The World Factbook. (2012). Academic Press.

ENDNOTES

1 According to the United Nations geographical region classification, South Asia comprises the countries of Afghanistan, Bangladesh, Bhutan, India, Maldives, Nepal, Pakistan and Sri Lanka

2 There is a small gender disparity in primary education completion rate in South Asia with 87% of boys completing primary school vs. 83% of girls in 2009. Among all other regions, South Asia had a large gender disparity in 1999 (14.5 percentage points) but decreased the difference to 3.2 percentage points in 2009 (UNESCO Institute for Statistics in EdStats, 2011).

3 The World Bank Enterprise Survey website provides details for how the survey was conducted. Enterprise Surveys (http://www.enterprisesurveys.org), The World Bank

Chapter 7

Why Credit Ratings Serve a Greater Role in Emerging Economies than Industrial Nations:

A Comparative Analysis between Family Firms and Concentrated Ownership Structures in South Asia

Marianne Ojo
North-West University, USA & Accounting Research and Legal Scholarship Networks, USA

ABSTRACT

The agency problem attributed to dispersed ownership is also principally regarded as being that of the control over powerful management. Whilst there are conflicting views in respect of the degree of agency problems which arise under dispersed and concentrated ownership structures, it appears that additional or greater agency problems will eventually necessitate the need for greater monitoring. In recommending the external auditor's expertise as appropriate for addressing agency problems, this chapter draws attention to the audit committee's roles, presenting them both as vital and complementary corporate governance tools.

INTRODUCTION

The agency problem attributed to dispersed ownership is also principally regarded as being that of control over powerful management. Whilst there are conflicting views in respect of the degree of agency problems which arise under dispersed and concentrated ownership structures, it appears that additional or greater agency problems will eventually necessitate the need for greater monitoring. Ownership of shares definitely also has a role to play in ensuring greater monitoring – however where a more harmonious

DOI: 10.4018/978-1-5225-0004-9.ch007

relationship exists between principal and agent – particularly based on trust and long term relationships, the principal may see no reason to undertake "unnecessary" levels of monitoring – which may be considered costly. In other words, the traditional professional business like principal-agent relationship is transformed over a long period of term during which the long term harmonious relationship is sustained. In this respect, the traditional principal agent relationship in concentrated ownership systems and structures, would exist not between dominant shareholders and the agent – rather between the agent and the minority shareholders. The minority shareholders, unfortunately, are unable to afford or commit the same level of control or funds (as that available to dominant shareholders), necessary to monitor the agent.

Emerging market corporate governance is typically characterized by high insider ownership and a predominance of family ownership. Emerging markets, where there is concentrated ownership, family ownership and weak legal protection, family members with majority shares, are able to engage in window- dressing, expropriating minority shareholders. The concentrated family ownership is the root cause of Principal-Principal-Agency (PPA) problems in Sri-Lankan public listed companies. (Wellalage & Locke: 2011)

Reasons highlighted for "prevalent inside ownership" in emerging economies are as follows:

- Founder managed firms being reluctant to share core competences and vital information with outsiders
- Weak legal protection
- Under developed nature of financial markets - which restricts access to external financing and results in family pre-dominant concentrated ownership.

According to Eun and Resnick (2009:81), in many countries with concentrated ownership, conflicts of interests are greater between large controlling shareholders and small outside shareholders, than between managers and shareholders. They also make reference to studies undertaken by La Porta, Lopez-de-Silanes, Shleifer, and Vishny (LLSV) which document „sharp differences between countries" in respect of:

- Corporate Ownership Structures
- Depth and Breadth of Capital markets
- Access of firms to External Financing
- Dividend Policies

It has been argued in many studies, that bank capital ratios and several other financial indicators do not serve as effectively in emerging market economies as is the case with industrial nations.

According to Rojas-Suarez (2002), the capital-to-asset ratio, has under-performed as an indicator of banking crisis related problems in Latin America and Asia. Two reasons which have been put forward as explanations for this are:

- Severe deficiencies in the accounting and regulatory framework in these jurisdictions;
- Lack of liquid markets for bank shares, subordinated debt and other bank liabilities and assets which are required to confirm and justify the actual worth of a bank – rather than merely its accounting value.

To which it will also be added that audits, which serve as vital signaling mechanisms in capital markets - as well as those nations which are pre-dominantly based on dispersed ownership structures, have limited roles in many emerging economies than is the case with industrial nations.

The Basel capital rules have evolved to address problems relating to regulatory arbitrage. There are still concerns that the present Basel III leverage/supplementary ratios may promote capital arbitrage since there are many loopholes to avoid grossing-up of the denominator component of the ratio, namely, the exposure measure component. With the presently revised Basel III leverage ratio (January 2014 revision) there are disallowances with the netting of certain activities (loans and deposits) - even though allowances have been permitted just in relation to certain cash variation margins. Further, netting has been permitted and re-instated in association with Securities Financing Transaction exposures (cash payables and receivables). Hence the January 2014 revision allows for greater flexibility - in comparison with the June 2013 revision since the revision of June 2013 disallowed offsetting of securities financing transaction exposures

However the major issue has always related primarily to the exclusion of certain derivative exposures, counter party risk related exposures - and of course, Off Balance Sheet items. The aim of the revisions to Basel III leverage ratios is to capture as accurately the derivative exposures, SFT exposures, as well as other components of the exposures measures - hence resulting in a greater denominator component of the leverage ratio.

In response to a central question being addressed by this chapter, namely why credit ratings serve a greater role in emerging economies than industrial nations, the response would primarily relate to the reduced role served by audits in these nations than their more oriented capital market based economies. Audit markets in many emerging economies which are based on family run concentrated ownership structures, being "thin" and commonly referred to as thin audit markets.

Hence data generated from family firms as well as other firms whose systems and structures are regarded as synonymous to those of concentrated ownership, are also therefore of vital importance and do indeed provide fertile ground for future research. It will also be vital for such concentrated ownership structures, upon which many jurisdictions in South Asia are based, to review and upgrade the status accorded to audits and audit committees if they are to effectively and maximally achieve goals and objectives of the Basel Committee's risk based adequacy framework, leverage ratios - as well as improve on attributes of good corporate governance practices - namely accountability, adequate supervision, monitoring, transparency and disclosure.

BACKGROUND

This chapter hence illustrates - by way of reference to selected jurisdictions from South Asia - these jurisdictions being emerging economies, which are also based on family firms (concentrated ownership structures), why corporate governance measures - including the operation of audit committees, as well as greater focus on audits as signaling mechanisms - are crucial for purposes of facilitating the achievement of regulatory aims, as well as the development of accounting and regulatory structures.

A key issue relating to the efficiency of corporate governance mechanisms in dispersed ownership systems and concentrated ownership systems principally revolves around effective monitoring. Whilst the model based on concentrated ownership systems and structures has been proposed by many to constitute a means of addressing agency problems, flaws inherent in the monitoring undertaken by dominant shareholders, such as banks, in concentrated ownership systems and structures, to the detriment of minority shareholders, necessitate a role for the involvement of other actors such as regulators and external auditors.

Insufficient disclosure and opacity are considered to be major problems with concentrated ownership systems and structures – particularly complex concentrated ownership structures. External sources of corporate governance control – such as take overs, are also much rarer in concentrated ownership systems. Whilst dispersed ownership systems are also not immune from certain flaws, recent developments around the globe, from globalization to liberalization, as well as the Asian Financial Crises of the nineties have resulted in a re-think of a shift to the Anglo American system of corporate governance. Many publications have advocated a more favorable move to the Anglo American system of corporate governance – particularly in respect of jurisdictions such as China, Germany and Japan. Such a move not being attributed not only to recent development in the financial markets, liberalization, but also the need to ensure greater disclosure and transparency in the bid to mitigate principal agent problems related to information asymmetries.

Concentrated ownership structures have frequently being cited as means of addressing agency problems so the above remarks may appear surprising. However, evidence also exists to bolster the claim that insider dealings are better facilitated in environments involving concentrated ownership structures. Furthermore, external corporate control mechanisms appear to function better and more frequently in Anglo American dispersed ownership systems. The most recent Financial Crisis has illustrated that since the Efficient Markets Hypothesis cannot be relied upon, regulation is a necessary complement to effective monitoring. Complementary to such effective monitoring is also the need for the involvement of external auditors in the regulatory process – since there exists every likelihood for regulatory capture to occur.

If perfect markets and perfect competition existed, and if there had been a world without externalities, perhaps markets would have been able to regulate themselves effectively and there would have been no need for regulation or external auditors.

MAIN FOCUS OF THE CHAPTER

This chapter is aimed at specifically directing the need for greater focus on regulations, compliance and enforcement processes in the financial system. Many instruments require complements – as this chapter will also illustrate. The essential role of external auditors in financial regulation has already been discussed extensively in many publications. This chapter is also aimed at illustrating that certain capacities exist whereby the dual role of the external auditor (in undertaking internal audit roles as well as skilled persons roles) could be exercised to the optimal and maximum benefit of an entity or organization. It also aims to accentuate on why a return to and focus on traditional auditing techniques, as well as auditing techniques which focus on internal controls is a much needed move. In so doing, it contributes to the extant literature by highlighting why such a move should be facilitated, as well as proposing means whereby such a move would be facilitated - namely, through a focus on benefits which could be derived where the external auditor is able to incorporate certain internal audit responsibilities. Attention should also be drawn to safeguards which require due consideration if the ever important attributes of objectivity and independence, in auditing, are not to be compromised.

Further, the roles assumed by capital regulations will be considered in this chapter. Furthermore, the vital roles which these regulations and ratios could play in facilitating greater transparency and disclosure when features embracing greater objectivity, comparability and consistency are incorporated and become the norm in the application of Basel rules across several jurisdictions, will be highlighted.

Greater consistency, comparability and objectivity would not only facilitate consistent application of rules, ratios, standards and regulations, but also serve to mitigate incidences of information asymmetries since greater transparency and disclosure will result in the process.

Just as it is virtually impossible to eliminate risks in their entirety, it is also difficult to ensure absolute objectivity, comparability and consistency in the application of Basel rules across jurisdictions – given the uniqueness of legal, regulatory and institutional structures and frameworks operating in respective jurisdictions.

An important aspect of the introduction of the (relatively new) two Basel liquidity standards, as well as the leverage ratios, is that they are intended to be complementary to the capital requirements. The application of either one or the other in isolation may not yield desirable results – as is indicative of lessons drawn from Northern Rock. Compliance or even over compliance with the individual ratios or standards may not necessarily avert a crisis from occurring. Retaining the appropriate levels of capital may prove futile where such is not complemented with the necessary liquidity ratios, standards or leverage ratios. What makes the introduction of the new leverage ratios particularly important are those contents that are to be accounted for in the numerator and denominator components. Such approach also mitigates regulatory arbitrage – even though it has also been argued that it could encourage regulatory arbitrage. Where such leverage ratios apply consistently across jurisdictions, then the tendency for regulatory arbitrage should be mitigated. Some financial institutions use the law to disguise or avoid what should be the appropriate treatment for assets. Regulations should be designed in such a way that assets intended to be addressed are covered, and that little room exists for transferring such assets in such a way that they evade the "regulatory trap."

Fair value measurements and its rise as facilitated through the Finance Theory provide a source of concern. Particularly its use with the ongoing adoption of International Financial Reporting Standards (IFRS). The issue really does not also relate to how to address certain "creative accounting practices". It is believed that enough incidences of off balance sheet activities have taken place over the past decades to equip regulators, standard setters and other policing authorities with how to detect and address these. The greater problem lies with how to effectively deter certain risk taking activities – an inevitability for certain professional spheres where risk taking is a must.

Fair values provide greater flexibility than historical cost accounting – and such flexibility is required in the financial markets just as incomplete contracts provide more flexibility between principals and their agents (even though more complete contracts would also address agency problems). Uncertainties, market failures and other anomalies (which are unavoidable and are a fact of life) make the need for certain contingencies and flexibility necessary.

One would then ask whether such flexibility is worth the potential costs which could arise – in cases where serious imbalance is struck in the process of maximization of the resource allocation or investment opportunities.

The engagement of market participants in the corporate reporting process, a process which would consequently enhance market disclosure, constitutes a fundamental means whereby greater measures aimed at facilitating prudential supervision, could be extended to the securities markets. Furthermore, as a result of the influence and potential of market participants to determine capital levels, such market participants are able to assist regulators in managing more effectively, the impact of systemic risks which occur when lending criteria is tightened – particularly owing to pro cyclical effects.

Two opposing views regarding the worth and informational value of credit ratings have been put forward by Kräussl (2003:9):

The first view:

- That credit agencies only have access to publicly available information and that these agencies lag behind financial markets in processing such information. Further, Kräussl adds that credit rating changes should not affect market prices if financial markets are efficient in semi-strong form.

The opposing view not only argues that credit rating agencies are „specialists in obtaining and processing information", but that sovereign credit changes, as well as negative credit ratings announcements are likely to generate more significant impacts in emerging markets – owing to the level of severity of problems attributed to asymmetric information and transparency.

Issues, Controversies, Problems

Addressing Information Asymmetries

The chapter seeks to address gaps in the literature - gaps in the current and previous literature which support the fact that family firms, concentrated ownership systems and structures suffer from less problems and issues associated with information asymmetries than pre-dominantly based dispersed ownership systems and structures, as well as the above claim relating to the worth and informational value of credit ratings agencies - in particular that relating to the negative impact of credit ratings announcements and their more "significant" impacts in emerging markets. Can audits be effectively relied upon to provide better and more reliable information than credit ratings agencies?

If indeed, it could be demonstrated that credit agencies only have access to publicly available information and that they "lag behind financial markets" in processing such information, then there are fundamental reasons to justify the role of audits in the selected jurisdictions - as well as reasons to discredit the claim that concentrated ownership systems and structures suffer from less problems and issues associated with information asymmetries than pre-dominantly based dispersed ownership systems and structures.

One of the best arguments to justify the fact that perfectly efficient markets cannot exist is the ambiguity relating to the quantification and perceptions of risks in markets. If perfectly efficient markets did exist, then there would probably be no justification for the need to regulate. The growing importance of risk in regulation and the increasing connection between risk and regulation is becoming more ever more apparent.

Three forms of the Efficient Market Hypothesis which have generally been identified are:

- The Weak Form of the EMH whereby current stock prices fully reflect what is knowable from a study of historical share patterns.
- The Semi Strong Form of the Efficient Market Hypothesis whereby it is argued that current stock prices reflect only all public information about a stock – Fama' Fair Game Theory.
- The Strong Form of the EMH which holds that share prices reflect not only what is publicly known about a stock but what is also knowable.

Finally, the chapter seeks to propose rules and recommendations whereby the current legal and regulatory challenges faced by financial markets in South Asia could be addressed. A pre dominantly based empirical and case study focus, contrasted with a theoretical based framework, will constitute the basis of the review of the literature.

Empirical Studies

Chen and Lu (2009:8) contend that empirical studies involving relationships between family ownership and performance do not generate conclusive and consistent results and that whilst there are reasons to expect that firms with concentrated ownership structures may be efficient than other firms (given the incentives whereby concentrated ownership compels the owners to monitor managers - resulting in reduced agency costs (Schleifer & Vishny, 1997), that there are also reasons for arguments favoring the fact that family-owned firms may be less efficient than non-family run firms. Further, they add that since "there is typically no equity market for minority family owners to cash in and go their way" given the fact that concentrated ownership denotes "limited diversification of financial risk and a higher cost of capital due higher risk premium" (Demsetz & Lehn, 1985), these all contribute in reducing "core competencies and performance" of family firms.

In further illustrating and consolidating on the inconclusiveness of empirical literature and evidence, Chen and Lu make reference to studies carried out by Gorriz and Fumes (1996) whose results revealed that even though on average, family firms generated higher productivity than non family firms, there was no difference in profitability. Wall's analysis (1998) is also referred to - whereby the impact of family ownership on productivity amongst private firms is considered - an analysis whose results revealed that "family firms are less productive than non-family firms" - having made adjustments for industry, labor input and age of the firm."

According to Bennedsen, Gonzalez and Wolfenzon, the main governance issue facing family firms is "balancing the benefits associated with having a controlling family with the challenges the structure imposes on minority shareholders." They are of the opinion that common governance mechanisms are less likely to be effective whenever control and decision rights are concentrated around a family.

Indeed there is growing consensus to support the view that common corporate governance mechanisms are not capable of mitigating governance issues relating to concentrated ownership based structures. Certain reasons which have been propounded for the inability to simply „extrapolate" experiences of corporate governance in developed countries into developing countries are as follows (Sarkar, 2011: 223)

Some of the institutional specificities of developing countries – such as a less developed capital market, less active takeover markets, absence of well developed managerial market, may impact costs and benefits of large shareholdings in countries uniquely (Sarkar & Sarkar: 2000);

Monitoring by large shareholders in developing countries may not be as effective as in developed countries because of poor availability of information on performance parameters of firms – owing to inadequate disclosure standards and weak enforcement mechanisms, as well as opaqueness associated with insider ownership and concentrated ownership structures.

The problem relating particularly to the inadequacy of disclosure standards and lack of transparency will be illustrated in the following section. In contrast to dispersed ownership structures and systems where greater agency problems are widely agreed to persist, the main issue relating to concentrated ownership structures - whereby a dominant shareholder is a distinctive feature, is the conflicts of interests between controlling and non- controlling shareholders.

Case Studies

Through this comparative analysis, this chapter also aims to investigate whether information provided through credit ratings agencies in South Asia, is considered superior to those of micro economic indicators - hence the rationale for greater reliance on these agencies than signaling mechanisms such as audits.

All countries involved in the study highlighted here, are predominantly based on family run concentrated ownership structures. According to an investigation by Butt and Hasan (2009) as regards Pakistani listed companies, "managerial ownership has negative relationship with debt to equity ratio indicating that concentration of ownership induces the managers to lower the gearing levels. Institutional ownership has positive relationship with capital structure which is consistent with corporate governance philosophy but this relation is statistically insignificant."

Based on "Five Year Average Composite Scores" obtained by Sophastienphong and Kulathunga (2010), which comprise of data from Afghanistan, Bangladesh, Bhutan, India, Nepal, the Maldives, Pakistan and Sri Lanka, with eight dimensions being incorporated into the study, results indicate the following:

Dimensions

1. Access to Finance
2. Performance and Efficiency
3. Financial stability
4. Capital market development
5. Market concentration and competitiveness
6. Payment systems development
7. Savings mobilisation
8. Corporate governance
    1. Access to Finance: The Maldives performed best - in relation to Access to Finance - with Sri Lanka performing second best.
    2. Performance and Efficiency: The Maldives also performed best under this dimension - with Pakistan performing second best
    3. Financial stability: India performed best under this dimension - with Pakistan and Bhutan following each other, separated marginally in terms of their performance. Micro economic indicators used by Sophastienphong and Kulathunga for this dimension include capital adequacy ratio, leverage ratio, gross non performing loans ratio, provisions to non performing loans ratio, liquid assets ratio, liquid assets to liability ratio.
    4. Capital market development: India performed best - with Pakistan performing second best
    5. Market concentration and competitiveness: India performed best - with Bangladesh following second.
    6. Payment systems development: Sri Lanka performed best - outstandingly well - with India coming second. In comparison to the other dimensions, the margin between the leading performing country and other jurisdictions was considerably wide.
    7. Savings mobilization: India performed best - with Bangladesh coming second
    8. Corporate governance: Pakistan performed best - with India and Sri Lanka coming jointly second

Micro economic indicators incorporated into the study include ownership structure and influence of external stakeholders, investor rights (shareholder meetings, basic ownership and voting rights), transparency and disclosure, board structure and effectiveness.

In relation to this dimension, the micro economic indicator which gave rise for concern was that relating to transparency and disclosure.

Overall, it can be ascertained that India generated the best overall performance. This is also reflected in relation the implementation of Basel regulations. According to their report, Sophastienphong and Kulathunga (2010:18) also highlighted the fact that whilst Afghanistan, Bhutan and the Maldives had not yet implemented Basel II - even though they were in compliance with Basel I, that Bangladesh, India, Nepal, Pakistan and Sri Lanka had adopted Basel II and were at various stages of implementation.

Further problems identified relate to discrepancies involved in the comparison of capital adequacy ratios of the countries:

- Differences in the pace at which South Asian countries were progressing with the adoption of Basel II standards, along with differences in the capital guidelines adopted by each country - which have resulted in differences in the capital adequacy ratio;
- Differences in the methods used to calculate the capital charges - which have further contributed to disparities.

In response to the question which introduces this section, namely, whether information provided through credit ratings agencies in South Asia, is superior to those of micro economic indicators, and having regard to the problems and inconsistencies involved with the above dimensions and micro economic indicators, reasons for resorting to information provided by credit ratings agencies is quite evident. The fact that information relied on through the above micro economic indicators such as transparency and disclosure, is not very reliable does not necessarily mean that such information provided by micro economic indicators could not prove to be more superior to that provided by credit ratings agencies.

Audit committees are appointed in the majority of countries which constitute the focus of the above case studies - even though according to the case study results, clarity is required as regards whether the committee chair attends shareholder meetings and whether chair is available to address questions on audits in certain jurisdictions such as Afghanistan, Bangladesh, Pakistan and Sri Lanka.

SOLUTIONS AND RECOMMENDATIONS

Placing Greater Reliance on Audits and Auditors

One of the determining factors in successfully harnessing the external auditor's roles involves the extent to which harmonisation can be achieved. The implementation of International Standards on Auditing, along with other numerous regulatory rules not only requires close cooperation between national regulators but also, the achievement of stipulated targets.

Improved transparency and comparability of accounting and financial information, as well as other benefits of high quality standards which should be derived from the adoption of IFRS: benefits such as improved attributes of information (such as relevance, reliability, understandability), will certainly ensure that users of financial information benefit from better decision making as well as restoring the confidence of investors in the aftermath of economic, capital market and financial crises, which have damaged the credibility of audits, and financial reporting.

The significance of Enron's collapse lies not only in the fact that its collapse affected Arthur Andersen and therefore resulted in further concentration within the audit industry, but also because of its impact on the financial markets. Threat of litigation to auditors could lead to further concentration in the audit industry and also increase incidences of "defensive auditing" - whereby audit partners tend to interprete rules prescriptively rather than exercising subjective judgment. Following the collapse of Arthur Andersen, only the "Big Four" and few medium sized auditing firms are capable of auditing major stock corporations (Doralt and others, 2008). Regulators are concerned about having a situation whereby only 3 of the present "Big Four" accounting firms exist, as this would result to increased audit concentration within the industry which could generate a "too big to fail" moral hazard problem amongst audit firms.

Traditional auditing techniques focus on internal controls and demonstrate the auditor's thorough reputation as compared to the lax and complacent attitude which has been evidenced through recent increases in creative accounting practices and the widespread use of off balance sheet instruments as illustrated in the case of Enron. For this reason, a return to and focus on traditional auditing techniques, as well as auditing techniques which focus on internal controls is a much needed move - whilst also supporting audits which also take into consideration, strategic and operational controls. Such a stance would be greatly facilitated in cases where an external auditor is able to undertake certain permitted internal audit responsibilities.

A return to traditional auditing techniques is also advocated for, since, as argued, many Post Enron reforms, notably the Sarbanes Oxley Act, do not go far enough in their efforts to address the issue of independence – primarily through the prohibition of particular non audit services.

Past and recent financial crises have illustrated that firms' compliance with capital adequacy ratios, on their own, are not sufficient to prevent such a firm from experiencing distress or financial difficulties. The introduction of the two new Basel liquidity standards, namely the Liquidity Coverage Ratio and the Net Stable Funding Ratio, as well as the Basel leverage ratios are a consequence of the need to supplement and complement the risk based capital adequacy ratios.

As is particularly the case with external auditors, the reliability of internal controls also plays a huge and crucial role in the audit process - as well as those in charge of those internal controls. Where safeguards such as the segregation of duties and other measures are incorporated into the process to reduce instances or situations whereby such controls could be manipulated, then benefits of having an external auditor serve in a dual role capacity may well extend beyond its stated disadvantages.

Benefits accruing from having a dual role include namely the acquisition of knowledge and expertise gained during the latter stages of the process - which could assist in providing more accurate judgments during latter stages of the process. This is also similar to the position which exists with external auditors: whereby the mandatory rotation of audit firms, whilst serving to ensure that independence and objectivity is not compromised, could also be detrimental where the external auditor leaves the firm shortly/prematurely after having been employed by the firm. In the case of internal audit outsourcing, the efficiency of financial audits is bolstered because the auditor is able to benefit from knowledge gained during the performance of internal audit functions. The auditor is able to gain a better understanding of the client's internal controls because the auditor has had close experience with the internal control environment as part of the client's internal audit function.

The firm incurs greater costs in employing a new auditor in re acquiring the knowledge which the previous auditor had acquired - having left the firm prematurely. Further, the knowledge which could have been employed by the departing/outgoing auditor is not fully maximized in the process.

As a result, the dual role capacity of the external auditor is able incorporate a greater degree of stability, more accurate judgments – which serve to foster comparability and consistency in the determination and performance of audit functions and responsibilities. Furthermore, the vital requirements stipulated by Basel Core Principles for effective supervision is also complied with, where external auditors are incorporated into a firm or enterprise's accounting procedures.

FUTURE RESEARCH DIRECTIONS

As highlighted in the previous section, the firm incurs greater costs in employing a new auditor in re acquiring the knowledge which the previous auditor had acquired - having left the firm prematurely. Further, the knowledge which could have been employed by the outgoing auditor is not fully maximized in the process.

Such knowledge spillovers are frequently cited as reasons for permitting the auditor to permit certain categories of non-audit services, as well as the argument that audit rotation should not be mandatory in every individual firm case. Some jurisdictions such as Malaysia and South Africa adopt partial mandatory audit rotation in a sense, whilst over the years, many other jurisdictions have switched from mandatory audit firm rotation to a more principles based accounting whereby rules are more relaxed to take into account individual circumstances of a particular firm. This being particularly the case where the costs of mandatory audit firm rotation are particularly high for medium or smaller sized firms who may not have sufficient funds to address re-training a new auditor or audit firm.

Given the above mentioned points, a focus on other measures which are aimed at facilitating auditor independence, namely those non audit services which auditors should be specifically prohibited from providing, is advocated.

Title II section 201 of SOX lists those services which lie outside the scope of practice of auditors, namely, non audit services and these include (amongst other services):

- Book keeping or other services related to the accounting records or financial statements of the audit client
- Financial information systems design and implementation

Other prohibited non audit services are as follows:[1]

- Appraisal or valuation services, fairness opinions, or contribution-in-kind reports
- Actuarial services
- Internal audit outsourcing services
- Management functions or human resources
- Broker-dealer, investment adviser, or investment banking services
- Legal services and expert services unrelated to the audit

Given the inconclusive nature of studies which have been undertaken in respect of whether the provision of certain categories of non-audit services by an audit firm, actually results in a compromise of audit independence, given the benefits of knowledge spillovers to be derived from the provision of certain non-audit services, more research in this area is recommended. Particularly from the perspective of those non audit services which actually compromise audit objectivity and independence.

Further research in this area would not only serve to justify more specific requirements in relation to mandatory audit firm rotation, but also foster more formidable corporate governance mechanisms.

CONCLUSION

Even though there have been initiatives by the World Bank, as illustrated under the studies that have been undertaken, as conducted by Sophastienphong and Kulathunga, to develop indicators which are standardized for purposes of measuring performance and soundness, inconsistencies still persist in terms of calculation methods, as well as modes of comparing capital adequacy ratios.

As identified by the Basel Committee on Banking Supervision (2013) in its discussion paper The Regulatory Framework: Balancing Risk Sensitivity, Simplicity and Comparability,“ the disadvantages attributed to undue complexity and reduced comparability in the capital framework, potentially” include:

- Increased difficulties for bank management in understanding the regulatory regime;
- The challenges arising in capital planning;
- Less accurate risk assessments;
- The creation of regulatory gaps and opportunities for arbitrage;
- An undermining of the ability of supervisors to effectively assess the capital adequacy of banks;
- Impediments presented to the effective review of the capital management process by supervisors.

Improved initiatives aimed at adopting recent Basel III reforms - in particular, the Basel III leverage ratios, as well as liquidity standards will be required of South Asian countries and jurisdictions. The need for consistency in the implementation of Basel requirements and regulations is all the more vital and necessary if practices relating to regulatory capital arbitrage are to be minimized and controlled.

Inconsistencies between regulatory and accounting policies are areas which are in need of redress. These embrace harmonizing views relating to accounting and regulatory definitions - as proposed by recent Basel III Leverage and Supplementary Leverage revisions. Expected losses and non expected losses being vital areas - with capital constituting a means of addressing expected losses.

Reforms and revisions to Basel III leverage ratios have resulted in new eligibility criteria for Tier 1 Capital and adjustments to capital being introduced. Further, revised definitions of regulatory capital, new - as well as higher minimum Tier One capital requirements have been introduced.

Information disclosure should be encouraged for several reasons, amongst which include the fact that imperfect information is considered to be a cause of market failure – which “reduces the maximization of regulatory competition,“ and also because disclosure requirements would contribute to the reduction of risks which could be generated when granting reduced capital level rewards to banks who may have poor management systems.

The risk coverage of the previous Basel II capital framework has been consolidated immensely through Basel III. In addition to the trading book and securitization reforms, the Basel Committee proposals on consolidation of the capital requirements for counterparty credit risk exposures arising from derivatives and securities financing activities have been implemented. Such exposures have also constituted a point of focus as regards the Basel III Leverage and Supplementary Leverage Ratios.

Consolidated counterparty capital requirements also being aimed at increasing incentives to transfer OTC derivatives exposures to central counterparties and exchanges.

Regulators are able to respond and to manage with greater efficiency, systemic risks to the financial system during periods when firms which are highly leveraged, become reluctant to lend. This constitutes one of the reasons for the introduction of Basel III's leverage, supplementary leverage ratios – as well as liquidity standards – which serve as complementary measures to the risk based capital adequacy framework.

In order for external auditors to effectively carry out their tasks, the use of fair value measures, in certain instances, as the basic measure for IFRS, merits reconsideration. Where particularly complex and difficult to value financial products are involved, other measurement bases could be employed where greater relevance and certainty would be derived. Other measures such as historical cost. Where vital characteristics of accounting information, characteristics such as understandability, relevance, comparability, faithful representation, prudence and predictability inter alia, would be compromised then a combination of measures such as the historical cost, current cost, realizable value and present value could be incorporated to achieved the best results which would enhance the value of accounting information.

The influence and role of Finance Theory in the use of off-balance sheet instruments during Enron, as well as other creative accounting practices is ironically, partly, contributory to the decision to introduce IFRS – a post Enron consequence. However, it appears that part of the underlying problems in the case of Enron – namely the need for greater attention in respect of value relevance of accounting information, appears, to a large extent, to have been ignored.

Kirkpatrick states that "another area where accounting standards have been put to the test concerns fair values of assets which either trade in thin markets or in no markets at all." Since markets with relatively few large clients are considered to be thin markets, it could inferred that such capital markets which operate in concentrated ownership systems (insider systems) which are typical of Europe (excluding the UK), and which are less developed than those of the UK and the U.S, will be more affected by fair value measures.

Hence the „short termist behavior" relating to compensation appears to affect outsider (dispersed ownership) systems, to a larger extent, whilst fair value measurements, it appears, will present greater problems for insider (concentrated ownership) systems – features of such concentrated ownership systems being less transparency and greater opacity. Hence incorporating more actors such as banks might appear to be the logical solution to addressing „short termist" executive compensation issues with outsider systems – whilst the involvement of external auditors through banks, as well as through audits and reports which are relied upon in capital markets, could also facilitate a greater degree of monitoring and accountability to the shareholders.

As regards insider systems, executive compensation still requires redress – even if not really at the same scale as that required by outsider systems. Fair values as primary bases for the adoption of IFRS will require careful consideration – given many flaws which have also been revealed from the recent Financial Crisis.

The role of executive compensation in exacerbating levels of risk taking by executives, as well as the contribution of fair values to risks and uncertainties, have been demonstrated in the recent Financial Crisis. The external auditor has roles to play in both situations – through an engagement with banks whose involvement not only mitigates instances of „short termist" behaviors, but also incorporates greater monitoring and accountability in the corporate governance process.

Additionally, external auditors and audits provide very reliable sources of information which capital markets and investors rely upon. Furthermore, through the application and incorporation of appropriate measures and accounting policies, the external auditor is able to influence financial reporting in such a way as to ensure that bases of measurement reflect the desirable qualities and attributes of accounting information and credible information provided to investors – particularly in capital markets.

In facilitating and promoting greater transparency and more efficient markets, the role of regulation and external auditors cannot be over emphasized. The need for essential attributes in incorporating accounting information, attributes such as greater comparability, accurate, relevant, reliable, consistency, become all the more important given the role of the audit as a signaling capital market mechanism to investors. Such desirable attributes of accounting information ensure that information asymmetries are mitigated, as well facilitate greater transparency – an essential and vital feature which is less prominent in systems and jurisdictions where concentrated ownership structures are the order of the day.

The Efficient Markets Hypothesis is also very much dependent on the degree of transmission of complete, accurate, and timely information, and such practices as insider dealing would be better addressed where information is more transparent. In this context the role of rules and regulations which facilitate and prohibit insider trading also come into play. Even though the withholding of insider information may be beneficial in certain cases – for instances to avoid potentially disastrous consequences such as systemic contagion and order detrimental results resulting from the premature release of certain highly sensitive information, an appropriate balance needs to be struck between the matters relating to the timing of the release of such highly sensitive information.

Hence the role of the external auditor in ensuring the credibility of the information which is conveyed to investors via the vital signaling mechanism in the form of audits. An authentic verification of such audits provides confidence to investors that information being conveyed to them is credible and can be relied upon. The role of the external auditor and the importance of such a role and relevance in respective jurisdictions is also crucial in evaluating the benefits which effective corporate governance mechanisms are able to provide.

Factors such as the growth of financial conglomerates and the derivatives markets, which have been facilitated by the impact of information technology and increased competition within the financial services industry, have instigated a change in the way financial regulation is carried out around the world.

A more globalized world has become more susceptible to globalized crises, partly owing to the ease of transfer of risks (systemic contagion) through highly interconnected conglomerates as well the increasing embeddedness of risk in regulation – whereby the increased connection between risk and regulation is becoming more apparent.

It is very well the case that certain well intended initiatives such as bank regulations, highly targeted compensated performance related incentives, as well as long term relationships aimed at fostering better communication between the principal and agency could either result in higher risk taking levels or serve as barriers to take over threats.

With the case of long term relationships between the principal and agent, there is always the need to retain a relationship which whilst conducive in fostering better communication – as well as trust, does not become so proximal that it also fosters insider dealings and the abuse of minority shareholders' rights.

Bank regulations could also result in higher or lower risk taking levels by the agent. In the above cases, the crucial issue revolves round achieving the right balance to ensure that principal agent relationships do not become too proximal or that regulations do not generate excessive risk taking incentives. Where remuneration incentives are inappropriately targeted, there is every likelihood that such remuneration packages may become so attractive that they induce higher risk taking levels by the agent or where stock options are involved, increased insider dealings. The danger of a threat of take over becomes mitigated or secondary as the incentives to undertake higher risk taking ventures is fuelled through performance related remuneration packages.

Even though monitoring costs – unlike agency costs, cannot be avoided (as is the case with 100% owner management scenarios), they could be minimized. The external auditor would facilitate a situation whereby managers are encouraged or compelled to be held more accountable. Through an appropriate application of accounting policies, the external auditor could help facilitate a position whereby creative accounting practices and hyper inflation/inflation of figures are discouraged. Penalties could be imposed on managers and directors who intentionally or recklessly inflate or manipulate accounting figures and financial statements. Such penalties could arise in the form of a reduction of such managers' (and directors') annual bonuses, remuneration or even pensions. The likelihood of a qualified audit opinion (as regards the auditor's findings on the financial statements) is considered to be less effective as a deterrent to such managers – particularly where an individual manager or few managers are held responsible for fraudulent related acts. In such a case, a "scapegoat" or few scapegoats would be held to account for the negligent acts of others who should also have been brought to book for their actions.

In order for external auditors to effectively carry out their tasks, the use of fair value measures, in certain instances, as the basic measure for IFRS, merits reconsideration. Where particularly complex and difficult to value financial products are involved, other measurement bases could be employed where (and if) greater relevance and certainty would be derived. Other measures such as historical cost, that is. Where vital characteristics of accounting information, characteristics such as understandability, relevance, comparability, faithful representation, prudence and predictability *inter alia*, would be compromised then a combination of measures such as the historical cost, current cost, realizable value and present value could be incorporated to achieve the best results which would enhance the value of accounting information.

The rise in the use of valuation procedures such as fair value accounting is considered to be attributed to Finance Theory – which is premised on the Efficient Markets Hypothesis. Whilst fair value accounting certainly has its merits and is considered by many as a justifiable basis for the adoption of IFRS, its inability to contribute the desired level of relevance to the value of accounting information – so called value-relevance characteristics which are essential and vital for information within capital markets (as well as information essential to other corporate and business spheres), are flaws not only associated with its implementation, but also attributes which increasingly link it to the Finance Theory.

The influence and role of Finance Theory in the use of off-balance sheet instruments during Enron, as well as other creative accounting practices is ironically, partly, contributory to the decision to introduce IFRS – a post Enron consequence. However, it appears that part of the underlying problems in the case of Enron – namely the need for more value relevance of accounting information, appears, to a large extent, to have been ignored.

The Audit Expectations Gap, that is, what stakeholders or the general public expect of an audit and what auditors actually do, provides a clear explanation for the existence and magnitude of information asymmetries within the capital markets. The audit is a vital signaling mechanism that should convey to the market and investors, that information being provided can be relied on. From this perspective, it may be questioned, whether accurately conveying information about the financial position of a firm to the markets or investors, prevents or mitigates the likelihood of the occurrence of systemic risks. Would the mitigation of information asymmetries within capital markets, the banking industry, or the entire financial sector, reduce the possibilities that systemic risks would occur?

It could be argued that conveying accurate and credible information about the financial position of a firm, enterprise or entity, to its investors, could actually trigger bank runs – with potentially devastating consequences for the entire financial industry. This being the case where the audit generates a negative signal – that is, if the auditor provides a qualified opinion on the financial statements. Timing, as well as the manner whereby the opinion is conveyed to investors then becomes crucial in preventing bank runs. Hence it could be argued that it is not actually the accuracy of the audit that generates adverse reactions on the capital markets, but negative signals conveyed about the financial statements. However, the inaccuracies or creative cover- ups of an audit, though initially manageable or avoidable, would eventually generate greater and more devastating consequences and risks - where no timely solution is found to address the deficits and inconsistencies in the financial reporting process. It was the inability of Enron to address the build-ups of cover- ups over the years that eventually and inevitably resulted in its demise – as well as those of its auditors, Arthur Andersen.

Regulatory convergence – with the adoption of Basel III globally, as well as strict compliance with, and enforcement of Basel capital and liquidity standards, would not only facilitate consistency in the application and interpretation of regulatory standards, but would also introduce greater degree of certainty and comparability which would greatly assist the ambit and scope of the application of international accounting standards.

Furthermore, the adoption of International Financial Reporting Standards (IFRS) globally – a post Enron consequence, would also facilitate greater convergence and harmonization through the external auditor's involvement in accurately interpreting and implementing such standards.

External auditors and audit committees have significant roles to play in ensuring directors' accountability. The Auditing Practices Board (APB), notes the potential importance of audit committees in both enhancing the value of external audit to shareholders and helping to re-inforce auditor's objectivity and commitment to high quality auditing (Beattie, 1999). The Hampel Report also notes that audit committees constitute an essential safeguard of auditor independence.

REFERENCES

Auditing Practices Board. (2011). *Enhancing the Value of Auditor Reporting: Exploring Options for Change*. Author.

Basel Committee on Banking Supervision. (2013). *Regulatory Framework: Balancing Risk Sensitivity, Simplicity and Comparability*. Bank for International Settlements Publications.

Basel Committee on Banking Supervision. (2015). *Eighth progress report on adoption of the Basel regulatory framework*. Bank for International Settlements Publications.

Beattie, V., Brandt, R., & Fearnley, S. (1999). Perceptions of auditor independence: U.K. evidence. *Journal of International Accounting, Auditing & Taxation*, *8*(1), 67–107.

Bennedsen, M., Perez Gonzalez, F., & Wolfenzon, D. (2010). The Governance of Family Firms. *Corporate Governance*.

Benston, G. J. (2006). Fair-Value Accounting: A Cautionary Tale From Enron. *Journal of Accounting and Public Policy*.

Brown, P., Preiato, A. J., & Tarca, A. (2014). Measuring Country Differences in Enforcement of Accounting Standards: An Audit and Enforcement Proxy. *Journal of Business Finance & Accounting*.

Butt, S. A., & Hasan, A. (2009). Impact of Ownership Structure and Corporate Governance on Capital Structure of Pakistani Listed Companies. *International Journal of Business and Management*, *4*(2). Retrieved from http://papers.ssrn.com/sol3/papers.cfm?abstract_id=1732511

Chakrabarti, R. (2002). *Corporate Governance in India - Evolution and Challenges*. Retrieved from: http://unpan1.un.org/intradoc/groups/public/documents/apcity/unpan023826.pdf

Chrisman, J. J., Chua, J. H., & Litz, R. A. (2004). Comparing the Agency Costs of Family and Non-Family Firms; Conceptual Issues and Exploratory Evidence, Entrepreneurship. *Theory into Practice*, *28*(4), 335–354.

Claessens, S., Djankov, S., & Lang, L. (2000). The Separation of Ownership and Control in East Asian Corporations. *Journal of Financial Economics*, *58*(1-2), 81–112. doi:10.1016/S0304-405X(00)00067-2

Demsetz, H., & Lehn, K. (1985). The Structure of Corporate Ownership. *Causes and Consequences Journal of Political Economy*, *93*(6), 1155–1177. doi:10.1086/261354

Eun, C. S., & Resnick, B. G. (2009). *International Financial Management* (2009th ed.). London: Mc-Graw Hill.

Fama, E. F., & Jensen, M. C. (1983). *Separation of Ownership and Control. Journal of Law and Economics*, *26*, 301–325.

Gorriz, C. G., & Fumas, V. S. (1996). Ownership Structure and Firm Performance. *Some Empirical Evidence from Spain Managerial and Decision Economics*, *17*(6), 575–586. doi:10.1002/(SICI)1099-1468(199611)17:6<575::AID-MDE778>3.0.CO;2-N

Horton, J., Serafeim, G., & Serafeim, I. (2013, Spring). Does Mandatory IFRS Adoption Improve the Information Environment? *Contemporary Accounting Research*, *30*(1), 388–423. doi:10.1111/j.1911-3846.2012.01159.x

Kershaw, D. (2005). Evading Enron: Taking Principles Too Seriously in Accounting Regulation. *The Modern Law Review*, *68*(4), 2005. doi:10.1111/j.1468-2230.2005.00552.x

Kräussl, R. (2003). *Do Credit Rating Agencies Add to the Dynamics of Emerging Market Crises?* CFS Working Paper No 2003/18 August 2003. Retrieved from: http://www.frbatlanta.org/news/conferen/fsc04/kraeussl.pdf

LaPorta, R., Lopez-de-Silanes, F., Shleifer, A., & Vishny, R. (1997). Legal Determinants of External Finance. *The Journal of Finance*, *52*(3), 1131–1150. doi:10.1111/j.1540-6261.1997.tb02727.x

LaPorta, R., Lopez-de-Silanes, F., Shleifer, A., & Vishny, R. (2000). Investor Protection and Corporate Governance. *Journal of Financial Economics*, *58*(1-2), 3–27. doi:10.1016/S0304-405X(00)00065-9

Nobes, C. (2004). *Rules-based Standards and the Lack of Principles in Accounting*. Retrieved from: http://www.econ.upf.edu/docs/seminars/nobes.pdf

Ojo, M. (2006). Audit Independence: Its Importance to the External Auditor's Role in Banking Regulation and Supervision. Retrieved from http://econpapers.repec.org/paper/pramprapa/231.htm

Ojo, M. (2006). Avoiding Another Enron: The Role of the External Auditor in Financial Regulation and Supervision. ICFAI University Press.

Ojo, M. (2009). The Role of the IASB and Auditing Standards in the Aftermath of the 2008/2009 Financial Crisis (September 2009). *European Law Journal, 16*(5).

Ojo, M. (2013). *Audits, Audit Quality and Signaling Mechanisms: Concentrated Ownership Structures*. Paper presented at the 2014 IBFR Conference, San Jose, Costa Rica. Retrieved from: http://www.theibfr.com/ARCHIVE/ISSN-1941-9589-V9-N2-2014.pdf

Ojo, M. (2013). *Why the Traditional Principal Agent Theory May No Longer Apply To Concentrated Ownership Systems and Structures*. Paper Presented at the PSRC Conference, Johannesburg, South Africa.

Rojas-Suarez, L. (2002). *Rating Banks in Emerging Markets: What Credit Agencies Should Learn From Financial Indicators.* Retrieved from: http://papers.ssrn.com/sol3/papers.cfm?abstract_id=300891

Sarbanes Oxley Act 2002

Sarkar, J. (2011). Ownership and Corporate Governance in Indian Firms. In N. Balasubramanian & D. M. Satwalekar (Eds.), Corporate Governance - An Emerging Scenario (pp. 152-89). National Stock Exchange of India.

Sarkar, J., & Sarkar, S. (2010). „Large Shareholder Activism in Corporate Governance in Developing Countries: Evidence from India. *International Review of Finance*, *1*(3), 161–194. doi:10.1111/1468-2443.00010

Schultze, W. G., Lubatkin, M. H., & Dino, R. N. (2003). *Exploring the Agency Consequences of Ownership Dispersion Among the Directors of Private Family Firms. Academy of Management Journal*, *46*(2), 179–194.

Sophastienphong, K. & Kulathunga, A. (2009). *Getting Finance in South Asia 2009 Indicators and Analysis of the Commercial Banking Sector*. World Bank.

Sophastienphong, K. & Kulathunga, A. (2010). *Getting Finance in South Asia 2010 Indicators and Analysis of the Commercial Banking Sector.* World Bank.

Tysiac, K. (2013). Europe Takes Step Toward Mandatory Audit Firm Rotation. *Journal of Accountancy*, *2013*(April). Retrieved from http://www.journalofaccountancy.com/news/20137862.htm

Wellalage, N. H. & Locke, S. (2011). *Corporate Governance and Principal-Principal Conflict in Emerging Market Family Firms*. Academic Press.

Wellalage, N. H. & Locke, S. (2012). Ownership Structure and Firm Financial Performance: Evidence from Panel Data. *Sri Lanka Journal of Business Systems, Governance and Ethics, 7*(1).

Young, M. N., Peng, M. W., Ahlstrom, D., Bruton, G. D., & Jiang, Y. (2008). Corporate Governance in Emerging Economies: A Review of the Principal–Principal Perspective. *Journal of Management Studies*, *45*(1), 196–220. doi:10.1111/j.1467-6486.2007.00752.x

ENDNOTE

1 See Sarbanes Oxley Act section 201 and also U.S Securities and Exchange Commission, Audit Committees and Auditor Independence: Specific Prohibited Non Audit Services https://www.sec.gov/info/accountants/audit042707.htm

Chapter 8
Volatility and the Regulation of Stock Markets:
Evidence from South Asia

Filiz Eryilmaz
Uludag University, Turkey

ABSTRACT

In recent years, one of the most important topics related to stock market volatility which is attracting attention, is stock returns, or in other words, the relationship between stock price volatility and trading volume. The aim of this study was to obtain information about the financial market structure of Bangladesh, India, Pakistan by applying Granger Causality Analysis to the relationship of trading volume and stock returns volatility in the period 1980–2012. The study then examines some of the stock market regulations that have been proposed in South Asia to attenuate stock market volatility, which have usually included proposals to limit volatility by imposing temporary trading halts, limiting the legal leverage available to investors in financial assets, altering exchange trading practices to accommodate volume, and by raising the transactions costs of financial trading.

1. INTRODUCTION

Financial market volatility is the volatility shown to the financial market by any asset worth or index in a specific period. Financial market volatility expressed as financial asset yield variability is an important measurement used in the determination of risk of investments in the financial market. Therefore, there has been increasing interest recently in studies related to volatility, which have the same meaning as the concepts of risk and uncertainty, which have an important place in traditional financial theory. When financial markets are effective markets, changes in asset prices and yield of the financial markets reflect the changes in the basic variables of the economy. When the financial markets are not effective, two conditions will arise.

The first is that agents external to economic factors start to affect financial market volatility, such as wrong financial policies and irrational behavior of investors. The second is that this volatility created

DOI: 10.4018/978-1-5225-0004-9.ch008

in the financial markets starts to affect the real economy. In both situations, the volatility observed in the financial markets is an independent indicator of the economic balance and requires intervention by policy-makers. The volatility, which is initially an internal variable, over time starts to affect the economy as a dependent external variable. Financial market volatility showed an increase in general after the 1980s. The most significant reason for this was the increase in worldwide financial liberalization after the 1980s. In this context, the collapse experienced in the USA in October 1987 is extremely noteworthy. Increased financial market volatility is highly significant in respect of both the market investors and the policy-makers. When increased volatility means increased risk for investors, the situation arises where investors may review their investment decisions. In the same way, as a result of increased volatility, policy-makers may fall into the idea that the increased volatility of the financial markets will damage the economy by reflecting the real economy. At the same time, the policy-makers may think that increased financial volatility may damage the financial institutions and the regular functions of the financial market. In this situation, structural and organizational changes may be required to be made by the policy-makers for the market to function more regularly and to increase the flexibility of the market. Therefore, the determination of the causes of the waves experienced in the financial markets and particularly in the stock markets and predictions made by the best modeling are of great importance in respect of both investors and policy-makers.

In recent studies, it has been accepted that there is a connection between the general state of the economy and the financial markets. Especially in developing markets, the general macroeconomic variables of the economy have an effect on securities prices. In financial markets experiencing high volatility, lower risk resources are generally seen as Treasury bonds and foreign currency. Therefore, modeling of the volatility in the financial markets is extremely important in the formation of healthy markets be able to provide depth and flow of resources in the financial markets. When financial market volatility is spoken of, the focus is generally on stock market volatility, which can be considered an indicator of the pricing of stocks not being effective and the financial markets not functioning adequately. There are two reasons why volatility in the stock market has become so important in recent years. The first is that stock market volatility is closely related to the performance of option and derivatives markets, and the second is the financial crisis experienced in the USA on 19 October 1987. At that time, stock prices fell by 40% on average and the fall of 508 points on the Dow Jones Index was a record-breaking crash. This volatility damaged economy transfer channels and caused serious crises in the financial markets. Just as there are negative aspects to stock market volatility, so there can also be said to be positive aspects. Therefore, both the positive and negative directions of stock market volatility should be well considered. Sometimes what can be characterized as positive can also be expressed as negative when volatility is looked at from a different angle. In this sense, with high volatility of stock prices, just as it has been emphasized that the stock may rise excessively, so it can also fall dramatically. Thus, investors with highly volatile stocks may make large profits and when prices fall, may lose large amounts. On the other hand, manipulation to protect investors who are active in the market from volatility risks is one of the negative aspects of volatility and damages the market.

While that is the negative aspect of volatility, that high returns can be provided in the short-term by long-term investment means is the positive aspect of volatility. Volatility in the stock market provides increased possibility of accumulation in the short-term without investors having to wait for a long period and thus the transfer of these accumulated funds to the market increases demand. Although there is general agreement among economists on how stock volatility should be measured and the factors affecting stock volatility, there does not seem to be a general consensus on the factors affecting stock returns volatility. When the factors affecting stock returns volatility are taken into consideration, one of the most important factors seems to be trading volume. As a result of previous studies, it has been established that there is a strong relationship between trading volume and stock return volatility. However, it is difficult to determine exactly what has led to this relationship. While some researchers have reported that trading volume has an indirect effect on stock return volatility, others have stated that the effect is direct. According to this, if all those trading in the market wanted to buy or sell stock, this would have a direct effect on stock prices. The relationship between trading volume and price volatility has long been a subject of interest in the financial economy. There are many studies in literature on this subject which have many perspectives on the relationship between these two variables. In these studies, the empirical findings obtained related to the relationship between these two variables are extremely important. However, the difficulty of testing these empirical explanations by standard routes constitutes the greatest problem in the process of examining the relationship between the two variables.

According to Karpoff (1987), the relationship between trading volume and price is important for four reasons. The first is that the relationship between trading volume and price provides information about the structure of the financial markets. Previous studies related to this subject have associated the relationship between the two variables with how the information is distributed in the market, whether or not the knowledge of the market is reflected in the market prices, the size of the market and whether or not there are restrictions on short-term sales. Thus, the information flow and communication mechanism of the market itself is helpful in understanding the relationship between the two variables. Therefore, several studies on this subject have associated the flow of information in the market and differences in opinion between investors with trading volume. The observed trading volume includes both business of liquidity origin and business based on information. If fixed rates of liquid commerce are assumed in the market, the price changes of stock will originate from information reaching the market. On the other hand, excessive differences in the opinions of different investors will create an excessive amount of trading volume. It is necessary to make a more accurate estimate; the price-trading volume relationship may be useful in understanding mechanisms such as the spread of the flow of information, prices reflecting the information and prices carrying this information. Thus, experimental observations between trading volume and price also provide differentiation between different hypotheses about market structures. Secondly, the price-trading volume relationship is important in studies of events, which have used combinations of price-trading volume data. If price changes and trading volume are defined together and at the same time on the market, the difficulty of testing the trading volume-price relationship is increased just as in studies including such an event. Thirdly, the relationship between these two variables is important for studies related to speculative price distribution. Finally, the price –trading volume relationship provides significant information for research into futures markets. At the same time, the price-trading volume relationship highlights the importance of public information compared to personal information in the demands of the investors.

In this context, the aim of this study was to determine the place and importance of financial market volatility in the financial economy by going to the roots of the concept of volatility. Then by explaining the factors affecting stock market volatility, which is accepted as the most important component of financial volatility, the relationship between stock market volatility and trading volume will be explained. After consideration of the theoretical basis of this relationship, the markets of Bangladesh, India and Pakistan in the period 1989-2012 will be tested for the relationship between trading volume and volatility.

2. BACKGROUND

2.1. The Relationship between Stock Returns Volatility and Trading Volume

Stock return volatility is an indicator used to represent the frequency and size of the waves occurring in the stock return market index or in the price of a specific stock. Just as in all financial markets, the increasing volatility in recent years in the stock markets has increased interest in terms of stock investors becoming extremely important. Besides the sources of the volatility, measurement and modeling are of importance in respect of specialist and portfolio investors. Although it can be defined in different forms, the most commonly used method in the definition of volatility is standard deviation. According to this, in observations related to a specific stock price or index, if the statistical distribution of these observations is collected around the average then this means that the volatility of this stock is low. If the observations are spread over a wider area, then the volatility and therefore, the risk, can be said to be higher. Two general methods are used to be able to calculate volatility. In the first of these, retrospective volatility is obtained using previous prices and indexes. In the other method, volatility is obtained directly with the help of estimates made from option prices of future markets. To be able to calculate the price or index volatility of any stock, it is firstly necessary to define a time period. Interday volatility is obtained using the change in price or index from the closing of the market on one day to the closing on the next day. Volatility calculated using changes at specific hours of the day is known as intraday volatility.

The most basic method in the calculation of stock return volatility is the standard deviation method as shown in Equation (1.1). Besides facilitating the calculation, because this method uses daily data, when daily data cannot be obtained, it cannot be used to calculate monthly variance. The estimate of monthly return variance according to this method is equal to the total of the daily variances calculated after subtracting the mean daily return rate of the current month.

$$\sigma_t^2 = \sum_{i=1}^{N_t} r_{it}^2 \tag{1.1}$$

Here R_{it} is the return rate of the day *i* of the month *t*. When R_t shows the mean of all the days return rates of this month, $r_{it} = R_{it} - R_t$. Here, N_t is the number of daily returns in the month of *t* (r_{it}). Another monthly volatility method was developed by Schwert. With an autoregressive model of 12 degrees, Schwert estimated monthly return rates. The model, named the Schwert Index, was developed as shown below:

$$R_t = \sum_{j=1}^{12} \alpha_j D_{jt} + \sum_{i=1}^{12} \beta_i R_{t-i} + \varepsilon_t \tag{1.2}$$

Here, R_t, shows the stock return rate of the month t and D_{jt}, shows the monthly dummy variable. In this formula, R_t, is defined as a direct function of the stock return rate of the 12 months prior to month t and 12 months of dummy variables. The error terms obtained as a result of the prediction of equation (1.2) ε_t, is used as a predictor of monthly volatility with equation (1.3):

$$|\varepsilon_t| = \sum_{j=1}^{12} \gamma_j D_{jt} + \sum_{i=t}^{12} \rho_i |\varepsilon_{t-j}| + u_t \quad (1.3)$$

The value, $|\varepsilon_t|$ obtained as a result of this regression, is an estimate of the standard deviation of the stock market return of month *t*. The absolute ε values, that is $|\varepsilon_t|$, calculated with the help of the parameters γ_j and ρ_i, obtained as a result of the regression shown in Equation (1.3) are the data set of the month prior to t, and the estimated values (of R_t) with standard error conditions are formed from the stock return (Schwert, 1989: 1117-1118).

In recent years, one of the most important topics related to stock market volatility which is attracting attention, is stock returns, or in other words, the relationship between stock price volatility and trading volume. In addition to important individual studies on this subject explaining the relationship between price changes and trading volume, there are also some inter-related theories which explain the relationships between these two variables. The first of these is the 'information theory'. In this group of theories, information is the power of the administrator, which determines both trading volume and volatility. The information theories are separated into the Mixture of Distributions Model and the Sequential Information Arrival Model. The second theory of the Noise Trader Model was presented by De Long et al (1990). In the Epps (1975, 1976) model of the Mixture of Distributions Hypothesis, a proxy trading volume is used as a variable to measure the disagreement created as a result of traders reconsidering their own conservative prices on the basis of new information reaching the market. In this context, as disagreement between investors increases, so the trading volume increases. Therefore, their model supports the view that the positive causality relationship certainly extends from trading volume towards stock returns (Leon, 2007: 177). Clark (1973) however, accepted the flow of information as a variable affecting trading volume and accepting the common shadow factor of trading volume as an indicator of the rate of information, reported that a positive relationship was formed simultaneously between variance of price changes and trading volume. It was also stated that no relationship of causality could be found between trading volume and stock prices (Yılancı & Bozoklu, 2014: 212). The Information Sequential Arrival Hypothesis of Copeland (1976), Jennings, Starks and Fellingham (1981) supports the asymmetric information approach and states that the new information reaching the market is perceived as simultaneous by the investors while, in contrast, the process of perception of the new information was monitored as a pipeline process. Therefore, until a definitive balance is reached, there will be intermittent balances. According to the Information Sequential Arrival Hypothesis, there is the question of positive causality in both directions between stock returns and trading volume. Trading volume in the past through the sequential flow of information may be the predictive power for present stock returns, and vice versa (Ong & Hoo, 2011: 46).

The basic difference between the Mixture of Distributions Hypothesis and the Information Sequential Arrival Hypothesis lies in the speed at which new information results in the market adopting a new balance. In the Mixture of Distributions Model, the new balance is reached quickly whereas in the Information Sequential Arrival Hypothesis a definitive balance can not be reached. As the Information Sequential Arrival Hypothesis contains information which will explain current prices of past values of trading volume and current trading volumes of past prices, a positive causality of the relationship between the two variables is predicted. In addition, it is accepted that there is symmetry between the positive and negative changes of the variables in both models. According to the Noise Trader Model, which is the other model, the activities of noise traders are not supported by economic principles and these traders cause a deviation from the balance value in the short term which leads to the inclusion of a temporary component. In the long-term, there is a tendency for this temporary component to disappear and stock returns return to the average. Thus, this model states that a positive autocorrelation of stock returns is seen in the short-term and a negative autocorrelation in the long-term. Observations of the strategies of noise traders which lead to price fluctuations cause a positive causality relationship from trading volume towards returns and decisions taken depend on past price movements, so in other words, the trading of noise traders including positive reverse feedback results in a positive causality from stock returns towards trading volume (Yılancı & Bozoklu, 2014:213). The trading strategy in question is that noise traders buy and sell dependent on past price movements (Chen et. al., 2004: 90).

3. REGULATION AND STOCK MARKET VOLATILITY

Volatility is important issue for many studies as stock markets have experienced ever-increasing interaction during the past decade. Volatility and returns have been closely synchronized across national stock markets as a result of economic integration, the development of stock markets, financial deregulation and liberalization, and reduced information and transaction costs (Gahlot, 2013: 20). Since the early 1980, South Asian countries have been introducing far-reaching reforms to the financial sector in their respective economies. These reforms cover several areas, including the promotion of competition in the financial sector, in particular in the banking sector, strengthening regulations, improving disclosure requirements and auditing and accounting standards, developing payment and settlement systems and strengthening the legal framework. The reforms undertaken thus far have helped South Asian economies to significantly increase domestic savings, attract foreign capital, and raise economic growth rates. For example, India, the largest South Asian economy, has successfully become a global growth promoter during recent years as a result of financial reforms in the 1990s. Financial reforms have also supported greater economic integration of South Asia and several new regulatory measures have been introduced to strengthen the regulatory and supervisory framework. Central banks have moved away from compliance-based supervision to risk-focused supervision. Considering the fiduciary responsibility of the Boards towards their stakeholders and in the interest of wider financial system stability, central banks have issued directions on corporate governance requiring banks to streamline their governance practices. The implementation of the Basel II framework is another enhancement to the regulatory structure. It has contributed to improving the financial industry's risk management mechanism. With the adoption of Basel II, most of the leading banks have taken steps to set up independent risk management units and compliance divisions to monitor bank-wide risks. Major banks are now focusing on implementing advanced approaches under the Basel II framework and have set up data warehouses and sophisticated IT systems which will contribute to better risk management and compliance. Similarly, the adaptation of Basel II will enhance disclosures, presentation and measurement practices in relation to financial instruments (Mohanty 2014).

There are two contrasting debates about the possible impact of foreign investors on stock market volatility. The first argument suggests that foreign investors can destabilize the market, making prices more volatile than they otherwise would be. For example, the short-termism of foreign investment is often said to be a potential danger to the stability of local stock markets. Underlying the fear of this adverse effect of increasing foreign investment on a local stock market's stability is the belief that foreign investors are the major sources of stock market volatility and that without their participation the market would be better off in the hands of local investors. In contrast the second argument relating to the impact of foreign investors views such investors as having a positive effect on the market by increasing the information flow to the market and reducing the impact of noise trading. This view is based on the belief that foreign investors who decide to participate in emerging stock markets are likely to be well-informed traders rather than uninformed speculators or noise traders. The increased participation of well-informed investors in emerging stock markets should improve market efficiency, increase the rate of information flow, improve the quality and reliability of information and reduce the impact of noise traders on price volatility (Holmes & Wong, 2001: 373).

In this study, as a result of the analyses applied to Bangladesh, India and Pakistan, it was observed that the information flow of the foreign investors in the market increased, thereby decreasing noise trade in the stock markets of these countries. The most probable reason for this is that the increased information of foreign investors in the stock markets rendered the market more effective. Therefore, it can be said that the regulatory practices and financial reforms in those 3 countries have contributed to the effectiveness of the market.

4. DATA SET AND MODEL

In this study, the relationship between trading volume and stock return volatility was examined for the period 1989-2012 in Bangladesh, India and Pakistan. To do this, the trading volume data and stock return volatility logarithm taken for each year were used for each country. The data were obtained from the World Bank. Granger Causality Analysis was applied for each country to understand whether or not there was a relationship between trading volume and stock return volatility. To be able to apply Granger Causality Analysis, the series must be stationary. To understand whether or not the series was stationary, the Augmented Dickey-Fuller (ADF) test, Philips-Perron and Kwiatkowski–Phillips–Schmidt–Shin (KPSS) test was applied. Series which were not found to be stationary as a result of the ADF test, Philips-Perron and Kwiatkowski–Phillips–Schmidt–Shin (KPSS) test were made stationary then the Granger analysis could be applied.

4.1. Bangladesh

The results of the stationary analysis of the stock and trading volume data of Bangladesh are shown below.

According to the results in Table 1, the stock return volatility series of Bangladesh is not stationary at all three levels of significance. Therefore, the series was made stationary. The results of the ADF, Philips-Perron and Kwiatkowski–Phillips–Schmidt–Shin (KPSS) test for trading volume for Bangladesh are shown in Table 2.

From Table 2, the trading volume series of Bangladesh is seen to be stationary, so there was no requirement to take the difference of the series.

From Table 3 it can be seen that there is a one-way causality relationship between stock return volatility and trading volume for Bangladesh and the direction of this relationship was seen to be from trading volume towards stock return volatility. Therefore, the Mixture of Distributions Hypothesis was accepted as valid for Bangladesh. Another meaning of this result is that the Bangladeshi stock markets can be balanced quickly.

Table 1. Unit Root Test Results of Bangladesh stock return volatility

	Intercept	Trend and Intercept
ADF	2.46 (-3.10)	1.20 (-3.64)
Philips-Perron	0.04 (-2.99)	-1.40 (-3.62)
KPSS	0.51 (0.46)	0.18 (0.14)

Table 2. Unit Root Test Results of Bangladesh trading volume

	Intercept	Trend and Intercept
ADF	-2.09 (-3.00)	-3.99 (-4.57)
Philips-Perron	-1.83 (-2.99)	-2.34 (-3.62)
KPSS	0.48 (0.46)	0.04 (0.14)

Table 3. Granger Test Results of the Bangladesh Series

Dependent Variable: Trading Volume			
Excluded	Chi-sq	df	Prob
Return	0.167573	1	0.6823
All	0.167573	1	0.6823
Dependent Variable: Return			
Excluded	Chi-sq	df	Prob
Trading Volume	9.509618	1	0.0020
All	9.509618	1	0.0020

4.2. India

Before testing the causality relationship between the two variables, whether or not the series for India was stationary was tested. Firstly, whether or not the stock return volatility series for India was stationary was investigated.

From Table 4 it can be seen that the stock return volatility series for India was not stationary at a significance level of 5%. Therefore, the series was made stationary, taking the difference into account. The results of the ADF, Philips-Perron and Kwiatkowski–Phillips–Schmidt–Shin (KPSS) test of the trading volume series for India are shown in Table 5.

Table 4. Unit Root Test Results of India stock return volatility

	Intercept	Trend and Intercept
ADF	2.72 (-3.08)	0.74 (3.75)
Philips-Perron	-0.36 (-3.01)	-2.50 (-3.64)
KPSS	0.59 (0.46)	0.18 (0.11)

Table 5. Unit Root Test Results of India trading volume

	Intercept	Trend and Intercept
ADF	-1.56 (-2.99)	-1.41 (-3.62)
Philips-Perron	-0.56 (-2.99)	-1.41 (-3.62)
KPSS	0.15 (0.46)	0.13 (0.11)

According to the unit root tests in Table 5, the India trading volume series is not stationary. Therefore, taking the first difference of the series into account, the series was made stationary and the Granger Causality analysis was applied. The results of the Granger causality analysis for both series are shown in Table 6.

According to the results in Table 6, no relationship was found between the two series for India. In this case, the Mixture of Distributions Hypothesis of Clark (1973) is valid for India.

4.3. Pakistan

Before applying Granger Causality analysis for Pakistan, whether or not the series was stationary was tested. The results of the unit root test of the stock return volatility series for Pakistan are seen in Table 7.

From Table 7 it can be seen that the stock market volatility series for Pakistan was not stationary. Therefore, taking the first difference of the series into account the series was made stationary. The results of the unit root tests for the trading volume series of Pakistan are shown in Table 8.

From Table 8 it can be seen that the trading volume series of Pakistan was not stationary. Therefore, taking the first difference of the series into account, the series was made stationary. When both series had been made stationary, Granger Causality analysis was applied. The results of the Granger Causality analysis for the series for Pakistan are shown in Table 9.

According to the results shown in Table 9, just as for India, in Pakistan also, there was no relationship between stock return volatility and trading volume and therefore the Mixture of Distributions Hypothesis

Tablo 6. Granger Test Results of the India series

Dependent Variable: Trading Volume			
Excluded	**Chi-sq**	**df**	**Prob**
Return	0.920377	1	0.3374
All	0.920377	1	0.3374
Dependent Variable: Return			
Excluded	**Chi-sq**	**df**	**Prob**
Trading Volume	0.017705	1	0.8941
All	0.017705	1	0.8941

Table 7. Unit Root Test Results of Pakistan stock return volatility

	Intercept	**Trend and Intercept**
ADF	-1.65 (-2.99)	-2.85 (-3.62)
Philips-Perron	-1.43 (-2.99)	-2.89 (-3.62)
KPSS	0.53 (0.46)	0.09 (0.11)

Table 8. Unit Root Test Results of Pakistan trading volume

	Intercept	**Trend and Intercept**
ADF	-1.79 (-3.02)	-1.23 (-3.65)
Philips-Perron	-1.65 (-2.99)	-1.35 (-3.62)
KPSS	0.22 (0.46)	0.15 (0.11)

Table 9. Granger Test Results of the Pakistan series

Dependent Variable: Return			
Excluded	**Chi-sq**	**df**	**Prob**
Trading Volume	1.123774	1	0.2891
All	0.123774	1	0.2891
Dependent Variable: Trading Volume			
Excluded	**Chi-sq**	**df**	**Prob**
Return	2.078525	1	0.1494
All	2.078525	1	0.1494

was accepted as valid for Pakistan. Another meaning of this result is that the stock markets of Pakistan can be balanced quickly.

5. FUTURE RESEARCH DIRECTIONS

As daily stock return volatility and trading volume data were not available for Bangladesh, India and Pakistan, it was necessary to consider annual data. Further studies on this subject would provide more reliable findings with the use of daily, weekly, monthly or quarterly data of countries.

6. CONCLUSION

In this study an evaluation was made of the relationship between stock return volatility and trading volume in Bangladesh, India and Pakistan and the connection of regulations made in those three countries. The relationship between stock return volatility and trading volume and the relationship direction benefitted from Granger Causality Analysis. As a result of the analysis, it was seen that the relationship between the two variables for Bangladesh was seen to be in the direction of from trading volume towards stock return volatility. Therefore The Mixture of Distributions Hypothesis was accepted as valid for Bangladesh. This means that the information coming to the Bangladesh stock market is spread to the market immediately. Therefore the Bangladesh stock market is an effective market.

No relationship was determined between trading volume and stock return volatility for India or Pakistan and therefore, as for Bangladesh, the Mixture of Distributions Hypothesis was valid for these two countries and the conclusion was reached that the stock markets were effective. Another meaning of the results obtained is that in all three countries the regulations and reforms made to the stock markets have made a positive contribution to the flow and distribution of information in the market and have made the markets more effective.

REFERENCES

Chen, G., & Firth, M., & Xin, Y. (2004). The Price-Volume Relationship in China's Commodity Futures Markets. *Chinese Economy*, *37*(3), 87–122.

Clark, P. K. (1973). A Subordinated Stochastic Process Model with Finite Variance for Speculative Prices. *Econometrica*, *41*(1), 135–155. doi:10.2307/1913889

Copeland, T. E. (1976). A Probability Model of Asset Trading. *Journal of Financial and Quantitative Analysis*, *12*(4), 563–578. doi:10.2307/2330332

Epps, T. W. (1975). Security Price Changes and Transaction Volumes: Theory and Evidence. *The American Economic Review*, *65*(4), 586–597.

Epps, T. W. (1976). The Demand for Broker's Services: The Relation Between Security Trading Volume and Transaction Cost. *Bell Journal of Economics*, *7*, 163–194.

Gahlot, R. (2013). Capturing Volatility and its Spillover in South Asian Countries. *Journal of International Business and Economics*, *1*(1), 20–36.

Gayğusuz, F. (2008). Hisse Senedi Piyasalarında İşlem Hacmi- Volatilite İlişkisi ve İMKB'ye Ait Bir Uygulama. *Çukurova Üniversitesi İİBF Dergisi, 12*(1), 34- 55.

Gayğusuz, F. (2008). *Hisse Senedi Piyasa Volatilitesi ve İşlem Hacmi ile İlişkisi*. Uludağ Üniversitesi Sosyal Bilimler Enstitüsü, Yayınlanmamış Yüksek Lisans Tezi.

Holmes, P., & Wong, M. W. (2001). Foreign investment, regulation and price volatility in South-east Asian stock markets. *Emerging Markets Review*, *2*(4), 371–386. doi:10.1016/S1566-0141(01)00025-5

Jennings, R. H., & Barry, C. (1983). Information Dissemination and Portfolio Choice. *Journal of Financial and Quantitative Analysis, 18*(1), 1–19. doi:10.2307/2330801

Karpoff, J. M. (1987). The Relationship Between the Price Changes and Trading Volume: A Survey. *Journal of Financial and Quantitative Analysis*, *23*(1), 109–126. doi:10.2307/2330874

Leon, L. K. (2007). An Empirical Study of The Relation Between Stock Return Volatility and Trading Volume in the BRVM. *African Journal of Business Management*, *1*(7), 176–184.

Mohanty, D. (2014). *Reforms to the Financial Sector in South Asian Countries to Promote Economic Growth with Financial System Stability*. Retrieved from: www.icrier.org/pdf/DeepakMohanty-PPT.pdf

Ong, Ş. H., & Mun, H. C. (2011). Testing For Linear And Nonlinear Granger Causality In The Stock Return And Stock Trading Volume Relation: Malaysia And Singapore Cases. *Labuan Bulletin of International Business & Finance*, *9*, 44–57.

Schwert, G. W. (1989). Why Does Stock Markets Volatility Changes Over Time? *The Journal of Finance*, *44*(5), 1115–1154. doi:10.1111/j.1540-6261.1989.tb02647.x

Schwert, G. W. (1990). Stock Market Volatility. *Financial Analysts Journal*, *46*(3), 23–34. doi:10.2469/faj.v46.n3.23

Yılancı, V., & Bozoklu, Ş. (2014). Türk Sermaye Piyasasında Fiyat ve İşlem Hacmi İlişkisi: Zamanla Değişen Asimetrik Nedensellik Analizi. *Ege Akademik Bakış*, *14*(2), 211–220.

KEY TERMS AND DEFINITIONS

Augmented Dickey–Fuller Test (ADF): In statistics and econometrics, an augmented Dickey–Fuller test (ADF) is a test for a unit root in a time series sample. It is an augmented version of the Dickey–Fuller test for a larger and more complicated set of time series models. The augmented Dickey–Fuller (ADF) statistic, used in the test, is a negative number. The more negative it is, the stronger the rejections of the hypothesis that there is a unit root at some level of confidence.

Granger Causality Test: Granger causality is a statistical concept of causality that is based on prediction. According to Granger causality, if a signal X1 "Granger-causes" a signal X2, then past values of X1 should contain information that helps predict X2 above and beyond the information contained in past values of X2 alone. Its mathematical formulation is based on linear regression modeling of stochastic processes. More complex extensions to nonlinear cases exist, however these extensions are often more difficult to apply in practice.

Regulation: A regulation is a legal norm intended to shape conduct that is a byproduct of imperfection. A regulation may be used to prescribe or proscribe conduct- command and control regulation- to calibrate incentives- incentive regulation- or to change preferences- preferences shaping regulation. In statist mechanisms it can also be extended to monitoring and enforcement of rules as established by primary and/or delegated legislation. In this form, it is generally a written instrument containing rules having the force of statist law. Other forms of regulation are self regulation. In general, regulations are written by executive agencies as a way to enforce laws passed by the legislature. Because of the actual or potential interference in choices, the idea of regulation and most issues related to regulation tend to be in controversy.

Stock Market: A stock market or equity market is the aggregation of buyers and sellers- a loose network of economic transactions, not a physical facility or discrete entity- of stocks- also called shares; these may include securities listed on a stock exchange as well as those only traded privately.

Time Series Analysis: Time series analysis comprises methods for analyzing time series data in order to extract meaningful statistics and other characteristics of the data. Time series forecasting is the use of a model to predict future values based on previously observed values. While regression analysis is often employed in such a way as to test theories that the current values of one or more independent time series affect the current value of another time series, this type of analysis of time series is not called "time series analysis", which focuses on comparing values of a single time series at different points in time.

Unit Root Test: In statistics, a unit root test tests whether a time series variable is non-stationary using an autoregressive model. A well-known test that is valid in large samples is the augmented Dickey–Fuller test.

Volatility: In finance, volatility is a measure for variation of price of a financial instrument over time. Historic volatility is derived from time series of past market prices. An implied volatility is derived from the market price of a market traded derivative in particular an option. The symbol σ is used for volatility, and corresponds to standard deviation, which should not be confused with the similarly named variance, which is instead the square, σ^2.

Chapter 9
Financial Market in Nepal:
Challenges of the Financial Sector Development in Nepal

Narayan Prasad Paudel
Kathmandu University School of Management, Nepal

ABSTRACT

The Nepalese financial sector is attributed of banking sector and non-banking sector. There is exponential growth in the number of financial institutions in Nepal in the last decade. The existing legal framework and institutional setup in Nepal is not conducive to the overall financial sector and private sector development and thus there is an urgent need for reformation in these sectors. The major impediments to private sector involvement in infrastructure development projects include the political and administrative instability; lack of consistent planning; lack of effective institutional support in designing and development of private sector infrastructure projects. Talking about the capital market and capital gains In Nepal, capital gains on securities transactions are taxed as ordinary income to corporations and individual investors while in most of the emerging markets capital gains on investments in stocks and bonds are not taxed, which need to be reformed as per the international practices.

BACKGROUND

The major obstacle to the private sector capital formation and economic development in Nepal is the high cost of capital which is associated with the lack of competition in the financial sector and the poor performance of government owned-banks. In this regard, it can be observed that gap between lending and borrowing rates has widened in recent years while the overall performance of the banking system has showed little improvement despite the growth of private banks in the 1990s. In line with above reference The Nepal Bank Limited (NBL) retrenched its operations, consequently, the market share of private banks doubled more than 37 percent, while the market share of the Rastriya Banijya Bank (RBB) remained unchanged at about 32 percent. Nevertheless, some members of the business community believe that the private joint venture banks have not contributed sufficiently to the economic well-being of the nation. Instead, these institutions are sometimes viewed as benefited from the inefficiency in the

DOI: 10.4018/978-1-5225-0004-9.ch009

financial sector (i.e., wide-loan deposit spreads). If this is the case, the Nepalese economy could benefit from the added competition that would be provided from the development of a money-and-bond market for private issues of securities. In Nepal, universal banking is permitted whereby commercial banks and quasi-banks (i.e., deposit-taking finance companies) may perform investment banking services within the same organization. Commercial banks, however, are not actively involved in capital markets. While authorized to act as underwriters they ordinarily do not participate in this line of business as extensively as finance companies. Commercial banks do not act as money managers or instead, sponsor mutual funds. They do not serve as brokers or market-makers on the floor of the stock exchange either. Commercial banks, however, are active participants in the markets for treasury bills and government bonds. Since the secondary market is relatively inactive, their role is largely limited to primary market transactions.

Over the past 20 years Nepal's financial system has become wider and consequently the number and the type of financial intermediaries have grown rapidly. In addition, recent reforms have made banks more stable, yet the access to financial services remains limited for many people in many parts of Nepal and in recent years it has been declining. During the last 40 years, Government of Nepal has tried much to increase access to formal financial services for small business and low-income households.

The government has introduced directed lending programs for small businesses and low-income households and it has required/encouraged banks to open branches outside Kathmandu Valley. Also it has created specialized wholesale and retail institutions, and lowered market entry to foster the development of different types of financial institutions.

The Nepalese financial sector is composed of banking sector and non-banking sector. The banking sector comprises Nepal Rastra Bank (NRB) and commercial banks. The non-banking sector includes development banks, micro-credit development banks, finance companies, cooperatives and non-government organizations (NGOs) that regulate limited banking activities and other financial institutions such as insurance companies, employee's provident fund, citizen investment trust, postal saving offices and Nepal stock exchange.

There is tremendous growth in the number of financial institutions in Nepal in the last decade. In the beginning of the 1980s, when financial sector was not liberalized, there were only two commercial banks, and two development banks performing banking activities. There were no micro-credit development banks, finance companies, cooperatives and NGOs. After the liberalization of the financial sector, it has made a hall-mark of progress both in terms of number of services. After 1984, there was rapid entry of joint venture commercial banks in to the Nepalese financial market. In the first phase, the Nepal Arab Bank (presently known as NABIL) (1984), the Nepal Indo-Suez Bank (1985) and the Nepal Grindlays Bank (1987) entered the market. In the second phase these banks were followed by the Himalayan Bank, the Nepal SBI Bank, the Nepal Bangladesh Bank, the Everest Bank, the Bank of Kathmandu and the Kumari Bank. In the third phase many development banks have emerged in the market.

In Nepal, the banking sector is one of the sectors which have been able to sustain by facing the test of time due to political instability in the country and it has established itself as the most profitable sector. Currently, with the increased rate of various problems in the country, banking sector is able to prosper with less difficulty. But the growth of financial institutions seems to be slowing down due to the entry of new players leading to a harsh competition. One of the signs of such problems has been the credit crunch faced by financial institutions in recent months. As a result, banks are looking for new geographic locations in order to diversify the portfolio of customers.

Despite government efforts, the access to formal financial services is declining in Nepal. Financial intermediation is stagnating, the number of bank deposits and loan accounts per citizen is falling, and lending targets for low income households have generated excess liquidity among microfinance institutions without significantly increasing their outreach.

The use of bank services in Nepal is limited. Therefore, financial NGOs and cooperatives play a vital role in providing both deposit accounts and loans, and informal borrowing has exceeded formal borrowing to a greater extent.

About 26 percent of Nepalese households have their bank accounts. To assists this job, financial NGOs and cooperatives run as close as the second largest provider of deposit accounts, serving about 18 percent of households. These institutions are the preferred providers for low-income households. Also, they are close to banks even for wealthier households. Microfinance and regional rural development banks are distant third providers for deposit accounts, serving only 4 percent of households– mainly the poor in the rural areas.

Increasing financial access to small business and low-income households requires that financial institutions be able to serve these segments in a financially sustainable manner. Lending profitably to small businesses requires a high level of efficiency, while operating microfinance institutions with large outreach requires a high level of professionalism and technical skills. Nepalese financial institutions are struggling to meet these requirements.

To serve small business profitably, banks need to minimize transaction costs and generate a large number of high-quality loans. But Nepal's financial sector finds it difficult to serve small and micro businesses profitably due to the following reasons:

1. Banking procedures for small business loans are too complex because such a lending process is unnecessarily long and expensive for business and bank both.
2. The most popular bank product, i.e. overdraft, (line of credit) is inappropriate for many small businesses, which do not deposit their revenues in banks.
3. The interest rates that banks charge on loans to the small business do not adequately reflect the cost of serving them.
4. Banks require a high level of immovable collateral, while small businesses tend to have only movable assets.
5. Although Nepalese banks have sophisticated management information system, they generally do not use it to measure staff and loan performance; which is crucial for profitable small business lending. Since the legal and regulatory framework is not a binding constraint on bank lending to small businesses, it could be improved to facilitate such loans.

Challenges of the Financial Sector Development in Nepal

The prudential regulations and supervision laws; process for foreclosure and bankruptcy, credit information on borrowers, valuation of collateral, and recovery of loan payment system constitute the basic financial infrastructure for any country. But in Nepal's case there are many problems.

The following points indicate the existing problems of the financial sector development in Nepal, (GMA, 2000):

1. The inefficient and in-competitive commercial banking system has been pointed out as the main cause for high interest rates in Nepal. The governmental protection granted to the dominant but inefficient government owned/managed banks that maintain a large spread by charging a high rate

of interest to meet their high cost of operation, and bad debt provisions has been pointed as the main reason for the in-competitiveness of the banking system. This has resulted in the borrower's paying high rate of interest to maintain inefficient government banks. It has an adverse impact on investment and growth.

2. The financial infrastructure is weak. It has contributed to financial sector inefficiency in Nepal. Prudential regulations for commercial banks are lax compared to the international standards in some crucial aspect. The lack of basic financial infrastructure, the unequal supervisory enforcement of the existing regulation, and the undue protection given to government owned banks are regarded as the major impediment to the investment and economic growth of Nepal.
3. Nepal's legal framework is inadequate in regard to the land record, bailment and bankruptcy. Moreover, court procedures for payment defaults or collateral recoveries tend to be excessively slow, unpredictable and inefficient. Banking activities are regulated by at least six different Acts, while a number of small savings and credit cooperatives are not licensed by the central bank to conduct banking operations. They are not compelled to fulfill prudential regulations, including "fit and proper" assessment.
4. Banking supervision practices in Nepal do not comply with Core Principles defined by the Basle Committee. Regulations on banking activities, in many cases, are inadequate, too lenient and inconsistent. Enforcement is particularly weak. Most of the regulations allow for long delays in correcting non-compliance. They do not set mandatory financial or legal penalties nor do they prescribe actions to be taken by banking authorities
5. Regulations relating to the internal control and audit, interest rate risks and foreign exchange transactions, concentration of credit exposure, capital definition, liquidity, loan classification and provisions, single borrower limit, and accounting policies need to be revised and harmonized with international standards.
6. The Nepal Rastra Bank (the Central Bank of Nepal) has no statutory independence from the Ministry of Finance. Being on the board and as a shareholder of various commercial and development banks, the government of Nepal faces a conflict of interest which it has been unable to resolve.
7. The banking supervision system does not provide legal protection for supervisors, nor operational independence and adequate resources.

Some of the Critical Problems of Financial Sector Development in Nepal

The critical problems of financial sector development in Nepal include the following:

A. In-competitive commercial banking system;
B. Weak financial infrastructure,
C. Weak and inadequate legal framework;
D. Undue protection given to government owned commercial banks;
E. High rate of interest to maintain the inefficient government banks;
F. Weak supervision and enforcement of financial regulations;
G. Lack of independency of the Nepal Rastra Bank and the lack of statutory protection to supervisors responsible for the enforcement of existing financial regulations.

The existing legal framework and institutional setup is not conducive to the overall private sector development and thus there is an urgent need for reformation. There is lack of effective and appropriate institutional arrangement for the enforcement of existing legislation dealing with regulatory, disciplining, disclosure and corporate governance mechanism. The status of the enforcement of legislation relating to the redress of grievances of investing public in the matter of financial irregularities, malpractices and capital market operation is very poor. The mechanism for settlement of commercial and business disputes, and the issues relating to privatization and liberalization in general is inefficient. The following are the additional major impediments to private sector development:

- Lack of legal framework meeting the international standard,
- Lack of forward-looking attitudes on the part of the government,
- The political instability, political interference,
- Lack of commitment to develop the system of governance,
- Lack of trained professionals in civil service, judiciary (legal, account) and audit professional to deal with issues related to commercial and business matters.
- The slow process of liberalization,

Furthermore, the lack of trained manpower, and physical facilities in the institutions and authorities responsible for surveillance and enforcement of financial, corporate and securities regulations such as the Nepal Rastra Bank, the Office of Company Registrar, the Securities Board, and NEPSE etc. can also be taken as an a serious impediment to private sector development.

Prospective Measures of Financial Sector Development in Nepal

The financial sector is the backbone of the economy. It works as a facilitator for achieving sustained economic growth by providing efficient financial intermediation. The Modern financial system is important in the economy in order to pool and utilize financial resources, to reduce costs and risks, to expand and diversify opportunities, to increase the allocative efficiency of resources and to promote the productivity and facilitate economic growth. While a sound and healthy financial system contributes to the growth of the real sector on a sustainable basis, uncertainty and fragility in the financial system adversely affect the targeted objectives of economic development.

The following points signify the possible measures of financial sector development in Nepal:

A. Empowerment of the Nepal Rastra Bank (NRB) by removing the control of the Ministry of Finance;
B. Removal of the undue protection given to government banks by eliminating branching and other restriction on private banks;
C. Enforcement of prudent regulation on all banks equally;
D. Enhancement of the supervision capacity and modernization of NRB;
E. Treatment all financial institutions equally;
F. Improvement in the accounting and audit standards;
G. Establishment of an effective and efficient credit information bureau;
H. Enactment of new legislation to strengthen financial infrastructure.

Role of Private Sector in Financial Sector Development in Nepal

The establishment of parliamentary democracy in 1990 opened the way for sweeping economic reforms, and a program of great scope was carried out, between 1991 and 1994. This embraced policies on finance; foreign and domestic trade and investment, industry and foreign exchange; and a start to privatization. A change of government, then, led to a hiatus in privatization and a setback in macro-economic stabilization, but the governments which have ruled since September 1995 have re-launched both.

The government which took office in April 1998 did not have a majority of seats in the Parliament but, significantly, it apparently had the necessary support to move forward with privatization and stabilization. The Prime Minister said his party aimed at winning the confidence of the other parties in the Parliament "and move ahead with a common agenda".

The approach paper drafted by the National Planning Commission for the Ninth Plan, whose implementation reaffirms very clearly the strategy of transition to a more market-oriented and private sector-led economy pursued since the early 1990s. It also offers support for privatization through wide share-issuance to public investors.

Nepal's own liberalization has been greatly reinforced by that of India, with which its economy is very closely linked.

Problems and Prospects of Private Sector Investment

Regarding the investment environment in the sectors of electricity, telecommunication, transportation and water supply, the major impediments to attract private investment are the absences of stronger private sector involvement in infrastructure. The major impediments to private sector involvement in infrastructure development are: the political and administrative instability; lack of consistent planning; lack of effective institutional support in designing and development of private sector infrastructure projects; reliance on unsolicited proposals; difficulty in obtaining commercial lending and the lack of government support arrangements.

Problems Relating to the Private Sector Development

A. Lack of matching procedural and institutional structure designed to attract as many interested investors as possible. The present passive approach by the government carries the danger of not making the use of the private financing option to the extent possible.
B. Lack of a proactive and strategic approach to the involvement of private investment in infrastructure. The government is treating private sector development participation as the last resort means of financing a project.

Ways for Effective Development of the Private Sector in Nepal

The following could be the possible measures for effective development of the private sector in Nepal:

A. Reformation of existing legal framework conducive to the private sector development which matches the international standards.

B. Establishment of some new institutions and strengthening the capability of the existing institutions to ensure effective enforcement and supervision of the regulatory measures under various legislation for the efficient operation of the capital market, financial system, implementation of the infrastructure projects and smooth operation of private sector development activities in general.
C. The government should follow the competitive tendering system while awarding the infrastructure project in the private sector and to accept direct or contingent financial responsibility to support commercial credibility of a specific infrastructure project which is not otherwise commercially viable.
D. Appropriate training for the staffs of different regulatory institutions and for professionals involved in the dispute settlement process such as judges, lawyers etc.

The appropriate legal framework required for efficient functioning and the operation of the International Finance Services Centre should be developed as domestic legislation. While developing such legislative incorporation, internationally accepted standards and practices should be taken into consideration.

There are important areas of the private sector development suffering due to the lack of appropriate legislation. New legislation is required to cater the need of the private sector development which requires the legal framework to come at par with the international standards for the purpose of: (i) building the confidence of the investing public including foreign investors, (ii) for the establishment of new institutions providing effective mechanisms for the enforcement of the capital market legislation and effective regulation of financial transactions and (iii) for providing an effective mechanism for the settlement of disputes relating to various commercial and financial transactions, issues relating to privatization and matters relating to, or arising in course of formulation and implementation of infrastructure development projects. In addition to new legislation, some of the related existing legislation requires reformation. Some of these may be amended and some should be replaced by new legislation.

Issues for the Private Sector Development in Nepal

The tax system can be reformed to encourage disclosure and stimulate capital formation. The government can accelerate the sale of the shares of the National Insurance Company which remain in the hands of the state. With this in view, the government should review the adequacy of existing regulations. In the interim, period, the government should also review existing insurance procurement practices in order to create a level playing field between the state-owned company and the private sector.

Private sector support measures should be taken to strengthen certain agencies and organizations which play a key role in the enabling environment for private sector development.

It can be noticed that the Improvement is essential for the following fields:

1. A careful consideration should be given in creating a Small Business Executive Agency to handle licensing and registration requirements for small businesses as a self-regulatory organization under Federation of Nepalese Chambers of Commerce and Industry (FNCCI).
2. NRB should publish guidelines granting greater flexibility to joint venture banks and finance companies in staffing headquarters office in Nepal, in order to encourage continuity in management and the transfer of state-of-the-art technical and operational skills.

3. Foreign lawyers and accountants (individual and companies) should be permitted to practice in Nepal. It will be necessary to abolish current restrictions on the right of foreign lawyers and chartered accountants to practice in Nepal, amending relevant legislation.
4. It is necessary to review the adequacy of the regulatory framework for various industries (insurance, banking, airlines, energy, communications, etc.) as the process of privatization moves forward.
5. There is a need to develop a competition policy. It will be necessary to review current policies, laws, regulations and practices to eliminate privileges for state owned enterprises as compared with the private sector. The government should consider the institutional arrangements for the regulation and enforcement of a competition policy.

Practical Problems of the Private Sector in Nepal

The high cost of capital to private business enterprises can be attributed as a major constraint on the private sector development. While there are many impediments to be overcome, it was widely believed that the further development of the capital market in Nepal could contribute to a more efficient allocation of savings, expansion of the private sector, and economic growth. Thus, several studies noted that the development of the Nepalese capital market is important for several reasons:

First, the primary or the newly issued market has the potential to provide a source of urgently needed long-term funding for the private sector. In order to avoid a mismatch in assets and liabilities, the Nepalese banking sector should most appropriately concentrate on short-term funding for business.

Second, the creation of an efficient secondary market with prices determined in a fair and transparent manner would instill public confidence and facilitate the allocation of capital to its most productive uses. This requires that investors have access to the accurate and timely information, improvement in the capital market infrastructure, and a more competitive environment in the delivery of financial services to issuers and investors.

Third, capital markets can facilitate the privatization of state-owned enterprises in a manner that allows broad public participation and provides an ownership structure that will support the long-term goals of the privatization program, including greater efficiency, transparency, sound corporate governance, good management practices, and increased revenues to the government. Finally, strengthening the capital market could help reduce the current dependence on external finance supplied by international lending agencies.

Asian Development Bank (ADB) estimates that the external financing for Nepal's development will account for 8.0 percent of GDP in 2008 while internally generated financing by bank and non-bank sources will account for 1.1 percent of GDP. In order to reduce the over-dependence on foreign assistance for Nepal's development requirements, ADB recommends further efforts to mobilize domestic resources more efficiently, including "major tax reforms and further measures to improve efficiency in the financial sector as well as to revitalize the capital market".

Under the primary securities market, macroeconomic conditions, political uncertainty, and the policy environment toward privatization have not been conducive to the expansion of the share market through public offerings.

Private Sector and Strategic Opportunities in Nepal

Nepal's greatest opportunities for private sector development include (GMA, 2000) hydro-power sector and tourism sector, both derive principally from the Himalayas. The potential supply of hydroelectricity far exceeds Nepal's own present and projected future demand. Schemes that would have a total capacity as great as 40,000MW have been economically and environmentally judged feasible. This compares with some 600MW of hydropower generating capacity now installed in Nepal, another 280MW under construction and projected demand in the country of 4000MW in the year 2014. But, by the same year, India's northern grid is expected to face a power deficit of around 20,000MW.

However, the Indian market for Nepalese power is more theoretical than actual at present. The Nepalese government understands this well and has taken a major step forward by concluding a Power Trade Agreement with India. This provides a legal framework which permits private parties in the two countries to enter into cross-border power sale/purchase agreements with each other. The conclusion of an agreement with India on the integrated use of the waters of the Mahakali river has established another landmark in relations between the two countries; and will open the way to a project which combines hydropower, irrigation and flood control once the arrangements for implementation have been finalized.

The Nepalese authorities are well aware that a constraint on Indian purchases at present is the financial weakness of the State Electricity Boards in India. But restructuring of these has begun, in some states, and the problem should prove to be one of transitions as India moves to a more market-oriented system.

The cost of eight schemes that account for half of the 40,000MW of potential installed capacity has been estimated at US$11,500 million, of which the vast majority would have to come from abroad because Nepal's total gross fixed capital formation in the year 2007 was less than US$2,000 million.

The government has enacted legislation to permit private investment, including foreign, in this sector and private investors are already playing an essential role in both large and small schemes.

Public and private sector investors from Norway, the US and Australia played a leading role in three hydropower projects at varying stages of development, the most advanced being Khimti-I (Norway), Bhote Kosi (Harza Engineering of the US), and the third being West Seti (the Snowy Mountain Corporation of Australia). The cost of these projects estimated at US$138, US$98million and US$ 1,000 million, and their generating capacity at 60MW, 36MW and 750MW respectively.

After pursuing a proposal to the government of Nepal for two years, the Enron Corporation of the US withdrew its application for a survey license for the 10,800MW Karnali-Chisapani project, in which it had calculated that it would have to invest US$6-9,000 million. According to the company, its investment alone would have added 43 percent to Nepal's GNP. In 1995, the World Bank withdrew from the 402MW Arun III project. These two decisions, and the intense political controversy which has been aroused by the Mahakali project, as mentioned above, have demonstrated that the difficulties and risks inherent in projects of such magnitude in Nepal are many and great. They are financial, commercial, economic, environmental, social, administrative and political ones. Indeed, the mismatch between the size of these projects and Nepal's own economy and the financial and administrative capacity are so great that it may be more realistic for Nepal to pursue a program of lesser projects, and develop a record of success in that before attempting mega-projects.

Feasibility studies for some seven medium-sized schemes selected for expansion of the domestic power system were due for completion by the end of year 2001. Their total cost was estimated to be worth US$1,039 million, with individual costs ranging from US$ 39 to 65 million. If they could be partly financed through the Nepalese capital market, this would provide a powerful dynamic to the development of that market, much as railway building helped drive the growth of capital markets in Europe and America in the 19th century.

Electricity generation was a state monopoly managed by the Nepal Electricity Authority until 1992. Since then a considerable legislative effort has been made by the government to open the sector to private ownership and investment, both domestic and foreign. An Electricity Development Centre has been established to facilitate foreign investment. Foreign lawyers have paid tribute to the quality and pragmatic responsiveness of the Nepalese officials with whom they have dealt on the Khimti project, which demanded creative solutions to legal problems not encountered in Nepal before.

The government has asked the Foreign Investment Advisory Service (FIAS) of the World Bank group to review the institutional, legal and regulatory environment for the private sector investment in infrastructure (including electricity, airports, dry ports, roads, telecommunications, water and waste disposal) and to provide recommendations on how to make these sectors more attractive to foreign investors. The FIAS report is likely to contain important indicators for follow-up work, including technical assistance requirements.

The strengthening of Nepal's regulatory regime for electricity and other utilities deserves high priority as a target for technical assistance.

The potential of the Himalayas for the growth of tourism has only begun to be exploited. Tourism itself is in private hands, and foreign investment is permitted, except in activities which lend themselves most readily to small-scale enterprise. The strengthening of this sector was the objective of a tourism infrastructure development project financed by the Asian Development Bank approved in July 1996.

Economic Reforms

Conducting an event study is the most direct and transparent way of assessing the impact of stock market liberalization on emerging market equity prices. However, unlike the typical event study in finance where an econometrician can be reasonably certain that the event in question is isolated from other influential events, the shift from closed to open capital markets usually coincides with four equally important changes in an economic policy: macroeconomic stabilization, trade liberalization, privatization, and the easing of exchange controls.

The theory used to explain the stock price effects of capital market liberalization assumes that everything else is held constant when this change is made. To construct an estimate that we can use to test the theory, it is necessary to hold constant the other reform measures and isolate a pure capital market effect.

To the extent that stock market performance depends on economic conditions, the decision to liberalize depends on the economy's current and expected future performance.

Prospects of Financial Service Centre in Nepal

The study report prepared by Professor Howell E. Jackson of Harvard Law School and Professor William W. Park of Boston University contains two components. The study report begins with the two premises. Firstly, in order to provide a viable legal structure, Nepal must develop not only the substantive legal standard and regulation but also the enforcement mechanism to ensure compliance with those regulations; and secondly, that Nepal presently lacks the legal and regulatory infrastructure required to become an attractive and successful financial centre. It is supportive to the cause for setting up an International Financial Services Centre in Nepal as proposed by Ms. Collins & Associates Inc. of Boston, USA.

Professor Jackson has suggested three options for overcoming the deficiency of Nepal's legal system required for the establishment of an attractive and successful International Centre. The first option is to establish a unique Nepalese legal and regulatory structure (the indigenous model), the second is to adopt an existing foreign legal and regulatory structure for application in Nepal (the domesticated foreign model) and the third, and the most preferred option by him, is the selection of one or more established laws and regulatory systems and incorporate those systems by reference directly into Nepali law. He calls this third option the Selective Incorporation of Foreign Legal System.

Three ways of incorporating foreign regulations into domestic laws have been suggested: (i) the incorporation of foreign regulation as a screening device, (ii) the incorporation of foreign regulation into domestic laws as a complete or near-complete substitute for domestic regulation and (iii) the incorporation of foreign regulatory structure through the contractual choice of the legal provision.

Investment Environment in Nepal

The Foreign Investment Advisory Services (FIAS) has analyzed the environment for investment in the sectors of electricity, telecommunication, transportation and water supply based on the Nepal government's intention to attract private investment in these sectors. The report prepared by the FIAS team is based on the review of the legal and institutional arrangements in the various infrastructure sectors and the response received from the key government representatives, senior executives of the major infrastructure projects as well as private investors interested in infrastructure projects.

The FIAS report examines the present environment for private sector investors in infrastructure, pointing out the major impediments to the stronger private sector involvement. The political and administrative instability, lack of consistent planning, lack of effective institutional support in designing and developing of private sector infrastructure projects, reliance on unsolicited proposals, difficulty in obtaining commercial lending the lack of government support arrangements, etc. have been identified as major impediments to private sector involvement in infrastructure development.

Three major problems can be pointed out as impediments to private sector involvement in infrastructure development, (Paudel, 2010).

1. The government's heavy reliance on investors' initiation to develop projects except in the telecommunication sector in which the new regulation prescribes a competitive tendering process among the interested parties,
2. Lack of an appropriate strategy that establishes private sector investment as the preferred option for the development of infrastructure project; and lack of matching a procedural and institutional structure designed to attract as many interested investors as possible. The present passive approach by the government carries the danger of not making the use of the private financing option to the extent possible, and
3. Lack of a proactive and strategic approach to the involvement of private investment in infrastructure. The government is treating private sector development participation as the last resort means of financing a project.

The Foreign Investment Advisory Services (FIAS) has advised the government to give up the present practice of introducing tax benefit as a strategy for attracting foreign investment in infrastructure projects. Since the private infrastructure projects seem to be more location independent, the general availability of benefits such as tax holding will generally not create attraction to investors. Instead of tax incentive, the government should focus on providing support to alleviate the specific risk element burdening the individual project.

FIAS recommends that the government should develop a more comprehensive strategy across all infrastructure sectors integrating the private financing option into the government's overall development efforts to make better use of private financing, and specially foreign direct investment. More specifically the following course of action has been suggested: (i) the government should adopt a comprehensive capital expenditure planning procedure in which private financing is explicitly considered and analyzed. The process should be driven by the potential for commercial viability. Such projects should be taken off from the public sector priority list. Different alternatives should be explored to make the project commercially viable, which do not seem otherwise commercially viable; (ii) the model of the Electricity Development Centre (EDC) may be adopted with required modification to strengthen institutional capacity to handle a private infrastructure project. The process of developing the private sector project could be strengthened if EDC were to be formally involved in all major steps of the process, including the project identification, the preparation of feasibility study and tender documentation; and the negotiation of crucial element such as power purchase agreements. In establishing EDC as a key authority responsible for the implementation of private infrastructure projects across all sectors, while its focus should remain on electricity sector given its tremendous potential. Other sectors could benefit in this way from the skills and expertise available. A key requirement is that such an agency should be politically independent to function as an effective and neutral advisory body to the government as a whole. It needs to enhance its capacity by hiring financial and legal experts; (iii) the government should make much more use of competitive tendering techniques. It would limit the danger of corruption allegations by challenging the awards of a project and improve the number of structure of private infrastructure projects. In some cases when the specific project structure is less clear or in which indigenous proposals by private sector experts are required, unsolicited proposals might still remain the most appropriate approach. Ultimately, these proposals may be converted into competitive tenders by paying the proponent in case he could not win in the competitive award process; (iv) the government should develop a more proactive approach to support the private infrastructure project. The support may take the form of the service/product guarantee and/or a specific support to individual projects to enhance their commercial viability. Possibly, even minor contribution from budget or donor sources might be sufficient to structure a project in such a way that it becomes commercially viable.

Recently, Investment Board Nepal has been established to initiate the bigger projects. Through the Investment Board Nepal Detail Project Report, of the few of the bigger project including Upper Karnali Hydropowr Project with the participation of Indian GMR Company has been finalized and signed.

Despite of above development and investment opportunities, the existing legal framework and institutional set-up in Nepal is not conducive to the overall private sector development and thus there is an urgent need for reformation. The following are the major observations in this area.

1. The legal framework required for the overall private sector development is inadequate. In some areas the existing legislation is redundant, while in some important areas there are no appropriate statutes and regulations, in some areas there is a hiatus between different types of legislation, whereas in some areas the existing legislation is not up to the international standards;
2. There is a lack of effective and appropriate institutional arrangement for the enforcement of existing legislation dealing with regulatory, disciplining, disclosure and corporate governance mechanism;
3. The status of the enforcement of legislation relating to the redress for grievances of the investing public in the matter of financial irregularities, malpractices and capital market operation is very poor; and

4. The mechanism for the settlement of commercial and business disputes and the issues relating to privatization and liberalization in general is inefficient, outdated, dilatory and highly unpredictable.

Way Forward for the Overall Private Sector Development and Investment in Nepal

The remedial measures for the above problems can be classified into the following major categories:

A. Reformation of the existing legal framework conducive to private sector development which matches the international standards.
B. Establishment of some new institutions and strengthening the capability of the existing institutions to ensure effective enforcement; and supervision of the regulatory measures under the legislation for the efficient operation of the capital market, financial system, implementation of the infrastructure projects; and smooth operation of private sector development activities in general.
C. The government initiation of the competitive tendering system while awarding infrastructure projects in the private sector; and the accept once of the direct or contingent financial responsibility to support commercial credibility of a specific infrastructure project which is not otherwise commercially viable.
D. Appropriate training for staffs of different regulatory institutions and for professionals– such as judges, lawyers etc involved in the dispute settlement process.

Institutional Mechanism for Private Sector Development

The institutional mechanism for the effective enforcement of law is more important than the enactment of new law. Lack of an appropriate and effective institutional mechanism for enforcement of existing laws and regulations has been identified as one of the major impediments to private sector development in Nepal. It has two aspects. Firstly, in some areas there are institutions but these are not effective due to the lack of required legal authority, trained manpower and physical facilities. Secondly, in some areas there is no appropriate and effective institutional mechanism in place to enforce certain legislation. For example, there is no effective institutional mechanism to develop infrastructure projects to be financed by private sector fund; and to supervise the enforcement of regulation applicable to non-banking financial transactions. For the purpose of remedying this deficiency, there is an urgent need to establish some institutions at the same time. The One-Window Committee within the Department of Industries should also be given equal importance in strengthening the capabilities of the existing institutions such as the Securities Board, NEPSE, the Nepal Rastra Bank, the Office of the Company Registrar, (Paudel, 2007).

a. One Window Committee

The existing Industrial Enterprises Act 2049 has the provision of a One Window Committee. But the way it is functioning shows that it is not serving its purpose. There is an urgent need for its strengthening, clear-cut definition of its authority and the bindingness of its decisions on other government offices. The Committee may be developed into an Investment Centre having its final legal authority in the matter of granting all types of concessions, benefits and facilities under the Foreign Investment and Technology

Transfer Act 2049 and the Industrial Enterprise Act 2049. Its decision should be binding on the rest of the government offices for the aforementioned purposes.

b. Company Registrar/Company Law Board

1. The Office of Company Registrar at present registers the companies, receives annual reports from companies and grants permission to increase capital; and related amendments to articles and memorandum of association of the companies registered with it. It does not keep the follow-up of whether the company has filed the annual reports; held on annual general meeting or conducted proper accounting and auditing of the company's books and accounts. Due to this, the investors are left to the mercy of majority shareholders controlling the management.
2. The role of the Company Registrar requires massive restructuring. Its responsibility and accountability need to be clearly defined. The authority to register the charges of all types of movable assets should be given to the Office of Company Registrar. The Registrar should be vested with the clear cut authority to prosecute all types of defaulters under the Company Act; and the authority to adjudicate the matter of imposition penalty should be vested in the Commercial Court. The present system of the registration of mortgage of immovable assets in the respective District Revenue Office should continue.

c. Nepal Securities Exchange Limited (NEPSE)

1. As an strategy for providing the foundation for building of public confidence in the stock exchange, the ownership and the governance, the pattern of the existing NEPSE should be changed. A highly desirable option would be to privatize it at an early stage of market development. It can be done in two stages. Privatize the Board of Directors as the first step towards the gradual privatization of NEPSE. The new Board of Directors of NEPSE should develop, for the submission to the government, a plan for the proposed ownership, operation, funding and management of NEPSE under the proposed private ownership. The plan should also contain appropriate organizational structure of NEPSE. Such a privatized Board of Director would be constituted by the majority of members representing the private sector (non-member users of the exchange facility such as issuers and investors). The representation of the public should also be ensured in the Board. Such public representation could be drawn from a broad range of professionals and organizations, academics, associations of financial analysts, institutional investors, etc.
2. NEPSE should be developed as a self-regulatory body. Its authority vis a vis the Securities Board should be clearly defined to remove duplication of authority. The effective self- regulation of NEPSE requires vesting some specific authorities with it, such as (i) the authority to enforce members' compliance with laws and regulations and NEPSE's own rules, (ii) governing structure that reflects the public interest and provides fair representation to its members, (iii) the access to membership based on competency and financial responsibility, (iv) the authority to frame by-laws that are adequate to protect investors and facilitate the efficient execution of securities transactions, (v) the authority to fix fees, dues and other charges that are reasonable and allocated equitably among members, issuers and other users of its facilities, (vi) the authority to impose sanctions on violations of the rules and regulations it is charged to enforce subject to a fair disciplinary procedure,

(vii) the authority and resources for staff training in both regulation and operational matters and to design and implement investor education programs.

d. Securities Board

1. The Securities Board should, in general, have full and final regulating, supervisory and enforcement authority over the capital market operation under the new Securities Exchange Act. The existing physical facilities and human resources capabilities should be enhanced to commensurate to its responsibilities and authorities.
2. The authority of the Securities Board should include among others: (i) anticipatory power for the protection of investors, (ii) power to step in on the insolvency of a registered person and take over the business, to close up operations and to transfer remaining business to another registered person, (iii) sufficient and detailed investigatory powers, (iv) power to establish an inquiry and disciplinary process in respect of contravention by registered persons and to prosecute the violation of securities law before the court of competent jurisdiction, (v) power to impose conditions on the certificate of any registered person after initial registration, (vi) power to enter into the memorandum of understanding with the Nepal Rastra Bank to determine their respective supervisory responsibilities over commercial banks and finance companies registered to conduct any form of services business.

Empowering the Corporate Governance

The problems of corporate governance in Nepal is directly related to factors such as the lack of proper accounting and auditing standards; inadequate legal provision requiring disclosure and transparency in corporate governance; lack of effective remedy against the defaulting directors and auditors responsible for non-disclose and false-certification etc. This problem can be solved to a large extent if directors of a registered or listed company are made personally liable for non-compliance with its continuing disclosure obligations; and subjected to a financial penalty which should be paid by the directors personally. Similarly, accountants and auditors not fulfilling their statutory obligation of reporting the true and fair picture of the corporate governance and disclosure should be subjected to a penalty. This requires amendment in the Company Act. Similarly, accountants and auditors should be made personally liable for their negligence in performing audits and keeping account as per the existing law. The accounting and audit standards for public companies need to be strengthened through the effective implementation of provisions of the existing Chartered Accountants Act, 1997. This may also require amendment in the Company Act.

BANKING AND FINANCIAL SYSTEM IN NEPAL

Over the past 20 years Nepal's financial system has become deeper and the number and the type of financial intermediaries have grown rapidly. In addition, recent reforms have made banks more stable. Still, access to financial services remains limited for many people in many parts of Nepal and it has been declining in recent years. Much of the past 40 years the Government of Nepal has tried to increase access to formal financial services for small business and low-income households.

The government has introduced directed lending programs for small businesses and low-income households. It has required banks to open branches outside the Kathmandu valley, created specialized wholesale and retail institutions, and lowered market entry to foster the development of different types of financial institutions.

The Nepalese financial sector is composed of banking sector and non-banking sector. The banking sector comprises the Nepal Rastra Bank (NRB) and commercial banks. The non-banking sector includes development banks, micro-credit development banks, finance companies, co-operatives and non-government organizations (NGOs) performing limited banking activities and other financial institutions such as insurance companies, employee's provident fund, citizen investment trust, postal saving offices and the Nepal stock exchange.

In Nepal the banking sector is one of the sectors which have been able to stand up the test of time amid the political instability in the country, and yet be able to be a most profitable sector in the economy. With the increasing problem in the nation, this sector has been able to prosper with less difficulty till now. But the growth of financial institutions seems to be slowing down due to the entry of new players leading to stiff competition. One of the signs of problems has been the credit crunch faced by the financial institution in recent months, so banks are looking for new geographic locations and diversifying the portfolio of customers.

Competitiveness of the Banking Industry in Nepal

Due to the growing economic competition worldwide, Nepal's banking industry is sharpening its tools to face it. The Nepalese banking industry has opened the doors of modernization. It is striving hard to increase its market share, attract more customers, and to diversify deposits and loans portfolio to capitalize the untapped opportunities. As we can see from the recent trends of the growing number of commercial banks, there is a significant increase in competition. This is due to the banks present in the same market catering to the same target group. Not only is the number of commercial banks increasing but also there is a significant rise in the number of financial intermediaries such as development banks etc. Due to the untapped opportunities in the financial market of Nepal, the government is looking forward for deregulation of few rules and regulations due to which banks are trying to be more efficient in managing their interest rate ceiling, capital adequacy and loan rates.

The new Act has enabled other financial institutions to operate the services that were limited to commercial banks provided they meet the capital requirements as stipulated in the directives making competition even more intense in the small market. Similarly, the development banks have also started providing the remittance service which is assumed to be the major source of foreign currency inflow in the country. Some of the mergers and acquisitions that have taken place in the past few years have also increased the competitive intensity of the banks. NRB has been emphasizing the increase in the number of mergers and acquisitions among the banks in the few years ahead so as to slowly regulate the flow of money in the economy. The increased use of technology by the general public has compelled the bank today to move towards internet banking.

With the focus on globalization, these trends have increased competition in the banking industry in terms of the opening of number of branches and becoming customer centric. Besides competition, these trends have led to the economic growth of the country by enabling the simple and specialized banking services to reach the sector-wise population of the country. However, the competitiveness in the market has given rise to the concept of market leaders, followers and challengers.

The banking industry is one of the vital parts of the Nepalese financial sector. The banking industry has stood as the most vulnerable yet most profitable sector in the economy in the Nepalese context. Despite increasing problems in the nation, this sector has yet been prospering with much lesser difficulty. As mentioned earlier, there are 25 commercial banks, which cater to the society with banking services. Commercial banks have gained vital trust from the public side. With the wide reach and wide diversity of services, it has become one of the most important sectors of the economy.

Nowadays people seem to be getting much more attracted to the facilities provided by the banks compared to the past. The demand for banking services has also been increasing, which can be observed through the escalating numbers of branches of every bank. Despite the weak economy, with continuity of effort, formulating plans and selecting projects, the banking sector has been growing for past many years. Hence, despite the unfavorable economic environment, tremendous growth could be seen in the banking sector.

Regulatory Influences

NRB is the apex body for all the financial institutions to imply the regulatory influences. NRB has formulated different laws, rules, regulations, policies, etc. that have an impact on every financial institution established in the country. For example, NRB has formulated a banking regulation to address the institutions interested in opening offices in Nepal. They are required to submit applications to NRB. NRB then reviews the existing competition in the banking sector, likely contribution to the development of banking and its status in international banking and then only grants the permission for opening offices for foreign banks.

Legal Requirement for the Establishment and Operation of Commercial Banks in Nepal

NRB has made the rules and procedures for establishing commercial banks in Nepal. The existing legal framework of NRB establishing a commercial bank in Nepal states that:

Only on the recommendation of NRB, a bank shall be established as a company with limited liability under the Company Act. For obtaining such recommendation an application should be filled along with the particulars as specified by NRB. Only after receiving the recommendation of NRB, commercial banks can be registered according to the Company Act to functioning under the Act.

According to the Nepal Rastra Bank (NRB Act, 2002), financial institutions in Nepal can be classified into the following categories (Table 1):

Table 1. Categories of financial institutions in Nepal

Class	Minimum Required Paid-Up Capital
A	Rs.1000 Million
B	Rs.320 Million
C	Rs.200 Million
D	Rs.100 Million

All commercial banks fall under 'Class A' category, requiring minimum paid-up capital of Rs. 1000 million. In the present Nepalese context, banking regulations have been formulated and regulated by the following Acts:

- NRB Act, 2002
- Banking & Financial Institutions Act, 2006
- Directives/Circulars issued by NRB (for prudential regulations)

Classification of Bank

Ever since the first bank was established, the financial needs of people have been growing. There have been many changes around the world in regard to the banking sector. With every instant change in people's need, technological advancement, and changing world economy, there are many functions that bank needs to perform. A single bank is not able to perform with all the functions. So in the course of time many types of banks came into existence catering to the different needs of the public.

The Central Bank

The Nepal Rastra Bank (NRB), the Central Bank of Nepal, was established in 1956 under the Nepal Rastra Bank Act, 1955, to discharge the central banking responsibilities including guiding the development of the embryonic domestic financial sector. Since their inception, there has been a significant growth in both the number and the activities of the domestic financial institutions.

To reflect this dynamic environment, the functions and objectives of the bank have been recast by the new NRB Act of 2002. Its preamble lays down the primary functions of the bank as:

A. to formulate necessary monetary and foreign exchange policies to maintain the stability in price, and consolidate the balance of payments for sustainable development of the economy of Nepal;
B. to develop a secure, healthy and efficient system of payments;
C. to make an appropriate supervision of the banking and financial system in order to maintain its stability, and foster its healthy development; and
D. to further enhance the public confidence in Nepal's entire banking and financial system.

NRB is eminently aware that, for the achievement of the above objectives in the present dynamic environment, sustained progress and continued reform of the financial sector is of utmost importance. Continuously aware of this great responsibility, NRB is seriously pursuing various policies, strategies and actions, all of which are conveyed in the annual report on the monetary policy.

The Development Bank

After the enactment of the Development Bank Act 2052, many development banks were established in different places of Nepal. They are performing under the Development Bank Act 2052, the Nepal Rastra Bank Act 2058 and the Company Act 2053. These banks are helping the people as well as the nation in economic development directly or indirectly. The major functions of the development banks are to finance and support for the development of the country rather than personal use.

The Agricultural Development Bank

Developing the agricultural sector of the economy is the main motive or rationale behind establishment of these banks. With the motive the Agricultural Development Bank was established in 2013 B.S. under the Agricultural Development Act 2024. These banks were initiated to improve economic welfare of people and provide loans and capital for the agricultural sector. This bank provides agricultural production loan, agricultural facility loan, small and cottage industry loan, agro-profession loan, loan to buy land and loan for agricultural graduate. Usually, there are two types of banks prevailing under the Agricultural Development Banks. They are the land mortgage bank and the cooperative bank.

The Exchange Bank

The exchange bank provides financial assistance for conducting international trade. It buys and sells the foreign exchange bills. This type of bank exchanges different foreign and indigenous currencies and transfers the fund to foreign countries. It provides facility to send money to foreign lands. It has branches and sub branches in the country and abroad. In Nepal, the functions of this bank are performed by the Nepal Rastra Bank and the commercial banks.

The Industrial Bank

A bank, which is opened to support the industrial field of a country and it's all round development and expansion is an industrial bank. In the context of Nepal, the Industrial Development Corporation can be considered as the industrial bank. Its major functions are: to open new industries; to expand the present industries; to provide loan and technical assistances for small industries opened in the industrial areas; to encourage the possible investors to buy and sell shares, bonds or debentures; and to support the overall economic structure of a company.

The Rural Development Bank

A rural development bank is established with the objective of uplifting the living standard of the people of rural areas by encouraging them to start the possible income generating occupation; by providing loan without security; and by providing necessary training and bank service. The rural development banks opened in Nepal have adopted and followed the system of the Rural Bank Bangladesh, in order to provide loans to the people who were deprived of institutional loan facility in the lack of security and guarantee. Hence the banks that are established to improve the economic condition of the farmers, laborers, masons, etc. are called rural development banks. Some of the rural development banks are the Eastern Rural Development Bank Ltd, the Far Western Rural Development Bank Ltd, and the Western Rural Development Bank Ltd. These banks are established with some fundamental goals for the equal distribution of the resources to all people and all regions.

The Savings Bank

A saving bank is established with the objective of managing a huge amount of capital by collecting the small amount of money saved by the people in urban and rural areas. The main purpose of this type of bank is to encourage people to save more and develop lifelong saving habit. Thus, by collecting the fragmented small amount throughout the country a savings bank collectively invests it in the sectors which are productive and will yield good returns for the investors.

Rural Development Banks (RDBs) and Microfinance Activities in Nepal

In 1992, Nepal Government, closely based on the Grameen Banking Model of Bangladesh, established two regional level rural micro finance development banks with the major share participation of NRB (66.75 percent and 58.5 percent), one each in the Eastern and Far-Western development regions. By June 1996, other three RDBs, one each in the other three development regions were established. NRB altogether has invested Rs. 195.0 million as equity into these five development regions. Establishment of RDBs is a major breakthrough in the microfinance sector development in Nepal. The main objective of RDBs was to provide credit to poorer households, mainly to women. The RDBs credit is provided for micro level income generating activities on group guarantee basis, (www.bwtp.org).

Problems and Challenges

NRB has always been playing a crucial role in following resources to the deprived and poorer sector of the economy through development finance policy. It has undertaken various policies on development finance including rural and microfinance to generate employment and increase production and income of the poorer people.

The rural credit survey of 1991/92 has revealed that only 20 percent households have access to formal financial institutions and 80 percent had access to the services of the informal sector. This shows two important policy failures of the organized sector: one is the insufficient infrastructure and another is the insufficiency of the existing financial institutions to deliver rural credit.

In this background, at least two immediate policy measures are needed to implement in order to make microfinance institutions viable, competent and microfinance-friendly. Firstly, a policy is required for continued support from the government in social mobilization and group formation, as the primary objective of the microfinance institutions is to help alleviate poverty. Secondly, it is important to create a wholesale fund for financing microfinance in the longer term possibly at the minimum interest rate. Reaching out to remote places and motivating the rural people are other challenges to microfinance institutions in Nepal because the country has a diverse topography and thin population density.

The efforts of creating the regulatory environment in the microfinance sector are an advanced step towards remedying policy on microfinance operation. This policy correction has established Nepal as a pioneer in the microfinance sector development in the world.

The major challenge to microfinance is how to make this industry viable, sustainable and profitable. Reaching out to the majority of people with micro and rural finance, and making the financing institutions viable, sustainable and profitable are two different aspects of microfinance.

The Reform Program for Regional Rural Development Banks

In 2001 the Government of Nepal and the Nepal Rastra Bank committed to a five-year restructuring program for regional rural development banks. This program included recapitalization of four of the five banks (equivalent to NRs. 163 million), reforms of the banks' operating practice, and progressive privatization of profitable ones. Reforms include introducing productivity measures for each bank, appointing executive directors through open competition, and implementing cost reduction schemes, such as for voluntary retirement. Under the restructuring program, 40-50 percent of shares of profitable regional rural development banks are to be sold to bank clients, while the Nepal Rastra Bank keeps up to 10 percent and the government up to 20 percent. The remaining shares are to be split among employees, other banks, and other investors.

As a result of the recapitalization and reforms, Western Regional Rural Development Bank and Eastern Regional Rural Development Bank generated profits in 2005. Improvements have also been seen in the 3 other regional rural development banks.

As per the restructuring program, privatization was completed for Western Regional Rural Development Bank in 2005. The bank is now owned by its clients (40 percent) and employees (1 percent), five commercial banks (23 percent), the government (17 percent), the Nepal Rastra Bank (10 percent). Although the privatization was successful, the performance of the privatized bank has not been very good. In 2005, it made a profit only due to the income generated by depositing its share of the deprived sector lending in other financial institutions.

The other profitable regional rural development bank, covering the Eastern Region, started its privatization program in December 2004. Under the program, the Nepal Rastra Bank divested all but 10 percent of its 67 percent share in the bank. Of that 57 percent, 42 percent is allocated to the bank's clients, 5 percent to its employees, and 10 percent to the public. It is not known when the program will be completed.

Divestment of shares from the regional rural development bank is an important step toward increasing private sector involvement in the microfinance sector. Still, as a token of its commitment to the sector, the Nepal Rastra Bank continued to hold 10 percent equity in all five banks, even after their privatization.

Between 1999 and 2005, the average number of inhabitants per branch rose from 36100 to 54000. Although every district has at least one bank branch, access is skewed toward the Central Region, where there is one branch for roughly every 50000 inhabitants compared with one for every 111000 in the Mid-Western Region. This regional disparity is mainly due to the fact that private commercial banks are concentrated in the Central Region, which contains 46 percent of their branches.

Private banks offer far better services than public banks. Many branches of public banks cannot offer the same range of products as their private counterparts due to lack of computerization. They also have very long delivery times. Moreover, none of the public bank branches offers electronic payment facilities.

Microfinance and Services to Low Income Households

Nepal's formal microfinance institutions can play a key role in delivering financial services to low-income households. Yet many potential clients of microfinance institutions prefer to save with and borrow from informal sources. The microfinance sector's limited ability to serve low-income households is reflected in its narrow outreach, sluggish growth, high liquidity and low profitability.

The following points explain the unsatisfactory state of Nepal's microfinance sector:

A. A complicated geopolitical environment.
B. Weak technical capacity in key areas, such as accounting and auditing, strategic planning, financial analysis, and human resource management.

C. Lack of commercial orientation and slow professionalization– mainly because microfinance is often considered a charitable activity.
D. Distortion arising from the government's deprived sector lending program that generates high liquidity among many microfinance institutions, as these institutions are encouraged to borrow beyond their needs and invest these low-cost funds in other financial institutions.

Although often cited as an obstacle, Nepal's legal and regulatory framework is not a binding constraint on the growth of the microfinance sector.

Microfinance Institutions and Financial Services in Nepal

Microfinance institutions play a key role in providing financial services for low income households. Yet many microfinance clients prefer to save with and borrow from the informal sector. Financial NGOs and cooperatives, followed by microfinance development banks and regional rural development banks, are the largest providers of financial services for low income households. Still, many microfinance clients prefer to use the informal sector for deposit accounts and loans.

The reason is that informal providers offer products and services better suited to the needs of low-income households, that is, with quick availability and no requirement for immovable collateral. Low income households are much more likely than wealthier ones to have irregular incomes. In addition, many of their non-routine expenditures are for health care. Thus, they often require quick access to financial resources. Moreover, half of Nepal's low-income households cannot use their homes as collateral because they do not have required documents and because their dwellings are in a bad area, in poor condition, or both. Informal providers better serve the needs of such clients by offering faster services and requiring no collateral.

The limited ability of formal microfinance institutions to adequately serve low-incomc households is reflected in their poor outreach, sluggish growth, high liquidity, and low profitability. Although regulated microfinance institutions represent only the tip of the iceberg of Nepal's microfinance sector, they are broadly the representative of the sector, if not better performing.

Several factors explain the poor state of the formal microfinance sector in Nepal, including the complicated geo-political environment, weak technical capacity, lack of commercial orientation, and distortions arising from deprived sector lending policies. These factors affect the sector's profitability, which can be discussed under the following headings:

1. **Complicated Geo-Political Environment:** The geo-political environment of Nepal-- a mountainous country that has been experiencing conflict in past few years--poses significant challenges. The performance of many small farmers' cooperatives and financial NGOs and cooperatives has been severely affected by the political conflict and turmoil. The conflict has affected all formal microfinance providers, though to different degrees, depending on their location and ownership structure.
2. **Weak Technical Capacity:** Formal microfinance institutions suffer from limited capacity in key technical areas such as accounting and auditing, strategic planning, financial analysis, and human resources management. This weak technical capacity clearly shows the sector's growth. Most microfinance providers face similar challenges: lack of professionally trained staff in technical areas, weak internal control systems, no internal or external audit mechanisms, inadequate management

information systems, and low capacity for product development. In this regard, Rural Microfinance Development Center (RMDC) has provided crucial capacity building and "hand holding" support for its borrowers. It has limited resources for such activities. Significant additional efforts are required to build capacity in the sector– both for providers of technical assistance to microfinance providers and for the sector itself.

3. **Lack of Professional and Commercial Orientation:** Lack of professional and commercial orientation of the sector hampers its profitability, and many stakeholders still recognize microfinance a charitable activity. By design, NGOs do not have profit motives. In addition, they tend to have weak governance structures due to lack of a clear ownership structure.
4. **Distortion arising from deprived sector lending policies:** Priority and deprived sector lending has led to high liquidity and distorted capital adequacy ratios among formal microfinance institutions. The balance sheets of Nepal's licensed microfinance providers have extremely high levels of liquidity with investments and liquid funds accounting for more than 20 percent of assets in all these institutions. This situation is particularly striking for microfinance and regional rural development banks and financial NGOs.

Such a high level of liquidity and loans is the result of the deprived sector lending window. In some cases, because commercial banks are uncertain about the capacity of some microfinance providers they lend to, they ask the providers to invest these low-cost funds in fixed deposits. The microfinance providers earn a profit on these investments; the interest rate margin is usually 2-3 percent.

5. **Low Profitability:** These various obstacles translate into low profitability in the formal microfinance sector. During the period of 2005, 8 of 20 financial cooperatives and 4 of 47 financial NGOs recorded profits over NRs 1 million. Despite central bank's reform program, just two of the five regional rural development banks recorded profits that year.

Overall microfinance development banks perform better than other microfinance providers. But they also have weaknesses that hamper their growth. Their management systems have not improved in line with their outreach and experience, and their accounting and internal controls should be strengthened. Accordingly, microfinance development banks have not been able to keep pace with international best practices in microfinance.

Moreover, supervision of the microfinance sector is not robust: institutions that pose no systematic risk are supervised while large ones are not, and supervisory capacity is very weak. Out of 76 microfinance institutions that the Nepal Rastra Bank currently supervises, 47 are financial NGOs, which account for only 3 percent of the deposits of regulated institutions. Some of these NGOs have fewer than 200 clients. Moreover, as noted, the regulated microfinance sector only represents the tip of the iceberg: there are a lot more microfinance players about which little is known. In addition, the institutions currently regulated are not adequately supervised.

Microfinance Institutions (MFIs)

A microfinance institution is an organization that offers financial services to the low-income population. Almost all of them offer microcredit and only take back small amounts of savings from their own borrowers, not from the general public. Within the microfinance industry, the term 'microfinance institution' is used to refer to a wide range of organizations dedicated to providing these financial services. Such organizations include NGOs, credit unions, cooperatives, private commercial banks and non-bank financial institutions (some that have transformed from NGOs into regulated institutions) and parts of state-owned banks.

Clients of Microfinance

The typical microfinance clients are low-income persons that do not have access to formal financial institutions. Microfinance clients are typically self-employed, often household-based entrepreneurs. In rural areas, they are usually small farmers and others who are engaged in small income-generating activities such as food processing and petty trade. In urban areas, microfinance activities are more diverse and include shopkeepers, service providers, artisans, street vendors, etc. Microfinance clients are poor and vulnerable non-poor who have a relatively stable source of income.

Exposure of Microfinance in Nepal

Nepal is one of the poorest countries in the world, and the poorest in the South Asia region. Its poverty reduction rate is low. The main reasons for this low poverty reduction rate are: (i) low per capita income, (ii) concentrated urban growth, and (iii) high population growth rate. Out of a population of 29 million, 25% are in below the poverty line. Most of the poor people live in rural areas and have little opportunity. Microfinance can help poor people who have no collateral, but willingness to work and a desire to do some business activities from which they will acquire employment as well as income. Although many programs have been implemented for poverty alleviation in Nepal, only microfinance programs are seen as poor targeted and rural based.

In Nepal agro-based co-operatives were initiated in the 1950s as a first step in microfinance. Poverty alleviation rural based programs were initiated through the Small Farmers Development Program (SFDP) on a pilot test basis in 1975 by ADB/N. The success of the pilot tests in Dhanusa and Nuwakot districts encouraged policy makers to expand formal rural based microfinance programs.

SFDP is now being transformed into several autonomous, self-help organizations called Small Farmers Cooperatives Limited (SFCL) and these organizations are managed by farmers themselves. Other microfinance development programs, such as Priority Sector Lending Program (PSLP), Intensive Banking Programme (IBP), Production Credit for Rural Woman (MCPW) and Rural Self-Reliant Fund (RSF) have been implemented. After studying the pros and cons of various microfinance development programs the government began to rethink the delivery mechanisms of microfinance.

In 1992, the government set up two Grameen Bikash Banks as a replication of the Bangladesh Grameen model of microfinance delivery. The government also created a situation to encourage participation in the microfinance by the private sector. Subsequently, the organizations such as Nirdhan*, Centre for Self-help Development (CSD), Chhimek came into existence. Rural Microfinance Development Centre Ltd. (RMDC) was also established to support microfinance institutions by giving wholesale credit, initiating training and other necessary support to MFIs. MFIs are dependent on small savings from group members. As a part of development finance microfinance is targeted at specific groups of people, falling in the lower bracket of society. Financial services include savings, credit and other services such as micromoney transfer and microinsurance. These services were differentiated by types of service employment and income orientated objectives, target group, target community, target area and credit at home.

In the past decade, microfinance has been recognized as a particularly effective development intervention for three basic reasons:

1. The services provided can be targeted specifically at the poor and the poorest of the poor.
2. These services can make a significant contribution to the socio-economic status of the targeted community.
3. The institutions that deliver these services can develop, within a few years, into sustainable organizations with steadily growing outreach. In this context, it is important to make a couple of distinctions:
   a. Microfinance is more than the provision of credit. It involves the provision of other financial services (most usually savings and insurance) and recognizing that even the poor have a variety of needs, not just credit.
   b. Securing sustainable access to microfinance for low-income communities involves building (or reforming) microfinance institutions- not just the delivery of time-bound microfinance programs (such as offering short-term revolving funds).

In Nepal there are a wide range of institutions active in the microfinance sector, each with its own way of going about the task of making financial services accessible to the poor. Some writers distinguish between the so-called informal and formal sectors, but given that many of the informal organizations are in fact registered societies, the preferred terms to use are community-based sector and institutional sector.

The Regulatory Status of Microcredit Institutions

Microcredit institutions are regulated by various laws, such as the Nepal Rastra Bank Act (2002), the Agriculture Development Act (1967), the Cooperative Act (1972), the Finance Company Act (1985), the Development Bank Act 1996, the Social Welfare Act (1991), the Company Act (1947), the Financial Intermediary Act (1998) and the Insurance Act. It appears to be over regulated but in reality the situation is just the opposite. There is some difficulty to regulate all microcredit institutions because there are many MFIs established under different acts doing microfinance activities. The ultimate responsibility to develop, regulate, monitor and supervise is of NRB. NRB had issued regulations for the development banks which were engaged in microfinance, as a guideline to develop MFIs activities on 24th February, 2003.

NRB is going to issue an Umbrella Microfinance Act very shortly to streamline the regulation of microfinance. The issues were also discussed in the second National Microfinance Summit 2010. (Second National Microfinance Summit Declaration Feb 16, 2010)

Regulation of Microfinance in Nepal

The microfinance sector in Nepal is regulated by the Priority Sector Lending Program, Financial Intermediary Act 1998, Development Banks Act 1995 and Cooperative Act (1972).

1. **Priority Sector Lending Program:** The central bank (NRB) imposes 'priority sector' lending on commercial banks, which entails lending a certain percentage of their deposit liability to the deprived population. The ratio of priority sector lending has increased from 5% to 12%, of which, 0.25 to 3% must be invested in the 'deprived' sector, targeting at the poorest of the poor.

2. **Financial Intermediary Act 1998:** The NGOs providing microfinance services are registered under the Financial Intermediary Act 1998, which provides a limited banking license to NGOs. To date, fourty seven NGOs are registered under this Act and providing financial services.
3. **Development Banks Act 1995:** The two apex organizations as well as five Regional Micro finance Rural Development Banks (RRDBs) and four private rural microfinance banks are registered under Development Bank Act 1995. This Act was merged under Bank and Financial Institution Ordinance (BAFIO)-2004.
4. **Cooperative Act:** Cooperatives are regulated by the Cooperative Act and supervised by the Ministry of Agriculture, Department of Cooperatives. Out of various types of cooperatives, savings and credit cooperatives are providing microfinance services. There are 8000 registered Cooperatives of which 2700 are savings and credit cooperatives.

Regulation of Microfinance Institutions

Bangladesh is the first country in South Asia to start a modern microfinance revolution. Bangladesh and Sri Lanka made impressive results in reaching out to poor borrowers, mainly women. Even in the socially conservative country like Afghanistan, association and involvement of women in credit programs are accepted. The Indian progress in microfinance is based on the Self-Help Group Model. In Nepal and Pakistan, microfinance institutions are more aggressively regulated.

Challenges in Micro Credit Delivery in Nepal

Nepal has a varied topography at varied development stages, a mix of different cultures and different ethnic groups, which challenges the successful delivery of microfinance. The major challenges are:

1. Formulating a microcredit delivery mechanism that is better suited to the people in hills and mountains.
2. Successfully extending the outreach to the hills and mountains.
3. Redesigning existing programs of the formal MFIs to better target the poorest.
4. Unsustainable delivery mechanisms of government initiated MFIs and programs

Improving Access to Financial Services in Nepal

Stable, privately owned financial sectors do not necessarily create inclusive financial systems as evidenced by international experience. Hence, governments have a reason to be concerned about expanding access.

Although this is a relatively new area of economic development, general consensus has been reached on the following issues:

A. Every government is better placed to function as a facilitator rather than a direct provider of financial services. Facilitation involves creating an enabling environment and, if needed, supporting initiatives that can help private institutions increase access.
B. Any effort to expand access should address sustainability issues among providers of financial services -that is, help them profitably reach their desired market segments, rather than require them to lend to specific sectors or open branches in specific areas.

These principles have already been proven true in Nepal. Despite government efforts, regional rural development banks are the worst-performing microfinance institutions, and their branches remain concentrated in the Central Region. Meanwhile, as priority sector lending requirements have been reduced, banks have withdrawn from the sector, and despite its high liquidity, the microfinance sector's loan portfolio is stagnating.

Priority sector lending, which seeks to increase access to credit by small business, is considered a burden by banks. Almost 40 years after such lending was introduced, banks are reducing it, as the Nepal Rastra Bank lowers requirements for it. Banks perceive priority sector lending as a sort of annual tax that they must pay to do business, as they are not equipped with the right products, procedures, and lending technologies to serve small business profitably.

Public banks are struggling with negative equity, and profitable private banks have few incentives to seek out new markets or develop product for new market segments. If left to their own devices, banks would probably develop appropriate lending methods for small business, but only after a few years as competition increases in the corporate and consumer segments.

Capital Market and Regulation in Nepal

The main regulators of capital markets and intermediaries providing broker and dealer services for primary and secondary markets are the Securities Board, Nepal Rastra Bank (NRB), and Nepal Stock Exchange (NEPSE), a self-regulatory organization under the Securities Exchange Act, as amended. NRB is responsible for the supervision of securities market intermediaries (other than brokers) while the Securities Board is responsible for the supervision of NEPSE, the registration and supervision of stock brokers, and the granting of licenses to finance companies and others acting as issue managers, underwriters, market-makers, or portfolio managers. The Registrar of Companies, in conjunction with the Securities Board, is responsible for the supervision of prospectus and periodic disclosure documents filed by listed public companies. It should also be noted that the Insurance Board regulates the investment activities of insurance companies. Also, in many countries insurance companies have established subsidiaries to provide money management services or to engage in capital market activities normally provided by a securities broker-dealer. In Nepal, there is a need to establish a regulatory body to supervise private provident funds. It would appear advisable to establish an independent, self-funded, Financial Services Commission to regulate all non-bank financial services.

Under BAFIA, the Finance Company Act and the Banking Act; NRB supervises and regulates finance companies and commercial banks. In Nepal, these organizations are also permitted to provide investment banking type services (acting as underwriter and/or issue manager). In this regard, it is noteworthy that the risks associated with investment banking activities are quite different from those associated with commercial banking or the quasi-banking functions performed by deposit-taking finance companies. While such entities must also obtain a business license from the Securities Board to conduct capital market activities, the Securities Board is not directly involved in off-site supervision, or the on-site inspections program which is administered by NRB. In obtaining a license from the Securities Board, however, certain minimum capital requirements must be met by anyone proposing to act as an issue manager, underwriter, market-maker, portfolio manager or stock broker.

Barrier of Capital Market Development in Nepal

The development of the Nepalese capital market is important for several reasons. First, the primary or new issues market has the potential to provide a source of urgently needed long-term funding for the private sector. In order to avoid a mismatch in assets and liabilities, the banking sector should appropriately concentrate on short-term funding for business. Second, the creation of an efficient secondary market with prices determined in a fair and transparent manner would instill public confidence and facilitate the allocation of capital to its most productive uses. This requires that investors have access to accurate and timely information, improvement in the capital market infrastructure, and a more competitive environment in the delivery of financial services to issuers and investors. Third, capital markets can facilitate the privatization of state-owned enterprises in a manner that allows broad public participation and provides an ownership structure that will support long-term goals of the privatization program, including greater efficiency, transparency, sound corporate governance, good management practices, and increased revenues to the Government. Finally, strengthening the capital market could help reduce the current dependence on external finance supplied by international lending agencies. During the Inception Mission, the high cost of capital to private business enterprises was identified as a major constraint on private sector development. While there are many impediments to be overcome, it was widely believed that the further development of the capital market in Nepal could contribute to a more efficient allocation of savings, expansion of the private sector, and economic growth. This is in keeping with the findings of a recent IMF Country Report on Nepal. Thus, the IMF study noted that a well functioning capital market is important for Nepal to support the efficient channeling of private savings to investment, and facilitate the transition to indirect monetary control. While headway has been made through various reforms since the late 1980s, the capital market is still in an early stage of development with many structural weaknesses. At the very beginning of an emerging market economy, it is important that the Government create the right policy environment to facilitate the creation of a critical mass of financial instruments, issuers, and investors. The government can also create incentives for capital mobilization, remove impediments to private sector development, educate investors, and provide basic legal and regulatory reforms. Legal reforms must provide a securities law with adequate regulatory and enforcement powers to the government regulator. In Nepal, legal reforms are also necessary in order to harmonize the Securities Exchange Act with the Companies Act, the Banking Act and the Finance Company Act. Collectively, each of these acts, as well as the Provident Fund Act and the Insurance Act, has a significant impact on the development of the capital market, the securities industry, and institutional investment.

The following facts indicate hindrances to capital market development in Nepal:

A. Obstruction in relation to attracting foreign direct investment, mobilization of foreign as well as domestic capital, lack of investor confidence, restriction on foreigners to purchase shares in the local market, the non-liberal tax policy; shortcomings in accounting and auditing of non-financial companies.
B. Inconsistencies in and overlapping of securities related legislation related to public issue of securities and continuing disclosure obligations of public issuers and collective investment funds and the inadequacy of some key provisions in securities legislation.
C. Inadequate and unstructured existing Nepalese securities legislation to meet the international standard. There are provisions in the Act which should be relegated to the Regulations, and there are important provisions of substance in the Regulations which should have been contained in the

Act. There are also provisions that are duplicated in both the Company Act and Stock Exchange and the regulation which can create confusion and conflict.

D. The inadequate regulatory framework for non banking financial institutions (NBFIs), capital market activities including private pension funds, insurance companies, and bank trust services and venture capitals.

E. The inadequate legal provision to ensure prompt and complete disclosure on the part of directors and penal provisions for defaulters.

F. Absence of the securities investor protection fund for the protection of the investor.

For the capital market development, the followings actions need to be taken by the Government of Nepal and the private sector so that a critical mass of instruments, issuers and investors can be achieved.

Strengthen the legal and regulatory framework; encourage the development of full service investment banks and securities firms; link capital market development to privatization of state-owned enterprises; rationalization of tax policies towards capital formation and secondary market transactions; increase the quality and timeliness of information available to investors; improve governance requirements and minority shareholder rights; strengthen the capital market infrastructure; establish an efficient secondary market in government debt to provide a benchmark for the money and bond market; eliminate restrictions on foreign portfolio investment gradually; launch a country-wide investor education and awareness programs; and train regulator and market professionals.

Role of Non-Bank Financial Institutions in the Capital Market

There are two types of non-bank financial institutions (NBFIs) that are important to the proper functioning of the capital market. The first are securities market intermediaries such as broker-dealers, investment banks or merchant banks which are involved in the mobilization of financial resources through the capital market to meet the financing needs of business enterprises and the Government. They are in direct competition with the traditional commercial banking function of taking deposits and providing loans. In Nepal, these functions are currently performed by deposit-taking finance companies and commercial banks. At the present time, there are no full service securities broker-dealers or investment banks in Nepal. The second type of NBFI acts in the capacity of a fiduciary in managing the money of clients, usually by investing in financial market instruments. These include contractual savings and institutional investors such as provident funds, insurance companies and collective investment funds.

There are a number of NBFIs and market practitioners that are essential to the operation of a capital market. These include brokers, dealers, and underwriters of securities, investment advisors, credit rating agencies and institutional investors in the form of investment companies, pension funds, and bank trust departments. The functions of a broker, dealer, or underwriter may be performed by specialised securities firms, investment banks, or by diversified financial firms offering a wide array of financial products (i.e., universal banks or merchant banks). Depending upon the legal framework, regulatory considerations, and institutional arrangements, individual financial institutions (i.e., finance companies and commercial banks) are able to offer both bank and non-bank financial services. From a public policy standpoint, it is important to keep in mind that there are different risk factors and potential for conflicts of interest that must be taken into consideration in the regulation of such diverse financial entities.

One of the obstacles to private sector capital formation is the failure to mobilize the extensive savings already available for investment in the capital market. This pent-up demand could be released if legal and institutional obstacles to investment in the capital market were removed. Resource misallocation has been encouraged by practices in the insurance industry and in the administration of the Employee Provident Fund, which has contributed to excess liquidity in the banking sector and a shortage of long-term funds to finance private business expansion through the capital market. Also, private provident funds operate without the benefit of a Private Pension Fund Act, which would encourage investment diversification to meet fiduciary obligations and avoid conflicts of interest. In an appropriate legal and regulatory environment, private pension funds could be expected to experience rapid growth over the next decade. This has been the experience in both emerging and developed markets.

Structural changes and regulatory reforms in the Nepalese capital market would promote increased capital mobilization and demand for securities through contractual savings and institutional investment.

Information Disclosure Practices in the Nepalese Capital Market

In order to make effective, accurate and informed decisions, investors must have access to accurate and timely information. This is often not the case in Nepal. While banks, finance companies and insurance companies are perceived to provide meaningful information for investors on a timely basis, disclosure to investors is not adequate for many non-financial listed companies. It has been argued by some financial market analysts, leaders of private industry and independent authorities that a major reason why financial information is not presented correctly in disclosure documents is that the system of tax collection works against it. There are good grounds for believing this to be the case.

The lack of accurate and timely information is forwarded as an important reason why investors to a considerable extent have lost confidence in the stock market. In some cases, companies listed on the exchange may have ceased operations or at least are in non-compliance with reporting requirements to the Nepal stock exchange, Nepal Rastra Bank (NRB), the Registrar of Companies and the Securities Board.

In general, the quality of information available to investors in listed companies, or to financial institutions making loans to private limited companies or public limited companies is not adequate by international standards. Financial and investment professionals do not believe that they have access to timely and reliable information for the purpose of making investment or lending decisions.

The Nepal Stock Exchange should adopt appropriate policies, membership and fee structure to attract members outside Kathmandu, including introducing brokers that need not be present on the floor or carry customers' accounts. All types of securities firms, including broker-dealers, issue managers and full service securities firms should be eligible for membership. Following the enactment of the new Securities Law, listing rules should be amended to ensure that an adequate number of shares are available to public investors. Inactive securities should be de-listed or traded on the second section of NEPSE. Listed companies not meeting periodic disclosure requirements or holding annual meetings should be de-listed. Under the new Securities Law, over-the-counter trading in securities should be permitted. Also, the private placement of securities should be clearly defined. The tax system should be simplified and rationalised (i.e., equal tax treatment for dividends and interest on private and the government debt securities and bank deposits) to encourage private sector capital formation.

There should be no capital gains tax on securities transactions to encourage long-term investment through the capital market. Listed companies displaying good corporate governance practices should receive a lower corporate tax rate (i.e. 5 or 10 percent lower) than other companies. The Ministry of Finance (MOF) and NRB should prepare a paper considering options for the establishment of a secondary market in government debt instruments to enhance pricing efficiency and provide a benchmark for private issuers of debt securities. The government should foster the development of money and bond market for private issuers of securities. In order to prepare for privatisation, a level playing field in the conduct of the insurance business should provided for. Restrictions on foreign direct and portfolio investment should be reviewed with a view to the elimination of unnecessary impediments. The government should review existing restrictions on foreign portfolio investment to determine the speed at which such restriction can be liberalized. The time table for opening a local capital market to foreign investment should be established. In order to foster international best practices in securities regulation and enforcement, the Securities Board should join the International Organization of Securities Commissions (IOSCO). This should be done prior to the opening-up of the Nepalese stock market to foreign portfolio investment in order to facilitate international co-operation in enforcement.

Improve corporate disclosure and transparency. Strengthening public company disclosure by streamlining a regulatory process and granting clear authority to the Securities Board to administer a disclosure program and suspend listed companies for non-compliance. Amend securities law and companies act, as appropriate, to eliminate duplication of work effort and to transfer initial and periodic disclosure supervision to the Securities Board.

Amend the securities law to grant Securities Board clear enforcement power regarding disclosure by public companies and compliance with listing standards.

At the current level of development of Nepal's financial sector, banks and finance companies do not have sufficient power to demand high quality financial information from potential borrowers. At the same time, investors in the capital market in some instances do not have access to accurate and timely information. This has resulted in a high cost of capital to the private sector in the form of bank loans where spreads are traditionally wide. Also, the capital market has not been able to achieve its full potential in mobilizing capital for the private sector development or in the privatization of state-owned enterprises.

Furthermore, the accounting and information systems at many state-owned enterprises have hindered effective management of those enterprises and has slowed the process of privatization. In order to correct this problem, it is essential to improve the quality of information available to investors, lenders, and the government. In order to do this effectively, it will be necessary to have comparable disclosure, accounting, and audit standards for (i) listed companies, (ii) private limited companies and public limited companies seeking credit from banks and finance companies, and (iii) state-enterprises owned by the government. In the short run, improving information and disclosure may increase the cost of doing business but in the long run it can be expected to reduce the cost of capital to the private business sector and the Government. Indeed, the urgent need to approve accounting and audit standards was recognized by the Government with the enactment of the Chartered Accountants Act of 1997.

There is a perception that private commercial banks, finance companies, and insurance companies have a better track record concerning disclosure to investors than those enterprises operating in the non-financial sector. This may be due at least in part to the fact that the financial institutions are required to produce higher quality financial reports in order to adhere to the prudential and reporting standards of the regulatory authorities. Also, deposit-taking financial institutions are subject to on-site inspections by NRB on a periodic basis and on-going off-site monitoring. Furthermore, many of the finance companies and all private commercial banks are joint venture firms that are accustomed to the discipline of meeting international accounting standards. Finally, the financial regulators require that audited reports be produced on an annual basis by a qualified auditor. Failure to comply with this requirement could result in the loss of their business license.

Transparency in Corporate Reporting

Today the minority of shareholders and other stakeholders are demanding a much higher level of transparency and are no longer easily satisfied. The Securities Board must therefore recognize that transparency is necessary to create and protect share value.

Investors must bear the responsibility for understanding and analyzing the information they use while making judgments about risk and return. Should they not find the full information required they should refrain from such investments or hold only themselves accountable for their decisions? The answer to this question is yet to be identified.

Legal Framework on Dividend and Share Prices in Nepal

The consistent declaration of dividend exhibits the profitability and financial strength of the company. The dividend policy followed in between is vital for the company, especially those planning to be listed on the stock exchange. The steady dividend definitely assists the company to penetrate the stock market and generate cash through public issues. Dividend, to the companies already listed, is the foremost tool to measure the value of its share. It is not important whether the dividend is paid or not, but the declaration of dividend is the key word of whole gambit. The payment or nonpayment of dividend does not affect the creditworthiness of firm. The timely payment of dividend increases the attraction of investors affecting positively in the capital market, whereas the non-payment of dividend means the indirect reinvestment of the retained earning which ultimately is beneficial to investors.

Present Regulation on Dividend Policy in Nepal

Following are the relevant provisions made by various regulations and directives regarding dividend:

Nepal Rastra Bank Act, 2012, section 32 (1) (a)

The section authorizes the bank to put ceiling in the payment of dividend by commercial banks and finance companies. This we can take as authoritative provisions.

Nepal Rastra Bank Directive No. 13:

This directive requires certain conditions to be complied with by finance companies before the distribution of dividend as under:

1. that shares taken by the promoters are fully paid
2. That the share capital as stated in the memorandum and articles of association is issued to the public and listed in the Stock Exchange Market.

Finance Company Act, 2042

As per the Section 29 of the Act, a finance company, before declaring dividend, is required to transfer to the reserve fund, out of its net profit a sum not less than the amount as stated under:

Where the amount in the reserve fund is less than 50% of its paid up capital, then the amount to be transferred to reserve fund is not less than 50% of the net profit, and

Where the amount in the reserve fund is more than 50% of its paid up capital, then the amount to be transferred to the reserve fund is not less than 25% of the net profit.

Commercial Bank Act, 2031, Section 18

The section requires compliance with before the declaration and distribution of the dividend by the commercial bank as under:

- That adequate provision is made for the preliminary expenses not yet written off and accumulated losses of the previous years,
- That, provisions of loan loss, capital adequacy ratio, transfer of profit to reserve fund etc. are complied with the first.

Companies Act 2063, Section 140

This section contains the provision regarding the post declaration of the dividend as under:

Excluding the cases stated as under, a company is required to pay the dividend to its shareholder within forty days of declaration of dividend.

- Where any law prohibits for the payment of the dividend.
- Where the right to receive the dividend is disputed.
- Where the dividend could not be paid because of a natural cause.

If the dividend is not paid within forty days of declaration of same, it is to be paid with interest as prescribed.

Banks and Financial Institutions Act 2063

Banks and Financial Institutions Act (2063) has replaced the Agriculture Development Bank Act, 2024; the Banijya Bank Act, 2031; the Finance Company Act, 2042; the Nepal Industrial Development Corporation Act 2046 and the Development Bank Act, 2052. The section 46 of the Act requires the compliance with the following provisions before banks or finance institutions declare or pay the dividend to shareholders:

- That provisions for all preliminary expenses, accumulated previous years losses, risk assets are made.
- That the minimum capital fund as prescribed is maintained.
- That the statutory transfer to general reserve fund complied and
- That the shares appropriated for issues to the general public is issued and fully paid up.

Apart from the compliance with above provisions, banks or financial institutions are required to obtain prior approval from the Nepal Rastra Bank before the dividend is declared. The dividend should be paid only out of the realized profit. The notional profit, revaluation reserve should not be taken in account of the dividend purpose. Most importantly, the dividend should be paid only on the fully paid shares.

Government's Long Term Plan Regarding Capital Market Development in Nepal

The Tenth Plan (2002) document of the Government of Nepal has mentioned that the long-term approach of the capital market in Nepal is to avail financial resources for infrastructure development in the area including roads, electricity, communication, water management etc. by granting the opportunities to the general people in the share ownership of such developmental activities and institutions. The plan has further expressed its hope that the Nepalese Stock Exchange Market would be widened and broadened in such a way that at least five percent of the total population would be counted as real investors. The plan has also added that total transactions in the market share of institutional investors would be raised to a minimum of 25 percent of GDP.

1. In the Tenth Plan it has been clearly stated that the government is committed to create opportunity for a number of people to reap benefits from the return obtained by directing investment in income generating portfolio of assets.
2. The Plan has pursued some objectives to develop the capital market in the country. This include the following:
   a. The participation of the general public would be raised through the medium of the stock exchange in projects with the private sector involvement and the rate of return would be made available to them.
3. The quantitative targets set by the plan in terms of the capital market can be expressed as: The number of people investing in the share capital of organized institutions would be raised at least to three percent of the total population of the country.
   a. Organized institution to raise Rs.7 billion through primary issues.
   b. The amount of transactions in the secondary market to reach Rs.12 billion.
   c. The value of capitalization in the stock market to reach 15 percent of GDP.
   d. Additional 40 companies to be listed in the stock exchange market.
4. The Government of Nepal has stated that the following strategies would be adopted to accomplish the stated objectives of the capital market:
   a. The security exchange market would be modernized
   b. The regulatory system of the security exchange market would be made effective.
5. The policy adopted by the Tenth plan relating to the capital market:
   a. It has been stated that effective regulatory norms related to the organized sector and the capital market would be established as a measure to protect the interest of investors.
   b. Allocative and operational efficiency of the capital market would be enhanced.
   c. The stock market would be made transparent and reliable.
6. The Tenth Plan of GON has emphasized the following framework of the program and the implementation mechanism:
   a. One window system would be established for the public issue through the Security Board.
   b. Ownership change would be made instantaneously just after the dealing of security.
   c. A simple method would be developed for the share issuance and dealings of the public enterprises which have been privatized.

d. A permanent committee would be constituted encompassing the agencies i.e. the Ministry of Finance, The Nepal Rastra Bank, The Security Board, and the Insurance Board, for developing a healthy and competitive financial market in a coordinated way. This would ensure the development of regulatory agencies for future. The secretariat of the Committee would be in the Security Board.
e. Based on feasibility studies, stock exchange facilities would be expanded into other regions enabling savers of those regions to deal in such markets.
f. The regulatory benchmark would be established for the Security Board and the Nepal Stock Exchange.
g. Arrangement would be made to publicize procedures in different aspects relating to stock exchange activities.
h. A code of conduct would be in place for the employees of security market and also for the director, manger, auditor, advisor of organized enterprises and security dealers.
i. Institutional arrangement would be in place to impart training on several aspects of the capital market including regular study and research.
j. In order to check persons to take undue advantage out of dealing of securities and having access on unpublished sensitive information a sever penalty clauses would be enacted.
k. While privatizing, government enterprises shares would be sold through the Security Market to the maximum possible extent.
l. The Nepal Security Exchange Market would be privatized in the process of modernization and would be developed as a self-regulatory agency adopting the good governance practices.
m. The security deposit system would be established to save investors from possible forgery and fraud in security dealing and for the immediate ownership transfer system of the securities dealing.
n. In this issue, some provisions have been made in the Securities Act.
o. The investor's security fund would be established to save the investors against the possible loss through the security brokers or to minimize the loss and risk.
p. A legal system would be made to enable the dealings of government debenture and the collective saving program suitable for various investing groups.
q. Arrangement would be made to enable the dealings of government debentures through the security market thereby presenting the benchmark for returns and increasing liquidation.
r. Legal reformation and the development of an investment regulatory system, having security regulatory sectoral-right, would be pursued to encourage the incoming of contractual savings in the capital market.
s. Arrangement would be made for annually submitting 'compliance report' to confirm whether the securities issuing organized security dealings have complied with the act, law, rules or not.
t. The process of entrance and exit of security dealers would be made simple through the adoption of prudential norms.
u. The Necessary regulation of the capital market, market conduction, manpower development as well as educational training and information for investors would be provided.
v. The gradual automation of the dealings of the security exchange market would be carried on, on the basis of feasibility.

w. Developing procedures would be developed having the facility to conduct dealings from the local level and the OTC market would be established through the expansion of floor trading existing centrally.
x. The central deposit system would be instituted and applied to make the clearance of security account transparent and prompt as well as for the settlement, (Tenth Plan of the Government of Nepal, 2003-2007).

Financial Markets and Institutions in Nepal

A financial market is a market in which financial assets (securities) such as stocks and bonds can be purchased or sold. Financial markets facilitate financing and investing by households, firms, and government agencies. The main participants in financial market transactions are households, business (including financial institutions), and governments that purchase or sell financial assets. Financial markets facilitate the flow of funds from surplus units and to deficit units. Those financial markets that facilitate the flow of short-term funds (with maturities of less than one year) are known as money markets, while those that facilitate the flow of long-term funds are known as capital markets. Securities with a maturity of one year or less are called money market securities, whereas securities with the maturity of more than one year are called capital market securities. Money market securities generally have a higher degree of liquidity (can be liquidated easily without a loss of value). However, capital market securities are typically expected to generate a higher annualized return to investors.

The Securities Board, NRB, and NEPSE are the main institutions regulating capital markets and intermediaries. Under the Finance Company Act and the Banking Act, frequent supervision of finance companies and commercial banks is performed by NRB. While the responsibility of Securities Board is to supervise the activities of NEPSE, the registration and supervision of stockbrokers, and the granting of licenses to finance companies and others acting as an issue manager, underwriter, market-maker, or portfolio manager. Under the Securities Investment Trust Act of 1997, the Securities Board is also responsible for the registration and supervision of investment funds. The Registrar of companies, in conjunction with the Securities Board, is responsible for the supervision of prospectus and periodic disclosure documents filed by listed public companies. The Insurance Board of Nepal regulates the investment activities of insurance companies.

Nepal Rastra Bank (NRB) as a Capital Market Regulator

Under the current regulatory scheme, the supervision of finance companies and commercial banks acting as a underwriter, issue manager, market-maker or portfolio manager are supervised by NRB, which includes the administration of prudential standards, financial reporting, off-site monitoring, and on-site inspections for compliance with applicable rules and regulations. NRB is also responsible for the overall supervision of commercial banks and finance companies, including their activities in the markets for treasury bills and government securities. Since, finance companies and banks are permitted to underwrite the securities of private issuers, the central bank plays a significant role in the supervision of the establishment of prudential standards, intermediaries engaged in investment banking (issue managers and underwriters) and other capital market activities. At the present time, the Securities Board does not participate in the NRB's program to inspect and monitor the financial conditions of finance companies and commercial banks that are licensed to conduct capital market activities (GMA Capital Market Ltd., 2000) .

Securities Board Nepal as a Regulator of the Capital Market

The Securities Board of Nepal (SEBON) was established on 26 May 1993 under the provision of the Securities Exchange Act 1983 (first amended). It was established with the objective of promoting and protecting investors by regulating the securities market. Besides the regulatory role, it is also responsible for the development of securities market in the country. The main objectives of the Securities Board Nepal is to promote and protect the interest of general investors, to supervise and monitor the activities of the Nepal Stock Exchange and other related firms carrying on securities business and to render contribution to the development of the capital market by making securities transactions fair, efficient, healthy, and responsible.

Currently, SEBON is focusing on improving corporate governance, improving policy and procedures to make securities markets more attractive to private and closely-held corporate houses, enhancing professionalism of securities businesspersons, and developing a clear regulation for merchant banking business. The other prioritized works of SEBON include increasing market access to investors by upgrading market services, promoting debt markets by developing a clear regulation for a debenture trustee, introducing necessary provisions for the transferability of rights, and developing required regulations for mutual funds, (Annual Report SEBON, 2007/08).

Major functions of the Securities Board, Nepal

- To advise the government on the issues related to the development of the capital market and the protection of investors' interest.
- To approve the stock exchange for the operation and oversee them for healthy trading of securities.
- To regulate and register market intermediaries involved in the primary issue as well as in the secondary trading of securities.
- To regulate public issues of securities including the mutual and trust funds.
- To monitor and supervise the securities transactions.
- To conduct research and studies in the areas of capital market.

Financial Institutions in Nepalese Securities Market

Commercial banks are the important financial institutions in the economy. They are the vital medium for monetary policy transmission. The stability and profitability of commercial banks depend on the sound management of their assets and liabilities. Thus, the aim of every commercial banks management is to optimize the portfolio of assets and liabilities with regard to its specific business policy, (NRB Economic Report, 2003/04). Commercial banks are performing the key role in the Nepalese securities market. 'Among the 56 companies classified under group 'A', commercial banks hold 19.64% of 'A' group, which is, 11 in number. In the FY 2005/06, out of the total paid up capital Rs.20008.55 million recorded in NEPSE, commercial banks hold 42.60% weight. Regarding the annual turnover, out of total annual turnover Rs.3451.43 million transacted in NEPSE, commercial banks weight has been recorded 78.12%. Similarly commercial banks have contributed 70.96% of total market capitalization value of Rs.96813.74 million recorded in NEPSE transaction, in the FY 2005/06, (Annual Report SEBON, 2005/06).

Finance companies are mushrooming in Kathmandu Valley, whereas, their presence out of the Valley is very thin, (NRB Economic Report, 2003/04). Among the 56 companies classified under group 'A', finance companies hold 57.14% of 'A' group, which are, 32 in number. In the FY 2005/06, out of the total paid up capital Rs.20008.55 million recorded in NEPSE finance companies hold 12.82% weight. Regarding the annual turnover, out of total annual turnover Rs.3451.43 million transacted in NEPSE the weight of finance company has been recorded 8.86%. Similarly, finance companies have contributed 5.17% of total market capitalization value of Rs.96813.74 million recorded in NEPSE transaction in the FY 2005/06.

As of February 2014 as per the report prescribed on (nepalstocks.blogspot.com), Nepal Stock Exchange has classified altogether 130 companies as ´A´ class companies at the country´s sole bourse. NEPSE has been classifying listed companies since fiscal year 1996/97 as per the Securities Listing Bylaws 1996. At present there are 230 listed companies in NEPSE. In the last fiscal year, 120 companies were categorized as class ´A´ companies. As per the bylaws, only the companies having minimum paid-up capital of Rs 20 million and at least 1,000 ordinary shareholders can be categorized as class ´A´ companies. Likewise, they should have posted profit for three straight years. Also, the book value of their share should not be less than the paid-up value. Similarly, only those companies submitting their particulars of business and statements of income and expenditure of the concerned financial year within six months of the completion of the fiscal year can be categorized as class ´A´ companies. Like past year, banking and financial institutions have dominated the list of the ´A´ class companies. Twenty-five commercial banks, 58 development banks and 27 financial institutions have made it to the elite list. Similarly, 14 insurance companies and three hydropower companies have been categorized as class ´A´ companies. The list also includes one company each from Manufacturing and Production, Others and Hotel sectors. Thou the categorization of the companies are done on the basis of analysis and performance of the company, some stock investors and analysts does not fully agree to this categorization method.

The Primary Securities Market and Legal Arrangement

The primary market allows issuance of new securities helping the issuer companies to raise funds for starting new enterprise or for expansion and diversification of the existing ones. Normally, securities once issued get listed in the Stock Exchange enabling securities holders to dispose them at their convenience. Attraction for investing in new securities is interlinked with the liquidity provided by the stock exchange. The primary market is characterized by the overwhelming presence of retail investors and a very small role of institutional investors. This may be attributed to the limited size of the new issue market and non-availability of risk financing and merchant banking type of intermediary institutions to support the growth of the market, (Kafle, 2004).

The public issue activities through the primary market are regulated by the "Securities Exchange Act, 1983" and the regulation and guidelines made under the act as well as the Companies Act 1997". The related regulations and guidelines are "Securities Exchange Regulation, 1993", Securities Registration and Issue Approval Guidelines, 2000", "Issue Management Guidelines, 1997", "Bonus Share Issue Guidelines, 2002" and "Securities Allotment Guidelines, 1997". Similarly with the objective of providing the public issuance related services to the issuing companies in a professional manner, a mandatory provision has been made that the issuing company must take the services of issue manager registered in SEBON.

The Impact of the Changing Capital Market Structure

The changing structure of a capital market has had some positive impact on the volatility, liquidity, and transaction cost.

Volatility

Volatility plays a key role in assessing the risk/return trade-offs and forms an important input in asset allocation decisions. It is widely accepted that large fluctuations in market returns carry important negative effects on risk-averse investors. Besides, they have important economic implications, especially for the overall domestic investment, and for the flow of funds from abroad. Volatility is caused by a number of factors ranging from technical or short-term to fundamentals. Several macroeconomic variables like inflation, money supply, interest rates etc. also affect the movements in share prices directly or indirectly. The market microstructure too wields influence on volatility.

Liquidity

One of the most important outcomes on the equity market, particularly from the viewpoint of economic policy, is stock market liquidity. The term 'liquidity' is related to transactions costs. A liquid market is one where transactions can be done with low transactions costs.

Transaction Costs

Transaction costs have a significant bearing on returns as they can substantially affect the national gains from investments. Transaction costs also impact volumes and volatility and reduction in trading cost could induce the investor to trade more frequently leading to increased volumes. The empirical evidence suggests that increased trading volumes by increasing liquidity results in reduction in volatility. Transaction costs apart from including explicit cost, such as brokerage fees, etc. also include some implicit components, such as market impact cost, clearing and settlement cost arising due to counter party risk, paper work cost and bad delivery, etc. despite the growing popularity of stock markets during the eighties and the first half of the nineties, the transaction costs were high due to physical movement of papers, bad deliveries due to existence of securities in physical form, less transparent method of trading, etc. Changes in the market microstructure, such as automated trading, dematerialization. Increased liquidity, guarantee of trades and increased competition in the supply of brokerage services and resultant reduction on brokerage fees have brought about a significant reduction in transaction cost. The transaction cost in India now compares well with that in the best markets of the world. Reduction in the transaction cost is an excellent signal of improvement in the overall market efficiency and capital market growth.

The Nepalese Securities Market: Regulations, Trends and Challenges

The development of the securities markets is part of the development process of the overall economy. All countries with effective securities markets have the opportunities of attracting foreign players thereby increasing the level of foreign investment. It is a pathway to increased foreign investment. It would not be surprising if we came to find out that the investment of German-based companies listed in the New York Stock Exchange (NYSE) is higher than that of the American companies themselves.

When we look at the security market of Nepal, the only security we can think of its stocks. Our security market is still at a primitive stage and has to be improved in order to develop the capital market of the country. Publicly traded companies do not only run efficiently with higher economies of scale but also providc a framework for healthy and disciplined corporate governance. This further enhances the need for development of the security market and strengthening of the capital market.

It has already been explained that the Nepalese securities market mostly consists of publicly traded stocks. Therefore we can analyze the security market by looking at the trend in the Nepal Stock Exchange. It is disappointing to know that the NEPSE index has been showing a downward trend for quite a long period now. Due to the lack of corporate discipline, many companies have also been de-listed from the stock exchange. The stock trade volume also decreased which implies that the investors' confidence in the security market is decreasing.

Security exchange regulations were initiated in Nepal a decade after implementing the Security Exchange Act, 1983. In the same year, The Security Exchange Board Nepal (SEBON) was also established to promote and protect investors by regulating the security market. Apart from that, SEBON is also responsible for the development of the security market. To get the investors' confidence it is necessary to make the securities market healthy, transparent and efficient and with this view the government has provided SEBON with various authoritative powers. To make SEBON's operations more effective, the second amendment of the Security Exchange Act has brought the security market intermediaries under the jurisdiction of SEBON. This has made it mandatory for the security traders (brokers) to register with SEBON before starting security business and to submit their statements of financial and trading activities.

SEBON has been supervising the stock market since its establishment in 1993. Its supervisory role has wider scope and extends from the maintenance of company transparency to the monitoring of brokerage firms. A company that does not fulfill the requirements placed by SEBON is delisted from the stock exchange due to the failure to comply with the rules and regulations of the governing body.

Actions taken against companies that do not comply with the guidelines are some of the measures taken to protect investors. In the same manner, SEBON has also rated the listed shares in order to provide investor with more insight of the stock market. Though in other countries, private companies do the ratings after a detailed analysis, SEBON has been doing this under the provision of the Securities Listing Bylaws, 1996. Under this law, stocks are rated "A" if the company:

1. Has been profitable for the past three years,
2. Has a book value of shares more than the paid up value,
3. Has submitted financial reports within six months of the closing of the fiscal year,
4. Has paid-up capital worth Rs. 20.00 million,
5. Has at least 1000 shareholders, and
6. Has floated shares to the public as per the Security Listing Bylaws, 1996. If any of these provisions are not met with, the shares are rated B.

Why has the security market not flourished despite these measures? The current law and order situation of the country, economic slackness, inadequate private sector development, and low level of internal savings have adversely affected the security market. Apart from this, there are many other factors creating hurdles in the expansion and development of the security market. Implementation of the corporate and financial governance project has also been delayed. The governance system would enhance the institutional capability of SEBON. Another important factor is the limited size of the market due to the lack of policies regarding the promotion of public issues. The modern sectors of the country such as telecom, airlines, roads, hotels etc. are also under the government and private ownership, which has further limited the market. Public issues of such sectors would create wider choice for investors. Lack of infrastructure, the backbone of a well functioning capital market, is another prime reason. Unless necessary measures are taken to develop the existing unutilized resources (like standard audit systems, investment advisors etc.) and to introduce unavailable resources (like credit rating agencies, e-trading facilities etc.), we cannot intensify the development of the capital market. Lack of institutional investors, and professionalism, concentration only in stock markets security trading only in the capital city etc. have also laid back the development process. Lack of coordination between SEBON and other regulatory authorities while formulating policies that affect the security market is further hindering this market.

A good capital market is an essential requirement to give a better shape to our economy. Thus it is necessary to take various measures that can enhance the development process of the capital market. All the above mentioned drawbacks have to be looked upon and settled to create a strong capital market. Stability in the political situation and a good law and order situation are essential for the growth of the capital market. The infrastructures to promote the stock market and other securities have to be improved. Market expansion to other cities to accumulate the savings from investors in different regions is also essential to promote the security market. Creating regulatory jurisdiction for public issues from various regulatory authorities to a single authority will also promote the security market. Membership in the International Organization of Securities Commission (IOSCO) could help in getting information and new development practices. Collecting sufficient resources and getting the membership in IOSCO are urgent needs for developing the security market in Nepal.

The Primary Securities Market in Nepal

Securities available for the first time are offered through the primary securities markets. The issuer may be a brand-new company or one that has been in business for many years, whereas in the secondary market, existing securities are simply being transferred between parties, and the issuer is not receiving any new fund. After their purchase in the primary market, securities are traded subsequently in the secondary market.

The primary market for securities is the new issues market which brings together the supply and demand or sources and uses for new capital funds. In this market the principal source of funds is the domestic savings of individuals and business; other suppliers include foreign investors and governments.

The principal uses of funds are: the long term financing of the investment in housing, the long term investment of corporations and other business, and the long-term borrowing of the government.

In a highly developed capital market by far the largest proportion of individual's savings reaches the new issues market indirectly via a financial intermediary. Moreover, most individual investors are unfamiliar with the new issues market and its institutions, such as underwriters and selling syndicates which serve as middlemen between the corporate demanders of funds and the individual investors and financial institutions which supply the funds. To most investors the term securities market is synonymous with the stock exchange.

Investment Banking and Broker-Dealer Services

The functions of a broker, dealer, and underwriter are essential to the efficient operation of the money and capital market. In Nepal, there are no full service securities firms or investment banks. Stock brokers are small in size. There are not many branch offices outside Kathmandu Valley. Investment banking services are provided as an adjunct to other financial services provided by finance companies and to a more limited extent by commercial banks.

In Nepal, the functions of a broker and dealer have traditionally been separated in order to avoid the potential for conflicts of interest. While well intentioned, this approach to regulation has resulted in a highly segmented financial services industry. Under the securities law, broker, market-makers, dealers, issue managers, and underwriting services are defined. Furthermore, the Securities Board requires a separate license for each of the five types of broker-dealer activities. Under the current regulatory framework, a broker may only perform the function of a broker and firms engaged in the other four defined categories of securities activities may not act as a broker on the stock exchange. As a result, Nepalese finance companies are able to perform the relatively risky functions of a market-maker and underwriter but they are precluded from taking on the less risky function of acting purely as a broker, buying and selling stock on behalf of customers. This is because the functions of broker and dealer may not be combined. As a result, finance companies have chosen to perform the function of underwriter rather than act as broker on the floor of the stock exchange. At the present time, the broker can only participate in the new issues market by collecting application forms from potential investors on behalf of issue managers in return for a commission.

The complete separation of the functions of a broker and dealer has not allowed for the development of diversified securities firms which can offer a full range of broker, dealer, and investment banking services to meet the needs of issuers and investors. Furthermore, the brokerage business is not economically viable as a standalone business at the present time due to the low transactions volume of recent years. Since a stock brokerage firm may not perform the economic function of an issue manager or underwriter, this has limited the ability of brokers to participate in the distribution of securities in the new issues market and has resulted in the artificial separation of the primary (i.e., new issues market) and secondary market in securities. As a result, the stock market is deprived of additional potential sources of liquidity. While full service securities companies should be encouraged to develop in Nepal, individual brokers should not be permitted to perform the function of both broker and dealer in the same security. This is necessary in order to avoid potential conflicts of interest and possible attempts at market manipulation. Thus only securities companies with adequate capital and appropriate regulatory safeguards in place (i.e., compliance officers and adequate accounting and information systems) should be permitted to perform the functions of both broker and dealer. The Securities Board should also require that NEPSE develop appropriate guidelines for securities companies performing the dual function of broker and dealer.

The mobilization of savings for investment in productive sectors requires a more competitive and innovative financial sector. Government policy actions should encourage the development of financial service firms such as investment banks or full service securities firms that will perform the essential economic functions of broker, dealers, investment bankers, money managers, and related capital market services. It is essential to consider the role of existing institutions in the financial sector along with the possible need for new business entities such as diversified securities firms that might provide a full range of capital market services for the Nepalese economy. Also there is a need to allow for the creation and licensing of introducing brokers to service areas outside Kathmandu.

Roles of Investment Bankers in the Securities Market

Billions of dollars worth of new securities reach the market every year. The traditional middleman in the primary market is called an investment banker. The investment banker's principal activity is to bring sellers and buyers together, thus creating a market. He normally buys the new issue from the issuer at an agreed upon price and hopes to resell it to the investing public at a higher price. Usually a group of investment bankers join to underwrite a security offering and form what is called an underwriting syndicate. The commission received by the investment banker in this case is the differential or spread between his purchase and resale price. The risk to the underwriter is that the issue may not attract buyers at a positive differential.

Stock Market Liquidity

Turnover to market capitalization and turnover to the GDP ratio are two main indicators of market liquidity. Increased transaction costs are believed to make the market illiquid. In developing countries capital markets are not competitive comparable to goods market. This is mainly due to market imperfection resulting from government intervention in the financial market, a limited number of market participants, mismatch of demand and supply of securities, etc, as a consequences stock market fluctuation is a common feature in Nepal. The frequently changing price effect is fully-reflected in the turnover and market capitalization value. The term 'liquidity' in the stock market is quite different than financial liquidity or economic liquidity. It says that not only the adequacy of capital denotes the market in state of liquidity but also the willingness and ability to purchase the securities is equally required. Furthermore, the promptness of changing hands of securities or converting them in terms of cash denotes the degree of liquidity. The stock market also imparts liquidity to securities holders. (Paudel,2010).

Liquidity is one of the important factors to investors. This offers an opportunity for investors to invest in long-term ventures, while the market also enables them to convert their securities into liquid cash before the maturity of the project. The liquid stock market makes the investment less risky and more attractive. It encourages savers to invest in long-term projects, because they can sell the security quickly and easily if they want to get back their savings before the project matures. Stock market liquidity is positively and robustly correlated with contemporaneous and future rates of economic growth, capital accumulation and productivity growth.

In terms of securities, liquidity may be measured by the size of the spread between the bid and asked prices, with smaller spreads suggesting greater liquidity. Furthermore, it is reasonable to assume that many investors would find more liquid securities to be more attractive, keeping everything else the same.

An efficient capital market is a market that channels liquid capital quickly to where ever it will do the best. In a general term liquidity is defined as funds or money available for investment or an asset is said to be liquid that can be converted into cash readily. The term liquid asset is used to describe money and assets that are readily convertible into money. Different assets may be said to exhibit different degrees of liquidity. Money itself, by definition, is the most liquid of assets; other assets have varying degrees of liquidity. Depending on the ease with which they can be turned into cash. For assets other than money, liquidity has two dimensions: (a) the time necessary to convert the asset into money and (b) the degree of certainty associated with the conversion ratio, or price realized for the asset. It refers to those assets that can be converted into cash immediately like banks deposits, treasury bills, national saving certificate, shares, bonds, debentures, gold, foreign currencies. The safeguard and the fair return on investment define the size of liquidity. According to various researchers and studies the money market is in the state of excess liquidity and the main challenge is to the utilization of available resources or liquid funds in a productive sector. When the fund freezes, opportunities for investment are minimum and limited, and it supports to promote liquidity. However, in Nepal there are opportunities and likelihood but no effective steps are taken. As a result, such capital is being more and more passive on the one hand and losing the hope of economic development on the other. As a result investors are in "wait and see" position. For example, the Taragoan Regency Hotel Ltd. issued primary shares of Rs. 160 million and Rs. 260 million was collected within a week. Likewise, the Hotel Raddision issued primary shares of Rs. 125 million while there was a collection of Rs. 710 million, which is nearly six times more than required. In April 2010, the Agricultural Development Bank Nepal has issued primary shares nearly of Rs 1 billion, and about 3 times has been collected. The aforementioned examples demonstrate that the huge amount of capital is seeking better investment opportunities. Furthermore, as a result of deduction in the interest rate by commercial banks, the public hesitate to make deposits. Since no better alternatives are available other than the stock market, the public shifted towards stock market. The price of stocks as well as the mobilization of capital started to increase. It attracted the general public to invest in the stocks that pushed the price further. Consequently, the prices of some stocks were overvalued due to some imperfect practices and market rumors. But, as time passed by, the outcome was the drastic fall in stock prices and investors hesitated to invest in stocks of companies by reason of such movement of the price.

However, a change in the interest rate on deposits alone cannot affect the price of securities. There may have various reasons behind. The market capitalization is increasing continuously along with the fall in the average rate of interest. It was due to the increase in the number of enlisted companies in the stock exchange. At present, commercial banks occupy the topmost position in the market. Investors are investing mostly in the banking sector because most of them are performing very well and distributing handsome rates of dividend to shareholders. The capital gain due to the increase in share values is another reason.

Stock market sectors systematically react to different stage of the financial and business cycles, as measured by shifts in the liquidity environment. The response of the liquidity of money market is negative with stock trading. The fall in the prices of stock facilitates liquidity. There is a relationship between interest rates and liquidity. The change in the interest rate affects the supply of money. If the rate of interest is high, the demand for money is less than the supply. There is surplus liquidity. If the stock market is well developed and the corporate environment is brighter, individuals shift from the money market to the stock market. Interest rates act as an important factor in making investment decisions. Liquidity is deeply affected by the interest rate. As the interest rate goes up, the market price of existing securities falls, and vice versa. This happens because the buyers of securities are attracted towards bank deposits.

Though liquidity is identified as one of the major economic problems in the country but no effective steps have been taken to manage it.

The huge amount of funds is being inactive due to lack of investment opportunities. A numbers of factor are responsible for mounting liquidity. The major points are:

1. Failure to mobilize the funds in productive sectors
2. The unavailability of physical infrastructure
3. Fail to achieve investors' faith
4. No effective demand of capital for the long-term investment
5. Scarcity of a favorable environment for both national and foreign investors

6. Unable to develop the sense of safety and security in the mind of investors
7. Political uncertainty
8. Ineffective rules and regulations in order to support long-term investment policies
9. No strong vision of government and concerned bodies

The well-developed and organized stock market plays a vital role in the mobilization of savings. The more liquid stock market encourages savings mobilization in long run profitable projects. First, liquid stock markets make investment less risky and more attractive because they allow savers to acquire an asset (equity shares) and to sell it quickly and cheaply if they need to access to their savings or want to change their portfolios. Many profitable investments require a long-term commitment of capital, and investors are often reluctant to relinquish the control of their savings for a long period. This problem is solved by the stock market due to the freedom of entry and exit. Second, liquidity in the stock also improves the allocation of capital and increase prospects for long term economic growth by facilitating long-term, more profitable investment. Therefore, companies have permanent access to capital raised through equity issues. Third, liquid stock markets also lead to more savings and investments by making investment less risky and more profitable.

Process to Obtain Membership of the Stock Exchange

The corporate bodies wishing to be a member has to submit an application in a prescribed format within the time specified along with the certificate of incorporation, tax certificate, Memorandum of Association, Articles of Association and the concerned Act, rules and regulations in the case of a corporate body other than a company after the incorporation and the projected B/S and PL A/C for the next three years, last three years' audited financial statements, if the year of incorporation is less than three years, the B/S and A/C of investment in shares of subsidiary company or investment made in its parent company's share capital, details of share investment in any other company other than subsidiary, the name, address, number of shares subscribed and the amount invested by shareholders having more than 5% of the share capital need to be submitted, (www.nepalstock.com).

Board of Directors

The Board of Directors of NEPSE consists 6 directors in accordance with the Securities Exchange Act, 1983. Six directors are nominated by the Government of Nepal and different institutional investors. Two from among the licensed members, and the General Manager of NEPSE is the Ex-Officio Director of the Board.

Capital Structure

The authorized and issued capital of the exchange is Rs.50 million. Of this Rs.30.41 millions was subscribed by Government of Nepal, the rest by Nepal Rastra Bank, Nepal Industrial Development Corporation and licensed members.

Listing

Trading on the floor of NEPSE is restricted to listed corporate securities and government bonds. At present, 159 companies have listed their securities to make them eligible for trading. Besides this, the NCM Mutual Fund enlisted its units to make them eligible to trade on the floor.

Listing Fee

The listing annual fee to be paid by the listed company is based on the capital of the company.

Review of Studies on Nepalese Capital Market

Bhatta, G.P (1995) has concluded that many listed companies in Nepal have high unsystematic risk or specific risk. He realizes the need of an expert institution to provide consultancy services for the investors to maximize their wealth through rational investment decision. Bhatta's major findings were that investors expect higher returns from those stocks which associate higher risk. The Nepalese capital market is not efficient, so the stock price does not contain all the information relating to the market and the company itself. He again highlights that, neither investors analyze the overall relevant information of the stocks nor the members of stock exchange try to disseminate the information. So the market return and risk both may not represent the reality. He further asserts that investors in Nepal have not yet practiced to invest in the portfolio of securities. His analysis of two securities portfolios shows that the risk can be totally minimized if the correlation is perfectly negative. In this situation, the risk can be totally diversified but when there is perfectly positive correlation between the returns of the two securities, the risk is un-diversifiable. Finally, Bhatta concluded that the negative correlation between securities return is preferred for the diversification of risk. Bhatta D. (2003) found that without proper analysis of individual security, portfolio security, the industry and overall market, it is almost impossible to beat the stock market. Generally knowledge about political, economic and technological trends are more advantageous. He further found that stocks had greater volatility risk than other investments. Stocks take a random and unpredictable path. Obviously the stock market is risky in the short term. In most of cases, portfolio management of listed finance companies in Nepal is not systematically organized. He further asserts that for the effectiveness of portfolio management in Nepal, the stock market should be developed, computer-based technology and information systems should be adopted, training and development program about portfolio management should be conducted. Bhatta further concluded that the most of the finance companies had enough unsystematic risk that means there is no effective portfolio management of listed finance companies. One of the major problems to manage the portfolio is volatility of different securities in the capital market. Finally he concluded that, for the portfolio securities selection in Nepal, technical analysis does not work effectively but fundamental analysis can make difference. Shrestha, S.C (1999) concluded that, the stock market liquidity is positively and robustly correlated with contemporaneous and future rates of economic growth, capital accumulation and productivity growth.

Tuladhar, P. (2002) reported that, most of the listed companies in her sample were quite risky and the return on stocks was fluctuating every year. She had further documented that some companies' common stocks were experiencing a higher rate of return at relatively lower risk. Shrestha, A. (2004) concluded that there is a positive relationship between portfolio return and risk (in most of the cases). Adhikari, R. H. (2005) reported that all the commercial banks' stocks were under- priced, so all the banks had stocks with good investment opportunities. He further claimed that investors could be benefited by purchasing such under-priced stocks of a banking group.

CONCLUSION

The access of formal financial services is declining in Nepal. To increase the financial access to small business and low income households Nepalese financial institutions start serving them in a financial sustainable manner and hence must exhibit the high level of financial and professional efficiency. Despite of severe problems in financial sector development in Nepal, government and regulators need to think about enforcement of prudent regulations and enhance the supervisory role. Government of Nepal needs to think of reforming prevailing legal framework so that Nepalese private sector can evolve and grow at par with international standards. The capital market in Nepal forms a significant part of infrastructure development. Legal framework of capital market development in Nepal requires reformation in major important aspects. The efficient capital market can only facilitate the privatization of state-owned enterprises in a manner that allows broad public participation and provides an ownership structure that will support long-term goals of the privatization program, including greater efficiency, transparency, and sound corporate governance. One of the obstacles to private sector capital formation is the failure to mobilize the extensive savings already available for investment in the capital market. Structural changes and regulatory reforms in the Nepalese capital market would promote increased capital mobilization and demand for securities through contractual savings and institutional investment. Perception of the common people in Nepal is that private commercial banks, finance companies, and insurance companies have a better track record concerning disclosure to investors than those enterprises operating in the non-financial sector. Hence, non-financial sector in Nepal need to exhibit greater operational efficiency and professionalism to make existing and potential investors aware and happy.

REFERENCES

Adhikari, R. H. (2005). *Risk and Return Analysis with Reference to Listed Commercial Banks.* (Unpublished MBS thesis). Tribhuvan University, Nepal.

Bhalla, V. K. (2008). Investment Management: Security Analysis and Portfolio Management. Chand (S.) & Co Ltd, India.

Bhatta, D. (2003). *Portfolio Management of Listed Finance Companies in Nepal.* (Unpublished MBS thesis). Tribhuvam University, Nepal.

Bhatta, G. P. (1995). *Assessment of Performance of Listed Companies in Nepal.* (Unpublished MBS thesis). Tribhuvam University, Nepal.

Kafle, D. R. (2004). *Towards Good Corporate Governance. SEBON Journal Special Publication.* Security Board of Nepal.

Mahat, R. S. (1981). *Capital market, financial flows, and industrial finance in Nepal* (1st ed.). Sajha Prakashan.

Paudel, N. P. (2007). *Financial Market and Portfolio Management in Nepal*. Kathmandu, Nepal: Wangmaya Publishers and Research Center.

Paudel, N. P. (2010). Nepalese Financial System and Investment Environment. Ratna Pustak Bhandar.

Shrestha, A. (2004). *Portfolio management in Nepal a case study of Listed commercial banks in NEPSE*. (Unpublished MBS thesis). Tribhuvam University, Nepal.

Banks and Financial Institutions Act, 2063 (2006), 2063 (November 2006)

Citizen Investment Trust Act 1990

Commercial Bank Act, 2031

Employees, Provident Fund Act, 1962

Finance Company's Act, 2042

GMA Capital Market Limited (2000). *Capital Market Development II Supplementary Report for the Asian Development Bank*. Technical Assistance to the Kingdom of Nepal.

Nepal Chartered Accountants Act, 1997

Nepal Rastra Bank (2003/04). *Report on Monetary Policy*. Author.

Nepal Rastra Bank Act, 2012

Nepal Rastra Bank Economic Report, 2003/04

Nepal Rastra Bank (NRB) Act, 2058 (2002)

Nepal Rastra Bank (NRB) Involvement in Microfinance. (n.d.). Retrieved from http://www.bwtp.org/arcm/nepal/II_Organisations/Supporting_Organisations/Nepal_Rastra_Bank.htm

Securities Board of Nepal, Annual Report. (2005). *Fiscal Year 2005/2006, Jul 4, 2005*. Author.

Securities Board of Nepal, Annual Report. (2008). *Fiscal Year 2007/2008, Nov 14, 2008*. Author.

Securities Exchange Act, 1983

Shrestha, S. C. (1999). *Stock price behavior in Nepal*. (Unpublished MBS thesis). Tribhuvam University, Nepal.

Tenth Plan, 2002-2007. (2002). His Majesty's Government National Planning Commission Nepal 2002, March.

The Companies Act, 2063 (2006)

Tuladhar, P. (2002). *A study on risk and return analysis of common stock*. (Unpublished MBS Thesis). Tribhuvan University, Nepal.

KEY TERMS AND DEFINITIONS

Banking: Any task related to bank.
Capital: Investment made in any project.
Challenges: Possible future threat and opportunities.
Companies: Any institutions registered under the company act 2063.
Development: Infrastructural and human progress.
Disclosure: Making public.
Exchange: Place where commodities and product change the ownership.
Financial: Related to finance.
Government: That governs the state.
Institutions: Any types of organized entities.
Market: Place where the buyer and seller can make exchange of agreement and products.
Nepal: Developing country.
Plan: Road map to accomplish any goal.
Problems: Prospective challenges that need deep care and address.
Regulation: Mechanism of ensuring good governance.
Securities: Long term or short term instrument of investment.
Stock: Investment made in securities.

Chapter 10
Financial Market Reforms in Nepal and Its Presence in South Asia

Bishnu Prasad Gautam
Nepal Rastra Bank, Nepal

ABSTRACT

Financial market is the backbone of the economy, hence is crucial for the economic growth and development of any country. The financial sector also entails the seeds of financial crisis that can spill over across the rest of economy. Though the interaction between various economic sectors is crucial, it requires timely assessment of risks and redressed. This chapter attempts to capture the sequencing and implementation of financial market reforms in Nepal and briefly examine its consequences. The evidence confirms that reforms do not only mean the institutional and policy reforms but also manifests in terms of increase in the number of financial institutions, expansion in the outreach of financial services and products in terms of quality and quantity as well as improvement in the soundness of macroeconomic indicators. Finally, it argues for the continuation of reforms and consolidation in the financial markets to make the system resilient in changing contexts.

INTRODUCTION

Comparing to its neighboring countries, the history of the modern financial market is relatively short. It starts with the establishment of Nepal Bank Limited (NBL) in 1937. The process gained the momentum with the establishment of Nepal Rastra Bank (NRB), the central bank of Nepal in 1956. It took almost 28 years for the second commercial bank, Rastriya Banijya Bank (RBB) to come into existence. The establishment of the third commercial bank, Nabil Bank Ltd. (previously known as Nepal Arab Bank Limited) took another 20 years. However, during the last 25 years, there has been a moments of growth in the setting up of new banks and financial institutions in Nepal. Consequently, the market nowadays is composed of 30 commercial banks, 84 development banks, 53 finance companies and 37 microcredit development banks (NRB, 2014c). In addition, there are 15 financial cooperatives and 30 financial non-

DOI: 10.4018/978-1-5225-0004-9.ch010

government organizations licensed by the central bank to perform limited banking activities (NRB, 2014d; Gautam, 2014). Likewise, there are some other contractual saving organizations (popularly known as other financial institutions) in Nepal viz., insurance companies (25), employee's provident fund, citizen investment trust and Nepal Stock Exchange Limited (NRB, 2014d).

This chapter is designed to enumerate the pace and speed of financial market reforms in Nepal. Main objective is to discuss the conceptual issues and context of financial market reforms in Nepal. It starts with documenting the rationale of reforms and continues with discussion of status and progresses made in financial sector restructuring and reforms in Nepal. It uses the information received through a review of literature, progress reports and websites pertaining to financial market reforms in Nepal. In addition, it uses the information received from key-informants connected with the project implementation and author's personal experience in the project. Another thrust of this chapter is to account and examine the evolution and imperatives of the financial market in Nepal during the last three decades.

The chapter has been organized in seven sections. After a short description on background of financial market reforms in second section, section three enumerates the reform modalities undertaken in the financial market. Section four provides a brief assessment of achievements and impact of reforms whereas section five deals with the issues and challenges of financial sector reforms in Nepal. Section six opens up the issue on regional context and finally last section concludes the discussion.

Background of Financial Market Reforms

In Nepal, a formal and modern financial institution, Nepal Bank Limited was set up in 1937 AD. However, the process did not get momentum until the establishment of Nepal Rastra Bank, the central bank of Nepal in 1956. Until mid-1980s, there were only two commercial banks and two development banks (NRB, 1996). The country's developmental needs required rapid expansion of modern banking services throughout the country. The NRB has made paramount contribution in the establishment and expansion financial development in the country (Bhetuwal, 2005). Nevertheless, financial system continued to remain shallow and undiversified. It encountered with episodes of distress. The banks set up under public sector ownership result in episodes of insolvency and required massive extent of recapitalization. Non-performing loans peaked as high as 60 percent of the portfolio (Booz and Hamilton, 1990). Until the late 1980s, Nepal had a repressive financial system involving various controls on interest rate and exchange rates, reserve requirement and directed credit, complex rule for money and capital markets as well as confusing and contradictory regulation and supervision (Gautam, 2013).

Nepalese banking sector gained momentum only after the initiation of financial sector liberalization since the late 1980s and early 1990s. The government and central bank joined their hands together and provided more emphasis on the liberalization of the financial sector. They paved the way for the financial sector reforms in order to raise private sector's confidence and participation in the financial market. Earlier reforms were aimed to remove the ruins of financial repression and promote financial market efficiency in mobilization and allocation of resources. It entailed policy deregulation, institutional reforms, introduction of prudential regulation and supervision and encouragement to a competitive environment in banks and other financial institutions. Insightful efforts were made to develop capital markets and encourage the growth of other financial institutions. However, As the financial sector was dominated by the commercial banks, it has been the focal point of reforms (Bhetuwal, 2005). Later, the Nepalese financial system witnessed a significant growth in the number of financial institutions. Consequently, the number doubled within a decade and by the year 2000, the financial system in Nepal was reasonably developed, diversified and enriched (SANEI, 2007)[1].

The NRB regulates and supervises the commercial banks and financial institutions operating within the country. In addition, it also supervises those savings and credit cooperatives and non-government organizations, licensed to undertake limited banking transactions only. However as elsewhere, the regulation and supervision of Employees Provident Fund (EPF), Citizen Investment Trust (CIT), Insurance companies (life and non-life) and stock exchange, is outside the purview of the central bank. The Insurance Board (IB) regulates the insurance companies, Securities Board of Nepal (SEBON) regulates the capital market and so does government for EPF and CIT (Gautam, 2013). More importantly, more than twelve thousand saving and credit cooperatives have been undertaking huge financial transactions; operate outside the purview of any close supervision. This poses the challenge for the soundness of the financial system.

Financial market contributes to pool and utilize scattered financial resources, reduce costs and risks, expand and diversify opportunities, increase the allocative efficiency of resources and promote productivity. Banks and financial institutions play positive role in mobilizing financial resources, identifying good projects, monitoring managers, and managing risk (Levine, 2004; Bhetuwal, 2007). It is equally important for fostering economic growth in the country through the intermediation of financial services (Demirguc-Kunt & Levine, 2001). It basically pools the resources from the savers (surplus units) and lends such resources to the borrowers (deficit units). Likewise, financial market creates conducive environment for transforming a traditional economy into a modern one (Vitols, 2001). As the financial market is considered to be the backbone of the economy, it is expected to be competitive, broad based, accessible and affordable for the general public. It should be structured on the strong base and is expected to comply with healthy norms and best international practices.

The financial sector reform in Nepal should be reviewed in an overall macroeconomic context as well as against the backdrop of the overall strategy of reforms implemented during the last two decades. Financial Sector Reforms is indeed a continuous process. It essentially comprises of policy and institutional reforms. The speed and pace of reforms basically depends on the macroeconomic situation and changing market conditions. The main objective of reform program is to ensure the proper operation of the financial institutions and its positive feedback in the economy. Likewise, other objectives are to protect the consumers and investors from financial abuses; improve the transparency and fairness in their services; encourage using crises management tools that are emerging globally as well as ensure that the financial markets are strong enough to withstand both system-wide stress and the failure of the financial institutions.

Major Reforms in Nepalese Financial Market

In the late 1970s and early 1980s, most of the developing countries began to introduce financial liberalization, deregulation and privatization in their economic sectors[2]. Nepal started reforming its economic sectors since the mid 1980s by first opening-up financial sector for the private sector investment. Financial sector reforms entailed financial liberalization, institutional reforms to systems, introduction of prudential regulation and supervision and revitalization of distressed public sector banks (Acharya et al., 1998). As the banking system dominates the financial sector, it has been the major focus of the reforms. Nevertheless, the ambit of reforms also encompassed development of capital markets, nonbank financial institutions, such as leasing and finance companies and micro finance. Though, Financial Sector

Reforms was initially started under the conditions of IMF's structural adjustment program, it was later continued to overhaul and strengthen the financial sector (Shrestha, 2004). The liberalization process gradually started to produce the results in the economy.

As the reform process gained its momentum, it improved the functioning of financial system by increasing the availability of funds and allowing risk diversification and increased investment (Acharya, et al, 1998; Shrestha, 2006; Bhetuwal, 2007). The reengineering strengthened the Central Bank's regulation and supervision capacity. Similarly, the restructuring of technically insolvent public sector commercial banks, namely NBL and RBB showed significant improvement in their balance sheet. Legal, institutional and governance were other components of the financial sector reforms.

Initial Reforms

The initial reforms in financial sector of Nepal was initiated in mid 1980s. The initial process of reforms proceeded with the implementation of financial liberalization program under the Structural Adjustment Program of the International Monetary Fund (Shrestha, 2004; Shrestha and Chaudhury, 2006). The process continued with the graduation to Enhanced Structural Adjustment Program of World Bank and IMF. In fact, financial sector reforms were implemented on a phase wise basis in order to address the institutional deficiencies resulting from closed and repressed financial system. Various macro-economic policies were modified and adjusted to facilitate the liberalization process (NRB, 1996; Shrestha, 2004). The process took some momentum with the opening up of financial system to the private sector and the Joint venture banks (with foreign collaboration) in 1984. It was followed by the facility offered to open the foreign currency accounts in commercial banks in 1985 (NRB, 1996). The central bank imparted freedom to banks to fix the interest rates (first, in 1986 with certain limits and then in 1989 without any limit) and lowered the statutory liquidity requirement of commercial banks. The central bank then embarked on implementing indirect monetary instruments in 1988. The major breakthrough involved the introduction of current account convertibility in 1993. The process was intensified with the introduction of auctioning of the treasury bills. In order to provide the regulatory and supervisory power to the central bank enactment of new act and amendments of existing acts related to the banking and financial sector including the Commercial Bank Act, 1975; the Nepal Rastra Bank Act, 1955; and the NIDC Act, 1960 were undertaken (Table 1) (NRB, 1996).

Table 1. Reform activities before 1990

Permission to open Joint venture banks in Nepal	1984
Permission to accept foreign currency deposits in Commercial banks	1985
Enactment of Finance Company Act	1986
Initiation of indirect monetary control and Open market operations	1988
Auction of treasury bills on weekly basis	1989
Deregulation of interest rates in the financial sector	1989
Establishment of Credit Information Bureau	1989
Commercial banks need to maintain capital adequacy ratio	1989
Amendments in Commercial Bank Act, the NRB Act and the NIDC Act	1990

Source: Author's self-compilation based on NRB (1996), SANNEI (2007) and NRB (2012).

The NRB gradually strengthened its regulatory and supervisory role, introduced prudential regulation and enhanced supervision capacity over the banks and financial institutions. Consequently, it provided commercial banks with the directives to maintain minimum capital adequacy ratio of 2.5 percent by mid-July 1989 and 3.0 percent by mid-July 1990. It also issued the regulation on single borrower limit, refinance policy and reserve requirements (NRB, 1996).

After the restoration of democracy in 1990, the country entered into a new era. Democratic governments that came into the power further widened the range and depth of open-liberal economic policy. In order to raise the confidence of the private sector and encourage them to participate and invest in the financial markets, the government along with the central bank provided more emphasis on the liberalization of the financial sector. Some other liberalization measures were also initiated such as, use of indirect instruments of monetary policy through open market operations and privatization of government-owned banking and financial institutions (table 2).

In order to improve the performance of Nepalese banking system, a study named "Commercial banking problem analysis and strategy study" popularly known as CBPASS was undertaken in 1990. The report that came in 1992 identified several operational and structural problems[3] including the extent of non-performing assets and capital shortfall in NBL and RBB. These two banks suffered from negative net worth and insufficient capital. The human resource management was found to be extremely weak with low morale and skills of employees, low pay scales and excessive union-activities.

The report also recognized systemic problems in Nepalese financial sector including; poor governance in banking system, frequent political interference, insider lending, lack of proper strategies, skills, international banking practices; insufficient supervision; weak financial and management information system and inadequate legal and accounting practices. Therefore, the reforms program was initiated and government also injected capital to these banks.

Table 2. Reform activities during 1990s

Major Activities	Year
The commercial banks were required to increase CAR to 3.5 percent	1991
The credit ceiling was removed except for government and nonfinancial government enterprises	1991
Opening secondary market for treasury bills	1991
Issuance of NRB bond to mop up excess liquidity	1991
The commercial banks were required increase CAR to 4.0 percent	1992
Nepal entered into the Enhanced Structural Adjustment Facility (ESAF)	1992
Commercial Banking Problem Analysis and Strategy Study report	1992
Rediscounting of treasury bills with NRB	1993
Introducing a full convertibility in current account	1993
Abolishment of Statutory Liquidity Ratio requirement	1993
Introduction of loan classification, provisioning and liquidity norms	1996
Definitions of core capital and supplementary capital	1996
Policy to increase paid up capital of banks and financial institutions	1996

Source: NRB (1996) and author's self-compilation.

Exhibit 1: Summary of Recommendation made by CBPASS
The KPMG Barents Group recommended following actions to be taken for RBB and NBL:
1. Support Government efforts to create an independent, commercially-run banking system and declare banking reform policies fostering sound banking system.
2. Upgrade Board, senior management and staff skills, capabilities and processes
3. Design and invest in comprehensive bank restructuring programs
4. Support and assist in implementing long-range plans to correct environmental weaknesses
5. Support central bank strengthening and independence and provide full enforcement powers
6. De-politicize and commercialize the banking system

NRB directed financial institutions such as the Agriculture Development Bank (ADBN) and Nepal Industrial Development Corporation (NIDC) to issue the debentures (in 1987) so as to augment their resource base. In fact, these financial instruments seemed to be the catalyst in developing Nepalese financial markets and providing with a new security instruments in the country. Not only this, regional and rural development banks were established in five development regions to provide microfinance services to the poor and the ultra-poor women (first in 1993 then gradually); finance companies to provide consumer credit, merchant banking services of underwriting and market makers. In addition, saving and credit co-operative societies and financial NGOs were licensed by the NRB to provide limited banking services in the un-banked rural areas. The development of the capital market took a momentum with the establishment of the Securities Exchange Center in 1994. The centre started to trade the corporate shares in its floor since 1994. However, there was a limited activity of other contractual saving institutions such as the Employees Provident Fund and insurance companies as they were essentially operated without any regulatory institution.

Two largest commercial banks (RBB and NBL) and two largest development banks (ADBN and NIDC) were suffering with various problems. They were technically insolvent and urgently needed restructuring program. Not only this, there were some weaknesses in the regulatory and supervisory functions of the central bank. Likewise, there were some mandatory government requirement for the banks and financial institutions. Despite of some improvements in the financial market brought by the initial financial sector reforms the banking and non-banking sector continued to encounter problems. There was a lack of regulatory and supervisory mechanism especially for microfinance sector, cooperatives and other contractual saving organizations. Moreover, the whole financial market continued to be weak, fragmented and inefficient even after the initial reform initiatives.

Comprehensive Reforms

World Bank and the IMF conducted Financial Sector Assessment Program in various developed and developing countries in 1999. It highlighted that most of the developing countries were still in the vulnerable situation as they were not complying fully with Basel core principles. Nepal was not the exception and was to be compliant to one core principle and largely compliant to merely 7 core principles and norms out of 25 core principles and 30 norms of Basel Accord 1988 (Lacombe & Olaso 1999). Moreover, poor risk management skills, governance weaknesses and other several deficiencies were found in the Nepalese financial system. Hence, the indicators of the financial sector of Nepal as well as the procedures governing the system indicated that the system was weak, vulnerable and risky.

Despite of several reforms in financial market undertaken during the 1980s and 1990s, a clear road map could not be drawn and concrete understanding of the system could not be developed until 2000. In order to create a competitive, market friendly, well diversified and prudently managed financial market, it was extremely necessary to undertake a comprehensive reform program in Nepal. Not only this, the financial system of the country should be capable to lead to the desired growth as well as stability of the economy. It was also necessary to continue the ongoing reform programs in the financial market. Hence, the government of Nepal (GON) published Financial Sector Strategy Paper (statement) in December 2000 and disclosed the urgent need of reforms. The statement has clearly mentioned about the needs to strengthen the central bank and provide full autonomy to regulate and supervise the commercial banks and financial institutions. It has clearly pointed out the need to draft a new NRB Act to increase the autonomy of the central bank and another umbrella act to govern all deposit-taking financial institutions.

The government started the Financial Sector Technical Assistance Project under the financial assistance of World Bank (IDA) and Department for International Development (DFID), UK. Considering the existing situation of the financial market and its diversity, two types of modalities were implemented in the restructuring and reform of financial institutions; (i) Financial Sector Reform Program (FSRP) and (ii) Rural Financial Sector Development Cluster Program (RFSDCP). The main objectives of these programs were to support the on-going reform efforts to improve and upgrade the whole financial sector whereas other objectives were to maintain macroeconomic stability and to promote private-sector-led economic growth in the country. The detail of the comprehensive reforms is discussed under separate headings as follows:

Financial Sector Reform Program

The financial sector reform program encompasses various reforms measures that were basically confined into three major components viz.; (a) Re-engineering of NRB, (b) Restructuring of NBL and RBB and (c) Capacity development of the financial sector.

Re-Engineering of NRB

The government assigned the responsibility of executing the Financial Sector Technical Assistance Project to the NRB. Therefore, a committee entitled Monitoring and Surveillance Committee was formed under the co-ordination of Executive Director of the NRB. The committee was responsible to observe the processes and evaluate the performance, make suggestions and implement the policies under guidance of Top-level Co-ordination Committee.[4] Hence, the reform program was implemented with an active participation of the NRB.

Exhibit 2: Main elements of Financial Sector Strategy Paper
1. Implementing restructuring plans for the to large commercial banks-the RBB and NBL
2. Identifying restructuring strategies for the two development banks, ADB/N and NIDC.
3. Strengthening banking sector regulation and accounting and auditing standards.
4. Strengthening the NRB's supervisory capacities and its ability to enforce compliance with prudential regulations.
5. Improving the regulation and supervision on non-bank deposit taking institutions.
6. Modernizing the legislative framework with a view to reducing legislative overlap and the segmentation and fragmentation.
7. Strengthening corporate governance and the framework for loan recovery.
8. Phasing out the role of NRB and commercial banks in providing directed credit.
Source: NRB (1996) and author's compilation.

The program was focused on particularly in its core central banking functions; supervision, monetary policy, banking legislation, accounting and auditing, information technology, human resources, and training. In fact, the NRB started its own re-engineering process under the program. The NRB has strengthened its capacity by restructuring its organizational structure, upgrading the quality of the human resources adopting information and technology and re-engineering in its business processes. In order to strengthen human resource management capabilities it formulated a right-sizing strategy and designed a suitable voluntary retirement scheme; revised the existing human resources policies or systems to ensure appropriate incentives and financial rewards; developed and implemented a decompressed salary systems and introduced appropriate computer systems to manage human resource functions.

Similarly in order to strengthen the NRB's supervisory and regulatory capacity, various measures were undertaken including; enhancing a supervisory and regulatory system for banks and financial institutions; supporting the NRB's bank examiners in supervising and inspecting these institution and upgrading computer systems to ensure bank supervisors conduct off-site and on-site supervisory operations effectively and efficiently. The NRB issued prudential regulations to all banks and financial institutions. It also prepared and implemented both on-site and off-site supervision manuals. It started a special drive for the improvement of professionalism in the bank. It introduced Voluntary Retirement System in two phases. The bank formulated five-year strategic plan in order to modernize itself.

In addition, other programs such as supporting NRB's comprehensive legislative and regulatory reform efforts in the financial sector; supporting NRB's research activities, including, computerizing and developing library services; strengthening accounting and auditing capabilities to produce better quality and more timely financial and accounting information; supporting internal audit functions; strengthening information technology solutions and conducting a training program for professional development of bank staffs.

Restructuring of NBL and RBB

Second major focus of the Financial Sector Technical Assistance Project was particularly on restructuring of two large ailing commercial banks namely NBL and RBB through the recruitment of Management Teams and automation of the branches. In fact, the strategic reform was necessary in these banks as they were almost dysfunctional. Both these public sector banks were in deep financial trouble and were almost technically insolvent. KPMG, an International Auditor's Group studied these two banks and produced the report[5] in 2000 indicating very poor financial position. The study clearly portrayed the serious condition and urged for the early reforms (KPMG, 2000). Hence, the reforms appeared to be

Exhibit 3: Major Activities under Re-engineering Program
1. Strengthening NRB's human resource management capabilities;
2. Strengthening NRB's supervisory and regulatory capacity with respect to banks and non-banking financial institution ;
3. Supporting NRB's comprehensive legislative and regulatory reform efforts in the financial sector;
4. Supporting NRB's research activities, including, among other things, computerizing and developing NRB's library services;
5. Strengthening NRB's accounting and auditing capabilities to produce better quality and more timely financial and accounting information;
6. Strengthening information technology solutions of NRB;
7. Conducting a training program for professional development of NRB staff including in-house training and attendance at external seminars and conferences.
Source: NRB (1996) and author's compilation.

Exhibit 4: Major Activities under Re-structuring Program
- *Under the restructuring of the NBL, the contract was signed between the NBL and ICC Consulting Bank of Scotland (Ireland).*
- *The Management Team worked in the NBL from July 22, 2002 to July 21, 2007.*
- *After the expiry of the contract with the ICC Consulting Ireland Limited, the NRB deputed its staffs in NBL for management.*
- *During the period of restructuring, almost all branches had been computerized and deployed with Newton Software and major branches started Any Branch Banking Services.*
- *Under the restructuring of the RBB, Mr. Bruce F. Henderson was appointed as Chief Executive Officer of the Management Team on Jan 15, 2008. The NRB hired management team of two consultants, as a CEO and IT Manager.*

Source: NRB (1996) and author's compilation.

a concern as these two banks represented approximately half of the total assets of the banking system with wider branch network.

The NRB took over the management of the NBL on March 8, 2002 removing the existing Board of Directors and replacing with new NRB-appointed Board. It started to reduce the role and ownership of the government in banks and financial institutions. Consequently, the NRB handed over the management of NBL to ICC Bank, Ireland in mid-July 2002 (NRB, 2005). Similarly, in case of the RBB, the NRB selected the international banking experts after Deloitte Touche Tohmatsu broke the contract. New management teams in both the banks received support from several international and domestic banking and financial experts. With this, these banks have already completed HRD Plan, Credit Policy and Guidelines, Computerization Policy and Programs, Portfolio Review and Loan Recovery and Restructuring of RBB and NBL. Both of them have implemented Voluntary Retirement Scheme and reduced their staff considerably during the period.

Capacity Development of the Financial Sector

Finally, major focus of the Financial Sector Technical Assistance Project was particularly on supporting for the capacity building in the financial sector through improvments in legislation, establishment of regulatory framework and strenthening of the existing instituions. Similarly it was also focused to impart fundamental banking knowledge for the financial journalist, automation of Credit Information Bureau and establishment of Debt Recovery Tribunal. In fact, the reforms in the financial sector cannot bring substantial changes and improvements until the capacity of the financial sector is substantially improved. In this front, several programs were initiated with the drive of the government and active participation of the the central bank.

Consequently, a series of capacity development initiatives were started in terms of legal framework and other support. A new Nepal Rastra Bank Act, 2002 has been enacted replacing the existing Nepal Rastra Bank Act, 1955 (the charter). Similarly, in order to expedite the special cases of banks and financial institutions' loan recovery aspects, Debt Recovery Act, 2002 has been enacted whereas the Public Debt Act and the Foreign Exchange Regulation Act were amended in 2002. Later, an umbrella act - Banking and Financial Institutions Act, 2006[6] has been enacted to consolidate entire fragmented acts governing bank and financial institutions such as, Commercial Bank Act, Development Bank Act, Finance Company Act and so on. In order to address the weaknesses in the legal enforcement mechanism and judiciary capacity a draft for the Secured Transaction act was sent to the government for approval.

Similarly, in order to consolidate the financial market; upgrade the financial services and to govern and facilitate liquidation aspects of companies (i) Insolvency Act, 2006; (ii) Company Act, 2006[7]; and (iii) Secured Transaction Act, 2005 were enacted. Likewise, a study (strategic planning) was undertaken

Exhibit 5: Supporting Other Financial Sector Reform:
1. Strengthening the Banker's Training Center by (i) developing a strategic plan for the center ; (ii) designing appropriate course work; (iii) supporting enhanced training capabilities; and (iv) establishing and operating a modern information technology and computer system at the center.
2. Strengthening the Credit Information Bureau and the means through which credit information is disseminated.
3. Supporting training and capacity building among local journalists to assist them in conveying financial and business news and issue to the public.
4. Supporting the Coordination Support Team in implementing and supervising the Project, especially in relation to financial management, procurement and coordination capabilities.
Source: NRB (1996) and author's compilation.

to strengthen the Bankers Training Centre as a focal institution for improving staff capacity of banks and financial institutions. Credit Information Bureau was incorporated as a company and the capital base has been strengthened and the restructuring process was undertaken to improve its institutional strength in changing context.

Rural Financial Sector Development Program

The second modality, Rural Financial Sector Development Cluster Program implemented by the government of Nepal was confined into four major components viz.; (i) Supportive legal and regulatory framework, (ii) Institutional restructuring and reforms; (iii) Sector capacity development and (iv) Enabling infrastructure for rural finance. In fact, it was designed with the ultimate goal of expanding frontier of finance services adopting an integrated package of policy and institutional reforms measures. This program adopted a sector development cluster approach and facilitated the comprehensive reforms in the financial market. Its focus was on specific policy and institutional reform targets and thus implemented flexible reforms initiatives according to changing political and economic conditions in the country. The major objective was to support the on-going reform efforts in the whole financial sector. It was aligned with financial sector reform strategy paper of the government. The detail of the reforms is discussed under separate headings as follows:

Supportive Legal and Regulatory Framework

It focused on building a congenial policy environment to support the financial markets in the country. It implemented a reform strategy to expand its frontier of financial services through enhanced institutional co-ordination. It was also to develop appropriate supervision and regulation for improved outreach of financial services for the poor through formal and semi-formal micro-finance institutions. It also facilitated the creation of a favorable policy environment through various supports such as (i) establish a supervisory and regulatory system for rural financial institutions, (ii) divest NRB shares in rural financial institutions to legally defined level, (iii) phase out government ownership of technically insolvent rural financial institutions, and (iv) discontinue applications of interest rate ceiling to ADBN and SFDB. In order to facilitate such programs, the GON and the NRB approved the Micro-finance Policy, 2008. The NRB also drafted a Micro-finance Act and submitted for enactment to the government (Dhakal, 2011).

Likewise, the government divested its shares on ADBN, SFDB and GBBs in order to increase the participation of private sector. Not only this, the government realized that priority sector credit had created various distortions in rural financial market and decided to phase out the program. Instead, it expanded the scope of deprived sector landing requirements for the banks and financial institutions. The government supported to enhance the capacities of the Debt Recovery Tribunals and fully empowered them to enforce for the debt recovery.

The reforms program opened up the issue systematically in order to consolidate fragmented and ineffective supervisory and regulatory mechanisms for all financial intermediaries that were not supervised yet. It was also necessary to address the concerns of proliferating co-operatives that were not supervised and regulated effectively. A business plan was drafted to establish a Second-Tier Institution as a supervisory and regulatory authority.

Institutional Restructuring and Reform:

Institutional restructuring and reforms was confined basically on restructuring and reforms of ADBN, SFDB and GBBs. Asian Development Bank has carried out a study on ADBN and NIDC and recommended for the restructuring and privatization of these banks respectively. The program supported the reforms and restructuring of ADBN to transform it into a viable and efficient financial institution. The restructuring and reform exercise focused on progressive divestment of the government shares and eventually enable for the privatization. In this process, a series of reforms were initiated including: (i) adoption of the restructuring plan and the conversion of government's debt into preference share for recapitalization and (ii) incorporation and licensing it as a Class 'A' financial institution. Similarly, important reforms measures and performance indicators were determined under the restructuring plan, including: (i) divestment of government's shares, (ii) initiation of the initial public offering, (iii) completion of a voluntary retirement scheme and (iv) attainment of viable operation (Dhakal, 2011).

In order to supplement the ADBN's credit lending in rural sector and ensure for the rural and small framers credit needs, it was necessary to strengthen SFDB and Small Farmers Co-operative Societies. Likewise, it was necessary to transform Small Farmers Development Program into the cooperatives and establish linkage between SFDB and cooperatives. It was also required to redesign the structure in expanding its outreach to small farmers and local communities. In order to systematically undertake restructuring and reform, enhance its viability and expand outreach of financial services, its diagnostic review was completed in 2003 which provided basis for developing restructuring plan.

The restructuring plan of SFDB included specific performance indicators along with identification of restructuring assistance. More specifically, it prioritized restructuring assistance into: (i) strengthening of micro-finance and banking operations, (ii) staff capacity development and (iii) accounting and auditing. The program initiated series of reform measures since November 2006 to implement the restructuring plan and achieve reform targets. During the program implementation, three broader areas of support were envisaged: automation of management information system, restructuring and strengthening of the cooperatives and institutional development.

The cluster reform program also recommended for the complete divestment of NRB shares in regional GBBs. In this process, the NRB's share in Eastern and Western GBBs was divested in June 2007; that of Central was divested in 2008 and that of mid-western was divested in April 2009. Government and the NRB decided to initiate restructuring process in GBBs by adopting time-bound business plans. Later, the process of merging all these GBBs was initiated as distinct measure in the financial system. The central bank facilitated merger process and approved it to enable and emerge as a strong and efficient rural and micro-financial institution.

Sector Capacity Building

It was also necessary to undertake the capacity development of the financial sector to enhance the sustainable outreach of rural and micro-financial services. The cluster reform program supported for the establishment of National Banking Training Institute as an autonomous training institution to impart the banking knowledge and skills. It was founded as a company with all the commercial banks (Class 'A' banks) as founder shareholders. It is conducting training on comprehensive banking and finance subjects and addressing capacity development needs of formal and semi-formal financial institutions (including rural institutions). It was really necessary to enhance the access of financial services for rural communities. It was striving to be an imminent instructional institution and exploring partnership to accredit its training modules and curriculum from recognized training institutes and universities in Nepal and abroad (Dhakal, 2011).

Enabling Infrastructure for Rural Finance

The cluster reform program stated to strengthen credit information services in the whole financial market. In this front, it supported Credit Information Bureau to extend its credit information services to class D financial institutions. Capacity of the Bureau was strengthened and physical facilities were improved as it was necessary to develop a system to store the detail and large data and ensure its flow properly.

Likewise, to speed up the recovery and settle down the chronic and problematic credits, it was necessary to build up supportive as well as congenial infrastructure. Thus, a capacity development process was undertaken for Debt Recovery Tribunals. Several reform measures were undertaken to make it less costly through an improvement of skills and confidence of its staffs in legal and financial management, office automation and MIS aspects.

RECENT REFORMS IN FINANCIAL SECTOR

The discussion showed that a lot of activities were launched in the financial markets during the past. The earlier reform programs were mostly concentrated to bring major changes in policy areas and in building a strong financial architecture in the country. The reforms measures undertaken were successful in strengthening financial and operational performance, improving the legal and institutional environment, enhancing the capacity of the central bank to supervise the banking system, implementing the improved regulations and supervision, and rationalization of various policies related to the financial markets.

The financial market in Nepal has been developing and proliferating well. It went through various changes and improvements in the past. However, the capital base of banks and financial institutions was low in contrast to the high ratio of non-performing loans. There was no clear-cut policy for an exit of either banks and financial institutions or insurance companies. Banks seemed to take excessive risks in their lending in contrast to inefficient management of their assets. Likewise, insurance companies seemed vulnerable in various aspects, including the management and corporate governance. Stock market also lacked provisions on corporate governance and fair-play of companies. Further, the laws related to the capital market (including stock exchange) and insurance services also needed timely amendment.

Therefore, the recent reforms were mainly confined to achieve financial and macroeconomic stability. Basic emphasis of reforms was laid on increased financial intermediation, deepening of financial markets and increasing the role of market forces in the financial market. Various measures, including prudential regulation and supervision of financial institution and application of international financial standards as well as best practices (including capital adequacy, classification of loans, loan loss provisioning, and auditing and disclosure practices) were gradually implemented.

Nepal has joined the World Trade Organization in 2004 and opened its financial and insurance services to the foreigners. It is certainly difficult to compete with internationally competent financial institutions if the ailing banks and financial institutions are not timely improved and modernized. Nepalese financial system could not introduce new financial products and instruments that are familiar for years in other financial markets. Though, the banks and financial institutions are found to be mushrooming in Nepal in the last decade or so, they are not in par with other financial markets. They are found to be run by non-professional people, have high level of NPA, have traditional credit appraisal system and follow up procedure, over staffing and lack of corporate governance. It was not only necessary to continue the ongoing reforms but also introduce other measures of consolidation such as merger, restructuring and simplifying liquidation process. In this backdrop, the central bank introduced the Merger Bylaws, 2011 and eased various provisions to facilitate the process[8]. Later, it introduced acquisition rules to encourage them in undertaking the appropriate measure of reforms and consolidation.

Under the recent reforms, necessary amendments are proposed in NRB Act and Financial Institutions Act in order to make the role of the NRB more effective in maintaining financial stability, enhancing good governance and controlling financial crime and money-laundering activities. In addition, some other legislation are prepared and proposed to the government to strengthen the financial sector in changing times. More recently, an initiation was taken to formulate Financial Sector Development Strategy. It is expected that the strategy will be catalyst to achieve speedy economic growth, quality development of the banks and financial institutions and consolidation of the financial market (NRB, 2014b). Likewise, it would be critical in strengthening of capital market and all aspects of insurance sector through maintaining financial stability, increasing financial access and financial sector development.

Recent reforms are expected to be focused in delivering allowances of provident fund and social security allowances through bank branches and branch-less banking system. Similarly, micro finance would be developed as a strong means to expand the access to financial services specifically in rural areas. Capability of Rural Self-Reliant Fund would be enhanced to increase financial access in remote, rural and deprived areas. Likewise, under Rural Financial Sector Cluster Program, financial services would be delivered to thousands of poor and deprived families of Himalayan and mountainous region.

Until the establishment of a separate regulatory institution for financial cooperatives and NGOs, specific monitoring of saving and credit cooperatives would be carried out. Capability of Department of Cooperative of the government would be enhanced to monitor big cooperative institutions. It is also necessary to address the issues of problematic financial cooperatives and interest of depositors through the establishment of a certain mechanism. Establishment of Asset Management Company is felt necessary to expidiate the resolution process of problemed bank and financial insttutions. Merger would be encouraged and its process would be expedited for banks, financial institutions and insurance companies (MOF, 2014a).

Necessary legal and institutional arrangements would be initiated to establish re-insurance company within the country. Insurance services providers would be motivated to increase insurance services in micro insurance sectors. The capacity of Deposit Insurance and Credit Guarantee Corporation would be scaled up through legal and structural reforms including capital increase. Stock market transaction would be made simple and easy to widen the participation in capital market. Transaction of NEPSE would be operated through electronic means. Institutional and Non-resident Nepali's investment would be attracted in the capital market (MOF, 2014a). For the long-term investment in the infrastructure projects, necessary arrangements would be made to issue bonds in local currency for international agencies that have high ranking credit rating. Necessary arrangements would be made to regulate commodity market.[9]

REFORMS IN INSURANCE AND CAPITAL MARKET

The liberalization of economic sectors as well as the initiation of financial market reforms in Nepal also included the reforms in insurance market and stock market. Insurance services are very important because they provide many opportunities for the efficient allocation of resources, utilization, promotion of economic activities, and fair competition and attract the foreign direct investment. However, the progress so far is less than satisfactory. Following is the summary of major reforms undertaken in the insurance sector and the stock market respectively.

Insurance Market

The history of insurance business in Nepal is very short, as the first insurance company, Nepal Insurance Company Ltd. (initially, 'Nepal Mal Chalani Tatha Bima Company Ltd.') was established in 1961 AD. Considering the role of insurance business in the expansion of economic activities and alarming outflow of money from the country, the government of Nepal felt the need to establish a large and well organized insurance company within the country. Hence, Rastriya Beema Sansthan was established under the Insurance Act, 1968. Later, in open and liberal economic policies, various acts, including insurance acts were amended. Along with the promulgation of Insurance Act, 1992 and Insurance Regulation, 1992; Insurance Board (known as 'Beema Samiti') was established as the supreme authority to manage, regulate, develop and facilitate insurance business in the country. The Insurance Board provides various services including registration and renewal of insurer, surveyor, broker and insurance agent, expansion of branch of insurer, judgment of insurance claims arbitrate in the disputes, which arises between the insurer and insured and training for surveyor, insurance agent and others. Likewise, it provides services such as acceptance of insurance fund and policy, provides information and publication, set out guidelines for insurers to invest their fund and prescribe the priority sectors for such investment, issue necessary directives to the insurer and formulate necessary basis for the protection of interest of people with insurance schemes (Insurance Board, 2014).

The liberalization in financial markets, on one hand and the privatization of state-owned public enterprises, on the other, provided a premise for the growth of modern insurance companies from private sectors (Gurung, 2010). In fact, a golden period in the history of insurance business started only after the enactment of new legislation. Consequently, insurance business became emerging business in Nepal with a number of insurance companies established gradually.

Insurance Board issued various bylaws and directives including Corporate Governance Guidelines, 2012. The new guidelines provided with specific provisions including eligibility criterion of the CEO, limit in expenses related to incentive and promotional activities, indulgence in activities, provision of penalty etc. In fact, these were the reforms intended to discourage fraudulent practices such as violation of the corporate governance guidelines by presenting high expenses, poor claim settlement and lack of transparency in their transactions. The Guidelines also prohibits board of directors and promoters with large stakes from getting insurance coverage from their own companies for their other businesses and property. The guidelines also capped the salary of CEOs, keeping it at a maximum range of 15 times the salary of the lowest ranking employee. The board is empowered fully and can take over the management of the company in case of irregularities. It can dissolve the board of directors and suspend chief executive officer of the company. It can also intensify the monitoring and supervision to resolve the problems and ensure the rights and benefits of clients (Insurance Board, 2014). Recently, it is found to be focused on ensuring strict compliance of the corporate governance guidelines.

Stock Market

The liberalization of economic sectors accompanied by the privatization of state-owned public enterprises and reforms in financial market created a congenial environment for the growth of capital market in Nepal. As in many developing and emerging market countries, privatization programs stimulate the development of equity markets as well as to increase government revenues and promote economic efficiency. Capital market reform was initiated in Nepal as a part of broader financial liberalization program.

Under the financial market reforms program, various acts were enacted and amended. Along with the initiation of liberal policy and promulgation of acts; SEBON was established as an apex authority to manage, regulate, develop and control securities markets in the country. Similarly, NEPSE was established as a formal exchange market for securities[10]. The history of stock market is very short in Nepal. It took a long time for the formal trading of shares in the secondary market, only since 1994. However, Biratnagar Jute Mills and Nepal Bank Limited floated their shares in the market long before, in 1937 as isolated cases.

In the past, several policy and institutional impediments to capital market growth were identified. These include high entry barriers in the securities industry, lack of competition, restricted foreign access to domestic equity markets, and government control over operations of securities companies, weak regulatory frameworks, and inadequate supervisory mechanisms. Likewise, other problems include lack of good governance, poor information system and transparency. Several problems were identified even in accounting and auditing system. In fact, inadequate accounting and auditing system leads to serious apprehension in the fairness of financial transactions which discourages equity investment. It also leads to the loss of investors' confidence.

Government of Nepal moved towards stock market reforms specifically in 1990s, when it was under growing pressures to reform capital markets as part of broader financial liberalization programs. The reform programs were directed to expand the size of stock markets and enliven trading activities in the country. It took a momentum with the speed of privatization of public enterprises, reforms in banking sector, establishment of new banks and financial institutions and divestment of its shares over various financial institutions by the central bank. Many companies started to get listed in the market. It can also increase opportunities for investors to diversify their portfolios, reduce portfolio investment risks and enhance the depth of equity markets.

Further reforms encompassed both deregulatory as well as regulatory spheres. These interlinked reform measures were aimed to reduce the cost of capital, and increase the pool of financial resources available to local industrial firms, broaden investor base and make domestic financial sector more efficient. Initially, there were only 62 companies with 25 brokers. The trading system was very primitive i.e. 'open out cry' system. The most significant change in Nepali secondary market was the establishment of semi-automated system in 2007. Moreover, a separate company for central depository system was established as a full subsidiary of NEPSE.

IMPACT OF FINANCIAL MARKET REFORMS

The liberalization of economic and financial sector as well as the initiation of financial market reforms produced distinct picture of progress in the past. Liberalization in financial services resulted in many positive advantages like economic growth, introduction of advanced financial practices and market efficiency (NRB, 2002)[11]. Impact of financial market reforms can be assessed in terms of various indicators, such as the number of banks and financial institutions, volume of banking transaction, inflow of foreign investment, growth in deposit and credit, access of banking services and so on. The policy reforms introduced during the nineties yielded positive impacts on the development and deepening of the financial system. The prominent reforms include but not limited to (i) removal of government participation in banking, (II) strengthening of regulation, inspection and supervision, (iii) formulation of long-term policies, (iv) restructuring of troubled commercial banks, (v) introduction of new products and services, and (vi) formulation and enactment of various legislative frameworks and institutions (NRB, 2005).

These reforms had a far reaching impact in financial sector development which was clearly evidenced in the growth of the financial assets and banking activities in the country. In fact, the outcome of the reforms should be examined in an overall macroeconomic context, against the backdrop of the overall strategy of reforms implemented during the last two and half decades. Under the reforms, the NRB has strengthened its capacity by restructuring its organizational structure, upgrading the quality of the human resources adopting information and technology and re-engineering its business processes. The NRB started prudent banking regulation and risk-based supervision in banks and financial institutions. It issued various directives requiring banks and financial institutions to be fully compliant with the international standards and codes prescribed by Basel Committee. Similarly, risk management practices were modified to conform to Basel II principles. Likewise, a number of measures have been taken to put best corporate governance practices in the system by prescribing 'fit and proper' test/criteria for Chief Executives, Boards of Directors and top management positions. Accordingly, accounting and audit standards have been brought to the International Standards. Nowadays, the number of financial institutions has proliferated. As of mid-July 2014, there are 30 commercial banks, 84 development banks, 53 finance companies and 37 micro-credit development banks[12]. The progress is presented in Figure 1.

Exhibit 6: Major Reforms in Financial Market
1. Reforming the financial sector laws and regulations.
2. Strengthening of NRB's regulatory and supervisory functions.
3. Restructuring of RBB and NBL as well as partial privatization of NBL.
4. Enhancing competition in the banking sector.
5. Implementing international accounting standards.
6. Establishment of the Banker's Training Institute.
7. Restructuring of the Credit Information Bureau
8. Restructuring and privatization of rural development banks and their merger.
9. Restructuring of ADB/N and NIDC.
10. Broadening and deepening of financial system in Nepal.
Source: Rawal (2004) and NRB (2005)

Figure 1. Growth in Number of Bank and Financial Institutions
Source: Banking and Financial Statistics, NRB

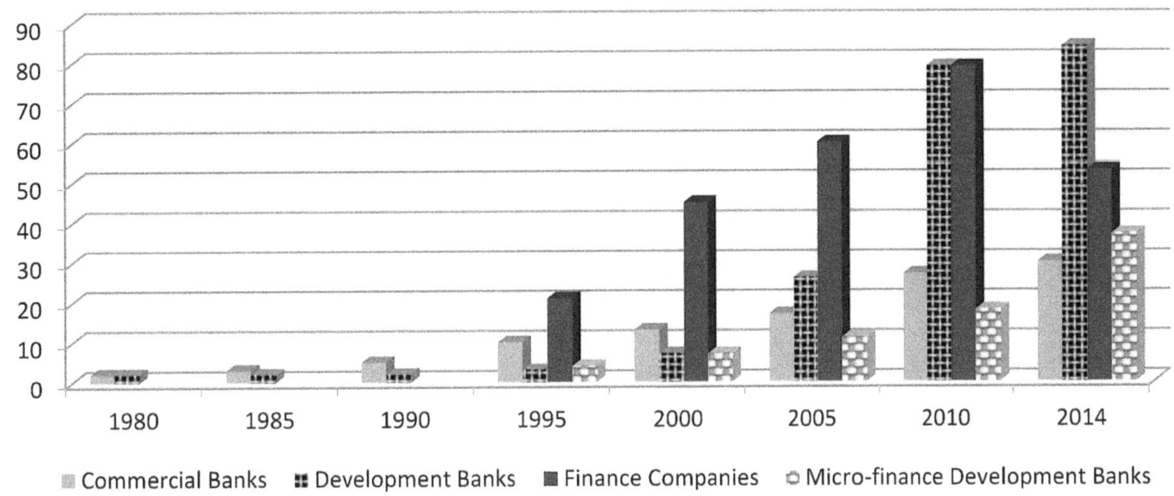

Banking sector has now diversified its product base and carried out a lot of innovation. They have expanded their outreach to rural and deprived sector, SMEs, and consumer financing. As exhibited in Table 3, the total number of BFIs branches (Class A, B, C and D) increased to 3,430 in mid-July 2014 from 1,153 in mid-July 2008 (also refer to Appendix Table). Similarly, there has been a tremendous increase in deposit accounts, loan accounts and cardholders In July 2014, there were more than 13 million deposit accounts, approximately 1.0 million borrowers and more than 4 million cardholders (NRB, 2014b).

The consequences of the reform can also be observed in macroeconomic indicators and hence the deposits/GDP ratio of bank and financial institutions rose to 76.6 percent at mid-July 2014 from 34.1 percent at mid-July 1998. Likewise, the credit/GDP ratio increased 58.6 percent from 22.8 percent during the same period. The RWA capital adequacy ratio improved to 12.7 percent from 4.8 percent during the same period. Similarly, the ratio of total banking sector assets to GDP rose to 132.7 percent in July 2014 from 35.0 percent in July 1994 and the ratio of private sector credit to GDP increased to 64.0 percent from 20.0 percent in 1994 (NRB, 2014d). Not only this, the financial soundness indicators showed a healthy and sound trend with high degree of financial stability.

Similarly, the insurance sector, securities market and corporate sectors are also being strengthened side by side. Insurance service has been developed and proliferated well along with the initiation of financial market reforms and establishment of IB. It facilitated for the establishment of joint-venture and private insurance companies in Nepal. As of mid-July 2014, there are altogether 25 insurance companies comprising of 6 life and 19 non-life insurance companies in the country. The total gross insurance premium increased to Rs. 24.85 billion and the sources and uses of insurance companies stood at Rs. 84.65 billion in July 2014 (NRB, 2014d). Similarly, the trading of shares has increased tremendously in the stock exchange. In July 2014, there were more than 237 listed companies (excluding 32 delisted companies), 50 stock brokers, and two market makers. It has Rs. 1,057.17 billion paid up capital and Rs. 1,057.17 billion market capitalization (NRB, 2014d).

Some prominent scholars and writers tried to measure the effectiveness and impact of financial sector reforms in Nepal. Adhikary (1989) and Kafle (1990) analyzed the process of monetary and financial

Table 3. Major Financial Indicators

		As of mid-July 2014			
Particulars		**Class "A"**	**Class "B"**	**Class "C"**	**Overall**
A. Credit, Deposit Ratios (%)					
1	Total Deposit/GDP	62.5	10.4	3.8	76.6
2	Total Credit/GDP	46.8	8.4	3.4	58.6
3	Total Credit/ Total Deposit	74.9	80.9	89.7	76.5
4	NPL/ Total Loan	2.9	4.2	14.3	3.8
B. Capital Adequacy Ratios (%)					
1	Core Capital/RWA	10.4	14.8	15.2	11.3
2	Total Capital/RWA	12.0	15.6	15.9	12.7
C. Number of BFIs Branches (including Class D branches of 826 in total)		1547	818	239	3430
D. Other Information					
1	No. of ATM	1,362	260	30	1,652
2	No. of Debit Card	3,641,960	465,640	23,642	4,131,242
3	No. of Credit Card	57,898	-	-	57,898
4	No. of Deposit Accounts	9,791,383	2,773,198	564,993	13,129,574
5	No. of Loan	647,701	244,362	47,942	940,005

Note: Nominal GDP(At Producer's Price) for 2013/14 Rs. 1928517 million
Source: Banking and Financial Statistics, NRB

sector reforms whereas Demitriades and Luintel (1996), Khanal (2003) and Bhetuwal (2005) attempted to examine the effectiveness of financial sector reforms in Nepal. Being a bit distinct, Basyal (2002) analyzed the prospects and challenges of capital account convertibility in Nepal whereas Shrestha and Chowdhury (2007) empirically assessed the role of financial liberalization in economic development. However, there is still dearth of literature on this particular subject in Nepal. Therefore, the conclusion of these papers should be analyzed with the grain of salt considering basic objectives, sample size, financial structure and level of development.

At the outset, the study of Adhikary (1989) pointed out three reasons motivating financial deregulations in Nepal such as (i) financial resources were unevenly distributed among different financial institutions and interest rate rigidity (ii) a wide interest rate spread between lending and deposits, and (iii) the introduction of joint venture banks and urge for developing competitive financial market in Nepal. Another study by Kafle (1990) analyzed the process of financial sector reform in Nepal after the implementation of the Structural Adjustment Program. Illustrating the background of reform as a basis; the paper argued about the main objectives of reforms. It concluded that the reforms were aimed to contribute to economic development, to maintain external as well as internal stability of the economy and to correct structural constraints for improving allocative efficiency of the economy. Likewise, the study of Demitriades and Luintel (1996) examined the effects of banking sector policies on the process of financial development and economic growth of Nepal over the period of 1960-1992. Using unrestricted error correction model, it constructed the index of financial repression through principal component method to quantify the influences of banking sector policies on financial development, among others.

They could not find support for real interest rate as determinant of financial development, but, came to a conclusion that financial depth influence economic growth and vice-versa.

Under the same context, Basyal (2002) chose a specific issue of capital account convertibility in Nepal. He analyzed the prospects and challenges of capital account convertibility. The study argued for the openness in the system so that international banks and financial institutions enter the domestic markets, compete and gain efficiency. Likewise, it asked for the convertability in capital account so that the residents can hold an internationally diversified portfolio thereby reducing the vulnerability in the income streams and wealth to domestic real and financial shocks. However, Khanal (2003) assessed economic and financial reforms in Nepal and criticized not only for absence of assessments on domestic conditions, lack of stakeholders' participation and cooperation but also for its prioritization and sequencing of policies. The study argued that as a result of reforms, there was a massive devaluation of domestic currency; tariff rates stood at the lowest in South Asia. Further, reforms are criticized for unbalanced liberalization where reform in some areas was far ahead without achieving concrete positive outcomes.

Bhetuwal (2005) examined the financial liberalization in Nepal by constructing index of financial liberalization and financial development. It revealed the bi-directional causality between these two set of indicators i.e. financial liberalization leading to financial development and vice versa. It observed that still there were some structural and institutional weaknesses, making reform efforts less effective. It argued that the reform had little impact on mobilization of financial saving, interest rate and currency stabilization. Notwithstanding, another study by Bhetuwal (2007) found a continuous and gradual process of financial liberalization was intact in Nepal. It found the presence of bi-directional causal relationship between the liberalization and level of financial development and concluded the effectiveness of financial sector reforms in Nepal.

Shrestha and Chowdhury (2006) empirically assessed the relationship between financial liberalization and economic development by constructing financial liberalization index for Nepal based on principal component methods. Representing eight major financial liberalization components,[13] their index examined the extent of financial liberalization in Nepal during 1984 to 2005. They found the degree of liberalization in Nepal was highest during 1984-1994. Further, in another study (Shrestha and Chowdhury, 2007), they examined the financial liberalization hypothesis by employing autoregressive distributed lag (ARDL) modeling approach on Nepalese data. Their results showed that the real interest rate affects both savings and investment positively.

Likewise, Kharel and Pokhrel (2012), investigated the role of financial structure on economic growth of Nepal during 1994-2011 using Johansen's co-integrating vector error correction model. They argued that the banking sector plays a key role in promoting economic growth compared to capital market in Nepal. They favored the policy to be focused on the banking sector reforms by enhancing its quality and outreach to promote economic growth in Nepal. Regmi (2010) explored the impact of financial development on economic growth in Nepal and found a weak link due to pervasive inefficiencies in the credit allocation mechanisms, poor quality of institutions, weak infrastructures and general shift of resources from productive investment to consumption. Similarly, Gautam (2013) examined the reforms and gradual consolidation process in Nepalese financial system whereas another study (Gautam, 2014) empirically assessed the nexus between financial development and economic growth in Nepal. Using Johansen's co-integration and vector error correction model, it supported both demand driven and supply leading hypotheses in case of Nepal. It is consistent with the results of Islam et al (2004) that used the data for Bangladesh, and Tahir (2004) that used data for Pakistan.

The reforms program indeed focused on developing a sustainable financial system and providing affordable services to the mass and to reduce poverty. It also focused on increasing rural financial outreach and facilitating small and marginal farmers with opportunities to generate income and employment. It was also expected to work on enabling policy environment, institutional restructuring and reforms, supporting legal and regulatory framework and capacity development. Consequently, it brought positive changes on bringing improved soundness, efficiency and outreach through policy, legal, regulatory and institutional reforms. It also provided with the favorable policy environment and effective supervision and regulation mechanism (Dhakal, 2008). Further, series of program interventions had been instrumental and quite efficient and support the program to achieve outcomes and outputs.

ISSUES AND CHALLENGES OF REFORMS

The financial market in Nepal is growing with several advancements in its operation. More specifically, the contribution made by the financial institutions on the economic development through creating employment opportunities, raising income level and providing saving and investment opportunities to the general people cannot be undermined. However, it still requires improvement in business operation, risk undertaking and asset management.

Despite of implementation of consolidation programs such as restructuring and merger, the inadequacy of the banks and financial institutions in providing increased benefits to the general public in rural areas is still a burning issue. Therefore, it is still necessary to create a healthy financial sector as a pre-requisite to sustained economic growth. It calls for continuation of further reforms measures. The burning issues and challenges of reforms are outlined as follows (MOF, 2014a):

- An alternative and robust mechanism should be developed to ensure enhanced credit supply to priority and productive sectors along with the continuation of credit to deprived sectors. It should be devised in such a manner that the financial institutions do not consider it as a burden; rather as a boon for their operation and sustainability.
- It is necessary to undertake timely amendments in Nepal Rastra Bank Act, 2002 and Banks and Financial Institutions Act, 2006 in order to empower NRB for timely resolution of problem banks and financial institutions. Similarly, for the smooth functioning and consolidation of financial market, Mergers and Acquisitions Act, Electronic Commerce (E-Commerce) Act, and Payments Act (or Cheque Act), etc are necessary to be enacted.
- It is equally necessary to transform Nepal Industrial Development Bank into the Infrastructure Development Bank by increasing capital, restructuring the organization and scaling up its capacity. It is still necessary to incorporate Asset Management Company to handle the problems arising in financial markets.
- It is imperative to establish a second tier institution to regulate and supervise the micro-finance sector. Likewise, there should be strong regulation and supervision for thousands of savings and credit co-operatives. The Department of Co-operative is handicapped with weak legal provision and inadequate human and other logistical resources.
- It is necessary to enhance the co-ordination among the regulators and supervisors so as not to transmit the problem of one sector into the other sectors. It is equally necessary to disseminate the information and share knowledge through a modern banking training institute.

- Insurance Board and Securities Exchange Board generally initiate event-driven approach on off-site supervision and on-site monitoring rather than following a forward-looking approach. Hence, it is necessary to introduce risk-based prudential regulation and supervision in non-bank financial sector.
- It is necessary to enhance the effectiveness of supervision in Non-Bank Financial System. It is imperative to address (i) insufficient resources and expertise of regulatory authorities, (ii) lack of independence in conducting monitoring and supervision, (iii) clarity on when or whether supervisory actions to be taken, and (iv) continuation of reforms.
- Insurance service is found to be growing recently. Therefore, it is necessary to (i) enhance the capacity and expertise in insurance services, (ii) strengthen capital base of the Insurers, (iii) establish re-insurance company (iv) promote the base of insurance market, and (v) educate general public.
- Stock market needs continuation of reforms. Hence, it is necessary to (i) make wide use of automation, (ii) promote the entry of institutional investors, (iii) attract non-resident Nepali and foreign capital (iv) encourage private limited companies to go public, (v) strengthen regulation and supervision, (vi) encourage foreign technical collaboration, and (vii) educate investors and general public.
- It is necessary to frame out a policy that can allow infrastructure construction companies to issue bonds and raise capital from the market. This will moderate unnatural fluctuations in the securities market and ultimately develop the bond market.
- There is no specific government institution or separate body to regulate and supervise the activities of pension funds. Lack of regulation and supervision has created a complex mix of multiple risks, such as mobilization of huge amount, open-end mutual fund operation, characterized by high leverage and large liquidity mismatches.
- It is necessary to devise new pension funds schemes because the existing mechanism does not seem to be sustainable in future.

Financial Market Reforms in South Asia: A Regional Context

Many developing countries implemented financial sector reforms, as part of broader market oriented economic reforms since the late 1980s or early 1990s. South Asian countries were not far from this. They also started reforming their economic sectors from the mid-1980s and consequently adopted financial markets[14] as an integral part of the reforms. They stated financial sector reforms mostly in the late 1980s and early1990s. Sri Lanka started it in the early 1980s, whereas India and Bangladesh introduced it in the early 1990s. Nepal and Pakistan introduced concrete reforms in late 1990s though some of reforms were introduced much earlier, since mid 1980s. However, it was different for Bhutan and Afghanistan where it was stated only after 2000s. Financial sector reforms basically entailed financial liberalization and institutional reforms though some were different in these countries. South Asian countries, though heterogeneous in terms of population and geographical size, political ideologies and level of development; they all nevertheless shared historical and cultural closeness, mass poverty and low level of human development. (Arora, 2010).[15] They had shallow and undiversified financial sectors with considerable financial fragility. The banking system had dominated their financial sectors and thus it had been the major focus of reforms. However, the reforms also intended to open market for private sector, develop capital markets and encourage the growth of non bank financial institutions.

The principal objective of financial sector reforms in South Asian Countries was to create an efficient and stable financial system and markets; to improve the efficiency of resources and to accelerate the growth in real sector by removing structural deficiencies. Therefore, main thrust of reforms both in the banking and non-banking financial institutions was on creating a deregulated environment and enabling free play of market forces. It was also focused on strengthening the prudential norms and the supervisory system, imparting operational flexibility, functional autonomy and strength to the system.

In contrast to big bang reforms approach adopted by the Latin American countries and transition economies, South Asians followed a gradual reform approach. It was basically focused on the improvement of allocative efficiency and profitability of the financial sector, at the same time it sought to maintain financial stability (Metzger, 2010). The banking sector was not only the most dominant financial intermediary in the region but also was suffering from serious problems over the years. It suffered from lack of competition, low capital base, low productivity, high intermediation cost, vast public ownership and rampant government interference. In addition, there was poor risk management system and weak prudential standards. All these resulted in poor asset quality and low profitability over the years and banks tended to face distress.

In contrast, nonbank financial institutions though grew rapidly over a short period of time; they rather played a minor role because of their number, size, resource base and networking. There was no proper regulation, they always faced control over pricing of financial assets, barriers to entry, high transaction costs and restrictions on movement of funds among the institutions. Moreover, these institutions operated in an over-protected environment with most of the funding coming from assured sources at concessional terms. The foreign exchange market was found to be highly controlled and regulated. There were various direct control measures on foreign exchange including the suppliers and users of foreign exchange. The case was not distinct for stock market (mutual funds) as it also suffered from lack of competition and was dominated usually by one institution with limited supply of securities. However, insurance sector had a little competition despite of limited scheme and products.

Most of the central banks in this region strengthened their capacity by acquiring new skills, upgrading the quality of their human resources, adopting technology and re-engineering their business processes. The banking regulation and supervision were made to be risk-based and fully compliant with the international standards and codes prescribed by Basle Committee. The risk management practices were modified to conform to Basle II rules (Husain, 2004). The financial soundness indicators showed a healthy and sound banking system with high degree of financial stability. Reforms in the financial market initiated various measures to put best corporate governance practices in the system by prescribing 'fit and proper' test/criteria for chief executives, members of the Board of Directors and top management positions. It was made possible through strong regulation, supervision and enforcement brought about by improved legal frameworks. Subsequently, accounting and auditing standards were updated in line with the International Accounting Standards and Codes. Interaction and training programs were conducted for external auditors and financial journalists when and wherever necessary.

The result of financial reforms has been evident in South Asian financial markets, themselves. For an example, despite prolonged global economic and financial crisis and subsequent turmoil in other parts of the world that surfaced in 2007, coupled with domestic unrest and political transition; South Asia experienced stability in their banking sector. In most of these countries, financial markets seemed less vulnerable. The reform was successful on removing structural bottlenecks, introducing new players/instruments, free pricing of financial assets, relaxation of quantitative restrictions, improvements in trading, clearing and settlement practices, creating transparency in the market. In almost all countries in the region, financial sector reforms reduced state ownership and led to significant changes in the financial sector.

CONCLUSION

Since financial sector plays a crucial role in the economic growth of the country, it is regarded as the engine of growth. Without a healthy and efficient financial system in the economy, credit delivery and allocative efficiency of the system will not be improved. Not only this, a high and stable economic growth cannot be achieved without a healthy financial system. Financial sector affects everyone in the country and beyond the extent of contagion though depends highly upon the interface of the economy with other economies. With the liberalization in the financial market and emerging globalization, there have been substantial inter-connections between the markets. There had been many ups and downs in the financial sector of several countries ranging from the financial crisis of Japan in early 1990s, Mexican crisis in mid 1990s, Asian economic and financial crises of 1997 and financial crisis of United States of America in 2007-08. These crises demonstrated their impact extensively to the rest of the world. In recent years, not only the Nepalese financial system but also the South Asian financial systems now stand well diversified and expanded their global footprint. Thus, it became difficult to be offline on global standards and international best practices and to withstand the alliance of emerging business.

Financial Crisis or any type of crises occurs at any moment in any country as and when the financial architecture and systems become weak. Likewise, any economy growing over a weak financial architecture is prone to collapse at any time without any warning. No matter, financial system can be vulnerable either it has many small institutions or it has a few big institutions, though there is growing debate over the optimal number of institutions in the country. The financial sector may invite financial crisis, when it is vulnerable, economy is weak or macroeconomic policies are not performing. The problem created in the financial system can easily be transferred to other sectors of the economy. Thus it is necessary for the financial regulators to think over the soundness of the system and to visualize early warnings in the system. It is equally important to get ready to absorb the risks, volatility and shocks arising from the system of its own or of contagion effect. Similarly, it is imperative to examine the health and solvency of the financial market, prudential norms and their compliance. The past crises provided the imminent lessons to several developed and developing countries and issued warnings to the governments to undertake timely assessment of their financial markets. They also opened up eyes to examine the system and to be ensured on the growth, stability and sustainability. The reform agenda produced several macroeconomic policies to improve business conditions and enhance economic activities in Nepal and South Asia too.

REFERENCES

Acharya, K. P., Nara, B. T., & Sharma, S. (1998). Economic Liberalization in Nepal: Sequence and Process. Kathmandu: OXFAM GB Nepal.

ADB. (2009). *Financial Sector in South Asia: Recent Developments and Challenges*. Manila, Philippines: Asian Development Bank.

Adhikary, G. P. (1989). *Deregulation in the Financial System in the SEACEN Countries*. Kuala Lumpur: South East Asian Central Banks Research and Training Centre.

Arestis, P., Demetriades, P., & Luintel, K. B. (2001). Financial Development and Economic Growth: The Role of the Stock Markets. *Journal of Money, Credit and Banking*, *331*(1), 16–41. doi:10.2307/2673870

Arora, R. U. (2010). *Regional Financial Cooperation in South Asia*. Griffith Asia Institute.

Basyal, T. R. (2001). *Reforming Nepal's Financial System: Rationale and Measures. Nepal Rastra Bank Annual Publication.*

Basyal, T. R. (2002). Financial Sector Reform: Need and Strategy. Arunodaya, 291-303.

Basyal Tula, R. (2002). *Benefits of Integrated Capital Markets. In Mirmire* (Vol. 200, pp. 297–302). Nepal Rastra Bank.

Bhetuwal, K. (2005). *Assessing the Effectiveness of Financial Sector Reforms in Nepal*. (Doctoral Thesis). Maharaja Sayajirao University of Baroda, Gujarat, India.

Bhetuwal, K. R. (2007). Financial liberalization and financial development in Nepal. *NRB Economic Review*, *19*, 23–42.

Booz, Allen & Hamilton. (1990). *CBPASS Strategic Workshop Materials: Developing Policy Assumptions for Bank Strategic Planning*. Author.

Booz, Allen & Hamilton. (1992). *CBPASS II: Final Report for CBPASS Committee*. Author.

Demirguc-Kunt, A., & Levine, R. (2001). *Financial Structures and Economic Growth: A Cross-Country Comparison of Banks, Markets and Development*. Cambridge, MA: MIT Press.

Dhakal, N. (2008). *Financial Sector Refroms in Nepal* (Vol. 2008). Arthik Mimansa.

Dhungana, B. R. (2004). Financial Sector Reforms. In Nepal Rastra Bank in Fifity Years- Part II Financial System. Kathmandu: Nepal Rastra Bank.

Gautam, B. P. (2013). Consolidation of Financial System in Changing Times: A case of Nepal. *Conference Proceeding of International Istanbul Finance Congress*. Istanbul: Turkey.

Gautam, B. P. (2014). *Financial Development and Economic Growth in Nepal*. NRB Working Paper 25/2013. Nepal Rastra Bank, Research Department.

Gurung, J. B. (2010). Insurance and Its Business in Nepal. *Journal of Nepalese Business Studies*, *7*(1), 70–79. doi:10.3126/jnbs.v7i1.6409

Husain, I. (2004). *Paper read at Italy-Pakistan Trade and Investment Conference, Rome on September 28, 2004*. Retrieved from http://ishrathusain.iba.edu.pk/ speeches/financialSector/2004/Financial_sector_reforms_in_Pakistan.pdf

Insurance Board. (2014). Retrieved from www.bsib.org.np

Kafle, P. K. (1990). *Monetary and Financial Reforms in Nepal: Implication for Adjustment and growth*. Economic Review Occasional Paper Number 4.

Khanal, D. R. (2003). *Why Economic Reform Failed in Nepal: 9 Reasons*. Kathmandu: New Business Age.

Kharel, R. S., & Pokhrel, D. R. (2012). Does Nepal's Financial Structure Matter for Economic Growth? *NRB Economic Review*, *24*(2), 31–46.

KPMG. (2000). *Final Report on Nepal Banking Reform Project: Nepal Bank Limited and Rastriya Banijya Bank*. Kathmandu: KPMG Barents Group.

Lacombe, A. V., & Olaso, R.-M. H. (1999). *Nepal: Assessment of Compliance with the BASLE Core Principles for Effective Banking Supervision*. Washington, DC: The World Bank.

Levine, R. (2004). *Finance and Growth: Theory and Evidence*. NBER Working Paper No. 10766.

Metzger, M. (2010). Trends in Financial Market Development in South Asia. New Delhi: MOF.

MOF. (2014a). *Budget Speech for the Fiscal Year 2014/15*. Kathmandu: Ministry of Finance.

MOF. (2014b). *Economic Survey for the Fiscal Year 2013/14*. Kathmandu: Ministry of Finance.

NRB. (1996). *Forty Years of the Nepal Rastra Bank (1956 - 1996)*. Kathmandu: Nepal Rastra Bank.

NRB. (2003). *Banking and Financial Statistics, No. 41*. Kathmandu: Nepal Rastra Bank, Bank and Financial Institution Regulation Department.

NRB. (2005). *Nepal Rastra Bank in Fifty Years. Part II: Financial System*. Kathmandu: Nepal Rastra Bank.

NRB. (2012). Quarterly. *Economic Bulletin*, *46*(4).

NRB. (2012). *Annual Report for the Fiscal Year 2011/12*. Kathmandu: Nepal Rastra Bank Research Department.

NRB. (2013). *Banking and Financial Statistics, No. 59*. Kathmandu: Nepal Rastra Bank, Bank and Financial Institution Regulation Department.

NRB. (2014a). *NRB, Then Now and Ahead*. Kathmandu: Nepal Rastra Bank.

NRB. (2014b). *Monetary Policy for Fiscal Year 2014/15*. Kathmandu: Nepal Rastra Bank.

NRB. (2014c). *Current Macroeconomic Situation (Based on Annual Data of FY 2013/14)*. Kathmandu: Nepal Rastra Bank, Research Department.

NRB. (2014d). *Annual Report for Fiscal Year 2013/14*. Kathmandu: Nepal Rastra Bank.

Qayyum, A. (n.d.). *Financial Sector Reforms and the Efficiency of Banking in Pakistan Islamabad*. Pakistan Institute of Development Economics. Retrieved from http://saneinetwork.net/Files/08_11.pdf

Rabiul, Wahidul, & Habib-uz-Zaman. (2004). Time Series Analysis of Finance and Growth. *The Bangladesh Development Studies*, *30*(1/2), 111-128. Accessed from http://www.jstor.org/stable/40795689

Rawal, T. B. (2003). *Corporate Governance and Financial Sector Reform in Nepal*. Kathmandu: Society for International Development.

Rawal, T. B. (2004). *Policy Paper on Financial Sector Reform*. Kathmandu: Nepal Rastra Bank.

Regmi, U. R. (2010). Relationship between Financial Development and Economic Growth in Nepal. *The Economic Journal of Nepal, 33*, 231–240.

SANEI. (2007). *Study on Financial Sector Reform in Nepal*. Islamabad: South Asian Network of Economic Institutes Pakistan Institute of Development Economics.

Shrestha, G. K. (2004). Financial Sector Reforms in Nepal. *Economic Review, 16*, 75–90.

Shrestha, M. B. & Chowdhury, K. (2006). Financial Liberalization Index for Nepal. *International Journal of Applied Econometrics and Quantitative Studies, 3*(1), 41–54.

Shrestha, M. B., & Chowdhury, K. (2007). Testing Financial Liberalization Hypothesis with ARDL Model Approach. *Applied Financial Economics, 17*(18), 1529–1540. doi:10.1080/09603100601007123

Tahir, M. (2008). An Investigation of the Effectiveness of Financial Development in Pakistan. *The Lahore Journal of Economics, 13*(2), 27–44.

Vitols, S. (2001). *The Origins of Bank-Based and Market-Based Financial Systems: Germany, Japan and the United States*. Discussion Paper FS I 01-302. Wissenschaftszentrum Berlin für Sozialforschung.

World Bank. (2002). *Nepal Financial Sector Study*. Washington, DC: The World Bank.

KEY TERMS AND DEFINITIONS

CAR: Capital Adequacy Ratio.
GON: Government of Nepal.
IB: Insurance Board.
NBL: Nepal Bank Limited.
NEPSE: Nepal Stock Exchange Limited.
NIDC: Nepal Industrial Development Corporation.
NPA/NPL: Non Performing Assets/ Non Performing Loans.
NRB: Nepal Rastra Bank.
RBB: Rastriya Banijya Bank.
SEBON: Security Board of Nepal.
SFDB: Small Farmers Development Bank.
WTO: World Trade Organization.

ENDNOTES

1. In 1990, there were only 5 commercial banks, 2 development banks, 2 insurance companies, and few other financial and quasi-financial institutions. As at mid-July 2000, there were 11 commercial banks, 2. development banks, 5 regional rural development banks (RRDBs), 44 finance companies, 2 insurance companies, 29 savings and credit co-operative societies and 30 NGOs licensed by the NRB.

2 A research based on an UNCTAD project undertaken during 1995-97, states that many developing countries implemented financial sector reforms, as part of broader market oriented economic reforms since the late 1980s (BROWNBRIDGE, Martin and Samuel K Gayi (No Date).

3 The KPMG report concluded that loan assets of RBB and NBL were highly overstated and extremely risky. As a result, both of them were technically insolvent. As of mid-1998, they had losses of around US$450 million, which was equivalent to around 46% of the annual budget of the government or 8.6 percent of GDP (NRB, 2005; SANEI, 2007).

4 The Committee was formed by the cabinet level decision of the government on March 26, 2001 under the coordination of Honorable Vice Chairman, National Planning Commission

5 The KPMG report highlighted various aspects of RBB and NBL including (i) Severe governance and management shortfalls, (ii) Dysfunctional lending processes, (iii) Extremely poor information systems, accounting and record keeping practices, (iv) Poor strategic planning, business planning and budgeting, (iv) Low morale of employees and numerous human resource issues, (v) A negative net-worth, and (vi) Technically insolvent (NRB, 2005).

6 At first it came as Banking and Financial Institutions Ordinance, 2004.

7 First it came as Companies Ordinance, 2006

8 Nepal Rastra Bank, Board of Directors approved Merger Bylawas, 2011 on May 2011 by it its meeting (2/2068).

9 Shanker M. Singh in his article attempted to analyze the prospects and consequences of share market and to address the fluctuations seen frequently in the share market of Nepal. Retrieved from http://www.sharebazarnepal.com.np/views/articles/219-capital-market.html

10 Securities Exchange Centre was established in 197* and was involved in limited securities transactions.

11 Dr. Maskay and Mr. Bhatta in their article have cited many positive aspects in their article, including (i) increased economic growth through the introduction of foreign capital (ii) adoption of advanced financial practices and know how, and (iii) greater financial market efficiency through increased competition.

12 Nepal Rastra Bank (2014) source: www:nrb.org.np

[13Xiii] Their index includes; interest rate deregulation, pro-competition measures, reserve requirements, directed credit, bank's ownership, prudential regulation, stock markets and international financial liberalization

14 Financial sector reforms were initiated in these countries as an integral part of economic reforms mostly in 1980s and 1990s.

15 It also states that South Asia is a unique and heterogeneous region that encompasses countries diverse in size, in the political ideologies under which they are governed, in their economies and their stages of economic development.

APPENDIX

Table 4. Structure of the Nepalese Financial Sector

Financial Institutions	2010	2011	2012	2013	2014
Nepal Rastra Bank	296,625.6	319,692.6	455,826.5	534,897.9	642,871.8
Commercial Banks	763,226.3	853,490.7	1,052,450.7	1,242,881.4	1,377,058.5
Development Banks	102,208.9	129,617.4	160,360.2	199,954.8	228,194.2
Microfinance Development Banks	17,681.6	20,862.9	29,815.5	35,774.9	108,377.1
Finance Companies	109,998.2	118,578.2	109,687.5	100,856.7	4,281.8
Financial Co-operatives	6,975.2	8,150.6	11,652.4	15,415.1	1,664.2
Financial NGOS	2,382.6	4,937.6	4,260.0	5,560.0	3,107.6
Contractual Saving Institutions					
Employees Provident Fund	90,390.3	106,584.5	125,752.8	145,283.4	160,327.1
Citizen Investment Trust	22,647.8	26,905.4	38,068.5	42,753.6	48,624.7
Insurance Companies	47,460.0	61,213.4	73,825.0	84,650.4	94,960.0
Postal Savings Bank	1,085.9	1,152.4	1,276.4	1,397.2	1,530.0
Total	1,460,682.4	1,651,185.7	2,062,975.5	2,409,425.3	2,670,997.0
Market capitalization	376,871.0	323,484.3	368,262.1	514,492.1	
Total (incl. market capitalization)	1,837,553.4	1,974,670.0	2,431,237.6	2,923,917.5	
Percentage Share					
Financial Institutions					
Nepal Rastra Bank	20.3	19.4	22.1	22.2	24.1
Commercial Banks	52.3	51.7	51.0	51.6	51.6
Development Banks	7.0	7.8	7.8	8.3	8.5
Microfinance Development Banks	1.2	1.3	1.4	1.5	4.1
Finance Companies	7.5	7.2	5.3	4.2	0.2
Financial Co-operatives	0.5	0.5	0.6	0.6	0.1
Financial NGOS	0.2	0.3	0.2	0.2	0.1
Contractual Saving Institutions					
Employees Provident Fund	6.2	6.5	6.1	6.0	6.0
Citizen Investment Trust	1.6	1.6	1.8	1.8	1.8
Insurance Companies	3.2	3.7	3.6	3.5	3.6
Postal Savings Bank	0.1	0.1	0.1	0.1	0.1
Total	**100.0**	**100.0**	**100.0**	**100.00**	**100.00**

(Total Assets/Liabilities)
(2010- 2014)
(Rs. in million)
Sources: Monthly Financial Statistics, Quarterly Economic Bulletins and authors calculation

Table 5. Number of BFI Branches

Type of Institutions	2008	2010	2013	2014
	Mid-July	Mid-July	Mid-July	Mid-July
Commercial Banks	555	987	1486	1547
Development Banks	117	495	764	818
Financc Companics	132	281	242	239
Microcredit Development Banks	349	425	634	826
Total	**1153**	**2188**	**3126**	**3430**
Population availing banking services per branch				**7724**

Source: Banking and Financial Statistics, NRB

Chapter 11
Financial Sector in Afghanistan:
Regulatory Challenges in Financial Sector of Afghanistan

Gunit Singh Marwah
Gujarat National Law University, India

Vishal Ladhani
Gujarat National Law University, India

ABSTRACT

In the following chapter, the authors have proposed to throw light on the scheme of financial sector prevalent in Afghanistan. The purpose of this chapter is to give the readers a brief insight on the financial background, policies and regulations in existence in Afghanistan. Adding upon, the authors have made an attempt to suggest a few recommendations to bring the Afghanistan's economy at par with the economy of other developing nations of the world. The authors received substantial amount of assistance from the top-managerial officials of Bakhtar Bank of Afghanistan and from a scholar named Abdul Samad Katawazy. The authors would like to thank AREU, AISA and ACCI for providing access to their published surveys and reports. This particular chapter as a whole focuses on ten basic factors which have the ability to make or break Afghanistan's financial structure and therefore aims to provide an insight into the same.

INTRODUCTION

Afghanistan is a country which has the capability of reaching unthinkable heights in all possible indices in general and financially in particular. This is because it is one of the very few countries of the world with a large resource base but its exploitation has been at a very rudimentary stage. The market in Afghanistan is very flexible and fluid and can be moulded in any way the authorities want it to be.

That is where the risk comes and uncertainty of the direction in which Afghanistan's financial market can go to. It either can follow a rational path by promoting inclusive growth and development of Afghanistan as a whole or it can move towards being a failed state and controlled by militia and various

DOI: 10.4018/978-1-5225-0004-9.ch011

terrorist organizations. This chapter tries to study the presence of various such factors for e.g. huge mineral resources, informal sources of dispute resolution etc which have the ability to either make or break the Afghanistan's economy. Through this chapter we also try to analyse the effect of various factors like ever-rising opium production, illiteracy, corruption and increase-in terrorism on Afghanistan's financial market and its economy and suggest a few measures to reduce their cascading effect in the short run and completely eradicate them in the long run.

Through this chapter, the authors also comment on the effectiveness of the Kabul Stock exchange and the challenges and opportunities it faces in one of the world's most unpredictable and resource rich economy. Through this chapter, the authors have also analysed the role of banking sector in Afghanistan which mainly revolves around factors like lack of government support, lack of financial assistance, inefficient leadership etc. The authors have also emphasised on the need to develop the ancillary facilities like credit worthiness, valuation of property, insurance values etc. The authors have also touched upon the dominance of Islamic cultures and values in the financial system of Afghanistan like for example Article 4 of the Islamic republic of Afghanistan's constitution which talks about making the application of Islamic law mandatory in case of commercial disputes and Article 130 of which talks about application of Hanafi Jurisprudence in case of non-application of any constitutional provision in a legal dispute. The Civil code of Afghanistan has also upheld the same provision as mentioned in Article 130. Finally the authors have analysed the overlapping of the formal and informal system of dispute resolution along with the pros and cons of integrating the two systems.

The last sub-section of this chapter gives an example of a successful pilot project by Norwegian refugee council in integrating the two systems of dispute resolution and thus brings out of possibility of expanding this particular project and introduction of more of such other projects. Therefore the main objective behind this chapter is to critically analyze the regulatory framework of Afghanistan's financial system and suggest some practical and feasible measures to assist it in giving neck-to-neck competition to other developing countries of the world.

STOCK EXCHANGE OF AFGHANISTAN

Stock exchange, also called the stock market or share market, is one of the most important constituent of capital market. It is an organized market for the purchase and sale of industrial and financial security. It's basically an investment intermediately which facilitates economic and industrial development of a country. It provides a platform for convenient and secured transactions for different securities as per certain well defined rules and regulations to prevent excessive speculation, scams and other undesirable and anti-social activities.

Stock exchange in Afghanistan also known as the Afghanistan Stock Exchange (ASE), is basically a private equity exchange with regards to initial listing, investing in private placements or secondary trading of securities in admitted companies. As far as naming of shares is concerned, private equity ownership shares are 'named' as opposed to public shares, keeping a complete track of the title of ownership in relation to shares on offer. A complete digital registry is maintained for keeping all the issued shares of listed companies securitized. The digital registry, Central Business Registry of Afghanistan performs a 'custodian role' of traditional exchanges and is supervised by the Kabul Chamber of Commerce and Industries. Afghanistan stock exchange has initiated efforts to get itself licensed from the financial market regulator of Afghanistan, i.e. Da Afghanistan Bank.

Any legal entity can opt for getting itself listed on the Afghanistan Stock exchange, where ownership and risks are distributed by means of musharakah (equity shares). All the legal entities which opt for getting listed are required to disclose the financial statements according to the ASE format every quarter(latest by two months after the quarter) and the audited financial report once a year(latest by five months from year-end). With regard to presence of a proper stock-exchange is concerned, the situation in Afghanistan doesn't seem absolutely hopeless but Afghanistan's financial system would be incomplete without the presence of a modern financial market. Some of the major problems which Afghanistan's financial system is facing without the presence of a modern financial market are as follows:

A. **Capital Outflow:** The introduction of currency and banking laws has helped in strengthening the currency against foreign currencies and also resulted in establishment of international banks but the lack of a modern financial market has forced the banks to invest the money overseas resulting in capital outflow and thus loss of funds which could have been used in nation re-building.
B. **State Owned Enterprises:** The National development Framework has articulated the need of complete privatisation as a central measure for reconstruction of the war-torn Afghanistan. For this measure to be fully implemented, it was planned to sell or disband the state-owned enterprises to the private sector. But the process has been substantially delayed due to the lack of clear mechanisms for transparently selling these organisations.
C. **Self-Sustaining Investment:** Out of all the investments made in Afghanistan, majority of them are made by the people who are already very rich. There is no mechanism to channelize the savings of the not-so wealthy individuals or the newly emerging middle class which severely limits the capacity of the country to shift towards self-sustaining investment/reinvestment cycles and results in increasing gaps between rich and poor.
D. **Foreign Investment:** Apart from all of the reasons mentioned above there is also a complete lack of mechanism for routing foreign investment in the country. There is no concrete law which can clearly describe the procedure for investment or rules which could regulate investments and their source.

Let us see a different perspective from the case of Sudan. The Sudanese Stock Market is dominated by the activities of Sharia dominated institutions. The Islamic Development Corporation is one of the most important public joint stock companies in Sudan having a nominal capital of one billion dollars divided into one billion shares.60% of the total capital is assigned to non-Sudanese Muslims whereas remaining 60% to Sudanese Citizens. Another noteworthy financial institution instrumental in development of Sudanese Stock Market is the Faisal Islamic Bank having a nominal capital of 100 million pounds divided into ten million shares of ten pounds per share.

One striking feature of Sudanese Stock Market is the levy of religious duty of Zakah, for which the Sudanese Government had enacted the Law of Zakah and Tax in 1984. In this regard, Sudan has been ahead of many other Muslim countries in the modern world. Rules and regulations specify types of intangible wealth and methods of assessing *zakah* on them including bank deposits, accounts, bonds and shares inside and outside Sudan.

In a survey conducted by the United States agency for international development, two hundred and fifty five large companies were surveyed in Afghanistan and found strong variations across sectors in capital markets activities and the following information regarding theier source of capital was computed (Table 1).

Table 1. [insert caption here]

Source of capital	Absolute amount of capital(total capital-($224.87)(in millions)	Percentage of total capital
Self	$148.17	65.89%
Others	$54.05	24.03%
Banks	$14.81	6.58%
Friends	$4.41	1.96%
Family	$2.18	0.96%
Sarafi	$1.19	0.52%
Donors	$0.06	0.026%

Nearly all industries relied on external capital far less than "self" capital. Out of all the sources of capital other than "self", friends, family, sarafi and donors combined also constituted a reasonable share of the total amount showing the presence of certain high-net worth individuals in the top cities of Afghanistan. Construction companies, retailers, trade/distribution companies and transportation are the categories of business with highest reliance on friends and family. Notably Sarafi, real estate, telecommunications and banks do not rely at all on friends or family for capital. A total 6.58% of the total capital raised was sourced from banks. Telecommunications, agriculture, construction, manufacturing and trade/distribution constitute the sectors which majorly rely on banks. Another finding which is not very surprising is that on an average people invested a total of $2,607,504 in banks, however those borrowing from banks, invested an average of $10.4 million, illustrating the use of the banking sector by large companies.

But in another survey conducted by "Investment Climate Assessment", it was found out that most of the commercial banks have their main focus only on the capital city of Kabul. They are involved in providing services mainly to donors, international businesses, foreign NGO's and foreign government agencies. Also there are no professional credit rating agencies or credit bureaus which could determine the level of proficiency or transparency in the banking operations and thus could motivate the banks in improving the way they carry out their functions.

Also apart from the regulated market, certain informal sources like Sarafi (Money changers), Hawala transfers play a very important role in supporting businesses in Afghanistan. Although not very popular, they are very valuable as they help in changing currencies and moving large sums of money around Afghanistan. Institutions like Sarafi, Hawala transfer even though mostly limited to small business have great prospects to grow in future because only about 30% of the total Afghan population have bank accounts and because of their conformity with the Afghan culture and rituals which make them to appear at least as efficient as bank transfers.

There is a great amount of difference in the factors upon which the growth of a stock exchange and the expansion of transactions related to it depend, in different countries. Infact, the growth and development of primary and secondary market in Egypt depends upon the following factors

- Trustworthiness of the issuing party
- Viability of the projects financed through them, together which in turn will lead to winning public confidence

The Afghanistan Stock Market can take example from the markets in Kuwait. The Kuwaiti stock market can be characterised for its large size, high rate of stock recycling and big volume of its operations. Even though from the Islamic perspective, ordinary shares are legally permissible since they share in the profit and loss but from Shariah point of view, what is need is a closer look. The funds raised through ordinary shares may fall in the hands of foreign companies that do not pay attention to the *shari'ah* tenets (*halal*, *haram* and the interests of the Muslim *ummah*) when utilizing these funds. Or, they may fall in the hands of national companies that do not care about investment priorities conforming to the Islamic methodology. On the other hand, these shares may be badly used and deviate from their objectives, when they are used in severe speculations aiming only at high and quick profits.

Initially, absence of a fully-fledged secondary market was a major obstacle in the growth of the security market in Kuwait. But after the introduction of secondary market along with the modern Kuwaiti banks have played a major role in the development and promotion of Interest based securities which are generally prohibited under Shari'ah point of view.

BANKING SECTOR IN AFGHANISTAN

The modern banking practice in Afghanistan is prevalent from the last 10 years. There seems to be a large scope of growth and development in this sector. The banking sector is majorly responsible for the fluctuations in an economy. Many issues like security, awareness, education, etc. are to be considered while discussing the banking sector. The fluctuations in the interest rate of the Afghani currency are a major area of concern for the banks. Both private and public banks are in operation in Afghanistan. The modern banking system is a relatively new sector with huge challenges in areas like experiences, skilled labour, technical knowledge, etc. The banking industry is an opportunity where various component units can be combined to reach the vision. Any kind of banking industry should develop in such a way that it helps the economy in the long run and create the culture of banking in short for developed and self-sufficient Afghanistan.

The economic reconstruction of Afghanistan is dependent upon government policies and frameworks. One of these should be to enhance the base of the banking sector across the country. The government should try to build such a structural framework which strengthens both the public and private sector banks and even make ways for new entrants in this sector. The banking culture is not well accepted by the people in Afghanistan because of the lack of education. Another reason of concern is the lack of savings because of unemployment. To cure the above points, awareness about banking and its good effects on the economy should be spread among the population.

Afghanistan is involved in a lot of trade activities across various countries like India, China and Pakistan. The traders deal in dollars while making payments for these transactions. Hence, they prefer to keep money in dollars and this makes the value of Afghani currency go down. The fluctuation rate of interest of dollar is very low and people tend to prefer dollar. This is one of the major reasons why people don't save Afghani currency and these results in lower amount of savings and non-expansion of banking sector. This is because in Afghanistan the number of borrowers is more compared to the number of depositors. These banks cannot only perform governmental functions like collecting taxes, making payments, etc. They have to expand their scope in order to earn higher returns.

There are various weaknesses in areas of banking governance in commercial banks. Internal controls should be proposed and implemented by the central bank of Afghanistan, Da Afghanistan Bank (DAB).

Any kind of help in banking sector by the US has been stopped since 2011. This makes it very difficult for the central bank to expand the proceedings of the commercial banks and to make up to the international standards. The International Monetary Fund does not currently have any advisors assisting DAB (SIGAR, 2014). The central bank has not been successful in its initial objectives. DAB was established in 1939, but by the end of 2001, the formal Afghan financial system (IMF, 2003) was nearly nonexistent. The Kabul Bank crisis is a very important example to indicate the failure of Da Afghanistan Bank. It almost came on the verge of closing and it was nowhere to the intended profits which it had predicted that it would make. This shows the weakness in the banking sector of the country.

The area of legislation is also a matter of concern for the banking sector. It has been argued that a lot of monetary transactions take place in the country which fund illegal forces in the country. For this purpose a draft bill has been proposed in the Parliament to curb counterfeiting and sponsoring of such activities. But till September 2013, these bills have not been passed. Any help given by the World Bank and IMF is moderately unsatisfactory. No real assistance in technical or financial area is received by the DAB, which is a major drawback for the development of the banking sector. The 2010 crisis of the Kabul Bank has resulted in loss of confidence among the people of Afghanistan. This has a huge impact on the long term economic growth of the country. For this reason, the Afghanistan government should look up to the developed nations for their support.

There is a banking law in Afghanistan which all banks have to adhere to. It deals with various chapters like:

- General Provisions
- Licenses and Permits
- Organization, Ownership and Administration
- Operational Requirements
- Accounts, Reports and Inspection
- Enforcement Measures
- Conservatorship
- Rehabilitation of Banks
- Liquidation of Banks
- Receivership of Banks
- Final Provisions

The deficiency in the banking sector is a major drawback for investments in a country. The Government has not been successful in providing enough opportunities to the banking sector and thereby, not realising the potential and importance of this sector. The lack of professional leadership, unavailability of financial resources and substandard service provision are areas of critical deficiencies with reference to the banking sector. This is the reason why various commercial banks in the country are hiring and employing foreign professionals in their banks, so that they can even achieve the same level as other reputed banks in various countries.

There is a certain substantive amount of difference between the commercial bank lending rates in Afghanistan and other sub-continent countries. Like for example in a survey in 2013, it was found out that the average bank lending rates by the end of December 2012, was 15% in Afghanistan compared to 12.41% in Pakistan. This clearly shows the reason why people in Afghanistan prefer taking loans from unregulated informal sectors as compared to the commercial banks.

One of the challenges faced by banking and microfinance organizations in Afghanistan is the development of ancillary facilities (Rod Monger, 2013). These ancillary facilities include valuation of property, acceptable risk, credit reporting, insurance values and credit worthiness. For the above purposes, one needs to have an effective accounting and auditing team of professionals. Both internal and external auditing is necessary for regulation of this sector. All the banks have to follow the regulations of both the Afghan banking laws and Da Afghanistan Bank, which can be easily done if an internal auditor is appointed. There are no means by which one can identify whether an auditor in Afghanistan is credible or not. It is just the claims of the few foreign companies who have acted as auditors in other countries, who claim to be good internal auditors. But a person who is a good auditor in some other country cannot be asserted to be a good auditor in Afghanistan, just for that reason. Thus, lack of efficient and educated professionals in Afghanistan is another hindrance for the development of the banking sector.

There have been arguments by various experts in favour of Islamic banking for the country of Afghanistan. They argue that in a nation where the modern banking system has failed to boost up the economy, the alternative of Islamic banking should be tried. It is said that Islamic banking might play an important role for the reconstruction and economic development of Afghanistan. By adding religious value in this sector, it could boost up this sector. For example, people following Islam think that interest is forbidden and hence, other products with some other feature could be more effective in attracting people towards banking. This will also boost investment as most people will be encouraged to take loans from the Islamic banking system leading to capital formation in the economy. By this way, the banking sector will be able to reach out low income level people, which form a majority of the population of Afghanistan.

The advancements in banking sector have not reached the majority of the areas in Afghanistan. Most of the daily transactions in Afghanistan are carried out through cash and banking is done through the old concept of passbooks. Most of the people do not have the access to online banking, ATMs or electronic cards. This creates a hindrance as the original process of banking is not user friendly and this makes less people become customers of banks. In countries like India and China, most of the banking sector is controlled by machines or user friendly custom softwares. This even tends to indicate that banking is less important than other occupations in the country. The banking sector has not yet received the confidence of the public. It is suggested that till date the banking sector in the country is not easy, efficient and trustworthy. This is one of the phenomenons which needs to be changed as early as possible for the country to flourish in the future, as banking contributes a large portion of the GDP of service sector in a developing country.

Foreign banks in China tend to invest in areas where there is proper flow of information. They tend to open operations and spread their services where finance is regulated by law. This clearly shows that lack of legal awareness in areas underpins the lending services in that areas. Many banks with its headquarters in China would not like to open up operations in majority of Afghanistan because of the lack of legislation relating to the banking sector that protects contract and property rights in the country. This is because these banks do no want to face contract enforcing problems at a later stage.

SOLUTIONS AND RECOMMENDATIONS

- **Financial Innovation:** New products should be introduced in the market which is different from the conventional system of banking. Transparency in transactions can be brought through efficient use of computer technology in areas where it is not available. New networks must be set up in order to reach the prospective customers. Most people are unaware of the banking facilities available in the country and to overcome this, the banks should set up booths to reach out to people and encourage them to deposit. The banks should hire survey agencies that study the habits of the consumers and help the bank in determining the needs of specific kinds of consumers. New products like smart cards and electronic cards (Merton & Robert, 1992) may also be issued to attract customers. Thus, financial innovation (Miller & Merton, 1986) is an integral part of any banking system.

- **Spreading Awareness:** Steps should be taken up by the banks to set up bodies who are involved in spreading awareness among the people about banking. Many people living in rural areas are unaware about the practices of modern banking. This sector can flourish only with the active participating and involvement of the public. This is possible only if the public is aware about the activities and schemes of these commercial banks.
- **Government Subsidy:** Government of Afghanistan should provide subsidy to the customers of the commercial banks to encourage them to deposit more. It is only when incentive is provided to a person that he invests more. Hence, if new schemes benefitting the people are introduced, it is going to boost this sector.
- **Foreign Model:** The banking practices in countries like USA, England, etc. should be taken into consideration while preparing the rules and laws regarding banking. All regulations regarding banking should be made in consideration with such laws prevalent in other countries.

FOREIGN INVESTMENTS IN AFGHANISTAN

The business climate in Afghanistan is a complex mix of great opportunity and the most difficult challenges. Outstanding, untapped natural resources, exceptional geographic location, and business friendly legislation sits behind lack of good governance, rampant corruption, high security risks, absence of skilled labour and dominance of informal arrangements. Since the fall of Taliban Regime the government of Afghanistan has planned a series of reforms to make the Afghanistan market look more attractive to investors but when it comes to their implementation, the progress has been slow and unsatisfactory which can be clearly seen through the rankings for "Ease of doing business" released by World bank periodically. For Afghanistan, it has slipped from 165th in 2010 to 183rd in June 2014 out of a total of 189 countries.(World Bank, 2014) When analysed on the criteria of trading across borders which is calculated based on import/export document, cost and time, the ranking for Afghanistan has been equally miserable even though it has slightly improved. It rose from being last in the list (189th) in 2010 to 184th in 2014.

In an attempt to come at par with other developing economies of the world, the Afghanistan Chamber of Commerce and Industries (ACCI) in coalition with eleven other business associations drafted the National Business Agenda and handed it over to the government of Afghanistan. It basically identifies laws, regulations and problems in six areas which hinder business activity and investment and aims to develop a system to gauge the progress of implementing policy recommendations through an active monitoring mechanism.

RECAP

The government of Islamic Republic of Afghanistan and the Government of Islamic Republic of Pakistan signed the Afghanistan and Pakistan Transit Trade Agreement (APTTA) in order to fulfil the following objectives:

A. Strengthening the economic ties between the two countries on a mutually beneficial basis
B. Recognizing the right of Afghanistan to freedom of access to the sea as an essential principle for the expansion of international trade and economic development.
C. Recognising the importance of the North-South Corridor for Pakistan in relation to trade with Central Asia and for Afghanistan in relation to trade with SAARC countries
D. Reiterating their commitment to ensure the smooth, rapid and efficient movement of goods and vehicles between and through the territories of the two countries
E. Recalling the WTO rules and provisions under the General Agreement on Tariff and trade concerning "Freedom of Transit"
F. Considering that the Afghan Transit Trade Agreement(ATTA) of 1965 does not take into account the current economic realities and the new international transit requirements

It was implemented on 12th June 2011 and trucks from both the countries crossed the border. The new agreement replaced the 1965 transit trade agreement which allows Afghanistan to import and export goods through Wagah, Karachi and Gawdar ports

OPPURTUNITIES AND CHALLENGES FOR FOREIGN INVESTORS

In a war-torn country like Afghanistan attracting foreign investment is central to the private sector development as it leads to inflow of foreign capital and funds but also transfer of skills, technology and job opportunities. Taking full note of the above mentioned requirement, the Afghan government has taken a number of measures to make the process of registering a business easier as can be seen from the rankings for ease in starting a business. Afghanistan stands at 24th place out of a total of 189 countries. Also the Afghan government has taken some steps to address issues of tax administration and labour law. But when one takes the full picture into account the situation isn't that rosy. A number of foreign companies in Afghanistan and a number of international organisations have cited security concerns, weak governance, pervasive corruption, dominance of informal arrangements etc as the main reasons for discouragement to enter the Afghan Financial Market. These uncertainties reduce confidence, discourage private investment, and also affect growth in construction, manufacturing and services.

The number of new firms registrations fell sharply in 2013 to its lowest level in five years with a reduction in both local and foreign new fixed investments.(From an average of 5000 registrations per annum to 3100 in 2013). There was a similar reduction in agricultural growth which came down from an average of 11% during 2007-11 to a little over 3% in 2013. There was an effect on the exchange rate too, prompting a switch out of local-currency-denominated assets. Inflation however stayed in single digits (5.3% in Feb 2014) due to good harvest and relatively benign commodity prices. Adding on there are some hidden and transient advantages to investing in Afghanistan simply because the failure of government to collect taxes and charge for public services. The MNCs that have made their presence felt in Afghanistan are in the transport and logistics sector (DHL), food processing (Coca Cola), banking (Standard Chartered Bank, National Bank of Pakistan, Habib Bank Ltd., and National Bank of Punjab), tourism (Hyatt Hotels and Serena Hotels), and trade (Toyota Motors and Alcatel Trade International).

Thus it can be seen that a number of multi-nationals have invested in Afghanistan but bulk of the economy still remains informal. Given below are a set of challenges and opportunities for investment in Afghanistan

- **Improving Legal Framework for Investment:** Afghanistan is in a stage of legal evolution where a number of laws related to various sectors of business are in various stages of enactment. Therefore a number of areas remain unregulated/poorly regulated along with limited capacity of judiciary. Also the existence of three overlapping systems Sharia(Islamic Law), Shura(Traditional law and practice) and the formal legal system instituted under the 2004 constitution can be confusing to both investors and legal professionals. This contributes to overall risk perception.
- **Developing Tax Regime and Custom Administration:** Like the legal framework, the tax regime is also in the developing stage which even though acts as an advantage for various businesses because they don't pay any taxes due to lack of clarity and enforcement but it also sometimes leads to large formal companies shouldering a disproportionate share of corporate tax burden in Afghanistan. Similar is the case with custom duties. Recent reforms even though have streamlined the process but there still exists lack of coordination in custom collection between the authorities and the central government. Also there is a major improvement needed in consistency and transparency in custom administration in various provinces of Afghanistan.
- **Developing Transport Infrastructure and Regularising Costs:** There is an urgent requirement to develop the transport infrastructure in Afghanistan. The roads are in a very poor condition, are freight is limited and most of the goods have to be shipped either through Pakistan or Iran. Afghanistan has a long way to go at coming at par with regards to transport facilities when compared with other developing nations of the world.
- **Complex Property Market:** Like many socialist economies of the world, most of the land in Afghanistan is held by government and acquiring/leasing land from the individual government agencies is generally a very frustrating task for various business organizations. This is because of the non-transparent and inconsistent methods of selling/leasing adopted by these agencies. Title disputes are pretty common and the inefficient judiciary adds to the woes of the business organisations.
- **Ability of the State to Provide the Basic Utilities:** Certain basic utilities like water, electricity are not commonly available to all. Majority of the business organisations have to make arrangements of these basic utilities privately which is not cheap. Improving their capacity to provide such basic utilities to all through collaboration with private organisations(PPPs) could be a step forward in this direction
- **Improving Security:** Security remains a major concern for the foreign investors in Afghanistan. Even though the regional extremist organisations have been weakened to some extent when compared to the situation prevalent during Taliban Regime, nevertheless a number of cities of

Afghanistan continue to face attacks. If Afghan government shows some initiative in improving the internal security of the country, it can do wonders to the investor confidence.

- **Strengthening Financial Markets:** Several international banks and the Central Bank provide conventional financial services to business, but standard financial products such as commercial loans and export financing are not yet available in Afghanistan for domestic investors. As a result, business finance is not fully developed and most loans seem to be informal sector transactions between family and friends.

SCOPE FOR IMPROVEMENT

At the July 2012 Tokyo conference, Afghanistan and the international community shared a vision to further consolidate their partnership in the areas of governance, security, peace process, economic and social development, and regional cooperation to help Afghanistan move from transition to attain sustainable economic growth and development and fiscal self-reliance through the transformation decade of 2015–24. The gradual withdrawal of troops from Afghanistan has definitely reduced the aggregate demand and increased the domestic spending which thus makes it really important to maintain the macroeconomic stability through a total structural reform in Afghan's financial structure, a continuing donor support, proper security measures and an encouraging business environment. The above mentioned factors could definitely play a major role in generating a 'peace dividend' for economic activity through higher activity across sectors, return of expatriates and more importantly foreign direct investment.

The Government of Afghanistan in the process of implementing the Afghanistan National Development Strategy which focuses government's activity in three main areas

- Agriculture and rural rehabilitation
- Human-capacity development
- Economic development and infrastructure through implementation of high priority programs chosen for their ability to contribute to significant to job creation, broad geographic impact, and likelihood of attracting additional investment.

Afghanistan has no formal regulations or laws governing performance requirements. There are no existing government-imposed conditions on investment, beyond the procedures required for establishing or acquiring a business. Also, faced with increasing uncertainty and a slowdown in the economic activity, the Union Cabinet has approved a series of measures which includes tax holidays up to 10years, subsidized loans, public loans with 5-10years maturity and automatic licenses to artisanal and small-scale mining activities without a bidding process. Along with favouring foreign investors by liberalising the business environment, the government of Afghanistan also encourages large business entities and foreign investors to contribute towards Corporate Social Responsibility (CSR) through investment in health, education, job creation, environmental protection and outreach to refugees. The American chamber of commerce in Afghanistan has identified CSR as one of the core focus areas.

Afghanistan has signed 31 bilateral trade and investment agreements/memoranda of understanding and a further 10 bilateral economic agreement/memoranda of understanding. Among these are the Afghanistan Pakistan Transit Trade Agreement (APTTA), which Afghanistan and Pakistan signed in October 2010 and investment-related agreements with China and Kazakhstan. Afghanistan signed a Trade and

Investment Framework Agreement (TIFA) with the United States in 2004. Afghanistan does not have a BIT or a bilateral taxation treaty with the United States. The European Union, the United States, India, Canada, and Japan have granted Afghan exports preferential treatment under their Generalized System of Preference schemes. Afghanistan is a member of the Economic Cooperation Organization (ECO), the South Asia Free Trade Area (SAFTA), the South Asian Association for Regional Cooperation (SAARC), and of Central Asian Regional Economic Cooperation (CAREC).

The Overseas Private Investment Corporation (OPIC) offers financing (from large structured finance to small business loans), political risk insurance, and support for private-equity investment funds. Since 2003, OPIC has committed more than $295 million in financing and political risk insurance to support 38 projects in Afghanistan. OPIC operates its programs in Afghanistan under the Investment Incentive Agreement ("IIA") signed in 2004 with the Government of Afghanistan. Nonetheless, during this past taxation year, the Government of Afghanistan, Ministry of Finance pursued a 20% withholding tax on interest paid to OPIC by several OPIC clients. Such taxation ignores the tax exemption explicitly provided to OPIC under the IIA. On January 10, 2014, OPIC President and CEO Elizabeth Littlefield sent a formal letter to the Afghan Minister of Finance, notifying the Afghan government that its efforts to tax loan recipients' on interest payments made to OPIC, which ignores the terms of the IIA, gave OPIC "no choice but to suspend consideration of and support for any new transactions in Afghanistan." Since then, after holding a series of cabinet meetings, the Afghan government issued a letter to the American Embassy with a diplomatic note indicating that loan recipients would not owe any taxes on their payments to OPIC for the 2013 tax year.

However, the diplomatic note also stated that the Ministers of Commerce, Foreign Affairs and Finance have been mandated by the Cabinet to review and make recommendations on the issue of whether the IIA is in the national interest of Afghanistan, and whether it should be (a) left as is, (b) modified, or (c) terminated (which either party has a right to do within certain parameters). Should the GOA elect to terminate the IIA, the provisions of the agreement (including the tax exemption) apply to OPIC investment support provided to loan recipients during the time the agreement was in force for so long as such investment support remains outstanding.

GOVERNMENT REGULATIONS IN COMPANY MATTERS

The Corporations and Limited Liability Companies law (CLLCL) provides Afghanistan with the legal rules for the organization of business enterprises in Afghanistan. The law defines two types of enterprises:

- **Corporation:** a business company whose capital is definite and divided into shares, with the share and responsibility of each shareholder limited to the proportion of his share; and
- **Limited Liability company:** It is a business company whose capital is not divided into shares with the responsibility of each shareholder limited to the amount of capital agreed to [by such shareholder] in the company.

Companies in Afghanistan have to get registered, a business license, Articles of Incorporation and Annual reports with the Central Registry. They have a two-tier Board of Directors including a board of supervisors that oversees the Board of Directors and can inspect Corporations books and records. Under the new law, the Board of directors are charged with a duty to disclose any conflict of interest whatsoever regarding transaction effected by corporation. The new law also makes it mandatory for companies to hold Annual general meetings and before such meetings; the corporations must deliver the financial statement (prepared in compliance with the international accounting standards) to all the shareholders.

With regards to transparency, the law provides privileges to shareholders like right to inspect the books of accounts, filing of a lawsuit in the name of corporation against the board of directors or other Key managerial personnel for failure to perform their duties etc. The new law also defines a limited liability company, i.e. a company having a minimum of 2 and maximum of 50 shareholders whose shares are not to be sold on a public stock exchange. A failure to meet these requirements results in terminations of the activities of corporation by the Central Registry.

The law relating to companies in Afghanistan in general has adopted western models and practices. But the law is not free of some lacunas and drawbacks.

First of all, the methodology for establishing a corporation in Afghanistan is incomplete. The primary agency for establishment of business in Afghanistan is the Afghan Investment Support Agency (AISA), for both domestic and foreign companies. But the agency hasn't been mentioned anywhere or given any power in the Corporations and Limited Liability Companies Law. (Shebergan, 2014) Another lacuna is the ambiguous way in which the law has been drafted. For example, the law provides for registration of Article of Incorporation with the Central Registry but it doesn't provide any information regarding where the central registry is located or any oversight of the business registration process. Fortunately the Afghan Investment Support Agency has suo-moto adopted the role of ensuring enforcement and administration of the law.

With regards to taxation matters the taxpayers are required to register with Large Taxpayers Office, Medium taxpayer's office and Small taxpayers Office respectively (according to size of capital and revenue of taxpayer). Tax returns have to be filed within three months of the end of the relevant tax year. A business receipt tax which varies from 2% to 10% is chargeable on gross revenue on quarterly basis within 15days of end of the quarter. In addition to that the taxpayers are required to prepare and issue to each employee an annual wage and tax withholding statement. Finally with regards to director's liability, his/her liability is limited to their shares and treated at the same rates as applicable to other taxpayers in the country.

ANALYSING THE MINING LAW IN AFGHANISTAN

Afghanistan is one of the few countries of the world which has been endowed with minerals worth millions of dollars. (James Risen, 2014)

This reservoir of resources presents a permanent solution to the excessive financial constraints faced by the Afghanistan government and the people living there. It possesses the capability of wiping out the extreme poverty, diminishing the dependence on foreign aid and making the country self-sufficient. But the same reservoir also possesses the ability to do more harm than any good because of the risk of increasing insecurity and corruption. To avoid such evils there was a need to introduce a powerful mining law.

After a two year long process of drafting, finally in the month of August 2014, the new minerals law was signed by President with the aim to achieve improved sector governance and greater investor confidence. Minerals like Hajigak(iron ore), Balkhab(copper), Badakhashan(gold), Shaida (copper) and Zarkashan(copper-gold) are examples of few minerals which are present in abundance and a step closer to be profitably extracted.(Adam Smith, 2014) Given below is a list of improvements introduced through the new minerals law

- Clarity on the types of mineral licenses, authorisations and what can be tendered
- The provision for joint bidding of Exploration and Exploitation (extraction) licenses
- Inclusion of a new provision for Community Development Agreements to be signed between the investor and the local community around sites of mining operation
- Clearer provisions on health, safety and environmental protection
- Increased transparency, with the requirement for non-confidential information on awarded contracts to be published.

This new legislation marks a major step by the Afghan government from an owner-operator of the country's assets to a policymaker, regulator and investment facilitator. But the advantages of this historic legislation come along with a few drawbacks too.

One of the major drawbacks is that this new legislation does not have some of the basic safeguards against the possibility of instability and corruption. For example, there is no provision which makes it mandatory for business houses to publish the contracts signed under this act opening up the possibility of potential abuses. For a nation where almost 1/3rd of the total population is below poverty line and mining is a major source of revenue for insurgents and armed groups, this particular omission could turn out to be quite dangerous.(Stephen Carter, 2014)

The political class of the state of Afghanistan is no less. In a study conducted by Mr. William A. Byrd and Mr. Javed Noorani on some of the major mining companies of Afghanistan, it was revealed that even though Afghanistan's mineral law explicitly prohibits elected politicians and selected government officials to own mining operations, a number of contracts were acquired by the relatives of politically influential people with some of them being acquired by a sitting member of parliament. Considering the political involvement, it isn't surprising that the contract holders do not comply with the statutory requirements regulating the mining operations in the country. Afghanistan's mineral and environment law requires the mining companies to prepare an environmental and social impact assessment (ESIA) and some other documents before beginning extraction. Out of the five major companies of all the politically influenced mining companies surveyed, none of them not only did not meet the above requirements but also neglected the safety measures for their workers and also have subjected them to low wages. Adding on most of them did not meet the necessary documentation requirements required to be submitted to National Environmental Protection Agency (NEPA).

The new Minerals law has defined the offences but hasn't clearly specified penalties. Even though a set of circumstances have been mentioned for holding the companies liable, there is a lack of strict enforcement measures.(William & Noorani, 2014) Therefore it lacks provisions for fair and affordable dispute resolution.

With the withdrawal of international troops there is an increasing chance of already loosened mining sector to go out of governments control because of the lacunas in the new legislation which would result in increasing confidence in the mind of insurgents. With that Afghanistan could lose almost US$1 trillion worth of mineral assets and petrochemicals worth around US$ 2 trillion into the hands of insurgents and thereby loose a great opportunity to prevent the economy from further slipping down. If there are lacunas in the mining legislation, then there is a great possibility that Afghanistan would deviate from its ambition "from war to peace" to from "military conflict to resource conflict" with the organizations like Taliban having an upper hand. Minerals being very valuable but non-renewable resources, a weak legislation, corrupt executive and inefficient judiciary could present a perfect opportunity for armed groups from within and outside the country to make an attempt to take over the control.

The new mineral law should include provisions for carrying out a full-fledged due-diligence on each and every bidder so that the most important revenue generating source in Afghanistan could stay free from political interference and corruption. The study also concluded that the MoMP and Ministry of Finance (MoF) should develop a mechanism (by forming a joint committee) for collecting revenues from mining companies when due and conducting follow-up in response to discrepancies and delays. Therefore it's a high time that Afghan government realizes that proper safeguards in the mining legislation, though might make the procedure a little complicated but they are not an obstacle to attract investment in the country, infact they are pre-conditions for the same.(Lynne, 2014)

THE FINANCIAL CULTURE IN AFGHANISTAN

Long years of conflict have devastated Afghan industry. It has completely destroyed most of Afghanistan's production capacity and has forced a large chunk of skilled workers/managers to flee from Afghanistan. Adding to the woes, the soviet backed government made the situation even worse by setting up a centrally planned economy which leads to closing down of many traditional industries including carpet weaving to close down and shift to neighbouring countries.

Agriculture was one sector which even though got badly handicapped but survived to exist after going through a severe drought of late 1990's. As a result, despite a recent resurgence, the Afghan economy remains agricultural based, mostly consisting of small farmers. Apart from agriculture, few small and medium enterprises and a handful of large firms, family owned micro-enterprises constitute a major portion of the private sector. The end of major conflict and the fall of Taliban regime led to an increase in private investment. But despite having the fortune of receiving certain high-profile investments, total investment has been relatively limited, compared to what had been hoped by the policymakers.

Till the year 2005 almost US$1.3 Billion had been approved in Afghanistan mainly in the construction and construction materials. This is mainly not only because there is a need of basic infrastructure but often investment is directed into construction because of lack of other opportunities. A portion of the investment was also diverted towards the industries in Afghanistan but the truth is that, Afghan enterprises are in the stage where they are emerging and not capable to in fact compete against imports or enter the exports market. A very little proportion of the total investments had been approved in agriculture which is very much predictable because of the insignificant scale at which agriculture is undertaken as an investment in Afghanistan. The presence of returnees in the investment process in Afghanistan is really important because besides bringing capital, they bring along understanding on diverse subjects like International business methods, financial markets which not many of the local afghan population are accustomed to. The presence of returnees can also lead to high firm productivity.

The financial certificates issued in Malaysia have the characteristics of local religion. Qard Hasan certificates are short-term certificates issued by Malaysian Government by virtue of a parliament decree, in order to obtain interest-free loans from banks, institutions and private individuals At the time of redemption, only the principal amount is repaid to its owners without any return or material benefit. The proceeds raised through Qard Hasan Certificate allows the government to continue with its projects without any need to undertake measures to increase money supply (inflationary financing) or to levy more taxes.

Same is the concept in Bangladesh, as in these countries culture is given prime importance. In the securities market of Bangladesh, Investment Council Fund Certificates are issued by the Investment Council in Bangladesh which is a governmental non-banking financing institution which mainly operate on interest basis but can also be arranged to operate on Mudarabah. The speciality of these types of securities is that each fund is totally independent in terms of underlying assets and liabilities and also has their own independent management. Under Investment Council Fund Certificates, funds are mobilised under two heads, i.e. ICB Unit Certificates (these certificates are redeemable as well as negotiable), ICB Mutual Certificates (these certificates are negotiable but not redeemable). The resources of the funds are used in investment operations whose returns are appropriated by certificate holders after deduction of a specific administrative charge for the Investment Council of Bangladesh (ICB).

Almost all of the private business enterprises in Afghanistan clearly understand the importance of obtaining external capital from the capital market. However important it may be, but raising capital is considered relatively challenging in Afghanistan. In a survey conducted by the Investment climate Assessment, 37% of the business interviewed had to face major obstacles in accessing finance and more specifically 78% of the large business interviewed had difficulties in raising finance therefore it's very easy to conclude that large business face much more difficulties in raising finance in Afghanistan. These results give a clear depiction of how the capital markets in Afghanistan, fail to meet the economic needs of the businesses and thus force them to opt for the informal sources of finance. Also apart from access to capital market there are even some other constraints which hinder the growth of private sector. Almost two-third of the businesses surveyed cited electricity as a major constraint. A number of businesses frequently face low voltage, intermittent supply and black-outs. Only 76% of the total businesses surveyed are connected to the power grid and even they get power for only about six-and a half hours a day. Even though the total power generation capacity of the power companies is over 420MW, only 270 MW is operational.

Over 60% of them said access to land was another troubling factor. Out of the total number of firms surveyed, over 56% of the firms said they couldn't get land even after making efforts for almost three years. And even if the businesses are able to get access to the lands, the registration process is so inefficient and cumbersome that a number of plots do not get registered and many a times the land records get destroyed or are inaccessible. The businessperson's have to go from one office to other to obtain a number of clearances without much hope that there document would get cleared.

Over and above there is widespread insecurity, a corrupt bureaucracy, cumbersome regime of rules and regulations, lack of critical infrastructure and lack of easy and secure transport facilities, lack of skilled workers and managers, no insurance and ineffective judiciary which add to the never ending foes(Mehdi, 2011). Firms in Afghanistan have to pay, on an average 8% of their sales as bribes. This is almost four times the average reported in Pakistan. These problems are spread all across Afghanistan with no city as an exception. Recently, a number of firms have started to cope up with security issues but these measures have come with a price. A recent survey by Investment climate Assessment suggests that the existing firms have to spend as high as 15% of their total sales to nullify security concerns as compared to just 2.2% of the total sales in Pakistan, 1.9% in Uzbekistan and 3.4% of the total sales in Tajikistan.

But even after these adverse difficulties, the private sector hasn't performed that badly. Over the last five years, there has been a 67% increase in employment (22% in last year alone). With regard to the manufacturing capacity, there has been a 60% capacity utilization which even though is slightly less than its neighbouring developing countries, but considering the level of armed conflict in the country is quite commendable. Where the median value of sales per worker in manufacturing is concerned, it is $3333 which is even higher than the median value of sales per worker in Tajikistan and Uzbekistan.

This shows that when compared to the countries which are at similar development stage, Afghanistan has fared pretty well. With regard to product line, out of the total business surveyed by Investment Climate, one-third of the total companies introduced a product line in last two years and more than 40% upgraded an existing product line in the last two years. It shows that despite the difficult business environment which the businesses in Afghanistan are subject to, Afghan industry is steadily recovering and existing firms are coping well. The country of Afghanistan needs to put in a tremendous amount of efforts to transform its economy from an aid-dependent, distributive system to a dynamic market economy. The recently elected president of Afghanistan who was also a former finance minister in the government of President Hamid Karzai said, "We have not woken up to the reality to make the economy function" He also said that "economic route could be an option to stabilize the country, mainly through many small and some big ticket investments. (Faiez & Heidi, 2011)

SOLUTIONS AND RECOMMENDATIONS

The country of Afghanistan is in dire need for a modern financial system. The key challenge in Afghanistan is to broaden participation in the market by removing barriers to new entry and creating conditions that will encourage those already in market to invest more. A certain set of steps have been recommended which together will increase the incentives to invest and perk up ability to carry out production activities.

- **Better Accesses to Inputs:** Industries/companies in Afghanistan are in direct need of an access to the basic inputs like land, finance, skilled labour and way better infrastructure. This would automatically reduce the over-dependence of the concerned parties on the informal sector and thus would lower down the probability of these industries/companies to enter into vicious cycle as it would be free from high interest rates and uncertainty in terms regarding payment. Also some quick reforms in the land sector could lead to freeing up of land which is at present locked up in non-performing assets (State-owned enterprises) and injecting more life in the banking sector by making them at par with the banks of more developing countries of the world could be a major progress towards supply of inputs. But what is the basic factor which would decide whether these measures would bring out the desired output is how transparently and efficiently the process is carried out.
- **Need to Strengthen Property Right:** A strong legal, judicial and regulatory framework would do a world of good to both the tangible property such as land and equipment and for intangible property such as licence to operate or permit to import raw materials. This would also reduce the increasing dependence on the informal means of dispute resolution. The above mentioned objectives like in case of 'improving access to inputs' could only be improved if the regulatory system becomes more predictable, transparent and less procedural in order to avoid the concept of resorting to informal contacts in order to get the necessary approvals.
- **Need to Improve the Flow of Information:** Urgent steps need to be taken to improve how quickly and efficiently the information regarding market 'opportunities and trends', 'quality of products', 'availability of resources', and 'government policies' is available in the market and thus reduce

the extent to which business enterprises would have to use their personal/informal contacts to get such information where always there is an element of uncertainty. There is a necessity to increase awareness of government policies, laws and regulations which would ensure that public contracts are even more transparent and competitive regulating utility standards and credit bureaus. Also there is a need to set up bodies such as private sector chambers and trade organizations which on a timely basis could notify rules and regulations on the method of functioning of its members. Adding on such organizations/chambers could play a role of initiating an effective public-private sector dialogue which could harmonise relations and could promote more and more public-private partnerships. It could also help in disseminating information about government policies to the various business organisations in the country.

- **Need to Improve the Provision of Business Services:** Any business enterprise in any country need certain basic services like for entering the business market they need 'assistance in preparing business plans' and to 'negotiate with creditors'. To operate and grow they need 'freight forwarding', 'accounting', 'market information', 'management services' and 'legal assistance'. To manage risk they need services like 'insurance'. The above mentioned services are majorly in almost all countries of the world, provided by public sector but the government needs to take measures to facilitate the entry of private sector, for example introduce public private partnerships to bring a sense of new life into the almost non-existing services sector.

This would encourage greater private sector investment and foster foreign investment in the form of foreign direct investment (FDI) or institutional portfolio investments which could direct flow of capital in the country, transform idle cash to capital then facilitate the investment of capital in the country's economy. With the establishment of the new government there is some the hope that each and every sector will show some progress. Till date Afghanistan Investment Support Agency (AISA) has approved more than US$520 Billion in FDI. Majority of the FDI has been directed towards the government-owned enterprises, donor-funded reconstruction projects or services where they can quickly recover their investment, to the long-term process of building markets for manufactured products. Almost 20% of the total FDI approved by AISA is routed from Turkey, 17% from the U.S, followed by China, UAE(10% each) and Pakistan, Iran(5% each) (World Bank, 2005).

When the performance and growth of the firms in Afghanistan is concerned, it is quite similar to that of the firms in other small Central-Asian countries but is considerably low when compared with Pakistan, India and China. When compared with other war-torn countries like Mozambique where even 3-4 years after the war, average utilization in manufacturing was only 48% compared to 62% in Afghanistan. Even when the question of how many firms (having 100 workers or fewer) invested in Equipment/machinery in the year 2003, 71% of the total firms (fulfilling the requirement) invested in equipment or machinery compared to 56% in Mozambique. Surprisingly the figure of 71% is even higher than what is prevalent even in India (38%), Pakistan (5%) and is very close to China (74%). Even though a large percentage of the investment in Afghanistan is going towards the most basic production process but the above mentioned figures clearly indicate that sincere efforts for rebuilding the country are definitely on. One area on which Afghanistan can definitely work upon is to improve their investment culture and environment and make it more acceptable to the foreign companies which would lead to increase in competition and would ensure that the local Afghan companies/firms thrive to improve their performance and would keep them at their toes.

As we are already talking about the measures on how to keep the Afghanistan capital market more competitive there are a certain set of investment opportunities which the firms in Afghan could look into or which they may already be indulging to but on a small scale and expand their area of operation and thereby diversifying their operations.

- **Import-Substituting Activities:** As Afghanistan never had a broad industrial base, a major portion of the economic demand has been met through imports. After the war, the situation has become even worse with industrial base getting completely destroyed making it even more important to import. Import mainly includes items like poultry, wheat based products, soaps, shampoo etc.
- **Traditional Exports:** Traditional exports mainly include items like carpets which are mainly catered by the rural women weavers. At the time of war many of the weavers migrated to neighbouring countries mainly to Peshawar. Post-war there is a possibility to re-cultivate the carpet-weaving culture in the villages of Afghanistan. Another item which had been hammered due to the war is raisins which were at one time one of the most successful Afghan exports. But more importantly the preferential trade agreement between the Republic of India and The Transitional Islamic State of Afghanistan under which Green Raisins, Black raisins, Red Raisins, Raisins Golden and Green Raisins except large have been placed in the list of items where preferential trade is granted by the government of India.
- **Exotic Exports:** These mainly include agro-based and mineral based products like cashmere, spices such as cumin and saffron, perfumes, gems etc
- **Construction Related Activities:** The post-conflict era can be a breeding ground for the entrepreneurs to come up and if they get a proper regularised and structured market to invest and full support from the government then this may lead to increase in construction-related activities to facilitate these budding entrepreneurs to convert their promising ideas into reality
- **Infrastructure and Utility Services:** A possible step could also be to look into diversified sectors such as small scale power generation, management contracts in power distribution, fixed line telephony, value-added services in telecommunications and construction and maintenance of roads and small-scale water systems.

DOMINANCE OF THE ISLAMIC CULTURE AND TRADITION IN DISPUTE RESOLUTION IN AFGHANISTAN

Post-war, there has come a sort of saturation point for the formal justice system because of its limited reach, lack on infrastructure, ineffective legal system and dominance of local powers over the supreme authorities. Three decades of war made the formal system almost bankrupt, and destroyed the power of the formal system to uphold rule of law. If one goes into the history of Afghanistan, it has been a country with a closely knit social environment with the village elders and tribal councils having the final decision making power for undertaking any steps for welfare of the local village population. Informal system of law expanded over-time with the new Sharia courts coming up adding on to the local tribal councils. However after the war there had been an increase in number of power-hungry militants and the army began to sort of exclude the traditional authorities and practice.

The inability of the central government to stop these militants added to the woes as it gave confidence to this new armed elite to take up power in their own hands and influence the distribution of local resources, including international relief. The disruptions caused by the war also gave rise to new representative institutions such as village shuras i.e. assemblies that were designed to represent local communities. Also the power of Islamic clergy(ulema) and of local assemblies(jigras and shuras) rose sharply compared to pre-war Afghanistan particularly when it came to administering religious law(sharia) in absence of central authority. But after the collapse of Taliban, it seems that the traditional practices and procedures are again gaining momentum. The new constitution enacted in 2004 calls for the formation of elected local governance councils at the provincial, district and village level. Despite demands from the local Afghani population to re-instate the traditional institutions for governance like 'jigars' to reduce the levels of factional fighting, the process for achieving that has been slow-paced because of strong militia commanders still holding power in various factions of Afghanistan.

Article 3 of the 2004 Constitution clearly states that all the commercial disputes in Afghanistan have to be governed by the Islamic law. Going more specific Article 130 of the 2004 Constitution says that when there isn't any law or any provision in the Constitution which provides for resolving of legal disputes then the Hanafi jurisprudence comes into existence. With regards to personal matters of followers of Shia Article 131 provides for the Shia version of Islamic jurisprudence. Not just the constitution, if one looks at other relevant statutes in Afghanistan like the Civil Code of 1977 which states that "where the law has a provision, the practice of religious jurisprudence is not permitted. "When there is no such provision in the law, *Hanafi* jurisprudence, public conventions, and precedent are to be followed, so long as laws are only repealed or amended through express legislative action."

It isn't surprising that the Afghan's financial law is dominated by Islamic practices and customs as even Prophet Muhammad was a merchant and a trader and since times as early as 7th century long distance trade, commerce and banking were carried on by Muslim traders. As Muslims are generally very strict with regards to conformity with the established practices followed by their ancestors, they generally tend to explore the commercial opportunities along similar beliefs and procedures. Quran is considered to be the supreme authority in Islam and is also the supreme authority when it comes to business transactions. There are numerous passages in Quran which specifically talk about contracts and the principles which govern them are similar to common beliefs shared by religions all over the world.

Islamic law encourages its followers to honour their contractual commitments. Islamic law also lays an equal footing on a person's wealth when compared to his life thus prohibits use of any illegal or unfair means to deprive a person of his right to enjoy his property. Like all commercial laws across the world, Islamic laws also days down certain restrictions on the commercial transactions. Interest charged on money loans, ambiguous contracts, contracts, monopolies and price fixing are banned under Islamic law. Islamic law also prohibits riba which means accumulation of interest or usury. But no exact definition of riba exists in Quran. The Federal Shariat Court in Pakistan in 1991 had declared that "bank interest" is included within the meaning of the term riba and thus made it illegal. However the Supreme Court of Pakistan in 2002 remanded the matter back to Shariat Courts for reconsideration as they felt that the earlier order of Shariat Court hadn't analysed every possible perspective behind the term riba and hence needed reconsideration. (Agha & Nazim, 2014)

As has been mentioned earlier in this paper almost 80% of all the transactions being carried out in Afghanistan are through the informal sector. With the formal sector still in the re-building stage, the informal system presents itself as a possible and an easy and efficient alternative. As already mentioned earlier, the Hawala system has been the most frequently used and dominated system of transfer operating in Afghanistan. There are almost 300 -400 registered Hawala dealers in the Afghanistan money market and upto almost 2000 unregistered hawala dealers. However because of the level of anonymity in such transactions it's a potential source of abuse by the criminals and terrorists to launder crime money across the world. Another major reason for the success of the informal system in Afghanistan is that the process of selection of judges/mediators is on the will of the parties and thus even though it increases the possibility of bribing the decision making authorities but it also increases their accountability as compared to the formal system.

The dominance of Islamic culture can be clearly seen in Muslim dominated countries throughout their security markets. This influence can be seen all over from their instruments to the way of charging interest. In the Securities market of Jordan, the most commonly purchased securities are the Muqradah Bonds. These bonds are issued by the Ministry of Endowments and Islamic Affairs and Sanctions in Jordan. A muqaradah bond is an instrument of a fixed value issued in the name of its holder against the amount of money he has contributed towards the implementation of the project with the aim of making profitable investment. The following instrument is transferable upon the condition that the issuing party has to be intimated to register the transfer of the title. The liability of the Security holder is limited i.e. upto the amount specified in the bond. As far as periodical income from the bond is concerned, the holders of the bonds cannot claim any interest income but are entitled to a fix percentage of the net profits at the end of the year arising from the underlying project after the completion of the necessary grace period for the implementation of the project. As stated earlier, these bonds are freely transferable, even outside Jordan and are exempt from income tax. For the purpose of redemption, the issuing party shall set aside a certain amount of net profits for redeeming the bonds.

Participation Term Certificates are the financial instruments issued by banks/financial institutions in Pakistan which are negotiable in nature and based on the principle of sharing of profit and loss by mobilizing medium as well as long term financial resources in the local currency for industrial as well as other projects. These certificates can be redeemed after a period of 10years (excluding the grace period) including within it the legal right of foreclosure to the underlying fixed assets and other collaterals in form of current assets. The certificate holders like in the case of shares have a right to a share in the total profits. Another benefit for the certificate holders is that they have a preferential right to profits as compared to shareholders and these profits are tax deductible. The entire amount obtained from term participation certificates is used for the implementation of the project under the commitment of the project sponsors to manage their operations according to the best known methods and in line with any other commitments they may have made towards the certificate holders. In order to protect the interests of the certificate holders, a board of trustees is elected to follow up the implementation of the project and to ascertain its genuineness through actual observation of operations and examination of records. The certificate holders have a right to convert a part of their holding into ordinary shares of the company and the shareholders may also be granted the right of purchasing participation term certificates.

Despite there being various advantages, the informal system isn't free of its weaknesses too. Women have been majorly excluded from participating in the informal system and every time they have to rely on male members of the family. Also the cultural norms and practices impose deep and unfair restrictions on women like for example, forced marriages as compensation. Another main reason why the informal system at times fails is that there is a lack of common feeling among the disputants that they both belong to the same nation and are subject to similar laws with similar restrictions. The more powerful party always tends to find a way to ensure that the ruling is in his/her favour.

CO-RELATION BETWEEN THE FORMAL AND INFORMAL (ISLAMIC) SYSTEMS OF JUSTICE IN AFGHANISTAN

The country of Afghanistan at present is currently wrapped in two overlapping dispute resolution systems. One is the target of state-building according to international standards and the other is the acceptance of the local norms and customs to make the process of dispute resolution more practical and in conformity with the needs of the circumstances. The reality, which each of the stakeholder needs to accept, is that none of the two systems can exist exclusively because these systems of justice overlap and the disputants have the option to shop for a forum according to their needs and claims.

Many a times the judges, prosecutors etc have referred to the cases to informal sector and have also recorded such decisions when brought on to them by the parties. But in general the formal system doesn't use much of either of Sharia law or customary law in its rulings as it doesn't recognise them. In order to achieve normality and stability in the dispute resolution process it would be preferable if the formal system recognises the local customs and practices and somehow co-exist with it. This is because the people of Afghanistan have been following jigras and shuras since traditional times and has embodied the citizens with a sense of justice. Cost could be another major reason as to why the customary practices can be recognised by the formal judiciary. This is because the formal system in

Afghanistan is still at its rudimentary stage and will require millions of dollars to come at par with the other developing countries of world. Till then the traditional courts could fill the vacuum in formal justice system. (Senier, 2006) But there are certain obstacles too. Customary law is not a single set of rules and regulations; rather it's a set of general principles which need to be interpreted according to the circumstances. Secondly the local authorities like jirgas and shuras work voluntarily and thus lack the coercive power which is a pre-condition to maintain rule of law. Thirdly the state might not be willing to allow the local authorities to adjudicate upon the criminal disputes along with civil disputes although in reality, even criminal disputes are resolved by these local informal authorities.

A POSSIBLE STEP AHEAD

After going through the possibilities and drawbacks of integration of formal and informal system of justice in Afghanistan, the question that comes up is what is the solution?

The Norwegian Refugee council since the year 2002 has set up seven Information and Legal Assistance Centres (ILACs) in Afghanistan in order to resolve cases relating to housing, land and property rights, civil documentation and other rights or social services of importance to displacement affected populations. Now the main idea behind these ILACs is that Afghan attorneys and judges with legal education and training, many of who have served in the government judiciary in the past have been made responsible for running them. They help the parties approaching them in selecting their representatives and explain those representatives the complete case, the possible remedies available and facilitate the meetings without having any right to vote. Like said above, at the time of settlement, they explain the possible remedies available and record the minutes of final settlement. A copy of the minutes is been handed over to the parties for future reference. This pilot project by NRC presents a possible durable solution to the tensions caused because of the conflict of formal and informal systems. As both the formal and informal systems of dispute resolution are at present in a very flexible and fluid state, it's the best time to test these pilot projects and mould the dispute resolution system in Afghanistan in the most favourable manner possible.

CASH TRADEOFFS AT LOCAL MARKETS

Post 9/11 and the U.S invasion of Afghanistan, the country has been in a continuous conflict originally in the name of security, locally known as "Jihad" has now got transformed into a war economy because of the ever growing illicit drugs industry in general and opium industry in particular. The opium economy and insurgency mainly thrive in an economy where there is insecurity, absence of rule of law and a weak and corruptible state. With Afghanistan providing 90% of the global opium supply, this industry is not only a source of deadly diseases but also a growing source of income for violent/criminal non-state actors and contributing towards corruption, criminality and global addiction levels.

The opium industry is one of the major sources of revenue for the rural population in Afghanistan and helps in living a comfortable livelihood for the producers by stimulating its demand and supporting balance of payments. Thus on the face of it, opium industry does have a major impact when considered from a micro-economic point of view. But when we look at it from a macro-economic point of view, its impact isn't that significant because much of the revenue received beyond the farm level never enters Afghanistan directly, mainly used for import finance or being stashed in various tax havens or used for conducting terrorist activities across the world.

On the one hand, opium cultivation is one of the most economically efficient cultivations as it doesn't require a lot of agricultural land, it can grow in harsh climates, and also its sales gives great returns but on the other hand this opium cultivation because of it being declared illegal fuels money into criminal and terrorist activities and also increases corruption. Thus it puts the nation into a great dilemma on how to tackle this illicit drug trafficking, how much to tackle and the counter-narcotics strategy to be adopted.

DATA ON THE LEVELS OF OPIUM PRODUCTION IN AFGHANISTAN

It's never an easy task to conduct a survey in Afghanistan and that too with regards to opium industry because of its uncertain nature and lack of documentation. But the United Nations Office on Drugs and Crime makes an attempt to conduct such a survey every year and here is a summary of the data collected by them in 2013. There has been a 36% increase in the area of agricultural land used for opium cultivation from 154,000 hectares to 209,000 hectares but a comparatively lesser 11% increase in average yield 23.7kg/ha to 26.3kg/ha probably because of unfavourable weather conditions or the fact that the rural population have also started to grow other agricultural products thus affecting the ability of the land to sustain high levels of opium. There has also been an increase in the number of provinces engaged in opium production from 17 in 2012 to 19 in 2013. The potential production of opium has increased by 49% from being in range of (2800-4200 tons) to (4500-6500 tons) being a major reason of 12% decrease in opium price in 2013 from the levels in 2012. In the area wise classification, none of the major opium producing provinces faced a drastic decline in opium production with only the province of Farah and Uruzgan facing 12% and 6% reduction in opium production respectively from 2012 whereas provinces like Nangarhar and Nimroz experiencing 397% and 392% of growth in opium production respectively.

OPIUM AS A CURRENCY

Opium is a type of drug, which on being processed can be converted into Heroin and Morphine which are much more refined. But still there hasn't been much information of this happening in Afghanistan. The main reason behind it is that unlike many other agricultural products, opium has a much larger shelf life which is even longer than that of heroin and morphine. This characteristic of Opium allows the traders in Afghanistan to use it as a saving and even as a currency. The durability factor also leads to fluctuation in total capital of opium traders from time to time which results in capital gains/losses.

PYRAMIDAL STRUCTURE OF OPIUM TRADERS

At the grass-root level there are numerous small traders with low margins engaged in opium production and selling. Along with opium trade they also generally carry on licit trade in-order to cover up and also to have a stable source of revenue in case there is a downfall in opium business. The margin of profits for the small traders is generally low. When one moves up the pyramid the number of traders gets lesser and lesser but more influential and powerful. They generally have trade-links with militia, top-government officials and big and powerful drug dealers all over the world. The organisational structure though Pyramidal, it also has traits of cooperation and regulation which clearly indicates that when it comes to common interests of both the small and large traders and other elements of drug industry, they can work together and that too even across ethnic lines. This is one of the main reasons behind the fact that unlike other drug business dominated countries; all out drug-wars aren't a common sight in Afghanistan. Thus it can be easily concluded that in whole Afghanistan presents an enabling environment for the opium industry because of insecurity, lack of rule of law, protection provided by armed militants etc.

A LIGHT ON THE HAWALA MODE OF MONEY TRANSFER

Even though a large number of banks have emerged in Afghanistan, the low literacy rate, high bank charges and interest rate, minimum balance requirements are major hindrances due to which opium trade in Afghanistan is generally carried on through the Hawala route which is an informal yet based on solid networks of trust. The agents which facilitate Hawala transfer have to only maintain small reserves of cash as the main transactions are carried on setting-off basis with only the balance amount being transferred. It also plays a major role in more and more drug money being laundered. But there are some positives out of it too. Like for example, it serves as an efficient vehicle for remittances during long period of conflict and also facilitates in providing money transfer services in certain parts of Afghanistan where no banks exist. It wouldn't be totally justified to say that all the money transfers made through the hawala system are generated from illicit activities because Afghanistan is a country where almost 80% of the economic activity is carried on through the informal sector and in reality, there are no departmentalised networks for licit and illicit activities because with the changing times both licit and illicit activities have developed with complex overlapping connections.

FINANCIAL IMPACT ON THE COUNTRY AND ITS PEOPLE

The Opium market in Afghanistan is at its highest levels with the drug-laden country producing almost 6062 tons of opium in 2013, a rice of almost 36% from 2012. No doubt, it's a bad news considering the increasing number of addicts in the country, but it isn't a very bad news from the economic and political stability point of view. The Opium industry employs a large number of people in the country till the harvest season and keeps them away from being distracted to join the insurgents. (Alice, 2014) Although not recorded in the official balance of payments data, the opium production also has a net positive impact on balance of payments. But the levels of corruption the top of the Pyramid is so high that the trickledown effect is very slow and ineffective that most of the small farmers remain debt-struck leading to suicides, increase in crime etc. With regards to savings, the drug traffickers earning a much larger share of total revenue and there total capital investment being much lesser than their share of revenues definitely makes us to assume that they have a lower propensity to consume. They have a much greater disposable income to invest in formal/informal assets within the country as well as abroad.

Now with regards to opium trade's effect on other goods and services, the drug economy contributes to higher consumer and asset prices by increasing the demand of goods and services (mainly non-tradable like rent etc). This drug economy also contributes towards increasing wages/salaries as it fuels demand for production factors and thus leads to increase in production costs. These factors thus have contributed to the enormous increase in the real interest rates over last few years and also to the limited competitiveness to Afghan's tradable sector. Moving on to the capital intensive sectors, illicit drug trade also has effect on Afghanistan's investment climate because of increase in insecurity, dominance of informal mode of carrying out transactions, high levels of corruption at grassroots level and weak and ineffective administration.

Drug trading because of its illegality is not directly taxed as most of the revenues generated by it go unrecorded. Thus with regards to direct tax, drug trading does not contribute much to fiscal revenue. Whereas when it comes to indirect tax, duties on imports or indirect tax charge on receipt of goods contribute a reasonable level of share to the government treasury. But still the amount mentioned above contributed is lesser than what the government spends on improving the security against the drug-traffickers, criminals etc involved in this industry plus the money spent on eliminating the drug economy.

Even though in recent times the share of opium industry in the total GDP is down to 15%, Afghanistan lacks the determination to do away with such profits despite the huge financial aid it receives from a number of countries across the globe. Investments abroad are mostly carried through the above mentioned Hawala system. This is because there are not much alternatives present. Mining could be considered as an alternative but its development is in very rudimentary stage and could take a few years to be fully set to replace or rather reduce its dominance in the Afghan economy. Graeme Smith, a senior analyst at International Crisis group based in Kabul told Vice news that "Right now, growing opium makes more money than anything else for Afghan farmers so it's going to be very hard to stomp out. The fact of the matter is that Afghanistan will continue to be the world's leading industry opium producer probably for many years to come and the international community will need to help Afghanistan get off the sauce when it comes to finding another way to bring in hard currency." Also the fact that drug-industry eradication has never been on the top-priority list of the Afghanistan's government has added to the woes. Most of the eradication has either been of political rivals or the small farmers with little or no resources making them lose their source of daily bread and forcing them to dislike the government and joining hands with the Taliban and other insurgent groups to fight injustice done to them by the government. This has made the drug dealers to realize that the best way to survive in Afghanistan is to maintain close relations with the authorities thereby leading to all sorts of criminals entering the Afghan executive. With more and more reasons for the people in Afghanistan to be vulnerable to addiction and the ever-increasing opium supply presents a very scary future for Afghanistan unless there is a complete overhaul in thinking of the Afghanistan's authorities.

The new government in Afghanistan has again raised some hopes in the minds of a lot of people and organisations and governments across the world. "We look forward to the new Afghan government assuming a leadership role in this regard." United Nations Officc on Drugs and Crime spoke of Kabul making "some very serious choices about the future it desires," with the prospect of success depending on "an integrated, comprehensive response to the drug problem, embedded in a long-term security, development and institution-building agenda." Many countries in the West have had faced the same issues as what the country of Afghanistan is facing right now but Kabul is much more vulnerable with a upcoming, under-financed and divided government therefore Afghanistan and its allies must understand the ground realities and abandon the futile and counterproductive campaign against opium trade.(Doug, 2015)

CORRUPTION INTERFERING IN FINANCIAL GROWTH

It has been argued by various authors and critics that in a post war country, the chances of corruption are very high. The eradication of corruption from the roots of such a country is highly difficult and it is even more difficult because of the presence of customs and traditions of a country like Afghanistan. The prevention of corruption and formal regulative framework to prevent it is one of the essentials to be executed in Afghanistan. The effects of corruption are that creeps into the growth of the economy and is one of the major threats to stability, peace building and state building (Hussmann, 2009). The example of corruption being prevalent in the country can be seen by the high rise in the cost of contracts, i.e. a person has to pay at least 20-25% of the cost of the contract to middlemen to bag the contract.

The Government of Afghanistan has taken steps in this regard to curb corruption in the country. The Government signed the United Nations Convention against Corruption (UNCAC) in 2004 and even ratified it in August, 2008. This convention gives a set of guidelines and measures, like debt recovery, law enforcement, etc. to be implemented by state authorities to prevent corruption. In 2001, just after the post conflict time, in order to take some steps towards the prevention of corruption, the Government of Afghanistan set up the General Independent Administration for Anti-Corruption. This body was set up to eradicate the growth of corruption which could lead to widespread imputed losses in the whole country.

One of the main reasons for this corruption is said to be the business dealings in counter narcotics narcotrade (Rubin, 2007). Various surveys carried out in Afghanistan tell that citizens refer the interaction between the state and citizens as 'bazaar economy' and they call corruption as the new currency of Afghanistan (Gardezi, 2007). By this the reader should understand that to get a contract or any work done by the state authorities we need to negotiate in the form of bribe. Giving of bribe is a type of customary currency which has to be given in order to get a work done, in the same way as an ordinary person pays currency to buy something from a bazaar i.e. market. The practices of corruption are present right from the grassroots of the country since a large number of the population lives in the rural areas. The practice of corruption in urban areas spreads like fire to the rural areas, since they always try to follow what is the trend in the urban areas.

To tackle the problem in urban areas, various shuras or jirgas were formed. It was found with the aim to resolve local conflicts. But slowly it came to be headed by anti-state structures which made it use for a different purpose, then for what it was set up. The term corruption is ever changing and it being dynamic, it has a different approach in various customs and cultures. The harmonization of local rules and international standards to prevent corruption is also a major problem. The predominant local norms, rules and expectations may stand in contrast with the umbrella of the United Nations Convention against Corruption (Hussmann & Tisne, 2010). Since, the term corruption itself does not have one particular meaning, how can one have a single set of rules in such a country to drive out corruption from the urban or even rural areas. High degrees of nepotism and red tapism in the government offices are a major concern and cause of corruption in the country. The bureaucratic difficulties or obstructionism and delays in government work are regarded as a normal fact of life by the Afghan citizens (Gardizi & Torabi, 2010).

The customs of Afghanistan come as an obstacle while preventing corruption. The concept of shukrana, shirini, bakshish, etc. is a blessing in disguise for the corrupt officials and people. The customs of Afghanistan allow all these kinds of monetary activities by virtue of which the people give bribes to the officials in the name of sweets for celebration or thanking. It is a practice of giving gifts which is used in a different sense in modern days. The former Ministry of Mines & Industries had been alleged in an article in Washington Post for taking a bribe of US$30 million (Joshua, 2009). The transfer of officials between ministries of the Government has also been seen as a source of corruption since high officials are ready to take bribes for changing position of an official to a much preferred post.

This has become such a practice in the country, that many people have started accepting the fact that civil servants take bribe and they say it to be justified since they are paid very low salaries. The point of major concern in Afghanistan is the introduction of institutionalized corruption, as it is becoming an accepted practice. This process involves a middlemen or agent known as commissionkari, who helps to speed up all kinds of administrative works for commission. His role is to carry out the speedy work of people in government offices by charging some commission from them. Even many government officials have recognized commissionkaris as formal agents for processing administrative work on behalf of the traders. Since, people are not much aware about the government process and the paperworks related to most of the businesses and transactions, these commissionkaris use this to their advantage and charge high commissions for a mere administrative help.

Corruption supported by businesses reinforces the informal economy and inhibits productive economic activity and growth, as businesses choose a strategy of low visibility to curb extortion and solicitation of bribes by government officials (Chechi, 2009). The enforcement of the regulatory framework behind driving out corruption is also one of the major challenges. A number of reforms have been introduced by the Government of Afghanistan but they are not much effective and the state of corruption among the traders goes back to the state when there were no such reforms. The licensing reform was introduced which reduced the complexity of signatures in obtaining a trade license. But as time progressed, this change was not appraised and renewal process of such licenses was made very complex which again introduced the role of commissionkaris in this field.

The contribution of public towards the Gross Domestic Product (GDP) in Afghanistan is less compared to that of other countries. This shows the reason why progress is not easy in the country. In Pakistan, taxes and other revenues make a contribution of 12.6% of the GDP, whereas in Afghanistan, it only makes a contribution of 11.3% of the GDP.

According to recent survey, unstable governments tend to dominate the lower rungs of the Corruptions Perceptions Index. With Afghanistan, North Korea and Somalia sharing the tied bottom spot. This clearly shows the level of corruption which is causing breaks and a kind of erosion in the economic development of the country. The number of regulations is very low in Afghanistan, this gives a greater power in the hands of the government officials to determine who receives government services and under what conditions. A remedy to this could be changing incentives within the government policy. Singapore is a good example for the same and Afghanistan should follow the policy of Singapore, so as to reduce corruption level.

The concept that culture is directly related to corruption is a myth. As one can look at the example of ethnic Chinese communities where culture has a major role to play, but the level of corruption in Hong Kong and Singapore is one of the lowest in the world as compared to a greater level in China. One can reduce the level of corruption by relaxing the intrusiveness of the government in various decisions. Such a change has made notable changes in the economy of different countries. Afghanistan can take examples from countries like Baltics, South Korea, Hong Kong, etc. These reforms will not be easy, as the beneficiaries who enjoy rewards from such a system will be strongly resisting these changes.

Many findings of the stay of US Army in Afghanistan say that Afghanistan presents an extremely difficult environment for military operations, logistics and business practices (Tierney, 2010). The sector of tax assessment and collection is also a major area of concern since most people try to maximize their profits by trying to evade taxes. But reconstruction and state building efforts are only possible if the business houses pay taxes on time and there is a clear chain of transparency in tax assessment, collection and deposition in the revenue department. This form of corruption even creates wealth disparities in the country since rich become richer by evading taxes whereas poor people are always under the scanner and face huge monetary difficulties.

For this problem, the Afghanistan government has established a body known as High Office for Oversight and Anti-Corruption under a special decree in 2008 by the then President of Afghanistan, namely Hamid Karzai. At the sub national level, efforts have been made in the form of Independent Directorate of Local Governance, established in 2007. Corruption is still considered by the IDLG as a secondary problem for governance and stability at the sub national level. The problems faced by the GIAA are also faced by the HOO, which makes the success of this body also very difficult. It is argued that the establishment of such body has been a failure once and hence, it is just a waste of the financial resources of the country. There have been no measures by the government to change the willingness of the people, as it is one of the main reasons for the growth of corruption in a country.

The challenge in post war environments is to target the types of corruption which, if not addressed, can derail the entire transition and to layer transparency, accountability and anti-corruption throughout the central state building processes in a way that reinforces stability.

RECOMMENDATIONS AND SOLUTIONS

- **To Merge the Anti-Corruption Process with Development:** One of the foremost goals of the anti-corruption campaign of the Afghanistan Government should be to increase the growth rate and development of the economy. The stability of the financial structure of the economy can only be attained if the corruption is driven out from the country in the areas which affect the economy the most.

- **The Use of HOO and ACCI Efficiently:** The purpose behind setting up these bodies is to eradicate corruption from the urban and rural areas, but it has failed to live up its expectations till now. The HOO should be given more powers to investigate into the matters directly without the interference of other government officials which raises the question of suspicion and even bias. The guidelines given by the Afghanistan Chamber of Commerce & Industry must have some sanctions and they should be followed by the trader community in unity. These guidelines will be effective only if the traders and their bodies follow it, since ACCI was developed as the voice of the traders in front of the government to tackle problems effecting their growth and development such as corruption.
- **Enforcement of Legal Provisions:** There must be a balance between sanctions and prevention, which is the two fold measure adopted by the Government of Afghanistan. Administrative sanctions and criminal sanctions must go hand in hand in order to prevent corruption. For e.g. A high official cannot be criminally charged for the offence of bribery and hence, an administrative sanction of demoting him to a lower or remote post would be an appropriate remedy. This kind of approach should be integrated into all the programmes of the government at both, national and sub national levels. Progress in this approach has varied depending on the existence of political will at the highest level of the state, the personality of the ministers responsible for implementing the reforms, and donor assistance (World Bank, 2005).
- **Accountability and Auditing:** The practice of maintaining true and fair accounts should be imbibed among the customers and business traders to create transparency and fairness in the system. It is only when the citizens become aware about corruption and take steps towards preventing it, then only it can happen. Businesses should be encouraged to set up auditable accounting systems. The concept of social accountability has to be introduced among the citizens of the country. There should be proper maintenance of the accounts of the funds given by international donors which is used towards preventing corruption. There is a need to decentralize the use of these funds, as these funds should also be used at rural and community levels to eradicate corruption from the grassroots.
- **Monitoring of Custom and Practices:** The practice of customary things like giving of bakshish and shirini should be monitored. They cannot be banned so the agencies should be appointed to look into the giving of such gifts among high officials and their agents. It is to make sure that money in the form of gifts is not used by the officials as bribery to clear contracts or any other such work. One of the goals of this approach is the replacement of warlords or their gradual conversion into controlled and controllable state authorities at the community level to stimulate political and economic development (Zakhiwal, 2005).
- **Defining Roles and Responsibilities of Anti-Corruption Agencies:** There should be a clear set of goals given to the agencies which they should follow while doing their work. The policy of the government should be directly linked with the anti-corruption goal, since they can be effective only when they work simultaneously or else it is a waste of both time and money of the government. The state-building perspective should always be integrated in the policies and programmes of the government.
- **International Donors:** The help of international agencies should be taken to remove corruption. These international donors should set examples for the government in order to promote their efforts towards removing corruption from the country. It is only with their aid and advice, the Government of Afghanistan will be successful in overcoming this problem in their economy.

INFORMAL SYSTEM OF TRANSACTIONS IN AFGHANISTAN

The local economy of most of the villages and rural areas in Afghanistan has got a drastic change since the 1990s. Most of the people are dependent upon agriculture in the country and most men live on daily wages which they got for the labour they do on lands. The informal nature of transactions is increasing because of the shift of confidence of the people from formal institutions to extended family networks. By the term informal the authors refer to any kind of institution which is not backed or regulated by a formal institution. If we see informality as a manifestation of the relationship between the state and economic agents (World Bank, 2007), informality matters because then various economic factors are disregarded from such benefits that are supposed to come from state actions.

When there are informal transactions, along with it various other costs come into picture like (Ana-Maria, 2009) unfair competition, low innovation, unprotected investors, etc. The growth of development is also hampered since all the government policies are directed towards formal instrumentalities. The concept of rationality comes into picture when it is the question of informality. This means that a person generally chooses to enter into an informal transaction when he knows that he is to achieve more benefits under such a transaction as compared to a formal one. Thus, this even acts as a check on the action of formal institutions and makes them analyze their costs, so as to advance the benefits of the citizens.

The government prefers the public to enter into transactions which are formalized since it will help in issues such as business registration, tax administration and labor law issues. Taxation is a problem which can plague the growth and economy of a state if it is not handled in a proper manner. If a rationale decision is not taken, then more interference of informality will result in a loss of economic opportunities and employment potential. The law makers should frame such laws which would help in having a clear and formal structure of all business related transactions. The government should make sure that requirements like tax filing should be seen by the citizens as a part of their duty rather than the government's strategy for accumulating financial resources.

The problem of both short term and long term debts is one of the major problems faced by the rural population. During the drought season there are reports if high debts being considered shameful (Lautze, 2002). Most of the business in Afghanistan is being conducted on personal terms because of personalized cliental relations and social networks. Such networks provide information, regular trade flows, trade credit and risk sharing (Fafchamps & Minten, 2002). This clearly directs the readers to think whether transactions in such kind of trade would follow all the rules and regulations being given by the state authorities. The rich traders are able to manipulate the market so much, that investors fear to invest in a company which is not dominant in the market. Since there is no such kind of security behind their investments, many of the investors are reluctant to risk the capital they have, since they are aware that only the dominant business houses can benefit from the business environment present in Afghanistan. This indirectly even results in development of various classes mainly on the lines of wealth.

The pattern of business found in Afghanistan is hereditary i.e. the class of people practicing the trade of carpets will keep on practicing the same trade even after many generations. This shows the dominance of a limited number of traders and the lack of formal financial systems. There are large numbers of illegal activities being carried on in Afghanistan, as various research studies have already pointed out the existence of narco trade in the country. The trade taking place in this field cannot be categorized as legal and hence, all transactions dealing in narco trade takes place by way of informal institutions or means. The dominance of rich business houses is another major factor for the growth of informal trade in the country. The business elite have strong and financial links with the government authorities, both at the state and national level. For power holders, they provide a means of investment, the potential for money laundering and an overall strengthening of influence by the linking of military, economic and political power (Sarah & Adam, 2004).

Though it is said that most of the markets do not follow formal regulations but they have to follow non-state regulations, which have come up because of the social norms prevalent from that time. The government tries to prevent such non formal transactions, but it is at an initial stage. Like the Income Tax Act, 2009 which was passed in the year 2009 tries to prevent tax evasion and any such transaction or deal. But the effect of such a law is not as desired by the legislature. The problem is with its enforcement since such tax laws are not properly enforced in all the areas. The same is the condition with tariff laws which was enacted to prevent evasion of duty and tariff on the recommended goods, but its success is nowhere near to the expectations.

When a person enters into contract, the level of scrutiny of such contracts and the legal relationship is very low. There is no kind of financial or technical backup in case if someone defaults a contract which is not made according to the formal rules laid down by the Government. This results in many powerful people repudiating the contract without any kind of legal action being taken against them nor is any payment of compensation given by them. This leads to poor quality of work done, along with the confidence of getting away easily. One of the reasons for people getting away easily is that the authorities look only for their benefit and they do not care about the government treasury. They have no interest in creating transparency in transactions for better of the whole public. Hence, it is said that there is always a difference in the level of regulation of an industry claimed by the government, than what actually is as people have experienced. The need of the day is growth with improving social indicators and without a significant deterioration in income distribution (TISA, 2004).

The concept of informal credit is also widely prevalent in the country, especially in rural villages of cities of like Herat, Kabul, etc. This is a give and take procedure, as almost all the village households are involved in the giving and taking of loans on informal lines. People fear to take credit from formal institutions because it generally involves the mortgaging of their house or land, which is not the same in cases of informal credit. Because of the general practice, credit can easily be obtained from family or neighborhood relations, without giving any kind of security. Use of muscle power to recover loans is another feature of formal institutions giving loan, which is feared by the people. Various such factors make the use of informal credit more favorable in villages and rural households.

Everybody wants to earn more from the credit they take and the point that people choose informal credit is because on most occasions it is interest free. This particular type of informal credit has grown up in the country because of the notion of the people that taking loans from such sources leads to low expenses in the form of interest payments. It is a kind of decision in which the public has to analyze whether the risk taken by them is equal or less than the monetary value of the lower amount of interest which they have to pay.

The amount of income, an Afghanistan family earns is much less as compared to a family in other countries. There is a notion in Afghanistan that only the senior male member in the family should work, whereas in other European Nations, there are working couples who both go to the workplace and earn for their livelihood. This creates an imbalance between the economy of different countries. This even creates a problem for the migrant population who migrate from Afghanistan to other countries. There is a huge change in the economic standards. Like in Afghanistan the concept of rented houses are very rare and education is free. Whereas in countries like India, Australia, etc. one has to pay for the education at higher levels, plus the rent for accommodation.

RECOMMENDATIONS AND SOLUTIONS

- **Cost-Benefit Analysis:** A rationale human being should compare the risk he is going to undertake with the amount that he is going to benefit with. If such a risk is much less than the benefit that he is going to derive from the transaction, then he should undertake such a transaction. This concept should be widely applied in Afghanistan so that there could be a balance between the nature of formal and informal transactions.
- **Village Programmes:** The Government of Afghanistan should take steps like conducting researches and camps in village sector. This will help them to find out whether the government backed low interest rate loan schemes are able to reach the people or are the people benefitted from it. If that is not the case, then the government should take measures to implement new schemes in this direction. There should be technical assistance given by the Government.
- **Simplified Tax Procedure:** The Government of Afghanistan should take steps to simplify the taxing rates and rules prevalent there. In countries like Afghanistan with a major rural population, most people are unaware about the tax schemes prevalent in their country, which creates a type of fear in them from entering into formal transactions.
- **Flow of Information:** There must be a clear flow of information about business opportunities and threats in the formal sector. This would help the people take a clear decision about the direction in which they want to proceed. This means that it will help the people to take crucial decisions as to where they should invest, from where they should get their loans or with which sources are they to enter into transactions.

MORTGAGE MARKET IN AFGHANISTAN

When we talk about the various mortgage schemes prevalent in a country, few of the factors which are to be essentially considered are modes of finance, regulatory barriers, etc. The central bank known as Da Afghanistan Bank has come up with a scheme in collaboration with a Afghanistan Investment Climate Facility Organization known as Harakat for the promotion of residential mortgage. The strategic intention behind this scheme is to encourage responsible investing in mortgage industry by reducing institutional and regulatory barriers. There is a general notion in Afghanistan that commercial banks do not like to indulge in this industry. Most of the loans circulated in and around Afghanistan are short term loans with high interest rates. There must be initiatives to invite foreign funds which can provide long term loans of up to 10-15 years. Mortgage is said to be an important part of the functioning of the economy.

Mortgage products will be very conducive to economic growth of the country and create jobs. There are various problems which have to be overcome to boost this sector like corrupt and inefficient courts, land titling issues and other problems like lack of mortgage problems. Many government schemes have come up which ask for the creation of an advisory board. This in turn would help in the better implementation of the scheme. Various agencies should be taken into the fold for the increase of mortgage products like Afghanistan Chamber of Commerce & Industries (ACCI), Afghanistan Builders Association and Afghanistan Banking Association (ABA).

There is a continuous need of mortgage for residential households as the instances of extended households including all unmarried and widowed females are large. The dominance of few major players and the concentration of risks within the narrow banking sector may inhibit competition and innovation

(Abdul Fitrat, 2010). The commercial banks are not in favour of taking risks in the mortgage sector because of the present law position. There is a lack of proper laws in the areas of bankruptcy, mortgage and contracts law (Jelena & Joshua, 2009). A very low percentage of Afghanistan's population has access to banking sector, which is one of the reasons of lower initiatives of investing in the mortgage sector.

Mortgage interest rate is another factor which has to be looked upon. The credit is given to a small number of people in Afghanistan, as compared to the majority of the society in countries like India and Pakistan. Like if we compare the mortgage interest rate of 4.66% in Malaysia to 8.50% in Afghanistan, we get to see the position of the mortgage sector in the country. When you get a loan at such a high interest even after keeping mortgage, this shows signs of lower investments, which in turn leads to lower rate of development. This is also the reason why people in Malaysia make a larger amount of money as compared to those in Afghanistan, even though both these countries follow the Islamic system of banking and other such instruments which are used in such economies.

There have been various initiatives in Afghanistan for the promotion of this sector. One of them being the Afghanistan Islamic Mortgage Project (AIM), a groundbreaking initiative taken up by the efforts of Wall Street Bankers, mortgage lenders and real estate professionals. It is the first step towards launching a multi-million dollar primary home finance institution called the Afghanistan Islamic Mortgage Company. They will try to integrate the banking system with technologically advanced features to promote the mortgage system prevalent in the country. There are many concerns which are to be addressed by this program like cultural dynamics and local systems of credit. This project needs the help of various international finance bodies and banks. The local customs have to also be followed because of Islamic Shariah Compliance which is a part and parcel of the transactions taking place in Afghanistan regarding any subject.

Most of the housing transactions in Afghanistan are on a cash basis and even if it is in credit, it is generally the informal system of credit from friends and relatives, which is prevalent throughout the country. Any kind of modern mortgage practice is virtually non-existent in Afghanistan. While the business case for sustainable housing finance in Afghanistan is strong, its attractiveness is significantly heightened by its potential contribution to help re-knit Afghanistan's torn social fabric. Many new ideas have come up in Afghanistan to promote this sector. One of them is like the owner need not pay interest bearing loans to the bank; rather he is in co-ownership program. In such a program, the owner has to pay back easy monthly installments and the end of it; he acquires the part of ownership which is with the bank. This kind of system has huge potential and can be a success in Afghanistan, if implemented properly.

There are many illegal transactions in Afghanistan which are barred by the Narcotics Bureau and hence, any profit earned through such a business have to be disposed of, so people use cash to buy houses and thereby reducing their dependence on mortgage loans for this purpose. Many difficulties are faced by banks preventing them from providing loans include recovery in cases of default, tracking individuals, corruption in court system, etc. There is even a gap between the huge demand and comparatively lower supply of housing, which acts as an incentive for banks too. But then lack of clear policies and an effective framework, makes them take a step backwards. Organizations in the past have suffered losses in this sector; this can be seen from the example of Afghanistan Mortgage and Reconstruction Bank (AMRB), which was dissolved in 2003.

The first step towards modern mortgage was taken way back in the 1950s when the Afghan Government had launched Mosessesa Keesa Omrani as a Finance Development Organization. There are some banks like the Pashtany Bank which do provide mortgage loans but of a short term, and they have a minimum impact. This makes the people take loans from informal sector but it is argued that informal financing is costly and not effective for the development of housing mortgage industry. Land titling (Gebremedhin, 2006) as mentioned earlier is a problem because if the complications in various laws like Shariah laws, customary laws and civil laws.

Another important problem faced by the banks is the scarcity of insurance companies. Afghanistan is prone to earthquakes and other such disasters. In such a country, even if you give a mortgage loan, the chances of the collateral being damaged is very high. Hence, all banking companies are redundant to give out loans with collateral which is not insured. Since the chances of them getting a loss because of damage to the collateral due to a natural disaster is very high. Another problem which is seen is inefficient financial intermediaries and a poor background behind them.

To promote the mortgage sector, the Afghanistan Parliament has passed the mortgage law in 2009. It was enacted with an objective to increase mutual trust in banking transactions and at the same time, expand trade and credit. Various experts say that the position of this mortgage law is neutral in regards to the balance between conventional mortgage system and Islamic compliance (May, Bell & Islam, 2008).

Even after so much growth of Islamic banking across various countries, still there is a large market which is untapped in Afghanistan. There are various products relating to mortgage where banks and other private institutions can do business, since a very low depth of penetration has been done till now. There is a growing need of mortgage loans among the low income level people as there is high demand of housing among them. But to equal such demand, an intractable challenge is being presented for the banking sector as only few banks till date provide mortgage for long term purposes.

The constraints of long term financial products and inefficient legal processes have discouraged the people from participating in this sector. But still there are many ways by which such transactions can be made transparent and cost effective.

SOLUTIONS AND RECOMMENDATIONS

- **Encouraging Developers to be Partners in Housing Schemes:** Various builders who undertake the activity of construction should be made active participants in housing finance schemes. They should try to provide housing to the lower income earning people by building a requisite number of low cost housing. The government along with the developers as partners should establish subsidized housing finance schemes to promote this sector.
- **Changes in Legal Framework:** The laws and legal framework prevalent in the country should be updated so as to provide some kind of security to people taking the risk of giving loans. Laws should be made in those areas where any legislation is absent in respect of default of giving loans and identification of such defaulters. Only when such laws are updated, more companies will be interested in giving mortgage loans, as they will feel much secured. Any step taken by the Government in this aspect will boost the economy and the business in this sector. Many of the banking companies want such changes in the laws so as to increase their business in this sector after having a balanced risk in analysis with the return.
- **Lower Interest Rates:** The general trend of mortgage trend in Afghanistan is connected with high rates of interest. These rates are comparatively higher to the compared interest charged in informal sector, if any. This causes most people to take up loans from informal sectors like friends, relatives, etc. People should be encouraged to loans from private companies and banks by providing them loans at subsidized interest rates.

- **Government Mortgage Schemes:** Government of Afghanistan should launch schemes whereby they develop housing societies and provide them to the public at an affordable cost. This should be accompanied by a Government backed mortgage guarantee scheme. The Government may either do this alternatively by supporting companies and institutions providing finance either directly to buyers or through local banks (Omar & Parwez, 2014).

CONCLUSION

After the war ended with Taliban and they were defeated, Afghanistan was complete tatters as if it had gone 50 years back in terms of development. The state of Afghanistan had to start from scratch and if one considers the fact that it's just been 10 years that the war ended and also considering the level of illiteracy, corruption and the level of insurgency it experiences, the situation in Afghanistan isn't absolutely hopeless. From being in a state of nothing, the Islamic Republic of Afghanistan has moved on to be recognised as democratic country, having a parliament, a constitution, a civil society and the new exciting private sector.

There is a new mining law to properly tap the huge mineral resources which have the ability to make Afghanistan's economy self-sufficient. Mohamamad Shafiq Hamadam, Chairman of the Afghan-Anti Corruption network wrote: "Many things are new for this country. Democracy is not very mature in Afghanistan and concepts like human and women's rights are still not well-developed after more than three decades of dictatorship and extremist and communist regimes. So it will take time for the people of this country to adopt the new culture of democracy, peace and stability.

What Afghanistan needs the most right now is a committed, sincere and a firm government because in present-times there have been increasing cases of militants/terrorists taking over the political government like ISIS in Syria and Iraq, Boko Haram in Nigeria etc. It's a common knowledge that Afghanistan along with parts of Pakistan is home to hardcore extremist organisations, therefore it's important that the government officials stay firm in their stand of completely eradicating terrorism and its other by-products like drug-trafficking otherwise the fate of this high potential country wouldn't turn out to be any better.

Afghanistan recently has been facing a decline in employment growth, according to World Bank Enterprise Survey 2014, employment growth dropped to almost 1/3rd(4.9%) of what it was in 2008. In a report by ACCI it was stated that approximately one-in ten managers reported cutting workforce size in the last three months, and that too in a season traditionally known for more hiring.

With the opium production also increasing every year there is a possibility of that the unemployed might join the business of opium trading or even worse out of frustration hold arms against the government. Therefore this is the time, the newly elected government in Afghanistan has to undertake measures to show that it's committed to the promise of not allowing Afghanistan to self-destruct and brining it at par with the other developing nations of the world.

The economy of Afghanistan is largely dependant on the donations it receives from abroad, as it needs a good resource of money in order to make amends to what has been lost in the many years of war which the country had to deal it. There is a difference in the amount of donations it receives from different countries. Like European Nations, Germany and Sweden have disbursed more amounts than what they had pledged, whereas United States and India had not disbursed the amounts which they had promised. By the end of the year 2008, Afghanistan had become the world's leading aid recipient and in the same year they had received the second largest amount ever received in a single year.

REFERENCES

Abdul Qadeer Fitrat. (2010). *Building an Efficient and Affordable Housing Finance System.* Da Afghanistan Bank.

Adam Smith International. (2014). The new mineral law: breaking new ground for Afghanistan. *The Guardian.* Retrieved 14th January 2015, from http://www.theguardian.com/global-development-professionals-network/adam-smith-international-partner-zone/2014/oct/30/new-minerals-law-afghanistan

Afghanistan Economy Update. (2014). *Poverty Reduction and Economic Management.* Retrieved 10th January 2015, from http://www.imf.org/external/pubs/ft/scr/2014/cr14128.pdf

Afghanistan Financial Services. (2010). *Afghanistan Capital Market Assessment.* Retrieved 7th October 2014, from http://www.ahg.af/data/work/stock-exchange/AFS%20-%20Afghanistan%20Capital%20Markets%20Assessment.pdf

Afghanistan Holding Group. (n.d.). Retrieved 6th October 2014, from http://www.ahg.af/work/stock-exchange

Afghanistan Investment Support Agency. (n.d.). *Investment in Afghanistan.* Retrieved 10th January 2015, from http://www.state.gov/documents/organization/226764.pdf

Afghanistan Legal Education Project. (2011). *An introduction to the commercial law of Afghanistan.* Stanford Research Paper.

Afghanistan Opium Survey. (2013). Retrieved 16th January 2015, from http://www.unodc.org/documents/cropmonitoring/Afghanistan/Afghanreport_Summary_Findings_2013.pdf

Afghanistan's Emerging Mortgage market Gets the Push Investors Were Waiting For. (2010). Retrieved January 14th 2015, from www.prweb.com/relcases/Afghanistan/Mortgage/prweb4122034.html

Agreements between Islamic Republic of Afghanistan and Islamic Republic of Pakistan. (2010). Retrieved 8th January 2015, from http://www.commerce.gov.pk/APTTA/APTTA.pdf

Ana-Maria Oviedo. (2009). *Economic Informality: Causes, Costs and Policies A Literature Survey of International Experience.* Country Economic Memorandum.

Bandow, D. (2015). *End the International drug war to control the Afghan Narco-State.* Huffingtion Post.

Bureau of Economic and Business Affairs of the United States. (2014). *Investment Climate Statement.* Retrieved 11th January 2015, from http://www.state.gov/e/eb/rls/othr/ics/2014/226588.html

Byrd & Noorani. (2010). *Exploitation of Mineral Resources in Afghanistan: What are the Government revenues or development benefits.* Academic Press.

Carter, S. (2014). *Gaps in new Afghan mining law pose a threat to stability.* Global Witness.

Chapter 3 Article 14: Certificate of Existence, Corporations and Limited Liability Companies Law of Afghanistan

Checchi. (2009). *Assessment of Corruption in Afghanistan.* Checchi & Company Consulting Inc.

Constitution of Islamic Republic of Afghanistan. Article 140

Expanding your horizons? A guide to setting up business across the Middle East, North Africa and South Asia Region. (2011). Retrieved 15th January 2015, from http://www.kpmg.com/Africa/en/Documents/ExpandingthehorizonMENASATaxGuid2011v2.pdf

Fafchamps, M. (2002). Returns to Social Network Capital Among Traders. *Oxford Economic Papers*, *54*(2), 173–206. doi:10.1093/oep/54.2.173

Faiez and Heidi Vogt. (2011). *Afghan President: West shares in Kabul Bank fiasco*. Retrieved 8th October 2014, from http://seattletimes.com/html/nationworld/2014736784_apasafghanistan.html

Faisal & Hazi. (2014). *Matter of Interest*. Retrieved 18th January 2015, from http://www.thenews.com.pk/Todays-News-9-270247-Matter-of-interest

Gardezi, M. (2007). *Afghans Experiences of Corruption: A study across seven provinces*. Kabul: Integrity Watch Afghanistan.

Gardizi, M., Hussmann, K., & Torabi, Y. (2010). *Corrupting the State or State-Crafted Corruption?* Afghanistan Research and Evaluation Unit.

Gebremedhin, Y. (2006). *Legal Issues Pertaining to Land Titling and Registration in Afghanistan*. LTERA Report.

Government of Afghanistan. (2008). *Strategy Paper on Launching of the Independent Directorate of Local Governance*. Kabul: Author.

Hussmann, K. (2009). *Joint Donor Responses vis-à-vis Corruption in Afghanistan: Myth or Reality*. OECD.

Hussmann, K., & Tisne, M. (2010). *Integrity in State-Building: Anti-corruption with a State-Building Lens*. OECD Paris.

Lautze, S. E., Stites, N., Nojumi, F., & Najimi. (2002). Qaht-e-Pool: A Cash Famine: Food Insecurity in Aghanistan. Tufts University.

Lister, S., & Pain, A. (2004). *Trading in Power: The Politics of Free Markets in Afghanistan*. AREU.

May, E., Bell, S.C., & Islam, R. (2008). *Housing Finance in Afghanistan: Challenges and Opportunities*. The World Bank Report.

Merton, R. C. (1992). Financial Innovation and Economic Performance. *Journal of Applied Corporate Finance*, *4*(4), 12–22. doi:10.1111/j.1745-6622.1992.tb00214.x

Miller, M. H. (1986). Financial Innovation: The last twenty years and next. *Journal of Financial and Quantitative Analysis*. Retrieved January 14th 2015, from http://countrystudies.us/afghanistan

Ministry of Commerce and Industries. (n.d.). *Islamic republic of Afghanistan*. Retrieved 15th January 2015, from http://moci.gov.af/en/page/550

Monger. (2013). *Why Accounting and Auditing Are Critical To Banking and Microfinance*. Academic Press.

NRCs Country Programme in Afghanistan. (n.d.). Retrieved 18th January 2015, from http://www.nrc.no/afghanistan

O'Donnell. (2014). *New Afghan mining law lacks transparency*. Retrieved 14th January 2015, from http://www.scmp.com/business/commodities/article/1579556/new-afghan-mining-law-lacks-transparency-say-experts

Partlow, J. (2009). Afghan Minister Accused of Taking Bribe. *Washington Post*.

Pavlovic, J., & Charap, J. (2009). *Development of Commercial Banking System in Afghanistan: Risks and Rewards*. International Monetary Fund.

Preferential Trade Agreement between India & Islamic State Of Afghanistan. (n.d.). Retrieved 12th October 2014, from http://commerce.nic.in/trade/international_ta_indafg.asp

Qargha, O., & Besmel, P. (2014). *Mortgage Market Assessment in 5 Major Cities of Afghanistan. Harakat*. Afghanistan Investment Climate Facility Organization.

Rezaie, M. (2011). *Afghanistan needs a modern stock exchange*. Retrieved 8th October 2014, from http://outlookafghanistan.net/topics.php

Risen, J. (n.d.). U.S. Identifies Vast Mineral Riches in Afghanistan. *New York Times*. Retrieved 14th January 2015, from http://www.nytimes.com/2010/06/14/world/asia/14minerals.html

Rubin, B. R. (2007). *Salvaging Afghanistan: Testimony before the United States Senate Armed Services Committee*. Washington, DC: U.S. Government Printing Office.

Senier, A. (2006). *Rebuilding the Judicial Sector in Afghanistan: The Role of Customary law*. The Fletcher School Online Journal.

Shakey Foundation. (2013). *Analyzing Afghanistan's Draft Mining Law*. Retrieved 11th January 2015, http://www.jordantimes.com/news/business/speculators-spoil-trading-activities-amman-stock-exchange-%E2%80%94-al-amin http://www.globalwitness.org/sites/default/files/library/SHAKEY_FOUNDATION_GW.pdf

Shebergan. (n.d.). *Legal and regulatory analysis report*. Retrieved 15th January 2015, from http://www.afghaneic.com/SheberghanFiles/AEAISFDPLegalandRegulatoryAnalysisReport.pdf

Special Inspector General for Afghanistan Reconstruction. (2014). *Afghanistan's Banking Sector: The Central Bank's Capacity to Regulate Commercial Banks*. Audit Report.

Speri, A. (2014). *Afghanistan's Opium Economy is doing better than ever*. Retrieved 15th January 2015, from https://news.vice.com/article/afghanistans-opium-economy-is-doing-better-than-ever

The, I. M. F. (2003). *An analysis of the informal Hawala system*. The IMF and The World Bank.

The Investment Climate in Afghanistan. (n.d.). *Exploring Opportunities in an Uncertain Environment*. Retrieved 7th October 2014 from http://www.aisa.org.af/presentations/InvestmentClimateAfghanistan.pdf

The United Nations Office on Drugs & Crime. (2013). *Afghanistan's Drug Industry Structure, Functioning, Dynamics and Implications for Counter-Narcotics Policy*. The United Nations.

The World Bank. (2014). *Doing Business and Measuring Business Regulations*. Retrieved 8th January 2015, from http://www.doingbusiness.org/rankings

Tierney, J.F. (2010). *Warlord, Inc.: Extortion & Corruption Along the US Supply Chain in Afghanistan*. Washington, DC: Academic Press.

TISA and International Agencies. (2004). Securing Afghanistan's Future: Accomplishments and the Strategic Path Forward. Kabul.

United States IP. (2006). *The clash of two goods, State and Non-State Dispute Resolution in Afghanistan*. Retrieved 18th January 2015, from http://www.usip.org/sites/default/files/file/clash_two_goods.pdf

World Bank. (2005). *Afghanistan: Managing Public Finances for Development*. Kabul: World Bank.

World Bank. (2005). *The State of the Private Sector*. Retrieved 10th October 2014, from http://siteresources.worldbank.org/SOUTHASIAEXT/Resources/223546-1151200078343/ch2.pdf

Zakhilwal, H. O. (2005). Extending Governance Structures beyond Kabul: Progress and Potential for Development Programs – the Case of NSP. Kabul.

KEY TERMS AND DEFINITIONS

Badakashan: Gold.
Bazaar: Market.
Haram: Sin.
Hawala: Money transfer without money movement.
Jirga: Traditional assembly of leaders.
Musharakah: Equity shares.
Riba: Interest.
Sarafi: Money changers.
Shahrak: Township.
Sharia Compliant: Non-interest based.
Shia: Muslim sect.
Shura: Consultation.

Chapter 12
Islamic Finance in India: Financial Regulations Challenges and Possible Solutions

Wasiullah Shaik Mohammed
B. S. Abdur Rahman University, India

Abdur Raqeeb H
Indian Center for Islamic Finance, India

Khalid Waheed
B. S. Abdur Rahman University, India

ABSTRACT

In order to provide financial services effectively to almost 1.21 billion people, India has adopted a comprehensive financial system governed under a number of financial regulations. These regulations, through regular amendments, are kept updated and inclusive of modern financial concepts that emerge in national and international markets. Islamic finance is one of such modern concepts emerged at global level. Growing with an annual growth rate of 15-20 percent the Islamic finance industry is holding total assets, value estimated to be more than USD 1.6 trillion. Hence, the authors, in this paper tried to study the feasibility of providing Islamic financial services in India, especially in the areas of Retail banking, Microfinance, Venture Capital financing. The objective of this paper is to identify the major regulatory challenges facing Islamic finance and to propose the possible solutions so as to make this emerging industry an internal part of the Indian financial system.

INTRODUCTION

India is a home to almost 1.21 billion people (Ministry of Home Affairs, Government of India[GOI], (2011) out which more than 500 million are estimated to be living as '*unbanked*' one (Chakrabarti, K.C., 2012). To tackle this issue the Government of India (GOI), under the policy of '*financial inclusion*' has launched a number of programs to provide financial services to this financially excluded population. Despite all the efforts, there still exists a gap from Demand & Supply perspective. To bridge this gap

DOI: 10.4018/978-1-5225-0004-9.ch012

the GOI should think of utilizing the alternative modes to provide financial services to these '*unbanked*' people.

India, on the other side, has emerged as an important economic player and is standing along with the nations such as United States of America (USA), the United Kingdom (UK), Europe, Russia and China at global economic platforms. To retain this position in long run, the policy makers are targeting an annual Gross Domestic Product (GDP) growth rate of around 10 percent in coming years. To achieve the targeted '*double-digit*' GDP growth India needs to upgrade its infrastructure facilities (energy & power projects, water projects, telecommunication, transportation, technology, etc). And, this process requires USD 1 trillion of investments in different sectors (Ministry of Finance, GOI, 2014). One of the most preferable ways to fulfill this huge capital requirement is to invite foreign investments using Venture Capital financing modes.

Islamic finance emerged as one of the profitable industry in global financial market, especially after the global financial meltdown. Due to the potential abilities it holds, the practices of Islamic finance has been adopted by a number of modern economies such as Indonesia, Malaysia, USA, UK, UAE, etc, as an internal part of their financial system.

It is in this context that this topic has been chosen by the authors. The objective of current study is to identify the major regulatory challenges facing Islamic finance in India and to propose the possible solutions to the identified issues.

BACKGROUND

Islamic finance is not a new concept in India. The researches available on this subject show that the origin of Islamic finance here goes back to the 1890s when an Interest-free loan providing institution was established in southern part of India. But the first formal Interest-free credit society was believed to be established in the year 1923 in Hyderabad (Zamir Iqbal & Abbas Mirakhor, 2011).

Initiated as the small community based institutions scattered in different parts of the nation, the Islamic finance practices have developed considerably in Indian market, especially in the last one decade. The establishment of Alternative Investments and Credits Limited- an asset financing company in Kerala (2000), establishment of Al-Khair Co-operative Credit Society- an interest-free microfinance institution in Bihar (2002), policy level discussions in the Anand Sinha Committee (2006)- a working group formed by RBI to examine the financial instruments used in Islamic banking under the chairmanship of Mr. Anand Sinha, the Raghuram Rajan Committee (2008)- a high level committee on financial sector reforms formed by the GOI under the chairmanship of Dr. Raghuram Rajan, launch of the Secura India Real Estate Fund- an Islamic Venture Capital Fund in Kerala (2009 & 2012), establishment of Sahulat Microfinance- a society established to promote the interest-free microfinance practices in India located in New Delhi (2010), launch of BSE-TASIS 50 *Shariah* Index- a *Shariah* Compliant Equity Index developed under the partnership of Bombay Stock Exchange and Taqwaa Advisory & Shariah Investment Solutions in Mumbai (2011), Cheraman Financial Services Private Limited- an NBFC under the partnership of M/s Kerala State Industrial Development Corporation in Kerala (2011) are some of the success stories.

Regardless of all these developments, the existence, operations and growth of formal Islamic Finance Institutions (IFIs) in Indian market is still a question that needs thorough exploration.

At the outset it is opined that due to the unfavorable legal framework it is impossible to provide Islamic finance services in India. Hence, the current study attempts to study the feasibility of providing Islamic finance services in the banking, microfinance and venture capital financing sectors. Therefore, the regulations that are governing these sectors in India such as the 'Banking Regulation Act, 1949', 'Multistate Cooperative Societies Act 2002', 'Reserve Bank of India Act, 1934', 'Securities and Exchange Board of India (Venture Capital Funds) Regulations, 1996', 'Securities and Exchange Board of India (Foreign Venture Capital Investor) Regulations, 2000' are considered for the present study. And, for the regulations related to Islamic finance, the authors relied upon the *Shariah* Standards published by the Accounting and Auditing Organization for Islamic Financial Institutions (AAOIFI).

ISLAMIC FINANCE AND INDIAN FINANCIAL REGULATIONS

Islamic Finance: An Introduction

Islamic finance is a wider term which includes retail banking, investments, bonds, insurance, non-banking services, etc. As per the report published recently, this industry is engulfing the international markets with a swift pace noting an annual growth rate of 15-20 percent. Moreover, the total assets of Islamic finance industry have been estimated to be USD 1.6 trillion by the end-2012 (Islamic Financial Services Board [IFSB], 2013).

Islamic finance is regulated under the '*Shariah*' (the Islamic Law) which is a derivative form of the Islamic principles derived from the primary sources of Islam i.e. the Holy *Quran* (the divine scripture) and the *Sunnah* (the sayings and traditions of the Prophet Muhammad [Peace be up on Him]). The *Shariah* prohibits charging of '*Riba*' (Interest) on any financial transactions. In terms of investments, the Islamic Finance Institutions (IFIs) are not permitted to take-up any business activity related to the commodities/items/subjects that are directly prohibited in the Holy *Quran* and the *Sunnah* such as pork, alcohol, gambling, etc. In addition, the IFIs should provide transparent services for the welfare of the society by following strict ethical and moral standards and by avoiding the unfair or exploitative practices (Karim Nimrah, Mechael Tarazi & Xavier Reille, 2008).

All the financial products introduced in the market by IFIs are designed using Islamic finance contracts. Such contracts form the foundation for the practice of Islamic finance. Therefore, it is worth to have a brief introduction to a few of the major Islamic finance contracts. They are:

1. Musharaka (Partnership)
2. Mudaraba (Joint Venture)
3. Murabaha (Cost Plus Sale)
4. Ijarah (Islamic Lease)
5. Istisna (Manufacturing Finance)
6. Salam (Share Cropping Finance)
7. Wakala (Agency)

1. **Musharaka:** *Musharaka* is a type of Islamic finance contract in which the Islamic Finance Institution (IFI) and the customer become partners in a (*Musharaka*) business or a project. Both the partners induct their capital and assets in the business. Profit (including income) is shared in a ratio mutually agreed between the partners. Loss, if any, will be shared only in the capital contribution ratio. In a Diminishing *Musharaka* (which is an extension of *Musharaka*), one of the partners, say the customer, would purchase the share of the other (say IFI) over a period of time and would become the full owner of the project. Basic principles and applications:
    a. The parties involved in *Musharaka* should be legally capable of entering into a contract. It means they should not be minor, insane, lunatic, etc.
    b. The subject matter of *Musharaka* like assets, nature of business, etc, should be *Shariah* compliant.
    c. Both the partners should contribute the money capital.
    d. Profit can be shared in mutually agreed ratio whereas the loss should be shared only in proportion to the capital contribution.
    e. One or all of the partners can manage the *Musharaka* Enterprise.
    f. Each of the partners has the right to terminate *Musharaka* but with a due notice to the other.
    g. In diminishing *Musharaka* the share price will be based on the market value or as agreed between the parties at the time of sale (*Shariah* Standards, Accounting & Auditing Organization for Islamic Financial Institutions (AAOIFI, 2010, pp. 204-218).
    h. The *Musharaka* contract is used in designing the products such as Bank accounts, Home finance, Project finance, *Sukuk*, Islamic funds, etc.
2. **Mudaraba:** In *Mudaraba* type of Islamic finance contract the IFI and customer as the partners initiate a (*Mudaraba*) business or a project. IFI (as a *Rab-al-Maal*) provide 100% of the capital whereas the customer (as the *Mudarib*) manages the business. The profit is shared in a ratio mutually agreed between the partners. Loss, if any, will be borne only by the IFI (*Rab-al Maal*) who has contributed capital. Basic principles and applications:
    a. The parties involved in *Mudaraba* should be legally capable of entering into a contract.
    b. The subject matter of *Mudaraba* such as assets, nature of business, etc, should be *Shariah* compliant.
    c. Only one partner (*Rab-al-Maal*) should contribute the money capital whereas the other (*Mudarib*) should manage the business.
    d. Profit can be shared in a ratio as agreed between the partners. Loss, if any, should be borne only by the partner who contributed the money capital (*Rab-al-Maal*).
    e. The partner who manages the business (*Mudarib*) will not be paid any salary or fee for managing the business.
    f. Each of the partners has the right to terminate the *Mudaraba* but with a due notice to the other (*Shariah* Standards, AAOIFI, 2010, pp. 235-241).
    g. *Mudaraba* contract is used in designing the Islamic financial products such as Bank accounts, Home finance, Project finance, *Sukuk*, Funds, Corporate products, Treasury products, etc.
3. **Murabaha:** *Murabaha* is a sale contract in which the IFI purchases certain goods/ assets required by the customer on its (customer's) request. The goods are generally purchased on spot and then sold to the customer on a higher price (after adding IFI's profit margin) usually on deferred payment

basis. Assets will be delivered to the customer on spot whereas the customer makes the payment later as per the agreement. Basic principles and applications:

a. The parties involved in *Murabaha* should be legally capable of entering into a contract.
b. The asset or goods should be *Shariah* compliant.
c. The subject matter of *Murabaha* like types of asset, cost, profit, payment terms, etc, should be clear to both the parties.
d. The seller should disclose the cost price and the profit margin to the customer (*Shariah* Standards, AAOIFI, 2010, pp. 115-124).
e. *Murabaha* is one of the widely practiced Islamic finance contracts. It is used in designing the products such as Bank accounts, Home finance, Vehicle finance, Working Capital finance, *Sukuk*, Funds, Project finance, Goods finance, Corporate products, Treasury products, etc.

4. **Ijarah:** *Ijarah* is similar to a conventional lease contract except a few technical and contractual differences. In *Ijarah* the IFI (as Lessor) purchases certain asset(s) on customer's request and leases out those assets to the customer (Lessee) against the lease-rent for a specific period as agreed between the parties. In a normal *Ijarah* financing, the customer at the end of the lease period would return the respective assets to the IFI. Whereas in '*Ijarah-Muntahia-Bi-Tamleek*' (which is an extension of *Ijarah*), the customer retains the assets once the ownership rights are transferred through a separate sale contract or in few cases, as a gift. Basic principles and applications:
   a. The parties involved in *Ijarah* contract should be legally capable of entering into a contract.
   b. The subject matter of *Ijarah* such as usufruct or benefits, lease period, lease rent and payment schedule, etc, should be *Shariah* compliant and clearly stated to both the parties.
   c. It is permitted to the lessor to ask a guarantee under lease contract from the lessee.
   d. The lease contract may be terminated when the lessor sells the leased asset or in case where there is total destruction of the leased asset or as per the mutual consent of the parties (*Shariah* Standards, AAOIFI, 2010, pp. 141-149).
   e. *Ijarah* is used in designing the products such as Home finance, Project finance, Vehicle finance, Goods finance, *Sukuk*, Funds, Corporate products, Treasury products, etc.
5. **Istisna:** *Istisna* is a type of Islamic finance contract in which the manufacturer (supplier) agrees to manufacture (supply) the assets (goods/ commodities) as per the specifications provided by the purchaser (customer). Payment towards the purchases of assets is made during the manufacturing (making process) in various installments normally linked to the stages of manufacturing. And, the assets will be delivered by the supplier on completion of the manufacturing process or on a specific date as agreed between the parties.

In banking practices, the IFIs use a Parallel *Istisna* arrangement (which is a modified version of *Istisna* contract). In this type of arrangement two separate *Istisna* contracts are signed among three different parties. The first *Istisna-1* contract is signed between the IFI and the customer in which the IFI acts as the manufacturer (builder/ supplier) and the customer as the ultimate purchaser. And, the second *Istisna-2* contract is signed between the IFI and the manufacturer (builder/suppler) in which the IFI acts as the purchaser and the manufacturer as the supplier. Usually the first *Istisna-1* contract signed between the IFI and customer precedes the second *Istisna-2* contract signed between IFI and manufacturer. Due the difference in price between the two *Istisna* contracts the IFI makes the profit. Basic principles and applications:

a. The parties involved in *Istisna* should be legally capable of entering into a contract.

b. The subject matter of *Istisna* like asset to be manufactured, raw material going to be used, cost, selling price, payment terms, delivery and disposable etc should be clear to both the parties.
c. Payment can be made in different installments as per the manufacturing stages.
d. In parallel *Istisna* both the contracts should be independent of each other (*Shariah* Standards, AAOIFI, 2010, pp.181-189).
e. *Istisna* contract is used in designing the Islamic finance products such as Home finance, Agriculture finance, Project finance, etc.

6. **Salam:** The mechanism of a *Salam* contract is similar to the mechanism of *Istisna* contract. The only difference is that in *Istisna*, the purchaser pays the purchase price in various stages linked to the manufacturing process whereas in *Salam* it is paid fully in advance.

In banking practices, similar to the parallel *Istisna*, the IFIs use a parallel *Salam* arrangement (which a modified version of *Salam*). In a parallel *Salam* arrangement, the purchase price is made in advance in both the *Salam* contracts (i.e. *Salam-1* and *Salam-2*). Due the difference in price between these two *Salam* contracts the IFI makes the profit. Basic principles and applications:

a. The parties involved in *Salam* should be legally capable of entering into a contract.
b. The subject matter of *Salam* like asset to be manufactured, the selling price, delivery and disposable etc should be clear to both the parties.
c. Payment should be made in advance at time of contract.
d. In case of parallel *Salam*, the two contracts should be independent of each other (*Shariah* Standards, AAOIFI, 2010, pp.165-169).
e. *Salam* contract is used in designing the Islamic finance products as Working Capital finance, Agriculture finance, Project finance, etc.

7. **Wakala:** *Wakala* is similar to the agency type of contract practiced in conventional finance. Under *Wakala* contract one party (principal) appoints the other party as its agent and delegates the authority to act on its behalf or in its interest. In banking practices, the IFI (as the principal) appoints a customer as its agent (known as *Wakeel*) to carry out some economic activities on its behalf. In the authority of an agent, the customer manages the business on behalf or in the interest of the IFI. The customer is paid a fee (known as *Wakala* fee and it can be a regular, lump sum or in terms of percentage of the return) for its management services. It is to be noted in *Wakala* the agent would neither share the profit (except if the *Wakala* fee is agreed to be a percentage of profit) nor bear the loss. Basic principles and applications:

a. The parties involved in *Wakala* should be legally capable of entering into a contract.
b. The subject matter of *Wakala* such as the nature of agency, the type of work, the financial contract, roles and responsibilities of the parties, etc, should be *Shariah* compliant and should be clear to both the parties.
c. *Wakala* contract expires when the agent has fulfilled his obligation or in the case of death of one of the parties i.e. principal or agent (*Shariah* Standards, AAOIFI, 2010, pp. 413-420).
d. *Wakala* is used in designing the products such as in Bank accounts, *Sukuk*, Funds, Corporate products, Treasury products, etc.

As said earlier, these contracts form the foundation for all the Islamic finance practices, products and services.

Financial Regulations in India

After a brief introduction to some of the Islamic finance contracts, let's move towards the laws and regulations that are governing the Indian financial system, especially the three major sectors, namely:

1. Banking Services
2. Microfinance Services
3. Venture Capital financing (Infrastructure finance)

1. **Banking Regulations in India and Challenges facing Islamic Banking:** The banking business in India is regulated under the Banking Regulation Act, 1949 (National Bank for Agriculture and Rural Development, 2014). The subjected act advances various conditions that help in smooth and effective functioning of the banks. But on the other side a few of these conditions have been identified as the legal hurdles to establish or to promote Islamic banking in India. The Reserve Bank of India (RBI) under the chairmanship of Dr. Anand Sinha has constituted a (high level) working group to examine financial instruments used in Islamic banking and possibility to include them in Indian banking practices in the year 2006. The working group after evaluating the Islamic banking instruments in the light of Banking Regulation Act, 1949 (BR Act, 1949) has submitted its report in 2007 (Khatkhatay, M.H., 2009a). The observations (which are the base for the current analysis) made by the working group are:
    a. Restriction on banks to involve in equity financing and trade under the definition "banking" provided in the Section 5(b) of the BR Act, 1949.
    b. Restriction on sale and purchase of property or assets as per the provisions of Section 8 & 9 of the BR Act, 1949.
    c. Restriction on practicing equity participation or joint venture type of financing in Section 19(2) of BR Act, 1949.
    d. Restriction on engaging in business Other than as prescribed under clauses (a) and (b) in Section 6 of BR Act, 1949, thereof.
    e. The constraints related to maintenance of CRR and SLR as per the provisions of BR Act, 1949.Similarly the issue of liquidity management.

These observations were reviewed by the Islamic experts, and the possible ways to tackle each of the identified issues has been proposed (Khatkhatay, M.H., 2009a). A summary of the discussion made on this subject is as follows:

To the issue of 'banking' definition and its other components (raised under the point 'a' of by the RBI Working group), the BR Act, 1949 itself defined banking as 'Lending' and 'Investment'. It means even in the eye of BR Act 1949, lending and investment are two separate activities. It is a misconception that both lending and investment are same in the regulatory context. Therefore, the RBI/GOI, through a special notification can clarify this issue and recognize 'Investment' as a separate activity linked to the market risk. To the issue of 'Deposits', by the definition itself, it implies that (in case of deposit) only principle is guaranteed and not the Return (on deposits). To make it viable for Islamic banking, the RBI/GOI can issue a notification stating in Islamic bank 'deposit' is the case where both principal as well as return are not guaranteed or subjected to risk. These two aspects can be tackled through notifications under Section 6 (1) (o) of the BR Act, 1949.

Table 1. Example to Tackling SLR, CRR & Liquidity Management Issue

iii. Example-1: Level Playing Field for Tackling SLR & CRR Issue: Assume that the prevailing returns of banks from prime customers are of the order of 12% and the returns available on specified SLR assets are of the order of 9%. Also assume that the current SLR & CRR ratios are 22% and 4% which comes to the total 26% (assumed on the basis of rates available on RBI website as on dated 27.09.2014). Hence, for every INR 100 of the bank's total time and demand liabilities it is suffering an opportunity loss of 26*(12-9) %, i.e., INR 0.78 on account of having to maintain the SLR & CRR. For there to be a level playing field between a conventional bank and an Islamic Bank, the Islamic Bank should therefore be required to maintain in (interest-free) current account with Central bank in lieu of the usual SLR & CRR, an amount equal to 0.78/(12-0), i.e. 6.5% of its total time and demand liabilities. iv. Expample-2: Level Playing field for Liquidity Management Issue: Assume that the repo rate is 8% and the reverse repo rate is 7% (assumed on the basis of rates available on RBI website as on dated 27.09.2014).Thus for every INR 100 Central bank lends to the bank against government securities it earns INR 8 and for every Rs. 100 it borrows from the bank it has to pay INR 7. If the Islamic Bank has to balance its interest earnings against its interest payments, the Islamic Bank can borrow for the same period from RBI 7/8*100, or 87.5% of the amount it has maintained for a given period with Central bank . Thus the relevant ratio is 87.5% and every INR 100 the Islamic Bank maintains with RBI for a single day should entitle the Islamic Bank to INR 87.5 of borrowings from RBI for a day. Hence, an account will need to be maintained of the Islamic Bank's dealings with the Central bank in terms of Rs-days. A positive balance of Rs-days will mean that the Islamic Bank has a balance of interest-free borrowings to its credit with the Central bank and a negative balance that it is liable to provide funds to the Central bank.

To the issues of impermissibility of purchase and sale of immoveable properties, prohibition of trading, and reservations regarding investment in equity of other companies (raised under the points 'b' 'c' &'d' by the RBI Working), under Section 9 of the BR Act, 1949, the banks are allowed to purchase and sale the immoveable properties. So this is not issue at all except an interpretation gap. And, under Section 19(2) of the BR Act, 1949, banks are allowed to investment in equity of the companies other than their own subsidiaries. Such investment is also in compliance to Islamic banking principles. Therefore, in this case as well there is no issue. To issue of restriction on trading, though BR Act, 1949 prohibits trading in section 8 but leaves an open provision to allow it by the way of notification under Section 6(1) (o) of the same Act. To tackle this issue there is a need to re-interpret the laws and more clarification can be sought through special notification issued by GOI/RBI.

To the issue of deploying funds in compliance to the CRR and SLR requirement (raised under the point 'e' by the RBI Working group), a Level-Playing field is proposed to maintain deposits with the central bank. And, the issue of liquidity management can be solved by using the Rs-Days mechanism for placing the liquidity with the central bank in case of surplus and borrowing the liquidity from the central bank in case of deficit. For more detail on this proposal please refer to the hypothetical (numerical) examples, Example-1 & Example-2 mentioned in the Table 1.

The discussion above the various proposals made by the Islamic finance experts indicate that it is possible to provide Islamic banking services in India. It requires only a few notifications to be issued from the concerned authorities without any major amendments in the BR Act, 1949.

2. **Microfinance Regulations in India and Regulatory hurdles for Islamic Microfinance:** Microfinance is the financial services provided at micro level to the individuals, small business, labours without any collateral security. Islamic Microfinance is the microfinance services provided within the *Shariah* norms. It is one of the important areas of Islamic finance industry. Islamic Microfinance Institutions (IMFIs) are providing efficient services in the countries such as Bangladesh, Iran, Indonesia, Malaysia, Pakistan, Sri Lanka, UK, USA, Yemen, etc, (Obaidullah, Mohammed, 2008).

IMFIs have been operating in India since the beginning of the 19th century. Patni Cooperative Society established at Surat in the year 1938, Muslim Fund at Tada Balvi in 1941, Islamic Welfare Societies established during 1950s, etc., are a few examples of such institutions (Bagsiraj, M. I., 2003, pp. 11-12). At present a good number of IMFIs, registered as Welfare societies, Charitable trusts, and Cooperatives, are operating in India in the states such as Andhra Pradesh, Bihar, Jammu & Kashmir, Karnataka, Kerala, Maharashtra, Tamil Nadu, Uttar Pradesh, etc.

In the present study only Multi-state Cooperative Society (MSCS) and Non-Banking Financial Corporation- Microfinance Institution (NBFC-MFI) models of microfinance is considered. The feasibility is studied in terms of MFI's capacity to mobilize funds, invest funds, provide insurance facility and provide training development services.

a. **Multi-state Cooperative (MSCS) Model:** The MFIs providing microfinance services through this model are regulated under the Multi-state Cooperative Societies (MSCS) Act, 2002 (Sahulat, 2012). Under Chapter-II, Section 10 (1&2) a MSCS is permitted to draft its own Bye-Laws in consistent with the provisions of the subjected Act. Such bye-laws should consists of the details related to the name, address, area of operation, sources of funds, application of fund, disbursement of Net Profits, etc. The bye-laws drafted by a MSCS should be registered with the Central Registrar. Once registered, the bye-laws stand as the legal document upon which the operations of the MSCS are judged.

Let's have a look on the various provisions provided in the MSCS Act 2002 for each of the parameters selected for the feasibility study.

i. **Mobilization of Funds:** Under Chapter-VII, Section 67 (1&2) of the MSCS Act 2002, a MSCS is allowed to receive deposits, raise loans and receive grants from both external sources (to such extent and under such conditions as may be specified in its bye-laws). There is no specific condition/discussion in the MSCS Act 2002 which directly restricts a MSCS from mobilizing funds in Islamic microfinance way (using contacts such as *Musharaka*, *Mudaraba*, etc). In the opinion of the authors, a MSCS can receive the funds in Islamic microfinance ways by including such provision in its bye-Laws. This would in no way effect the status of the MSCS Act, 2002.

ii. **Application of Funds:** Under Chapter-VII, Section 64 of the MSCS Act 2002, a MSCS can provide loan to a depositor on the security of his/her deposits, can deposit the fund in the bank, can invest fund in securities, shares (as specified in the law), and can invest or deposit its funds in such other modes as may be provided in its bye-laws. There is no specific condition/discussion in the MSCS Act 2002 which directly restricts a MSCS from investing its funds in Islamic microfinance way (using contract such as *Musharaka*, *Mudaraba*, *Murabaha*, *Ijarah*, etc). In the opinion of the authors, as similar to the mobilization of funds, a MSCS can deploy or invest its funds in Islamic microfinance modes by including such provision in its bye-laws. Even this would also not change the status of the MSCS Act, 2002.

iii. **Insurance Facility:** Under Chapter-VII, Section 64 (f) of the MSCS Act 2002 a MSCS is permitted to deposit its fund in any scheme as specified in its bye-laws. As it appears from the provision, that a MSCS can provide insurance facility to its customers by depositing its fund in an insurance company registered with Insurance Regulatory Development Authority (IRDA) of India. But from the Islamic microfinance perspective, the conventional insurance products usually involve in Riba (interest), Gharar (uncertainty) and Maysir (gambling) which is prohibited in Islamic finance or Islamic microfinance (Khatkhatay, M. H., 2009b). The possible ways to solve the issue of insurance can be explored or dealt in detail in future research.

iv. **Training/ Development Facilities:** Under Chapter-IV, Section 27 (1&2) of MSCS Act, 2002 a MSCS may allocate fund and also organize cooperative education programs for its members, directors, and employees. There is no issue in this aspect from the Islamic microfinance perspective.

It appears from the discussion above that providing Islamic microfinance services through MSCS model do not require any major changes in existing regulations. If any MSCS decided to provide Islamic microfinance services then it should include such provisions in its bye-laws.

After studying the feasibility of providing Islamic microfinance through MSCS model, let's move on to the NBFC-MFI model.

b. **NBFC-MFI Model:** According to the definition provided by the RBI, an NBFC-MFI is a non-deposit taking NBFC (other than a company licensed under Section 25 of the Indian Companies Act, 1956) with a minimum Net Owned Funds (NOF) of INR 50 million (for NBFC-MFIs registered in the North Eastern Region of the country, it is INR 20 million) and having not less than 85% of its net assets as 'qualifying assets' (Reserve Bank of India [RBI], 2011)

Under the same notification, the RBI has defined the 'Qualifying Assets' saying, "*Qualifying assets are those mobilized funds (Loan) that are disbursed to the customer without any collateral (security)*". RBI also laid some specific and additional conditions for the NBFCs providing microfinance services through NBFC-MFI model. The conditions are as follows:

i. An NBFC-MFI can lend fund to a borrower with a household annual income not exceeding INR 60,000 (rural) or INR 1, 20,000 (urban and semi-urban).
ii. Total indebtedness of an individual borrower under NBFC-MFI model should not exceed INR 50,000.
iii. Loan amount advanced to an individual under NBFC-MFI model should not exceed INR 35,000 in the first cycle and INR 50,000 in subsequent cycles;
iv. Total tenure of the loan advanced under NBFC-MFI model should not to be less than 24 months. At least 70% of the aggregate amount of loans should be given for income generation purpose.
v. The payment terms (weekly, fortnightly or monthly installments) should be as per the choice of the borrower.
vi. At least 15% of total funds should be invested in the interest based securities issued by the GOI.
vii. Not more than 12% per annum interest should be paid on public deposits.
viii. Not more than 26% per annum interest should be collected from a single borrower.

After a brief look on the various conditions laid by the RBI for the better functioning of NBFC-MFIs let's evaluate the feasibility of an NBFC-MFI providing Islamic microfinance services in terms of the parameters selected for this study. The authors have also considered the RBI Act, 1934 in which is applicable to the NBFCs operating in India (RBI Publication, 2014).

i. **Mobilization of Funds:** Towards the mobilization of funds, Chapter-III, Section 45-I of RBI Act, 1934, allows a NBFC to mobilize deposits (in any form but excluding demand deposits) from both internal and external sources. According to the definition provided in the Act, 'Deposit' includes any receipt of money by way of deposit or loan or in any other form, but does not include the deposits mobilized from the sources and means restricted in the Section 45I (bb) (i-vii) of the RBI Act, 1934. It is to be noted that for the NBFCs deposit mobilization is likened to the size of their Net Owned Fund (NOF). In addition to the NOF criteria they are also required to meet investment grade rating criteria.

Within the current regulation, an NBFC cannot mobilize funds in Islamic microfinance ways except as interest based deposits. Further, there is a condition that the depositors should be paid a fixed return i.e. 'Interest' at 12% p.a. (maximum) on their deposits.

In Islamic microfinance receiving interest based deposits or paying interest on deposits mobilized is prohibited. Therefore, to make a NBFC to be able to mobilize funds on Islamic microfinance ways (and also on demand or interest-free or current deposits) the RBI should provide some concessions through special notifications or by issuing specific directions. This is possible under the Section 45I (f) (3) & 45J (A) (1) of the RBI Act, 1934. To tackle the issue of 'Interest' rate ceiling, the RBI can issue a notification prescribing a variable rate of return between 0%-12% enabling the NBFC-MFIs to borrow and lend funds on a variable rate of return linked to linked to risk but within the range prescribed in the regulations. This type of notification can also be issued under the Section 45J (A) (1) of the RBI Act, 1934.

ii. **Application of Funds:** Towards the application of funds, under the Chapter-III, Section 45-I (c) of RBI Act, 1934', an NBFC is permitted to deploy its funds in financing (interest based lending), acquisition of shares, stock, bonds, debentures or securities issued by GOI, etc.

Within the existing regulations, the NBFC cannot deploy its funds in Islamic microfinance ways. An NBFC-MFI, in compliance to the regulatory norms laid through RBI notifications, has to deploy 15% of the total funds mobilized in the (prescribed) interest bearing securities. In addition, the RBI has also put a ceiling on 'interest' rate to be charged to the borrowers, which is at 26% (maximum).

In Islamic microfinance, neither it is permitted to deploy the funds in the avenues that earn the interest-based income nor is it permitted to charge interest on the funds lent. Therefore, in this case also, the RBI should provide some concessions through special notifications or by issuing specific directions to make a NBFC to be able to deploy funds in Islamic microfinance ways (and also on interest-free basis). This is also possible under the Section 45J (A) (1) of the RBI Act, 1934. And, to tackle the issue of deploying 15% of the total funds mobilized in, the RBI can issue a separate notification to include Equity shares in the list of specific securities and directing the NBFC-MFI to invest in them. This type of notification can also be issued under the Section 45J (A)(1) of the RBI Act, 1934. And, to tackle the issue of 'Interest' rate ceiling to be charged to the borrowers, the RBI can issue a notification prescribing a variable rate of return ranging between 0%-26% linked to risk enabling the NBFC-MFIs to deploy the funds in Islamic microfinance modes but within the existing regulations. This type of notification can also be issued under the provision provided in the Section 45J (A) (1) of the RBI Act, 1934.

iii. **Insurance Facility:** As far as providing insurance facility is concerned, the NBFCs are permitted to provide the insurance facility on their own and as the agent to any insurance company registered with IRDA (Sa-Dhan Microfinance Resource Center, 2006). And, from the Islamic microfinance perspective, similar to the MSCS the NBFC too have the same issues as identified earlier.

iv. **Training/ Development Facilities:** Towards the training & development facilities, the RBI Act, 1934 do not provide any specific restrictions. Therefore, it can be assumed that a NBFC-MFI may organize training & development programs for its all stake holders.

The discussion above reveals that a few of the provisions of the RBI Act, 1934 and the directions issued by the RBI for NBFC-MFI do not support the NBFCs to provide Islamic Microfinance services. But these issues can be solved through the special notifications and directions issued by RBI without making any changes in the prevailing regulations.

3. **Venture Capital Financing, *Sukuk* and Infrastructure Finance in India:** The practices of *Musharaka* and *Mudaraba* contracts reflect the relationship of Islamic finance with the concept of venture capital financing. Nevertheless, the Islamic venture capital financing formally appeared on the global financial market during the period 2000-2010 in the Middle East and Malaysian regions.

In India too there have been a few major Islamic venture financing transactions made by the Arab Islamic finance players such as Kuwait Finance House, Saudi Economic Development Company and Gulf Finance House during the same period. Furthermore, the first SEBI-registered Islamic venture capital fund i.e. Secura India Real Estate Fund, was launched in 2009 (Khatkhatay, M H, 2011). After the successful operation of the first fund, the same company has launched its second fund in 2012 (Business Line, 2012).

It is to be noted that *Sukuk* (an Islamic bond) plays a key role in Islamic venture capital financing. *Sukuk* (as part of Islamic capital Market) is one of the preferable means/avenue to raise funds to initiate and upgrade huge infrastructure projects. The report published recently on the growth of Islamic finance industry indicates that the *Sukuk* issuances between 2004 and end-2012 have charted a Compound Annual Growth Rate (CAGR) of 45.2% and a rise in value from just USD 6.6 billion to USD131.2 billion (IFSB, 2013).

Thus, in this section let's have brief introduction to the *Sukuk*, its structure, mechanism and various types. Further, the operations of a VCF and the regulations that are governing VCFs in India will also be studied in detail.

a. ***Sukuk* – An Islamic Bond:** According to AAOIFI (2010, p. 307) *Sukuk* are the "*certificates of equal value representing undivided share in ownership of tangible assets, usufruct and services or (in the ownership of) the assets of particular projects or special investment activity, however, this is true after receipt of the value of the Sukuk, the closing of subscription and the employment of funds received for the purpose for which the Sukuk were issued*". In legal terms, *Sukuk* reflects the participation/ownership rights in an underlying asset under which an investor has a right to the proportionate benefit, income, and return in the respective asset for a defined period.

i. ***Sukuk*- Basic Structure and Mechanism:** The structure and mechanism of a *Sukuk* issuance, except to a few key technical and contractual differences, is similar to the structure and mechanism of venture capital fund. In *Sukuk*, the promoter (usually the *Sukuk* Management Company or the Originator) who proposes to raise funds would establish a Special Purpose Vehicle (SPV) to facilitate *Sukuk* issuance in capital market. SPV helps in efficient management of *Sukuk* as well as acts as a bankruptcy remote to the promoter. Prior to the issuance of *Sukuk* in the market, the SPV drafts (submits) a prospectus containing the details of the proposed *Sukuk*, the fund mobilization methods, details of the projects in which the investment is to be made, *Sukuk* maturity period, cost and expenses details, income, return and profit distribution and sharing details, project exit plan, etc. Through placing the prospectus (in private) the SPV would invite investments from the investors. Investors would subscribe to the prospectus and pay the principal amount. After receiving the principle amount the SPV would issue the *Sukuk*. SPV would act as a trustee to the investor's funds. SPV transfers the funds to the promoter under any of the Islamic finance contracts (depending upon the type of *Sukuk* structured). Promoter as a partner or an agent of the SPV would invest the amounts in any of the *Shariah* compliant projects. The income returns and profits are shared as per the agreement between the promoter and the SPV. The SPV would transfer the return or income to the investors in proportion to their *Sukuk* holdings. At the maturity of *Sukuk*, the project or assets are either sold to a third party or purchased by the promoter itself on the market price. The sale realization received would be shared between the promoter and SPV as per the agreement. SPV would transfer the realization amounts to investors against redemption of the *Sukuk*.

The investor can have return on their investments in three forms, namely, a) Regular income such as rent and periodical profits associated with the underlined assets, b) Profit realized in *Sukuk* trading (subject to the condition) and c) Capital yield secured after sale-out of the underlined assets at the maturity of the *Sukuk*.

A typical structure of *Sukuk* is represented in the Figure 1.

Mechanism:

Step 1: Promoter (company or institution or a group of institutions) establishes a SPV to issue the *Sukuk*.

Step 2: An advisor, particularly a *Shariah* Board or a *Shariah* consultant is appointed to seek advises on various issues.

Step 3: Issuer SPV issues prospectus and the Investors subscribes and pays the proceeds as the Principal Amount.

Step 4: Issuer SPV after receiving Principal Amount issues the *Sukuk* to the Investors. The *Sukuk* represent an undivided ownership in an underlying asset going to be purchased. They also represent a right of the Investors to the Periodic Distribution Amount (an amount paid periodically as the share of Rental Income/Profit/ Return) and the Dissolution Amount (an amount paid on redemption of the Sukuk on maturity).

Step 5: Issuer SPV declares a trust over the proceeds and thereby acts as Trustee on behalf of the Investors.

Step 6: Issuer SPV enters into any of the Islamic finance contracts (such as *Musharaka*, *Mudaraba*, *Murabaha*, *Ijarah*, etc based on the type of *Sukuk* structured) with the promoter and both agree on certain conditions like contribution to the capital, allocation share investment, profit sharing ratios, etc. However, the promoter usually manages the SPV and Investment.

Step 7: Issuer SPV pays the Principal Amount to the Promoter as its contribution to the Total capital going to be invested.

Step 8: Promoter transfers the share to the Issuer SPV in accordance to its capital contribution.

Step 9: Promoter invests the Total Capital into a *Shariah* Compliant Investment Project/portfolio.

Step 10: On each Periodic Distribution Date, the Promoter collects the actual profits/income/ return generated by the Investment Project / Portfolio.

Step 11: Promoter after retaining its share pays of the actual profits/income/return to Issuer SPV in proportion to its capital contribution or in a pre-agreed ratio. It is to be noted that if the actual share of the Issuer SPV's profit exceeds its pre-defined expectation then it is permitted that the excess amount is given to the Promoter as an incentive for its good performance. In case of loss, both Issuer SPV and the Promoter shall share that loss in proportion to their capital contribution only (subject to the type of *Sukuk*).

Step 12: Issuer SPV pays each Periodic Distribution Amount to the Investors using the profit/income/return it has received from the Promoter.

Step 13: In the event of maturity or default the promoter would purchases the Assets from Issuer SPV exercising the Purchase Undertaking, at the applicable Exercise Price, which will be equal to the Principal Amount plus any, realize (earned) but unpaid Periodic Distribution Amounts owing to the Investors. **OR** in case of pre-payment or any other event as agreed between the parties, Issuer SPV would sells the Assets to promoter exercising the Sale Undertaking at the applicable Exercise Price, which will be equal to the Principal Amount plus any, realize (earned) but unpaid Periodic Distribution Amounts owing to the Investors.

Step 14: Issuer SPV Receives the Dissolution Amount from the Purchaser.

Step 15: In case of the maturity or default or pre-payment, the Investors would redeem the *Sukuk* to Issuer SPV against the Dissolution Amount.

Step 16: Issuer SPV pays the Dissolution Amounts to the Investors using the amount it has received from promoter or purchaser.

The financial calculation of *Ijarah Sukuk* is explained using a numerical Example-3 in the Table 2.

Figure 1. Sukuk Structure

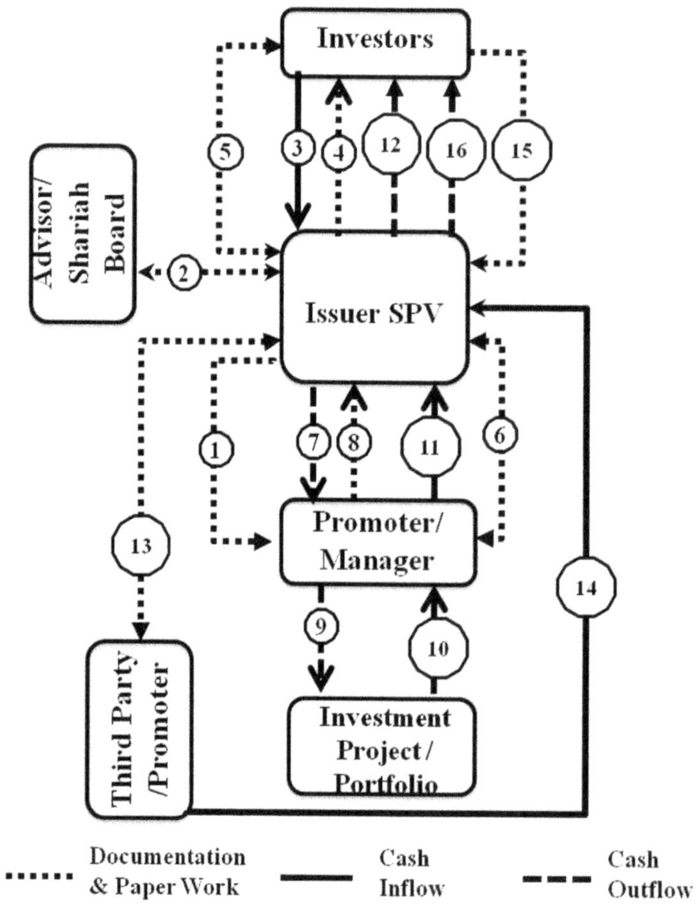

Table 2. Numerical Example showing Financial Calculation of Ijarah Sukuk

Numerical Exmaple-3: *Ijarah Sukuk*

Step-1: Suppose there are three investor **i-1**, **i-2** and **i-3.**

Step-2: Promoter wants to mobilize the Investment of USD 1000,000.

Step-3: SPV established by the promoter issues prospectus to the Investors.

Step-4: The investors subscribe to the prospectus and pay amounts in the following segregation:
Investment of **i-1** = 250,000/-, **i-2**=250,000 and **i-3**=500,000/- respectively.

Step-5: After receiving the Principal Amount from the Investors the SPV would issue 10,000 *Sukuk* in the following proportion:
i-1 would subscribe to 2,500, **i-2** would subscribe to 2,500, **i-3** would subscribe to 5,000 respectively representing the proportionate ownership of the investors in *Ijarah* assets going to be purchased.

Step-6: The SPV would forward the principal amount to the promoter to be invested in *Ijarah* assets.

Step-7: SPV then leases out the *Ijarah* assets to the promoter on annual rental 12% p.a.

Step-8: The rental income would be USD 120,000 as annual rent. It is calculated as follows: **Annual Rent= [(Total Cost of the assets*Rental Rate].** Which is [(1,000,000*12%] =120,000.

Step-9: Let us assume 2% would be the SPV management Expenses. Therefore, USD 20,000 shall be deducted as SPV Management Expenses.

Step-10: The SPV distribute the Net Rentals i.e. Annual rentals- SPV Management Expenses to the investors in proportion to their *Sukuk* holdings (as given below):

	Investment	**Rental @ 12%**	**SPV Management Expenses @ 2%**	**Net Profit**	**Net Profit in %**
Investor-1	250,000	30,000	5,000	25,000	10%
Investor-2	250,000	30,000	5,000	25,000	10%
Investor-3	500,000	60,000	10,000	50,000	10%
Project	**1,000,000**	**120,000**	**20,000**	**100,000**	**10%**

ii. **Types of *Sukuk*:** There are various types of *Sukuk* that are structured using different Islamic finance contracts. The key features of a few of the major types of *Sukuk* have been mentioned in the Table 3. It is to be noted that the key features mentioned here are in confirmation to the *Shariah* Standards, issued by AAOIFI (2010, pp. 307-317).

iii. **Important Legal Documents used in *Sukuk* Structuring:** A list of the important legal documents that are commonly used in *Sukuk* structuring is enlisted in the Table 4. In addition to the documents mentioned, there can be a number of other related documents that are used in structuring a particular type of *Sukuk*.

Since the last one decade there has been a significant development in *Sukuk* market and a good number of huge infrastructure projects have been financed using these instruments in the Gulf regions and South-East-Asian region. With a minimum alteration, *Sukuk* can be launched using VCF regime in the Indian capital market to mobilize required funds, particularly in the area of private equity funds.

After having a brief introduction to *Sukuk,* let's move to the regulations governing the venturing capital financing in India.

b. **Venture Capital Fund:** According to Shison (as citied by Mansoor Durran & Grahame Boocock, 2006, p. 36) a venture capital (VC) can be defined as an activity by which investors support entrepreneurial talent with finance and business skills to exploit market opportunities and thus obtain long term capital gains.

   i. **Operative Structure of Venture Capital Fund:** Promoter (the fund Management Company) who proposes to raise funds would establish a Special Purpose Vehicle (SPV) registered as a trust or a company or a body of corporate. Promoter would draft and

Table 3. Key features of different types of Sukuk

Type of *Sukuk*	Key Features
Musharaka Sukuk	■ Issuer SPV acts as the Trustee to the Investors ■ Issuer SPV & Promoter join as partners and both the parties contribute to the capital. ■ Promoter manages the SPV and also takes the Investment decisions. ■ Profit sharing ratio should be agreed at the time of contract. ■ Losses should be borne in proportion to the capital contribution. ■ As per *Shariah* rule it is necessary that at least 30% or 33% (based on the *Shariah* rule applicable in particular case) of the Total capital should be invested in tangible assets. ■ Assets of Investment Project should remain throughout the *Sukuk* maturity period. ■ Income is linked to the performance of the assets/project. ■ It is permitted to trade the *Musharaka Sukuk* on its face value.
Mudaraba Sukuk	■ Issuer SPV acts as the Trustee to the Investors. ■ Issuer SPV and Promoter join as partners where SPV (as *Rab-al Maal*) contribute the capital and Promoter (as *Mudarib*) will be Manage the Investment. Promoter will also take the Investment decisions. ■ As per *Shariah* rule it is necessary that at least 30% or 33% (based on the *Shariah* rule applicable in particular case) of the Total capital should be invested in tangible assets. ■ Profit sharing ratio between Issuer SPV and promoter should be agreed at the time of contract. ■ Losses, if any, should be borne only by the SPV (as *Rab-al- Maal*). ■ Assets of Investment Project should remain throughout the *Sukuk* maturity period. ■ It is permitted to trade the *Mudaraba Sukuk* on its face value.
Murabaha Sukuk	■ Issuer SPV acts as the Trustee to the Investors. ■ Issuer SPV (by itself or through appointing the promoter as its agent with a separate agreement) purchases certain assets from a Supplier on the request made by the promoter. ■ Issuer SPV sells the assets to the promoter on *Murabaha* basis on a mark-up to be paid in differed time in various installments. ■ Issuer SPV should disclose the cost and profit margin of the assets to the promoter at the time of contract. ■ Deferred price and payment schedule should be known and should be agreed between the parties at the time of contract. ■ *Murabaha* assets may not remain with the Issuer SPV till the maturity period of the *Sukuk*. ■ Income is not linked to the performance of the assets. ■ It is NOT permitted to trade the *Murabaha Sukuk* either on premium or discount except at par. However, *Murabaha Sukuk* is tradable only if the total receivable is less than 50% of the total *Murabaha* Sale price.
Ijarah Sukuk	■ Issuer SPV acts as the Trustee to the Investors. ■ Issuer SPV first purchases the assets from the promoter through an independent purchase & Sale contract. ■ Issuer SPV (as Lessor) leases out the assets to the promoter (Lessee) on a specified Rental and for a specific time period as agreed between the parties at the time of contract. ■ Ownership of the assets should remain with the SPV (trustee or lessor) and only the usufruct right should be transferred to the promoter (Lessee). ■ All the liabilities of assets arising from the ownership aspect should be borne by the Issuer SPV (as Owner). ■ All the liabilities relating to the use of the assets, however, rest with the promoter (as Lessee). ■ In the event of the total loss to the function of the asset, the lease contract may be terminated. ■ If the total loss is caused by the misuse or negligence of the lessee, then the lessee will be liable to compensate the Trustee for depreciation in the value of the affected asset. ■ Assets will remain with the Issuer SPV till throughout the *Sukuk* maturity period. ■ Income is linked to the performance of the assets. ■ It is permitted to trade the *Ijarah Sukuk*.
Wakala Sukuk (Hybrid *Sukuk*)	■ Issuer SPV (as Principal) enters into a *Wakala* arrangement with Promoter (as Agent or *Wakeel*). ■ The subject matter of the *Wakala* agreement that includes the duration of the *Wakala*, the type or criteria of assets that the *Wakeel* can select, the fees payable to the *Wakeel* for the services, etc., must be specific and clear. ■ Promoter will manage the assets and would be paid a fee for its services as agent. ■ As per *Shariah* rule it is necessary that at least 30% or 33% (based on the *Shariah* rule applicable in particular case) of the Total capital should be invested in tangible assets. ■ Assets may or may not remain with the Issuer SPV depending upon the type of Investment arrangement chosen. ■ Income to the investors is linked to the performance of the assets. ■ It is permitted to trade the *Wakala Sukuk* if at least 30% of the total assets are tangible assets. ■ If two or more Islamic Finance contracts (such as *Mudaraba & Ijarah*) are combined to form an investment portfolio in *Wakala Sukuk* (also known as Hybrid *Sukuk*) then the assets related to *Ijarah* contract in that particular portfolio should not be less than the 30% of total assets.

Table 4. List of the important documents used in Sukuk Structuring

Document	Parties	Details
Prospectus	Between Issuer SPV & Investors	This document contains the details of the contract, parties who are involved, different conditions with respect to each party, investment, project, etc.
Trusteeship Contract	Between Issuer SPV & Investors	This is the document under which the investors entrust their monies to issuer SPV for the purpose of investment.
Sale and Purchase Undertakings	Between Seller & Purchaser	These are the independent and unilateral promises based on which the sale and purchase contracts are signed in order to transfer the ownership of assets from one party to another against the payment.
Service Agency Contract	Issuer SPV and Promoter	Under this document the agent is entitled to act on behalf or in the interest of the Principal to carry out the investment and to manage the assets.
Partnership or Relationship Agreement	As per the applicable Islamic Finance contract	This document specifies the parties involved in the contact, their contribution, role, return, etc.

submit the required documents as per the applicable law. The document such as Trust-deed or the Partnership agreement should constitute the details of the proposed VCF, fund mobilization methods, details of the investment projects, time period of VCF, cost and expenses details, income, return and profit distribution and sharing details, VCF exit plan, etc,. It is to be noted usually the promoter makes investment decisions on behalf of the investors and also manages the VCF. And, for its services the promoter can charges certain fees and also claims a share in the profits generated by the fund. But all these details should be mentioned in the trust-deed or the partnership agreement even before the incorporation VCF. Promoter would invite investments from the investors placing the prospectus in private. After receiving the principle amounts from the investors the VCF would issue VCF-units. The incomes, returns and profits are shared as per the agreement between the promoter and VCF. VCF transfers the regular income, returns, and profit to the investors in proportionate to their VCF-units holdings. At the maturity of the VCF, the infrastructure project or portfolio or the assets are generally sold to a third party or purchaser on market price by the promoter itself. The sale realization received will be shared between the promoter and the VCF as per the agreement. And, on the redemption of VCF-units, the VSF transfers the realization/redemption amount to the investors.

After seeing the operative structure of VEC, let's see its regulatory aspects.

ii. **Regulations related to Venture Capital Financing /Funds in India:** There are two types of venture capital funds operated in India. They are Venture Capital Fund-domestic and Foreign Venture Capital Investor. Each of these two types of funds is regulated under a separate law. The domestic Venture Capital Fund (VCF-Domestic) is regulated under the Securities and Exchange Board of India (Venture Capital Funds) Regulations, 1996 (Securities Board of India [SEBI], 2014a). Whereas the Foreign Venture Capital Investor (FVCI) is regulated under the Securities and Exchange Board of India (Foreign Venture Capital Investor) Regulations, 2000 (SEBI, 2014b).According to Chapter-I, Section 2,(m) of the SEBI-VCF Act, 1996 the VCF (domestic) is "a fund established in the form of a trust or a company including a body corporate and registered under SEBI-VCF Regulations, 1996". It has three key features namely: a) It has a dedicated pool of capital; b) The fund is raised in the manner specified under the SEBI VCF Regulations; and c) The funds are invested in venture capital undertaking in accordance with the SEBI VCF Regulations. And, according Chapter-I, Section 2, (g) of SEBI-FVCI Act, 2000, a FVCI is the investor registered under this act but incorporated and established outside the India. In addition to the basic features and investment conditions, in terms of operations, the FVCI should appoint a domestic custodian. There are also certain reporting and disclosure requirements that need to be satisfied by a registered FVCI on a continuing basis.

Let's understand the difference between the VCF-Domestic and FVCI in terms of their establishment, regulations, management, mobilization of funds, application of funds and distribution of profits/income. The differences are given in the Table 5.

As it can be seen in the Table 5 that in compliance to the provisions of SEBI-VCF Regulations, 1996 and SEBI-FVCI Regulations, 2000, a VCF has to invest 25% of its investable funds into Debt-based securities or instruments which certainly invite 'interest-based' income. As said earlier, receipt of interest (*Riba*) is prohibited in Islamic finance. Therefore, an Islamic venture capital fund (or a *Sukuk* Fund) cannot deploy its funds into the avenue that brings interest-based income.

This issue can be dealt easily by seeking permission from the SEBI/ RBI to allow VCFs to deploy the 25% of investable funds in Equity based instruments. Apart from this issue, there are no other regulatory issues that can become a hurdle for Islamic venture capital financing (using *Sukuk*) in India.

In view of the enormous amounts of investment required to upgrade the infrastructure to raise to a level of economically developed nation it is important for India to access Islamic venture capital investment (Sukuk).

SOLUTIONS AND RECOMMENDATIONS

After discussing the issues facing Islamic finance in India in the banking, microfinance and venture capital financing sectors, the authors, in this section tried to summaries the proposed solutions and also made some recommendations to the GOI, RBI and other concerned authorities. Let's see the summary of solutions and recommendations in relation to each of the sector.

1. **Banking Sector:**
    a. To the issue where banks are not permitted to involve in any activity other than Lending on Interest. The authors recommend that the GOI/ RBI should issue a notification under Section 1 (1)(o) of the BR Act, 1949 recognizing 'Investment' as a separate activity liked to market risk and also should redefining word 'deposit' by stating that not only return but also principle is not guaranteed.
    b. To the issue where the banks are not permitted to engage in purchase and sale of immoveable properties, trading, and make investment in equities of other companies, in the opinion of the authors, BR Act, 1949 allows the banks to purchase and sale of immoveable properties, to investment in equity of companies other than its own subsidiaries and to trade by way of a notification under Section 6(1) (o). Hence, there is no issue in this case.
    c. To the issue of SLR, CRR and Liquidity Management mechanism the authors recommend the GOI and RBI to consider the Level Playing field and Rs-Days mechanism proposed by Islamic finance experts.

Table 5. Difference between VCF-Domestic and FVCI

Heads	Venture Capital Fund (Domestic)	Foreign Venture Capital Investor
Establishment	■ Trust, ■ Company, ■ A Body Corporate	■ Trust, ■ Company, ■ A Body Corporate
Regulations	■ Indian Trust Act 1882 ■ Indian Registration Act, 1908 ■ Companies Act, 1956 ■ SEBI-VCF Regulations, 1996	■ Indian Trust Act 1882 ■ Indian Registration Act, 1908 ■ Companies Act, 1956, ■ SEBI-FVCI Regulations, 2000 ■ Regulations of the country where it is operating
Document	■ Trust-deed [Chapter-IV, Section 14-17] ■ Partnership agreement [Chapter-IV, Section 14-17] ■ Any other document as required [Chapter-IV, Section 14-17]	■ Trust-deed [Chapter-II, Section 5 & Chapter-III 11 (a & b)]. ■ Partnership agreement [Chapter-II, Section 5 & Chapter-III 11 (a & b)]. ■ Any Other document as required [Chapter-II, Section 5 & Chapter-III 11 (a & b)].
Management	Promoter Manages the VCF	■ Offshore Promoter Manages the VCF in Foreign country ■ Local Custodian Manages the VCF in India
Mobilization of Fund	■ May raise fund (monies) from any investor whether Indian, Foreign or Non-resident Indian by way of private placement of VCF units [Chapter-III, Section 11 (1)]. ■ Minimum Investment that can be mobilized from Each Investor is INR 0.5 million [Chapter-III, Section 11 (2)]. ■ Minimum Capital Commitment from Each Investor is INR 50 million [Chapter-III, Section 11 (3)].	■ May raise fund (monies) from any investor whether Indian, Foreign or Non-resident Indian by way of private placement of VCF units (equity based). ■ Minimum Investment that can be mobilized from Each Investor is INR 0.5 million. ■ Minimum Capital Commitment from Each Investor is INR 50 million.
Application of Fund	■ Not permitted to invest more than 25% of its corpus in one VCU [Chapter-III, Section 12 (a)]. ■ Not less than 75% of the investable fund has to be invested in unlisted Equity shares or equity linked instruments [Chapter-III, Section 12 (d) (1)]. ■ Up to 25% of the investable fund has to be invested Initial Public Offer (IPO) of a Venture Capital Undertaking (VCU), Debt or Debt-linked Instrument of a VCU [Chapter-III, Section 12 (d)(2)]. ■ Not permitted to invest in its 'Associate Company' –a company in which the promoter holds equity shares in excess of 15% of its paid-up equity share capital of VCU [Chapter-I, Section 2, (aa)] & [Chapter-III, Section 12 (c)].	■ Permitted to invest 100% corpus in a domestic SEBI registered VFC [Chapter-III, Section 11 (b)]. ■ Not less than 75% of the investable fund has to be invested in unlisted Equity shares or equity linked instruments of a VCU [Chapter-III, Section 11 (c)(i)]. ■ Up to 25% of the investable fund has to be invested Initial Public Offer (IPO) of VCU, Debt or Debt-linked Instrument of a VCU, Preferential allotment of equity shares of a listed company, equity shares or equity linked instruments of a financially weak company, sick industrial company whose shares are listed, Special Purpose Vehicles which are created by an FVCI [Chapter-III, Section 11 (c)(ii)].
Distribution of Income/Profit	■ Regular Income ■ Annual Dividends ■ Capital Gains	■ Regular Income ■ Annual Dividends ■ Capital Gains

2. **Microfinance Sector:**
    a. To the issue of mobilization and application of funds in Islamic finance ways in a MSCS model the authors recommend the GOI and other concerned authorities to permit the MSCS to included provision in its bye-laws. To the issue of insurance the authors recommend the concerned authorities to permit the MSCS to provide Islamic Micro-insurance (Micro-*Takful*) products.
    b. To the issue of mobilization and application of funds in Islamic finance ways in an NBFC-MFI model the authors recommend the GOI and RBI to permit the NBFC-MFI to do so by issuing notification. The authors also recommend the RBI to issue notifications prescribing a range for rate of return between 0%-12% (variable) linked to risk to be paid to the depositors, a range for rate of return between 0%-26% (variable) linked to risk to be charged to the borrower and allowing the NBF-MFI to deploy 15% of its total funds in equity shares.
3. **Venture Capital Financing:**
    a. To the issue of deploying 25% of its investable funds into Debt-based securities or instruments by VCF and FVCI, the authors recommend the SEBI and RBI to issue a notification allowing the VCF to invest the prescribed proportion of the funds in equity based instruments.

Based on the solutions and recommendations made above it can be said that the practice of Islamic banking and finance is possible in India. But it requires the GOI, RBI, SEBI and other concerned authorities to take necessary steps at policy and regulation level to accommodate this industry. These types of measures have already been taken by some of the countries like France, Hong Kong, Japan, Singapore, UK, USA, etc, to explore the potentials of newly emerging Islamic finance industry (Lovells, 2009).

FUTURE RESEARCH

The present study is the part of various discussions that are going on to draw the feasibility of providing Islamic finance services in India within the existing financial regulations. It attempts to provide a base for the researchers, experts, practitioners, authorities to consider the Islamic finance industry seriously and utilize the opportunities and potential it holds for India. This study may help the researchers to set a direction for their future research and discussion on the subject matter considering the other regulations such as International Accounting Standards, International Financial Reporting Standards, Trust Act 1861, Various Societies Acts, Companies Act 1956, Insurance Regulatory & Development Act, 1999, Indian Income Tax Act, 1961, Commercial and Sales taxes, etc. Though providing a favorable regulatory environment is the need of hour and is the first requirement for Islamic finance to be practiced in India but it is not the end of the discussion. More research work, especially empirical research, on the aspects such as designing of innovative Islamic finance products specific to Indian market, creating the efficiency in the operations of existing IFIs, etc are expected to be taken up soon. All these points highlight that the discussion and research on Islamic finance should continue or has to continue till the entire questions raised and going to be raised are answered comprehensively.

CONCLUSION

Having discussed on the various regulations governing banking, microfinance and venture capital financing in India and studying the feasibility of providing Islamic finance services within the existing regulations, it can be concluded that the Islamic finance industry can become an internal part of the prevailing financial system in India. Islamic finance practices can be easily adopted through required notifications and directions issued by the concerned authorities without any major amendments in the existing regulations. It can be hoped that in the interest of the nation the GOI, RBI, SEBI and other stake-holders would take some positive and would utilize the opportunities that the Islamic finance industry holds for India.

REFERENCES

Accounting and Auditing Organization for Islamic Finance Institutions. (2010). *Shariah Standards*. Manama, Bahrain: Author.

Bagsiraj, M. I. (2003). Islamic Financial Institutions of India - Progress, Problems and Prospects. Jeddah, Saudi Arabia: Scientific Publishing Centre, King Abdulaziz University.

Chakrabarty, K. C. (2012, March). *M - Banking in India - Regulations and Rationale*. Speech delivered at International Banking Summit on Regulation of Cross-Border Mobile Payments and Regional Financial Integration organized by RBI, Mumbai, India.

Iqbal, Z., & Mirakhor, A. (2011). An Introduction to Islamic Finance. Singapore: John Wiley & Sons (Asia) Pte. Ltd. doi:10.1002/9781118390474

Islamic Financial Services Board. (2013). *Islamic Financial Services Stability Report*. Retrieved on September 29, 2014 from http://www.ifsb.org/docs/IFSB%20-%20IFSI%20Stability%20Report%20 2013%20%28Final%29.pdf

Khatkhatay, M. H. (2009a, August). *Road to Islamic Banking in India*. Paper presented at Seminar on Islamic Banking and Finance, Bhatkal, India.

Khatkhatay, M. H. (2009b, October). *Some Thoughts and Suggestions on Muslim Participation in the Finance Sector*. Paper presented at National Seminar on Economic Advancement of Indian Muslims: Situations, Scope and the Islamic Guidance, India.

Khatkhatay, M. H. (2011, May). *Islamic Real Estate Venture Capital in India*. Paper presented at Seminar on Venture Capital Financing organised by the Institute of Objective Studies (IOS), New Delhi, India.

Lines, B. (2012). *Secura Launches Real Estate Venture Capital Fund*. Kochi, India: Business Line. Retrieved on September 22, 2014 from http://www.thehindubusinessline.com/markets/secura-launches-real-estate-venture-capital-fund/article4139782.ece

Lovells. (2009). *Islamic Finance Regulations in Non-OIC Jurisdictions*. Indian Centre for Islamic Finance.

Microfinance, S. (2012). Multi-state Cooperative Society Act, 2002. New Delhi, India.

Ministry of Finance. (2014). *The Indian Infrastructure Debt Funds*. New Delhi, India: Government of India Publication. Retrieved on September 29, 2014 from http://www.finmin.nic.in/the_ministry/dept_eco_affairs/infrastructure_div/IDF_Brochure0062014.pdf

Ministry of Home Affairs. (2011). *Census of India 2011 Primary Census Abstract Figure at a Glance, India*. New Delhi, India: Ministry of Home Affairs, Government of India. Retrieved on September 29, 2014 from http://www.censusindia.gov.in/2011census/PCA/PCA_Highlights/pca_highlights_file/India/5Figures_at_glance.pdf

National Bank for Agricultural and Rural Development. (2014). *The Banking Regulation Act, 1949*. Mumbai, India: National Bank for Agricultural and Rural Development Publication. Retrieved on September 20, 2014 from https://www.nabard.org/pdf/India_Banking_BankingRegulationAct1949.pdf

Nimrah, K., Tarazi, M., & Reille, X. (2008, August). *Islamic Microfinance: An Emerging Market Niche*. Focus Note: 49. Washington, DC: Consultative Group to Assist the Poor (CGAP). Retrieved on September 29, 2014 from http://www.cgap.org/sites/default/files/CGAP-Focus-Note-Islamic-Microfinance-An-Emerging-Market-Niche-Aug-2008.pdf

Obaidullah, M. (2008). *Introduction to Islamic Microfinance*. Jeddah, Saudi Arabia: Islamic Research & Training Institute (IRTI), Islamic Development Bank (IDB).

Reserve Bank of India. (2011). *Guide Lines to NBFC-MFI* (Notification DNBS. PD. No. 234 dated December 02, 2011 enclosed with RBI Letter reference: RBI/2011-12/290 dated December 02, 2011). Mumbai, India: RBI Publication. Retrieved on September 22, 2014 from http://www.rbi.org.in/scripts/NotificationUser.aspx?Id=6857&Mode=0

Reserve Bank of India. (2014). *RBI Act, 1934*. Retrieved on September 22, 2014 from http://rbidocs.rbi.org.in/rdocs/Publications/PDFs/RBIA1934170510.pdf

Sa-Dhan Microfinance Resource Centre. (2006). *Existing Legal and Regulatory Frame work for the Microfinance Institutions in India: Challenges and Implications*. New Deli, India: Sa-Dhan. Retrieved on September 29, 2014 from http://www.sa-dhan.net/Adls/Microfinance/Article/Publications/ExistingLegalRegulatoryFramework.pdf

Securities Exchange Board of India. (2014a). *Securities Exchange Board of India-Venture Capital Fund Regulations, 1996*. Mumbai, India: SEBI Publication. Retrieved on September 22, 2014 from http://www.sebi.gov.in/cms/sebi_data/commondocs/vcregu_p.pdf

Securities Exchange Board of India. (2014b). *Securities Exchange Board of India-Foreign Venture Capital Investor Regulations, 2000*. Mumbai, India: SEBI Publication. Retrieved on September 22, 2014 from http://www.sebi.gov.in/acts/fvcregu.pdf

Shison, D. (1984). Venture Capital in the United Kingdom. Bank of England.

KEYWORDS AND DEFINITIONS

Accounting and Auditing Organization for Islamic Financial Institutions: A regulatory institution established in the year 1991 with an objective of regulating the Islamic financial institutions. It regulates the IFIs by issuing *Shariah* and Accounting standards. Its head quarter is located at Bahrain.

Banking: Banking means accepting deposits from the public for the purpose of lending and investment.

Financial Inclusion: A terminology used in India and around the globe to indicate the policy of providing financial services to the 'unbanked' population.

Indian Financial Regulations: Various regulations that are governing Indian financial system such as 'Banking Regulation Act, 1949', 'Multistate Cooperative Societies Act 2002', 'Reserve Bank of India Act, 1934', 'Securities and Exchange Board of India (Venture Capital Funds) Regulations, 1996', 'Securities and Exchange Board of India (Foreign Venture Capital Investor) Regulations, 2000', etc.

Infrastructure finance: A financing business under which the big infrastructure projects are financed.

Islamic Banking: A banking business regulated under *Shariah* norms. One of the widely known principles of Islamic banking is prohibition of 'Interest' (Riba) in financial transactions.

Islamic Microfinance: A Microfinance business regulated under the *Shariah* norms. It is an important area within the Islamic finance industry.

Islamic Venture Capital Financing: A type of partnership financing in which monies from investors are pooled together and invested in various profitable avenues. It is a key sector within the Islamic finance industry which is usually preferred to finance the big infrastructure projects.

Microfinance: Providing loans and other services to the small business men without any security or collateral.

Shariah: Islamic law and code of conduct derived from the divine principles mentioned in primary sources of Islam i.e. *Quran* and *Sunnah*.

Sukuk: A financial instrument that reflects the ownership right of the investor in an underlying asset. It is also known as Islamic bond.

Venture Capital Fund: A fund in which monies from investors are pooled together and invested in various profitable avenues.

Chapter 13
Recent Status of Capital Market Regulations in Bangladesh:
Capital Market Regulations in Bangladesh

Md Azizul Baten
Shahjalal University of Science and Technology, Sylhet-3114, Bangladesh & Universiti Utara Malaysia, Kedah, Malaysia

ABSTRACT

The capital market of Bangladesh perceived a self-important growth which is not in line with developed economy. The Securities and Exchange Commission (SEC) tried to correct the irregular behaviour observed in the market, lack of proper decisions from the regulator's side which has contributed to the creation of market instability. This study tried to identify the factors on market crash and regulatory failure. Government had reform SEC to soothe the market but unsuccessful as investors' confidence is in the bottom level. The reasons behind the stock market crash are found irrational market behavior, inconsistency in regulations, excess liquidity in the market, stock split by companies, faulty listing system, issuance of right shares and preference shares by companies at high price, stock manipulations by insider trading, serial trading and excessive greed of investors. Government and regulators should work together to detect the main speculators and should bring investors back to the market.

INTRODUCTION

Stock market is one of the most important financial institutions and it releases door for companies to nurture huge amount of capital from individual investors in and out of a country. Sound capital market is an indispensible part of an economy and without the efficient capital market; economic development could be hampered as capital market delivers long term funds to entrepreneurs. The capital market of Bangladesh is the third largest in South Asia and one of the smallest in Asia. There are two full-fledged automated stock exchanges namely Dhaka Stock Exchange (DSE) and Chittagong Stock Exchange (CSE). Bangladesh Securities and Exchange Commission (BSEC) was established in 1993 to regulate

DOI: 10.4018/978-1-5225-0004-9.ch013

the businesses of the exchanges, confirm proper issuance of securities and agreement with laws and protect the interests of securities investors.

The global economic crisis in 2008 and 2009 was known as a volatile year but during this year Bangladesh economy benefited from low prices of imported goods and was able to avoid negative pressure on its export of goods and services (CPD, 2011). Regulators had taken some measures to stabilize the market with the introduction of central depository, circuit breaker, online trading, etc. to attract investors. As a result, the market started to grow and investors started to invest again. Unfortunately, investors had lost their money when the bubble started to burst in December 2010. The Benchmark index came down to 3616 points in early February 2012 from its highest point of 8918. After the crush of the capital market in 2011, a continuous fall in turnover is observed. In FY 2011-12, the turnover in DSE dropped to Tk. 117145.07 crore from Tk. 325879.77 crore of the previous FY in 2010-11, which was a decrease rate of 65.05 percent. The regulators had failed to take proactive measures to avoid the market from crashing and caused losses for millions of investors.

The volatility of the capital market of Bangladesh is an abnormal phenomenon and such volatility tends to create economic instability. In the state of market growth, role of regulators has been questioned in two accounts. Firstly, whether regulators act promptly to address the volatility of the capital market and secondly, whether frequent changes in regulators' decisions contribute negative impact on the sustainable development of the market. Again, as volatility raises many questions on the regulatory capability of the Securities Exchange Commission (SEC), it is unknown whether the stock market fluctuation is due to regulatory failure or due to irrational behaviors of investors. It is necessary to determine the main reasons of the stock market crash in Bangladesh and the roles of the regulators. Eventually, some guidelines will be recommended for better regulations to strengthen the capital market of Bangladesh.

Background

The history of Bangladesh Capital Market started on the 28th of April, 1954 when Bangladesh was known as East Pakistan and the market was known as East Pakistan Stock Exchange. In April 28, 1954 where Bangladesh was still known as East Pakistan as East Pakistan Stock Exchange Association Ltd, the journey of stock market started while Bangladesh used to be ruled by Pakistan. But trading on this market started in 1956 with a total paid up capital of Taka 4 billion and 196 securities were listed on this market. The exchange was renamed on in June 23, 1962 as DSE Limited. Trading on DSE was suspended from 1971 to 1976 because of liberation war and its post-independence weak economy. Then the trading was resumed in 1976 with 9 listed securities having a total paid up capital of Taka 137.52 million (Hassan et al., 2000). By 1987, the number of listed companies in DSE increased up to 92 and the development of the market is noticeable in the 1990s since its establishment (Economy watch, 2010).

Dhaka Stock Exchange (DSE)

Dhaka Stock Exchange is the first stock exchange regulated by its Articles of Association rules & regulations along with the Securities and Exchange Ordinance 1969, Companies Act 1994 & Securities & Exchange Commission Act 1993. DSE was used to trade in the open outcry system, installed on 10th of August, 1998. The latest upgrading was done on 21st of December, 2008. There are 238 members and total of 507 listed securities in DSE. The working days of DSE are 5 days in a week excluding Saturday, Sunday, public holidays & other government holidays. The trading time is from 11:00 am to 15:00 pm (local time). Investment options for an investor are ordinary share, Debenture and Bond & Mutual funds. There are three different indices of DSE which are DSI (All share), DGEN (A, B, G & N) and DSE 20 (www.dsebd.org).

Functions of DSE:

A. Listing of Companies (As per Listing Regulations).
B. Providing the screen based automated trading of listed Securities.
C. Settlement of trading (As per Settlement of Transaction Regulations).
D. Gifting of share / granting approval to the transaction/transfer of share outside the trading system of the exchange (As per Listing Regulations 42).
E. Market Administration & Control.
F. Market Surveillance.
G. Publication of Monthly Review.
H. Monitoring the activities of listed companies (As per Listing Regulations).
I. Investor's grievance Cell (Disposal of complaint by laws 1997).
J. Investors Protection Fund (As per investor protection fund Regulations 1999).
K. Announcement of Price sensitive or other information about listed companies through online. (Source: www.dsebd.org)

Chittagong Stock Exchange (CSE)

Chittagong Stock Exchange is the 2nd stock exchange introducing modern technology & sophisticated logistic support. It was incorporated as a self-regulated non-profit organization on 1995 and started its automated trading on 2nd June, 1998 and internet trading service on 30th May, 2004. CSE has 147 members and 238 of listed securities. There are four different markets in CSE which are public, Spot, Block & Odd and Lot market. Five categories of company namely A, B, N, G and Z listed in CSE of which none company is in G category. The trading time of CSE is between 11:00 am to 15:00 pm. The working days & holidays of CSE are similar with DSE. CSE consists of 25 members of whom 12 are elected through election of its members, 12 members are elected from different major economic & social arena of Bangladesh. CSE has 3 indices in the stock exchange namely All Share Price Index (CASPI), CSE Selective Index (CSE30) and CSE Selective Categories' Index (CSCX) (www.cse.com.bd).

Security and Exchange Commissions (SEC)

The Government of Bangladesh is founded SEC on 8th of June, 1993 under the Securities and Exchange Commission Act, 1993. The commission is consists of a chairman and four members. The Chairman & members of security exchange commission are appointed by the government of Bangladesh. According to Securities and Exchange Ordinance, 1969 SEC has been empowered to control the self-regulatory institutions for instance Stock Exchanges.

Responsibilities of SEC:

A. Conducting transparent trading, stop fraudulent practices like market manipulation, insider trading, short selling.
B. Ensuring submission of transparent accounts as per rule, statements, reports and returns.

C. Carrying out inquiry to alleged irregularities and taking legal action for all kinds of violation of securities law and regulations.
D. Ensuring submission of annual financial statement in time containing balance sheet, profit and loss account, cash flow statement and notes to the accounts.
E. Examining audited financial statements, ensure that audit conducted in accordance with prescribed rules and take necessary action for deficiencies.

Functions of SEC:

A. Registering and regulating the business operation of DSE, CSE, stock brokers, merchant banks, underwriters, share transfer agents, portfolio managers and other intermediaries.
B. Developing investor`s education, providing training for intermediaries, executing market research and publishing.
C. Controlling every authorized self-regulatory organization.
D. Inspecting and controlling fraudulent and unfair trading in security markets.
E. Auditing and investigating of any intermediaries or stock exchanges.
F. Collective investment scheme registering & controlling.
(www.secbd.org)

Central Depository Bangladesh Limited (CDBL)

CDBL was incorporated as a public limited company on 20th August, 2000. The owners of CDBL are DSE, CSE, banks, Investment Corporation of Bangladesh and some other financial institutions.

Functions of CDBL:

A. Operate and maintain the Central Depository System (CDS) of Electronic Book.
B. Recording and maintaining securities accounts and registering transfer of securities.
C. Changing the ownership without any physical movement or endorsement of certificates.
D. Supervision of Depository participant activities.
E. Providing different investor services including providing a platform for the secondary market trading of Treasury Bills and Government Bonds issued by the Bangladesh Bank (www.cdbl.com).

MAIN FOCUS OF THE CHAPTER

Regulatory Renovations and Market Developments

From return perspective, the year 2012 seemed to be an unfortunate; it included some regulatory changes and progresses as follows:

A. Implementing Mandatory shareholding requirement from BSEC by corporate directors.
B. Development of draft guidelines on Research and Investment Advisor services.
C. Amending Margin Loan Rules.
D. Progress in Omnibus account closeout.

E. Developing BSEC Roadmap for capital market.
F. Initiation of demutualization process for the Exchange.
G. Implementing New MSA-Plus Software for Trading.
H. Amendment in the Mutual Fund Rules.
I. Inaugurating Surveillance system by BSEC.
J. Progress in introducing new Indices for DSE.

The impact of these changes in market development was not found significant for most of these events.

(Capital Market Review 2012, IDLC Investments Ltd., January 2013.)

Regulatory Problems

SEC could not identify and investigate many irregularities that happened in the process of the stock market bubble. To restructure SEC with skilled human capital is one of the major constraints. Both SEC and the stock exchanges failed to monitor the issue of IPO and rights shares. Overpricing through overstating EPS (earning per share) and NAV (net asset value) was found to be the problem. The SEC did not allow merchant banks to make forced-selling when share prices started to fall.

(Source: Bangladesh Economic Update, Volume 4, No. 3, 1-27, March 2013).

Comparison of Stock Market volatility of DSE with Other Markets

Price fall in DSE was sudden and persistent which caused a significant loss of paper wealth and was abnormal in nature as compared to other stock markets.

From Table 1, it was observed that during December 2011 to January 2012, Bombay Stock Exchange index (BSE-30) was fallen by 14% while SET index of Thailand increased by 55.62% and Dhaka Stock Exchange general Index (DGEN) was fallen by more than 50% during this period, i.e., DGEN lose its value by 50% during the period which indicated that this was not a simple volatility and it can be defined as a collapse. On the other hand, Standard deviations of index return for BSE-30 and SET index were recorded to be 7.8% and 5.84% respectively. But for DSE, the standard deviation of index return was 11% which was much higher than the other two indices.

Table 1. Comparison of DSE Volatility with Other Markets

Name of the Index	Index Return (Dec'10-Jan'12)	Std. Dev. of Index Return (Dec'10-Jan'12)
DSE	50%	11%
BSE-30	14%	7.8%
SET	55.62%	5.84%

SOLUTIONS

Rules and Stock Market Crash of Bangladesh in 2010-11

During the military-backed regime in 2007, investment in real sectors as well as in Foreign Direct Investment (FDI) decreased but the inflow of foreign remittance was increased. Banks & other financial institutions had a lot of excess liquidity due to less business opportunities in the recession period of 2009-10. These financial institutions & its officials as well as other people took loan and invested in the share market in order to minimize the cost of bearing excess liquidity. It was seen that the daily transaction in the share market was on an average from Taka 20,000 to Taka 30,000 million in 2010 and the figure was doubled comparing to 2009 (Raisa, 2011). Investors tried to find alternative investment sector to invest their savings and found stock market as an attractive alternative (Khaled, 2011).

The total number of BO Account holders on 20th December, 2010 reached to 3.21 million though the number was 1.25 million in December 2009. Internet-based trading operation, opening branches of brokerage houses across the country, easy access to the market information, arranging a countrywide 'share mela (fair)' are the factors for increasing investors. But supplies of new securities through IPOs were not enough to chase huge capital of too many investors in the market (CPD, 2011).

The directives of 6th & 7th December 2010 applied by SEC were cancelled on 8th December 2010. The reason of cancelling these directives was a significant fall of share prices on 8th December. SEC changed directive of margin loan ratio by increasing it from 1:0.5 to 1:1 on 13th December and later it was again hiked to 1:1.5 & 1:2 because of free fall of share prices (Bhuiyan, (2011). As the Institutions & banks started selling their shares from the beginning of December 2010, the turnover of DSE was the highest ever in its history on 5th December 2010. On 19th December 2010, DSE witnessed its biggest one day fall in 55 years history until the date with a loss of 551.76 points or 6.71 percent. The losing index was even higher than 284.78 points or 3.32 percent in 12th December 2010 (Raisa, 2011).

On 11th January 2011, market recovered 15.6 percent of General index by initiating with Institutional buyer for instance merchant banks, state owned banks & non-financial institutions and made a record in Bangladesh stock market history of gain (Chowdhury, 2011). Moreover, Ahmed (2011) mentioned that institutional buyers were asked not to sell shares rather to buy. Though steps were taken and applied by the government, BB and regulators to improve the market conditions and bring the investors' confidence, nevertheless market index declined heavily on 20th January 2011 DGEN by slipping 599.77 points or 8.68 percent. From 26th of January 2011 there was an increase trend of index. But finally Index stood at the lowest point which is 5579 from 7th to 14th February 2011. (Khalid, 2011)

Bangladesh Bank (BB) adopted accommodative monetary policy during the high inflation periods to support investment and pegged Taka against dollar to support exports. The policy that was adopted by BB to grow economy by increasing exports & investment eventually misguided and ended up blowing the mother of all bubbles. Government again fuelled the bubble after permitting whitening of black money through tax breaks and schemes (Rahman, 2011).

Due to the poor monitoring of SEC & market surveillance share prices of Z Category Companies and small companies increased dramatically. Some initiatives taken by SEC were not effective and changing directives frequently such as; it changed directives of margin loan ratio 19 times (Raisa, 2011).

Recent Trends in Capital Market and Regulators

The current most important problems of the capital market are lack of confidence of investors and lack of liquidity of the capital market. After the crush of the capital market in 2011, a continuous fall in turnover has been observed, revealing the crisis of liquidity in the capital market. In FY 2011-12, the turnover sunk to Tk. 117145.07 crore from Tk. 325879.77 crore, meaning a fall of 64 percentages. In FY 2012-13, the volatility capital market followed a declining trend. DSE index movement was found not normal and the fall was so abrupt that it caused huge loss for investors. In FY 2011-12, the market capitalization ratio was 21.12 percent, which sharply declined from 29.55 percent of the previous FY 2010-11. In January 2013 total market capitalization of DSE was Tk. 184545.2 crore, a less of 4.5 percent than that of previous FY 2011-12.

In FY 2012-13, the market capitalization and investment ratio witnessed a downward trend, reaching at 83.01 percent. This indicates the descent in ratio between capitalization and investments, revealing a continuous fall in the capital market. In January 2013, a declined trend of market capitalization was witnessed for the banking sector, reaching at Tk. 49251.80 crore, a sharp drop Tk. 1986.9 crore than in FY 2011-12 in which year the banking sector contributed a total amount of Tk. 51238.60 crore. From FY 2010-11 to January 2013 falling rate of contribution in banking sector in market capitalization was 2 percent which came down from 29 percent in FY 2010-11 to 27 percent in January, 2013 (Bangladesh Economic Update).

Factors Contributed to Capital Market Crash in Bangladesh

The contributed factors to the crash are commonly accused by different market analysts, economists and stakeholders. As Hossain (2011) evaluated "this time liable factors are -omnibus account, placement share, book building method, rumors and so on. Misuse of those factors causes the capital market debacle". Again Haque (n.d.) stated "Combination of wrong information to the investors, illegal participation of banks and institutions in the stock markets, weak accounting functions are at the core of the crisis that saw billions of Tk. wiped out".

The *"Ibrahim Khaled share market probe Committee"* identified the following factors that caused the capital market to crash:

A. Primary issue related problems
   - i. Direct listing in Primary issue.
   - ii. Abuse of Book Building Method of IPO.
   - iii. High premium for stock listing.
   - iv. Illegal Private placement market.
   - v. Asset Revaluation of Companies before listing to charge higher premium.

B. Secondary market related problems
   - i. Circular trading in Secondary market.
   - ii. Block trading.
   - iii. Stock Price Manipulation through Omnibus Accounts.
   - iv. Most of the market players are identified in the report.

C. Irregularities in issuance of Right Share/Preference Share/Repeat IPO etc.

D. Recommendation of Stock Dividend by companies against unrealized Profits.

E. Regulatory Failure
  i. Inconsistency in regulatory activities.
  ii. Supporting and legalization of unethical activities of Big Investors.
  iii. Irresponsible Behavior/Weakness in many areas.
  iv. Formulating policies to support market Players (Manipulators).
  v. Lack of Due Diligence.
  vi. Lack of Co-ordination between SEC and Stock exchanges.
  vii. Allowing Financial Institutions to invest in capital market aggressively.
  viii. SEC Failed to take measure against manipulation of financial statements.

F. Stock Exchange Demutualization
  i. Formulating policy for Capital Market financing by FI's.
  ii. Ensuring transparency in dealing with Omnibus Accounts.
  iii. Prohibit share trading by some Government Officials (e.g., SEC, DSE, CSE, Bangladesh bank, Commercial bank officials).
  iv. Asset Revaluation by companies should be reviewed by SEC.
  v. Review the Book-Building Method of IPO.
  vi. Restructuring of SEC.
  vii. Uniform face-value of all companies.
  viii. Legal actions against market players/manipulators.

RECOMMENDATIONS

The following recommendations for stronger capital market in Bangladesh are in line of this study.

A. Demutualization of Stock Exchanges.
B. Strengthening the Market Surveillance Systems.
C. Ensuring Integrity and Efficiency of SEC Members and Staffs.
D. Co-ordination between SEC and Stock Exchanges.
E. Bank Finance in Capital Market.
F. Introduction of Asset Revaluations Policy.
G. Consistency in Regulation.
H. Supply of adequate securities.
I. Transparency in listing procedure.
J. Serial Trading and Manipulation.

The *Ibrahim Khaled share market probe* Committee recommended some suggestions to the Government to recover the capital market crash. There are:

A. Restructuring of SEC
  i. Termination of SEC chief and some other corrupt members.
  ii. Comprehensive inspection of their corruption and necessary legal actions.
  iii. Recruiting qualified accountants/financial analysts/experts/Talents for SEC.
  iv. Increase the remuneration of SEC staff to attract talents.

   v. Ensuring integrity of SEC personnel.

B. Stock Exchange Demutualization
   i. Form Committee within DSE to give report regarding demutualization process within 3 months.
   ii. If DSE fails to give report on time, Government should take steps after 3 months.
   iii. Government can take advisory supports from World Bank or any other international organization.
   iv. Government can employ an "Administrator" to DSE to implement the demutualization process.

C. Co-ordination between SEC and stock exchanges for better regulation.

D. Capital Market financing by Financial Institutions (FI's).
   i. Formulate policy for capital market investment by FI's in the line of such policies in India and Pakistan.
   ii. Take measures against FI's who are involved with the recent stock market manipulation.
   iii. Central Bank should monitor FI's aggressive stock investment very strictly.

E. Formulate clear policy for Pre-IPO placement.

F. Ensure transparency in dealing with Omnibus Accounts.

G. Prohibit share trading by some Government Officials (e.g., SEC, DSE, CSE, Bangladesh bank, Commercial bank officials).

H. Asset Revaluation by companies should be reviewed by SEC.

I. Review the Book-Building Method of IPO.

J. Make uniform face-value of all companies.

K. Take legal actions against market players/manipulators.

L. Government should be more aware about the capital market and they should be free from influence of top market players (Salman F. Rahman, Rakibur Rahman etc.).

M. SEC should Open Investors advisory support services to avoid rumor-based trading.

FUTURE RESEARCH DIRECTIONS

The results of this study is of a great interest to academics, policy makers and local and foreign listed and unlisted companies and have an important practical implications to different capital market participants such as investors, managers and regulatory authorities. This study identified the factors on capital market crash and regulatory failure would be of a great benefit to investors at home and abroad. Researchers can further study in finding new tools, strategies, directives, rules and regulations for market development and to prevent the stock market from crash in future. Finally, it may also be useful for international organizations (such as the World Bank, IMF, WTO) and governments of development partners who are interested in the development of capital markets in the emerging countries.

CONCLUSION

The study endeavored to find out the major reasons for the stock market to crash of in Bangladesh and the role of different regulatory organizations including DSE, CSE, and SEC of the country. It reviewed the background of the capital market crash with reasons. The continuous fall in the capital market exhibited lack of confidence by the investors. In January 2013, the continuous fall in the contribution of banking sector was observable. The capital market could not revive after the crush and in certain circumstances the fall continued, despite the announcement of certain measures such as tax rebate, exemption of credit for marginal level investors. SEC did not come forward to stop while thousands of totally inexperienced investors open by the brokers from remote areas to the overpriced market. Most of promises by the government like Bangladesh fund, market stabilization fund, bank investments remained unfulfilled eroding investor confidence seriously and it was wondering why SEC did not come forward to take necessary action to stop these irresponsible comments and acts. Due to poor regulatory framework, capital market of Bangladesh was found to be highly speculative and lacks of market's transparency and the recommendations of Ibrahim Khaled committee have not been implemented. It was observed that developing faulty accounting practices and methods, recruiting honest officials, providing education on the stock market to the general investors and taking strict actions against manipulators are crucial.

In addition, it was observed that the stock market boom and fall was due to following reasons:

1. Direct Listing and Book Building in IPO, high indicative price for IPO, Misuse of Book Building method of IPO, and pre-IPO Private placement activity.
2. Circular trading, Block Trading and unusual trading of securities where few numbers of investors/ institutions are involved.
3. Issuance of Right Share, Preference share, Repeat IPO at excessive price.
4. Excessive Greed of Investors and Institutions.

SEC responsibility need to ensure in a market that where various kinds of manipulation, insider trading, circular trading, pump and dump practices may prevail and create market distortion. Again, they need to concentrate on transparent listing procedure, proper IPO pricing, adequate financial disclosure, market surveillance and monitoring and promote investor confidence. The regulators and government is required to introduce new tools, strategies, directives, rules and regulations for market development and to prevent the stock market crash in future. SEC should stop excess bank investment violating provision of law.

Actions should be taken against those who were involved in this stock market crash

1. Improving security laws and penalty for breaking those.
2. Balancing of demand and supply of shares.
3. Follow-up the market and protect against any kind of manipulation.

REFERENCES

Amadeo, K. (2012). *Stock Market Crash.* Retrieved from http://useconomy.about.com/od/glossary/g/Market_Crash.html

Bangladesh Bank. (n.d.). Retrieved from http://www.bangladesh-bank.org

Center for Policy Dialogue (CPD). (2011). *Independent Review of Bangladesh's Development (IRBD).* Retrieved from http://www.cpd.org.bd/downloads/IRBD%20FY11_First%20Reading.pdf

Central Depository Bangladesh Limited. (n.d.). Retrieved from http:// www.cdbl.com

Chittagong Stock Exchanges. (n.d.). Retrieved from http://www.cse.com.bd

Dhaka Stock Exchange. (n.d.). Retrieved from http://www.dsebd.org

Economy Watch. (2010). *A Brief Introduction to the Dhaka Stock Exchange.* Retrieved from http://www.economywatch.com/stockexchanges/dhaka.html

Fellowes, R. (2008). *The Complete Guide to Investing in the Stock Market.* Easy Way Guides.

Galbraith, J. K. (1979/1988). *The Great Crash 1929.* Boston: Houghton Mifflin.

Hassan, M. K., Islam, A. M., & Basher, S. A. (2000). *Market Efficiency, Time-Varying Volatility and Equity Returns in Bangladesh Stock Market.* Ibrahim Khalid Committee Sharer Probe Report. Retrieved from http://www.mof.gov.bd/en/index.php?option=com_content&view=article&id=169&Itemid=1

Khaled, K. I. (2011). *Investigation report of Probe Committee.* Academic Press.

Rahman, J. (2011). *Share Market Bubble -the Big Picture.* Retrieved from http://dpwriters.wordpress.com/2011/02/04/share-market-bubble-the-big-picture

Raisa, A. (2011). *Behind the Scenes The Stock Market Saga.* Retrieved from http://www.thedailystar.net/magazine/2011/01/03/cover.htm

Security and Exchange Commission. (n.d.). Retrieved from http://www.secbd.org

Smith, V., Suchanek, G., & Williams, A. (1988). Bubbles, Crashes and Endogenous Expectations in Experimental Spot Assest Markets. *Econometrica, 56*(5), 1119–1151. doi:10.2307/1911361

Sullivan, R., Timmermann, A., & White, H. (2003). Forecast Evaluation with Shared Data Sets. *International Journal of Forecasting, 19*(2), 217–227. doi:10.1016/S0169-2070(01)00140-6

Update, B. E. (2013). Economic Policy Unit. *Unnayan Onneshan, 4*(3), 1–27.

KEY TERMS AND DEFINITIONS

Capital Market: A capital market is a market for both debt and equity securities, where business enterprises and governments can raise long-term funds. It is defined as a market in which money is provided for periods longer than a year (Sullivan et. al., 2003). Bangladesh capital market has two full-fledged automated stock exchanges namely Dhaka Stock Exchange (DSE) and Chittagong Stock Exchange (CSE). It consists of a regulator, the Securities and Exchange Commission (SEC), since, it implements rules and regulations, monitors their implications to operate and develop the capital market. It consists of Central Depository Bangladesh Limited (CDBL), the only Central Depository in Bangladesh that provides facilities for the settlement of transactions of dematerialized securities in CSE and DSE.

Demutualization: Demutualization of a stock exchange is the process of transforming a non-profit member-owned mutual organization into a profit seeking Shareholder Corporation. Exchanges all over the world have been demutualizing due to increasing international competition and technological challenges to traditional modes of securities trading.

Generally speaking: crashes usually occur under the following conditions, a prolonged period of rising stock prices and excessive economic optimism, a market where P/E ratios exceed long-term averages, and extensive use of margin debt and leverage by market participants (Galbraith, 1979/1988).

Omnibus Account: Omnibus account is a type of account between two futures merchants (brokers). Transaction of individual accounts is combined in this type of account that allows easier management of portfolio by the futures merchant. But this type of account could be used to manipulate stock as many individual transactions are kept hidden over there.

Present Coverage: Chittagong, Dhaka, Sylhet, Rajshahi, Khulna, Barisal, Tangail and Coxsbazar.

Share Category: "A": Category Companies: Companies which are regular in holding the Annual General Meetings (AGM) and declared dividend at the rate of 10 percent or more in a calendar year. "B" Category Companies: Companies which are regular in holding the AGM but failed to declare dividend at least at the rate of 10 percent in a calendar year. "G' Category Companies: Greenfield companies. "N' Category Companies: All newly listed companies except Greenfield companies are placed in this category. "Z' Category Companies: Companies which failed to hold the AGM or failed to declare any dividend or which are not in operation continuously for more than six months or whose accumulated loss after adjustment of revenue reserve, if any is negative and exceeded its paid up capital.

Stock Market Bubble: A stock market bubble is one kind of economic bubble that takes place in stock markets when market participants drive stock prices above their value in relation to some system of stock valuation (Smith et.al. 1988).

Stock Market Crash: "Stock market crash is a sharp and unexpected decline of stock market prices for a very short period of time, usually accompanied with the decline of many other assets' prices" mentioned by stockmarketcrashes.net. Amadeo (2012) defined stock market crash as more than 10% loss within few days in a stock market. But stock market crash has differentiated from stock market correction where the loss is 10% or less.

Stock Market: Fellowes (2008) described that stock market has same features like a normal market with buyers, sellers and agreed price. There will bc a middleman who guides investor to deal offers of buying and selling shares in the stock market. Stock exchange, regulatory organizations, investors, listed companies with securities, broker houses, merchant banks, and other intermediary organizations are found in a stock market with co-operation of central bank and government of the country.

Trading System: Fully automated screen-based. Nation-wide online trading network.

Chapter 14
Economic and Financial Integration in South Asia

Piyadasa Edirisuriya
Monash University, Australia

Abeyratna Gunasekarage
Monash University, Australia

ABSTRACT

Many countries in the South Asia region are global players in many aspects due to the nature of emerging markets as well as being democratic countries irrespective of the fact that many people in the region are troubled by higher level of poverty. Many years of regulation in the South Asian region has hampered economic growth and reduced the level of efficiencies in almost all economic activities. However, implementation of market deregulations since the early 1980s in many sectors has benefited the majority of countries in the region in a number of ways. Among others, one of the most significant benefits is the integration of markets in the financial as well as other economic sectors generating better economic achievements. In this study, we examine the process of economic and financial market integration as well as cost/benefit of such a process. We find significant benefits of economic and financial market integration to the region.

1. INTRODUCTION

Examples from the European Union have brought to the attention of many academics, politicians and policy makers that integration of economic activities among countries may in fact, deliver economic benefits. There are many types of economic integration activities such as free trade agreements to closer economic relationships among many nations. Many economic and trade alliances such as Association for South East Asian Nations (ASEAN), Asia-Pacific Economic Cooperation (APEC), Common Market for Eastern and Southern Africa (COMESA), Gulf Cooperation Council (GCC) and Southern Common Market (MERCOSUR) are examples for alliances established mainly for economic benefit of nations. Globalisation has encouraged many countries to participate in efficient economic activities throughout the world. Widely accepted such benefits of successful examples of globalisation have created continued

DOI: 10.4018/978-1-5225-0004-9.ch014

support for economic integration among regions and countries around the world. In most cases, the process of integration basically comes from political agreements which are multilateral, regional or bilateral in nature. These agreements allow countries to do economic and business activities in a freer market environment. As mentioned above, the European Union is one such successful example that goes even beyond economic integration to a more powerful political block. ASEAN is another successful example. Going in a similar path, counties in South Asia have formed an alliance called South Asian Association for Regional Corporation (SAARC) in 1985 with the objective of improving economic corporation and economic growth in the region. Going further in the path of economic integration, in 2002, leaders of SAAARC have agreed to accelerate cooperation in the core areas of trade, finance and investment to realise the goal of an integrated South Asian economy in a step-by-step manner. They have also agreed to the vision of a phased and planned process eventually leading to a South Asian Economic Union (SAEU). Furthermore, they also have formed the SAARCFINANCE group which has been entrusted the responsibility of studying and making recommendations on the early and eventual realisation of SAEU, a development bank for the region, single payment system and ultimately a single currency. Though it may take a very long period to achieve all of these objectives, we can be satisfied that at least we are heading in the right direction.

All countries in the South Asian region have already begun reforming their financial markets to lay down a better foundation for achieving higher economic growth. Speeding up financial sector reforms is one major requirement to establish a deep financial sector. When countries in a region have deep financial markets, financial integration should take place naturally subject to government interferences. With financial market integration, investment and growth will improve through identifying opportunities for successful business activities by economic agents. Financial market integration generally could synchronise economic activities of countries in a region due to the impact of consolidation. Furthermore, financial integration will mobilise and pool savings in a more efficient way. When financial markets are integrated, corporate governance could improve further. All of these activities will result in a more efficient allocation of resources supporting the fundamental economic theory.

According to some studies, financial market integration could be defined as to have two main features such as free movement of capital and integration of financial services and markets (Perera and Wickramanayake, 2012, Chai and Rhee, 2005). Based on these, financial markets are said to be integrated when the law of one price holds, such as when securities with identical cash flows command the same price (Kleimeier and Sander, 2000). This is the theoretical explanation. Continues financial market sector reforms in the South Asian region will not only lead to financial integration but also to lower the cost of financial intermediation within the region and outside the region. Lower financial intermediary cost through increased competition is a gain for households as well as firms. Going beyond from financial market reforms, continuous expansion of regional trade agreements among the member countries in the region has helped to achieve further economic integration. As the South Asia has begun to march towards a more financially integrated market, next step would be to think about more integration in economic as well as monetary point of view. Regional financial integration in South Asia can also make regional financial systems to face global competition in a more effective way while not only minimising the risks of financial instability but also attracting domestic and foreign investors to the region. All of these points motivate us to examine in details the issue of economic and financial market integration in South Asia. Therefore, the objective of this study is to examine in depth the economic and finance integration in the South Asian region and measure the level market integration. It is also expected to examine the existing obstacle to market integration process and explore future expectations as well. This comprehensive analysis is followed by some policy recommendations which may be useful to SAARCFINANCE group in its efforts to form the SAEU.

2. SOUTH ASIA

It is generally regarded that Indian sob-continent as the South Asia region. However, different international organisations such as the World Bank, the International Monetary Fund and the Asian Development Bank have their own geographic boundaries. For example, Asian Development Bank identifies South Asia as Bangladesh, Bhutan, India, Maldives, Nepal and Sri Lanka. They do not take Pakistan or Afghanistan as South Asian countries. On the other hand, the World Bank identifies South Asia as Afghanistan, Bangladesh, Bhutan, India, Maldives, Nepal, Pakistan and Sri Lanka. For our purpose we use the World Bank geographic boundary. This is relevant as the South Asian Association for Regional Corporation (SAARC) Organisation also has all of the 8 countries as member states. The history of the SAAARC goes almost 30 years back. South Asian Counties have formed this alliance called South Asian Association for Regional Corporation (SAARC) in 1985 and have been attempting to improve economic corporation and economic growth in the region. As a leaders group, the organisation's leaders have met 17 times in the past. The last meeting was held in 2011. As noted before, the objective of the organisation is to have an integrated economic and finance market for the benefit of all countries. Going in these direction, the newly elected Prime Minister of India, proposed to setting up of a South Asian Development Bank for financing infrastructure development in the region at a meeting of trade ministers from SAARC countries in Bhutan in July, 2014. In addition, the SAARC Organisation in 2010 embarked on a programme to study further financial market and economic integration among member countries in a systematic way. Among many other things, the organisation is looking at taking actions to identify possible risks and impediments to strengthening regional economic integration, explore the scope of currency convertibility in the SAARC region and identify the scope of financial market integration among member nations. Appendix 1 shows some important macro-economic data for the region.

3. FINANCIAL MARKET LIBERALISATION IN THE SOUTH ASIAN REGION

Decades of under heavy government control, the liberalisation of finance and banking sector in the South Asian region has helped almost all countries in the region to achieve higher economic growth. For example, the World Bank reports that during the 10-year period to end-2010, South Asian economies, despite such characteristics as low per capita income and high population density, have received more than US$500 billion of foreign direct investment, while attracting a further US$300 billion in net equity inflows (ESCAP, 2010). During this period, these countries maintained steady economic growth (reporting average annual increases of 6.9% in real GDP), which has co-existed with programmes of deregulation and liberalisation. It may be worthwhile to have brief look at the deregulation measures taken in the each country of South Asia.

As Afghanistan has not implemented significant market deregulation reforms so far, we omit the country from number of analysis. There are significant data limitations too.

3.1. Bhutan

Apart from Afghanistan, Bhutan's financial sector could be regarded as the least deregulated sector among other South Asian countries. Although the process of deregulation under the structural adjustment programs of the International Monetary Fund (IMF) were began in early 1990s, the progress has been very slow. There are four major banks in Bhutan. They are the Bank of Bhutan (BoB), the Bhutan National Bank (BNB), the Royal Insurance Corporation of Bhutan (RICB) and the Bhutan Development Finance Corporation (BDFC). One of the strongest evidences regarding the policy changes in the financial market sector of Bhutan is the deregulation of interest rates in the country. Taking the competition to a higher level in June 2002 some government pension funds and corporations (stock corporations with the help of the National Pension and Provident Fund or NPPF) announced a special housing loan at a rate of 10% for its members. This rate was 3% below the commercial bank rates which was 13% at that time. As a result of this action the BNB announced a major reduction of its interest rates bring down their rates to the 10% level.

Lack of investment opportunities including infrastructure is hindering the country of getting benefits from financial market integration. Substantial amount of assets are just held with Royal Monetary Authority (RMA) due to lack of opportunities in the country. However, its private sector domestic borrowing appears to be increasing in recent times indicating that benefits of deregulation are on the way (IMF Country Report – Bhutan). Moving further in the direction of deregulation, the Bhutan National Bank (BNB) has introduced country's first international gold Visa card in September 2004. Two new banking licenses (Druk PNB and T bank) were issued in 2009. As the banking sector of the country is very small compared to other countries in the region, the interest on it among investors appears to be non-significant. For example, Bhutan has not a single bank representing largest 500 banks in Asia.

3.2. Nepal

Similar to Bhutan, Nepal is surrounded by mountains and is a landlocked country. The financial sector deregulation program in Nepal has begun about 15 years ago similar to the programmes of other countries in the Region. However, the progress has been very slow and as a result financial market has not been developed as anticipated. Nepal has 32 commercial banks, 90 development banks, 79 finance companies, 25 micro credit development banks and 16 savings and credit co-operatives. Since 2007 there were 12 new commercial banks were opened. Nepalese banking system has developed from two states banks namely the Nepal Bank Limited (NBL) and the Rastriya Banijya Bank (RBB). Two sates owned banks are leading the commercial banking sector of Nepal representing 83 percent of commercial bank branches (IMF Country Report No. 01/173). Nepal has been more slowly opened for competition than other partners within the SAARC region. However, since 1984 the government has allowed foreign banks to open offices in Nepal. Even with the given limited freedom for foreign banks (opened branches as partners of local companies), this can be taken as a significant development in the Nepalese financial system. In the year 2001, the government allowed foreign banks to own up two-third of joint ventures allowing for more competition. The IMF and the World Bank sponsored restructuring programs are still continuing in Nepal. It may be argued that the recovery of two largest commercial banks in Nepal (NBL and RBB) in 2004 from continued losses may have been a result of ongoing deregulation programmes and financial market integration in the country.

3.3. Sri Lanka

The Financial market in Sri Lanka is well developed compared to other financial markets in South Asia. Sri Lanka was the first country to implement financial sector reforms in the South Asia region. It was the new government which came into power in 1977 and began to dismantle the regulatory structure prevailed for decades. A number of policy changes were introduced since then and the process is continuing. Among the significant measures taken to deregulate the financial sector include interest rate deregulation, introduction of market based credit policies, relaxation of market entry for foreign and local banking firms and improved supervisory measures including taking appropriate legislative measures to safeguard the financial system. This financial market deregulation policy package could be regarded as the most comprehensive package among all South Asian countries. The establishment of the Colombo Stock Exchange (CSE) in 1984 could be regarded as another outcome of financial sector reforms in Sri Lanka. The CSE has opened its public trading floor for the ordinary public and modern share trading has now become a normal day to day activity of many ordinary people in the country.

As a result of expanding financial market activities due to reforms, there are money markets, capital market, electronic market activities and micro-financial market activities are spreading throughout the country. With financial reforms, the banking sector of Sri Lanka has made substantial gains within the Asian Region. As a result of relaxed market entry conditions to allow for more competition, there are number of new domestic and foreign banks operating in Sri Lanka competing against the dominant state owned banks. However, government owned Bank of Ceylon and the People's Bank still have the largest share of the traditional banking in Sri Lanka. Sri Lankan banking sector has more than 55% of total assets of the financial sector showing a significant improvement after financial reforms. In addition branch networks are growing with added electronic facilities regularly. Banks such as the Commercial Bank of Ceylon now has a branch in Bangladesh to suggest market integration within the South Asian region.

3.4. India

The Indian financial system was under regulations since almost its inception. Among other regulations, the main regulatory features were the interest rate regulation, credit restrictions, equity market controls and foreign exchange controls. Though some restrictions are still in operation, regulations, which are affecting banks, are being relaxed after implementing the Narasinham Committee report (1991). Second phase of deregulation was implemented after the review report by the same Narasinham Committee. There are other important reports, which were contributed to the present deregulated financial markets. Among them, Report of the Committee to Review the Working of the Monetary System (1985) and the Vaghul Report (1987) that examined the Indian money market activities are significant reports.

It is important to note that none of the deregulatory measures implemented were entirely strong enough to diminish the important role played by the largely inefficient public sector banks. While there are some improvements within the sector, the overall inefficiency remained the same (Verma Report 1999). One of the stumbling blocks towards full deregulation may be the public sector banks which are not open for full scale competition. One significant reason for Indian public sector banks to survive even while making losses is the stringent regulations imposed on general economic activities of the country.

India has more than 10000 bank branches, of which 60 percent are in rural areas. Among these banks there are more than 75000 branches of public sector banks and more than 16000 of private sector banks.

This may be due to the geographic factors but not necessarily a reason to have such a large number of branches. In relation to the number of commercial banks in India, the regional rural banks (more than 17000 offices) contribute 66 percent of the total number of commercial banks. There are 334 foreign bank offices in India. The public sector banks account for 80 percent of the total assets of the banking and financial institutions sector, while the private sector banks and foreign banks each account for 12 percent of the assets.

3.5. Bangladesh

When Bangladesh became independent from Pakistan, the banking system had State Bank of Pakistan and seventeen large commercial banks. There were fourteen smaller commercial banks. Almost all banking services were concentrated in urban areas. The State Bank of Pakistan later became the Central Bank (Bangladesh Bank). The management of banks was not up to the standard and banking system had been facing severe problems continuously. This led major donors to apply pressure to induce the government and banks to take firmer action to strengthen internal bank management and credit discipline. As a result of this, in 1987 the National Commission on Money, Credit, and Banking recommended broad structural changes in Bangladesh's system of financial intermediation.

In recent time, a number of actions were taken by the Bangladesh Bank (BB) to improve banking institutions. Among them, improving transparency is one of the major actions taken to establish the soundness of the banks in Bangladesh. Apart from this, there were number of measures such as de-regulating interest rates, strengthening loan classification standards and reducing the BB's control over financial transactions and loan recovery measures, have been taken to improve the competitiveness and efficiency of banks. However, the level of non-performing loans (28% of total bank loans) suggests that still there is a long way to go to improve the competitiveness of the banking system in Bangladesh. The dominance of the government owned banks (nationalized commercial banks) in the system appears to be declining making significant developments by private banks. According to the Bangladesh Bank, in recent times, state owned bank's share of deposits have fallen below 30% while private sector banks share has risen to more than 60%. The government has issued nine new banking licences in 2012, making the total number of banks to 56.

3.6. Pakistan

Pakistan financial market had been subjected to deregulation for about more than a decade now. As a result of deregulation new banks were allowed to enter the market, foreign exchange controls were relaxed and more market oriented banking system has been introduced. Similar to other countries in the region Pakistan still has favourable credit policies. However, these policies are being reviewed and more prudential supervisory measures are applied in Pakistan compared to the pre-deregulation era. Just like in other parts of South Asia, one of the biggest problems to improve competitiveness and efficiency in Pakistan is the dominance of government owned banks [United Bank Ltd (UBL), Habib Bank Ltd (HBL) and National Bank of Pakistan (NBP)] in the loans and deposit market. There are more than 40 commercial banks in operation in Pakistan. Political interferences and selective loan policies have hampered efforts to improve banking services of the country. One of the reasons for the prevailing higher interest rates in Pakistan is mainly due to inefficiencies and higher administrative costs associated with providing banking services to the general public.

To summarise, for example, India has initiated financial reforms together with economic deregulation such that foreign companies are now permitted to own majority stakes in quoted Indian firms in a number of industries while the Sri Lankan government has taken a number of steps toward the objective of creating an investor-friendly economic environment, such as repealing the business acquisition act and privatising government-owned business enterprises. Deregulation in Bangladesh has opened many industries to private investment, so that foreign investors are allowed to own up to 100% of outstanding equity in domestic companies. In Pakistan, liberalisation policies by the government have led to rapid deregulation of the economy and the removal of impediments to private investment. In the early stages of these deregulation and liberalisation processes, these countries concentrated on development of their capital markets and the financial system. As noted above, in India, with the implementation of the Narasimham Committee Report (1991), many regulatory features relating to interest rate determination, credit restrictions, equity market controls, and foreign exchange controls have been relaxed. Similarly, the deregulation of financial markets in Pakistan has resulted in relaxation of foreign exchange controls and introduction of a market-oriented banking system. Over the years, Bangladesh's financial system has undergone broad structural changes as a result of continues deregulation. These changes include an improvement in transparency of the financial system, deregulation of interest rate determination, strengthening of loan classification standards, and a reduction in the central bank's level of control over financial transactions and loan recovery measures. Equally, the Sri Lankan government has introduced a number of policy changes in recent time to develop its financial system. These changes include the deregulation of interest rate determination, the introduction of market-based credit policies, relaxation of market entry for foreign and local banking firms, and the introduction of necessary legislative measures to safeguard the financial system.

4. MARKET INTEGRATION

Many regulatory changes in the financial market sector have encouraged the private sector to enter the financial services industry. Most of these newly emerged private sector institutions have preceded rapidly to obtaining listing status in their respective stock exchanges. As an outcome, the region has proceeded to develop a competitive financial industry sector and fast-growing equity markets, and, simultaneously, producing a notable economic growth. The outcome has been a transformation of the financial services sector in this region from its previous domination by state-owned institutions.

Table 1 provides statistics highlighting the significance of the banking sector which is the dominant sector in the financial services industry, in the South Asian region. We observe that during the 16-year period from 1995 to 2010, countries in this region recorded significant growth in the number of operating banks, thereby contributing a significant (and much needed) level of competitiveness to the industry (Panel A). Asiaweek (www.asiaweek.com) reports that banks in the South Asian region now have a significant presence (Bangladesh: 12 banks; India: 54 banks; Pakistan: 12 banks; and Sri Lanka: 6 banks) among the largest 500 banks operating in Asia, where more than 70% of financial assets are controlled by the banking sector. Such growth in the number of banks operating in these countries has resulted in a notable increase in the domestic credit they are able to provide (Panel B), and an increase in the banking sector's contribution to GDP (Panel C). We also observe remarkable growth in the banking sector's contribution to market capitalisation during this 16-year period (Panel D). Typically, the banking sector has remained the dominant capital market sector constituent for these countries. For example, in Bangladesh and Sri

Lanka, the banking and finance sector possesses the largest market capitalisation (on the Dhaka Stock Exchange and the Colombo Stock Exchange, respectively). On the Indian stock market (the Bombay Stock Exchange), the banking and finance industry is the second largest industry following the oil and gas industry. In Pakistan, the Karachi Stock Exchange is dominated by banking- and finance-related firms. As a direct outcome of financial deregulation that brought market integration, the private banking industry now challenges previously dominant state-owned banking in the region.

The asset bases of private sector banks are more diversified than those of state-owned banks. Private sector banks in this region have followed a diversified approach that has taken advantage of the opportunities offered by the liberalised financial system. Primary modes of bank diversification have been in relation to both assets and income, as the banks have responded to the challenge of global competitive-

Table 1. Growth in Banking Sector in South Asian Countries

Country	Levels				Growth (%)	
	1995	2000	2005	2010	1995 to 2000	1995 to 2010
Panel A: Number of Banks						
Bangladesh	15	23	26	39	53.33	160.00
India	51	59	76	115	15.69	125.49
Pakistan	17	22	38	59	29.41	247.06
Sri Lanka	7	9	17	19	28.57	171.43
Panel B: Domestic Credit Provided by Banking Sector as % of GDP						
Bangladesh	26.76	34.26	54.91	66.12	28.03	147.08
India	44.11	53.01	58.45	71.08	20.18	61.14
Pakistan	51.02	41.60	46.51	48.80	-18.46	-04.35
Sri Lanka	40.91	43.74	43.61	40.51	06.92	-0.98
Panel C: Contribution of Banking Sector to GDP (%)						
Bangladesh	1.48	1.54	1.60	1.67	4.05	12.84
India	3.18	3.80	5.00	6.90	19.50	116.98
Pakistan	7.67	6.82	6.56	6.84	-11.08	-10.82
Sri Lanka	6.71	7.19	8.10	10.66	7.15	58.87
Panel D: Contribution of Banking Sector to Market Capitalisation (%)						
Bangladesh	9.01	25.21	43.09	53.02	179.80	488.45
India	4.76	4.52	9.59	12.74	-5.04	167.65
Pakistan	3.49	3.79	14.72	20.18	8.60	478.22
Sri Lanka	40.86	24.65	12.78	20.96	-39.67	-48.70

Note: This table reports statistics relating to the growth of banking industry in the South Asian region. It contains the information on the number of banks, domestic credit provided by the banks (as a percentage of GDP), the contribution of the banking sector to GDP, and the contribution of the banking sector to the capitalisation of stock markets for the each individual country investigated in the study. Data sources: BankScope, ADB, and Datastream.

ness. As a result, these banks now generate a substantial portion of their income from non-traditional banking activities, such as investment banking, leasing, merchant banking, factoring, hire purchase, mutual funds, and many other activities. For example Sampath Bank, a leading private sector bank in Sri Lanka incorporated in 1986, generated an operating income of US$129.6 million in 2010, of which US$52.8 million (41%) was generated from non-traditional banking activities such as foreign exchange transactions, investments in securities, securities dealing, professional services, trade-related services, foreign remittances, credit and debit card services, and other banking services. Similarly, ICICI bank, the second largest private bank in India, generated US$1.31 billion in revenue for the 2010/11 fiscal year, of which US$0.91 billion (or 70%) came from non-interest income sources such as foreign exchange income and margin on customer derivative transactions. The outcome is that strategic diversification decisions are now a major factor in determining the performance level of banks in this region. All these measure indicate higher level of market integration within the region.

In relation to trade between the South Asian nations, market integration in the region is further visible by when examine the number of Free Trade Agreements (FTAs) signed by countries in the region. These agreements are to allow free trade among participating courtiers and it strengthen further economic corporation in the region. While India and Pakistan are dominating trade activities in the region (32 and 26 free trade agreements respectively), they also have signed the highest number of FTAs. Sri Lanka and Bangladesh have signed 8 and 6 free trade agreements respectively. All these evidence support continues market integration among the member nations of South Asia.

Another measure we could use to examine the depth of market integration is to observe the cost of business start-up procedure index developed by the Asian Development Bank. Figure 1 shows data from 2005 to 2012 and all countries are showing improvements. Under a regulatory system businesses spend more money and time to start a business as there are so many 'approvals' to be obtained and too many 'red tapes' to be passed. When the system is more liberal businesses could start easily without spending more money and time. Still, in countries like India, it may be costly to start a business compared to the other countries in the region. However, declining cost indicates improvements and integration in the region.

Figure 1. Cost of business start-up procedure (% of GNI per capita)

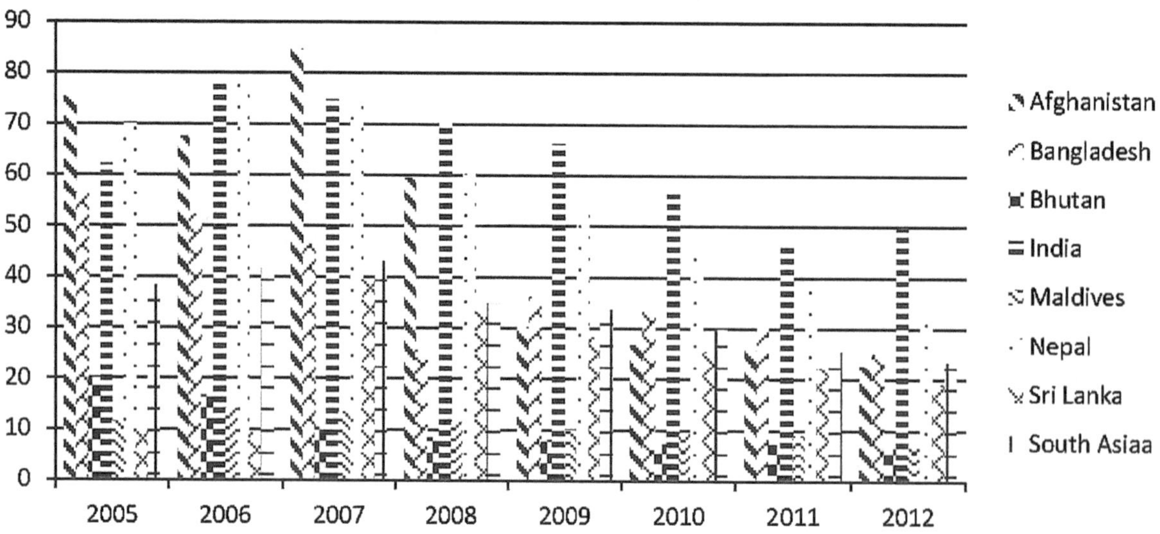

5. CAPITAL MARKET DEVELOPMENTS

Within the South Asian financial market sector banks are the dominating players. However, over the years, equity markets have become increasingly important for many countries in the region. Three decades ago there were no equity markets or very little markets were active in the region. Continues financial sector reforms have helped equity markets in the region to grow significantly. (Table 2 lists stock exchanges in all South Asian countries.) Foreign market participants are still not very common but increasingly their participation is becoming significant. Encouraging broader equity market integration in the region, exchanges have already formed an organisation called South Asian Federation of Exchanges (SAFE). This has helped bourses in South Asia to boost securities markets activities in a significant way. The members of countries have agreed to work towards common standards including international accounting standards and best business practices in capital markets. Stock market capitalisation within the region has been remarkable for all countries however India has been the dominating player in the region. Sri Lanka with a 125% increase in yield has become one of the best performers in the world in 2009 while India was not far behind.

It is notable that among the all nations, Indian equity market has been experiencing a significant growth in recent years except 2008 in which it had some impact of Global Financial Crisis (GFC). One significant measure to identify equity market integration in the regions is the examination of equity market returns correlation data. Equity market returns correlation is a pair-wise measure of co-movement in the stock markets. A higher correlation indicates a higher degree of integration in the markets. Figure 2 shows stock market correlation returns for Bangladesh, India, Pakistan and Sri Lanka. Due to data deficiency Afghanistan, Bhutan, Maldives and Nepal were omitted. Compared to 2001, all countries have shown improved correlation statistics indicating market integration within the region. It appears that in most countries, over the years, correlation has improved. However, between some countries there is no continues increase in correlation. This may be due to internal factors of such as civil unrest/war or political volatility which are highly sensitive to equity market activities.

Table 2. Equity Markets in the South Asian region

Country	Name of the Stock Exchange
Bangladesh	Chittagong Stock Exchange (CSE)
	Dhaka Stock Exchange (DSE)
Bhutan	Royal Securities Exchange Bhutan
India	Bombay Stock Exchange (BSE)
	National Stock Exchange (NSE)
Maldives	Maldives Stock Exchange (MSE)
Nepal	Nepal Stock Exchange
Pakistan	Islamabad Stock Exchange (ISE)
	Karachi Stock Exchange (KSE)
	Lahore Stock Exchange (LSE)
Sri Lanka	Colombo Stock Exchange (CSE)

Source: www.safe-asia.com

Figure 2. Stock market returns correlation 2001-2012

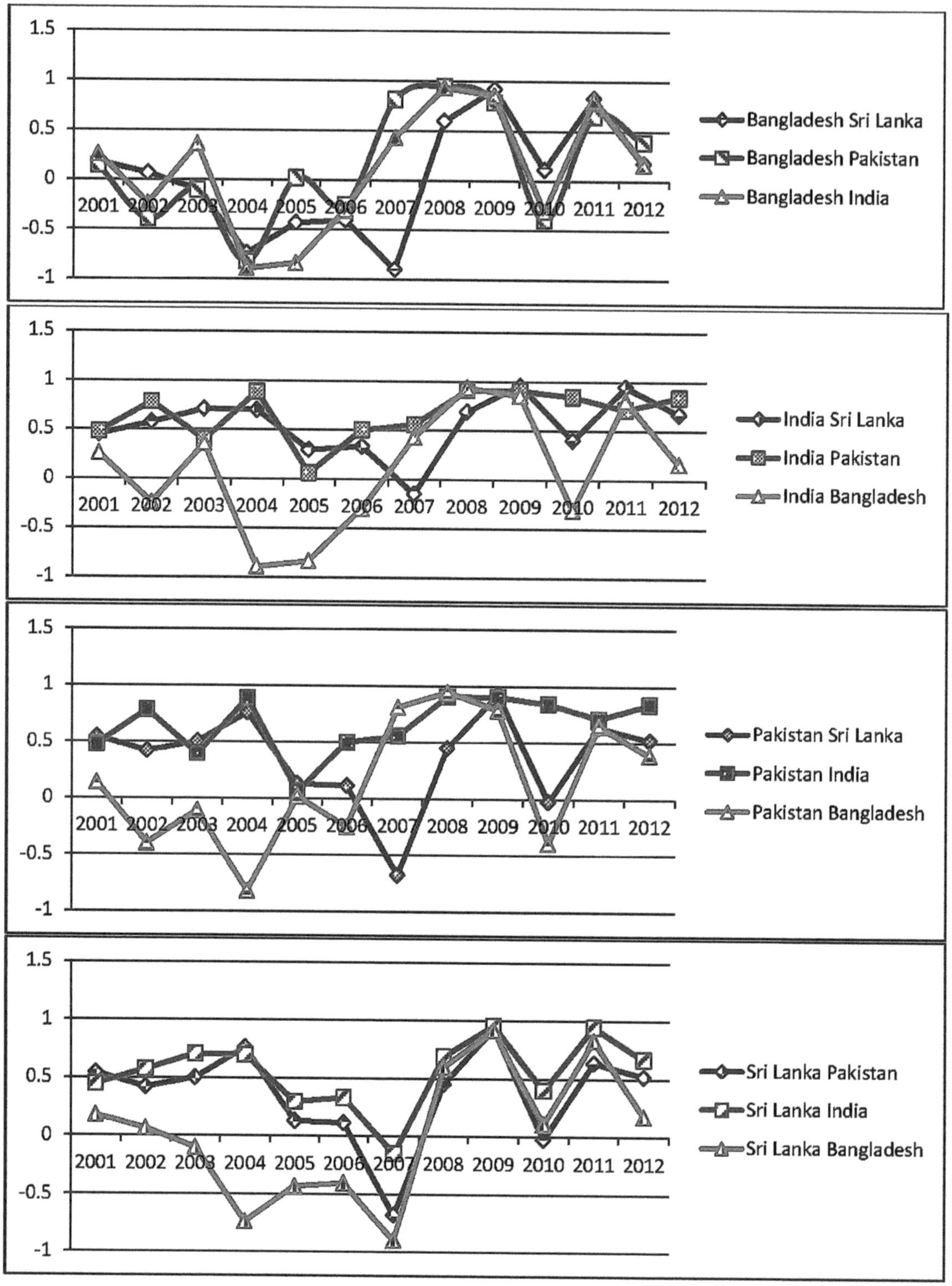

6. BENEFITS OF MARKET INTEGRATIONS

According to the World Bank data, in the year 2012 South Asia's share of GDP was India = 81%, Pakistan = 9%, Bangladesh = 5%, Sri Lanka = 2.5%, the all other countries = 2.5%. This proves us the Indian dominance of economic activities in the region and the necessity of plying a significant role in financial and economic integration activities by India to achieve better results. The annual export growth rate (year to year change) of India has increased from 9.1% in 1990 to 43% in 2010 showing significant benefits of market integrations. Similar results could be found for other countries except Sri Lanka. Due to the internal war activities, Sri Lanka's annual export growth rate was declining for many years but now recovering as the conflict has come to an end.

Theoretically, the cost of capital should decline within the region due to market integration and investment should improve. Almost all countries in the region experienced improvement in investments during the last two decade. For examples, according to the IMF's World Economic Outlook Database, India's total investment as % of GDP has improved from 1981-1990 average of 20.78 to 34.73 in 2013. For Sri Lanka, the same indicator shows an improvement from 21.18 to 32.66 for the same time period. For Bangladesh, for the same period, figures show an improvement from 16.9 to 26.56. Most of these achievements are the due to market integration within the region.

Reduction in tariffs and duties among nations, due to the signing of trade agreements, are significant benefits for exporters, producers as well as consumers. Similarly, due to Visa relaxation among member nations for a specific activity such as businesses has benefitted many countries as travel between the nations have increased over the years. As a result, increased tourism has benefitted all countries. Joint-ventures in manufacturing, agriculture and services industries are increasing in recent times among many countries. Irrespective of all these developments, there are many issues to be addressed to achieve higher benefits from economic and financial market integration.

7. MAJOR ISSUES

To get the maximum benefit of financial market and economic integration in the region there are some important measures to be implemented. Apart from political, religious, ethnical, cultural and social issues in each country, other issues such as corruption, institutional deficiencies, lack of transparency, inefficiency and regulatory problems are needed to be looked at.

7.1. Political Factors

Irrespective of being democratic nations, the major obstacle to economics and financial market integration in South Asia would be the underlying political factors in the region. For example, disputes among nations on many issues are substantial and ongoing discussions would not be able to give a clear solution in the immediate future. Apart from the well-known historical conflict between India and Pakistan, all countries in the region have internal political issues as well as issues with neighbouring nations. For instance, still many issues between India and Pakistan need permanent solutions, irrespective of military and political victories, countries such as Sri Lanka and Nepal both have long-run ongoing ethnical issues within their countries. When there is no political stability in a country, it is a difficult task to introduce significant structural changes though such countries have democratic political systems. Many countries in Asia, specifically in East Asia, have been able to achieve remarkable economic growth during the past, irrespective of the political system they had. After achieving notable economic development, many of these countries have now introduced democratic political systems. Irrespective of these on-going issues in the South Asian region, it is apparent that there is a political will to continue with economic deregulation measures. The progress of the SARRAC organisation is a good example for this.

7.2. Poverty

Regardless of becoming emerging market nations, Indian sub-continent is one of the poorest parts in the world, having substantially low per-capita income levels. This could be regarded as one of the barriers to faster economic and financial integration in the region. However, market deregulation policies would help these countries to lower the level of poverty and achieve higher economic growth levels. According to the World Banks's Poverty and Equity database, regions level of poverty is declining showing positive results of market liberalisation policies. For example, in Sri Lanka and in Bangladesh, from 2002 to 2010, the level of poverty has declined on average by 1.7%. For India, the figure for the period of 2005-2010 shows a decline of average 1.5%. For Pakistan, the level of poverty has not declined as in other countries but by 1.2% for the period of 1999-2006. For Nepal, figure shows a decline of just 0.8% for the period of 2004-2011. While there are obvious improvements in the level of poverty, it may take some times for many people to come out of poverty in many nations in the region. Faster economic growth should help in this process.

7.3. Corruption

Based on the Transparency International's Corruption Perception Index, the level of corruption in the region has been declining over the years. For example, in the year 2000, India's index value was 2.9 and in 2013 this figure has increased to 3.6. (lower the index value, higher the level of corruption) This shows an improvement not only from social point of view but also from economic benefits. It's widely accepted that corruption is a hindrance to economic growth or higher accelerated economic growth could increase the level of corruption. However, it appears to be that in South Asia, financial deepening has not positively contributed the level of corruption but the other way. The Corruption Perception Index values for other countries are showing similar improvements. For example, for Pakistan, it has improved from 2.25 in 1995 to 2.8 in 2013. In Bangladesh, it has improved from 0.4 in 2001 to 2.7 in 2013. Regardless of the improvement in corruption indicators, the region still has higher level of corruptions compared to other Asian nations such as Singapore and Hong Kong. Figure 3 shows the level of corruption in the South Asian region.

7.4. Institutional Deficiencies

Many countries have failed in the past in reforming their institutions once the financial market is deregulated. With deregulation, existing institutional setup will not be able to supervise or monitor deregulated institutions such as financial institutions. For example, central banks or reserve banks are the usual supervisor of financial institutions. As banking and other financial services institutions expand beyond their traditional business models after deregulation, existing supervisory arrangements will be inadequate in monitoring them. While deregulating there financial market sector, almost all South Asian

Figure 3. Level of corruption in South Asia

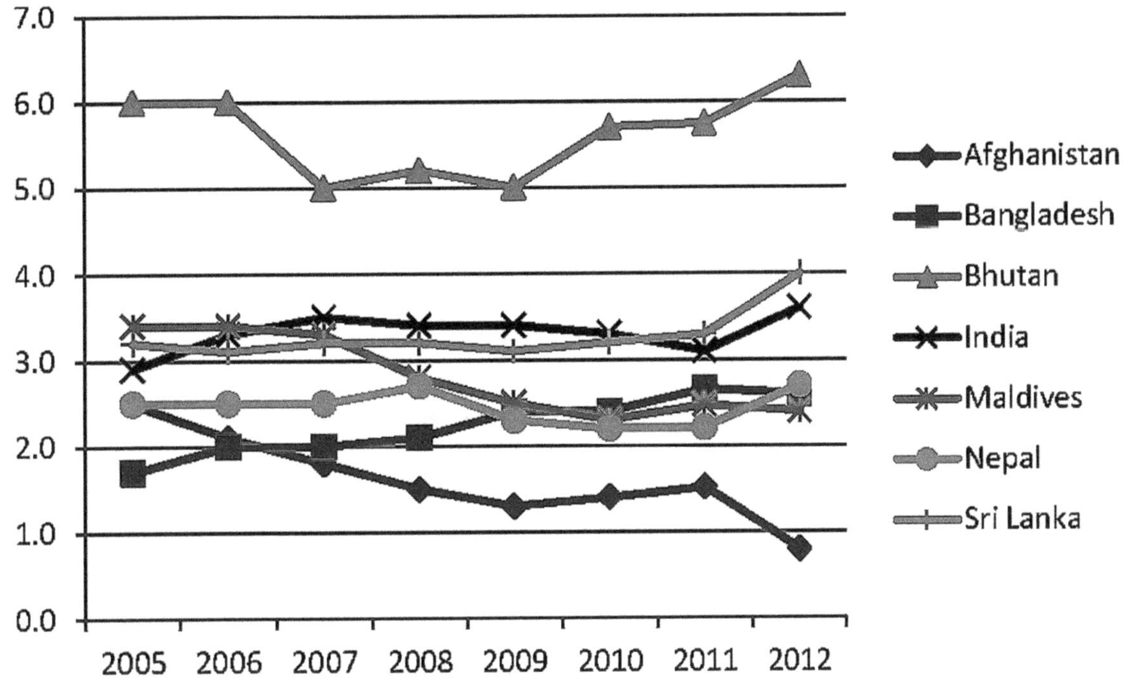

nations have failed restructuring their supervisory structure except doing minor adjustments. Lack of institutional arrangements to cope-up with the newly liberalised market activities may hinder economic and financial market integration significantly.

7.5. Lack of Transparency

South Asia needs to improve transparency and disclosure regime of their financial institutions further for the market to understand finance and economic activities in a better way. Lack of disclosure could affect money markets, capital markets, equity markets, foreign exchange markets as well as derivative markets in the region. If the South Asian nations have sufficient institutional arrangements, the level of transparency and disclosure among financial institutions could be improved.

8. POLICY RECOMMENDATIONS

One of the most important steps needed to be taken immediately is to expedite already agreed projects and programmes by the member nations of the SAARC. For example, there are plans in areas of agriculture and rural, biotechnology, culture, economic and trade, education, energy, environment, finance, information and media, poverty alleviation, science and technology, social development and tourism to improve cooperation among member nations of the SAAARC organisation. Giving priority to areas such as finance, economic and trade, agriculture and science and technology could deliver significant benefits to all nations in the South Asian region. As most countries in the region are producing below the capable capacity level, cooperation among member nations could improve efficiency substantially. Since there is a political will for cooperation among nations, it will not be a difficult task to expedite many programmes already started. Since its inauguration on 9 September 1998, SAARCFINANCE has not achieved much for the last 16 years. Only notable events so far were the establishment of the SAARC Payment Council (SPC) in 2008 and continues dialog between central bankers among member nations. Therefore, we suggest that all those planned activities by the SAARC organisation should be expedited to achieve common goals for all nations in the South Asian region. These planned activities are necessary to improve economic and financial market integration in the region.

9. CONCLUSION AND FUTURE EXPECTATIONS

South Asia has come a long way in the path of deregulation and now there are visible signs of economic and financial market integration. Irrespective of political differences and internal conflict among number of nations, deregulation policies implemented so far have helped economic and financial markets to integrate significantly. Foreign direct investments in the region have significantly increased. For example, the largest economy India has reported a massive $32 billion investment in the year 2011. The same figure for the year 2000 was just above $3 billion (see Table 3). This shows economic and financial market improvements in India. The rest of the South Asia is no different except few countries where political uncertainties have had negative impacts on investments. The level of foreign direct investments in Bangladesh has increased from just $280 million in 2000 to $1.1 billion in 2011.

As the South Asian region is expected to be a 'union' one day, there may be benefits but there could also be costs. It is important to have common characteristics among countries, who are expected to be members of a monetary union (monetary union referred to countries in which they have a common currency), to be successfully integrated. For example, European Union had number of common features such as political, social and cultural apart from economic features. One of the major problems arising in South Asia in this regard is the diversity or discrepancies each country inherited. From political point of view, almost all countries are democracies. However, India has substantial political problems with Pakistan and almost all countries in the region are fighting with insurgents, terrorists, rebels or secessionists. Religious and ethnic issues are predominant in many parts of South Asia. One of the most significant factors in relation to the benefit of financial integration is the level of financial literacy among

Table 3. Foreign Direct Investments in South Asia (in million US dollars)

Country	1995	2000	2005	2007	2010	2011
Bangladesh	2	280	813	653	918	1138
Bhutan	...	...	9	74	19	16
India	2144	3584	7606	25483	26502	32190
Maldives	7	22	53	91	216	282
Nepal	0	0	2	6	88	94
Pakistan	723	308	2201	5590	2018	1309
Sri Lanka	56	173	272	603	478	956

Source: Asian Development Bank

the population in the South Asian region. It has been found out that even in highly developed financial market nations the majority of population is very poor in financial literacy. As the level of financial literacy is low among the majority of population in the South Asian countries, expected benefit may not be easily achievable. Irrespective of this, money and capital market developments in the region helping the general population gradually to understand market concepts. Having a monetary union similar to the European Monetary Union in which number of countries has a single currency (EURO) in use may have some benefits. South Asian countries have different currencies in use at present. Among the possible outcome of a monetary union improving exports, less transaction cost, lower interest rates and less volatility in nominal exchange rates could be regarded as beneficial to the region while loss of monetary policy independence, loss of seigniorage income, political cost and small country disadvantage for some countries could be regarded as costs. Specifically, the need for tougher fiscal policies could be regarded as a significant cost associated with a monetary union. Obviously, a single currency could encourage intra-trade activities significantly as there are no exchange rate issues but these benefits could be limited by taxes and tariffs in each country. As what we learned from the European Union experience, better coordination among nations in respect of fiscal policies is vital in improving efficiencies. The problem with South Asia is how far the nations are willing to go politically to achieve common goals, as at this point of time, it looks like there is nothing happening soon. The bright side is that nations are organised under the SAARC umbrella and at least have a vision to achieve such a monetary union states.

REFERENCES

Asian Development Bank. (2014). *Database*. Author.

Chai, H.-Y., & Rhee, Y. (2005). *Financial integration and financial efficiency in East Asia*. Paper presented at the Claremont-KIEP International Conference.

ESCAP (2010). *Capital flows and development: Lessons from South Asian experiences*. MPDD working papers WP/10/11.

International Monetary Fund. (n.d.). *World Economic Outlook database*. Author.

Kleimeier, S., & Sander, H. (2000). Regionalisation versus globalisation in European financial market integration: Evidence from cointegration analysis. *Journal of Banking & Finance*, *24*(6), 1005–1043. doi:10.1016/S0378-4266(99)00116-8

Narasimham Committee Report. (1997). *Report of the Committee on Banking Sector Reform*. Reserve Bank of India.

Narasimham Report. (1991). *Report of the Committee on the Financial System*. Reserve Bank of India.

Perera, A., & Wickramanayake, J. (2012). Financial integration in selected South Asian countries. *South Asian Journal of Global Business Research*, *1*(2), 210–237. doi:10.1108/20454451211252741

Verma Report. (1999). *Report of the Working Group on Restructuring Weak Public Sector Banks*. Reserve Bank of India.

APPENDIX

Appendix 1. Some Important macro-economic data for the South Asian region

Selected macro-economic variables for South Asian countries							
Country	Subject	1981-1990	1991-2000	2001-2010#	2011	2012	2013
Afghanistan	GDP Growth rate (%)	n.a.	n.a.	9.13	6.11	7.90	4.23
Bangladesh	GDP Growth rate (%)	3.73	4.80	5.82	6.71	6.23	6.03
Bhutan	GDP Growth rate (%)	10.10	5.00	8.75	8.55	4.62	4.98
India	GDP Growth rate (%)	5.57	5.60	7.54	6.64	4.74	5.02
Maldives	GDP Growth rate (%)	n.a.	5.31	7.76	6.48	1.33	3.71
Nepal	GDP Growth rate (%)	4.79	5.00	3.93	3.42	4.85	3.78
Pakistan	GDP Growth rate (%)	6.29	3.96	4.22	2.79	4.02	6.07
Sri Lanka	GDP Growth rate (%)	4.20	5.22	5.20	8.25	6.34	7.25
Afghanistan	Total investment as % of GDP	na.	na.	35.46	23.57	18.61	18.00
Bangladesh	Total investment as % of GDP	16.90	20.38	25.64	25.90	26.70	26.56
Bhutan	Total investment as % of GDP	25.93	35.46	44.26	50.00	52.00	52.59
India	Total investment as % of GDP	20.78	23.66	32.07	35.53	34.70	34.73
Maldives	Total investment as % of GDP	26.28	25.41	19.53	20.00	20.00	20.00
Nepal	Total investment as % of GDP	15.70	20.48	27.66	33.17	33.78	31.78
Pakistan	Total investment as % of GDP	15.57	14.71	16.05	14.12	14.92	14.22
Sri Lanka	Total investment as % of GDP	21.18	23.56	23.81	29.95	30.63	32.66
Afghanistan	Gross national savings as % of GDP	na.	na.	30.44	26.71	22.54	20.85
Bangladesh	Gross national savings as % of GDP	56.44	70.94	85.34	29.00	29.36	28.15
Bhutan	Gross national savings as % of GDP	7.31	14.22	18.62	31.97	32.20	31.73
India	Gross national savings as % of GDP	394.27	484.74	576.59	31.37	29.96	32.74
Maldives	Gross national savings as % of GDP	13.14	11.50	6.24	0.02	-2.95	-0.62
Nepal	Gross national savings as % of GDP	15.57	20.05	27.07	32.22	38.58	35.06
Pakistan	Gross national savings as % of GDP	55.71	68.92	85.31	14.22	12.85	13.18
Sri Lanka	Gross national savings as % of GDP	16.24	19.10	20.97	22.15	24.04	28.53
Afghanistan	Current account balance	na.	na.	3.14	3.14	3.93	2.85
Bangladesh	Current account balance	3.36	1.89	4.51	-1.17	0.85	1.83
Bhutan	Current account balance	-14.40	1.22	-1.36	-23.69	-17.62	-22.21
India	Current account balance	3.16	3.27	3.29	-4.16	-4.74	-1.99
Maldives	Current account balance	4.13	-0.15	-5.34	-19.98	-22.95	-20.62
Nepal	Current account balance	-0.19	1.07	3.54	-0.95	4.79	3.28
Pakistan	Current account balance	0.96	1.36	1.67	0.10	-2.07	-1.05
Sri Lanka	Current account balance	-8.49	-5.55	-3.03	-7.80	-6.59	-4.13
Afghanistan	Population (million)	na.	na.	12.773*	29.11	29.83	30.55

continued on following page.

Appendix 1. Continued

Selected macro-economic variables for South Asian countries							
Country	**Subject**	**1981-1990**	**1991-2000**	**2001-2010#**	**2011**	**2012**	**2013**
Bangladesh	Population (million)*	107.39*	132.38*	151.13*	152.86	154.70	156.30
Bhutan	Population (million)	0.56*	0.57*	0.73*	0.74	0.74	0.75
India	Population (million)	847.44*	1029.19*	1194.62*	1210.98	1227.19	1243.34
Maldives	Population (million)	0.21*	0.27*	0.32*	0.33	0.33	0.34
Nepal	Population (million)	18.11*	23.18*	26.85*	27.16	27.47	27.92
Pakistan	Population (million)	108.4*	137.53*	171.73*	175.31	178.91	182.59
Sri Lanka	Population (million)	16.27*	18.47*	20.40*	20.54	20.66	20.82

*Population figures are for 1990, 2000, 2010
#For Afghanistan 2003-2010
na: Not available
Source: IMF

Compilation of References

Abdul Qadeer Fitrat. (2010). *Building an Efficient and Affordable Housing Finance System*. Da Afghanistan Bank.

Accounting and Auditing Organization for Islamic Finance Institutions. (2010). *Shariah Standards*. Manama, Bahrain: Author.

Acharya, K. P., Nara, B. T., & Sharma, S. (1998). Economic Liberalization in Nepal: Sequence and Process. Kathmandu: OXFAM GB Nepal.

Adam Smith International. (2014). The new mineral law: breaking new ground for Afghanistan. *The Guardian*. Retrieved 14th January 2015, from http://www.theguardian.com/global-development-professionals-network/adam-smith-international-partner-zone/2014/oct/30/new-minerals-law-afghanistan

ADB. (2009). *Financial Sector in South Asia: Recent Developments and Challenges*. Manila, Philippines: Asian Development Bank.

Adhikari, R. H. (2005). *Risk and Return Analysis with Reference to Listed Commercial Banks*. (Unpublished MBS thesis). Tribhuvan University, Nepal.

Adhikary, G. P. (1989). *Deregulation in the Financial System in the SEACEN Countries*. Kuala Lumpur: South East Asian Central Banks Research and Training Centre.

Afghanistan Economy Update. (2014). *Poverty Reduction and Economic Management*. Retrieved 10th January 2015, from http://www.imf.org/external/pubs/ft/scr/2014/cr14128.pdf

Afghanistan Financial Services. (2010). *Afghanistan Capital Market Assessment*. Retrieved 7th October 2014, from http://www.ahg.af/data/work/stock-exchange/AFS%20-%20Afghanistan%20Capital%20Markets%20Assessment.pdf

Afghanistan Holding Group. (n.d.). Retrieved 6th October 2014, from http://www.ahg.af/work/stock-exchange

Afghanistan Investment Support Agency. (n.d.). *Investment in Afghanistan*. Retrieved 10th January 2015, from http://www.state.gov/documents/organization/226764.pdf

Afghanistan Legal Education Project. (2011). *An introduction to the commercial law of Afghanistan*. Stanford Research Paper.

Afghanistan Opium Survey. (2013). Retrieved 16th January 2015, from http://www.unodc.org/documents/cropmonitoring/Afghanistan/Afghanreport_Summary_Findings_2013.pdf

Afghanistan's Emerging Mortgage market Gets the Push Investors Were Waiting For. (2010). Retrieved January 14th 2015, from www.prweb.com/releases/Afghanistan/Mortgage/prweb4122034.html

Agreements between Islamic Republic of Afghanistan and Islamic Republic of Pakistan. (2010). Retrieved 8th January 2015, from http://www.commerce.gov.pk/APTTA/APTTA.pdf

Ahluwalia, M. S. (1999). Reforming India's Financial Sector: An Overview. *India: A financial sector for the twenty-first century*, 29-54.

Ahmed, M. N., & Chowdhury, M. I. (2007). *Non-Bank Financial Institutions in Bangladesh: An Analytical Review.* Working Paper Series- WP 0709. Bangladesh Bank.

Akhtar, S. (2006). *Financial Sector of Pakistan – The Roadmap. Speech, Dawn Asia Finance Conference - Asian Banking: A Paradigm Shift.* Karachi, Pakistan: Academic Press.

Akhter, N., & Ghani, E. (2010). Regional Integration in South Asia: An Analysis of Trade Flows Using the Gravity Model. *Pakistan Development Review*, 105–118.

Akshatha, B. G. (2014). Cheque truncation system: Innovative mechanisms for effective payment. *International Journal of Logistics & Supply Chain Management Perspectives*, *2*(4), 767–771.

Ali, M. J., & Ahmed, K. (2007). The legal and institutional framework for corporate financial reporting practices in South Asia. *Research in Accounting Regulation*, *19*, 175–205. doi:10.1016/S1052-0457(06)19009-8

Allen, F., Chakrabarti, R., & Shanker, D. (2007). *India's Financial System.* Available at: http://fic.wharton.upenn.edu/fic/papers/07/0736.pdf

Amadeo, K. (2012). *Stock Market Crash.* Retrieved from http://useconomy.about.com/od/glossary/g/Market_Crash.html

Amuedo-Dorantes, C., & Pozo, S. (2006). Migration, Remittances, and Male and Female Employment Patterns. *The American Economic Review*, *96*(2), 222–226. doi:10.1257/000282806777211946

Ana-Maria Oviedo. (2009). *Economic Informality: Causes, Costs and Policies A Literature Survey of International Experience.* Country Economic Memorandum.

Ang, J. B. (2010). Finance and Inequality: The Case of India. *Southern Economic Journal*, *76*(3), 738–761. doi:10.4284/sej.2010.76.3.738

Anwar, S., & Cooray, A. (2012). Financial development, political rights, civil liberties and economic growth: Evidence from South Asia. *Economic Modelling*, *29*(3), 974–981. doi:10.1016/j.econmod.2012.02.009

Arestis, P., Demetriades, P., & Luintel, K. B. (2001). Financial Development and Economic Growth: The Role of the Stock Markets. *Journal of Money, Credit and Banking*, *331*(1), 16–41. doi:10.2307/2673870

Ariyarathna, T. W. (1993). Changes in the Banking and the Financial Sector in Sri Lanka Since 1985. *Sri Lanka Economic Journal*, *8*(1), 1–29.

Arora, R. U. (2010). *Regional Financial Cooperation in South Asia.* Griffith Asia Institute.

Aruna Kumar, D. (n.d.). *An Overview of Indian Financial System.* Available at: http://ww.indianmba.com/Faculty_Column/FC177/fc177.html

Asian Development Bank. (2014). *Database.* Author.

Aterido, R., Beck, T., & Iacovone, L. (2011). *Gender and Finance in Sub-Sahran Africa: Are Women Disadvantaged?* Policy Research Working Paper: 5571.

Athukorala, P., & Rajapatirana, S. (2000). Liberalization and Industrial Transformation: Lessons from the Sri Lankan Experience. *Economic Development and Cultural Change*, *48*(3), 543–573. doi:10.1086/452610

Atreya, B. (2015). Financial Sector Regulation in SAARC Countries. In Research Department International Finance Division, Economic Integration in South Asia (pp. 41–49). Kathmandu, Nepal: Nepal Rastra Bank. Retrieved from http://red.nrb.org.np/publications/special_publication/Special_Publications--Economic_Integration_%20in_South_Asia_%282005%29.pdf

Atyeh, M. H. (2012). The Theoretical Considerations of Financial Markets Integration: The case of Arab countries. *Journal of Economics and Sustainable Development*.

Auditing Practices Board. (2011). *Enhancing the Value of Auditor Reporting: Exploring Options for Change*. Author.

Ayuso, J., & Blanco, R. (1999). *Has financial market integration increased during the nineties?* Research Department, Banco de Espana.

Bagsiraj, M. I. (2003). Islamic Financial Institutions of India - Progress, Problems and Prospects. Jeddah, Saudi Arabia: Scientific Publishing Centre, King Abdulaziz University.

Bandow, D. (2015). *End the International drug war to control the Afghan Narco-State*. Huffingtion Post.

Bangladesh Bank (BB). (2008). Article. *Financial Sector Review, 3*(2).

Bangladesh Bank. (n.d.). Retrieved from http://www.bangladesh-bank.org

Basel Committee on Banking Supervision. (2013). *Regulatory Framework: Balancing Risk Sensitivity, Simplicity and Comparability*. Bank for International Settlements Publications.

Basel Committee on Banking Supervision. (2015). *Eighth progress report on adoption of the Basel regulatory framework*. Bank for International Settlements Publications.

Basyal Tula, R. (2002). *Benefits of Integrated Capital Markets. In Mirmire* (Vol. 200, pp. 297–302). Nepal Rastra Bank.

Basyal, T. R. (2002). Financial Sector Reform: Need and Strategy. Arunodaya, 291-303.

Basyal, T. R. (2001). *Reforming Nepal's Financial System: Rationale and Measures. Nepal Rastra Bank Annual Bulletin*, 7–13.

Basyal, T. R. (2001). *Reforming Nepal's Financial System: Rationale and Measures. Nepal Rastra Bank Annual Publication*.

Basyal, T. R. (2002). *Financial Sector Reform: Need and Strategy*. Arunodaya.

Beattie, V., Brandt, R., & Fearnley, S. (1999). Perceptions of auditor independence: U.K. evidence. *Journal of International Accounting, Auditing & Taxation, 8*(1), 67–107.

Beck, T., Demirguc-Kunt, A., & Maksimovic, V. (2008). Financing Patterns Around the World: The Role of Institutions. *Journal of Financial Economics, 90*, 467–487.

Beck, T., Demirgüç-Kunt, A., Soledad, M., & Pería, M. (2010). Bank Financing for SMEs: Evidence Across Countries and Bank Ownership Types. *Journal of Financial Services Research*.

Bekaert, G., Harvey, C., & Lundblad, C. (2001). *Does Financial Liberalization Spur Growth?* NBER Working Paper No. 8245. Cambridge, MA: National Bureau of Economic Research.

Bennedsen, M., Perez Gonzalez, F., & Wolfenzon, D. (2010). The Governance of Family Firms. *Corporate Governance*.

Benston, G. J. (2006). Fair-Value Accounting: A Cautionary Tale From Enron. *Journal of Accounting and Public Policy*.

Berkmen, P., Gelos, G., Rennhack, R., & Walsh, J. P. (2009). *The global financial crisis: Explaining cross-country differences in the output impact*. International Monetary Fund.

Bernardo, A. E. (2001). Contractual Restrictions on Insider Trading: A Welfare Analysis. *Economic Theory*, *18*(1), 7–35. doi:10.1007/PL00004135

Bhalla, V. K. (2008). Investment Management: Security Analysis and Portfolio Management. Chand (S.) & Co Ltd, India.

Bhatta, D. (2003). *Portfolio Management of Listed Finance Companies in Nepal.* (Unpublished MBS thesis). Tribhuvam University, Nepal.

Bhatta, G. P. (1995). *Assessment of Performance of Listed Companies in Nepal.* (Unpublished MBS thesis). Tribhuvam University, Nepal.

Bhetuwal, K. (2005). *Assessing the Effectiveness of Financial Sector Reforms in Nepal.* (Doctoral Thesis). Maharaja Sayajirao University of Baroda, Gujarat, India.

Bhetuwal, K. R. (2007). Financial liberalization and financial development in Nepal. *NRB Economic Review*, *19*, 23–42.

Bhoi, B. K., & Dhal, S. C. (1998). Integration of Financial Markets in India: An empirical evaluation. *RBI Occasional Papers, 19*(4), 345–380.

Bhole, L. M. (2004). *Financial Institutions and Markets: Structure, Growth and Innovations*. Tata McGraw-Hill Education.

Booth, L., Aivazian, V., Demirg¨uc¸-Kunt, A., & Maksimovic, V. (2001). Capital Structures in Developing Countries. *The Journal of Finance*, *56*(1), 87–130. doi:10.1111/0022-1082.00320

Booz, Allen & Hamilton. (1990). *CBPASS Strategic Workshop Materials: Developing Policy Assumptions for Bank Strategic Planning*. Author.

Booz, Allen & Hamilton. (1992). *CBPASS II: Final Report for CBPASS Committee*. Author.

Brown, P., Preiato, A. J., & Tarca, A. (2014). Measuring Country Differences in Enforcement of Accounting Standards: An Audit and Enforcement Proxy. *Journal of Business Finance & Accounting*.

Buigut, S., & Rao, V. K. (2011). International Financial Integration of the Indian Money Markets. *International Journal of Economics and Finance*, *3*(4). doi:10.5539/ijef.v3n4p170

Bureau of Economic and Business Affairs of the United States. (2014). *Investment Climate Statement.* Retrieved 11th January 2015, from http://www.state.gov/e/eb/rls/othr/ics/2014/226588.html

Burki, A. A., & Niazi, G. S. K. (2010). Impact of financial reforms on efficiency of state-owned, private and foreign banks in Pakistan. *Applied Economics*, *42*(24), 3147–3160. doi:10.1080/00036840802112315

Burton, M., Nesiba, R. F., & Brown, B. (2015). *An Introduction to Financial Markets And Institutions*. Academic Press.

Butt, S. A., & Hasan, A. (2009). Impact of Ownership Structure and Corporate Governance on Capital Structure of Pakistani Listed Companies. *International Journal of Business and Management*, *4*(2). Retrieved from http://papers.ssrn.com/sol3/papers.cfm?abstract_id=1732511

Byrd & Noorani. (2010). *Exploitation of Mineral Resources in Afghanistan: What are the Government revenues or development benefits*. Academic Press.

Calvo, G., & Mendoza, E. (2000). Rational Contagion and the Globalization of Securities Markets. *Journal of International Economics*, *51*(June), 79–113. doi:10.1016/S0022-1996(99)00038-0

Carter, S. (2014). *Gaps in new Afghan mining law pose a threat to stability*. Global Witness.

Carter, S., & Rosa, P. (1998). The Financing of Male- and Female-owned Businesses. *Entrepreneurship & Regional Development, 10*(3), 225–241. doi:10.1080/08985629800000013

Carvalho, A. (2008). *The Effect of Institutions on the External Financing of Brazilian Firms*. Academic Press.

Cavalluzzo, K. S., Cavalluzzo, L. C., & Wolken, J. D. (2002). Competition, Small Business Financing, and Discrimination: Evidence from a New Survey. *The Journal of Business, 75*(4), 641–676. doi:10.1086/341638

Cavalluzzo, K., & Wolken, J. (2005). Small Business Loan Turndowns, Personal Wealth, and Discrimination. *The Journal of Business, 78*(6), 2153–2177. doi:10.1086/497045

Cbsl.gov.lk. (2007). *Financial System Stability Review*. Retrieved 30 December 2015, from http://www.cbsl.gov.lk/pics_n_docs/latest_news/press_20071206e.doc

Center for Policy Dialogue (CPD). (2011). *Independent Review of Bangladesh's Development (IRBD)*. Retrieved from http://www.cpd.org.bd/downloads/IRBD%20FY11_First%20Reading.pdf

Central Depository Bangladesh Limited. (n.d.). Retrieved from http:// www.cdbl.com

Chadrasekhar, C. P. (2013, May 18). Redistributing Regulatory Power: Financial Sector Legislative Reform Commission. *Economic and Political Weekly*.

Chai, H.-Y., & Rhee, Y. (2005). *Financial integration and financial efficiency in East Asia*. Paper presented at the Claremont-KIEP International Conference.

Chakrabarti, R. (2002). *Corporate Governance in India - Evolution and Challenges*. Retrieved from: http://unpan1.un.org/intradoc/groups/public/documents/apcity/unpan023826.pdf

Chakrabarty, K. C. (2012, March). *M - Banking in India - Regulations and Rationale*. Speech delivered at International Banking Summit on Regulation of Cross-Border Mobile Payments and Regional Financial Integration organized by RBI, Mumbai, India.

Chakravarty, S., & Xiang, M. (2011). Determinenets of profit reinvestment by small business in emerging economies. *Financial Management, 40*(3), 553–590. doi:10.1111/j.1755-053X.2011.01153.x

Chandratre, K. (1993). *Bharat's law relating to insider trading*. New Delhi: Bharat Law House.

Chapter 3 Article 14: Certificate of Existence, Corporations and Limited Liability Companies Law of Afghanistan

Checchi. (2009). *Assessment of Corruption in Afghanistan*. Checchi & Company Consulting Inc.

Chen, G., & Firth, M., & Xin, Y. (2004). The Price-Volume Relationship in China's Commodity Futures Markets. *Chinese Economy, 37*(3), 87–122.

Chittagong Stock Exchanges. (n.d.). Retrieved from http://www.cse.com.bd

Cho, Y. (2013). *Why do countries implement Basel II? An analysis of the global diffusion of Basel II implementation. The London School of Economics and Political Science*. LSE.

Chrisman, J. J., Chua, J. H., & Litz, R. A. (2004). Comparing the Agency Costs of Family and Non-Family Firms; Conceptual Issues and Exploratory Evidence, Entrepreneurship. *Theory into Practice, 28*(4), 335–354.

Ciarli, T., Parto, S., & Savona, M. (2010). *Entrepreneurship under conflict in Afghanistan: Determinants and Motivations of Small Business Owners*. Retrieved from http://pagesperso.dial.prd.fr/dial_pagesperso/dial_eve_shocks/pdf/59_Ciarli%20Tommaso.pdf

Ciccaglione, K. R. (2014). *From Inclusion to Empowerment: The Political Implications of Microfinance*. Academic Press.

Claessens, S., Djankov, S., & Lang, L. (2000). The Separation of Ownership and Control in East Asian Corporations. *Journal of Financial Economics*, *58*(1-2), 81–112. doi:10.1016/S0304-405X(00)00067-2

Clark, P. K. (1973). A Subordinated Stochastic Process Model with Finite Variance for Speculative Prices. *Econometrica*, *41*(1), 135–155. doi:10.2307/1913889

Coleman, S. (2000). Access to Capital and Terms of Credit: A Comparison of Men- and Women-Owned Small Businesses. *Journal of Small Business Management*, *38*(3), 37–52.

Collier, P. (1999). On Economic Consequences of Civil War. *Oxford Economic Papers*, *5*(1), 168–183. doi:10.1093/oep/51.1.168

Committee on Financial Sector Assessment. (2009). *India's Financial Sector - An Assessment*. Mumbai: RBI and GoI Database on Indian Economy. Available at: http://www.rbi.org.in

Constitution of Islamic Republic of Afghanistan. Article 140

Cooray, A. (2015). *The Impact of Deregulation On Financial Market Efficiency In Sri Lanka*. Retrieved 30 December 2015, from https://www.researchgate.net/publication/268328371_

Copeland, T. E. (1976). A Probability Model of Asset Trading. *Journal of Financial and Quantitative Analysis*, *12*(4), 563–578. doi:10.2307/2330332

Cowen, D. (2006). *Financial Integration in Asia: Recent Development and Next Steps*. IMF Working Paper No. 169.

Cull, R., & Xu, L. C. (2005). Institutions, Ownership, & Finance: The Determinants of Profit Reinvestment Among Chinese Firms. *Journal of Financial Economics*, *77*(1), 117–146. doi:10.1016/j.jfineco.2004.05.010

D'Espallier, B., Guérin, I., & Mersland, R. (2010). Women and Repayment in Microfinance: A Global Analysis. *World Development*, *39*(5), 758–772. doi:10.1016/j.worlddev.2010.10.008

Das, D. J. (2000). *Problems Faced by Women Entrepreneurs* (K. Sasikumar, Ed.). Women Entrepreneurship.

Dee, P. (2012). *Economic Reform Processes in South Asia: Toward Policy Efficiency*. Abingdon, UK: Routledge.

Delis, M. D. (2012). Bank competition, financial reform, and institutions: The importance of being developed. *Journal of Development Economics*, *97*(2), 450–465. doi:10.1016/j.jdeveco.2011.05.012

Demirguc-Kunt, A., & Maksimovic, V. (2001). *Firms and financial intermediaries: Evidence from Trade Credit Data*. Research Working Paper 2696: The World Bank Development Research Group.

Demirguc-Kunt, A., & Levine, R. (2001). *Financial Structures and Economic Growth: A Cross-Country Comparison of Banks, Markets and Development*. Cambridge, MA: MIT Press.

Demsetz, H., & Lehn, K. (1985). The Structure of Corporate Ownership. *Causes and Consequences Journal of Political Economy*, *93*(6), 1155–1177. doi:10.1086/261354

Dhaka Stock Exchange. (n.d.). Retrieved from http://www.dsebd.org

Dhakal, N. (2008). *Financial Sector Refroms in Nepal* (Vol. 2008). Arthik Mimansa.

Dhungana, B. R. (2004). Financial Sector Reforms. In Nepal Rastra Bank in Fifity Years- Part II Financial System. Kathmandu: Nepal Rastra Bank.

Doing Business. (2011). Retrieved from http://www.doingbusiness.org/rankings/

Economy Watch. (2010). *A Brief Introduction to the Dhaka Stock Exchange*. Retrieved from http://www.economywatch.com/stockexchanges/dhaka.html

Edirisuriya, P. (2007). Effects of Financial Sector Reforms in Sri Lanka: Evidence from the Banking Sector (SSRN Scholarly Paper No. ID 1536035). Rochester, NY: Social Science Research Network; Retrieved from http://papers.ssrn.com/abstract=1536035

Edirisuriya, P. (2007). Effects of Financial Sector Reforms in Sri Lanka: Evidence from the Banking Sector. *Asia Pacific Journal of Finance and Banking Research*, *1*(1), 45–64.

Enterprise Surveys . (2013). Retrieved from http://www.enterprisesurveys.org/

Epps, T. W. (1976). The Demand for Broker's Services: The Relation Between Security Trading Volume and Transaction Cost. *Bell Journal of Economics*, *7*, 163–194.

Epps, T. W. (1975). Security Price Changes and Transaction Volumes: Theory and Evidence. *The American Economic Review*, *65*(4), 586–597.

ESCAP (2010*). Capital flows and development: Lessons from South Asian experiences.* MPDD working papers WP/10/11.

Eun, C. S., & Resnick, B. G. (2009). *International Financial Management* (2009th ed.). London: McGraw Hill.

Expanding your horizons? A guide to setting up business across the Middle East, North Africa and South Asia Region. (2011). Retrieved 15th January 2015, from http://www.kpmg.com/Africa/en/Documents/ExpandingthehorizonMENA-SATaxGuid2011v2.pdf

Faccio, M. (2006). Politically Connected firms. *The American Economic Review*, *96*(1), 369–386. doi:10.1257/000282806776157704

Fafchamps, M. (2002). Returns to Social Network Capital Among Traders. *Oxford Economic Papers*, *54*(2), 173–206. doi:10.1093/oep/54.2.173

Faiez and Heidi Vogt. (2011). *Afghan President: West shares in Kabul Bank fiasco*. Retrieved 8th October 2014, from http://seattletimes.com/html/nationworld/2014736784_apasafghanistan.html

Faisal & Hazi. (2014). *Matter of Interest*. Retrieved 18th January 2015, from http://www.thenews.com.pk/Todays-News-9-270247-Matter-of-interest

Fama, E. F., & Jensen, M. C. (1983). *Separation of Ownership and Control. Journal of Law and Economics*, *26*, 301–325.

Federal Government of United States of America. (2012). *Securities exchange act of 1934*. Washington, DC: Federal Government of United States of America.

Federal Government of USA. (2002). *Sarbanes–Oxley Act*. Washington, DC: Federal Government of USA.

Federal Government of USA. (2013). *Jumpstart Our Business Startups (JOBS) Act* (pp. 1–22). Washington, DC: Federal Government of USA.

Fellowes, R. (2008). *The Complete Guide to Investing in the Stock Market*. Easy Way Guides.

Ferrarini, B., Ramayandi, A., & Jha, R. (2012). *Public debt sustainability in developing Asia*. Routledge.

Financial reforms in Sri Lanka and their influence on the banking industry. (n.d.). Academic Press.

Financial Sector Regulation in Pakistan: The Way Forward. (2011). *SBP Research Bulletin, 1*(1), 31-44. Retrieved from http://iba.edu.pk/News/speechesarticles_drishrat/dec2011/Financial_sector_regulation.pdf

Firth, M., Lin, C., Liu, P., & Wong, S. (2009). Inside the black box: Bank credit allocation in China's private sector. *Journal of Banking & Finance, 33*(6), 1144–1155. doi:10.1016/j.jbankfin.2008.12.008

Gahlot, R. (2013). Capturing Volatility and its Spillover in South Asian Countries. *Journal of International Business and Economics, 1*(1), 20–36.

Galbraith, J. K. (1979/1988). *The Great Crash 1929*. Boston: Houghton Mifflin.

Ganesh Kumar Shrestha. (n.d.). *Financial Sector Reforms in Nepal*. Retrieved from http://www.nrb.org.np/ecorev/pdf-files/vol16_art3.pdf

Gardezi, M. (2007). *Afghans Experiences of Corruption: A study across seven provinces*. Kabul: Integrity Watch Afghanistan.

Gardizi, M., Hussmann, K., & Torabi, Y. (2010). *Corrupting the State or State-Crafted Corruption?* Afghanistan Research and Evaluation Unit.

Gautam, B. P. (2014). *Financial Development and Economic Growth in Nepal*. NRB Working Paper 25/2013. Nepal Rastra Bank, Research Department.

Gautam, B. P. (2013). Consolidation of Financial System in Changing Times: A case of Nepal.*Conference Proceeding of International Istanbul Finance Congress*. Istanbul: Turkey.

Gayğusuz, F. (2008). Hisse Senedi Piyasalarında İşlem Hacmi- Volatilite İlişkisi ve İMKB'ye Ait Bir Uygulama. *Çukurova Üniversitesi İİBF Dergisi, 12*(1), 34- 55.

Gayğusuz, F. (2008). *Hisse Senedi Piyasa Volatilitesi ve İşlem Hacmi ile İlişkisi*. Uludağ Üniversitesi Sosyal Bilimler Enstitüsü, Yayınlanmamış Yüksek Lisans Tezi.

Gebremedhin, Y. (2006). *Legal Issues Pertaining to Land Titling and Registration in Afghanistan*. LTERA Report.

Gevurtz, F. A. (2002). Globalization of Insider Trading Prohibitions. *The. Transnat'l Law, 15*, 63.

Gill, S. S., & Madaan, D. K. (2015). *Understanding Non-Tariff Trade Barriers between India and Pakistan*. Academic Press.

Goldsmith, R. W. (1969). *Financial Structure and Development*. New Haven, CT: Yale University Press.

Gopalan, S., & Rajan, R. S. (2015). *How Does Foreign Bank Entry Affect Financial Inclusion in Emerging and Developing Economies?* HKUST Institute for Emerging Market Studies.

Gopinath, S. (2008). Financial Markets in India: Recent Developments and Challenges. Cairo: RBI and FIMMDA-PDAI. Available at http://rbidocs.rbi.org.in/rdocs/Speeches/PDFs/85236.pdf

Gorriz, C. G., & Fumas, V. S. (1996). Ownership Structure and Firm Performance. *Some Empirical Evidence from Spain Managerial and Decision Economics, 17*(6), 575–586. doi:10.1002/(SICI)1099-1468(199611)17:6<575::AID-MDE778>3.0.CO;2-N

Government of Afghanistan. (2008). *Strategy Paper on Launching of the Independent Directorate of Local Governance*. Kabul: Author.

Government of Nepal. (2007). *Securities Act, 2007*. Kathmandu: Government of Nepal.

Goyal, A. (2012). *The future of financial liberalization in South Asia*. Academic Press.

Green, P. G., Brush, C. G., Hart, M. M., & Saparito, P. (2001). Patterns of Venture Capital Funding: Is Gender a Factor? *Venture Capital*, *3*(1), 63–83. doi:10.1080/13691060118175

Griffith-Jones, S., & Ocampo, J. A. (2009). *The financial crisis and its impact on developing countries*. Working Paper. International Policy Centre for Inclusive Growth.

Guérin, I., & Palier, J. (Eds.). (2006). *MicroFinance Challenges: Empowerment or Disempowerment of the Poor?*

Gunathilake, W., De Zoysa, A., & Chandrakumara, P. M. K. (2011). *Corporate governance in Sri Lanka: the status quo*. Academic Press.

Gupta, D. (2015). *Key Barriers Faced in Implementing Financial Inclusion*. Academic Press.

Gupta, L. C. (1969). *The changing structure of Industrial Finance in India*. Oxford University Press.

Gupta, L. C. (1998). What Ails the Indian Capital Market? *Economic and Political Weekly*, *23*(29-30).

Gupta, S. C. (2003). Banking Industry Vision 2010. *Risk Management*, *23*, 25.

Gurley, J., & Shaw, E. (1955). Financial Aspects of Development and Growth. *The American Economic Review*, (September), 515–538.

Gurung, J. B. (2010). Insurance and Its Business in Nepal. *Journal of Nepalese Business Studies*, *7*(1), 70–79. doi:10.3126/jnbs.v7i1.6409

Hameed, F. (2006, December). Fostering the corporate bond market in Pakistan. In *IInd SBP International Conference on Fixed Income Market Development in Emerging Market Economies. State Bank of*PakistanLearning Resource Center.

Har-An, & Maimbo, S. (2003). *The Money Exchange Dealers of Kabul: A study of the Hawala System in Afghanistan*. World Bank Working Paper No. 13.

Hassan, M. K., Islam, A. M., & Basher, S. A. (2000). *Market Efficiency, Time-Varying Volatility and Equity Returns in Bangladesh Stock Market*. Ibrahim Khalid Committee Sharer Probe Report. Retrieved from http://www.mof.gov.bd/en/index.php?option=com_content&view=article&id=169&Itemid=1

Hassan, M. K., Sanchez, B., & Yu, J.-S. (2011). Financial development and economic growth: New evidence from panel data. *The Quarterly Review of Economics and Finance*, *51*(1), 88–104. doi:10.1016/j.qref.2010.09.001

Hindustan Times. (2014, August 17). *RBI forms committee to monitor shadow banking; realty in focus*. Retrieved from http://www.hindustantimes.com/business-news/rbi-forms-committee-to-monitor-shadow-banking-realty-in-focus/article1-1253148.aspx

Holmes, P., & Wong, M. W. (2001). Foreign investment, regulation and price volatility in South-east Asian stock markets. *Emerging Markets Review*, *2*(4), 371–386. doi:10.1016/S1566-0141(01)00025-5

Hommes, M., Khan, A., Gerber, C., Kipnis, H., & Hamm, K. (2014). Out of the shadows and into the banks: Financing very small and informal enterprises. *Enterprise Development and Microfinance*, *25*(3), 211–225. doi:10.3362/1755-1986.2014.020

Horton, J., Serafeim, G., & Serafeim, I. (2013, Spring). Does Mandatory IFRS Adoption Improve the Information Environment? *Contemporary Accounting Research*, *30*(1), 388–423. doi:10.1111/j.1911-3846.2012.01159.x

Hoskisson, R. E., Lau, L., & Wright, M. (2000). Strategy in emerging economies. *Academy of Management Journal*, *43*(3), 249–267. doi:10.2307/1556394

Howe, J. (2006). The rise of crowdsourcing. *Wired Magazine*, *14*(6), 1-4.

http://www.ibsl.gov.lk. (2007). *Annual Report 2007: Strengthening. Regulating. Protecting. Colombo.* Retrieved 30 December 2015, from http://www.ibsl.gov.lk/images/annual_reports/IBSL%20Annual%20Report%202007.pdf

Husain, I. (2004). *Paper read at Italy-Pakistan Trade and Investment Conference, Rome on September 28, 2004.* Retrieved from http://ishrathusain.iba.edu.pk/ speeches/financialSector/2004/Financial_sector_reforms_in_Pakistan.pdf

Hussain, M. A. (2013). *Effect of Dividend Policy on Market Return Empirical Evidence from South Asia.* Available at SSRN 2206819.

Hussmann, K. (2009). *Joint Donor Responses vis-à-vis Corruption in Afghanistan:Myth or Reality.* OECD.

Hussmann, K., & Tisne, M. (2010). *Integrity in State-Building: Anti-corruption with a State-Building Lens.* OECD Paris.

Ibrahim, T. M., & Shuaibu, M. I. (2013). Financial Development: A Fillip or Impediment to Nigeria's Economic Growth. *International Journal of Economics and Financial Issues, 3*(2), 305–318.

India Times. (2014a, January 20). *RBI sets up a panel to review banks' corporate governance.* Retrieved October 31, 2014, from http://articles.economictimes.indiatimes.com/2014-01-20/news/46374817_1_private-banks-banking-licence-shubhalakshmi-panse

India Times. (2014b, March 3). *RBI switches 30 banks to risk-based supervision.* Retrieved October 31, 2014, from http://articles.economictimes.indiatimes.com/2014-05-03/news/49594370_1_risk-based-supervision-riskbased-supervision-asset-quality

Indian Council for Research on International Economic Relations. (2013). *Reforms to the Financial Sector in South Asian Countries to Promote Economic Growth with Financial System Stability.* Retrieved from http://icrier.org/pdf/DeepakMohanty-PPT.pdf

Insider Trading Regulations - A Primer. (2013). Retrieved from http://www.nishithdesai.com/fileadmin/user_upload/pdfs/Research%20Papers/Insider_Trading_Regulations_-_A_Primer.pdf

Institute for Development and Research in Banking Technology. (2014). *Technology in Banking Towards Improving Business Performance and Customer Engagement.* Retrieved from http://www.idrbt.ac.in/publications/Frameworks/Technology%20in%20Banking%20(2013).pdf

Insurance Board. (2014). Retrieved from www.bsib.org.np

International Monetary Fund. (n.d.). *World Economic Outlook database.* Author.

Iqbal, Z., & Mirakhor, A. (2011). An Introduction to Islamic Finance. Singapore: John Wiley & Sons (Asia) Pte. Ltd. doi:10.1002/9781118390474

Islamic Financial Services Board. (2013). *Islamic Financial Services Stability Report.* Retrieved on September 29, 2014 from http://www.ifsb.org/docs/IFSB%20-%20IFSI%20Stability%20Report%202013%20%28Final%29.pdf

Jadhav, N. (2003). *Financial Sector Reforms and Role of RBI.* Retrieved from http://drnarendrajadhav.info/drnjadhav_web_files/speeches/NDC-speech.pdf

Jain, R. (2013). *Overview of the International Financial Instruments Issued from Sri Lanka.* Available at SSRN 2312253.

Jain, S., & Bhanumurthy, N. R. (2005). Financial Markets Integration in India. Asia-Pacific Development Journal, 10(2).

Jalil, A., & Feridun, M. (2011). Impact of financial development on economic growth: Empirical evidence from Pakistan. *Journal of the Asia Pacific Economy, 16*(1), 71–80. doi:10.1080/13547860.2011.539403

Jennings, R. H., & Barry, C. (1983). Information Dissemination and Portfolio Choice. *Journal of Financial and Quantitative Analysis*, *18*(1), 1–19. doi:10.2307/2330801

Jones, K., & Tullous, R. (2002). Behaviours of Pre-Venture Entrepreneurs and Perceptions of Their Financial Needs. *Journal of Small Business Management*, *40*(3), 233–249. doi:10.1111/1540-627X.00053

Joseph, E. (1989). Financial Markets and Development. *Oxford Review of Economic Policy*, *5*(4).

Judge, W. Q., Douglas, T. J., & Kutan, A. M. (2008). Institutional antecedents of corporate governance legitimacy. *Journal of Management*, *34*(4), 765–785. doi:10.1177/0149206308318615

Kafle, P. K. (1990). *Monetary and Financial Reforms in Nepal: Implication for Adjustment and growth*. Economic Review Occasional Paper Number 4.

Kafle, D. R. (2004). *Towards Good Corporate Governance. SEBON Journal Special Publication*. Security Board of Nepal.

Kaminsky, G., & Schmukler, S. (2002). *Short and Long-Run Integration: Do capital controls matter*. Publication at World Bank Discussion.

Kane, M. T. (1983). Evidence that protease action is not specifically involved in hatching of rabbit blastocysts caused by commercial bovine serum albumin in culture. *Journal of Reproduction and Fertility*, *68*(2), 471–475. doi:10.1530/jrf.0.0680471 PMID:6688094

Kapadia, J. (1992). Insider Trading: SEBI on Test. *Economic and Political Weekly*, 2571–2572.

Karpoff, J. M. (1987). The Relationship Between the Price Changes and Trading Volume: A Survey. *Journal of Financial and Quantitative Analysis*, *23*(1), 109–126. doi:10.2307/2330874

Kaur, R., & Bawa, S. (1992). Psychological Correlates of Entrepreneurial Performance among Women. *The Journal of Entrepreneurship*, *8*(2), 195–205. doi:10.1177/097135579900800204

Kemal, A. R. (2002). Economy and the Government: Privatisation and Regulation in Pakistan. Islamabad: Pakistan Institute of Development Economics.

Kershaw, D. (2005). Evading Enron: Taking Principles Too Seriously in Accounting Regulation. *The Modern Law Review*, *68*(4), 2005. doi:10.1111/j.1468-2230.2005.00552.x

Khaled, K. I. (2011). *Investigation report of Probe Committee*. Academic Press.

Khan, H. (2013). *Indian Financial Markets: Fuelling the Growth of the Indian Economy*. Speech, inaugural session of the conference on Indian Financial Markets: Fuelling the Growth of the Indian Economy organized by the Confederation of Indian Industry at the ADB Annual Conference, Delhi, India.

Khanal, D. R. (2003). *Why Economic Reform Failed in Nepal: 9 Reasons*. Kathmandu: New Business Age.

Khan, M. Y. (1997). *Financial Services*. New Delhi: Tata Mc-Graw Hill.

Kharel, R. S., & Pokhrel, D. R. (2012). Does Nepal's Financial Structure Matter for Economic Growth? *NRB Economic Review*, *24*(2), 31–46.

Khatkhatay, M. H. (2009a, August). *Road to Islamic Banking in India*. Paper presented at Seminar on Islamic Banking and Finance, Bhatkal, India.

Khatkhatay, M. H. (2009b, October). *Some Thoughts and Suggestions on Muslim Participation in the Finance Sector*. Paper presented at National Seminar on Economic Advancement of Indian Muslims: Situations, Scope and the Islamic Guidance, India.

Khatkhatay, M. H. (2011, May). *Islamic Real Estate Venture Capital in India.* Paper presented at Seminar on Venture Capital Financing organised by the Institute of Objective Studies (IOS), New Delhi, India.

Klapper, L., Laeven, L., & Rajan, R. (2006). Entry regulation as a barrier to entrepreneurship. *Journal of Financial Economics*, *82*(3), 591–629. doi:10.1016/j.jfineco.2005.09.006

Kleimeier, S., & Sander, H. (2000). Regionalisation versus globalisation in European financial market integration: Evidence from cointegration analysis. *Journal of Banking & Finance*, *24*(6), 1005–1043. doi:10.1016/S0378-4266(99)00116-8

Kohli, R. (2001). *Capital Flows and their Macroeconomic effects in India.* Indian Council for Research on International Economic Relations. Available at http://www.icrier.org/pdf/renu64.pdf

Kohli, R. (2001). *Capital Flows and their Macroeconomic effects in India.* Indian Council for Research on International Economic.

KPMG. (2000). *Final Report on Nepal Banking Reform Project: Nepal Bank Limited and Rastriya Banijya Bank.* Kathmandu: KPMG Barents Group.

Kräussl, R. (2003). *Do Credit Rating Agencies Add to the Dynamics of Emerging Market Crises?* CFS Working Paper No 2003/18 August 2003. Retrieved from: http://www.frbatlanta.org/news/conferen/fsc04/kraeussl.pdf

Krishnan, K. P. (2011). *Financial Development in Emerging Markets: The Indian Experience.* ADBI Working Paper 276. Tokyo: Asian Development Bank Institute.

Kuchhal, S C. (n.d.). *Industrial Economy of India* (18th ed.). Chaitanya Publications.

Kumar, M. (n.d.). Banking Sector reforms in India. *International Research Journal of Commerce Arts and Science.*

Kumar, M. (n.d.). Banking Sector reforms in India. *International Research Journal of Commerce Arts and Science.* Available at http:www.casirj.com

Kumari, S. S. M. (2014). Determinants of Interest Margins of Banks in Sri Lanka. *South Asia Economic Journal*, *15*(2), 265–280. doi:10.1177/1391561414548952

Kutan, A. M., Muradoglu, G., & Sudjana, B. G. (2012). IMF programs, financial and real sector performance, and the Asian crisis. *Journal of Banking & Finance*, *36*(1), 164–182. doi:10.1016/j.jbankfin.2011.06.015

Lacombe, A. V., & Olaso, R.-M. H. (1999). *Nepal: Assessment of Compliance with the BASLE Core Principles for Effective Banking Supervision.* Washington, DC: The World Bank.

LaPorta, R., Lopez-de-Silanes, F., Shleifer, A., & Vishny, R. (2000). Investor Protection and Corporate Governance. *Journal of Financial Economics*, *58*(1-2), 3–27. doi:10.1016/S0304-405X(00)00065-9

La-Porta, R., Silanes, F. L., Shleifer, A., & Vishny, R. W. (1997). Legal Determinants of External Finance. *The Journal of Finance*, *52*(3), 1131–1150. doi:10.1111/j.1540-6261.1997.tb02727.x

Lautze, S. E., Stites, N., Nojumi, F., & Najimi. (2002). Qaht-e-Pool: A Cash Famine: Food Insecurity in Aghanistan. Tufts University.

Lemmon, G. T. (2012). *Entrepreneurship in Postconflict Zones.* Working Paper.

Leon, L. K. (2007). An Empirical Study of The Relation Between Stock Return Volatility and Trading Volume in the BRVM. *African Journal of Business Management*, *1*(7), 176–184.

Le, V., Venkatesh, S., & Nguyen, T. V. (2006). Getting bank financing: A study of Vietnamese private firms. *Asia Pacific Journal of Management*, *23*(2), 209–227. doi:10.1007/s10490-006-7167-8

Levine, R. (2004). *Finance and Growth: Theory and Evidence.* NBER Working Paper No. 10766.

Levine, R. (1997). Financial development and economic growth: Views and agenda. *Journal of Economic Literature, 35*, 688–726.

Levine, R., Loayza, N., & Beck, T. (2000). Financial intermediation and growth: Causality and causes. *Journal of Monetary Economics, 46*(1), 31–77. doi:10.1016/S0304-3932(00)00017-9

Lines, B. (2012). *Secura Launches Real Estate Venture Capital Fund.* Kochi, India: Business Line. Retrieved on September 22, 2014 from http://www.thehindubusinessline.com/markets/secura-launches-real-estate-venture-capital-fund/article4139782.ece

Lister, S., & Pain, A. (2004). *Trading in Power: The Politics of Free Markets in Afghanistan.* AREU.

Lovells. (2009). *Islamic Finance Regulations in Non-OIC Jurisdictions.* Indian Centre for Islamic Finance.

Mahalingam, G. (2015). *Some Thoughts on Forex Markets in India.* Speech, Key Note Address on February 25, 2015 at the India Treasury Summit, Mumbai, India.

Mahat, R. S. (1981). *Capital market, financial flows, and industrial finance in Nepal* (1st ed.). Sajha Prakashan.

Map, R. (2008). *Monetary and Financial Sector Policies 2008 and beyond.* Colombo.

March, J., & Olsen, J. P. (1989). *The Organizational Basis of Politics.* New York: The Free Press.

Marlow, S., & Patton, D. (2007). All Credit to Men? Entrepreneurship,Finance and Gender. *Entrepreneurship Theory and Practice, 29*(6), 717–735. doi:10.1111/j.1540-6520.2005.00105.x

Masuduzzaman, M., Rahman, M. H., & Ahammed, S. (2013). *Integration of Financial Market and its implication of Stock Market Development in Bangladesh: An evaluation.* Working Paper Series- WP 1304. Policy Analysis Unit, Bangladesh Bank.

May, E., Bell, S.C., & Islam, R. (2008). *Housing Finance in Afghanistan: Challenges and Opportunities.* The World Bank Report.

McKinnon, R. I. (1973). *Money and capital in economic development.* Brookings Institution Press.

Mead, D., & Liedholm, C. (1998). The Dynamics of Micro and Small Enterprises in Developing Countries. *World Development, 26*(1), 61–74. doi:10.1016/S0305-750X(97)10010-9

Merton, R. C. (1992). Financial Innovation and Economic Performance. *Journal of Applied Corporate Finance, 4*(4), 12–22. doi:10.1111/j.1745-6622.1992.tb00214.x

Metzger, M. (2010). *Trends in Financial market development in South Asia.* Available at: http://www.icrier.org/pdf/martina%20metzger-paper.pdf

Metzger, M. (2010). Trends in Financial Market Development in South Asia. New Delhi: MOF.

Meyer, K., & Nguyen, V. H. (2005). Foreign investment strategies and sub-national institutions in emerging market: Evidence from Vietnam. *Journal of Management Studies, 42*(1), 63–93. doi:10.1111/j.1467-6486.2005.00489.x

Microfinance, S. (2012). Multi-state Cooperative Society Act, 2002. New Delhi, India.

Miller, M. H. (1986). Financial Innovation: The last twenty years and next. *Journal of Financial and Quantitative Analysis.* Retrieved January 14th 2015, from http://countrystudies.us/afghanistan

Ministry of Commerce and Industries. (n.d.). *Islamic republic of Afghanistan*. Retrieved 15th January 2015, from http://moci.gov.af/en/page/550

Ministry of Finance and Planning. Sri Lanka. (2012). *Annual Report*. Retrieved from http://www.treasury.gov.lk/reports/annualreport/2012/7-Rerorms.pdf

Ministry of Finance, Government of Pakistan. (2007). Pakistan Economic Survey 2006-07. Islamabad: Finance Division, Economic Advisor's wing, Ministry of Finance, Government of Pakistan.

Ministry of Finance. (2014). *The Indian Infrastructure Debt Funds*. New Delhi, India: Government of India Publication. Retrieved on September 29, 2014 from http://www.finmin.nic.in/the_ministry/dept_eco_affairs/infrastructure_div/IDF_Brochure0062014.pdf

Ministry of Home Affairs. (2011). *Census of India 2011 Primary Census Abstract Figure at a Glance, India*. New Delhi, India: Ministry of Home Affairs, Government of India. Retrieved on September 29, 2014 from http://www.censusindia.gov.in/2011census/PCA/PCA_Highlights/pca_highlights_file/India/5Figures_at_glance.pdf

Mishra, S. K. (n.d.). *Money, Income and Financial Institutions* (5th ed.). Pragati Publications.

MOF. (2014a). *Budget Speech for the Fiscal Year 2014/15*. Kathmandu: Ministry of Finance.

MOF. (2014b). *Economic Survey for the Fiscal Year 2013/14*. Kathmandu: Ministry of Finance.

Mohan, R. (2004). *A Decade of Reforms in Government Securities Market in India and the Road Ahead*. Mumbai: Reserve Bank of India. Available at: http://rbidocs.rbi.org.in/rdocs/Speeches/PDFs/60551.pdf

Mohan, R. (2007). *Development of Financial Markets in India*. Mumbai: Reserve Bank of India. Retrieved from http://rbidocs.rbi.org.in/rdocs/Speeches/PDFs/77375.pdf

Mohan, R. (2007). India's Financial Sector Reforms: Fostering Growth While Containing Risk. BIS Review, 145, 1-24.

Mohan, R. (2011). Growth with Financial Stability: Central Banking in an Emerging Market (OUP Catalogue). Oxford University Press. Retrieved from http://ideas.repec.org/b/oxp/obooks/9780198070207.html

Mohan, R. (2013). Financial Sector Reforms and monetary policy. *Economic Reform in India: Challenges, Prospects, and Lessons*, 139.

Mohan, R. (2005). Financial sector reforms in India: Policies and performance analysis. *Economic and Political Weekly*, 1106–1121.

Mohanty, D. (2012). *Money Market and Monetary Operations in India*. Mumbai: RBI. Available at: http://rbidocs.rbi.org.in/rdocs/Speeches/PDFs/SMMIED171212.pdf

Mohanty, D. (2014). *Reforms to the Financial Sector in South Asian Countries to Promote Economic Growth with Financial System Stability*. Retrieved from: www.icrier.org/pdf/DeepakMohanty-PPT.pdf

Molyneux, P., Nguyen, L. H., & Xie, R. (2013). Foreign bank entry in South East Asia. *International Review of Financial Analysis*, *30*, 26–35. doi:10.1016/j.irfa.2013.05.004

Monger. (2013). *Why Accounting and Auditing Are Critical To Banking and Microfinance*. Academic Press.

Mu, Y. (n.d.). *South Asia Bond Markets South Aisa Bond Markets: Bangladesh*. 10.2139/ssrn.999713

Muravyev, A., Talavera, O., & Schäfer, D. (2009). Entrepreneurs' gender and financial constraints: Evidence from international data. *Journal of Comparative Economics*, *37*(2), 270–286. doi:10.1016/j.jce.2008.12.001

Muzaffar, A. T., & Chowdhury, A. (2014). The IMF and the policy of low inflation: A review of Article IV consultations for selected Asian developing countries. *Economic and Labour Relations Review*, *25*(3), 435–454. doi:10.1177/1035304614544272

Narasimham Committee Report. (1997). *Report of the Committee on Banking Sector Reform*. Reserve Bank of India.

Narasimham Report. (1991). *Report of the Committee on the Financial System*. Reserve Bank of India.

National Bank for Agricultural and Rural Development. (2014). *The Banking Regulation Act, 1949*. Mumbai, India: National Bank for Agricultural and Rural Development Publication. Retrieved on September 20, 2014 from https://www.nabard.org/pdf/India_Banking_BankingRegulationAct1949.pdf

Nayak, G. (2014, October 22). *Credit information bureaus rely on counselling to expand footprint*. Retrieved October 30, 2014, from http://economictimes.indiatimes.com/industry/banking/finance/banking/credit-information-bureaus-rely-on-counselling-to-expand-footprint/articleshow/44903908.cms

Nguyen, C. V., Islam, A. M., & Ali, M. M. (2011). *The Current State of the Financial Sector of Bangladesh: An Analysis* (AIUB Bus Econ Working Paper Series No. AIUB-BUS-ECON-2011-03). American International University-Bangladesh, Office of Research and Publications (ORP). Retrieved from http://econpapers.repec.org/paper/aiuabewps/89.htm

Nicholas, C., et al. (n.d.). *Economic Reform India Challenges Prospects And Lessons | Economic development and growth | Cambridge University Press*. Retrieved July 28, 2014, from http://www.cambridge.org/us/academic/subjects/economics/economic-development-and-growth/economic-reform-india-challenges-prospects-and-lessons

Nimrah, K., Tarazi, M., & Reille, X. (2008, August). *Islamic Microfinance: An Emerging Market Niche*. Focus Note: 49. Washington, DC: Consultative Group to Assist the Poor (CGAP). Retrieved on September 29, 2014 from http://www.cgap.org/sites/default/files/CGAP-Focus-Note-Islamic-Microfinance-An-Emerging-Market-Niche-Aug-2008.pdf

Nobes, C. (2004). *Rules-based Standards and the Lack of Principles in Accounting*. Retrieved from: http://www.econ.upf.edu/docs/seminars/nobes.pdf

NRB. (1996). *Forty Years of the Nepal Rastra Bank (1956 - 1996)*. Kathmandu: Nepal Rastra Bank.

NRB. (2003). *Banking and Financial Statistics, No. 41*. Kathmandu: Nepal Rastra Bank, Bank and Financial Institution Regulation Department.

NRB. (2005). *Nepal Rastra Bank in Fifty Years. Part II: Financial System*. Kathmandu: Nepal Rastra Bank.

NRB. (2012). *Annual Report for the Fiscal Year 2011/12*. Kathmandu: Nepal Rastra Bank Research Department.

NRB. (2012). Quarterly. *Economic Bulletin*, *46*(4).

NRB. (2013). *Banking and Financial Statistics, No. 59*. Kathmandu: Nepal Rastra Bank, Bank and Financial Institution Regulation Department.

NRB. (2014a). *NRB, Then Now and Ahead*. Kathmandu: Nepal Rastra Bank.

NRB. (2014b). *Monetary Policy for Fiscal Year 2014/15*. Kathmandu: Nepal Rastra Bank.

NRB. (2014c). *Current Macroeconomic Situation (Based on Annual Data of FY 2013/14)*. Kathmandu: Nepal Rastra Bank, Research Department.

NRB. (2014d). *Annual Report for Fiscal Year 2013/14*. Kathmandu: Nepal Rastra Bank.

NRCs Country Programme in Afghanistan. (n.d.). Retrieved 18th January 2015, from http://www.nrc.no/afghanistan

Nseindia.com. (2015). *NSE - National Stock Exchange of India Ltd.* Retrieved 30 December 2015, from http://www.nseindia.com/int_invest/content/regulatory_framework.htm

O'Donnell. (2014). *New Afghan mining law lacks transparency.* Retrieved 14th January 2015, from http://www.scmp.com/business/commodities/article/1579556/new-afghan-mining-law-lacks-transparency-say-experts

Obaidullah, M. (2008). *Introduction to Islamic Microfinance.* Jeddah, Saudi Arabia: Islamic Research & Training Institute (IRTI), Islamic Development Bank (IDB).

Obsfeld, M., & Taylor, M. A. (2002). *Globalization and Capital Markets.* National Bureau of Economic Research (Working Paper Number 8846).

Ojo, M. (2006). Audit Independence: Its Importance to the External Auditor's Role in Banking Regulation and Supervision. Retrieved from http://econpapers.repec.org/paper/pramprapa/231.htm

Ojo, M. (2006). Avoiding Another Enron: The Role of the External Auditor in Financial Regulation and Supervision. ICFAI University Press.

Ojo, M. (2009). The Role of the IASB and Auditing Standards in the Aftermath of the 2008/2009 Financial Crisis (September 2009). *European Law Journal, 16*(5).

Ojo, M. (2013). *Audits, Audit Quality and Signaling Mechanisms: Concentrated Ownership Structures.* Paper presented at the 2014 IBFR Conference, San Jose, Costa Rica. Retrieved from: http://www.theibfr.com/ARCHIVE/ISSN-1941-9589-V9-N2-2014.pdf

Ojo, M. (2013). *Why the Traditional Principal Agent Theory May No Longer Apply To Concentrated Ownership Systems and Structures.* Paper Presented at the PSRC Conference, Johannesburg, South Africa.

Ong, Ş. H., & Mun, H. C. (2011). Testing For Linear And Nonlinear Granger Causality In The Stock Return And Stock Trading Volume Relation: Malaysia And Singapore Cases. *Labuan Bulletin of International Business & Finance, 9*, 44–57.

Overview of Fuller Capital Account Convertibility and the Committee's Approach. (2011). Retrieved from https://rbidocs.rbi.org.in/rdocs/PublicationReport/Pdfs/72252.pdf2007

Padmanabhan, G. (2011). *Forex market development: Issues and challenges—Thoughts of a returning forex market regulator.* Singapore: RBI and Forex Association of India. Retrieved from http://rbidocs.rbi.org.in/rdocs/Speeches/PDFs/EDGPS110811.pdf

Partlow, J. (2009). Afghan Minister Accused of Taking Bribe. *Washington Post.*

Pathak, B. V. (2003). *Indian Financial System.* Pearson Education India.

Paudel, N. P. (2007). *Financial Market and Portfolio Management in Nepal.* Kathmandu, Nepal: Wangmaya Publishers and Research Center.

Pavlovic, J., & Charap, J. (2009). *Development of Commercial Banking System in Afghanistan: Risks and Rewards.* International Monetary Fund.

Peng, M. W., & Heath, P. S. (1996). The growth of the firm in planned economies in transition: Institutions, organizations, and strategic choice. *Academy of Management Review, 21*(2), 492–528.

Perera, A., & Wickramanayake, J. (2012). Financial integration in selected South Asian countries. *South Asian Journal of Global Business Research, 1*(2), 210–237. doi:10.1108/20454451211252741

Pethe, A., & Karnik, A. (2000). Do Indian Stock Market Indices and Macro Economic Variables. *Economic and Political Weekly*, *35*(5), 349-356.

Pope, N. D. (2010). Crowdfunding Microstartups: It's Time for the Securities and Exchange Commission to Approve a Small Offering Exemption. *U. Pa. J. Bus. L.*, *13*, 973.

Prakash, B. A. (n.d.). The Indian Economy Since 1991: Economic Reforms and Performance. Pearson Education.

Prasad, E. S. (2010). *Financial Sector Regulation and Reforms in Emerging Markets: An Overview* (Working Paper No. 16428). National Bureau of Economic Research. Retrieved from http://www.nber.org/papers/w16428

Prasad, E., Rajan, R., & Subramanian, A. (2016). *Finance and Development. Finance and Development F&D*. Retrieved on 8 August 2015, from http://www.imf.org/external/pubs/ft/fandd/2007/03/prasad.htm

Preet Bharara. (2010). *The Future of White Collar Enforcement: A Prosecutor's View*. New York Bar Association.

Preferential Trade Agreement between India & Islamic State Of Afghanistan. (n.d.). Retrieved 12th October 2014, from http://commerce.nic.in/trade/international_ta_indafg.asp

Qargha, O., & Besmel, P. (2014). *Mortgage Market Assessment in 5 Major Cities of Afghanistan. Harakat*. Afghanistan Investment Climate Facility Organization.

Qayyum, A. (n.d.). *Financial Sector Reforms and the Efficiency of Banking in Pakistan Islamabad*. Pakistan Institute of Development Economics. Retrieved from http://saneinetwork.net/Files/08_11.pdf

Rabiul, Wahidul, & Habib-uz-Zaman. (2004). Time Series Analysis of Finance and Growth. *The Bangladesh Development Studies*, *30*(1/2), 111-128. Accessed from http://www.jstor.org/stable/40795689

Rahman, J. (2011). *Share Market Bubble -the Big Picture*. Retrieved from http://dpwriters.wordpress.com/2011/02/04/share-market-bubble-the-big-picture

Raisa, A. (2011). *Behind the Scenes The Stock Market Saga*. Retrieved from http://www.thedailystar.net/magazine/2011/01/03/cover.htm

Rajan. (2009). The Global Crisis and Financial Sector Reforms in India. *Business Standard India*, *2009*, 142.

Rajan, R. G., & Zingales, L. (1995). What Do We Know about Capital Structure? Some Evidence from International Data. *The Journal of Finance*, *50*(5), 1421–1460. doi:10.1111/j.1540-6261.1995.tb05184.x

Rangarajan, C. (1998). *India's Financial Markets changes and challenges*. Available at: http://www.iief.com/Research/tushar_chp1.pdf

Rawal, T. B. (2003). *Corporate Governance and Financial Sector Reform in Nepal*. Kathmandu: Society for International Development.

Rawal, T. B. (2004). *Policy Paper on Financial Sector Reform*. Kathmandu: Nepal Rastra Bank.

Ray, P., & Prabhu, E. (2013). *Financial Development and Monetary Policy Transmission Across Financial Markets: What Do Daily Data Tell for India?* Mumbai: Department of Economic and Policy Research, Reserve Bank of India.

Read, L. (1998). *The Financing of Small Business: a Comparative Study of Male and Female Business Owners*. New York: Routledge. doi:10.4324/9780203024942

Real Interest Rate (%). (2013). Retrieved from http://data.worldbank.org/indicator/FR.INR.RINR

Reddy, Y. V. (2006). Reforming India's Financial Sector – Changing Dimensions and Emerging Issues. Address at the International Centre for Monetary and Banking Studies. BIS Review, 39, 1-6.

Regmi, U. R. (2010). Relationship between Financial Development and Economic Growth in Nepal. *The Economic Journal of Nepal*, *33*, 231–240.

Renu, K. (2005). *Liberalizing Capital Flows: India's Experience and Policy Issues.* Oxford University Press.

Reserve Bank of India. (2011). *Guide Lines to NBFC-MFI* (Notification DNBS. PD. No. 234 dated December 02, 2011 enclosed with RBI Letter reference: RBI/2011-12/290 dated December 02, 2011). Mumbai, India: RBI Publication. Retrieved on September 22, 2014 from http://www.rbi.org.in/scripts/NotificationUser.aspx?Id=6857&Mode=0

Reserve Bank of India. (2013). *Non-Banking Financial Institutions.* Retrieved October 29, 2014, from http://www.rbi.org.in/scripts/PublicationsView.aspx?id=15442

Reserve Bank of India. (2014). *RBI Act, 1934.* Retrieved on September 22, 2014 from http://rbidocs.rbi.org.in/rdocs/Publications/PDFs/RBIA1934170510.pdf

Rezaie, M. (2011). *Afghanistan needs a modern stock exchange.* Retrieved 8th October 2014, from http://outlookafghanistan.net/topics.php

Risen, J. (n.d.). U.S. Identifies Vast Mineral Riches in Afghanistan. *New York Times.* Retrieved 14th January 2015, from http://www.nytimes.com/2010/06/14/world/asia/14minerals.html

Rodriguez, P., Uhlenbruck, K., & Eden, L. (2005). Government corruption and the entry strtergies of multinationals. *Academy of Management Review*, *30*(2), 383–396. doi:10.5465/AMR.2005.16387894

Rojas-Suarez, L. (2002). *Rating Banks in Emerging Markets: What Credit Agencies Should Learn From Financial Indicators.* Retrieved from: http://papers.ssrn.com/sol3/papers.cfm?abstract_id=300891

Ronald, J. L., & Meyer, J. W. (1991). *The Public Order and the Construction of Formal Organizations.* Chicago: University of Chicago Press.

Rubin, B. R. (2007). *Salvaging Afghanistan: Testimony before the United States Senate Armed Services Committee.* Washington, DC: U.S. Government Printing Office.

Sa-Dhan Microfinance Resource Centre. (2006). *Existing Legal and Regulatory Frame work for the Microfinance Institutions in India: Challenges and Implications.* New Deli, India: Sa-Dhan. Retrieved on September 29, 2014 from http://www.sa-dhan.net/Adls/Microfinance/Article/Publications/ExistingLegalRegulatoryFramework.pdf

Saha, M. (2012). *Indian Economy and Growth of Financial Market in the Contemporary Phase of the Globalization Era.* Academic Press.

Sahoo, P., & Dash, R. K. (2013). Financial sector development and domestic savings in South Asia. *Economic Modelling*, *33*, 388–397. doi:10.1016/j.econmod.2013.04.018

SANEI. (2007). *Study on Financial Sector Reform in Nepal.* Islamabad: South Asian Network of Economic Institutes Pakistan Institute of Development Economics.

Sarbanes Oxley Act 2002

Sarkar, J. (2011). Ownership and Corporate Governance in Indian Firms. In N. Balasubramanian & D. M. Satwalekar (Eds.), Corporate Governance - An Emerging Scenario (pp. 152-89). National Stock Exchange of India.

Sarkar, J., & Sarkar, S. (2010). „Large Shareholder Activism in Corporate Governance in Developing Countries: Evidence from India. *International Review of Finance, 1*(3), 161–194. doi:10.1111/1468-2443.00010

Sbp.org.pk. (2015). *State Bank of Pakistan - Annual Report 2001-2002*. Retrieved 30 December 2015, from http://www.sbp.org.pk/Reports/Annual/arFY02/qtr-index-eng.htm

Scalera, D., & Zazzaro, A. (2001). Group reputation and persistent (or permanent) discrimination in credit markets. *Journal of Multinational Financial Management, 11*(4-5), 483–496. doi:10.1016/S1042-444X(01)00037-8

Schultze, W. G., Lubatkin, M. H., & Dino, R. N. (2003). *Exploring the Agency Consequences of Ownership Dispersion Among the Directors of Private Family Firms. Academy of Management Journal, 46*(2), 179–194.

Schwert, G. W. (1989). Why Does Stock Markets Volatility Changes Over Time? *The Journal of Finance, 44*(5), 1115–1154. doi:10.1111/j.1540-6261.1989.tb02647.x

Schwert, G. W. (1990). Stock Market Volatility. *Financial Analysts Journal, 46*(3), 23–34. doi:10.2469/faj.v46.n3.23

SEBI. (2002). Securities and exchange board of India (prohibition of insider trading). *Regulations, 1992*, 1–21.

SEBI. (2013). Report of the high level committee to review the SEBI (prohibition of insider trading). *Regulations, 1992*, 1–78.

Securities and Exchange Commission of Pakistan. (2001). *Listed companies (prohibition of insiders trading) guidelines*. Islamabad: Securities and Exchange Commission of Pakistan.

Securities and Exchange Commission Sri Lanka. (2003). Company Take-overs and Mergers Code 1995, as amended in 2003. Colombo: Securities and Exchange Commission, Sri Lanka.

Securities and Exchange Commission v. W. J. Howey Co, 163 A.L.R 1043 (US Supreme Court 1946).

Securities Exchange Board of India. (2014a). *Securities Exchange Board of India-Venture Capital Fund Regulations, 1996*. Mumbai, India: SEBI Publication. Retrieved on September 22, 2014 from http://www.sebi.gov.in/cms/sebi_data/commondocs/vcregu_p.pdf

Securities Exchange Board of India. (2014b). *Securities Exchange Board of India-Foreign Venture Capital Investor Regulations, 2000*. Mumbai, India: SEBI Publication. Retrieved on September 22, 2014 from http://www.sebi.gov.in/acts/fvcregu.pdf

Security and Exchange Commission. (n.d.). Retrieved from http://www.secbd.org

Seelanatha, L., & Wickremasinghe. (2009). Financial reforms in Sri Lanka and their influence on the banking industry. *Banks and Bank Systems, 4*(4).

Seelanatha, L. (2010). Market structure, efficiency and performance of banking industry in Sri Lanka. *Banks and Bank Systems, 5*(1), 20–31.

Sen Kunal and Vaidya R.R. (1997). *The process of Financial Liberalisation in India*. Oxford University Press.

Senier, A. (2006). *Rebuilding the Judicial Sector in Afghanistan: The Role of Customary law*. The Fletcher School Online Journal.

Shah, A., & Patnaik I. (2011). *Reforming the Indian financial System and India's Financial Globalization*. Academic Press.

Shahbaz, M., & Islam, F. (2011, January 15). *Financial development and income inequality in Pakistan: An application of ARDL approach*. MPRA Paper. Retrieved July 28, 2014, from http://mpra.ub.uni-muenchen.de/28222/

Shakey Foundation. (2013). *Analyzing Afghanistan's Draft Mining Law*. Retrieved 11th January 2015, http://www.jordantimes.com/news/business/speculators-spoil-trading-activities-amman-stock-exchange-%E2%80%94-al-aminhttp://www.globalwitness.org/sites/default/files/library/SHAKEY_FOUNDATION_GW.pdf

Sharma, R., & Sharma, D. (2008). *Role of Stock Exchange in the Development of Indian Capital Market: A Study of National Stock Exchange*. Indianmba.com. Retrieved 4 April 2015, from http://www.indianmba.com/Faculty_Column/FC708/fc708.html

Shaw, E. S. (1973). *Financial Deepening in Economic Development*. New York: Oxford University Press.

Shebergan. (n.d.). *Legal and regulatory analysis report*. Retrieved 15th January 2015, from http://www.afghaneic.com/SheberghanFiles/AEAISFDPLegalandRegulatoryAnalysisReport.pdf

Shison, D. (1984). Venture Capital in the United Kingdom. Bank of England.

Shrestha, G. K. (2004). Financial Sector Reforms in Nepal. *Economic Review*, *16*, 75–90.

Shrestha, G. K. (2004). Financial Sector Reforms in Nepal. *NRB Economic Review*, *16*, 75–90.

Shrestha, M. B. & Chowdhury, K. (2006). Financial Liberalization Index for Nepal. *International Journal of Applied Econometrics and Quantitative Studies*, *3*(1), 41–54.

Shrestha, M. B., & Chowdhury, K. (2007). Testing Financial Liberalization Hypothesis with ARDL Model Approach. *Applied Financial Economics*, *17*(18), 1529–1540. doi:10.1080/09603100601007123

Siddiqui, J., & Ferdous, C. S. (2014). The Regulatory Conundrum: Achieving Corporate Governance Reforms in Developing Countries. In S. Boubaker & D. K. Nguyen (Eds.), *Corporate Governance in Emerging Markets* (pp. 445–464). Springer Berlin Heidelberg. doi:10.1007/978-3-642-44955-0_18

Singh, A. (1997). Financial liberalisation and economic development. *The Economic Journal*, *107*(May), 771–782. doi:10.1111/j.1468-0297.1997.tb00042.x

Sinhal, S. (2005). *Developing Women Entrepreneurs in South Asia: Issues, Initiatives and Experiences*. Trade and Investment Division: ST/ESCAP/2401.

Smithies, A. (1953). Review of The Rate of Interest and Other Essays. *The American Economic Review*, *43*(4), 636–641. Retrieved from http://www.jstor.org/stable/1812414

Smith, V., Suchanek, G., & Williams, A. (1988). Bubbles, Crashes and Endogenous Expectations in Experimental Spot Assest Markets. *Econometrica*, *56*(5), 1119–1151. doi:10.2307/1911361

Sofia, A., Ghulam, S., & Zakir, H. (2011). Relationship between Financial Sector Development and Sustainable Economic Development: Time Series Analysis from Pakistan. *International Journal of Economics and Finance*, *3*(1). doi:10.5539/ijef.v3n1p262

Sophastienphong, K. & Kulathunga, A. (2009). *Getting Finance in South Asia 2009 Indicators and Analysis of the Commercial Banking Sector*. World Bank.

Sophastienphong, K. & Kulathunga, A. (2010). *Getting Finance in South Asia 2010 Indicators and Analysis of the Commercial Banking Sector.* World Bank.

Sorenson, O., & Stuart, T. E. (2001). Syndication Networks and the Spatial Dis-tribution of Venture Capital Investments. *American Journal of Sociology*, *106*(6), 1546–1588. doi:10.1086/321301

Special Inspector General for Afghanistan Reconstruction. (2014). *Afghanistan's banking sector: The central bank's capacity to regulate commercial banks remains weak*. Author.

Special Inspector General for Afghanistan Reconstruction. (2014). *Afghanistan's Banking Sector: The Central Bank's Capacity to Regulate Commercial Banks*. Audit Report.

Speri, A. (2014). *Afghanistan's Opium Economy is doing better than ever*. Retrieved 15th January 2015, from https://news.vice.com/article/afghanistans-opium-economy-is-doing-better-than-ever

Srivastava, A. (2013). *Foreign Exchange Risk Management in India - FICCI Blog*. FICCI blog. Retrieved 19 September 2016, from http://blog.ficci.com/foreign-exchange-india/2834/

State Bank of Pakistan. (2007). *Pakistan Banking Sector Reforms: Performance and Challenges*. Retrieved from http://www.sbp.org.pk/about/speech/governors/dr.shamshad/2007/Banking-Reforms-01-Feb-07.pdf

Stemler, A. R. (2013). The JOBS Act and crowdfunding: Harnessing the power—and money—of the masses. *Business Horizons*, *56*(3), 271–275. doi:10.1016/j.bushor.2013.01.007

Stiglitz, J. (1993). The Role of the State in Financial Matters. In *Proceedings of the World Bank Annual Conference on Development Economics*. Academic Press.

Sullivan, R., Timmermann, A., & White, H. (2003). Forecast Evaluation with Shared Data Sets. *International Journal of Forecasting*, *19*(2), 217–227. doi:10.1016/S0169-2070(01)00140-6

Tahir, M. (2008). An Investigation of the Effectiveness of Financial Development in Pakistan. *The Lahore Journal of Economics*, *13*(2), 27–44.

Taku, Y. (2012). Crowdfunding: Its Practical Effect May Be Unclear Until SEC Rulemaking is Complete. *Bus. L. Today*, 1.

The Economic Times. (2011, March 13). *Number of foreign banks' branches up in India in FY10*. Retrieved October 29, 2014, from http://articles.economictimes.indiatimes.com/2011-03-13/news/28686069_1_new-branches-foreign-banks-royal-bank

The Economic Times. (2014, May 15). *Shares of state-owned banks rally up to 12% after RBI panel moots lower government stake*. Retrieved October 29, 2014, from http://articles.economictimes.indiatimes.com/2014-05-15/news/49873347_1_psu-banks-state-run-banks-public-sector-banks

The Hindu. (2012, May 3). RBI to implement Basel III from January 1, 2013. *The Hindu*. Retrieved from http://www.thehindu.com/business/rbi-to-implement-basel-iii-from-january-1-2013/article3377762.ece

The Indian Capital Market. (2010). *Growth & Governance*. Retrieved from https://www.pwc.in/assets/pdfs/publications-2010/india-captial-market.pdf

The Investment Climate in Afghanistan. (n.d.). *Exploring Opportunities in an Uncertain Environment*. Retrieved 7th October 2014 from http://www.aisa.org.af/presentations/InvestmentClimateAfghanistan.pdf

The United Nations Office on Drugs & Crime. (2013). *Afghanistan's Drug Industry Structure, Functioning, Dynamics and Implications for Counter-Narcotics Policy*. The United Nations.

The World Bank. (2014). *Doing Business and Measuring Business Regulations*. Retrieved 8th January 2015, from http://www.doingbusiness.org/rankings

The World Factbook . (2012). Academic Press.

The, I. M. F. (2003). *An analysis of the informal Hawala system*. The IMF and The World Bank.

Thomas, S. (2006). How the Financial Sector Was Reformed. In Documenting Reforms: Case Studies from India (S. Narayan, ed.). Bangalore, India: Macmillan Publishing India.

Tierney, J.F. (2010). *Warlord, Inc.: Extortion & Corruption Along the US Supply Chain in Afghanistan*. Washington, DC: Academic Press.

TISA and International Agencies. (2004). Securing Afghanistan's Future: Accomplishments and the Strategic Path Forward. Kabul.

Tomar, A. S., & Kashyap, A. K. (2013). Corporate Governance In Indian Capital Market: An Appraisal. *Journal of Business Management & Social Sciences Research*, *2*(5), 5–12.

Tsang, E. (1994). In Search of legitimacy: The private entrepreneur in China. Entrepreneurship Theory and Practice, 21(1), 21–30.

Tysiac, K. (2013). Europe Takes Step Toward Mandatory Audit Firm Rotation. *Journal of Accountancy*, *2013*(April). Retrieved from http://www.journalofaccountancy.com/news/20137862.htm

Uddin, S. M. S., & Suzuki, Y. (2011). Financial Reform, Ownership and Performance in Banking Industry: The Case of Bangladesh. *International Journal of Business and Management*, *6*(7), 28. doi:10.5539/ijbm.v6n7p28

UN Women's flagship report: 2011-2012 Progress of the World's Women: In Pursuit of Justice. (2013). Retrieved from http://progress.unwomen.org/

United States IP. (2006). *The clash of two goods, State and Non-State Dispute Resolution in Afghanistan*. Retrieved 18th January 2015, from http://www.usip.org/sites/default/files/file/clash_two_goods.pdf

Update, B. E. (2013). Economic Policy Unit. *Unnayan Onneshan*, *4*(3), 1–27.

Varma, J. R. (1992). *Commercial Banking; New Vistas and New Priorities*. Paper presented at the seminar on Reforming Commercial Banking, New Delhi, India.

Varma, J. R. (1997). *Indian money market: market structure, covered parity and term structure*. Academic Press.

Varma, J. R. (1997). *Indian Money Market: Market Structure*. Covered Parity and Term Structure.

Verma Report. (1999). *Report of the Working Group on Restructuring Weak Public Sector Banks*. Reserve Bank of India.

Vishwananthan, R. (2001). *Opportunities and challenges for women in business*. Retrieved from http://indiatogether.org/women/business/renuka.htm

Vitols, S. (2001). *The Origins of Bank-Based and Market-Based Financial Systems: Germany, Japan and the United States*. Discussion Paper FS I 01-302. Wissenschaftszentrum Berlin für Sozialforschung.

Vyas, P., & Zaveri, B. (2016). Banking sector reforms in India: Some reflections. Varanasi: School of Management Studies. Retrieved from http://www.smsvaranasi.com/insight/banking_sector_reforms_in_india_some_reflections.pdf

Wellalage, N. H. & Locke, S. (2011). *Corporate Governance and Principal-Principal Conflict in Emerging Market Family Firms*. Academic Press.

Wellalage, N. H. & Locke, S. (2012). Ownership Structure and Firm Financial Performance: Evidence from Panel Data. *Sri Lanka Journal of Business Systems, Governance and Ethics*, *7*(1).

Welter, F., & Smallbone, D. (2011). Institutional Perspectives on Entrepreneurial Behavior in Challenging Environments. *Journal of Small Business Management*, *49*(1), 107–125. doi:10.1111/j.1540-627X.2010.00317.x

Wikipedia. (2016). *Money market in India.* Retrieved 19 July 2015, from https://en.wikipedia.org/wiki/Money_market_in_India

Williams, J., & Nguyen, N. (2005). Financial liberalisation, crisis, and restructuring: A comparative study of bank performance and bank governance in South East Asia. *Journal of Banking & Finance*, *29*(8–9), 2119–2154. doi:10.1016/j.jbankfin.2005.03.011

Women Entrepreneurs in Asia and the Pacific . (2013). Academic Press.

World Bank. (2002). *Nepal Financial Sector Study*. Washington, DC: The World Bank.

World Bank. (2005). *Afghanistan: Managing Public Finances for Development*. Kabul: World Bank.

World Bank. (2005). *The State of the Private Sector*. Retrieved 10th October 2014, from http://siteresources.worldbank.org/SOUTHASIAEXT/Resources/223546-1151200078343/ch2.pdf

World Bank. (2014a, October 6). *Led by India, South Asia Economic Growth to Accelerate, World Bank*. Retrieved October 29, 2014, from http://www.worldbank.org/en/news/press-release/2014/10/06/led-india-south-asia-economic-growth-accelerate

World Bank. (2014b, October 29). *India leads South Asian countries in "doing business" easier: World Bank*. Retrieved October 30, 2014, from http://news.oneindia.in/international/india-leads-south-asian-countries-doing-business-easier-world-bank-1548324.html

World Bank. (2014c). *South Asia Economic Focus Fall 2014: The Export Opportunity*. World Bank Publications.

World Finance. (2016). *Afghanistan Financial Market*. Retrieved 12 January 2015, from http://finance.mapsofworld.com/finance/market/afghanistan.html

Yılancı, V., & Bozoklu, Ş. (2014). Türk Sermaye Piyasasında Fiyat ve İşlem Hacmi İlişkisi: Zamanla Değişen Asimetrik Nedensellik Analizi. *Ege Akademik Bakış*, *14*(2), 211–220.

Young, M. N., Peng, M. W., Ahlstrom, D., Bruton, G. D., & Jiang, Y. (2008). Corporate Governance in Emerging Economies: A Review of the Principal–Principal Perspective. *Journal of Management Studies*, *45*(1), 196–220. doi:10.1111/j.1467-6486.2007.00752.x

Zakhilwal, H. O. (2005). Extending Governance Structures beyond Kabul: Progress and Potential for Development Programs – the Case of NSP. Kabul.

About the Contributors

Amit Kashyap is Director of Centre for Banking Investment & Taxation in Gujarat national law University & Asst. prof of Securities Law. He post Graduate in Law & Finance from National law University, Jodhpur. He is also Consultant to various firms like cyberra legal services Ahmedabad, IIFS pvt. ltd. Ahmadabad & EEIG-Global Commercial Licence, Europe. He has experience of working in prestigious institutes like IIM, Ahmedabad & companies like Kotak Mahindra Bank, Mumbai.

* * *

Md. Azizul Baten currently is working as a Visiting Associate Professor in Department of Decision Science, School of Quantitative Sciences, Universiti Utara Malaysia, 06010 Sintok, Kedah, Malaysia. Previously he had been working in Department of Statistics as a full Professor, School of Physical Sciences, Shahjalal University of Science and Technology (SUST), Bangladesh (on leave). Since 1995, Dr. Baten had about 19 years teaching and research experiences in Bangladesh, Japan, and Malaysia. He completed his Master of Science, B.Sc. (honors) in Statistics from University of Dhaka, Ph.D. in Statistics from Jahangirnagar University, Dhaka, Bangladesh and Post-Doctorate in Operation Research from Universiti Sains Malaysia. His areas of interest are in Stochastic optimization models in control and growth theory; Inventory production models; Stochastic frontier and Meta-frontier production function models; Data Envelopment Analysis. Dr. Baten published over 123 research works including 90 Journal articles into different international journals including ISI science citation and Scopus index, 30 Conference Proceedings and 3 book chapters/books. Earlier he was awarded doctoral Fellowship (MONBUSHO-2000, Japanese Govt. Scholarship) in Japan since October 2000 to March 2004 and at a time he was studied as a research student at Ehime University, Department of Mathematical sciences, Matsuyama, Japan. Dr. Baten is holding the editorial position of different Journals such as World Research Journal of Fuzzy Systems, Journal of Statistics and Mathematics, Agri Crop Science, International Journal of Biotechnology Applications, Continental Journal of Applied Sciences, Cell and Plant Sciences. He is also working as a Managing Director of Center for Research & Training (CRT), Dhaka, Bangladesh. He is also overseas expert of Professor Selection (BPS-21) board in Management Studies in Gomal University, D.I. Khan, Pakistan. Dr. Baten is a member of the following committee (1) Research, Consultation and Publication (2) Promotion and Internationalization in School of Quantitative Sciences, Universiti Utara Malaysia. Having enjoyed Statistics, Mathematics, Econometrics, Operations Research in both the academic and research settings, it is with enthusiasm that he pursued a career in Stochastic optimization models; Stochastic frontier production function models and Inventory models. The area of stochastic optimization, to which, he contributed a fast growing area of research having important applications. As an invited author and speaker he has already presented many articles relevant to my expertise in the department, national and international conferences in Bangladesh and abroad. His research publications include papers in prestigious journals such as IEEE Transactions on Automatic Control, Stochastic Analysis and Applications, Journal of Applied Mathematics and Stochastic Analysis, Journal of Mathematical Sciences, Journal of Probability and Statistics, PLoS ONE, Journal of Intelligent & Fuzzy Systems, International Journal of Applied Mathematics and Statistics etc.

Anchit Bhandari is student of Institute of Law, Nirma University, Ahmedabad & is Student Research Scholar with Centre for Corporate Law Studies, Nirma University. He has authored many articles in the field of corporate law & IPR & part various committees in University & has interned with leading law firms like AZB & Partners and Jyoti Sagar Associates, to name a few, in India. He is also student chairperson of Centre for IP in Nirma University, Ahmedabad.

Aaron Busary is a Director of Operations and Software at Hyveminds Pty Ltd. He is a Management Consultant with MarsHill Solutions.

Michael D'Rosario is a Lecturer and Chair of Financial Markets at Deakin Business School. He is a management consultant with MarsHill Solutions.

Piyadasa Edirisuriya is a Lecturer in the Department of Banking and Finance at Monash University, Australia. He is the Chief Examiner for several undergraduate and post-graduate courses and he conducts research on financial markets and banks in South Asia. His publications have appeared in many refereed academic journals, articles, books, book chapters and book translations. He has a Master's degree in Economics from the University of New England and a PhD in Economics from La Trobe University, Australia. Before becoming an academic, he served as an Economist for the Ministry of Finance, Sri Lanka, for more than 12 years.

Filiz Eryılmaz is affiliated as a research assistant at the Faculty of Economics and Administrative Sciences of Uludağ University in Bursa/Turkey. She graduated with a bachelor's degree in economics department of same university. She holds a Ph.D. degree from Uludağ University. Her current research is focused on fields of new political economy, political business cycles, macroeconomy and financial economy.

Bishnu Prasad Gautam – Doctor of Philosophy (Ph. D.) _ Masters' Degree in Business Administration (MBA): Working Experience and Major Responsibilities Current Position: Deputy Director, Research Department Nepal Rastra Bank, the Central Bank of Nepal. (Apr. 2011-Continue): Updating and applying macroeconomic model and generating other sector-specific models. Conducting both short and long-term research reports and special studies as per the requirement of the bank and look after the various publications. Deputation: Ministry of Finance, Government of Nepal from Nepal Rastra Bank (Apr. 2010 – Jul. 2010 and Feb. 2009 – Aug. 2009) National Cooperative Development Board, Government of Nepal from Nepal Rastra Bank (Feb. 2000 – Jul. 2000): Academic Experience: External Expert (Ph. D. and M. Phil. - Thesis Evaluation and viva-'voce): (i) Tribhuvan University Kathmandu Nepal, LBEF (Sikkim Manipal University India). Faculty Member and Visiting Lecture: Masters Degree in Business Administration (MBA), Presidential Business School affiliated to International American

University and Herald International College affiliated to Anglia Ruskin University and London School of Marketing. Session Chair in International Istanbul Conference (IIFC) – 2013 Contact Person for the International Conference on Economics and Finance Presented Papers in various International Conference/seminars. Publication: various Books and Articles

Abeyratna Gunasekarage is a Senior Lecturer in the Department of Banking and Finance of Monash University, Australia. Prior to joining Monash university he has worked at the University of Canterbury and the University of Waikato in New Zealand. Abey received his BSc Honours from the University of Sri Jayewardenepura, Sri Lanka and MAcc & PhD from the University of Dundee, UK. He has published widely on dividend policy, performance of investment strategies, efficiency of emerging capital markets, Mergers and acquisitions and corporate governance.

Abdur Raqeeb H. is the General Secretary of Indian Center for Islamic Finance. He is a well known expert in India in the area of Islamic banking and Finance. He delivered lectures and presented papers in this subject.

Nirosha Hewa-Wellalage is a Senior Lecturer at The University of Waikato, Department of Finance.

Urvashi Jaswani is Student of Law at Institute of law Nirma University, Ahmedabad. She has authored many papers on Financial market regulations in National Journals. Urvashi is also Student Research Scholar at Centre for Corporate Law Studies, Nirma University, Ahmedabad & is working as a Legal Intern High Court of Rajasthan. She is also Editor of various journals lke Libertatem Magazine, Journal of Centre for IP, Corporate Research Law Journal to name a few.

Vishal Ladhani is a 4th Year B.Com LL.B (Hons.) student at Gujarat National Law University.

Stuart Locke is Professor of Finance at the University of Waikato, New Zealand. Professor Locke's research interests lie in the area of corporate finance, especially relating to governance as it impacts return and risk; microfinance in relation to outreach performance; State and Private ownership performance; financial structure and social performance. Professor Locke has several PhD students from South, South-East and North Asia and Africa and he is particularly interested in research relating to emerging and low income countries. His non academic interests relate to a small property with livestock, cricket and trekking.

Amir Manzoor holds a bachelor's degree in engineering from NED University, Karachi, an MBA from Lahore University of Management Sciences (LUMS), and an MBA from Bangor University, United Kingdom. He has many years of diverse professional and teaching experience working at many renowned national and internal organizations and higher education institutions. His research interests include electronic commerce and technology applications in business.

Gunit Singh Marwah is a 4th Year BBA LL.B (Hons.) student at Gujarat National Law University.

Tanya Nayyar is a BCom LL.B. (Hons.) graduate from Gujarat National Law University, Gandhinagar and is an Associate at a leading Indian law firm.

Marianne Ojo has authored over 80 books, journals and book chapters accredited with ISI credentials. She currently works as a lecturer, Visiting Professor and Scholar at several universities which include North-West University.

Narayan Prasad Paudel, Ph. D. Assistant Professor Kathmandu University School of Management, Lalitpur, Kathmandu, Nepal. Teaching experience: 19 years of teaching experience on graduate and undergraduate programs as a lecturer and assistant professor of Accounting, Project Management and Finance (under Tribhuvan University and Kathmandu University). Corporate and consulting work experience: More than 12 years of corporate and consulting work experience under various government and none-government entities. Research article: published 2 articles in International Peer reviewed Journal and Conference proceedings, 4 articles in national journals. Conducted research on micro finance under University Grants Commission faculty research grants program. Books: Published 2 books in the field of finance.

Kairav Raval is an Associate Director of Information Technology at Hyveminds Pty Ltd.

Khalid Waheed is an Assistant Professor at Crescent Business School, B S Abdur Rahman University, Chennai. He teaches Economics and Islamic Finance. He has completed his Ph.D in Economics and a specialization course in Shariah-Islamic Law.

S. M. Wasiullah, currently pursuing Ph. D in Management in the area of Interest-free Microcredit (Microfinance) at B. S. Abdur Rahman University, Chennai. He has four years of experience working as a Financial Analyst and Financial Research Analyst in different firms. He earned his MBA specializing in Finance from the prestigious Osmania University, Hyderabad in the year 2009. He produced an explorative research paper on the topic "Islamic Finance: Developments and Opportunities in India" as a part of his MBA curriculum in 2009. S M Wasiullah is keenly interested in the field of Islamic Economics and Finance and started studying the subject when he was yet in the early years of his college life. Based on his study and research he has been contributing research papers and articles on various issues to local and national level magazines. Among his research works "Impacts of taxation on Islamic finance contracts in India" presented at Monad University, Uttar Pradesh in 2013, "Review of Literature on Islamic Economics and Finance" submitted to Centre for Study and Research, Hyderabad in 2012 and "Islamic Finance in India: Prospects and Challenges", submitted for the International Seminar on Islamic Finance in India at Kochi in 2010 are most notable one. He has also lectured on the subject of Islamic Finance at some institutions and colleges in India.

Index

A

B

D

E

F

G

H

I

S

T

U

V

W

www.ingramcontent.com/pod-product-compliance
Lightning Source LLC
LaVergne TN
LVHW062136300926
849161LV00010B/2544